THE ROUTLEDGE COMPANION TO POLITICS AND LITERATURE IN ENGLISH

The Routledge Companion to Politics and Literature in English provides an interdisciplinary overview of the vibrant connections between literature, politics, and the political.

Featuring contributions from 44 scholars across a variety of disciplines, the collection is divided into five parts: Connecting Literature and Politics; Constituting the Polis; Periods and Histories; Media, Genre, Techne; and Spaces. Organized around familiar concepts—such as humans, animals, workers, empires, nations, and states—rather than theoretical schools, it will help readers to understand the ways in which literature affects our understanding of who is capable of political action, who has been included in and excluded from politics, and how different spaces are imagined to be political. It also offers a series of engagements with key moments in literary and political history from 1066 to the present in order to assess and reassess the utility of conventional modes of periodization.

The book extends current discussions in the area, looking at cutting-edge developments in the discipline of literary studies, which will appeal to academics and researchers seeking to orient their own interventions within broader contexts.

Matthew Stratton is Associate Professor of English at the University of California, Davis and the author of *The Politics of Irony in American Modernism* (2014).

ROUTLEDGE LITERATURE COMPANIONS

Also available in this series:

THE ROUTLEDGE COMPANION TO LITERATURE OF THE U.S. SOUTH
Edited by Katharine A. Burnett, Todd Hagstette, and Monica Carol Miller

THE ROUTLEDGE COMPANION TO LITERARY URBAN STUDIES
Edited by Lieven Ameel

THE ROUTLEDGE COMPANION TO WORLD LITERATURE, SECOND EDITION
Edited by Theo D'haen, David Damrosch, and Djelal Kadir

THE ROUTLEDGE COMPANION TO MEDIEVAL ENGLISH LITERATURE
Edited by Raluca Radulescu and Sif Rikhardsdottir

THE ROUTLEDGE COMPANION TO ROMANTIC WOMEN WRITERS
Edited by Ann R. Hawkins, Catherine S. Blackwell, and E. Leigh Bonds

THE ROUTLEDGE COMPANION TO GLOBAL LITERARY ADAPTATION IN THE TWENTY-FIRST CENTURY
Edited by Brandon Chua and Elizabeth Ho

THE ROUTLEDGE COMPANION TO POLITICS AND LITERATURE IN ENGLISH
Edited by Matthew Stratton

For more information on this series, please visit: www.routledge.com/Routledge-Literature-Companions/book-series/RC4444

THE ROUTLEDGE COMPANION TO POLITICS AND LITERATURE IN ENGLISH

Edited by
Matthew Stratton

LONDON AND NEW YORK

Designed cover image: Robert Delaunay, *Political Drama*, Gift of the Joseph H. Hazen Foundation Inc.

First published 2023
by Routledge
4 Park Square, Milton Park, Abingdon, Oxon OX14 4RN

and by Routledge
605 Third Avenue, New York, NY 10158

Routledge is an imprint of the Taylor & Francis Group, an informa business

© 2023 selection and editorial matter, Matthew Stratton; individual chapters, the contributors

The right of Matthew Stratton to be identified as the author of the editorial material, and of the authors for their individual chapters, has been asserted in accordance with sections 77 and 78 of the Copyright, Designs and Patents Act 1988.

All rights reserved. No part of this book may be reprinted or reproduced or utilised in any form or by any electronic, mechanical, or other means, now known or hereafter invented, including photocopying and recording, or in any information storage or retrieval system, without permission in writing from the publishers.

Trademark notice: Product or corporate names may be trademarks or registered trademarks, and are used only for identification and explanation without intent to infringe.

British Library Cataloguing-in-Publication Data
A catalogue record for this book is available from the British Library

ISBN: 978-0-367-48103-2 (hbk)
ISBN: 978-1-032-43023-2 (pbk)
ISBN: 978-1-003-03800-9 (ebk)

DOI: 10.4324/9781003038009

Typeset in Bembo
by codeMantra

For Ambrose Stratton-Miller and Giacomo Stratton-Miller.
Es la hora de luchar.

CONTENTS

Notes on contributors   *xi*
Acknowledgments   *xviii*

   Introduction   1
   Matthew Stratton

PART I
Connecting Literature and Politics   9

 1 Aesthetics and Affect   11
    Tyler Bradway

 2 Forms   22
    Ingrid Nelson

 3 Realism and Representation   32
    Regina Martin

 4 Symptoms   42
    Benjamin Kohlmann

 5 Reforms and Revolutions   53
    John S. Garrison and Kyle Pivetti

 6 Rights Catalogue   64
    Juno Jill Richards

7	Empires, Decolonization, and the Canon *Maryam Wasif Khan*	74

PART II
Constituting the Polis — 85

8	Citizenship and Enslavement *Elizabeth J. West*	87
9	Humans and Posthumans *Jennifer Rhee*	98
10	Animals *Mario Ortiz Robles*	109
11	Workers *Benjamin Balthaser*	118
12	Debtors *Robin Truth Goodman*	128
13	Refugees *Hadji Bakara*	138
14	Nations and States *Jessie Reeder*	148

PART III
Periods and Histories — 159

15	On or about 1066 *Mary Rambaran-Olm*	161
16	On or about 1400 *Susan Nakley*	172
17	On or about 1616 *Urvashi Chakravarty*	183
18	On or about 1789 *John Owen Havard*	194

19	On or about 1885 *Padma Rangarajan*	204
20	On or about 1914 *Tanya Agathocleous*	214
21	On or about 1945 *Claire Seiler*	225
22	On or about 1989 *Ian Afflerbach*	236
23	On or about Now *Rachel Greenwald Smith*	247

PART IV
Media, Genre, Techne — **257**

24	Sound and Print *Anthony Reed*	259
25	Photography, Literature, and Time *Emily Hyde*	269
26	Art, Propaganda, and Truth *Melissa Dinsman*	280
27	Criticism *Thom Dancer*	291
28	Digital Platforms *J. D. Schnepf*	302
29	Translation *Roland Végső*	312
30	Comics *Daniel Worden*	323

PART V
Spaces   **339**

31 Archives   341
    Megan Ward

32 Homes   352
    Natalie Pollard

33 Cities   364
    Ameeth Vijay

34 Streets and Highways   375
    Myka Tucker-Abramson and Sam Weselowski

35 Nature   387
    Steven Swarbrick

36 Oceans   397
    Alison Maas

37 Borders   408
    Anne Mai Yee Jansen

38 Planets   419
    Gerry Canavan

39 Utopia   430
    Deanna K. Kreisel

40 Classrooms   441
    Laura Heffernan and Rachel Sagner Buurma

Index   *453*

CONTRIBUTORS

Ian Afflerbach is Associate Professor of American Literature at the University of North Georgia, where he researches and teaches in modern American fiction, intellectual history, African American studies, and periodical culture. His first book, *Making Liberalism New: American Intellectuals, Modern Literature, and the Rewriting of a Political Tradition*, appeared with Johns Hopkins UP in 2021. His essays have appeared in *PMLA*, *Modernism/Modernity*, *ELH*, *Modern Fiction Studies*, and *African American Review*.

Tanya Agathocleous is Professor of English at Hunter College and the Graduate Center, CUNY, where she teaches and researches nineteenth- and early twentieth-century Anglophone literature and culture in colonial, postcolonial, and transnational contexts. Among other works, she is the author of *Disaffected: Emotion, Sedition, and Colonial Law in the Anglosphere* (Cornell UP, 2021) and *Urban Realism and the Cosmopolitan Imagination* (Cambridge UP, 2011); co-editor of *Teaching Literature: A Companion* (Palgrave, 2003); and editor of a Broadview edition of Joseph Conrad's *The Secret Agent* and two Penguin editions: *Great Expectations* and *Sultana's Dream and Padmarag*. Alongside these works and academic articles, she has also written for *Public Books* and *Los Angeles Review of Books*.

Hadji Bakara is Assistant Professor of English Language and Literature at the University of Michigan. He is the editor of a special issue of *JNT: Journal of Narrative Theory* on "Refugee Literatures" (2020), and his writing on human rights and migration can be found in *PMLA*, *American Literary History*, *German Quarterly*, the *Routledge Handbook of Refugee Narratives*, and *The Los Angeles Review of Books*.

Benjamin Balthaser is Associate Professor of Multi-Ethnic Literature in the United States. He is the author of *Anti-Imperialist Modernism: Race and Radical Culture from the Great Depression to the Cold War* (U of Michigan P, 2016) and *Dedication* (Partisan Press, 2011). His critical and creative work has appeared in *American Quarterly*, *Boston Review*, *Minnesota Review*, and elsewhere.

Tyler Bradway is Associate Professor of English at SUNY Cortland and author of *Queer Experimental Literature: The Affective Politics of Bad Reading* (Palgrave, 2017). Bradway co-edited

Queer Kinship: Race, Sex, Belonging, Form (Duke, 2022) and *After Queer Studies: Literature, Theory and Sexuality in the 21st Century* (Cambridge, 2019). His essays appear in *PMLA, MLQ, GLQ, Textual Practice,* and *College Literature*.

Rachel Sagner Buurma is Associate Professor of English Literature at Swarthmore College. She is co-author, with Laura Heffernan, of *The Teaching Archive* (U of Chicago P, 2021), a new disciplinary history that places classrooms at the center of the history of literary study to show how teachers and students invented many of its core practices and methods. She has published essays on book indexes, Anthony Trollope, literary metadata, and reading in the digital age.

Gerry Canavan is Associate Professor of English at Marquette University, specializing in twentieth- and twenty-first-century literature. An editor at *Extrapolation* and *Science Fiction Film and Television*, he has also co-edited *Green Planets: Ecology and Science Fiction* (2014), *The Cambridge Companion to American Science Fiction* (2015), and *The Cambridge History of Science Fiction* (2019). His first monograph, *Octavia E. Butler,* appeared in 2016 in the Modern Masters of Science Fiction series at U of Illinois P.

Urvashi Chakravarty is Associate Professor of English at the University of Toronto and works on early modern English literature, critical race studies, queer studies, and the history of slavery. Her first book, *Fictions of Consent: Slavery, Servitude, and Free Service in Early Modern England* (U of Pennsylvania P, 2022), explores the ideologies of Atlantic slavery in early modern England; her current project is titled *From Fairest Creatures: Race, Reproduction, and Slavery in the Early Modern British Atlantic World*. Her articles appear in *English Literary Renaissance, Shakespeare Quarterly*, the *Journal of Early Modern Cultural Studies, Spenser Studies, postmedieval, Literature Compass,* and the edited collections *Queering Childhood in Early Modern English Drama and Culture, Shakespeare/Sex: Contemporary Readings in Gender and Sexuality,* and *The Cambridge Companion to Shakespeare and Race*.

Thom Dancer works at the University of Toronto. He is the author of *Critical Modesty in Contemporary Fiction* (Oxford UP, 2021) as well as various other articles and chapters on contemporary fiction, novel theory, and literary criticism.

Melissa Dinsman is Assistant Professor of English at York College-CUNY and author of *Modernism at the Microphone: Radio, Propaganda, and Literary Aesthetics during World War II* (2015). Her research focuses on WWII women writers, the politics of the domestic, propaganda, and information networks. Dinsman's work can be found in *ELN, Women's Writing, Modernism/modernity, International Yeats Studies,* and the MLA's *Teaching Modernist Women's Writing in English*. She serves as co-President of the Space Between society.

John S. Garrison is Professor of English at Grinnell College. His books include *Shakespeare at Peace* (with Kyle Pivetti, Routledge, 2018) and *Shakespeare and the Afterlife* (Oxford UP, 2019). In 2021, he was named a Guggenheim Fellow.

Robin Truth Goodman is Professor of English at Florida State University. Her publications include *Feminism as World Literature*; *Gender Commodity: Marketing Feminist Identities and the Promise of Security*; *Understanding Adorno, Understanding Modernism*; *The Bloomsbury Handbook of 21st Century Feminist Theory*; *Promissory Notes: On the Literary Conditions of Debt*;

Gender for the Warfare State: Literature of Women in Combat; *Literature and the Development of Feminist Theory*; *Gender Work: Feminism after Neoliberalism*; *Feminist Theory in Pursuit of the Public: Women and the "Re-Privatization" of Labor*; *Policing Narratives and the State of Terror*; and *World, Class, Women: Global Literature, Education, and Feminism*.

John Owen Havard is the author of *Disaffected Parties: Political Estrangement and the Making of English Literature, 1760–1830* (Oxford UP, 2019) and *Late Romanticism and the End of Politics: Byron, Mary Shelley and the Last Men* (Cambridge UP, forthcoming). His articles and essays on literature and party politics, political emotion, and the future of democracy have appeared in *ELH*, *The Eighteenth Century: Theory and Interpretation*, *Nineteenth-Century Literature*, *The New Rambler*, and *Public Books*.

Laura Heffernan is Professor of English at the University of North Florida. She is co-author, with Rachel Sagner Buurma, of *The Teaching Archive* (U of Chicago P, 2021), a new disciplinary history that focuses on how and what twentieth-century English professors taught at a range of twentieth-century institutions of higher education. At UNF, Heffernan is project lead on the NEH-funded Viola Muse Digital Edition, which publishes the notes and draft essays that local salon owner Muse made for the Negro Writers Division of the Florida Federal Writers Project (1936–1940).

Emily Hyde is Associate Professor of English at Rowan University. Her articles and reviews on comparative modernisms, postcolonial literature and theory, contemporary literature, and photography appear in *PMLA*, *Literature Compass*, *Post45: Peer Reviewed*, *Modernism/Modernity*, *Public Books*, and *Post45: Contemporaries*. Other writing has appeared in the collections *The Pocket Instructor: Literature*, *Auden at Work*, *Around 1945*, and *B-Side Books*.

Anne Mai Yee Jansen is Associate Professor of Ethnic Studies and Literatures and the director of US Ethnic Studies at the University of North Carolina at Asheville. Her research revolves around the intersections of literature, activism, and genre in multiethnic and Indigenous texts. She is particularly interested in the ways literature sometimes aims to engage with and impact the world we live in, especially regarding its potential to disrupt settler colonialism and racism.

Maryam Wasif Khan is Associate Professor of Comparative Literary and Cultural Studies at the LUMS University, Lahore. Her first book, *Who Is a Muslim? Orientalism and Literary Populisms* (Fordham University Press, 2021), argues for a renewed interrogation of the European scholarly discipline and cultural practice, orientalism, and its influence on modern vernacular literatures. Her second project revisits her undergraduate studies in literature at Princeton and engages with her present teaching to think through the possibilities contained in canonical Western texts once they are dislocated from the Euro-American academy.

Benjamin Kohlmann teaches English literature at the University of Regensburg, Germany. He is the author of *British Literature and the Life of Institutions: Speculative States* (Oxford UP, 2021), *Committed Styles: Modernism, Politics, and Left-Wing Literature in the 1930s* (Oxford UP, 2014) and articles in *PMLA*, *ELH*, *Modern Fiction Studies*, *Modernism/Modernity*, and elsewhere.

Deanna Kreisel is Associate Professor of English and Co-Director of Environmental Studies at the University of Mississippi. She is the author of *Economic Woman: Demand, Gender, and*

Narrative Closure in Eliot and Hardy (2012) as well as essays in *PMLA*, *Representations*, *ELH*, *Novel*, *Victorian Studies*, *Nineteenth Century Literature*, and elsewhere. She is co-editor, along with Devin Griffiths, of *After Darwin: Literature, Theory, and Criticism in the Twenty-First Century* (Cambridge UP, 2022). Her academic work can be found at www.deannakreisel.com and her creative non-fiction at doctorwaffle.substack.com and *3 Quarks Daily*.

Alison Maas is a PhD candidate in English with a Designated Emphasis in Critical Theory at the University of California, Davis. Her research focuses on early twentieth-century transatlantic literature, global shipping infrastructure, and the ecological crisis of coastal erosion and has appeared in *Atlantic Studies* and *Comparative American Studies*. She is the creator of the podcast series "California's Eroding Coastline" (funded by the Bilinski Fellowship at Bodega Bay Marine Lab), co-editor of the Searchable Sea Literature website run by Williams Mystic, and co-organizer of the University of California Humanities Research Institute working group "Coast as Crisis: Narratives, Ecologies, and Politics of the California Coast."

Regina Martin is Associate Professor of English at Denison University, where she teaches British literature, Caribbean literature, literary theory, digital humanities, and global commerce. Her research focuses on intersections between economic history/theory and British literature, with a specific focus on how those intersections manifest in literary form. She has published articles in *PMLA*, *Modern Fiction Studies*, *Modern Language Studies*, *Criticism*, and other journals.

Susan Nakley is Professor and Associate Chair of English at St. Joseph's University, Brooklyn and author of *Living in the Future: Sovereignty and Internationalism in the* Canterbury Tales (U of Michigan P, 2017). Her second monograph project is tentatively titled *Libelous Reorientations: Orientalism and Antisemitism in Middle English Literature*. Nakley has published in venues like *The Journal of English and Germanic Philology* and *Literature and Medicine*.

Ingrid Nelson is Associate Professor of English and European Studies at Amherst College. She is the author of *Lyric Tactics: Poetry, Genre and Practice in Later Medieval England* (U of Pennsylvania P, 2017). She has published essays in *ELH* and *NLH*, among other journals.

Kyle Pivetti is Associate Professor of English at Norwich University. His first book is titled *Of Memory and Literary Form: The Making of Nationhood in Early Modern England* (University of Delaware Press, 2015). He is also co-author, with John Garrison, of *Shakespeare at Peace* (Routledge, 2018). His research on adaptation, memory, and political identity has also been featured in *Shakespeare*; *Studies in Ethnicity and Nationalism*; *Modern Philology*; and *Explorations in Renaissance Culture*.

Natalie Pollard is Senior Lecturer in Contemporary Literature at University of Exeter, UK. Her research specialisms are in contemporary writing and visual culture at the intersection of the arts, humanities, and social/natural sciences. She is the author of two monographs: *Fugitive Pieces: Poetry, Publishing and Visual Culture from Late Modernism to the 21C* (Oxford UP, 2020) and *Speaking to You: Contemporary Poetry and Public Address* (Oxford UP, 2012). Natalie's areas of research include global and trans-local poetics, academic refusal and irreverence, ecocriticism and erasure, and anti-colonial pedagogy.

Mary Rambaran-Olm specializes in the literature, language, culture, and history of pre-conquest England. Her research focuses on race in the early medieval period and medieval misappropriation. She has published widely in *NLH*, *postmedieval*, *Notes & Queries*, *English Studies*, *Digital Medievalist*, as well as in a number of compilations. As a public literary historian, her work has been featured in Public Books, TIME, Smithsonian, History Workshop Online, and elsewhere. Her second book co-written with Dr. Erik Wade is *Race in Early Medieval England* (Cambridge UP, 2023). She spends extra time helping burn down her field.

Padma Rangarajan is Associate Professor of English at the University of California, Riverside, where she specializes in nineteenth-century British literature and colonial epistemologies. She is the author of *Imperial Babel: Translation, Exoticism, and the Long Nineteenth Century* (Fordham, 2014). She has published essays in *English Literary History*, *English Language Notes*, *Studies in Scottish Literature*, *Nineteenth Century Literature*, *Romanticism*, *Keats-Shelley Journal*, and *Romantic Circles*.

Anthony Reed is Professor of English at Vanderbilt University. His publications include *Soundworks: Race, Poetry, and Sound in Production* (Duke UP, 2021) and *Freedom Time: The Poetics and Politics of Black Experimental Writing* (Johns Hopkins UP, 2016). He is co-editor, with Vera M. Kutzinski, of *Langston Hughes in Context* (Cambridge UP, 2022).

Jessie Reeder is Associate Professor of English at Binghamton University, specializing in nineteenth-century British literature, imperialism, and form. Her book, *The Forms of Informal Empire: Britain, Latin America, and Nineteenth-Century Literature* (Johns Hopkins UP, 2020), won the Sonya Rudikoff Prize for the best first book in Victorian studies from the Northeast Victorian Studies Association. Her essays appear in *Victorian Literature and Culture*, *Studies in English Literature*, *Studies in Romanticism*, and more. Jessie is also an organizing member of Anglophone Chile, a project to digitize the newspapers printed by anglophone settlers in mid-nineteenth-century Chile.

Jennifer Rhee is Associate Professor in the Department of English at Virginia Commonwealth University. She has written about race, gender, and labor in robotics and artificial intelligence technologies in her book *The Robotic Imaginary: The Human and the Price of Dehumanized Labor* (U of Minnesota P, 2018). She is co-editor of *The Palgrave Handbook of Twentieth and Twenty-First Century Literature and Science* (2020), which was edited by a group of scholars working under the name "The Triangle Collective." Her scholarship on artificial intelligence and on speculative fiction has also appeared in numerous journals and edited volumes.

Juno Jill Richards is Associate Professor of English and affiliated faculty in Women, Gender and Sexuality Studies at Yale University. They are the author of *The Fury Archives: Female Citizenship, Human Rights, and the International Avant-Gardes* (Columbia UP, 2020) and a co-author of *The Ferrante Letters: An Experiment in Collective Criticism* (Columbia UP, 2020).

Mario Ortiz Robles is the Nancy C. Hoefs Professor of English and a Senior Fellow at the Institute for Research in the Humanities at the University of Wisconsin, Madison. His work is situated at the intersection of nineteenth-century European literature, literary theory, and the environmental humanities. He is the author of *The Novel as Event* and *Literature* *and Animal Studies*, and the co-editor of *Narrative Middles*. He has published extensively on Victorian literature and culture, animal studies, and literary theory.

J. D. Schnepf is Assistant Professor of American Studies and Co-Director of the Research Centre for the Study of Democratic Cultures and Politics at the University of Groningen. Her writing has appeared in *Contemporary Literature, Feminist Media Studies, Media and Environment, Modern Fiction Studies*, and other venues. She is the recipient of the Emory Elliott Prize from the International American Studies Association (2019) and has edited an issue of *Review of International American Studies* entitled "Gender and Surveillance," with Molly Geidel (2022). She holds a PhD in English from Brown University.

Claire Seiler is Associate Professor of English at Dickinson College. She is the author of *Midcentury Suspension: Literature and Feeling in the Wake of World War II* (Columbia UP, 2020). Her articles and essays have appeared in *Contemporary Literature, Modernism/Modernity, Twentieth-Century Literature*, and elsewhere. Seiler's work focuses on the global cultural imprint of polio and, more broadly, on the literary history of public health from the influenza pandemic of 1918–1920 through the AIDS crisis.

Rachel Greenwald Smith is Professor of English at Saint Louis University. She is the author of *On Compromise: Art, Politics, and the Fate of an American Ideal* (Graywolf Press, 2021) and *Affect and American Literature in the Age of Neoliberalism* (Cambridge UP, 2015) as well as an editor of *American Literature in Transition: 2000–2010* (Cambridge UP, 2018) and, with Mitchum Huehls, *Neoliberalism and Contemporary Literary Culture* (Johns Hopkins UP, 2017).

Matthew Stratton is Associate Professor of English at the University of California, Davis.

Steven Swarbrick is Assistant professor of English at Baruch College, CUNY. He is the author of *The Environmental Unconscious: Ecological Poetics from Spenser to Milton* (U of Minnesota P, 2023) and numerous articles on ecocriticism, critical theory, and the political imagination. His scholarship has appeared in journals such as *Critical Inquiry, Discourse*, and *Postmodern Culture*.

Myka Tucker-Abramson works at the University of Warwick. Her research focuses on the road novel and the built environments of American hegemony.

Roland Végső is Professor of English at the University of Nebraska-Lincoln, where he teaches literary and critical theory and twentieth-century literatures. His primary research interests are contemporary continental philosophy, modernism, and translation theory. He is the author of *The Naked Communist: Cold War Modernism and the Politics of Popular Culture* (Fordham UP, 2013) and *Worldlessness After Heidegger: Phenomenology, Psychoanalysis, Deconstruction* (Edinburgh UP, 2020). In addition, he is the translator of numerous philosophical essays as well as two books: Rodolphe Gasché's *Georges Bataille: Phenomenology and Phantasmatology* (Stanford UP, 2012) and Peter Szendy's *All Ears: The Aesthetics of Espionage* (Fordham UP, 2016). He is the co-editor of the book series *Provocations* published by University of Nebraska Press.

Ameeth Vijay is Assistant Professor of Literature at the University of California, San Diego. He specializes in global anglophone literature, modern and contemporary British literature, postcolonial studies, and urban studies.

Contributors

Megan Ward is Associate Professor of English at Oregon State University. She is the author of *Seeming Human: Artificial Intelligence and Victorian Realist Character* and co-director of the digital archive *Livingstone Online*. She writes about the influences of realism from the Victorian era to the present. Her work has appeared in scholarly journals and edited collections, as well as more popular venues such as *The Atlantic*, the *Los Angeles Review of Books*, and *The Washington Post*.

Sam Weselowski is a PhD candidate in the Department of English and Comparative Literary Studies at the University of Warwick. His research focuses on postwar poetry and the urban form of extraction.

Elizabeth J. West is Professor of English and John B. and Elena Diaz-Verson Amos Distinguished Chair in English Letters at Georgia State University. She serves as Director of Academics for Georgia State University's Center for Studies on Africa and Its Diaspora (CSAD), Advisory Board member of the Obama Institute for Transnational American Studies (Johannes Gutenberg University), and member of the University of Mississippi Medical Center's Asylum Hill Research Consortium. She is PI for "Intersectionality in the American South," a Mellon Foundation Grant fostering cross-institutional collectives in Intersectionality Studies. Her work focuses on interdisciplinary studies of early to contemporary African American and African Diaspora Literatures of the Americas with emphasis on connections of spirituality and gender. She is the author of *Finding Francis: One Family's Journey from Slavery to Freedom* (U of South Carolina P, 2022).

Daniel Worden is Associate Professor of Art at the Rochester Institute of Technology. He is the author of *Neoliberal Nonfictions: The Documentary Aesthetic from Joan Didion to Jay-Z* (U of Virginia P, 2020), the editor of *The Comics of R. Crumb: Underground in the Art Museum* (UP of Mississippi, 2021), and the co-editor with Jesse W. Schwartz of *New Directions in Print Culture Studies: Archives, Materiality, and Modern American Culture* (Bloomsbury, 2022).

ACKNOWLEDGMENTS

Reading widely across fields and periods as a preface to soliciting contributors, and then engaging these writers in sustained scholarly dialogue, has been one of the most invigorating and sustaining experiences of my intellectual life. This volume was conceived just before and then populated during the latest global pandemic and the latest financial crisis. Contributors not only amazed by accepting my invitation, but persisted through tribulations and tragedies of the kind that are never distributed equally or equitably across populations: illness, pain, loss of dear ones, closing of schools, closing of minds, dramatically transformed conditions of pedagogical labor, insurrection, murder by police, the caretaking of selves and kin and students and others. So, to all of you who stayed with the project, I salute you with sincere and deep admiration and gratitude and debt. To the significant number who were forced by circumstance to bow out early or late, I salute you with sincere admiration and gratitude and regret and hope for future collaboration. To those who swept in to save entries at the last minute, I stand in awe and arrears. For the entries that finally just couldn't make it, I'm really sorry.

I take responsibility for flaws and shortcomings and errata, but can't take credit for the shape of the whole. At Routledge, it was Polly Dodson's original inspiration and Chris Ratcliffe who brought it home. Just in my own home department, Elizabeth Freeman, Mark Jerng, Tobias Menely, Parama Roy, Matthew Vernon, and Michael Ziser talked about this thing and read parts early and late and ate and drank and helped. Just in my own home, Elizabeth Carolyn Miller, Ambrose Stratton-Miller, and Giacomo Stratton-Miller put up with way more than they should and offer way more than they have to.

Two then-graduate students, now Dr. Thomas Hintze and Dr. Jessica Hanselman-Gray, did a lot of key work and offered a lot of sound advice, all while writing dissertations and teaching and caring for families and being generally lovely humans. Tom helped get the ball rolling, handling reams of early e-paperwork while producing his own, genuinely excellent, original research on the politics of laughter in African-American modernism and working to remind everybody that "There is Power in a Union" is more than the title of a Joe Hill song. Jessica took the ball and ran with it, and it is absolutely no exaggeration to say that the whole thing would have been sunk without her exceedingly keen critical eye and intellect, her nigh-heroic mastery of the blue pencil and the new MLA format, her ability to finish her own great dissertation and other scholars' works-cited pages simultaneously, and her general sympathetic cool under the obnoxious conditions of Winter-Spring 2022.

Recent research has demonstrated quantitatively what many of us, students and faculty alike, knew all along: that "the professoriate is, and has remained, accessible disproportionately to the socioeconomically privileged."[1] Academia has too frequently remained a family business whose members are, at this late date, still impressed by baronial escutcheons on university letterhead and mother-tongue fluency in the argot, demeanor, and social networks that reproduce hidden curricula from elite secondary schools through elite graduate programs. This fact is just part of why I am fortunate to work at a public research university—with all its many flaws and frustrations and shortcomings, located on land that for thousands of years has been the home of the Patwin people—where more than 40% of undergraduates are first-generation to college, where more than 40% of students come from low-income families, where more than 30% of students belong to groups of people who are underrepresented in higher education (African-American, Hispanic and Latina/o and Chicana/o, and Native American). My work there is part of how I know, from research and conversations and common sense, that these undergraduate students bore the damaging brunt of the past few years in ways that I didn't have to. They often did so with grit and grace I couldn't hope to muster. With thanks to those who won't allow the online state of exception to be made permanent, I'm genuinely glad to be back in the classroom with these students. I hope that many and more of them will choose to lead classrooms of their own, especially in elementary schools and middle schools and high schools where their wit and judgment and fortitude and experience can make a real difference. With hopes that higher learning becomes more widely accessible and legible and attuned to those who were neither to the manor nor the manner born, I salute and thank them most of all.

Note

1 Morgan, A.C., LaBerge, N., Larremore, D.B. et al. "Socioeconomic Roots of Academic Faculty." *Nature: Human Behavior* (August 2022). https://doi.org/10.1038/s41562-022-01425-4

INTRODUCTION

Matthew Stratton

Among academic literary critics, the general proposition that writing literature, reading literature, analyzing literature, and teaching literature are frequently "political" tasks is well established. This is true even when texts are not obviously concerned with representing laws or wars or elections or institutions or the distribution of goods and services: the traditional realms of traditional "politics," of action, of V. I. Lenin's and Joseph Stalin's "who does what to whom" and Harold Lasswell's "who gets what, when, how." Even literary movements that most famously repudiated overtly political understandings of literature—e.g., fin de siècle Aestheticism or the New Criticism—have long been understood as deeply political in their repudiation of competing forms of politics. Bluntly, "literature and politics" is not really a sub-discipline of literary studies today; "literature and politics" is literary studies today. Indeed, as Sandra MacPherson observes, "nothing runs deeper in the recent history and practice of literary criticism than the presumption that criticism is politics by other means" (1215).[1]

Of course, presumptions are frequently untrue. But set aside whether the claim is actually true or false, whether writing or teaching literature and literary criticism do or should qualify as "real" political acts; that seemingly intractable knot can be cut by defining key terms and distinguishing between theoretical and empirical claims. Because true or false, depending on where you sit in the classroom or the faculty meeting or the job market or what self-segregated space of social media you inhabit, different texts and readings and authors and curricula are indeed championed as politically salubrious or attacked as politically noxious or—perhaps worse—anodyne. Entirely disinterested aesthetic judgments don't exist except as an influential theoretical proposition; neither do literary judgments entirely divorced from the political, whether way deep down or right up there on the supposed surface.

To be clear, "the political" here and elsewhere signifies and entails more than merely an adjectival form of politics.[2] The idea that both literature and literary criticism are not just political but substantively "the political"—that is, bound to the realm of meaning that precedes and constitutes the conditions for perceiving, representing, understanding, and performing those particular acts that qualify as political acts—is shared across populations that are much wider and more diverse than the relatively narrow academic world.

This fact has become both obvious and ominous in a moment when politicians and parents and pundits ferociously object to what they see as the transformation of a previously apolitical set of practices into a menacing tool for indoctrination. Reading fiction and poetry was once a source of inoffensive aesthetic pleasure (we are told), or a resource for easily digestible moral instruction (they say), or a luminous connection to transcendent, transhistorical truths (of course), and a usefully instrumental tool to help future workers read and write lucid memos and reports (if only). And they are not messing around: as PEN America reports, between January 2021 and January 2022, 122 "educational gag orders" were introduced by U.S. legislative bodies, largely to criminalize the teaching of "controversial subjects"—transparent code for teaching "sex, race, ethnicity, religion, color, national origin, or political affiliation" in a way that acknowledges and engages historical facts about colonialism, white supremacy, and the violent suppression of facts, identities, and experiences more diverse than Donald Trump's and Boris Johnson's. During the 2021-2022 school year, more than 2500 books were banned in the U.S. alone, affecting 1,648 individual titles.[3] In the U.K., human rights groups like Amnesty International warn of the chilling effect of "Prevent Duty," where teachers are legally obliged to identify warning signs of undesirable political actors.[4] Moreover, as the work of PEN International reminds us by highlighting the brutal suppression of texts and writers around the globe, this situation in U.K. and U.S. schools and libraries might still reasonably be described as comparatively gentle.[5]

Of course, the idea that literature and teaching have only recently become politicized is flatly absurd. As Laura Heffernan and Rachel Sagner Buurma show in their contribution "Classrooms," "[s]tudents and teachers have discussed the politics of literature in classrooms since at least the nineteenth century," and these are scenes from a very old story indeed: debates about the proper relationship between literature and politics lie at the very foundations of Western conceptions of how societies are and should be organized. From the role of poetry in Plato's *Republic*, through and beyond Salman Rushdie's claim that "description itself is a political act," the particulars are hotly contested even as precisely what qualifies as "politics" and "criticism" and "literature" remains unsettled. The definition of what qualifies as "literature" worthy of academic study has expanded from poetry and drama to include popular genre fiction, digital media, comics, and texts written by authors who were long considered unworthy of academic analysis. So too have definitions of "politics" expanded, if perhaps less dramatically: from "war by other means" to the organization of institutions and states, to the election of representatives, all the way to the fundamental ways that things and people and other animals are organized, experienced, represented, narrated, and understood to be embodied agents with public and private desires, commitments, biases, and significance. As part of this vexed and sometimes vexing history, the best academic presses publish stacks of articles and monographs addressing the particular politics of particular authors, texts, periods, identities, styles, genres, and so forth. To navigate the secondary world of criticism and theory thus means navigating a more general, dynamic, conceptual, and semantic terrain that is not always explicit about its fundamentals. This is a task not only for professional scholars but for anyone who wants to understand or join ongoing critical conversations about texts they love, hate, or simply want to know and understand more profoundly.

Almost a decade ago, writing about the complicated relationship between the terms "democracy" and "the novel," Nancy Ruttenburg elaborated key questions that can and must be posed equally strongly today about the relationship—presumed or assumed or breezily mentioned or explicitly stipulated—between "politics" and "literature" more broadly:

> [W]hat are the criteria for identifying and evaluating evidence for this relationship in order to establish its legitimacy? What is the nature of the gravitational pull that keeps these enormous abstractions…orbiting one another? Is it historical, formal, discursive,

ideological, structural, metaphorical, or some combination of these, depending on the inclinations, methodologies, and disciplinary field(s) of the analyst? (1)[6]

The chapters in this volume collectively and respectively answer these questions with "multiple," "complicated," and "yes." And they do so as a coherent collection of views, a demi-chorus of variously consonant and dissonant claims that seek, in different ways and with different styles, both to explain and to instantiate the importance of continuing to think and write and read and act within and beyond the boundaries of a discipline that may be singular but has never been uniform.

The scholars in this volume do not always mean the same thing when they use the word "politics" and its adjuncts. Yet the fact that so many perspectives and concrete deployments are at play is not a conceptual obstacle to be overlooked and overcome, but rather a democratic political value that is embedded in the organization of this volume. What has emerged from the original process of soliciting contributions, and thus from this collection, is not simply the summary of what one endogamous ideological cohort thinks about what literature and people should do in the world, but a constellation of diverse perspectives and archives and methodologies and commitments that unapologetically oppose those who would ban books, discourage free inquiry and discomfiting questions, scold instead of argue, or prosecute teachers for introducing students to ideas and facts.

Relying on multiple, shifting meanings of a single term within a single text can make for exceptionally good poetry and does make for exceptionally weak arguments. Thus, to avoid the objectionably familiar "fallacy of conceptual equivocation," the writers of these chapters have made clear what they mean and when they (and their archives) mean it. In "On or about 1616," for example, Urvashi Chakravarty reminds us that the "very word 'politics'... recalls its etymological association with the *polis*, the state—and who might be said to belong, and who is excluded. It places pressure on the question of the polity, and who constitutes it." In "Forms," Ingrid Nelson follows "Aristotle's account of the formation of the *polis*" to stipulate politics as "the discipline of constituting and governing the *polis* that organizes itself around turning the biological fact of human life into a set of norms and practices that conduce to 'the good life,' a culturally contingent ethical concept." Susan Nakely, in "On or about 1400," emphasizes the particularly ethical valence of the word when she asserts that politics "is the negotiable part of human responsibility that instantiates power shifts as it draws writers and readers into an intellectually and ethically charged public sphere." These are but a few examples from a volume running to a quarter-million words, and compiling a lexicographical summary of 40 different chapters would accomplish precisely and perversely what this preface (let alone this volume) is not intended to do: maximize efficiency or suggest that summary can be a healthy substitute for carefully elaborated argumentation. And while there is a striking amount of intersection and overlapping interest among the different chapters, they are roughly divided into sections delineating the deceptively simplified fact that politics comprises acts performed or represented by agents in time and space.

As "politics" partially designates actions within a symbolic and discursive field of meaning that is conventionally termed "the political," and as the *polis* is constituted by a process of exclusion and inclusion, much depends upon how political actors are represented (or not). Represented here involves both the most familiar, institutional sense of elected officials' "representation" and extra-institutional voices speaking "for" or "on behalf of" others, and also the "representation" of painting and plots and poems (German helpfully distinguishes between these senses as *Vertretung* and *Darstellung*). Thus, for example, in "Refugees," Hadji

Bakara distinguishes between political actors as "participants in shaping the societies they enter and the futures they will inhabit" and "apolitical subjects," by which he "mean[s] supplicants to sympathy and moral feeling or the sovereignty of a receiving nation." Considering the key role of "sympathy" in the history of political philosophy and also in ordinary conversations about what affective responses we imagine literature to activate in readers, a specifically political understanding of literary characters acting in history becomes both legible and compelling. And, as Mario Ortiz-Robles in "Animals" and Jennifer Rhee in "Humans and Posthumans" show, a genuinely ethical reexamination of fundamental categories will require more than the presumption that humans serve as the sole and stable political species.

Of course, actions are necessarily executed by agents in physical, legal, social, and virtual spaces. Thus, many contributors engage the exceptionally thorny philosophical and historical question of how "agents" have been distinguished from "non-agents," dating back to early modernity (as in Elizabeth J. West's chapter "Citizenship and Enslavement") and through present crises of perception, action, and governance. Indeed, the representational process whereby agents are defined and conceptualized (and thus perceived and understood) is itself a process that is frequently and explicitly both political and literary. This becomes both pressing and clear when, for example, Anne Mai Yee Jansen invokes politics as "the complex national (both inter- and intra-) power dynamics that arise from and around geopolitical borders and the spaces they intend to delineate" in her chapter "Borders." Some spaces in literary history have been inextricably associated with conventional political history for a few millennia; as Deanna Kreisel shows, this is the case for "Utopia," a genre where the venerable question of "how representation relates to praxis is particularly fraught." Other genres and histories press us to understand how politics, as Ameeth Vijay writes in "Cities," constitutes "the way that power, resistance, and conflict come to shape the different ways that space is experienced, apportioned, conceptualized, and expressed." These and the other definitions deployed by this volume's contributors are sometimes in tension, sometimes identical, sometimes congruent, but collectively insist on spaces as both a source and a function of the literary-political.

If political agents necessarily act in and around and on spaces, they also act in and outside of time. The ways that our relationships to the past are perceived, experienced, apportioned, delineated, regulated, and narrated both produce and are produced by the concept of "historical periods." Literature plays a role in producing and maintaining these periods and vice versa. Thus, the "Periods and Histories" part of the volume is dedicated to and predicated upon a paradox: we experience the present through a set of conceptual/temporal filters even as we recognize the material and ideological damage done when conceptual constructs are understood to be natural or inevitable. That section is structured to highlight the ongoing work of conceptualizing and reconceptualizing our basic disposition toward literary history. Hardly new but no less vital for all that, iconic dates serve as recognizable nodes in literary history (and undergraduate curricula, and graduate preliminary exams, and job advertisement prose) precisely in order to call them into question. As Mary Rambaran-Olm writes in "1066,"

> literary historians and other scholars in the humanities [must] challenge our perceptions, our nomenclature, and our use of periodization. Anchoring a systemic understanding of English history in dates like 1066 has served to familiarize and accustom people with the history of 'the English' as an imperial superpower spreading the supposed virtues of white 'civilization' at the point of the sword and into the hull of the slave ship.

Introduction

In manifold ways, contributors provide different access points to and around these dates—from the Battle of Hastings and the death of Chaucer to the French Revolution, the fall of the Berlin Wall to now—to teach and provoke readers about how these dates persist within history, why these dates matter to a specifically literary or cultural understanding of the world, and why they should matter differently as a result of scholarly intervention.

We frequently discuss literature as necessarily entangled with the value-laden ways we imagine and act in pursuit of a "good life"—for ourselves, for others in the present and the future—and thus a studied orientation to "the politics of literature" seemed to fill an obvious need. Yet an organized stab at the central questions addressed by the most compelling literary scholarship could not, in my opinion, usefully take the form of a list, a map, or a taxonomy of disciplinary methodologies with a summary of pre-existing conditions. This volume might have imitated traditional guides to literary theory, for example, by including a chapter "Marxism and Literature," followed by "Literature and Feminism" and "Literature and Race" or "Gender and Literature" or "Ecocriticism." While quotable and comfortably, lucidly tidy, such an organization would misrepresent the best of literary studies by artificially segregating—and paradoxically delimiting and containing—diverse interpretive methodologies and commitments and archives from one another. In literary studies, classrooms and research programs regularly employ multiple frameworks simultaneously; "interdisciplinary" or "postdisciplinary" are really more well-established facts than distinctively innovative or aspirational characteristics of newly formed or reformed scholarly dispositions and methodological protocols.

Moreover, the world has increasingly recognized what many scholars have known for decades: categories such as "race" and "gender" and "class" and "sexualities" and "environment" are not indicators that work has suddenly "become" political. This is the vision of reactionary anti-intellectuals who seek to repeal the past century, to create a public sense that stable, unchanging traditions are under attack, and to raise the alarm that the democratic aspirations of educators are a danger to be defunded. I approached the daunting task of populating a roster of writers without an open call for contributors and, for the most part, without drawing upon people I knew from school or conferences or life. Instead, with the combined advice of colleagues and strangers and a compulsive habit of seeing where intriguing citations will lead me, I read hundreds upon hundreds of articles and book chapters in areas far afield from my own. One of the things I learned is that most interesting and compelling scholarship employs multiple frames and methodologies for understanding politics and culture and cannot be cleanly sequestered into discrete analytical categories. Thus, in different ways, the scholars in this collection are attuned to central terms that subtend and extend into questions of representation, narrative, praxis, race, space, gender and sexual identity, class, history, affect, media, and more. Some are avowed in their formal political affiliations and some are not. In this, and despite some key absences, they represent literary criticism and politics as more than homogenous, as more than a single centimeter on an academic yardstick or an annual reunion of friends at a favorite conference.

In keeping with what I understood to be an animating principle congruent with this volume's tacit political logic, contributions were solicited without instructions on specific themes to be covered, archives to be explored, rhetorical approaches to be employed, authors to include, or (with the exception of "Periods and Histories") temporal ambit to be delineated. I reached out to scholars with a sincere statement of admiration for their scholarship, shared my vision for an alternative to standard guidebooks, and explicitly promised the total freedom to do what they wanted to do with the word, words, or moment in time that I suggested—including changing that word or date. Sometimes they did, sometimes they didn't, but the choices were finally and rightly theirs.

Ultimately, choices about archive and period and focus and terminology had to belong to the contributors because the expertise was and is theirs; a responsible and representative companion to "politics and literature in English" could only be constituted inductively, from particular thinkers in all their rich diversity of convictions, fields, trainings, tastes, experiences, backgrounds, and commitments. Thus, while I feel confident that readers of this volume will gain significantly from reading individual chapters, I encourage you to connect concepts and related discourses and terms as they become visible by reading and understanding multiple pieces together, for no individual scholarly voice, perspective, or intervention can be exhaustive, final, or located outside of much larger conversations. Chapters are not adequate metonyms.

Anthony Reed reminds us in his chapter "Sound and Print" that "aesthetic autonomy rooted in group practice does not necessarily translate into political freedom." Neither does literary-critical autonomy, whether rooted in practices of the group or the individual. While neither the humanities nor democracy seem to be on the upswing, authoritarianism around the globe most certainly is, with theocratic and anti-democratic agendas that have moved very quickly from speculative dystopias to sickening headline news in the rearview mirror. And perhaps it must be observed that the many reactionary victories over basic democratic freedoms have been achieved by right-wing forces relying very little on the presumed political powers of poetry, fiction, and literary criticism. There is no program of direct action to be derived from the organization, theory, and practice of this volume. If there is a persuasive theme to be found, however, let it be one that encourages knowledge and argumentation in place of presumption; that recognizes and resists the signal dangers of mistaking private convictions for general conditions; and that acknowledges how much is lost when a spirit of free and generous scholarly inquiry is replaced by the momentary pleasures of heresy hunting, ideological parochialism, sectarian groupthought, and shrill ignorance denying the virtues of honest and informed disagreement.

Finally, a word to those who rightly object that this gigantic volume has gigantic, even unforgivable, lacunae: yes, and some of them keep me up at night. I agree completely, even as the title of the volume (which I chose) itself raises doubts. This is partially because of all the great literatures in English that don't appear between these covers, and partially because the selective criterion of English itself is fundamentally reductive. In "Nations and States," Jessie Reeder compellingly makes this point and quite justly calls into question the primary delimiting linguistic factor of the volume. Pointing to "the widespread assumption of a unity between nation, state, and language," she not only laments the fact that "many scholars remain themselves unilingual and thus ill-equipped to grapple fully with the nonalignment of their fields with a single literary language" but shows concretely and compellingly—in English and Spanish—the implications of this status quo. She is right, of course, especially in the United States and especially now, when opportunities and incentives and requirements for learning second (let alone third) languages are disappearing not just from elementary schools but from English PhD programs. And as Roland Végső shows in his chapter "Translation," necessary and transformative conjunctions of literature and politics will require more than an expanded marketplace for English-language versions of texts from around the world.

As for the essays not included here, at this late date I can only offer another 40 entries for some other editor's consideration: Continents, Territories, Novel, Lyric, Kinship, Memory, History, Intention, Agriculture, Democracy, Speculation, Authoritarianism, Reproduction, Choice, Health, Incarceration, Death, Allegory, Institutions, Tribes, Toxins, Intoxication, Suicide, Atmosphere, Fire, Food, Violence, Migration, Domesticity, Prohibition, Disability, Religion, Epistemology, Ontology, Style, Anthologies, Militaries, Monarchies, Obscenity, and Conclusions. Until those entries are written, I hope you take as much from these essays as I did.

Notes

1. Macpherson, Sandra. "The Political Fallacy." *PMLA*, vol. 132, no. 5 (October 2017): pp. 1214–1219.
2. While Fred Moten famously raises the possibility that "the political is nothing other than a public slippage into the self" (104) that presents radically different challenges and requires radically different tactics for differently racialized populations, I mean to evoke the more ordinary disciplinary usage familiar to political scientists and political theorists (in English) since at least the 1980s: what Cedric J. Robinson and others stipulated "as an ordering principle arranging the relationship of things and of people within society" (229). Moten, Fred. *The Universal Machine* (Duke UP, 2018); Robinson, Cedric J. *The Terms of Order: Political Science and the Myth of Leadership* (State U of New York P, 1980). The task of distinguishing between "politics" and "the political," which is central to many strains of political science and political theory that entered English-language academic discourse in the 1980s, is too frequently ignored in literary studies and beyond the scope of this introduction. For an efficient overview, see: Wiley, James. *Politics and the Concept of the Political: the Political Imagination* (Routledge, 2016), especially pages 3-17.
3. Sachs, Jeffrey. "Steep Rise in Gag Orders, Many Sloppily Drafted." *PEN* 100 (January 2022), https://pen.org/steep-rise-gag-orders-many-sloppily-drafted/. See also "Banned Book Data Snapshot" https://pen.org/report/banned-usa-growing-movement-to-censor-books-in-schools/
4. See Busher, Joel and Lee Jerome, editors. *The Prevent Duty in Education: Impact, Enactment and Implications* (Palgrave MacMillan, 2020).
5. See Dondo, Aurélia, et al. *Chaos, Conflict, Impunity: PEN International Case List, 2021*, https://pen-international.org/app/uploads/Chaos-Conflict-Impunity-PEN-International-Case-List-2021.pdf
6. Ruttenburg, Nancy. "Introduction: Is the Novel Democratic?" *Novel: A Forum on Fiction*, vol. 47, no. 1 (Spring 2014): pp. 1–10.

PART I

Connecting Literature and Politics

1
AESTHETICS AND AFFECT

Tyler Bradway

Affect theory has revolutionized the way that literary and cultural scholars understand the politics of art.[1] Broadly, affect theory is a philosophy of sensation, which is distinct from the personal "feelings" that are conventionally associated with emotions. Inspired by the philosopher Baruch Spinoza, affect theory literally attends to the body's capacity "to affect" and "to be affected." Defined in the most expansive terms, bodies are nothing more or less than their affective capacities and their unlimited potential for change. Indeed, Spinoza scandalously asserts that we do not yet know what a body can do. His point is that the body has agencies of its own, which are not determined by nor fully accessible to the mind. In this way, affect theory challenges rationalist philosophies that center consciousness as the essence of being, perhaps most familiarly exemplified by René Descartes' mantra, "I think, therefore I am" (25). Affect theory contributes to posthumanism, new materialism, eco-criticism, and other theories that reject anthropocentrism. After all, ticks, rats, and whales have affects that enable them to sensually navigate a material lifeworld. Affect theory's displacement of the human subject also converges with existing theories of embodiment in cultural studies and critical theory, especially feminism, queer theory, critical race theory, psychoanalysis, and performance studies. They too understand affect as a force that has been repressed within the humanist tradition and, in turn, weaponized against minoritized groups marked as too emotional or too unruly in their embodiments. Affect theory responds by affirming sensation as a pre-subjective current of potential that connects bodies directly to social power and to the unfolding of life itself.

Given this ontology, affect theory sees the aesthetic as not fundamentally different from any other assemblage of affects. As Gilles Deleuze and Félix Guattari contend, "the work of art is a being of sensation and nothing else" (164). Art is thus affective in two senses: it composes a "bloc of sensations" through its own materials, such as words, paint, or rhythm; and these compositions "directly impact living bodies, organs, nervous systems," stimulating affects in unpredictable ways (Grosz 4). In the tradition inaugurated by philosopher Immanuel Kant, aesthetics are understood as involving a particular power of judgment, which evaluates objects (including the objects conventionally understood as "art," but also naturally occurring objects such as flowers); when certain criteria are met certain sensations are experienced, and those objects may then qualify as "beautiful" or "sublime" (and for theorists after Kant, "good" or "bad" art).

Affect theory, however, is less interested in judgment itself than in understanding art's imbrication with the means by which life transforms itself. For this reason, it may seem to let the specificity of art slip through its fingers. A Picasso, a commercial, and a coffee cup are all "blocs of sensation" that stimulate the body. Who is to say which is better or worse, or even which is art? This is a familiar problem in postmodernity, where firm distinctions between popular culture and art have been eroded by mass commodification (Jameson). Yet, for affect theory, aesthetics are a question of pragmatics: theory does not stand outside the work and assess from above; rather, it plunges into the artwork to trace what does, unleashes, and realizes through its own forms and within its social situation.

Affect theory thus rethinks art as a live event in the present rather than a representation, symptom, or mediation of a prior reality. Art is a visceral and fundamentally relational encounter with its own agencies to act on us. Such an approach dethrones the critic as a special interpreter of the aesthetic object. In fact, art is understood to produce its own affect theories (Frank), which can be gleaned through style, surface, and form. This is why aesthetics play a vital role in affect theory. Like tuning forks, aesthetics vibrate with feelings, resonances, and intensities that cascade through the social field prior to being codified as signs, symbols, or ideologies. Hence, affect theorists create new taxonomies to grasp emergent or ignored "structures of feeling" (Williams), such as "ugly feelings" (Ngai), "cruel optimism" (Berlant), "wallflower aesthetics" (Glavey), "brown feeling" (Muñoz), or "side affects" (Malatino). Across these taxonomies, affect opens a window onto unarticulated antagonisms and intimacies that give shape to the social field.

At the same time, the aesthetic *intervenes* in the social by recalibrating sensation. We can see this affective politics, for example, in the work of Jacques Rancière, who highlights the aesthetic's capacity to rupture the "distribution of the sensible." For Rancière, the aesthetic wields the unruliness of sensation against the demarcation of sensibilities, comportments, and feelings, which are wedded to structures of social inequality and naturalize their relations of power. Think, for example, of the tears of white fragility that recenter whiteness at the moment it is challenged; or the "mansplaining" that boisterously delegitimizes women's authority even before it has been voiced; or the toxic positivity that shoves aside any "unredeemed" sadness, suffering, or trauma. Such moments show that affect always has a political (or "biopolitical") dimension, even when it seems merely personal. Politics coordinates and entrains bodies through their affects, which may feel natural even though they are highly regulated by social norms and systems of power.

Despite its imbrication with power, affect cannot be easily constrained. For Brian Massumi, affect actually is potential as such. In his metaphor, affect is an "overspill" (*Parables* 215) that leaks out from any container. Affect endlessly outpaces the ideological structures and discursive scripts that cohere social life. From this vantage, affect theory can sound more hopeful than other poststructural accounts of power, which tend to emphasize how agency is inevitably bound up with whatever it opposes (Butler). But the tension between affective potential and structural determination remains an unsolved problem within affect theory. Some critics (Berlant 2011; Ngai 2015; Dango) situate affect as a symptom and negotiation of crises in contemporary capitalism. Others (Sedgwick; Flatley; Snediker) turn to affect to articulate the "middle-ranges of agency," which counter theories of power caught between the extremes of repression and liberation (Sedgwick 13). And still others (Muñoz; Freeman; Dinshaw) see affect as a shimmering crystal of untapped potential that transports bodies beyond a claustrophobic present—into a future to come or a past yet to be.

Because it locates agency in residues and overspills, ruptures and unfurlings, affect theory has been understandably critiqued for romanticizing formlessness, both political (Kornbluh) and aesthetic (Brinkema).² I will demonstrate, to the contrary, that affect theory embraces form as a necessary and enabling constraint immanent to a body. Aesthetics help us to see the vital tension between affect and form, which gives shape to intimate and social bonds. Still, it is true that a rhetorical overemphasis on viscerality can make it hard to specify the affective qualities and relations of an aesthetic object. Intensity starts to seem like an end in itself, and escape the necessary answer to any social problem. After all, if affect's power lives outside of language, then how can we think of form as anything other than a diminishment and capture of potential? How can we read for affect if it is, by definition, non-signifying and non-linguistic?

To answer these questions, this chapter resuscitates narrative as an affective form. Affect theory critiques narrative as too representational, linear, and subjective to render the mobility of affect.³ Anything less than "pure" abstraction seems to contain affect within bodies or persons that feel.⁴ By entirely dispensing with bodies, however, we risk losing sight of affect theory's foundational contribution to the politics of aesthetics—namely, the importance of relationality. Affect is relational in the sense that it passes between bodies, opening them to sociality itself. Affect is contagious and promiscuous, pre-personal and hypersocial (Freeman 2019). Affect composes collectives through its bodily circulation and uptake. This is why affect can be so effectively wielded in cultural politics (Ahmed), such as the Right's weaponizing paranoia at trans people to cement the bonds of cis-white-Christian nationalism. Thus, affect theory needs formalist methods to trace the dynamism of affect as it weaves social bonds into particular patterns.

I locate such a method in affect theory's unappreciated reliance on narrative. In particular, I develop Berlant's theory of "the scene" to grasp the relationalities that affect and aesthetics unfold. Reading for the "unfolding scene" decenters the "rupturing event," which overemphasizes punctual flights from representation. By contrast, the unfolding scene foregrounds a crisis of social relationality and illuminates the structures of affective attachment that emerge to manage that crisis. To highlight the political stakes of these attachments, I juxtapose brief readings of *Midsommar* (2019) and *Detransition, Baby* (2021), which narrate queer and trans relational forms in opposition to hetero-patriarchal kinship. Together, these texts push affect theory to reevaluate narrative as an aesthetic form, because it can render the pliability and durability of affective relations as well as their imbrication with the politics of race, gender, and sexuality. Narrative shifts us from a focus on "the body" to "bodies-in-groups," defined less by identity than by the affective labor, or group work, they undertake to transform themselves into a scene of belonging.

Scene Theory and the Crisis of Relationality

At first glance, affect theory seems to draw a sharp line between affect and narrative. For example, Brian Massumi argues that emotion is "qualified intensity," inserted into "semantically and semiotically formed progressions, into narrativizable action-reaction circuits, into function and meaning" (*Parables* 28). By contrast, affect is neither "ownable [n]or recognizable" by a subject, because it is a "never-to-be-conscious autonomic remainder… disconnected from meaningful sequencing, from narration" (25). The disconnect between affect and narrative is key to Massumi's resuscitation of the event within cultural theory, which portrays structure as atemporal. For Massumi, structure is "the place where nothing ever happens, that explanatory heaven in which all eventual permutations are prefigured in a self-consistent set of invariant generative rules" (27). It may seem strange to equate narrative—an irreducibly temporal form—with stasis. Yet structuralism theorizes narrative as a rule-bound system that combines a finite set of elements to generate stories. Narrative may be temporal, but its temporality is understood as teleological, as driving toward a predetermined outcome such as birth, marriage, or death. In this view, narrative is a paradigmatic structure. It straightens affect's recursive nonlinearity, its boundless potential for change, into predictable sequence.

Yet affect theory also needs narrative to render the autonomy and potentiality of affect. Massumi's chapter is organized around four "stories," and he relies on narrative idioms, such as suspense, incipience, and unfolding, to recover the affective potentials that overspill linear causality. By highlighting affect theory's rhetorical and conceptual reliance on narrative, I am not catching it in a contradiction. Rather, I argue that affect theory offers a distinct theory of narrative, which is easy to miss because of its understandably strong critique of structuralism. Massumi playfully acknowledges this distinction when he observes that "the feedback of 'higher'" functions can take such forms as the deployment of narrative in essays about the breakdown of narrative" (39). Here, Massumi underscores that the putatively "higher functions" of the mind (cognition, subjectivity, narrative) are not divorced from sensation. Like the Freudian unconscious, they depend on and feed back "into the realm of intensity and recursive causality" (30). Narrative is not only a dampener of affect, then, but also a resonance machine in its own right, with effects uncontained by its organizing principles.

By foregrounding such effects on the body, affect theory counters postmodernity's "crisis of representation," or the waning faith in language to represent an exterior social reality. For some poststructural theories, language is a closed system of signifiers that refers only and endlessly to itself. By contrast, affect theory sees the body as a pleated fold of affect and thought, a place where intensity and sociality meet. As Massumi writes, the body "infolds *contexts*, it infolds volitions and cognitions that are nothing if not situated" (30). Thus, affect theory is not an uncritical fetish for unmediated experience outside of discourse, as some contend (Leys). Rather, affect registers the dynamic relations among bodies, signs, and contexts as they transform one another. This is why affect is key to grasping the shapeless "impasse" (Berlant 2011, 4) that defines the contemporary. As Lauren Berlant contends, the endless upheavals of mass precarity unravel any sense of stability or futurity. In response, we flail, experiment, and adjust (Berlant 2018). We hunt for forms to sustain ourselves and our worlds. Affect takes the pulse of an incoherent, or semi-coherent, body politic as it stumbles along in search of a footing.

To give form to this undulating social field, affect theory needs narrative because it can render the scattershot volatilities of agency and constraint in densely populated scenes of embodiment. Take, for example, Berlant and Kathleen Stewart's public feelings project, *The Hundreds*, which organizes itself around brief narrated scenes of "hundred-word units or units of hundred multiples" (ix). The word count is a simple constraint, but it underscores that the aesthetic is not a realm of "unconstrained expression" (Massumi, *Politics* 174). Rather, aesthetic affect is bound up with and emerges from its formal limits.[5] Agency thus lies in "playing with the constraints, not avoiding them" (12). For Berlant and Stewart, this play emerges as narration in search of "points of precision where something is happening. We don't presume what's going on in a scene but look around at what might be" (28). Narrative shifts from a retrospective form that orders events after the fact to an event that lacks a single or definitive horizon. "To convert an impact into a scene, to prehend objects as movement," Berlant and Stewart write, "retains a scene's status as life in suspension, the way an extract in cooking conveys the active element in a concentrated substance" (8). Narration is the mechanism of conversion, the means by which Berlant and Stewart distill the potency of a situation. Hence, their writing strives to "stretch out a scene, hold up a world's jelling, and register change, which is not the antithesis of chains" (117). In other words, affect theory dilates scenes with narrative, returning them to a threshold that refuses oppositions between change and stasis, event and sequence, cause and effect, freedom and constraint.

Of course, the "scene" is a unit of analysis in theories of performance, rhetoric, narratology, film theory, and dramaturgical sociology. Yet affect theory has a specific definition of the scene worth highlighting. For Silvan Tomkins, scenes need "at least one affect and at least one object of that affect" (qtd. Frank and Wilson 102). Recall that, for Tomkins, "any affect may have any 'object'" (qtd. Sedgwick 19). This is one of affect theory's foundational insights. In Eve Sedgwick's words, "Affects can be, and are, attached to things, people, ideas, sensations, relations, activities, ambitions, institutions, and any number of other things, including other affects. Thus, one can be excited by anger, disgusted by shame, or surprised by joy." For this reason, it is rarely obvious which affects form a scene, or to which objects they attach, especially since affects can attach to themselves, like taking pleasure in pain. In short, scenes narrate a drama of affective relationality as it unfolds. This is why Berlant contends that scenes, such as the Freudian primal scene, are provoked by "over-presence of affect that makes it impossible to narrate it away and to narrate yourself away from it" (Poletti and Rak 269). Narration is not so much obliterated as twisted around, pressurized by, and snagged on the affective relations that compose a scene. The scene presents a disturbance, but it may not be disturbing; it might be surprising, titillating, boring, or some strange mix of these and other feelings.

The scene unfolds a crisis in relationality that takes shape as a narrative problem. By turning to the unfolding scene, we move away from the rupturing event as definitive of affect's relationship to aesthetics. Phrased differently, affect does not only start where representation stops. Affects inhere within and as scenes of relationality that have narrative form. Understood as a "vibrant tableau" (Berlant and Stewart 8), the scene is a place where affect and aesthetics meet to confront unsettled relations: where one stands in relation to an event; how affects and objects attach to one another; when an event becomes, or fails to become, a sequence; and how the scene of narration relates to the scene it narrates. Scenes beckon for a method of affective reading that can trace the circuits of relation that overlay and unfurl through them.

Yet, as the next section shows, it will not be enough to approach a scene as if its relations are entirely self-contained or self-constrained. Rather, reading for unfolding scenes attends to the torsions between affective relations and social forms, which organize bodies into certain collective modes. Famously, Massumi redescribes walking as "controlled falling" (*Politics* 12) to stress that the body cannot simply escape its constraints, whether internal (lung capacity, stride) or external (gravity, accessible architecture). Yet a focus on "the body" singular obscures the fact that sociality is less like a solitary body out for a stroll and more like a three-legged race: bodies, forms, and contexts impinge on and constrain one another in a vibrating field. The frictions between affect and form thus point to a politics of relationality.

Bodies That Gather

Ari Aster's horror drama, *Midsommar* (2019), unfolds a crisis of relationality that moves from the nuclear family toward a queer engroupment that is simultaneously reparative and oppressive. The film centers on Dani Ardor, whose last name is one of many nods to affect. Dani's sister commits suicide by attaching a long hose to an exhaust pipe and taping it to her mouth. At the same time, she murders their parents by filling their room with the carbon monoxide fumes; the hose connects the family's bodies like an umbilical cord, or the lines in a genealogy. Distraught with grief, Dani looks for support from her boyfriend, Christian, an anthropology graduate student. But Christian diminishes Dani's pain and gaslights her about their relationship. Rather than breaking up, as he desires, Christian invites Dani on a trip to Sweden with his male friends. The group is guided by Pelle, who takes them to the Hårga, an isolated commune where he was raised. Once there, they witness the midsummer celebration, which takes place every 90 years. The celebration entails ritual senicide of two elderly members, a maypole dance among the women to anoint the May Queen, an impregnation ceremony with an outsider, and, finally, a sacrifice of nine humans: four outsiders, four Hårga, and one selected by Dani, the newly crowned May Queen. Dani chooses Christian as the final sacrifice, and in an infamous final shot, she smiles as he is consumed in flames.

Clearly, *Midsommar* is a horror film. However, the narrative weds us so tightly to Dani's grief that her slow initiation into a cult feels more like a fairy tale where her desperate wish for a loving family is realized. Indeed, the film's horror lies less in flayed skin and smashed skulls, although those images appear. Rather, it emerges through a narrative parallax: we (the audience and eventually the characters) know the commune intends to sacrifice innocent lives against their will; yet the Hårga's culture of collective belonging is presented as a nourishing contrast to the alienation of the heteronormative couple and the modern nuclear family. Rather than judge the Hårga from a transcendent position of morality, the film plunges into the commune's cosmology to a degree that it seems utopian. This parallax generates the eerie mood of *Midsommar* even more than its clever subversion of horror tropes, such as setting nearly every scene in the bright sun or locating most of the murders off-screen.

What makes the Hårga reparative is not simply that they replace Dani's lost family. On the contrary, the Hårga live, conceive, and experience affective relations in ways that radically redefine "family." These relations take conventional social forms, such as communal child-rearing, meals, and labor. But they also structure the Hårga's relationship to their own bodies. When a member fails to commit suicide, for example, everyone wails and writhes in a shared expression of his suffering. Each body echoes and amplifies the individual's pain. The cry becomes collective, a hypersocial affect not consigned to interiority or the self. Rather, affect circulates in public and constitutes these bodies as a group. In fact, the Hårga do not have clear distinctions between public and private, or self and other, a point made clear when an outsider's question, "What do you do when you wanna jerk off?" goes unanswered. Masturbation—understood by outsiders as an isolated and solitary act—does not make conceptual, social, or architectural sense, because every body is implicated in every other body.

Thus, *Midsommar* emphasizes that Dani's suffering is not simply the result of one toxic relationship but a toxic social order that stigmatizes negative affect. Note, for example, an early scene where Pelle empathizes with Dani. He is the only person to acknowledge her loss, and she instantly becomes upset. As she rushes into the bathroom to cry, the camera tracks above so we cannot see her face. In an unbroken shot, Dani opens the door to the apartment's bathroom and enters an airplane bathroom. There is no cut, yet the narration elides the scene of breakdown. We are plunged into a different moment without a clear sense of what has triggered Dani. She stifles her cry and silently returns to her seat on the plane next to Christian. The transition underscores that such triggering happens to Dani frequently. But the elision of the cry intensifies Dani's anguish and her internalization of it—the pain she feels in not being able to let it out. There is no scene of belonging for her feelings to unfold.

Such a scene emerges after Dani discovers Christian in the reproduction ritual. Dani witnesses him having sex with a female Hårga as a group of women surround them, breathing, chanting, singing, and literally guiding Christian to orgasm. Dani collapses, heaving. A group of women ushers Dani to bed, where she curls into a fetal position. She crawls to the floor, gasping, as one woman holds Dani's face in her hands and six others surround them. Breath by breath, they sob in unison. The cries layer so that they resonate and crescendo into a rhythmic shout.[6] We could call this catharsis by way of Lamaze; after all, Dani is being "reborn" into a new family. But rather than read for signifiers, I wish to note that an elided affect has now been dilated in narrative time and space. Until this moment, the film, like Dani, has choked an affect that now breathes as a scene. It is an unfolding scene in the precise sense that we cannot easily demarcate which affects and objects are in play or how they attach to one another. Certainly, there is Dani's loss of the allegorically named Christian, redoubling the loss of her family. Her dread, fear, rage, and sadness at being abandoned are manifest—and perhaps so too is Dani's unspoken resentment of and desire to abandon her sister. Yet these affective relations overlay Dani's yearning to be held by a group that does not simply recognize her pain but literally experiences it. Could these women be sisters like the one she lost? Might they be sisters in an entirely different sense? At stake in the scene is a qualitative and structural change in Dani's affective relations: the potential for attaching to different objects and attaching differently to objects.

Midsommar seems to present the outcome as a given, like a fairy tale or structuralist narratology. The breathing scene cuts to an illustration of the May Queen, as if Dani's fate is pre-ordained. Indeed, the film opens with a tableau that illustrates every event of the narrative. Such moments adopt the Hårga's cosmology of cyclical repetition and social rituals keyed to the seasons and the stars. They do not share modernity's conception of linear progress. Yet the Hårga do have a notion of change, uniquely linked to affect. Each letter of their runic alphabet "represents one of the 16 affects, which are graded from most holy to unholy." Their sacred texts, which they compare to "emotional sheet music," are "always evolving" as "intuitive" members add new affects. In other words, affects are not static or known in advance; affect is the site of ontological and social change. Notably, the authors of these affects are "deliberate product[s] of inbreeding," underscoring the Hårga's queer distance from normative kinship. Their queerness is by no means utopian: bloodlines—strictly white—are "well preserved" by elders; social life is structured around a rigid gender binary; and the bonds of the group rely on a sharp distinction between insiders and outsiders. The Hårga also seem to repeat modernity's suppression of affect in a different form. Sewn into a bear skin for his sacrifice, Christian is told: "Mighty and dreadful beast. With you, we purge our most unholy affects. We banish you now to the deepest recesses, where you may reflect on your wickedness." To be sure, Christian is odious, and like many characters in horror, we are urged to desire his death. Yet his narrative function converges with the Hårga's belief that "unholy" affects can be bound to an object and cast out through violence that purifies and renews their collective bonds.

Midsommar thus poses a philosophical and political question about relationality: is it possible to detach from patriarchal heteronormativity without reproducing its violence? Can a different economy of affective and social belonging be sustained? Rather than answer these questions, I want to underscore how reading for the unfolding scene illuminates them in a distinct way. When confronted with a narrative ending, as Caroline Levine argues, critics "spin out implied stories in which new forms take shape beyond a narrative's end" (110). For Levine, such stories extend the "political ordering principles that are at work in the text to understand its implied rules for ordering the extratextual world." Beyond the film's ending, we can easily project Dani's role in the ritualized white supremacist and hetero-patriarchal world of the Hårga, from her daily meals to her death at 72. Harder to grasp, however, is her affective relation to this social structure. Affect, by definition, changes. It cannot stay the same. Extending narrative time requires that we also account for affect's inevitable qualitative changes. Therefore, Dani's infamous smile in the final shot cannot simply be read as a signifier of narrative closure. Of course, we might ask of this moment: Is she happy? Sane? Does she smile alone, or with the Hårga who are just outside the frame? Is this a feminist triumph or tragedy? But answering these questions does not account for the scene's continued unfolding. While the form this social world will take is predictable, Dani's affective relation to it is much less so. Dani's smile will transition to another (and another) affect, which may even attach to the smile itself. Affective relations extend into the future and the past, which *Midsommar* stresses by literally overlaying the Ardors' corpses in the landscape of Dani's present. An unfolding scene can be hard to escape, even as its unfolding keeps the potential for change alive.

Narrative is a form, then, that illuminates the durability and dynamism of affective relations. We become affect theorists, by necessity, when confronting the politics of a text. This is because affect and form co-constitute the social, as *Midsommar* illuminates. Dani has been liberated from a toxic social order and entered one that genuinely nourishes her; but as a queer social form, the cult is no less violent and equally (if not more) invested in the regulating the body's affects. *Midsommar* answers a crisis of relationality with a relational form—cult—that ironically reproduces the violence of hetero-patriarchal kinship. In the next section, I turn to an ending that, instead, stretches out a crisis in relationality to foreground the desire for a social form that sustains queer and trans kinship—and to stress the pain of its absence.

Queer Belonging as Design Problem

Like *Midsommar*, Torrey Peters' comic realist novel *Detransition, Baby* (2021) confronts a crisis in relationality. Where *Midsommar* may seem to resolve this crisis, *Detransition, Baby* stretches it out to an almost excruciating degree. Peters, a trans woman, dedicates her novel to "divorced cis women, who, like me, had to face starting their life over without either reinvesting in the illusions from the past, or growing bitter about the future" (1). This dedication captures two key affective relations in the novel: those between trans and cis women, and those between trans women and time. The novel centers on the queer relational form of the "triad," or throuple, in which three partners coordinate their intimacy together. Unlike the classic heteronormative triangle, where one partner (usually a woman) serves as the object of exchange between two others (usually men), the throuple names a yearning for reciprocal exchanges among partners that also sustain the group (110). *Detransition, Baby* upends the conventional focus on sex as the glue for triadic bonds. Instead, three people attempt to reconcile their conflicting desires to have a child and raise a family together: Reese, a white trans woman who desperately yearns for a child but fears the opportunity is lost; Ames, formerly Amy, Reese's ex-girlfriend, also white, who detransitioned and unwittingly impregnated his cis-girlfriend; and Katrina, Ames' mixed-race girlfriend and boss, who is unfamiliar with queer and trans cultures but is curious about non-normative kinship. The novel's 11 chapters are all marked by their position in time relative to Katrina's date of conception (i.e., "Eight years before conception"). Shifting between their narratives, *Detransition, Baby* struggles with what Reese calls "The *Sex and the City* Problem," which is that "women still [find] themselves with only four major options to save themselves, options represented by the story arcs of the four female characters of *Sex and the City*" (9). The options are: find a partner, have a baby, have a career, or "express oneself in art or writing." In Reese's view, "Every generation of women reinvented this formula over and over... blending it and twisting it, but never quite escaping it." This is a problem of unfolding a new plot for queer and trans life as much as it is of "re-narrativiz[ing]" one's affective relations to these existing plots (56).

As the novel stresses, the *Sex and the City* problem is exponentially harder for trans women due to stigma, precarity, and transphobic violence. Indeed, Ames believes that "trans women knew what trans women were, they know how to *be*, but they didn't know how to *do*... there's almost nothing out there on how to actually live" (99). This is both an affective and social problem. Trans women of his "cohort" are a "lost generation" (99, 101): "We have no elders, no stable groups, no one to teach us to countenance pain." Without stable bonds, trans suffering ricochets and intensifies. This is why Ames insists that "part of being queer can be a design problem. I mean, Jesus, just look at our sex toys" (274). To think of queerness and transness as a design problem means entwining affect and form: pleasure and the toys to elicit it, or care and the infrastructures to sustain it. Ames exuberantly dreams that, together, the triad can "break the pattern of typical two-parent, even queer two-parent nuclear families" by confronting the "logistics of the replacement." The novel shares this aspiration, despite critiquing Ames' "eagerness to fix problems rather than feel them." Yet his designs fizzle as the plot turns on potent misunderstandings and affective damage between Ames and Reese, Reese and Katrina, Katrina and Ames—and, by extension, between trans women, trans and cis women, and white women and women of color. Rather than just accumulate more damage, however, the frustration of Ames' plans is narratively important. As its dedication suggests, *Detransition, Baby* deflates unfettered idealism *and* refuses crushing bitterness—it craves a future for trans desires to be satisfied and trans bond to be sustained, even if it knows that future may not come any time soon.

This is why the novel ends in the present tense as the time ticks away toward Katrina's decision to have, or not have, an abortion. In this context, time is a biological, ontological, juridical, and normative constraint on Katrina's body—and time is running out. Once naively idealistic and fetishistic about queer and trans kinship, Katrina is now uncertain. The difficulty of the triad's design has dawned on her: they cannot all be equal partners, or equal in the sense experiencing the same power and privilege as mothers in a cis-heteronormative world. Still, Ames makes a last-minute pitch that their frustrated affect testifies to the validity of their relational experimentation: "Maybe this is so awkward and hard and without obvious precedent because we're trying to imagine our own solution, to reinvent something for ourselves, whatever kind of... women we are" (337). Katrina and Reese reply, "Maybe," and they sip tea as the clock ticks. The narration ends by gathering their affective relations into an unfolding scene:

> They are together, and miles from each other, their thoughts turning to themselves, then turning to the baby, each in her own way contemplating how her tenuous rendition of womanhood has become dependent upon the existence of this little person, who is not yet, and yet may not be.

Their fantasies share the same object, but they do not share the same fantasy. Affect circulates into a scene of queer and trans attachment shot through with specific feelings—desire, fear, disappointment, shame, regret—enabled and constrained by a generational struggle, a cis- and hetero-patriarchal social order, and the passing of time itself. The unfolding scene stretches out this crisis of relationality in the hopes that affective messiness (in all its overlaying weaves of relation) could itself be the basis for a new kind of queer engroupment.

Whereas *Midsommar* displaces the violence of heteronormativity only to resurrect it as a cult, *Detransition, Baby* knows better. Its suspension of narrative closure might seem hopeful, but only if we forget Reese's and Amy/Ames' desperate need for relational forms in their present (and their past) that can endure, preserve, sustain, and enable trans bonds. Affect theory can grasp these middle ranges of relationality, which lie between the subject and the mass, between utopia and more of the same. Between these thresholds, there are groups that work, and that must *do work*, to transform relationality from a passive background into a dynamic scene of agency.

Group Work

Aesthetics intensify affects, but they also transform sensations into scenes. Minimally, a scene needs an affect, object, and a relation that unfolds in time. Unfolding has a pace: slowed down, scenes reveal potentials that exceed a script; ramped up, scenes illuminate patterns beyond the scales of human perception. A scene is thus an acute site to witness the composition of relationality as affective labor, as group work. Narrative foregrounds the aesthetic and political constraints that make group work possible, fraught, and potentially transformative as a social practice. Spinoza is right: we do not yet know what a body can do. But we also do not yet know what bodies can do together. Narrative gives us a place to start.

Notes

1. For helpful overviews of affect theory, see Grattan; Gregg and Seigworth; Clough and Halley; and Houen.
2. See also Ingrid Nelson's chapter "Forms" in this volume.
3. See Breger for an important synthesis of affect and narrative theories.
4. See Brinkema.
5. For a convergent accounts, see Grosz and Levine.
6. On the biopolitics of breath, see Tremblay.

Works Cited

Ahmed, Sara. *The Cultural Politics of Emotion*. Routledge, 2004.
Barad, Karen. *Meeting the Universe Halfway: Quantum Physics and the Entanglement of Matter*. Duke UP, 2007.
Berlant, Lauren. *Cruel Optimism*. Duke UP, 2011.
———. "Genre Flailing." *Capacious: Journal for Emerging Affect Inquiry*, vol. 1, no. 2, 2018, pp. 156–162.
Berlant, Lauren and Kathleen Stewart. *The Hundreds*. Duke UP, 2019.
Bradway, Tyler. *Queer Experimental Literature: The Affective Politics of Bad Reading*. Palgrave, 2017.
———. "Queer Narrative Theory and the Relationality of Form." *PMLA*, vol. 136, no. 5, 2021, pp. 711–727.
Bradway, Tyler and Elizabeth Freeman, editors. *Queer Kinship: Race, Sex, Belonging, Form*. Duke UP, 2022.
Breger, Claudia. "Affects in Configuration: A New Approach to Narrative Worldmaking." *Narrative*, vol. 25, no. 2, 2017, pp. 227-251.
Brinkema, Eugenie. *The Forms of the Affects*. Duke UP, 2014.
———. *Life-Destroying Diagrams*. Duke UP, 2022.
Butler, Judith. *Bodies That Matter: On the Discursive Limits of "Sex."* Routledge, 1993.
Clough, Patricia, and Jean Halley, editors. *The Affective Turn: Theorizing the Social*. Duke UP, 2007.
Cvetkovich, Ann. *Depression: A Public Feeling*. Duke UP, 2012.
Dango, Michael. *Crisis Style: The Aesthetics of Repair*. Stanford UP, 2021.
Deleuze, Gilles and Félix Guattari. *What Is Philosophy?* Translated by Hugh Tomlinson and Graham Burchell, Columbia UP, 1994.
Descartes, René. *Discourse on Method and Related Writings*. Translated by Desmond M. Clarke, Penguin Books, 1999.
Dinshaw, Carolyn. *How Soon Is Now? Medieval Texts, Amateur Readers, and the Queerness of Time*. Duke UP, 2012.
Flatley, Jonathan. *Affective Mapping: Melancholia and the Politics of Modernism*. Harvard UP, 2008.

Frank, Adam. *Transferential Poetics, from Poe to Warhol.* Fordham UP, 2014.
Frank, Adam J. and Elizabeth A. Wilson. *A Silvan Tomkins Handbook: Foundations for Affect Theory.* U of Minnesota P, 2020
Freeman, Elizabeth. *Beside You in Time: Sense Methods and Queer Sociabilities in the American Nineteenth Century.* Duke UP, 2019.
———. *Time Binds: Queer Temporalities, Queer Histories.* Duke UP, 2010.
Glavey, Brian. *The Wallflower Avant-Garde: Modernism, Sexuality, and Queer Ekphrasis.* Oxford UP, 2015.
Grattan, Sean. "Affect Studies." *Bloomsbury Handbook of Literary and Cultural Theory,* edited by Jeffrey R. di Leo, Bloomsbury, 2018, pp. 333–342.
Gregg, Melissa, and Gregory J. Seigworth, editors. *The Affect Theory Reader.* Duke UP, 2010.
Grosz, Elizabeth. *Chaos, Territory, Art: Deleuze and the Framing of the Earth.* Columbia UP, 2008.
Houen, Alex, ed. *Affect and Literature.* Cambridge UP, 2020.
Jameson, Frederic. *Postmodernism, or The Cultural Logic of Late Capitalism.* Duke UP, 1991.
Kornbluh, Anna. *The Order of Forms: Realism, Formalism, and Social Space.* U of Chicago P, 2019.
Leys, Ruth. "The Turn to Affect: A Critique." *Critical Inquiry,* vol. 37, no. 3, 2011, pp. 434–472.
Massumi, Brian. *Parables of the Virtual: Movement, Affect, Sensation.* Duke UP, 2002.
———. *Politics of Affect.* Polity, 2015.
Malatino, Hil. *Side Affects: On Being Trans and Feeling Bad.* U of Minnesota P, 2022.
Midsommar. Directed by Ari Aster, performances by Florence Pugh, Jack Reynor, William Jackson Harper, and Vilhelm Blomgren. A24, 2019.
Muñoz, José Esteban. *Cruising Utopia: The Then and There of Queer Futurity.* New York UP, 2009.
Ngai, Sianne. *Our Aesthetic Categories: Zany, Cute, Interesting.* Harvard UP, 2015.
———. *Ugly Feelings.* Harvard UP, 2007.
Peters, Torrey. *Detransition, Baby.* One World, 2021.
Poletti, Anna and Julie Rak. "The Blog as Experimental Setting: An Interview with Lauren Berlant." Identity Technologies: Constructing the Self Online, edited by Anna Poletti and Julie Rak. U of Wisconsin P, 2014, pp. 259–272.
Rancière, Jacques. *The Politics of Aesthetics: The Distribution of the Sensible.* Translated by Gabriel Rockhill, Bloomsbury, 2004.
Sedgwick, Eve Kosofsky. *Touching Feeling: Affect, Pedagogy, Performativity.* Duke UP, 2003.
Snediker, Michael D. *Queer Optimism.* U of Minnesota P, 2009.
Spinoza, Benedict de. *Ethics.* Translated by Edwin Curley, Penguin Books, 1994.
Tremblay, Jean-Thomas. *Breathing Aesthetics.* Duke UP, 2022.
Williams, Raymond. *Marxism and Literature.* Oxford UP, 1978.

2
FORMS
Ingrid Nelson

Bringing "forms" into a discussion of politics and literature may seem to muddy already murky waters. What are forms in the first place, and what do they have to do with either of the two main concepts of this volume? Can't we bypass abstruse musings on form and get right to the concrete materialities where literature and politics intersect? But as Aristotle reminds us, matter can only exist with a shaping form; indeed, the philosopher asserts that matter *desires* form (*Physics* 31). Forms are not fixed abstractions, things "out there" waiting to be occupied, like empty vessels. They are more like the rules of a game, meaningless until tested, followed, and adapted to specific circumstances. As we shall see, forms are the means by which literature is political and politics are literary.

Forms, as abstract patterns that make possible the articulation of disciplines, are not only shared in common by literature and politics; in fact, forms make possible expression and action in both domains. At the same time, the concrete practices of literature and politics can resist formal abstraction. This chapter examines how forms are central to a particular branch of politics known as "biopolitics," the political regulation of life, and how literature can both express biopolitics in its use of forms and use forms to shape it. It does so through a process the philosopher Giorgio Agamben has called "form-of-life," after the medieval monastic *forma vitae*. This is a set of rules for communal living that, in Agamben's interpretation, can be not so much restrictive as creative and facilitate an alternative political structure to repressive juridical rule. This discussion of form in literature and politics will focus especially on two case studies of poetry, as the literary genre most explicitly focused on form: Elizabeth Barrett Browning's nineteenth-century protest poem "The Cry of the Children," and an excerpt from Nathaniel Mackey's ongoing serial poem "Song of the Andoumboulou." These radically different examples suggest how poetic form can constitute a kind of form-of-life for challenging, subverting, and living within political hegemonies. More, they suggest that form's very constraints may offer a kind of freedom from political oppression that literature is uniquely suited to provide. But first, what is form?

A Brief Account of Form

A form is a shape or pattern that gives structure to matter. It can also be an agglomeration of qualities or their distillation. In other words, "form" is the name for commonalities among groups of things that, tautologically, we understand as related *because of* their common traits. Think of a tree. In thinking of it, you probably see a shape in your mind. That shape is determined by all the trees you have seen in your life, real or depicted, but is not identical to any of them. When philosophers understand the real world as ultimately constituted by minds, it is called "idealism," and when they conceive of the real world as ultimately constituted by non-mental things, they call it "materialism." The concept of "form" crosses the supposed boundary between the abstract realm of ideas and the realm of concrete matter to make structure apparent. In the words of the scholar Christopher Cannon, "Form is that which thought and things have in common" (5).

This border-crossing quality of form is at the heart of the two Classical theories of form that influence how we think about it today. For Plato, forms existed strictly in the realm of the ideal. They are the perfect abstractions that the tangible things of our world can only aspire to imitate. As such, Plato's concept of the relationship of form to matter to art is strictly hierarchical: the material world consists of imperfect imitations of the world of forms, and works of art (including literature) are one step further removed, imperfectly imitating the material world. In Plato's theory, forms exist in untouchable isolation, apart from the constant flux and change of the material world. Aristotle's philosophy of forms, by contrast, puts them in direct contact with matter. His theory of *hylomorphism*, a portmanteau of the Greek words for form and matter, asserts that no material object can exist without a shaping form. Thus, the flux we observe in the material world is a consequence of matter passing from one form into another (*Physics*; Ainsworth).

In literature, the word can take on different scales. "Form" might refer to particularities of rhyme or meter in poetry, but it might just as easily refer to genre: novels, plays, and epic poems are all distinct literary forms. Forms also interact with each other. We identify a literary work as a novel, its macroscopic form, in part because of its microscopic forms: prose sentences, a narrator, characters, plot actions; or we identify it as a play when characters speak in dialogue and settings and actions are described in stage directions. When we read literature in a classroom, we are often encouraged to look for literary forms, especially if we are reading poetry.

Ideas about form have powerfully shaped how we read literature, yet historically the concept of form largely ignores literature until modernity. In a sense, the concept of form is at the foundation of the Western tradition of political philosophy; after all, recall that some of Plato's key discussions about form appear in *Republic*, where he theorizes the ideal state. As the literary critic Caroline Levine puts it, "It is the work of form to make order. And this means that forms are the stuff of politics" (3). In this model, forms are not static patterns but active agents in political life. Levine identifies five qualities of forms: they are "*containing, plural, overlapping, portable, and situated*" (6). Her point is that mental abstraction is necessary for imagining and understanding forms; once imagined, however, their qualities of containment and boundedness give them power to influence the world. They are, in short, the means by which art and literature not only influence but indeed constitute politics.

Like "form," "politics" is a capacious term. In using it, I follow Aristotle's account of the formation of the *polis*, which states that "while it comes into existence for the sake of life, it exists for the good life" (*Politics* 1252b 28–30). That is, politics is the discipline of constituting and governing the *polis* that organizes itself around turning the biological fact of human life into a set of norms and practices that conduce to "the good life," a culturally contingent ethical concept. Agamben notes that Aristotle thus separates "a community of the simply living"—those without political agency, like enslaved persons or animals—from "a political community" (*Use of Bodies* 197). As we shall see, this construction of politics has implications for the ways that literary forms shape and are shaped by a politicization of life.

Literary Politics and the Persistence of Form

One aspect of what we now think of as literary form, rhetoric, was originally conceived and articulated as a political instrument. Classical treatises on rhetoric, such as Quintilian's *Institutiones Oratoriae* and pseudo-Cicero's *Rhetorica ad Herennium*, teach readers how to persuade others toward political action. To do so, the orator must master the forms of language that we now think of as characteristic of literary expression: everything from the sound of words in alliteration and rhyme, to the cadence of phrases, to figures like metaphors and antithesis. Used masterfully, these rhetorical techniques can, the treatise writers assert, effect political change by converting your opponents to your point of view and inspiring them to act, collectively, toward a political end. Shakespeare famously illustrates the power of this concept in *Julius Caesar*. Marc Antony, facing a crowd that viewed Caesar as a tyrant and Brutus as the hero who assassinated him, gives a funeral speech that, as a masterpiece of Ciceronian rhetoric, gradually turns his audience against Caesar's killer and inspires mob violence. In a moment where democracies across the globe are threatened by forms of authoritarianism, it is perhaps no longer possible to consider representations of politicized mob violence without hearing disconcerting echoes of the American Capitol riots on January 6, 2021. We are thus reminded that when detached from concrete examples, the intersection of rhetorical, aesthetic, and political forms can seem abstractly neutral, perhaps aesthetically even positive. Pragmatically, however, forms equally have the power to incite violent and repressive political action.

Politics, of course, has forms that are not only literary. Broadly speaking, political systems use several forms to organize people into categories. Medieval feudalism organized people in pyramidal hierarchies that were highly localized, for example, with a single lord controlling many serfs; modern Western democracies organize regional voting blocs to elect representatives, a structure meant to encapsulate and adjudicate the voices of all citizens in a smaller deliberative body. Again, we must be careful to recognize the repressive potential within forms, even those that purport to include or liberate. The writer Nathaniel Mackey, whose poetry I will examine later in this chapter, associates systems of classification with murderous imperialism when he warns of "the exclusionary, conquistadorial uses to which classificatory schemes tend to be put" (*Discrepant Engagement* 5). For example, the pseudo-scientific classification of the races in early modernity created a formal basis for acts of political oppression and atrocity that were themselves codified and perpetuated in a form: the political and economic structure of race-based slavery.

But it is important to observe that even forms that seem entirely aesthetic or entirely political continually cross these boundaries. As the philosopher Jacques Rancière has observed, aesthetic forms determine what is visible to a political community, and thereby delimit the horizons of political action. Nonetheless, Western aesthetic theory from the Classical to the modern periods has typically isolated aesthetic forms from their political entanglements. For example, Aristotle located tragic drama in the realm of aesthetics, thereby associating the form with ethics while isolating it from politics. One ideological strain of artistic modernism, emphasizing pure formalism and a credo of "art for art's sake," elides its reification of the revolutionary politics of the early twentieth century that was, in fact, espoused by many of its most prominent creators (Rancière 12–23). By way of illustration, Ezra Pound was once one of the most celebrated of modernist poets, winning the prestigious Bollingen Prize in 1948 even as he was institutionalized on criminal charges of treason for his role in disseminating Fascist propaganda in Mussolini's Italy. In one view, Pound's formal commitments align with his totalitarian politics; his masterwork, *The Cantos*, for example, emphasizes rupture and regeneration, and rejects what he sees as a decadent Western poetic form: "To break the pentameter, that was the first heave" (81.55). This example suggests the ways in which aesthetic and political forms can be mutually constitutive, with what Rancière calls "aesthetic regimes" supporting and insinuating political ideologies into our sensoria.

Biopolitics: Norms and Forms

But forms are not only top-down impositions; they also arise from more localized impulses to organize. In fact, the absence of hierarchically imposed forms creates a vacuum that forms rush in to fill, an insight as old as Aristotle's theory of hylomorphism. It is also at the heart of political theories of biopolitics. In fact, thinking of form as a conceptual intersection between literature and politics invites us to think about biopolitics because this branch of political theory addresses how the forms of matter shape and respond to the forms of politics—and vice versa.

The twentieth-century philosopher Michel Foucault identified biological life as a central category in modern politics. In *The History of Sexuality* vol. 1, Foucault describes what he sees as a seminal shift in Western politics that emerges around the seventeenth century. Political sovereignty, which had previously revolved around the power to take life as a response to threats or offenses to power, came to have an organizing, regulatory force that instead controlled the conditions of subjects' lives: "One might say that the ancient right to *take* life or *let* live was replaced by a power to *foster* life or *disallow* it to the point of death" (Foucault 138). The shift coincides with the overthrow of monarchical and aristocratic regimes throughout the West; their replacement with representative governments provides an administrative structure suited to overseeing and controlling the operations of bodily life. For Foucault, this meant largely replacing the power of laws, whose telos was the death penalty, with the power of *norms*, a set of "continuous regulatory and corrective mechanisms" that structured subjects' modes of living, including their habitations, health, and sexuality (144).

Norms permeate life much in the way that forms structure matter. They create a structure within which subjects self-regulate, often unaware of the political interests that created the norms they live by. But this does not mean that biopolitics is more innocuous or less deadly than premodern sovereign power; in fact, quite the contrary. The philosopher Giorgio Agamben, in the eponymous first volume of his *Homo Sacer* series, describes how a government based in biopolitics leads directly to the kind of horrific but utterly bureaucratic violence of genocide. Disagreeing with Foucault's historicizing of a shift from sovereign rule to biopolitics in modernity, Agamben identifies the origins of all Western models of governance in the sovereign's ability to define the "exception" to the law, the person who is outside the law's recognition while still living within the polis and thereby subject to acts of violence committed by the state. This power rests on a distinction between two kinds of life, expressed in the Greek terms *zoè*, biological life, and *bios*, political life. The sovereign's ability to separate human lives into one or the other category creates the *homo sacer*, the person who can be "killed but not sacrificed" because he has a biological but not a political life (*Homo Sacer* 83). Examples include slaves in the American antebellum South, and Jews in Nazi Germany. Agamben sees the violence visited on these groups not as aberrant with respect to Western liberalism, but as inevitably developing from the roots of biopolitics in the tradition of Western political thought going back to Aristotle.

Searching for an alternative biopolitics that could escape the logic of the sovereign exception and its horrors, Agamben explores a model of what he calls "form-of-life" or "a life inseparable from its form" (*Use of Bodies* 207). He finds a precedent for form-of-life in the medieval Benedictine monastic rule, known as the *regula vitae* (rule of life) or the *forma vitae* (form-of-life.) Two features of it are most salient to Agamben. First, Benedictine life occurs in community; its monasteries are founded on the principle of communal living rather than the kind of isolation one finds in eremitic religious orders. Second, the monastic rule prescribed activities for every hour of the day. While this may appear on the surface to cohere with Foucault's sense of totalitarian control over biological life, Agamben interprets it differently. In his reading, the Benedictine rule creates

> a zone of undecidability with respect to life. A norm that does not refer to single acts and events, but to the entire existence of an individual, to his *forma vivendi* [form of living], is no longer easily recognizable as law. […] Just as precepts that are no longer separable from the monk's life cease to be "legal," so the monks themselves are no longer "regular" but "vital."
>
> (*Highest Poverty* 26)

Agamben then extends the medieval religious context of "form-of-life" to a broader political imaginary, which in its very structure resists the separation of *zoè* and *bios*. Rather than understanding life as a set of acts and events that can be regulated by laws, a life that cannot be separated from its form is centered on potential and becoming. As we recall, Aristotle asserted of the *polis* that "while it comes into existence for the sake of life, it exists for the good life" (*Politics* 1252b 28–29). Form-of-life is political precisely in an Aristotelian sense because it is about "anthropogenesis—the becoming human of the human being" (*Use of Bodies* 208). Thus, Agamben's development of the political form-of-life is a recuperative model that, rooted in the premodern history of the West, has the potential to replace the repressive biopolitics founded in the sovereign's ability to create the *homo sacer*. Form-of-life does not create the state of exception that deprives *zoè* of *bios*; rather, it permits every life to exist in a perpetual state of becoming that unites them.

In short, the Foucauldian and Agambenian histories of biopolitics differ not only in their historicism but also in their implications for literature. Foucault scholars generally divide his thought into his earlier work on discourse, with its implications for literature, and his later work on politics and especially biopolitics. Against such a division, however, Judith Revel argues for a "literary birth of biopolitics," understanding Foucault's entire corpus to emerge from a core set of concerns that the philosopher explored through different conceptual lenses (29). Among these core concerns are the idea that the critique of the subject as the origin of language that Foucault revised with his discourse theory (which asserts that any subject is a subject of discourse) is in fact a theory of ongoing creation. Foucault's biopolitics, likewise, is fascinated with the possibility of the creative responses to power that life makes possible (Revel 44–45). Put in conversation with Agamben's emphasis on "becoming" as central to form-of-life, we see that despite their disagreement both philosophers locate a creative power in biopolitics.

Forms are perforce necessary to enact this creative power and to enable literary works both to represent political circumstance and to imagine alternatives. With this in mind, let us consider two poetic case studies that are deeply invested in form, life, and relationships between the two. These studies show us ways in which poets have explored the centrality of forms—poetic, political, and material—to the political powers of literature.

Poetic Forms-of-Life

Literature has long used forms to intervene in politics. We might think, for example, of how playwrights from Sophocles to Tony Kushner address political questions by means of the dramatic forms of character, dialogue, and spectacle. From Homer's epics to the American tradition of the presidential inaugural poem, nondramatic poets have also long turned to specific forms to make literary sense of political events. The following two case studies explore how poetic forms can create new forms-of-life and thereby shape a personal biopolitics, which not only addresses but resists a state-sanctioned biopolitics of repression.

Elizabeth Barrett Browning is best known today as a love poet, for her sonnet cycle *Sonnets from the Portuguese* dedicated to her husband, the poet Robert Browning. But during her lifetime in the reform-minded Victorian era, the famous poet also dedicated her energies and genius to political causes. Her poem "The Cry of the Children" was inspired by a report of the Children's Employment Commission that described the execrable labor conditions of children working in the mines of West Yorkshire. Browning adapts many of the details from the report into a poem that draws on classical Western forms of poetic meter and rhetoric. "The Cry of the Children" invokes Greek tragedy with an epigraph from Euripides' *Medea*: "Alas, my children, why do you look at me?" The poem is largely composed of stanzas ranging from 12 to 16 lines, themselves based on hexameter-tetrameter verse pairs. The epigraph and hexameter line, typical of Classical epic, write the children's story into the literary tradition of great tragedy. Yet the alternating hexameter-tetrameter lines invoke another tradition: that of song and, in particular, the ballad. While ballad meter typically consists of alternating tetrameter-trimeter lines, the cadence of the longer-shorter verse pairs inflects "The Cry of the Children" with a similar kind of immediacy as a performed song posing hard questions about the relationship of suffering individuals within the political state:

> Do you question the young children in the sorrow
> Why their tears are falling so?
> The old man may weep for his to-morrow
> Which is lost in Long Ago;
> The old tree is leafless in the forest,
> The old year is ending in the frost,
> The old wound, if stricken, is the sorest,
> The old hope is hardest to be lost:
> But the young, young children, O my brothers,
> Do you ask them why they stand
> Weeping sore before the bosoms of their mothers,
> In our happy Fatherland?
>
> (13–24)

Browning uses metrical forms (and, as this excerpt shows, other Classical rhetorical techniques like antithesis, anaphora, and isocolon) to shape the political message of the poem. But she also engages with literary forms that are more explicitly political. The contrasting images of the "mothers" before whom the children weep and the "happy Fatherland" that exploits their bodies remind the reader of the biopower in which these children are ensnared. In the poem's most trenchant image, a factory wheel figures the pitiless, implacable form-of-life the child workers endure:

> "For, all day, the wheels are droning, turning;
> Their wind comes in our faces,

> Till our hearts turn, our heads with pulses burning,
> And the walls turn in their places:
> Turns the sky in the high window blank and reeling,
> Turns the long light that drops adown the wall
> Turn the black flies that crawl along the ceiling,
> All are turning, all the day, and we with all."
>
> (77–84)

The wheel's formal properties include its lack of origin or telos, a mechanical cycle that overtakes and replaces the organic cycles that determine form-of-life in agrarian, pre-industrial cultures. Not coincidentally, these are also the cycles of an idealized childhood that Browning invokes in the poem: "Go out, children, from the mine and from the city,/Sing out, children, as the little thrushes do;/Pluck your handfuls of the meadow-cowslips pretty,/Laugh aloud, to feel your fingers let them through!" (57–60). The children, though, identify their form-of-life with the form of the wheel's motion: "and we with all."

Replacing the organic cycles of light and darkness, growth, death, and rebirth with the endless motion of the wheel, Browning evokes what Foucault would later identify as an anatomical biopolitics that "centered on the body as a machine: its disciplining, the optimization of its capabilities, the extortion of its forces, the parallel increase of its usefulness and its docility, its integration into systems of efficient and economic controls" (139). This is not the fateful Roman wheel of Fortuna, which offers good and bad by turns, but a millstone grinding human grist into profit. If Agamben imagines that the monastic form-of-life offers a political form that evades the repressive juridical control of Foucault's biopolitics, Browning's poem squelches the possibility that child laborers can participate in such a redemption: in Agamben's formulation, they are the exception. The poorly educated children know only a curtailed version of prayer, the two words "Our Father," and reject the imagination of a divine order that offers an escape from the wheel:

> "But, no!" say the children, weeping faster,
> "He [God] is speechless as a stone:
> And they tell us, of His image is the master
> Who commands us to work on.
> Go to!" say the children,—"up in Heaven
> Dark, wheel-like, turning clouds are all we find."
>
> (125–130)

As bleak and wrenching as Browning's poem is, it is also imbued with the sentimentality of reform: the affective idea that the outsider, observing and sympathetic to the plight of the oppressed, can and should use her voice to ventriloquize it. My second example turns to a poetry that takes not only contrasting forms but a contrasting subject position as its foundation. The poet and critic Nathaniel Mackey has, since 1985, been writing a serial poem called "Song of the Andoumbolou," a masterpiece of epic scope to which the following brief remarks can hardly do justice. But approaching Mackey's poem as a riposte to Browning's along a biopolitical axis illuminates how non-Western forms can express an alternative politics of form-of-life.

"Song of the Andoumboulou" has evolved over many volumes: *Blue Fasa*, *Whatsaid Serif*, and *Splay Anthem* all include extensive sections of the work, and Mackey continues to add to the serial poem. Its name comes from a figure of West African Dogon mythology: "The

Andoumboulou are a failed, earlier form of human being in Dogon cosmogony" whom Mackey understands as "a rough draft of human being, the work-in-progress we continue to be," whose

> lost ground, lost twinness, lost union and other losses invariably inflect that aspiration, a wish, among others, to be we, that of the recurring two, the archetypal lovers who visit and revisit the poems, that of some larger collectivity an anthem would celebrate.
>
> (SA xi)

The poem in its many parts indeed turns from the lyric "I" toward what we might call the "serial we" as its central voice.

In Mackey's poem, new forms-of-life continually emerge from cataclysm and undoing. He rewrites the myth of the Andoumboulou as still present, part of our human "becoming" that offers a narrative counter to that of evolutionary progress. Predating Agamben's work on form-of-life, Mackey's exploration of the figure of the Andoumboulou anticipates the philosopher's interest in "becoming" as a political form. Mackey's poetic form, too, resists the progressivism of a Western poetics built on accentual-syllabic rhythms and linear rhymes and stanzas. Instead, Mackey takes the recursive, improvisatory musical forms of jazz and blues as poetic scaffolding. But music is more than form for Mackey; it is also a metaphysics. In his essay "Sound and Sentiment, Sound and Symbol," Mackey speaks of music as an expression of the reality that exists beyond sense perception: "The world, music reminds us, inhabits while extending beyond what meets the eye, resides in but rises above what is apprehensible to the senses" (DE 232). But music, like poetry, also emerges from loss, and specifically from the loss of social ties symbolized by the figure of the orphan. As such, Mackey finds that the intersection of music—especially Black music—and poetry creates a space where the social and metaphysical intersect, where the social amputation that gives rise to music also makes it a "phantom limb" that allows us to reach beyond an oppressive and damaging social reality toward a transcendent reality accessible in music's formal patterns (DE 232–236).

Black music, in short, is a form-of-life in Mackey's poetry, one that is in relation and response to the oppressive biopolitics specifically oriented to black and brown bodies in American political regimes. Excerpts from "Song of the Andoumboulou" demonstrate how these bodies can reshape their forms in ways both distorting and filled with potentiality. The title of one book-length installment of the poem, *Splay Anthem*, captures the frisson of putting divergent movement into dialogue with imagined political unity: the "splay" body, spread across space, belies the unitary "anthem" that asserts, in music, centrality of rule that aims to govern and regulate bodies. In the poem itself, these bodies are figured in the evocative images of "limbo" and "crab." "Song of the Andoumboulou: 51," an excerpt in *Splay Anthem*, roughly centers on a driving trip and car crash of the poem's central we, and the ways their bodies accommodate their circumstances:

> Nunca was at the wheel, namesake
> chauffeur we made-believe
> we believed in, stiff-backed
> ecstatics that we were…
>
> It wasn't limbo what we did,
>   we
> sat up straight, backs ironing-board

> stiff,
> not limbo where we were, a kind of
> loop we were in....
> ...
> We were inland. Crab amble called out
> from hills we saw in the distance,
> ...
> No sooner Spain than it was
> somewhere known as Adnah we came to
>   next,
> everyone went around on all fours. Animal
> surmise local parlance proclaimed it.
> No sooner were we there than we moved on....
>
>   ...
>
>   an
> ambulance whatever it otherwise was, wounded
>   crew
> that we were, an ambulance not withstanding we
> sat up straight...
> ...
> Leaned inward, sat up straight, crab
> auspices outward list compensated, Nunca's
> demiurgic wheel....
> ...
>   Crash we'd have
> remembered gone blank...Anansic
>   bend
> we'd have been caught in, webbed
>   had we
> not leaned
> in

(*SA* 74–75)

Mackey's hermetically dense style resists the symmetries of for consistency with earlier usage Browning's syllogisms. Like jazz and blues music, his poetry is one of recursion and iteration, returning to themes and phrases, different every time, that evoke new meanings. Reading Mackey's poetry encourages association and induction rather than definition and deduction, noticing and inhabiting patterns rather than interpreting symbols.

    The scope of this chapter prevents doing justice to even a short excerpt of Mackey's poetry, but this selection nonetheless suggests how its literary forms shape its implied biopolitics. Although it almost certainly is not a direct response to Browning's poem so much as to the longer reformist tradition to which she belongs, the image of the "wheel" in Mackey's reimagines the biopolitics visible in "Cry of the Children." The steering wheel of this poem is first an image of liberation offering escape on the open road; then of an imagined loss of control, as we learn an imaginary (but believed-in) "Nunca" is at the wheel; and later of creation: "Nunca's demiurgic wheel." But the Gnostic connotations of "demiurgic" also imply Nunca's malevolence. As the literal driver of this segment of the poem, Nunca figures as much a metaphysical force as a political one, moving the bodies of the central "we" at once toward progress and destruction. Yet the embodiment that renders the "we" vulnerable is also their mode of resistance. They are largely defined in this excerpt by postures, sitting bolt upright, "stiff-backed" by contrast with not only the turning of the wheel but the other postures and movements they observe: "Crab amble," the people who go on all fours.

The conclusion of "Song of the Andoumboulou:51" supplants the image of the wheel with the twin images of the road and the ride: "The/road was all there was and ride was all/we did" (*SA* 80). The road is form and the ride is life; the two together constitute a form-of-life that is an endless becoming, at once constrained and generative. Like the complementary forms of myth and serial poem that structure the longer, ongoing work (the latest installment of "Song of the Andoumboulou" was published in 2021), road and ride together both do and do not constitute a life.

In very different ways, Browning's and Mackey's poems show how literary forms can heighten our attention to repressive forms-of-life, but also have creative power. They can imagine new political circumstances not only through their images but through the creations of new forms that, in turn, suggest new forms-of-life. Yet much poetry that treats repressive forms-of-life finds it difficult to escape representing them, and thereby reinscribing them. This is to say that forms encode neither repression nor liberation, in politics or in literature. They are powerful tools whose effects depend on use.

Works Cited

Agamben, Giorgio. *The Highest Poverty: Monastic Rule and Form-of-Life*. Translated by Adam Kotsko. Stanford UP, 2011.

———. *Homo Sacer*. Translated by Daniel Heller-Roazen. Stanford UP, 1998.

———. *The Use of Bodies*. Translated by Adam Kotsko. Stanford UP, 2015.

Ainsworth, Thomas. "Form vs. Matter." *The Stanford Encyclopedia of Philosophy*, edited by Edward N. Zalta, Summer 2020. Metaphysics Research Lab, Stanford University, 2020. https://plato.stanford.edu/archives/sum2020/entries/form-matter/.

Aristotle. *Physics*, edited by Bostock, David. Translated by Robin Waterfield. Oxford UP, 1996.

———. *Politics*. Translated by H. Rackham. Harvard UP, 1977.

Browning, Elizabeth Barrett. *Elizabeth Barrett Browning: Selected Poems*. Johns Hopkins UP, 1988.

Cannon, Christopher. *The Grounds of English Literature*. Oxford UP, 2004.

Foucault, Michel. *The History of Sexuality*. Vol. 1. 3 vols. Pantheon Books, 1978.

Levine, Caroline. *Forms: Whole, Rhythm, Hierarchy, Network*. Princeton UP, 2015.

Mackey, Nathaniel. *Discrepant Engagement: Dissonance, Cross-Culturality, and Experimental Writing*. Cambridge UP, 1993.

———. *Splay Anthem*. New Directions, 2006.

Pound, Ezra. *Selected Cantos of Ezra Pound*. New Directions, 1970.

Rancière, Jacques. *The Politics of Aesthetics: The Distribution of the Sensible*. Translated by Gabriel Rockhill. Continuum, 2004.

Revel, Judith. "The Literary Birth of Biopolitics." *Biopower: Foucault and Beyond*, edited by Vernon W. Cisney and Nicolae Morar. Translated by Christopher Penfield. The U of Chicago P, 2016, pp. 29–47.

Silverman, Allan. "Plato's Middle Period Metaphysics and Epistemology." *The Stanford Encyclopedia of Philosophy*, edited by Edward N. Zalta, Fall 2014., n.p. Metaphysics Research Lab, Stanford University, 2014. https://plato.stanford.edu/archives/fall2014/entries/plato-metaphysics/.

3
REALISM AND REPRESENTATION

Regina Martin

In 1886, novelist William Dean Howells declared that "Realism is nothing more and nothing less than the truthful treatment of material."[1] The idea that a literary genre unblinkingly and unromantically represents an ontological world beyond language—what philosophers call "the philosophical real"—is from its inception tied up in politics. Since politics denotes struggle over the distribution of social power, this seemingly simple definition of a literary genre is also a complex and increasingly contested claim to a privileged position outside of political struggle: if realism merely and clearly represents what exists, it is by definition apolitical. It is not a participant in the struggle; it simply and innocently records the struggle. But realism is not simply a mode of representation; it is not merely mimetic. Rather, like any act of communication, it is a semiotic mode: a system of signs whose meaning grows out of its own internal logic as well as a relationship to the external world. Importantly, a semiotic mode that lends the impression of and is credited with mimesis has a great deal of power to define and even help to create what comes to seem real, and what seems real has the power to shape human behavior and social relations. Therefore, those who have the ability to attach the label of realism to a text or perceived family of texts have a great deal of power to define what is "real," and, by extension, what is worth contesting and what is not.

Anglo-American literary studies has long identified the Victorian era as the golden age of literary realism. Recently, however, Elaine Freedgood has shown that understanding to be a revisionist myth traceable to literary criticism of the 1980s and beyond. Prior to that time, Anglo-American critics tended to understand the "triple-decker" novels by nineteenth-century authors such as Charles Dickens, George Eliot, and Anthony Trollope as actually breaking with the primary characteristics of literary realism. For these earlier critics, Victorian novels were not so much mimetic as diagetic; mimesis was an externally imitative function of "dramatic form" as envisioned by Aristotle, whereas the ostensibly diagetic novels revealed, via narrative processes, an imaginary world created by an author. Eventually, the argument goes, narrative theory gained traction and critics began to appreciate the dramatic elements of novels; Victorian novels came to epitomize the genre of realism and were increasingly "watched" rather than "listened to" (Freedgood 9). The project of positioning Victorian novels as the ideal examples of realism and re-inventing them as "polished forms," Freedgood writes, required collectively forgetting the general messiness of the "hastily written novels"; for novels written by those in the margins of the colonial metropole to be considered great literature, they had to reproduce Victorian realism's imagined formal unity (141). Thus, the definition of literary realism, the texts that have historically fit those changing definitions, and the value literary critics have attached to realism have plainly shape-shifted throughout the history of literary studies. At the same time, what constitutes literary realism at any given moment serves as a gatekeeper for admitting certain texts and traditions to the realm of "great" literature.

Freedgood's argument illustrates how changing definitions and attitudes toward realism track with shifting political contours and schisms in literary studies. For example, during the "canon wars" of the 1980s through the early 2000s, scholarship on realism focused on how at certain historical moments realism has been leveraged as a movement to legitimate particular texts and authors at the expense of what Suzanne Clark calls the "unwarranted discourses" of sentimentalism, sensationalism, and naturalism in the nineteenth century and the romances of the seventeenth and eighteenth centuries. The invention of realism's prestige also marginalized women novelists, who were pigeonholed as writers of sentimental and romance fiction. Edith Wharton, now considered one of the great American literary realists, felt the pressure of gendered discourses of realism and sentimentalism as she toiled to align her work with the prestige and power associated with realism and to militate against gendered charges of either romance or Romanticism.[2] Thus, scholars concerned themselves with the ways in which realism, a label with a fluid referent, was wielded as a political weapon—one whose efficacy derived from its ostensibly apolitical nature—to distribute power unequally within gendered and racialized social hierarchies.

After the millennium, the primary political debate within literary studies shifted away from questions of inclusion and exclusion and toward questions about the value of literature under an intensifying neoliberal global-economic consensus, in which value is increasingly recognized exclusively in economic terms. As John Guillory points out in *Cultural Capital*, while literary critics were debating which literature should be included in the curriculum, the rest of the world was wondering why universities should be teaching literature at all: for the "professional-managerial class... the reading of great works is not worth the investment of very much time and money" (46). Thus, scholars redirected their interests toward promoting the value of literature and literary studies and efforts to positively theorize the epistemological contributions of realism emerged.[3] Rather than defining realism or developing a method for qualifying a text as "realism," this scholarship strives to understand the cultural work performed by literary realism by asking, "what does literary realism do?" This chapter answers that question in two parts. The first part analyzes post-millennial theories of realism to identify some key problematics and points of conflict and contradiction among these theories. The second part takes Paule Marshall's realist novel *Brown Girl, Brownstone* (1959) as a case study that simultaneously illustrates and provides the opportunity to question and refine these theories.

Theorizing Realism after the Millennium: What Does Realism Do?

One effect of post-millennial approaches to theorizing realism as a type of cultural work is to transfer the definition of realism from text to method. A text *per se* is not realistic; rather, certain texts—especially those, like *Brown Girl, Brownstone,* that follow a linear narrative and feature recognizable human beings in a natural (as opposed to a romanticized, supernatural, or futuristic) environment—invite us to read in certain ways such that literary realism becomes an interpretive lens rather than a feature of the text itself. A few related problematics emerge in these investigations into the cultural work that happens when we read a text as an example of literary realism. The first concerns realism as a philosophical problem, the conjecture or claim that a reality exists beyond language. The label of literary realism derives from the tradition of philosophical realism as it purports to capture that world; but of course literary realism, by definition, is an effect of language. As a semiotic mode, literary realism presents a paradox that questions the very philosophical conjecture that inspires it. Does a philosophical real exist beyond language? Or is it actually constituted by language insofar as our concepts of the world are themselves fundamentally linguistic? Rather than simply dismissing literary realism as making a false claim, however, recent scholars view this paradox as a source of productive tension encouraging readers to interrogate the contact zones between the semiotic and the real.

This productive tension is manifest in the second problematic, which grows out of the work of György Lukács, an early twentieth-century theorist of the novel. Lukács theorized literary realism as an attempt to think reality as totality—that is, to try to render visible the complex ways that society (including social practices, language, modes of subjectivity, structures of identity, educational, medical, economic, and other modern institutions, as well as geopolitical events and structures) interact with each other to shape the lived experience of individuals. In this vein, "realism derives from the need of human subjects, would-be agents, to look for 'the real factors that relate their experience to the hidden social forces that produced them'" (Lee 419). Far from Howell's simple "truth" about visible "material," then, realism's virtue is to expose otherwise invisible structures of power.

To some critics, however, realism's vice lies in its inability to see past the structures of social power it exposes; in attempting to represent social power mimetically, realism reproduces those structures materially. Realism has thus been condemned by some as "the cultural brother of ideology" by "naturalizing socially and historically produced systems of meaning" (Prendergast 2). The notion that realism critically exposes power structures but ultimately reproduces them is the focus of a third problematic called "fatalist realism." Fatalist realism is exemplified by the connotation of inevitability contained in the phrase "capitalist realism"—that is, "the widespread sense that not only is capitalism the only viable political and economic system, but also that it is now impossible even to *imagine* a coherent alternative to it" (Shonkwiler and La Berge 2).

More recently, in diametrically opposed ways, Freedgood and Kornbluh resist the notion that literary realism merely reproduces the status quo by representing it. Thus, they locate a utopian impulse—the desire to think beyond the horizons of what is immediately possible—in literary realism in their break with the tradition of criticism that takes for granted the representational purport of literary realism. In their arguments, realism becomes a kind of "laboratory" for utopian thinking in the Jamesonian sense, in which utopia is not a place but an orientation toward the world that engages the hard work of imagining more just and equitable ways of being.[4]

Freedgood resurrects the seeming formlessness of Victorian realism—the ruptures in narrative, the authorial intrusions into narrative voice, the seemingly unrealistic coincidences that create drama—that was erased by the revisionism of late-twentieth-century literary criticism. For example, metalepsis—the "rupture of one ontological or diegetic layer into another" (103)—is a characteristic of realism's "twin commitments to fictionality and reference" in which historical characters, locations, and events collide with fictional characters, locations, and events (100). Metalepsis is a literary convention that allows two worlds to exist in tandem. Historically, metalepsis has served a very dystopian function; for example, she argues that it enables the cognitive dissonance that is constitutive of the "liberal subject," which has proven adept at celebrating ideals of liberty and freedom and exploiting enslaved labor. However, Freedgood argues that metalepsis also offers the possibility of adding "a collective 'what if' to the collective thinking about history. It opens a passage to counterfactuality, an exercise that reminds us that historical events might have unfolded otherwise" (104–105).

Where Freedgood sees a tendency in scholarship on Victorian literature to impose formal unity on unwieldy novels, Kornbluh sees a trend in postmodernist literary studies more generally to celebrate "fragmentation, unmaking, [and] decomposition" (4). She sees a tendency to "Privileg[e] modernism over realism, openness over closure, transgression over synthesis, irony over telos"; this privileging of "forms that undo their own formedness" has created a situation in which politics is "imagined... as demolition" and the "value of what forms build recedes" (4). Kornbluh calls for a renewed effort to understand how formalism, rather than formlessness, must be part of any "struggle to create a just collective" (6).

To theorize how literary realism, a mode that ostensibly is condemned to reproduce status quo political structures, can play a role in imagining new forms of social collectivity, literary realism must be wrested from the grip of representation. Kornbluh argues that realism should be read as an internally consistent semiotic system whose meaning is derived from a relationship between elements within the system (diegesis) rather than as an imitative relationship to the philosophical real (mimesis). Just as mathematical formalism provides the raw materials for economists to build models of human behavior, for climate scientists to model possible climate scenarios, and for political scientists to model election outcomes, literary realism provides the raw material to model various social forms, and in this way it participates in the struggle over power that defines politics.

In Kornbluh's account, architecture stands in as a metaphor for how literary realism models sociality: "architecture does not represent, depict, denote, or refer — it rather takes place, makes space, composes shape, inaugurates contour" (43). Kornbluh goes on to analyze how architectural tropes are used in various examples of Victorian fiction to "open projects of building, drafting, sheltering, and structuring that found the constituent commitments of political formalism" (18). By turning to architecture as metaphor and trope, Kornbluh wrests literary realism not only from representation but also from critique—an analysis of what is wrong in the world—and locates in literary realism an opportunity to imagine and build new possibilities.

This overview of post-millennial theories of realism highlights a number of conflicts and contradictions among individual works in the corpus. Does realism represent? Or does it model? Is realism characterized by formal unity or is its best feature its refusal (or inability) to abide by measures of formal consistency? Is realism destined to reproduce status quo social structures or can it have a utopian impulse? Is its purpose to critique or to imagine and build? If the purpose of post-millennial theories of realism were to define realism and taxonomize texts into categories of realism and not-realism, we might need to answer these questions and resolve these contradictions. But the main thrust of post-millennial theories of realism has not been to explain what realism is; rather, it is to theorize what realism does, so that theories of realism become an interpretive framework for reading instead of guidelines for categorizing. The contradictions that enrich (some would say plague) theories of realism are intrinsic to realism itself. Indeed, the capstone on Jameson's decades-long study of realism is entitled *The Antinomies of Realism* to emphasize the degree to which contradiction is the seedbed of realism: it is both fiction and representation; it is a "chronological continuum and the eternal affective present" (83); it is "epistemological claim" and "aesthetic ideal" (6).

Aesthetic Formalism, Literary Realism, and Paule Marshall's *Brown Girl, Brownstones*

As an Afro-Caribbean diasporic and Black-American novel, Paule Marshall's *Brown Girl, Brownstones* (1959) exemplifies what Jed Esty and Colleen Lye call "peripheral realism," a literature composed in the margins of the metropolitan colonial context. Much of the work on realism comes out of a metropolitan context because of the revisionism Freedgood describes, which identifies Victorian England as the golden age of literary realism. Writing about realism in a postcolonial context, Simon Gikandi pushes back against Jameson's *The Political Unconscious*, which periodizes romanticism, realism, and modernism according to historically shifting modes of production and class structures. While Jameson's periodizing project makes sense in a metropolitan context, the practice of chronologizing has the effect of positioning realism as a less developed mode of writing compared to a more complex and sophisticated modernist mode of formal experimentation. In a postcolonial context, the periodizing schema appears to parallel the economic development schema of first, second, and third world, in which countries teleologically proceed through stages of production (preindustrial, industrial, and postindustrial) and modes of writing (romance, realism, and modernism) to realize full development. To illustrate, Gikandi reads Marshall's oeuvre as an effort to construct a "distinctly Afro-Caribbean notion of modernism," but such a notion of modernism does not include the formal experimentation of European modernism (*Writing* 168). Marshall's oeuvre is an example of how non-metropolitan writers use "inherited forms" to a variety of ends as it deploys realist techniques to imagine Afro-Caribbean modernism.

Modes of writing do not represent stages of economic or cultural maturity; they perform different kinds of cultural work. As an example of peripheral realisms appearing at the liminal cusp between imagined periods of late modernism and postmodernism, *Brown Girl* provides the opportunity to refract the three post-millennial problematics of realism—philosophical realism, totalizing realism, and fatalistic realism—from a non-Eurocentric context that also exposes the patriarchy and white supremacy capitalism has always comprised.[5] Well before Freedgood's and Kornbluh's recent monographs, the novel pushes back against the notion that literary realism is destined to merely reproduce status quo systems of power. That said, the novel is not interested in jettisoning the mimetic potential of realism as it embraces the totalizing critique mimesis makes possible. Rather, the utopian impulse of the novel lies in how it thematizes one of Jameson's primary antinomies of literary realism: realism both presents an epistemological claim and expresses an aesthetic ideal.

Published in 1959 but set in New York City during World War II, *Brown Girl* tells the coming-of-age story of Selina Boyce. She lives in a Brooklyn brownstone with her parents, Deighton and Silla, and her older sister Ina. Deighton and Silla immigrated from the British colony of Barbados in their early adulthood. They met and married in New York City and settled in Brooklyn's growing Barbadian community. At the beginning of the novel, the family lives in a rented Victorian "brownstone" (a U.S. term for a style of townhouse/terraced house), which was originally built for middle-class white families who are leaving the neighborhood as Barbadian immigrants move in. The primary conflict driving the novel's narrative is Silla's desire to purchase the brownstone, so an architectural image stands at the center of the novel's realism. To be sure, architectural imagery is not unique to realism; rather, as I will show, *Brown Girl* organizes its interrogation of what I have identified as the three problematics of realism around the brownstone house.

Silla, along with many members of the Barbadian community, sees property ownership and rentierism as the only means of class mobility and method of acquiring social power in a white supremacist world. Selina witnesses the way her mother's relentless pursuit of property tears her parents apart and participates in a system in which the class mobility of Barbadian property owners depends on the exploitation of other Black and immigrant families. She recognizes that Black experience is caught in a fatalist system of white-supremacist capitalist realism in which Black people either live in immiserating poverty or participate in and reproduce the same systems of exploitation that are the sources of their oppression. The novel's utopian rather than reformist gesture lies in Selina's growing interest in artistic formalism and a longing for alternative social forms, a longing that leads her to flee the architectural formalism of her mother's world and set sail as a dancer on a Caribbean cruise ship. Though far from a utopian outcome, the novel's ending refuses the reformist impulse of Silla's desire for her to become a doctor and improve her position in an exploitative system.

In Kornbluh's argument, architectural formalism stands in as a metaphor for realist formalism, which engages in processes of imaginatively building rather than merely critiquing. However, in *Brown Girl*, the literal architecture of the novel's built environment provides the raw material for the novel's totalizing critique. For Selina, whiteness continues to haunt the house her family is currently leasing and her mother hopes to buy. Ten-year-old Selina entertains herself by imagining

> the white family who had lived here before... glid[ing] with pale footfalls up the stairs. Their white hands trailed the bannister... as they crowded around, fusing with her, she was no longer a dark girl alone and dreaming at the top of an old house, but one of them, invested with their beauty and gentility.
>
> (5)

But, "As Selina entered [the parlor]... the mirror flung her back at herself. The mood was broken... The illusory figures fled and she was only herself again" (5). "The room was theirs, she knew" (6). Selina expresses a desire for the "gentility" that is coded as white in the social space of white supremacy, but when she catches a glimpse of herself in the mirror, the illusion disappears, and she is reinserted into the racial hierarchy. In the novel, the house is the central node that figuratively connects the lived experiences of Selina and her family to the totality of historical processes, institutions, and cultural practices that have built white-supremacist capitalism. Kimberly Benston has argued that the novel's "architectural imagery" is the source of its formal unity. Compared to classics of Victorian realism like *Great Expectations*, however, the novel itself is an ideal of formal unity. Its narrative voice, cast of characters, tone, style, and narrative threads are consistent throughout. That Benston felt the need to conjure evidence for the novel's formal unity says less about the novel and more about its status as an example of peripheral realism, which created the need to associate it with characteristics of "great" literary realism. I argue that the architectural imagery of the brownstone functions instead as a kind of centrifuge for the novel's totalizing critique.

In imaginatively building a fictional world to serve as a model for reimagining the "real" world, the novel cannot turn to the architecture of the built environment for inspiration because it is too thoroughly implicated in white supremacy; rather, the architecture of the novel's utopian desire grows out of the dialectic represented by the conflict between Silla and Deighton. While Silla orients every aspect of her life toward the singular goal of owning the brownstone, Deighton refuses to save money to put toward the home; he instead spends money first on an accounting course, with the hope of entering the professional classes, and, when that fails, he buys a trumpet with the hope of becoming a jazz musician. Whereas the mother seeks dignity and respect in property and accumulated wealth, the father seeks it in the meritocratic ideal of professional society. His mother took pains to make sure he could get an education in Barbados, and as a young man he sought employment as a clerk in one of the white-owned shops but was met with "incredulity,... disdain and indignation" (39). He is similarly turned away from the major accounting houses, so he takes up the trumpet, a skill and profession that, due to the long history of racism in the United States, has been one of the few professional pathways toward social mobility for black Americans. Like realism, accounting masquerades as a system of representation—its purpose is to represent the financial situation of an organization—but in fact, as Mary Poovey has argued, it is a rhetorical system that creates the reality it is supposed to represent (30–40). It is an ordering system, with its own internal logic, that lends credibility to an organization. Jazz, by contrast, makes no pretense at representation. It is expressive rather than representative, and it is an aesthetic whose beauty and expressiveness grow out of a non-representative internal architecture of chords and scales. Whereas property makes up the architecture of Silla's realism, jazz makes up the architecture of Deighton's alternative formalism: "he held the trumpet as if it were the wand which had finally ordered life around him" (84–85).

Deighton's dream of becoming a jazz musician is not the only source of order in his life; early in the novel, he learns he has inherited a two-acre piece of land in Barbados. Silla wants to sell the land to make a down payment on the brownstone, but Deighton refuses. The undeveloped land becomes a kind of blank screen on which Deighton projects his fantasies of escaping white-supremacist structures of power. He repeatedly regales Selina with tales of their future: he imagines himself becoming a wealthy jazz musician and building a house "out of good Bajan coral stone" (86). Meanwhile, Ina, Selina's sister, dismisses her father's ambitions as "nothing but silly dreams" (89). Part of Selina's coming of age is the realization that her father's dreams are not realistic, but instead of dismissing them as "silly," she embraces the myth of the Barbados land over what the novel casts as her mother's realistic, methodical march toward ownership of the brownstone.[6]

For Silla, the brownstone represents a kind of realist formalism. It represents a realistic route to social mobility. Deighton, by contrast, looks toward the non-representational formalism of jazz and the undeveloped land in Barbados. When he loses use of his arm in a workplace accident, he turns to a religious cult, which has a strict organizational structure with a man called "Father Peace" at the center. The cult is another example of non-representational formalism onto which Deighton projects a desire, albeit an ironically tragic one, for something beyond the immediately possible, in this case the promise of spiritual transcendence.

Selina is the synthesis that emerges from this dialectic. She is repulsed by her mother's fatalist realism, which leads her to sell her father's land without his knowledge and exploit other immigrant renters; Silla insists that "People got to make their own way. And nearly always to make your way... you got to be hard and sometimes misuse others, even your own" (224). By contrast, Selina's "own small truth... dimly envisioned a different world and a different way; a small belief—illusory and undefined still—which is slowly forming out of all she had lived" (225). Selina sympathizes with her father's tendencies to chase the unrealistic, but she also recognizes the tragic, self-defeating nature of those tendencies. In an act of self-assertion, she rejects her mother's realistic desire for her to pursue a medical degree and follows her father's path, taking to the sea as a dancer on a cruise ship. But unlike her father, who fantasized about the material wealth his fame as a successful jazz musician and land-holder would bring him, Selina locates freedom from white-supremacist capitalism in the aesthetic itself.

Thus, phrased differently, Marshall's novel offers a kind of meditation on representational readers (like Silla) vs. non-representational readers (like Deyton). Realism invites readers to read novels as mimetically representational; however, realism can and should also be read non-representationally because doing so illuminates how the genre may resist a simplistic reproduction of the status quo. The political power of Marshall's novel lies in how it dramatizes the two modes of reading; and it is precisely in the architecture of that drama, in the juxtaposition of Silla and Deyton as readers and as characters, where we find the novel's utopian resistance to status quo politics. This is not simply a quietist retreat into pleasure often associated with Aestheticism, and the novel does not naively assume that the aesthetic offers any kind of true liberation. Far from it. In a novel so openly constrained by the fatalism of white-supremacist capitalist realism, however, aesthetics provides the architecture for imagining something new. For Selina, aesthetics offers the epistemological space for a personal escape from the racist realities that constrain her real existence. The novel persuasively suggests that people must find sources of emotional and cognitive resilience under conditions of material oppression; for Selina, aesthetics serve that function.

As she matures from a girl to a young woman, Selina begins to aestheticize the world around her. As a teenager, Selina walks the streets of her neighborhood in Brooklyn:

> To Selina the colors, the people seemed to run together. Dark, lovely little girls in straw bonnets flowed into little boys with their rough hair parted neatly on the side; into women in sheer dresses which whipped around their brown legs... Life suddenly was nothing but this change and return... Those colors, those changing forms were the shape of her freedom, Selina knew.
>
> *(56)*

As a college student, she roams the streets of Manhattan at night: "To Selina it was a new constellation, the myriad lights hot stars bursting from chaos into their own vivid life" (213). She "would feel sucked into that roaring center, the lights exploding inside her, and she would be free of the numbness" (214). For Selina, "freedom" from white supremacist capitalism emerges not from the literal architecture of her built environment, which is bound up in the fatalist realism of her mother; rather it is in aesthetic architecture that, like her father's non-representational formalism, gestures toward other possible ways of being in the world. Aesthetics, not the architecture of her built environment, is her model.

Her realist novel seems to agree. The final scene has Selina strolling past a landscape of demolished brownstones that the city plans to replace with a new architectural formalism: housing projects. As she passes, she removes "two silver bangles she had always worn... hurled them high over her shoulder. The bangles rose behind her, a bit of silver against the moon then curved swiftly downward and struck a stone. A frail sound in that utter silence" (310). On the one hand, Selina's removing the bracelets that she, like all Barbadian girls, had worn since birth symbolizes her renunciation of the formal institutions of family and nation. On the other hand, however, the final image of the novel is an aesthetic one that asks the reader to contemplate a "frail sound" with "utter silence." In this final image, architectural formalism and the social forms of family and nation, which are bound up in white-supremacist capitalist realism, are displaced by an image of aesthetic formalism grown from the juxtaposition, proximity, and constellation of forms and media rather than signs.

The dialectic between Silla and Deighton suggests that the philosophical real of Selina's lived experience provides little raw material for imagining alternative social and political forms. Kornbluh sees architectural formalism as a model for how literary realism can perform positive cultural work beyond the totalizing critique it had come to be appreciated for. But for Marshall, architecture is the built environment of white-supremacist capitalist realism, and it locks her characters into a series of fatalist impulses; architecture is a metonym for the political structures of white-supremacist capitalist realism. But the novel does not abandon formalism for abstraction and fragmentation in its utopian impulse. Instead, it embraces and thematizes the fundamental antinomy of realism—it is both truth claim and aesthetic object—as its utopian impulse. In the novel, it is aesthetic formalism—the juxtapositions of sounds, colors, shapes, and sensations—that provides the raw material for Selina's "freedom" and for modeling new social forms. As an example of literary realism, Marshall's novel interrogates the contact zones between aesthetic and social-political formalism in an effort to move beyond the fatalist realism that limits the scope of what is possible. In so doing, it offers us the opportunity to reconsider evolving theories of realism, which continue to explore the political limits and opportunities of realism as semiotics, model, representation, epistemology, and aesthetic form.

Notes

1 Howells, William Dean. "Editor's Study." *Harper's Monthly*, vol. 73 (May 1886), p. 973.
2 See Hoeller for an explanation of how Wharton strategically aligns herself with literary realism.
3 See *Adventures in Realism* (2007) and *Reading Capitalist Realism* (2014), a double special issue of the *Journal of Narrative Theory* entitled *Realism in Retrospect* (2006 and 2008), a *Modern Language Quarterly* special issue, *Peripheral Realisms* (2012), a *Novel* special issue, *Worlding Realisms Now* (2016), Fredric Jameson's *Antinomies of Realism* (2013), Freedgood's *Worlds Enough* (2019), and Anna Kornbluh's *The Order of Forms* (2019).
4 See Fredric Jameson's *Archaeologies of the Future: The Desire Called Utopia and Other Science Fictions* (London: Verso, 2013).
5 When critics address the form of *Brown Girl*, they tend to discuss it as a *Bildungsroman*. See Buma.
6 See Dupoin for an extended analysis of how Barbados functions as a mythic place in Deighton's and Selina's imaginations. Dupoin is interested in Deighton's myths as fantasies, but I am interested in how the myths are examples of non-representational formalism that give shape to other possible ways of being in the world.

Works Cited

Benston, Kimberly A. "Architectural Imagery and Unity in Paule Marshall's *Brown Girl, Brownstones*." *Negro American Literature Forum*, vol. 9, no. 3, 1975, pp. 67–70.
Buma, Pascal P. "Paule Marshall's *Brown Girl, Brownstones*: A Nexus Between the Caribbean and African-American 'Buildungsromane'." *CLA Journal*, vol. 44, no. 1, 2001, pp. 303–316.
Clark, Suzanne. *Sentimental Modernism: Women Writers and the Revolution of the Word*. Indiana UP, 1991.
Coykendall, Abby, ed. *Realism in Retrospect. Journal of Narrative Theory*, vol. 38, no. 1, 2008.
Duboin, Corinne. "Paule Marshall's Reconstruction of Barbados in *Brown Girl, Brownstones*." *Commonwealth*, vol. 18, no. 2, 1996, pp. 90–98.
Esty, Jed and Colleen Lye. "Peripheral Realisms Now." *Modern Language Quarterly*, vol. 73, no. 3, 2012, pp. 269–288.
Freedgood, Elaine. *Worlds Enough: The Invention of Realism in the Victorian Novel*. Princeton UP, 2019.
Gikandi, Simon. "Realism, Romance, and the Problem of African Literary History." *Modern Language Quarterly*, vol. 73, no. 3, 2012, pp. 309–328.
———, *Writing in Limbo: Modernism and Caribbean Literature*. Cornell UP, 1992.
Goodlad, Lauren, ed. *Worlding Realisms Now. Novel: A Forum on Fiction*, vol. 42, no. 2, 2016.
Guillory, John. *Cultural Capital: The Problem of Literary Canon Formation*. U of Chicago P, 1993.
Hoeller, Hildegard. *Edith Wharton's Dialogue with Realism and Sentimental Fiction*. U of Florida P, 2000.
Jaffe, Audrey, ed. *Realism in Retrospect. Journal of Narrative Theory*, vol. 36, no. 3, 2006.
Jameson, Fredric. *The Antinomies of Realism*, Verso, 2013.
Kornbluh, Anna. *The Order of Forms: Realism, Formalism, and Social Space*. U of Chicago P, 2019.
Langbauer, Laurie. *Women and Romance: The Consolations of Gender in the English Novel*. Cornell UP, 1990.

Lee, Yoon Sun. "Type, Totality, and the Realism of Asian American Literature." *Modern Language Quarterly*, vol. 73, no. 3, 2012, pp. 415–432.

Marshall, Paule. *Brown Girl, Brownstones*. Chatham, 1959.

Poovey, Mary. *A History of the Modern Fact: Problems of Knowledge in the Sciences of Wealth and Society*. U of Chicago P, 1998.

Prendergast, Christopher. "Introduction: Realism, God's Secret, and the Body." *Spectacles of Realism*, edited by Margaret Cohen and Christopher Prendergast. U of Minnesota P, 1995, pp. 1–10.

Shonkwiler, Alison and Leigh Claire La Berge, editors. *Reading Capitalist Realism*. U of Iowa P, 2014.

4
SYMPTOMS

Benjamin Kohlmann

"Today," a philosopher observed, "it is normative to read literature, film, and other cultural texts primarily as evidence about the societies that made them—evidence that necessarily requires our hermeneutic labor in order to yield its significance." This aesthetic "evidence" frequently goes by a specific name drawn from long, intertwined traditions in Marxism and psychoanalysis: "symptom" (Dean 20). This had been true for at least 20 years before it was written, and perhaps remains equally true 20 years later. While clearly normative, however, such protocols were never exhaustive, and literary-theoretical debate has long been energized both by the political possibilities and by the limits of such "symptomatic reading."[1]

As scholars ranging from queer theorist Eve Kosofsky Sedgwick to critical theorist Rita Felski have pointed out, the hermeneutic protocols of symptomatic reading, at least as they came to be codified by psychoanalytic and Marxist critics from the 1960s and 1970s onward, instruct us to look past and through the surface structure of literary texts in order to search out their hidden, latent, or repressed meanings. The norms of symptomatic reading also prompt us—even urge us—to distrust the phenomenal content of aesthetic experience as well as any readerly attachments (e.g., to characters or situations in the story-world) that form during the experience of reading. As critics interested in the limits and problems of symptomatic reading have observed, this mode of engaging with texts has given rise to hegemonic types of critique that often entail negative moods of "paranoia" or "suspicion."[2] The language of literary and cultural studies, Felski writes in her influential book *The Limits of Critique*, "has grown weighty with references to symptoms and repressions," but at the same time there is

> something perplexing about the ease with which a certain style of reading has settled into the default option. Why is it that critics are so quick off the mark to interrogate, unmask, expose, subvert, unravel, demystify, destabilize, take issue, and take umbrage? What sustains their assurance that a text is withholding something of vital importance, that their task is to ferret out what lies concealed in its recesses and margins? Why is critique so frequently feted as the most serious and scrupulous form of thought? What intellectual and imaginative alternatives does it overshadow, obscure, or overrule? And what are the costs of such ubiquitous criticality?
>
> *(Limits 5)*

Felski's question might be equally asked of most practitioners of critique far outside the discipline of literary studies. Furthermore, the obvious fact that many texts don't transparently offer stable, clear, and indisputable meanings has for centuries provided the basic foundation for every form of "close reading," ranging from Biblical exegesis to international systems of law and jurisprudence. Finally, while debates about symptomatic reading in literary studies have been undeniably important and useful, I want to suggest that the fixation on symptomatic reading has eclipsed alternative theories and practices of literary politics, many of which predate the institutional rise of symptomatic reading in the second half of the twentieth century. As an ironic result, many literary theorists have too quickly propounded a myth propagated by the most influential symptomatic readers of the 1970s and 1980s, including Louis Althusser, Jacques Rancière, and Fredric Jameson: that theoretically sophisticated conversations about literary politics really started with them.

One way to trace the implications of dispelling this myth is to pay sustained attention to literature that engages explicitly and politically with their own historical moment at the level of "manifest," overt content rather than "repressed," hidden content. These overtly politicized texts are interesting precisely because it is hard to think of them through a hermeneutic model of political latency; that is, in terms of a political unconscious that becomes symptomatically visible in the cracks and interstices of texts, just waiting to be probingly and patiently dug out by demystified analysts. How can we talk about texts which don't seem to require this kind of decoding? What kinds of theoretical resources do we have to talk about works that demand to be read not only as indices of social formations but as moments of actual or attempted intervention? My focus here will be on the interwar years of the early twentieth century, although my field of historical reference extends roughly from 1920 to 1980: right up to the moment when symptomatic reading begins its ascendancy in the Anglo-American academy.

Theorizing Causality: Literature and Activism before the "Political Unconscious"

There is perhaps no better or more sustained articulation of the protocols of symptomatic reading than Fredric Jameson's *The Political Unconscious: Narrative as a Socially Symbolic Act* (1981). The book famously opens by sketching three different models of historical causality, which are foundational to the book's overarching argument that politics are encoded within literary forms rather than being somehow external to those forms.[3] Thus, revisiting the three types of causality that Jameson presents—the one type that is privileged and the two that are quickly discarded—highlights some theoretical, and ultimately political, blind spots of his influential model.

The first type of causality, "mechanical causality," is described by Jameson as "the billiard-ball model of cause and effect" (9). This version of causality comes closest to what most people intuitively understand by the term "causality"—a cue ball strikes and thereby causes an eight-ball to move—but Jameson warns that in literary historiography there is something "scandalous" or narrowly empiricist about this way of relating cause and effect:

> That a material and contingent 'accident' should leave its trace as a form-'break' (and 'cause' modification in narrative categories)—this is no doubt a scandalous assertion. In this type of causality, rifts cannot ultimately be grasped 'from the inside' or phenomenologically, but must be reconstructed as symptoms whose cause is of another order of phenomenon from its effects.
>
> *(10–11)*

By "rifts" Jameson means breaks within the generic structures of individual texts; what he finds so "scandalous" about this model of causation is that textual "effects"—e.g., the hybrid admixtures of realism and romance in the novels of Joseph Conrad—seem to be of only secondary importance compared to the external material factors which are held to "cause" them. Literature, that is to say, seems incapable of truly incorporating history, which remains both ontologically distinct from and external to it.

Althusser's second type of causality is "expressive." For Jameson, expressive causality maintains that economic infrastructure is "expressed through" the elements of the superstructure: art, religion, law, and so on. Althusser and Jameson criticize this type of causality by pointing to the various forms of reductionism which it implies. This includes the vulgar-Marxist version of economic reductionism, according to which socio-cultural phenomena can be traced back (i.e., are "reducible") to economic causes: "expressive causality," notes Jameson, claims that "all cultural levels are somehow 'the same' and so many expressions and modulations of one another" and of hidden economic causes (22).

Finally, the third form of causality is termed "structural," and presents a powerful alternative to the previous two types. "Structural causality" suggests that the "cause" of social reality lies not in an essence behind things, but in the relations that pertain between the elements of the superstructure. As Jameson explains, the "political unconscious" of a literary work can be described precisely in terms of the relations that obtain between the formal and generic structures that make up a text: we accordingly need to describe the political unconscious "not by abandoning the formal level for something extrinsic to it—such as some inertly social 'content'—but rather immanently, by construing purely formal patterns as a symbolic enactment of the social within the formal and the aesthetic" (63). On this view, politics is intimately woven into the texture of the literary work itself: the text carries politics within itself as its immanent or intrinsic subtext. As Jameson's rich and suggestive readings of a series of canonical literary works (ranging from Honoré de Balzac to George Gissing and Joseph Conrad) demonstrate, the real political meaning of these texts is to be found not outside them, but rather in the "symptomatic" formal instabilities and semantic opacities of the works themselves.

Jameson and Althusser devote a good deal of attention to the ideas of expressive causality and, especially, to structural causality. Strikingly, however, both give short shrift to the first, mechanical type, as though mechanical causality offered too crude and simplistic a notion of cause-and-effect to merit detailed refutation. It is futile, Althusser and Jameson seem to say, to imagine that a set of extra-textual causes can sufficiently explain changes in literary history or an author's particular stylistic choices: to imagine, for instance, that the historical occurrence of a single food riot would or could cause a significant shift in the generic structure of a given set of novels or poems. Jameson's dismissal of mechanical causality would also seem to include texts which take a different view of their own socio-political agency, i.e., texts which suggest or openly declare that literature can intervene directly in history by "causing" political change. And yet, Jameson is repeatedly drawn back to what he calls the "scandal" of mechanical causality—after all, the avowed main task of his book is "to invent ways of opening the text onto its hors-texte or extratextual relationships in less brutal and less contingent fashion than is the case with the mechanical causality touched on above" (27). Relegated to the background of these arguments are texts which in some respects do resemble the model of mechanical causality: texts which attempt not only to represent but to intervene literally—mechanically—in the world in which they appear. Pointedly, even committed symptomatic readers would find it difficult to think of these works primarily in terms of a political unconscious because politics is precisely what these works are so centrally and self-consciously about. In Jameson's book, we could say, the idea of mechanical causality plays the role of an undertheorized, even partially repressed, explanatory model for literary historiography and literary theory. In short, I am suggesting that Jameson's own argument could and should be subjected to a form of symptomatic reading, which can help us make visible the models of literary politics that Jameson's book inadvertently or strategically eclipses.

The Politics of Despair: Symptomatic Reading as Symptom

Administering a dose of its own medicine to Jameson's masterwork might proceed from Alex Woloch's recent book-length study of George Orwell. As Woloch notes in the introduction to his book, *The Political Unconscious* can be read as a response to the "Anglo-American reaction" of the early 1980s—"the era of Reagan and Thatcher" that signified "the death of liberal intentionality in US politics and culture" as well as the foreclosure of more radically utopian political horizons (xi). On this reading, Jameson privileged the model of historical causality that most closely responded to the left's political crisis of the 1980s by depriving politics of its concrete historical specificity and urgency. By insisting that literature's engagement with history is oblique (indirect, latent, symptomatic), Jameson effectively negates the idea that literature can become an instrument of social and political change. One the most intensely politicized works of late-twentieth-century critical theory thus appears to betray an awareness that what it is doing is not (or not quite) politics, that true historical agency is located beyond its grasp.

Scholars are not generally accustomed to reading (critical) theory for the affective charge it carries, yet Woloch's comments helpfully ask us to consider the broader structures of feeling in which some of our most cherished critical practices are embedded. On Woloch's account, the governing affect of works such as Jameson's would not be suspicion (as Felski and Kosofsky Sedgwick would claim) but rather a form of despair that is rooted in concern about critique's own lack of political efficacy. As Robyn Marasco has recently noted in her reassessment of the emancipatory project of critical theory, such "despair" grows out of an "external loss," namely the barring of access to Marxist theory's desired field of external reference: reality, history, revolutionary social change, and so on (12). When it is read in this light, Jameson's adoption of Althusser's structural causality has a paradoxical double effect: it places texts in closer proximity with history by showing how history shapes a text's structure, but at the same time it also distances literature from history by insisting that the latter can only be known indirectly, insofar as it is encoded in literary texts. Partly as a result of the historical conditions that conditioned its emergence, symptomatic reading has tended to foreclose important ways of thinking about literature's political efficacy and agency.

Interwar Literary Politics and Beyond: The Long 1930s

In what follows, I want to recover some of the force of the model of mechanical causality which Jameson so roundly dismisses. To do so, I turn to the politicized literature of the later interwar years, although my argument could easily be extended to include examples from other historical contexts before, up to, and including the present moment.[4] By turns championed and reviled for the attempt to harness art in service of radical politics, few periods have provided a more hotly contested ground for literary historiography than the later interwar years. Starting with the New Critics of the 1950s, the bulk of interwar politicized literature has been excluded from the canon of aesthetically "good" twentieth-century writing, and subsequently left off of "Best of" lists and university syllabi alike.

This form of writing, the story often goes, keeps its eye fixed too intently on its immediate historical moment to achieve the sort of immortality attained by truly successful literature. This view was even shared by some now-canonical authors of the interwar years, who derided writing which seemed to draw its energies too directly from the political struggles of the present moment. For example, W. H. Auden dismissed such writing as the art of "the flat ephemeral pamphlet" ("Spain 1937" 212): this was the artistic trap that awaited writing which sought to become socially and politically active and effective, texts which the British left-wing poet Stephen Spender described in 1933 as being "complementary to action" (63).

In the Anglophone context, these exclusion mechanisms have pushed many writers (e.g., the British proletarian writers Jack Lindsay, Edward Upward, Storm Jameson, and B. L. Coombes; or their American analogues Mike Gold, Jack Conroy, and Josephine Herbst) to the period's artistic sidelines. The same mechanisms have also led to the near-total eclipse of entire genres—such as the Living Newspaper or the Mass Declamation[5]—which were conceived as artistic responses to the twists and turns of contemporary politics. We should learn to take the concept of mechanical causality more seriously as a category of literary-historical and theoretical inquiry, partly because the politically engaged writing of the interwar period can prompt us to suspend categories such as "formal complexity" that continue to be central to our understanding of interwar modernism.[6] The concept of mechanical causality captures the fact that many politically committed writers of the interwar years sought to open their texts onto the sheer messiness of day-to-day politics, e.g., by exploring the footholds for political action that are created by specific material conjunctures; but the model of mechanical causality can also help us describe the reverse process, whereby many engagé writers attempted to turn their works into instruments that were intended to "cause" social change.

It is worth reminding ourselves in this context that Jameson's work forms part of a longer critical history that privileges formal complexity and perhaps unintentionally discounts activist writing. The loose affiliation of American New Critics, who rose to prominence in the 1930s and ascended to something like institutional dominance in the early 1950s, presented their protocols of "close reading" as a response to 1930s politicized writing: for these critics, praising formal complexity was a way of dismissing the politicized writing of the later interwar years as a literary-historical aberrance. "For the poet as a public performer," the New Critic William K. Wimsatt pointed out, "poetic language is a complex and treacherous medium" (243). Literature, Wimsatt warns, is constitutively incapable of realizing W. H. Auden's wish, expressed in a well-known 1935 poem to Christopher Isherwood, that poetry "make action urgent and its nature clear" ("August" 157). The New Criticism, we could say, tried to contain the radical energies of the interwar period's politicized writing by translating its instrumental logic of (artistic) means and (political) ends into a complex internal dialectic: "Inside the poem," Wimsatt concludes, "there are no ends and means, only whole and parts" (243). Here, formal complexity intercepts the attempt to make literary writing do urgent political work that seeks to intervene in social reality. Pushing back against this tendency, I want to suggest that we can experimentally remobilize the instrumental (i.e., "mechanical") logic of literary means and political ends: this move, I argue, helps us reclaim parts of the literary-historical map which are eclipsed by the habitual privileging of formal complexity (and the politics of form) in literary studies. Against both Jameson and Felski, then, I want to direct our attention away from theoretical disputes about symptomatic reading (important as these are) and toward earlier ways of thinking about the relationship of literature and politics.

The attempt by many interwar authors to treat their texts as weapons in the political struggle gave rise to particular artistic difficulties. Above all, the fast pace of the period's politics required a constant rethinking and readjustment of what it meant for a text to become politically active in a specific time and place. In his important essay on the 1930s communist critic and activist Christopher Caudwell, the British Marxist historian E. P. Thompson aptly noted that the instrumental understanding of literary politics formed part of the period's "interactionist epistemology": this "interactionism," Thompson explains, "was carried over from epistemology to poetics and historical and cultural analysis" (90, 99). Thompson quotes a passage from Caudwell to illustrate this line of thinking: "ideas are causally linked with material reality, and are not only determined but also determine: in their turn exerting a causal influence on their matrix" ("Caudwell" 100). In a closely related vein, Jean-Paul Sartre's essay "Materialism and Revolution" (1946) provocatively suggests that political activism in literature can be reduced to the status of an efficient cause: "the relation of cause to effect is revealed in and through the efficacy of an act which is both plan and realization" (242).

Contemporary critics have tended to resist such arguments: they have instead worked hard to distinguish literature's complex and multiply mediated agency from mechanical causality's starkly instrumentalist cause-and-effect logic. For example, the literary theorist Gabriel Rockhill insists that "it is crucial to rethink the operative logic of political efficacy outside of the instrumentalist framework that tends to predominate by reifying a one-to-one relationship between an artistic work and a political effect": the production and reception of artworks, Rockhill insists, always take place within a complex "conjuncture of determinants with multiple tiers, types, and sites of agency" (53–54). In pointed contrast to such arguments, Thompson's and Sartre's essays hark back to a large body of interwar "interactionist" thought that involves a thinking along (rather than against) the grain of mechanical causality. But it is also important to remember that Thompson identified this strand of interactionist thought in 1977: that is, that he looked back to interwar conversations about literary politics just when symptomatic reading was gathering institutional momentum in the academy. This was a process that was beginning to shut down the space available for such acts of theoretical recuperation on the part of radical theorists, activists, and cultural practitioners. Put plainly, the rise of symptomatic reading as political reading—or indeed as politics tout court—actually foreclosed political horizons of reading under the guise of disclosing them: it did so at the precise moment that the reactionary counterrevolution of Ronald Reagan and Margaret Thatcher was about to take place.

Activist Modernism

The poem "Autumn on Nan-Yüeh" by the writer and critic William Empson exemplifies what this interactionist thought looked like in practice. Empson wrote his poem in China's Yunnan Province in the autumn of 1937, after the Japanese invasion of mainland China had forced Empson and his colleagues of National Peking University into exile. There are several reasons why Empson's poem has long occupied a place on the margins of the '30s literary canon, which is otherwise populated by writers of the so-called Auden Generation (Cecil Day-Lewis, Stephen Spender, Christopher Isherwood, and Auden himself): the text is insistently fixated on contemporary political and military developments, especially the unfolding of the Sino-Japanese war; it explicitly invokes, reflects, and insists upon its own politics of writing; and finally, it questions the stance of cool political detachment which Empson had famously cultivated in some of his earlier poems as well as in the criticism on which his career was built. While Empson is usually celebrated as one of the exemplary political "neutrals" of the interwar decades, "Autumn on Nan-Yüeh" indicts the aloofness of his earlier verse:

> This passive style might pass perhaps
> Squatting in England with the beer.
> But if that's all you think of, what
> In God's name are you doing here?
>
> (ll. 195–202)

Empson's poem concludes that "Politics are what verse should/Not fly from, or it goes all wrong." Instead of celebrating the mental poise which Empson had earlier associated with Buddhism, the poem recognizes the growing nationalist sentiment among Empson's Chinese students: "the Chinese have caught nationalism like a bug," Empson noted in a letter to Robert Herring as he was writing the poem (111). "Autumn on Nan-Yüeh" reflects the political and aesthetic adjustments that were pressed on Empson during those crucial weeks of 1937. In the end, the poem fails to maintain a neutral stance, as the universities are once again forced to escape from the Japanese invaders. The poem's final stanza conveys a keen sense of how political action pushes beyond, or runs ahead of, poetic language:

> Claiming no heavy personal cost
> I feel the poem would be slow
> Furtively finished on the plain.
> We have had the autumn here. But oh
> That lovely balcony is lost
> Just as the mountains take the snow.
> The soldiers will come here and train.
> The streams will chatter as they flow.
>
> (ll. 226–234)

Empson later confessed that "my war started in 1937," and the closing stanza of "Autumn on Nan-Yüeh" gives the impression of having been scribbled down hastily on departure, putting an abrupt end to the poem's abstract contemplation of war ("Letter to Ricks" 598). The poem's coda presents a view of the world as it will be like when the speaker is no longer there to see it, while the unintelligible "chatter" of the water offers a disconcerting image of an empty and chaotic future. In response to this scenario of historical disarray, the speaker decides to relinquish the position of solitary observer and to join the exodus of the Chinese universities. The desire to belong, to take sides in the war, ultimately trumps the possibility of political detachment.

"Autumn on Nan-Yüeh" begins to illustrate how closely literary texts of the interwar years—even those by professed neutrals like Empson—responded to the contingencies of a particular historical situation, and how intensely they reflected on what it meant to commit to a particular political cause and to express that commitment in poetic terms and forms. Of course, there are countless other examples. I already mentioned that there are entire genres of activist art—such as the Living Newspaper and the Mass Declamation—which were dedicated to registering the course of historical events and to proposing routes for revolutionary political action. Another useful resource might be the unpublished notebooks kept by communist writers such as Jack Lindsay or Edward Upward, which offer material for micro-historical accounts of the politicized writing of the later interwar years. These notebooks record in painstaking detail the confusions to which the seemingly simple actions of "going over" (to the proletariat) and "taking sides" (with Communism or Fascism) invariably gave rise. Upward, for example, obsessively rewrote his fictional works over the course of the '30s, and his fascinating diaries (now in the British Library) would make it possible to trace these formal revisions as they respond to specific historical events and to Upward's studies in Marxism-Leninism.

Perhaps unbeknownst to Jameson and Althusser, there is a rich body of theoretical work about mechanical causality—from the interwar years and beyond—that can usefully defamiliarize the protocols of symptomatic reading contemporary literary critics so often default to. This neglected canon of theoretical production includes books from the 1930s such as Christopher Caudwell's *Crisis in Physics*, as well as Thompson's work from the 1970s on "interactionist epistemology." We could also think of early works of Soviet art theory such as Yevgeny Zamyatin's 1923 essay "On Literature, Revolution, Entropy, and other Matters," which imagines literature as one type of material cause (or effect) among others. Revolution, on Zamyatin's account, is the outcome of matter working on matter:

> the law of revolution [...] is a universal, cosmic law. [...] Two stars collide with an inaudible, deafening crash and light a new star: this is revolution. A molecule breaks away from its orbit, and, bursting into a neighbouring atomic universe, gives birth to a new chemical element: this is revolution.
>
> *(107)*

This passage derives its considerable rhetorical force from a utopian belief that the inner-worldly workings of cause-and-effect will be able to bring about radical and qualitative change. Zamyatin's essay indicates the vitality and force of the model of literary politics that is inadvertently foreclosed in Jameson's work: indeed, even if contemporary literary theorists find it difficult to share the exuberant futurism of Zamyatin's Bolshevik politics, they should be able to distill from his thinking a more capacious and generative view of literary politics than has been available to generations of symptomatic readers.

Coda: Efficient Causes

The logic of mechanical causality forms part of a neglected tradition of radical artistic production that has continued to be reactivated in revolutionary or semi-revolutionary conjunctures. For example, Nanni Balestrini's *The Unseen* (1987), an important novel about the Italian Autonomia movement of the 1970s, features several passages that resonate with the mechanicist politics of Zamyatin's essay. Early on in his novel, Balestrini introduces a character, known as Scilla, who at first glance seems singularly uninterested in questions of theory and qualitative historical change:

> Scilla and his kind never took part in the internal debates of the movement in the meetings and mass meetings they were largely silent [...] they experienced the stage of intensified conflict in merely mechanical terms of escalating the conflict.
>
> *(21)*

Balestrini reminds us that while Scilla's thinking remains limited to the "merely mechanical" (i.e., non-dialectical) cause-and-effect logic of the physical struggle, this attention to mechanical causality still helps to drive the larger historical dialectic of (material) force and (qualitative) social change. Indeed, Balestrini's novel itself can be understood as embodying a dialectic of activist practice (governed by the instrumental, cause-and-effect logic of physical struggle) and speculative reflection (an attempt to think through the ways in which this same struggle helps to effect qualitative historical transformations).

While Balestrini's and Zamyatin's texts highlight the importance of thinking about mechanical causality as a model for current and future activist struggles, the present chapter has been more specifically concerned with mechanical causality insofar as it poses a challenge to prevailing tendencies in contemporary literary theory. Importantly, repositioning mechanical causality at the center of debates about politicized literature does not mean that we should simply dispense with questions of (aesthetic, social, cultural) mediation and symptomatic form altogether: rather, this move is intended to unsettle our understanding that the work of mediation is all we should be paying attention to, especially when it comes in the modernist guise of artistic "complexity" or "difficulty." My aim here has accordingly been a modest one, namely, to highlight one account of literature's political uses that Jameson's theory of historical causality leaves out of the picture. Jameson's *Political Unconscious*, I have been suggesting, marks the precise moment in the institutional history of critical theory when a richly theorized older account of historical causality became eclipsed in favor of a narrower scholarly attention to the political work of literary form.

In concluding, I briefly want to invoke Althusser's final essays, written around the same time as *The Political Unconscious*. In these essays, Althusser intriguingly revisits the idea of mechanical causality while also developing a politically charged version of that idea. In essays such as "The Underground Current of the Materialism of the Encounter," Althusser proposes the concept of an "aleatory materialism" that is distinct from what Althusser calls Marxism's "idealist materialism" (168, 171). While "idealist materialism" seeks to identify underlying structures of historical movement, Althusser claims, aleatory materialism is not intended as a coherent theory or system; it relies not on a new set of abstractions but on the close empirical analysis of a given historical conjuncture. Thus, for example, Althusser enjoins critics to question communist assumptions about the proletariat as the meta-subject of history, and instead to look precisely at the unfolding of concrete material conjunctures in the hope of creating openings for site-specific political interventions. In these late essays, Althusser describes history as the continuous transformation of provisional forms by new events; and art, too, Althusser argues, can be understood as a response to "the necessary contingency of history" (187).

Althusser's last essays advance a form of materialist monism which suggests that causation is immanent to a vast and distributed network of causes-and-effects—this model has also proved influential for more recent proponents of the "New Materialism" who posit "flat ontologies" that radically decenter the primacy of the human in favor of types of material immanence.[7] The political theorist Banu Bargu contends that Althusser's aleatory materialism is capable of "unlocking a new materialist understanding of revolutionary political transformation" (88). Indeed, as I have been suggesting in this chapter, the attempt by many interwar writers to imagine their texts as interventions in the material configuration of the world invites theoretical thinking precisely along these lines. Jameson is certainly right when he notes that to think about history in terms of mechanical causality is to conceive of history as a sequence of events which are both "brutal and contingent" (27). But perhaps this is not such a bad way to describe how the historical cataclysms of the 1920s and 1930s appeared to those politicized writers who were forced to live through them.

"The Underground Current of the Materialism of the Encounter" crucially indicates that Althusser felt the need to modify his earlier emphasis on structure (as in "structural causality") by insisting once more on the transformative efficacy of individual events—that is, by returning to a mode of pre-symptomatic causality. Even so, Jameson's resounding dismissal of mechanical causality as too "brutal and contingent" has proved hugely influential in the field of literary studies, and there is a real sense that new debates about the relative merits and demerits of symptomatic reading have remained beholden to anti-mechanistic models of historical causality. It is true that the work of some recent critics of symptomatic reading, such as Rita Felski (2008) and Toril Moi (2017), has begun to shift theoretical discussion back toward the question of literature's "uses"—yet even these reactivations of the concept of instrumental "use" have tended to eclipse the specifically political valences of the term. As I have been suggesting here, the writing of the later interwar years can help us restore to view broader twentieth-century debates about the ends of politicized literature that we have ignored to our own political loss.

Acknowledgment

I am grateful to the Heisenberg Programme of the German Research Foundation for funding research relating to this chapter.

Notes

1. See Slavoj Žižek, "Part I: The Symptom." *The Sublime Object of Ideology* (London: Verso, 1989), pp. 9–84.
2. For critiques of symptomatic reading, see Eve Kosofsky Sedgwick's *Touching Feeling: Affect, Pedagogy, Performativity* (Durham, NC: Duke UP, 2003), which calls for synthetic practices of "reparative" reading at the expense (psychoanalytic, Marxist, poststructuralist) "paranoid reading"; Stephen Best and Sharon Marcus, "Surface Reading: An Introduction", *Representations*, vol. 108, no. 1 (2009): pp. 1–21; as well as Rita Felski's loose postcritical trilogy *Uses of Literature* (Oxford: Wiley-Blackwell, 2008), *The Limits of Critique* (Chicago: University of Chicago Press, 2015), and *Hooked: Art and Attachment* (Chicago: University of Chicago Press, 2020).
3. Jameson borrows them in outline from Althusser's influential contribution to *Reading Capital*. For Althusser's discussion of the three types of causality, see *Reading Capital* (186–190).
4. See, e.g., Yates McKee's important situated analysis of "the *reinvention* of art as direct action" by the Occupy movement: *Strike Art: Contemporary Art and the Post-Occupy Condition* (London: Verso, 2017), p. 6.
5. "Mass Declamation", according to *The Continuum Companion to Twentieth-Century Theatre*, is a "-non-naturalistic, group performance used by working-class theatre troupes in Europe and America between the world wars [...] Distinguished by its use of chanting and choral speech, singing and choreographed movement, the mass declamation belongs to Agitprop theatre." See *Continuum Companion*, ed. Colin Chambers (London: Continuum, 2002), pp. 483–484. The Living Newspaper also originated with interwar Agitprop troupes: here, source material, which was taken from newspapers and updated on a daily or weekly basis, "was used in highly theatrical ways, often using the amplified 'Voice of the Living Newspaper' to underline points." See *Continuum Companion* (451).
6. This method could also be applied to now-canonical writers such as Ezra Pound, whose works possess an aesthetic complexity that is sometimes held to rescue or redeem the questionable politics of their authors.
7. See Diana Coole and Samantha Frost's *New Materialisms: Ontology, Agency, and Politics* (Durham, NC: Duke UP, 2010), pp. 33–35.

Works Cited

Althusser, Louis. "The Underground Current of the Materialism of the Encounter." *Philosophy of the Encounter: Later Writings, 1978–87*, edited by Matheron, François, and Oliver Corpet. Verso, 2006, pp. 163–207.

———, Pierre Macherey, et al. *Reading Capital*. Verso, 1979.
Auden, W. H. "August for the People." *The English Auden*. Faber and Faber, 1977, pp. 155–157.
———. "Spain 1937." *The English Auden*. Faber and Faber, 1977, pp. 210–212.
Balestrini, Nanni. *The Unseen*. Translated by Liz Heron. Verso, 2011.
Bargu, Banu, "In the Theater of Politics: Althusser's Aleatory Materialism and Aesthetics." *Diacritics*, vol. 40, no. 3, 2012, pp. 86–111.
Dean, Tim. "Art as Symptom: Žižek and the Ethics of Psychoanalytic Criticism." *Diacritics*, vol. 32, no. 2, 2002, pp. 20–41.
Empson, William. "Autumn on Nan-Yüeh." *Complete Poems*. Penguin, 2001, pp. 91–98.
———. "To Christopher Ricks." 19 January 1975. *Selected Letters of William Empson*, edited by Haffenden, John. Oxford UP, 2006, pp. 598–599.
———. "To Robert Herring." 14 July 1938. *Selected Letters of William Empson*, edited by Haffenden, John. Oxford UP, 2006, pp. 110–112.
Felski, Rita. *The Limits of Critique*. U of Chicago P, 2015.
———. *The Uses of Literature*. Blackwell, 2008.
Jameson, Fredric. *The Political Unconscious: Narrative as a Socially Symbolic Act*. Routledge, 2002.
Marasco, Robyn. *The Highway of Despair: Critical Theory after Hegel*. Columbia UP, 2015.
Moi, Toril. *Revolution of the Ordinary: Literary Studies after Wittgenstein, Austin, and Cavell*. Duke UP, 2017.
Rockhill, Gabriel. *Radical History and the Politics of Art*. Columbia UP, 2014.
Sartre, Jean-Paul. "Materialism and Revolution." *Literary and Philosophical Essays*. Collier Books, 1955.
Spender, Stephen. "Poetry and Revolution." *New Country*, edited by Roberts, Michael. Hogarth Press, 1933, pp. 62–67.
Thompson, E. P. "Christopher Caudwell." *Persons and Polemics: Historical Essays*. Merlin Press, 1992, pp. 77–140.
Wimsatt, William K. *The Verbal Icon*. U of Kentucky P, 1954.
Woloch, Alex. *Or Orwell: Writing and Democratic Socialism*. Harvard UP, 2016.
Zamyatin, Yevgeny. "On Literature, Revolution, Entropy, and Other Matters." *A Soviet Heretic: Essays by Zamyatin*. Translated by Mira Ginsburg. Northwestern UP, 1992, pp. 107–112.

5
REFORMS AND REVOLUTIONS

John S. Garrison and Kyle Pivetti

Percy Bysshe Shelley famously concludes his "A Defence of Poetry" with a stirring proclamation: "The most unfailing herald, companion, and follower of the awakening of a great people to work a beneficial change in opinion or institution, is Poetry" (716). But does the change ever come, and can literature actually claim credit? Does the emotional and memorial power of literature imply an inherent possibility for social transformations, and do those possibilities tend toward the gradual amelioration of conditions associated with "reform" or the total upheaval and inauguration of new ways of political being implied by the word "revolution"? In what follows, we consider an unlikely pair of texts that begin to answer these venerable questions—William Shakespeare's *Henry VI, Part 2* (England, 1591) and Keith Hamilton Cobb's *American Moor* (United States, 2015)—as well as some of the influential accounts of why one might seek reform or revolution and what, after all, imaginative literature has to do with either.

A Case in Point: Cade's Rebellion

The middle of *Henry VI, Part 2* dramatizes the largest popular revolt of medieval England: Jack Cade's Rebellion, the 1450 uprising of laborers and commoners that stormed into the heart of London in an uninvited visit to the seat of monarchical power. Working from historical accounts, Shakespeare gives voice to a number of real-world complaints of the early modern period: a citizen approaches the king to denounce "my lord Cardinal's man, for keeping my house and lands and wife and all from me" (1.3.19–20); another citizen objects to "enclosing the commons of Melford" (1.3.23–24), referring to the process where previously public land held in common was concentrated into private ownership by the upper classes. When Jack Cade marshals his troops for the inevitable class conflict, one soldier proclaims, "it was never merry in England since gentlemen came up" (4.2.7).

The embryonic revolt thus takes aim at an entire history of class division, and the followers understand the radical possibilities. "I tell thee," says another soldier, "Jack Cade the clothier means to dress the commonwealth, and turn it, and set a new nap upon it" (4.2.4–5). That is, the laborer will "turn" the political structure and dress it in the clothing of the populace. Cade joins in with a bold proclamation of freedom and equality: "And henceforward all things shall be in common" (4.7.16). In the middle of this history play—performed in the public theaters of London—the vision of a possible Utopia emerges, governed as a "commonwealth" by those who may very well watch from the floor of the Globe theater.

Fifty years later in 1642, these rebellious impulses would manifest again as England entered a period of Civil War. Culminating in the execution of the King Charles I and the institution of the English Commonwealth, the conflict was saturated with revolutionary literature of its own. John Milton, for example, argued in *The Tenure of Kings and Magistrates* (1649) for the inherent right of the people to depose their monarch. Gerard Winstanley founded the Diggers in 1649 with a yet more radical proposal for the abolition of private property. Far from mere verbal afterthoughts to historical events, Nigel Smith argues that "without literature" to make available new ideas of self-determination and liberty, "the 'English Revolution' as we know it could not have been" (2). That is, an English era of revolution not only came in the wake of Shakespeare's play, but historical actors perceived a causal relationship between literature and revolution. But just as the Earl of Essex's failed 1601 uprising against Elizabeth I was linked to a performance of Shakespeare's *Richard II*, the Commonwealth of the 1650s and the dreams of the Diggers also ended in failure. Tragically, the same is true for Jack Cade and his followers.

In the play, Cade reveals himself to be a cruel hypocrite, no different from the lords he overthrows: they both allow violent punishments of suspected enemies and he sanctions sexual assaults. Cade also declares himself part of the noble Mortimer family and so not only revives but reinforces the very class structures he had earlier denounced. For every proclamation of class revolt, Cade also inflicts vicious and farcical punishments against those who can read, those who print books, and those who run grammar schools. And he does so with dreams of being named King himself. It is little wonder that Cade's followers betray him as the tide of fighting in London turns, but Cade can only cry at their fickleness, "I thought ye would never have given out these arms till you had recovered your ancient freedom. But you are all recreants and dastards, and delight to live in slavery to the nobility" (4.7.168–70). If Cade briefly imagines a state of natural and original freedom, reality reverts quickly to the familiar condition of lower classes exploited and abused by their supposed "betters."

Cade dies in a poetic image of failure, alone and desperately searching for food. Shakespeare dramatizes the collapse in the garden of Alexander Iden, a local landowner who knows that the "small inheritance my father left me" (4.9.16) secures his place in the social hierarchy. When Iden finds Cade hiding in this echo of the Garden of Eden, the rebel leader has turned into a pathetic vagrant invading the scene of innocence. A swordfight follows and Cade dies a traitor, with Iden promising that he will "drag thee headlong by the heels/Unto a dunghills, which shall be thy grave" (4.9.77–78). This brutally postlapsarian Garden of Eden tolerates disobedience no better than the scriptural one. Rebellion ends at great cost, and the shame permeates Cade's monologue and Shakespeare's stage. If Eve attempted to seize power in claiming the tree of knowledge, she ultimately fails in supplanting her superiors. Cade did as well, for this particular form of revolution has never ended well. In the Renaissance, an era so-named because it has been imagined as a rebirth and a period of social upheaval, where exactly are the revolutions? And why is the stage so often remembering the dramatic, Utopian visions gone wrong?

If such fatalistic questions were posed to seventeenth-century theatergoers, they reach an apotheosis in the new historicists of the 1980s. For Stephen Greenblatt, Louis Montrose, Catherine Gallagher, and numerous others, the change was never going to come, whether from Cade, Brutus, Hotspur, or Caliban. Their pessimism derives from what Frederic Jameson identified as "strategies of containment," wherein the narrative inevitably ends by reaffirming political systems (37). For Jameson, this is the function of ideology, to incorporate dissent into the formal structures of narrative. In the case of Shakespeare, the monarch will always remain. The petitioners may get a chance to speak, but they seemingly will not—cannot—escape from the king's throne room and all that it represents.

Revolution and Memory

We know that literature has inspired real change, that it has dramatized successful moments of revolution and reform. In *Uncle Tom's Cabin* (1852), Harriet Beecher Stowe explicitly pursued an abolitionist agenda, and the novel did play its part in stirring anti-slavery sentiment well ahead of the American Civil War (Reynolds 380). Scholars continue to cite the role played by Thomas Paine's *Common Sense* (1776) in fomenting revolution; Steven Blakemore places it among a "textual war" (9) of subversive political writings in the Revolutionary period. That language echoes in Colin Wells' analysis of literary texts that constituted the "poetry wars," both terms turning literature into the literal battleground of political change.[1] Across the Atlantic, the French Revolution inspired its own series of textual wars, with responses permeating British and American society alike, to the degree that John Mee finds a British "radical culture" emerging from the social upheaval. Katherine Astbury goes further to show that the seemingly apolitical works of the era, like the sentimental novel of the eighteenth century, reacted to the events in France and perpetuated political debate. Socially conscious literature followed in the nineteenth century with the realist novels of Charles Dickens, William Dean Howells, and Elizabeth Stoddard. Amada Claybaugh shows that this "novel of purpose came to encompass all novels that sought to intervene in the contemporary world. And nearly all novels sought to do so" (34).

In representing their world, these writers pursued reform; their visions of the social world surpassed entertainment or fantasy to seek out real change. Yet these works too have been labeled failures, far less committed to the promise of reform than they seem. Amy Kaplan follows Jameson and treats the realist genre not so much as a subversive model of political critique but rather a "strategy for imagining and managing the threats of social change" (9). Nor was Kaplan alone in making these charges in the 1980s. Mark Seltzer similarly discovered in these novels complicity with systems of power. D. A. Miller equates the novel with the police, or a detective working to maintain discipline over a world order. The novel of reformation, in this perspective, becomes the very means of withholding reformation. So what is the legacy of the revolutionary text? A spur to change, or a symptom of failure? Why and how should we remember these kinds of texts?

We find that this complex dynamic of revolution and failure relates to memory in at least three ways. First, literary texts—not just plays or novels but a broad array of speeches, pamphlets, and other media—often function retrospectively to document periods of significant cultural change. Second, literature might commemorate past events in a way not just to document what has happened but to try and influence what might happen next, often by stirring the emotions of an audience that has been taught (truly or not) what mistakes were made. But literature can do more than that. In yet a third way that memory and revolution intersect, literature can compellingly depict historical events happening otherwise, through alternate histories in which the losing side actually wins the war or disaster never comes. Past wrongs and unjust systems can fall as authors dare to envision new histories and possible utopias. Cade might not be widely quoted today, but for a brief moment, this historical figure reimagined the present of Shakespeare's audience. That same impulse to reimagine the present still persists in the slogans of revolutionary movements today; consider the real-world example of the World Social Forum (an annual gathering of civil societies working to imagine an alternative to globalization). "Another world is possible," they pronounce. The slogan associated with the Zapatista movement in Mexico, "¡Exigid lo imposible!," goes even further to urge us to divorce ourselves from what we remember as possible paths and to demand the impossible.[2] Such phrases from those who imagine new social orders could just as easily describe the work of the author who conceives a work of fiction.

There is even a fourth way that literature ties to real-world efforts toward dramatic social change. We refer to the philosophical uses of literature, in which thinkers look to the texts as statements on the likelihood of change, and whether that change was ever likely in the first place. Writing from a range of thinkers gives us access to debates about the nature of revolution and reformation, of the sort that animates the manuscript source for Shakespeare. For all of his flaws (and for all of North's protestations), Shakespeare's Cade still asks whether the upheaval is both possible and desirable and presents the test case for revolution. In what follows, we first consider familiar touchstones of the debate about whether revolution is possible before moving to complicate that debate by considering the role of memory in this question. We end by providing two brief case studies that model how literary adaptation might offer new directions, and new modes of recollecting the past, in old debates.

The Impossibility of Revolution: First as Tragedy, Then as Farce

Major thinkers of the modern period have long considered the nature and possibility of revolution. Writing in 1851, Karl Marx was poised for the moment of reflection. He had just witnessed the Revolutions of 1848, a series of uprisings that saw the Second Republic of France. As the French monarchy fell, "The springtime of the peoples" (Roberts 6) gave renewed promise, with revolts spreading across Germany, Italy, and Austria. By 1851, though, Marx would have understood the failed promises. The political parties quickly splintered within a year, and in France, Napoleon's nephew declared himself emperor, leaving Marx to consider yet another revolution that had not remade the world. In a now-famous passage in *The Eighteenth Brumaire of Louis Bonaparte*, Karl Marx captures why:

> Men make their own history, but they do not make it as they please; they do not make it under self-selected circumstances, but under circumstances existing already, given and transmitted from the past. [...] And just as they seem to be occupied with revolutionizing themselves and things, creating something that did not exist before, precisely in such epochs of revolutionary crisis they anxiously conjure up the spirits of the past to their service, borrowing from them names, battle slogans, and costumes in order to present this new scene in world history in time-honored disguise and borrowed language.
>
> *(595)*

If Marx offers the possibility that we might be free to author our own futures, only too quickly does he snatch away that possibility. He argues that revolutionaries claim to be enacting a new way of living and being, but unwittingly recreate the past and thus cannot bring about a more desirable future. In turn, social change agents only reinforce those very structures that the revolution sought to overthrow. Note how he describes this cycle in explicitly literary terms. Revolutionaries look like stage actors—with their new "names, battle slogans, and costumes"—as they stage a "new scene." Marx seizes upon literary genres in one of his most damning phrases when he claims revolutions ultimately fail in their first attempt and then repeat those failures in any subsequent attempt: "the first time as tragedy, the second time as farce" (594). Feel sorry for those failed nobly minded change-makers the first time, Marx says, and laugh at those who try again.

The notion that revolutionaries simply cannot escape the gravitational pull of history finds its way into Walter Benjamin's essay "On the Concept of History" (1940), composed just after he fled Nazi Germany. In it, he describes the "angel of history":

> His face is turned toward the past. Where a chain of events appears before *us*, *he* sees one single catastrophe, which keeps piling wreckage upon wreckage and hurls it at his feet. The angel would like to stay, awaken the dead, and make whole what has been smashed. But a storm is blowing from Paradise and has got caught in his wings; it is so strong that the angel can no longer close them. This storm drives him irresistibly into the future, to which his back is turned, while the pile of debris before him grows toward the sky. What we call progress is *this* storm.
>
> *(392)*

Benjamin, like Marx, sees history not as progressing through a series of radical breaks but rather as one big, messy swirl of repetition. Any hope we might have for "progress" is just a delusion that makes it impossible to see how the wreckage of failed efforts in the past only foreshadows the same wreckage that awaits in the future. In the wake of history, there is no opportunity to "make whole" what is broken.

Another important thinker for this topic is Roland Barthes, who asserts that our inability to break free from patterns of the past rests at the level of language itself. He claims the writing of a novel and the writing of history differ little because "language is a corpus of prescriptions and habits common to all writers of a period" (9). That is, when we sit down to conceive and communicate new ideas or visions of how things might be different, we ultimately use formulations and terms that we know or that will be familiar to our audience. Both Benjamin and Barthes are less derisive toward failed change-makers, but both reinforce the idea that it is impossible to avoid repeating the past. How, then, does one make sense of this seemingly unbreakable chain that connects the weight of past to the present? How might literature offer a means to reconcile with the path and move forward in a new way? Indeed, might literature have a special capacity for showcasing revolutionary ideas and possible worlds?

The Future as Recuperation, as Emotional Memory

More recent writers are keen to note how the emotional aspects of memory, at least cultural memory, are crucial in the struggle to make revolution possible. Svetlana Boym has argued that our visions of the future are always the work of memory, remarking that "fantasies of the past determined by the needs of the present have a direct impact on the realities of the future" (xvi). At first, this might sound like the same arguments coming from Marx and Benjamin, wherein political futures are necessarily reformulations of corrupt pasts. Yet Boym also shows that imagining the future can be an opportunity to reconcile emotionally with the past because "consideration of the future makes us take responsibility for our nostalgic tales" (xvi). In other words, we must acknowledge how the stories we tell ourselves about the past are just that—stories, narrative inventions—meant to reassure us or allow us to place blame on others.

It is then up to us whether we tell more honest stories about the past. Sara Ahmed nicely articulates how the unsavory elements of past regimes can become either built-in or exorcized in the process of the continual building of the nation:

> What is striking is how shame becomes not only a mode of recognition of injustices committed against others, but also a form of nationbuilding. [...] Recognition works to restore the nation or reconcile the nation to itself by "coming to terms with" its own past in the expression of "bad feeling."
>
> *(102)*

By these lights, literature has the power to put such shame on display in order for the national collective to look critically at the past to see how it was unjust, unsavory, even downright embarrassing. Cade meets his "shameful" end in Iden's garden, but the emotional memory of that moment need not resurrect only the old power structures against which he railed. His shame might also signal change.

So how do we balance the hope for a different future against the recognition that the rebellion is already in so many ways failed? In *Cruel Optimism*, Lauren Berlant captures this ambivalent, paradoxical experience of looking forward. Optimism, to hope for the fulfillment of some sort of desire, is so often already impossible (like hoping that this time Cade will resist stupidity and cruelty and thus might live up to his own promises). Berlant puts the experience in terms of emotion and desire. "All attachments are optimistic," she writes, meaning that to relate to someone or something is to hope that a promise will be fulfilled. She does not mean this naively. She admits, "That does not mean that [attachments] all feel optimistic: one might dread, for example, returning to a scene of hunger or longing or the slapstick reiteration of a lover or parent's typical misrecognition" (47). Nevertheless, attachments and optimism are always intertwined. Even remembering the moment before it went wrong contains revolutionary potential: "But the surrender to the return to the scene where the object hovers in its potentialities is the operation of optimism as an affective form" (20). Literature provides that return. It refashions the attachment in each iteration, in each return to the text. In remembering, the revolution becomes possible again. Cade might do better, and as we will see, maybe the time for change was always there.

Othello, American Moor, and the Promise of Reform

So we come to reform. With that word we look beyond particular moments like the transformation of medieval Christianity called "The Reformation," or the nineteenth-century "Reform Bills" that expanded the franchise in the United Kingdom. Rather, the word poses a larger question: can moments of failure be re-formed in and through new emotional attachments?

Shakespeare's *Othello* might seem like a very unlikely place to go looking for the possibility of social change. Even though *Othello* features a Black man married to a white woman, the play culminates in the traumatic vision of Othello's suicide, terminating the figure most challenging to Venetian social, sexual, and economic norms. As a successful Black military leader, his very presence in Venice contradicts ideals of whiteness that shore up the Italian city-state's (and early modern London's) claims to exceptionalism. His challenge, then, cannot last. Stephen Greenblatt famously meditates on the "improvisation of power" in the play, before coming to the foretold conclusion, wrapped in Jameson's language of containment.

He writes, "for Othello there is no escape – rather a still deeper submission to the narrative" (252). The story has been written already, and Othello dies as the outsider who could never actually belong.

Greenblatt even applies that same language around the playwright himself: "Shakespeare approaches his culture not ... as rebel and blasphemer, but rather as dutiful servant, content to improvise a part of his own within its orthodoxy" (253). The profound work of recent decades on early modern constructions of race might imagine some relief.[3] For example, Ian Smith has helped us see the tragedy in a new way when he showed that the famed handkerchief was most likely black, a symbol of the character's own black skin. Yet still, this newly imagined version of the handkerchief underscores "an idea of blackness and race that place severe constraints on black subjectivity" (3). And if readers of Shakespeare have always wanted to see the handkerchief as white, it is because "as readers we are subjected to reproduce a dominant 'white' ideology that defines what we see and how we read" (Smith 25). So constrained are audiences that the possibility for difference, and so the possibility for change, is fundamentally invisible.

And yet, just when it seems as if there is hope for early modern literature to speak productively and politically to a twenty-first-century audience, along comes Keith Hamilton Cobb's *American Moor* (2020), a largely one-actor show in which the speaker reflects on a lifetime of playing Othello. Simmering with energies of rebellion, the monologue challenges the traditions of performance and the power structures that suffuse the play. The play begins with Cobb waiting to begin another audition for the part, fidgeting onstage. Cobb gives detailed instructions for this awkward preamble:

> He "prepares," moves, stands, stretches, sits again, perhaps recites, or mumbles ... but mostly he waits... Always he waits. From time to time he checks his watch...the way one might if perhaps an appointment had been scheduled for noon and it is now 12:20.
>
> (3)

This set-up foregrounds the actor's lack of agency. He can pace and work over his prop—a worn copy of *Othello*—but "always he waits" for something to change rather than inhabiting the conditions to be a "political actor" in the non-theatrical sense. In the case of *American Moor*, this actor literally mills about until he begins his audition for a "disembodied voice" that comes "about two-thirds back and center" (10). For the man onstage, the white director manifests only as a presence "omnipresent, answerable to, and impossible to ignore" (10). The construction of the theater echoes the circumstances of the play, once again throwing constraints in the way—immaterial as they may be. First Cobb must wait, and then he performs for an authority that offers direction, critique, and commentary on the legacy of *Othello*.

The scene on hand is Othello's first monologue to the senate, in which he recounts his journey to Venice. That choice bears ominous relevance to Cobb's own position as the actor; both he and Othello perform for a dominant power structure. The director, that disembodied voice of "a little white man," tells Cobb that Othello

> really needs to charm the senate with this gift of oratory and tale-weaving that he has in order to prevail. So, let me see him ingratiate himself a little more to them, I mean, the senate thrives on ... uh ... obeisance ... Right?
>
> (16–17)

The request comes in the form of a question, as if the director offers the possibility for refusal. Cobb understands the implicit directive and thinks aloud to the audience,

> But you see, in matters of race, throughout my American life, whenever some white person, well-meaning or otherwise has asked me to 'be open' they have invariably meant, 'See it my way.' And in this instance, in *this* play, that is unacceptable.
>
> *(17)*

Cobb forcefully defends his reading of the scene; Othello in Cobb's understanding grows weary of the performance and angry at the constraints. *American Moor* thrives on that irony, of the Black actor identifying with Othello at the moment of performance and knowing still that the play ends with the Moor's death. Cobb gives voice to his anger and makes claim to his own agency against the director: "You're gonna enlighten me? Fuck you, white boy! Shut up and listen. ... You think any American Black man is gonna play Othello without being in touch with his anger ... at you?" (22). The scene transforms: Othello and the actor are both going through the motions, made subservient for the possibility of landing a temporary job. In the case of Cobb, he would also understand that for much of the play's history, an American Black man was not in the part. Instead, Othello was played by white actors in blackface, meaning Cobb's anger could also be erased with a simple matter of recasting.

As the monologue continues, Cobb merges his reading of the character as a frustrated actor into the longer history of *Othello*'s performance. When Cobb wants to use Shakespeare to explore and to share "Black consciousness" (31), the stage has already seemed to stop him. Cobb captures the frustration of a Black actor struggling to earn the right to play this paradigmatic Black character:

> He'll tolerate you because he wants the job; because absurdly – to his horror – after ages, and generations, after four hundred years he *still* finds himself beholden to likes of *you* for the opportunity to do the thing that he does better than anything else he's ever done.
>
> *(41)*

Cobb's consciousness extends beyond the immediate audition, taking in Othello's multiple perspectives in which the performance never changes, much less the possibility for rebelling against the Venetian senate's power over his body, voice, and performance. Four hundred years and counting, Cobb—the character and the actor—confronts the impossibility of revolution and pivots toward another approach: reformation.

If he cannot change the script of the play, Cobb can alter the way it is interpreted by the audience. "He is wholly human," says Cobb of Othello, "But he is Black. And to be Black here has only ever meant to be more misread, misrepresented, misinterpreted" (37). The anger and conviction of Cobb's monologue marks another of *American Moor*'s central ironies: the value and potential of affect. The director avoids confronting the racist implications of the play's events by turning to Othello's individual emotions. He tells Cobb, "What fascinates us is not only the size of the man, but the size of his emotion, his passion the Early Moderns would call it. I think we need to see it" (24). In his way, Cobb gives exactly that: his emotion. The problem is the nature of the Black actor's rebellious anger. It is not "the time or place" for that. Cobb says to the director, "I can offer you the Moor from the inside out, and, standing before you, let what I feel be everything ... Then you see whatever you see. And what you feel *about* me will be everything else" (37). His emotion comes through, in direct confrontation but also in an invitation for the audience to hear, to share, to participate in a different monologue by a Black actor.

But the director is right about one thing, because the early moderns did call it "passion." They also recognized the theater as a place remarkably well suited to cultivate the passions. In fact, Steven Mullaney says of the public theaters that emerged in era of Shakespeare's career: it was "an inhabited affective technology, if you will, within which, and with which, they could think and feel things not always easy or comfortable to articulate" (74). Such passions also carried with them risky potential in Shakespeare's day, for the emotional outburst was unstable and was an implicit moment of rebellion. The antitheatricalist John Rainolds in *The Overthrow of Stage-Playes* (1599) captured how passion and memory come from—and come together because of—theater. He tells the story of how playgoers

> as soon as they were abroad out of their beds, did fall into a strange distemper and passion of a light frenzy. The which exciting them to say and cry aloud such things as were sticking freshly in their memory, and had affected most their mind.
>
> *(118)*

The playgoers, overwhelmed with the dramatic performance, forget themselves and become the characters onstage. Their own social positions vanish, and the "strange distemper and passion of a light frenzy" takes over. Othello, of course, suffers his own "strange distemper," and Cobb's passion—indeed, his anger—may consume a new group of playgoers, watching Othello anew in 2020. He brings his own memory of playing Othello, of being a Black man in the United States, into Shakespeare's narrative. And, after seeing this new play, audience members will never see *Othello* the same way again.

As *American Moor* resolves, Cobb reflects on his own aging body. He recalls, "So about a year ago, I start feelin' this shoulder when I liftin' heavy stuff. The doctor says, 'EEh, you're older. A little arthritis, a little tendonitis… Shit's gonna start to break.'" (34). The end is coming, Cobb implies. And with that breaking, the immediacy of the moment becomes more apparent: "What about all my unrealized dreams? I've been struggling after them for so long" (34). Just like Othello, the general who approaches the Venetian senate and must perform the same recollection of his "obeisance" one more time. Cobb says, "[Othello] knows he is old… He knows he is epileptic… He knows by now that no one is going to erect a statue on the Rialto to the memory of the great General Othello, the Moor" (35). How will Othello be remembered? This performance, in all of its passion, can erect a new statue by getting the playgoer to remember the past in a different way. It can, in its way, forestall the aging, even transform the 400 years of performance history. "Talk with me," Cobb implores, "We got so much to talk about. We ain't gotten past Othello's first speech and everything they told you is a lie" (41).

That talk, of course, will be passionate, an affective experience. In his final lines, the director gives a polite dismissal, "Thank you … Thanks for coming in" (42). The actor who began by waiting for the audition responds, "Sure… Any time" (42). The possibility for affective transformation hangs in the air. Any time the audience can feel and "go deep," the theater is there. In her introduction to *American Moor*, Kim Hall writes of the play's potential:

> we can stop the racism in theater and in our lives, if we can make the space and time for learning and listening. We don't have to passively play roles as others imagine them. What's past need not be prologue.

She seizes onto *The Tempest*, but in recreating the past, the reformation emerges. It isn't a new idea that the past charts the events of the future. After all, the familiar phrase "what's past is prologue" comes from Shakespeare and is engraved on the National Archives Building in Washington, DC. The new idea that Hall captures so perfectly is that the future has the power to re-chart the past by actively re-forming how we memorialize it, and thus open the possibility for changing the future. Theater can make new memories of old texts and past events, shaping them in light of the passions that seize the time of performance.

The story may remain the same, but the audience does not. A revolution is not just an overturning but a recurrent transformation: the word itself enters the English language first as "circular movement" or "a convolution; a twist, a turn; a loop." From the mechanistic and fatalistic Roman wheel of fortune effecting sudden change in events, to the political concept arising in the sixteenth century, revolutions are circular movements looping back around, upheavals in the past and always to come. When the revolution failed yesterday or the reform doesn't materialize today, consider the event a turn toward another beginning sure to come.

Notes

1 See Wells on the ongoing debates in American verse.
2 For more on the implications of this evocative slogan, see Rabasa.
3 See Urvashi Chakravarty's chapter "On or about 1616 or 1619" in this volume.

Works Cited

Ahmed, Sara. *The Cultural Politics of Emotion*, Second Edition. Routledge, 2015.
Astbury, Katherine. *Narrative Responses to the Trauma of the French Revolution*. Legenda, 2012.
Barthes, Roland. *Writing Degree Zero*, translated by Annette Lavers and Colin Smith. Hill and Wang, 2012.
Benjamin, Walter. "On the Concept of History." *Selected Writings of Walter Benjamin, Vol. 4: 1938–1940*, edited by Howard Eiland and Michael W. Jennings. Translated by Edmund Jephcott et al. Harvard UP, 2003, 389–400.
Berlant, Lauren. *Cruel Optimism*. Duke UP, 2011.
Blakemore, Steven. *Literature, Intertextuality, and the American Revolution: From Common Sense to Rip Van Winkle*. Fairleigh Dickinson UP, 2012.
Boym, Svetlana. *The Future of Nostalgia*. Basic Books, 2001.
Claybaugh, Amanda. *The Novel of Purpose: Literature and Social Reform in the Anglo-American World*. Cornell UP, 2007.
Greenblatt, Stephen. *Renaissance Self-Fashioning*. U of Chicago P, 1984.
Hamilton Cobb, Keith. *American Moor*. Methuen, 2020.
Jameson, Frederic. *The Political Unconscious: Narrative as a Socially Symbolic Act*. 1981. Routledge, 2002.
Kaplan, Amy. *The Social Construction of American Realism*. U of Chicago P, 1988.
Marx, Karl. *The Eighteenth Brumaire of Louis Bonaparte*. 1852. Reprinted in *The Marx-Engels Reader, Second Edition*, edited by Robert C. Tucker. W.W. Norton & Co., 1978, pp. 594–617.
Mee, John. "Popular Radical Culture." In *The Cambridge Companion to British Literature of the French Revolution in the 1790s*, edited by Pamela Clemit. Cambridge UP, 2011. 117–128.
Miller, D.A. *The Novel and The Police*. U of California P, 1988.
Mullaney, Steven. "Affective Technologies: Toward and Emotional Logic of the Elizabethan Stage." In *Environment and Embodiment in Early Modern England*, edited by Mary Floyd-Wilson and Garrett A. Sullivan. Palgrave Macmillan, 2007, pp. 71–89.
Rabasa, Jose. "Of Zapatismo: Reflections on the Folkloric and the Impossible in a Subaltern Insurrection." *The Latin American Studies Reader,* edited by Ana del Sarto, Alicia Ríos, and Abril Trigo. Duke UP, 2004). 561–583.
Rainolds, John. *The Overthrow of Stage-Playes*, Second Edition. Richard Shilders, 1599.

"revolution, n." *OED Online*, Oxford University Press, June 2022, www.oed.com/view/Entry/164970. Accessed 9 June 2022

Reynolds, David S. "Harriet Beecher Stowe's Uncle Tom's Cabin." In *The American Novel to 1870*, edited by J. Gerald Kennedy and Leland S. Person. Oxford UP, 2014.

Roberts, Timothy Mason. *Distant Revolutions: 1848 and the Challenge to American Exceptionalism*. U of Virginia P, 2009.

Scott-Warren, Jason. "Was Elizabeth I Richard II?: The Authenticity of Lambarde's 'Conversation.'" *The Review of English Studies*, vol. 64, no. 264, 2013, 208–230.

Seltzer, Mark. *Henry James and the Art of Power*. Cornell UP, 1984.

Shakespeare, William. *The Second Part of Henry VI*. In *The Norton Shakespeare*, Second Edition, edited by Stephen Greenblatt et al. W.W. Norton & Co., 2008, 229–316.

Shelley, Percy Bysshe. "A Defence of Poetry." In *The Norton Anthology of Literary Criticism*, edited by Vincent B. Leitch. W.W. Norton & Co., 2001, 695–717.

Smith, Ian. "Othello's Black Handkerchief." *Shakespeare Quarterly*, vol. 64, no.1, 2013, 1–25.

Smith, Nigel. *Literature and Revolution in England 1640–1660*. Yale UP, 1994.

Wells, Colin. *Poetry Wars: Verse and Politics in the American Revolution and Early Republic*. U of Pennsylvania P, 2018.

6
RIGHTS CATALOGUE
Juno Jill Richards

In the most basic sense, "right" signifies an entitlement or protection afforded to individuals by law. But rights are notoriously slippery and unstable, their value depending on the identity of the person or entity that claims them. This slipperiness emerges from the relational quality of rights and injuries, as a kind of intractable thicket wherein the rights of some are premised on the unfreedom of others. Rather than a universal force of emancipation, rights can be a source of harm, granting some individuals and governments the authority to regulate, police, and surveil others. Rights have been a propulsive organizing vehicle for some social movements, but also continue to offer legal justification for racial and sexual violence in the name of property protection, self-defense, safety, or conjugal entitlement.

Consider, for instance, the right to vote, the right to intimidate others from voting, the right to marriage, the right to rape one's spouse, the right not to be raped, the right to housing, the right to own property, the right to stand one's ground, the right to remain silent, the right to free speech, the right to hate speech, the right to asylum, the right to vigilante border control, the right to poison rivers, and the right to clean drinking water. My use of the catalogue draws on a footnote from Wendy Brown's "Rights and Losses," an essay that stresses the status of rights as "protean and irresolute signifiers," rather than a uniform social good (*States* 97). In the footnote, Brown asks us to consider a list of opposed possibilities:

> Consider: rights as boundary, and as access; rights as markers of power, and as masking lack; rights as claims, and as protection; rights as organization of social space, and as defense against incursion; rights as articulation, and as mystification; rights as disciplinary, and as antidisciplinary; rights as a mark of one's humanity, and as a reduction of one's humanity; rights as expression of desire, and as foreclosure of desire.
>
> (Brown, *States* 97)

The footnote is a catalogue of rights in opposing modes, offering a specific version of freedom and domination, entitlement and impoverishment, depending on the identity and historical positioning of the rights claimant. Each example offers a more concrete instance of what Brown, drawing on Marx, refers to as the paradoxical quality of liberal rights, which convey a universal, formal equality upon an abstract human subject, while disavowing the material constituents of lived personhood—including race, gender, sexuality, class, and nation—that practically constrain this freedom.

Catalogues make for an unwieldly grammar (and so are often relegated to footnotes). But there is something about the list as form that is important here. What constitutes the literary, in my analysis, is the catalogue itself, as a portable form that can be read very closely across a variety of genres, from canonical theories of rights to experimental memoirs, short stories, and novels. Across these works, the catalogue usually organizes a series of similar contents; for the grammar of a list to be correct, all the enumerated parts must have parallel structures. This grammatical sameness informs our readerly expectations, creating a general habit to skim over the set as a whole. Reading a catalogue usually lulls us into a pattern of sameness, each part a different version of the others. When we read lists, we tend to speed up. But when the contents of the list are not similar, when they scale up or down, or shift across the political spectrum from left to right, between utopian horizons for universal healthcare and white supremacist claims on border safety, the catalogue does a different kind of work, highlighting the frictions between grammatical similarity and vastly different contents.

An example of this second, more dissonant mode, Brown's list is a catalogue of paradoxical rights claims, separated by a series of colons. It is long and awkward (the sort of enumeration that usually gets edited out). But the list form allows us to hold each possibility in tension, unresolved, so that rights can signal a version of freedom or injury, at the same time. The footnote is a kind of preview for a later, major essay, "Suffering the Paradoxes of Rights," which expands more fully on the contradictory political valences of rights discourse. Once again, it does so with a catalogue.

> It would appear that a provisional answer to the question of the value of rights language for women is that it is deeply paradoxical: rights secure our standing as individuals even as they obscure the treacherous ways that standing is achieved and regulated; they must be specific and concrete to reveal and redress women's subordination, yet potentially entrench our subordination through that specificity; they promise increased individual sovereignty at the price of intensifying the fiction of sovereign subjects; they emancipate us to pursue other political ends while subordinating those political ends to liberal discourse; they move in a transhistorical register while emerging from historically specific conditions; they promise to redress our suffering as women but only by fracturing that suffering—and us—into discrete components, a fracturing that further violates lives already violated by the imbrication of racial, class, sexual, and gendered power.
>
> (Brown, *"Suffering"* 430)

Here again, the catalogue offers a mode of elaboration, drawing out structurally parallel propositions with different local specifics. Each entry is a different version of paradox, spun out like a fan. Each clause of the list holds together two incommensurable truths that threaten to undo the other. However, Brown argues for a secondary understanding of paradox, not as a container for opposites but as transformative action. Paradox becomes the structure that can accommodate the incommensurability between claims on rights and therefore the limiting possibilities of the existing juridical system. As Brown goes on to argue, paradox is not just a logical structure than holds together opposites; it can also mean to be against doxa, or orthodoxy, and so have a more active, transformational quality. To argue for rights that cannot be obtained within the current legal system changes the fundamental nature and quality of rights altogether. In this schema, rights are not legal reforms, but transformational demands, in that their attainment necessitates an entirely different social order.[1] Consider, for instance, the right to universal basic income, the right to free healthcare and housing, the right to abolish the prison industrial complex, and the right to freedom of movement across all borders. These more capacious versions of right would necessitate a wholescale restructuring of the social order across international lines. To name such demands as basic human rights sets a paradox in motion, allowing for a radical transformation of what rights can mean.

The language of mystification and the seemingly magical, transformative quality of rights paradox are also a central current in Patricia J. Williams' inimitable collection, *The Alchemy of Race and Rights*. Here alchemy does not just suggest the lasting intertwinement of race and rights, but their seemingly miraculous transubstantiation from dead, lifeless forms of exclusion into something vital and new. This transformation begins with a shift of perspective, turning to the experience of the historically disenfranchised in order to accommodate a different sort of paradox, this time understood through the language of desire. "To say that blacks never fully believed in rights is true," writes Williams.

> Yet it is also true that blacks believed in them so much and so hard that we gave them life where there was none before; we held onto them, put the hope of them into our wombs, mothered them and not the notion of them
>
> *(163)*

Rather than ask for rights to be doled out or protected more fully, Williams offers an alchemic narrative of bodily incorporation, putting the lifeless legal formula literally into the body and gestating it anew through the force of communal hope and desire. This transformative vision becomes, for Williams, a manifesto for future scholarship:

> The task for Critical Legal Studies, then, is not to discard rights but to see through or past them so that they reflect a larger definition of privacy and property: so that privacy is turned from exclusion based on self-regard into regard for another's fragile, mysterious autonomy; and so that property regains its ancient connotation of being a reflection of the universal self. The task is to expand private property rights into a conception of civil rights, into the right to expect civility from others. In discarding rights altogether, one discards a symbol too deeply enmeshed in the psyche of the oppressed to lose without trauma and much resistance. Instead, society must *give* them away. Unlock them from reification by giving them to slaves. Give them to trees. Give them to cows. Given them to history. Give them to rivers and rocks. Give to all of society's objects and untouchables the rights of privacy, integrity, and self-assertion; give to them distance and respect. Flood them with the animating spirit that rights mythology fires in this country's most oppressed psyches, and wash away the shrouds of inanimate-object status, so that we may say not that we own gold but that a luminous golden spirit owns us.
>
> *(Williams 164–165)*

Here too is a catalogue, but it does not just enumerate; it makes demands. The list form shifts, moving from the more academic language of "what we can do" to an imperative mode: *unlock, give, flood, wash away*. There is, in this shift, a kind of grammatical alchemy, a transformational magic at work, in the turn to the reader. The reader is not the subject of rights, the person who asks for rights. In the turn to the imperative, the reader becomes the giver of rights, the benefactor of freedoms to rocks and rivers. This turn shifts the foundational character of rights more generally. Rights are not something that we ask for from the state, but something that is ours to collectively reimagine and, in this imagining, transform.

Another version for this alchemy, for the transformation of what a rights claim might mean or do, can be located in a wider shift of critical emphasis, from an individual rights framework to the wider field of racial justice. In some cases, as Williams notes, critical legal and race theorists advocated for a wholescale rejection of rights language, arguing instead for more emancipatory and informal frameworks, outside the limiting purview of the state, law, and the current social order. One lineage for this tendency can be found in Black feminist organizing, through the work of the SisterSong Women of Color Reproductive Collective in the 1990s. In contrast to the American Birth Control Movement, which had primarily focused on the right to contraception, the SisterSong Collective argued for a shift from individual choice to a wider field of race and reproductive justice.[2] Rather than focus on an individual right to bodily privacy, which has been historically defined through the experience of white women, the SisterSong Collective organized around a project that moved beyond contraceptive choices to consider the racialized social forces that inhibit these choices, including an outsized vulnerability to violence, premature death, and state-sponsored medical oversight. This wider field begins with the right to bear a child or not, but also includes fundamental needs for raising that child, including the right to affordable housing, healthcare, childcare, and childhood education; the right to a living wage; the right to local access to clean water and affordable food; the right to parent without prejudicial interference from children's welfare services; and the right to raise children without the threat of racialized police violence and juvenile incarceration.

In this activist reimagination of individual rights, what began as a singular defense of contraception formulated around white heterosexual womanhood shifts, to accommodate an ever-expanding rights catalogue. This begins with prejudicially allocated entitlements, like housing and food, but also imagines entitlements that do not yet exist in the current social order, beginning with the perspective of populations most vulnerable to legalized forms of harm and inequality. Through the organizing efforts of Wages for Housework, Lesbian Due Wages, and Black Women's Wages for Housework, rights hold ground for newly possible futures: the right for wages for housework; the right to universal free healthcare, childcare, or basic income. In this case, the rights catalogue is also a set of demands for a different distribution of life chances, for a different relation between the state and its populace, and so for collective social forms that do not yet exist.

The rest of this chapter focuses on calls for recognition that use the language of rights to imagine forms of freedom and equity beyond the purview of the nation-state. My emphasis of this tactical use of rights emerges as an extension of the research in my first book, *The Fury Archives*, which offers a counter-history to more traditional accounts of human rights through queer and feminist organizing. Rather than begin with the League of Nations or the U.N., my work takes up a more illiberal use of rights, or the ways that feminist and queer activists have appropriated human rights language as a tactic. In these histories, what is significant is not so much the achievement of a demand for rights, but the daily worldmaking practices that emerged around such demands. Instead of the narratives of failure or success through legal reform, a turn to these practices reveals modes of intimacy, care, kinship, and freedom far exceeding what might be achieved through a juridical framework.

In what follows, I extend this consideration of rights athwart or beyond the status quo of the law. In the wake of the intervention of critical legal theory, critical race theory, and postcolonial studies, almost no interdisciplinary considerations of rights and literature are satisfied with the existing practices of legal and human rights. Whether they believe literature is complicit in, or an alternative to, the limitations of legal rights varies, but most begin with a dialectical accounting of the ways rights and the legal systems that ensure them have worked as systems of knowledge and power that distribute unequal life chances across the lines of race, gender, class, and nation. This body of work takes up questions of rightlessness, most famously through Hannah Arendt's consideration of "the right to have rights" in the wake of the refugee crisis produced through the World Wars. Arendt's key thesis, elaborated in *The Origins of Totalitarianism*, focuses on the exception to rights and the stateless person to draw out the paradoxes of a system that promises universal human rights through the limited purview of citizenship. Scholars focusing on the transatlantic slave trade often underline states of racialized rightlessness, through what Orlando Patterson has theorized as social death, as the counterpart to enlightenment ideals of universal equality and the category of the human.[3] Postcolonial scholars note the ways that human rights posit Western models of freedom that look to speak for or rescue subaltern populations, often while maintaining unequal balances of power in an international world order.[4] As Inderpal Grewal has argued, human rights have emerged in the past 25 years as a dominant ethical language across national borders, as "a regime of truth and as an ethic that was believed to lie at the heart of a normative state and a transnational civil society," while effectively functioning as a mode of transnational governmentality, allowing state actors to defend and maintain a hierarchical international order (122).

Though I will not offer a full survey of the interdisciplinary consideration of rights and literature, what follows tracks out three key tendencies. The first includes the ways that narrative genres, including testimony, the *Bildungsroman*, the war novel, and the family saga, have shaped both the drafting of rights declarations and the literary imagination of a human subject of rights. The second tendency emphasizes embodiment and vulnerability as a corrective for the abstract imagination of universal personhood in legal doctrines. Finally, a third strain of criticism focuses on the status of sympathetic identification in narrative representations of suffering rights abuse. Drawing together questions of genre, bodily vulnerability, and vexed sympathy, my conclusion returns to the catalogue as a structuring modality of rights critique.

Critical Methods in Rights and Literature

Interdisciplinary considerations of rights and literature often begin with the ways that particular genres of writing have shaped the popular and legal imagination of a human subject of rights. One thread in this tradition turns to the ways that testimony, including fact-finding missions, tribunals, inquests, and other modes of writing, functions in the governmentality of human rights organizations, from truth commissions to NGOS. In *Human Rights and Narrated Lives*, Kay Shafer and Sidonie Smith argue for the importance of life writing as a genre in human rights campaigns, highlighting the ways that first-person testimony became a key organizing modality for humanitarian intervention and the recognition of injustice.

Considerations of testimony necessitate a closer study of the ethics and politics of witnessing trauma, alongside the ways its representation can produce discourses of sentimentalism, wherein sympathetic identification papers over material differences as a kind of symbolic reparation, erasing existing structural inequalities in the act of reading. Nicole Rizzuto offers one intervention in this model through a rendering of testimony as an insurgent genre, moving beyond the more canonical site of the World Wars to consider histories of colonial insurrection across the modernist and postcolonial period. In her reading of the literary afterlives of Jamaica's Morant Bay rebellion, Rizzuto positions the use of testimony in the work of V. S. Reid and H. G. de Lisser as a way critique "the legal concept of necessity that was at the foundation of British emergency law and at the heart of the debates about whether the counterinsurgency was justifiable" (11).

Given the long history of right resting upon accounts of the putatively universal subject, it is not surprising to find indispensable theoretical interventions drawn from the Global South. Focusing more particularly on the contexts of Latin America, for example, John Beverly describes a particular branch of collaborative life writing, *testimonio*, as a combination of a first-person narrative of someone who was a witness to atrocity and the work of editor, who mediates between the narrative voice of the witness and a Western reading public. Writing on the particular case of Rigoberto Menchú, Beverly has positioned the *testimonio* as a singular voice that overrides the Quiché-speaking indigenous community, an "absent polyphony of other voices" (34). Hearing this absence in Menchú's testimony, Arturo Arias sees this inscription of the narrative witness into the historical record as a mode of disappearance, through the failure to translate subaltern voices into Western models of representation.

If first-person writing brings to the fore questions of authenticity, cross-cultural empathy, and witness, scholarship on the novel tends to focus more closely on the construction of the human personality named as a subject of rights. In *Human Rights Inc.*, Joseph Slaughter positions the eighteenth century *Bildungsroman* and human rights law as "mutually enabling fictions," which emerge from German idealism's nomination of the bourgeois white male citizen as a universal subject. In Slaughter's accounting, the *Bildungsroman* and human rights discourses collaboratively construct the development of the human personality articulated by law as an individual that develops out of any refractory impulses, growing into a harmonious relation with existing civil society and the nation-state.

More recently, a number of critics have shifted from the individualist emphasis of the *Bildungsroman* to related genres that focus on wider populations. In *The People's Right to the Novel*, Eleni Coundouriotis highlights the specificity of the war novel, seeing in the genre a way to address collective rights. Rather than focus on the confrontation between individual and society that runs throughout the long tradition of Western democratic theory, the African war novel offers "a collective account of ordinary people in the historical transitions from colonialism to independence" (1–2). Here Coundouriotis's sense of collective history is not just a point of thematic emphasis, but a historiographic method. Through richly detailed case studies, chapters set internationally recognized war novels alongside a range of lesser-known, more local responses to war aimed at African readers, allowing for a wider-ranging construction of both war and its aftermaths.

Through a study of U.S. authors of color, Crystal Parikh similarly shifts our focus from the *Bildungsroman*, turning instead to the family saga as a way to represent the construction of the human person as a part of a political community. Drawing on the work of Jhumpa Lahiri and Ana Castillo, Parikh positions the family saga as a way to reconsider affiliation beyond biological kinship "in order to grant recognition to the *desiring* subjects that modernity produces, subjects who want otherwise than either traditional, patriarchal forms of communal life" (190). Parikh reads Lahiri and Castillo alongside the 2006 U.N. Convention on the Rights of Persons with Disabilities (CRPD) as a way to rethink the human right to health, not as a universal norm but as "the political sign under which subjects lay claims to protections and privileges they have not been granted, transforming themselves as political agents in the process" (205).

A second, alternative tendency in the interdisciplinary consideration of rights and literature sets aside the development of specific genres to consider embodiment as an alternative to the universalizing, abstract registers of rights discourses. In *Fictions of Dignity*, for example, Elizabeth S. Anker argues for an "embodied politics of reading," tracing the ways that human dignity and bodily integrity work together in a symbolic economy, rendering violated, broken, or irregular bodies illegible within dominant legal norms. Against an Enlightenment-based lineage of rights, Anker surveys a more proliferating, diffuse tradition through phenomenological attention to fleshiness, porosity, and bodily incoherence.

This turn to embodiment often begins from the perspective of subjects historically excluded from universalizing discourses as key figures for the reimagination of freedom. Working in this vein, Samantha Pinto's *Infamous Bodies* opens with a rights paradox: the notorious visibility of early Black women celebrities, alongside the ways these women were not historically legible as subjects of rights. Pinto's work explores the history of Black women celebrities as a reckoning with the failures of rights discourse, shifting from the heroics agency to a more careful consideration of shared vulnerability. This study turns to performances of law and rights as fictions that Black women celebrities embody to reimagine consent, contract, civic engagement, citizenship, and sovereignty. As Pinto notes, her focus on the vulnerable body relies on a wider tradition of African American studies, including the work of Hortense Spillers, Saidiya Hartman, and Alexander Weheiye, that theorizes the materiality of the flesh to expose the paradoxes of rights' abstract claims to equality.

Finally, a third critical tendency centers on the often spectacular representation of suffering rightlessness. This tradition turns against a more laudatory account of sympathetic identification with a suffering subject as a humanitarian good in itself.[5] These accounts consider the hierarchical relationship between spectator and spectacles of rightlessness, drawing out what Saidiya Hartman has called "the precariousness of empathy and uncertain line between witness and spectator" (4). The problem of the humanitarian gaze becomes a touchstone in Lyndsey Stonebridge's *Placeless People: Writing, Rights, Refugees*, which foregrounds the category of the stateless person as a limit case for the ethical claims of literary representation. Rather than attend to a specific genre, Stonebridge takes up the politics of humanitarian compassion across a variety of writerly modes to locate a shift in attention, away from the fact of suffering and toward the historical and political forces that produce rightlessness. In her consideration of journalist Dorothy Thompson's writing and advocacy surrounding the Palestinian documentary, *Sands of Sorrow*, Stonebridge draws out

> the capacity of humanitarian sentiment to miss its mark and be spat back at your feet not because you have failed to sorrow fairly but because you have confused your human ability to recognize suffering with a way of living with other people in the world.
>
> (165–166)

#MeToo and the Catalogue Form

My survey of critical methods is a catalogue of sorts, in that it draws together scholarship that turns to the question of rights, taking seriously histories of attachment, desire, and fantasy around what rights promise, while remaining critical of the ways legal systems of power have unequally distributed these freedoms. In this conclusion, I situate the catalogue more fully as an aggregative form. I started to think about the technologies of cataloguing in the wake of the #MeToo movement, through the use of the hashtag as a technology of aggregation on Twitter and through the publication of lists of serial perpetrators, like the crowdsourced spreadsheet, "Shitty Media Men." In these examples, the hashtag #MeToo suggests a narrative similarity, but not necessarily a sameness. It becomes a container for structural forms of harm that can also accommodate distinctions of individual experience. Part of the political weight of the catalogue becomes its unreadability: the list or group that is too long to consider, too many entries to possibly read.

With these organizing currents as a backdrop, I want to consider the ways more creative genres use catalogues to theorize gender-based harm. A number of recent memoirs eschew conventional narrative forms in favor of a catalogue-like agglomeration, as one way to account for the overwhelming prevalence of sexual violence in daily life. Rather than an isolated incident, or the crux or a narrative arc, sexual violence becomes, in these accounts, perpetual, nearly atmospheric. For instance, Myriam Gurba's *Mean*, an unclassifiable, utterly indelible blend of life writing, true crime, and ghost story, draws together multiple narratives of gender-based violence, the short chapters cycling through different forms of catalogue, including a court room deliberation report, undergraduate class schedule, Death Row Inmates list, and faux catechism on the omnipresence of rape. A key document of #MeToo activism, Seo-Young Chu's "A Refuge for Jae-In Doe: Fugues in the Key of English Major," cycles through genres bureaucratic and poetic, including a "Mutant Blazon," describing the author's rapist, and "A Kind of Census" that offers a portrait of the author, beginning with the number of spouses and children ("zero"), then turning to a reciprocal entanglement with an epically long serial drama: "Number of episodes of Law and Order: Special Victims Unit never seen: zero."

Indeed, *Law and Order SVU*, in its formulaic structure and abundant episodes, is a useful rubric for the ways that the catalogue of sexual harms might extend beyond the singular event, taking up the more diffuse temporalities of post-traumatic stress disorder and diminished life chances. If the rights catalogue can express a more transformative social vision, a serialized version of harm offers, instead, a narrative for the ways that sexual violence is utterly pervasive. In the chapter, "Omnipresent," Gurba begins with what she was taught about the nature of God and then, in cutting and unforgettable phrasing, turns to the similarly ubiquitous nature of rapists: "You never predict that rapists are lurking in the sun, sky, and trees" (111). This catechism for the omnipresence of sexual violence, in its turn to the second person, shifts our focus from the violent encounter to a technology of post-traumatic perception: "After a stranger ambushes you and assails your private parts, everything becomes new. Everything is reborn. Everything takes on a new hue, the color of rape. You look at the world through rape-tinted glasses" (111).

This rendering of the ways that sexual violence extends into the crevasses of everyday life takes on a similarly sardonic, somewhat fantastic register in Carmen Maria Machado's short story, "Especially Heinous: 272 Views of *Law & Order: SVU*." The story is a serial take on a serial form, each stanza-like paragraph sharing the title of the televised episode it ostensibly summarizes. These summaries of heinous violence are often irreverent, though sympathetic to the pull of salacious, violent detail. Sometimes they grow bored or petty, focusing on inane dialogue or surrealist reveries. These are not so much summaries, but metonymic fragments, parts taken for wholes. The complete entry for the episode "GHOST" reads: "A prostitute is murdered. She is too tired to become a spirit" (95). In many ways, "Especially Heinous" is an ironized rendition of the infamous catalogue of crimes in Roberto Bolaño's *2666*, a 284-page graphic account of femicide in the borderlands. Bolaño's narrative reads like a series of police files, detailing when and where the woman's body was found alongside a graphically detailed accounts of her injuries. If Bolaño's narrative looks to make visible the scale and scope of an ongoing atrocity, Machado is more interested in a narrative experiment in agglomeration, as a dizzying fracture of the police procedural, with its predictable staging of crime, investigation, juridical theater, and restitution. As a perspective of a prior serial form cycle that it re-writes, the story creates friction between what we know to have happened on television and the more arbitrary or irreverent fragment that appears on the page. In this way, Machado creates a technology for telling multiple, conflicting narratives at once. The catalogue is not about the subject of rights or the subject of injury, but the violent and prismatic ties between them.

> "SPECTACLE": On a Wednesday, they catch so many bad guys that Benson throws up seventeen girls in one afternoon. She laughs as they spill out of her, tumble into her vomit like oil slicks, and dissipate into the air.
>
> *(122)*

In this episode, Machado imagines girls metamorphized into vomit and air, expelled and inhaled. It is a different sort of imperfect substitution, a fairy tale of transubstantiation, as though the fantastic were the only mode that could properly accommodate this legal narrative of rescue and rehabilitation.

It would be possible to read these pages as a straightforward critique: on the prurient entertainment value of sexual violence; of a carceral feminism that necessitates the imprisonment of perpetrators in the name of safety and restitution, expanding a prison industrial system well known for its human rights abuses. But Machado's story is not really a judgment, true or false, right or wrong. It is an alchemy, a kind of technology for narrating multiple narratives from opposing perspectives, as the paradoxical content of gender-based rights. Two stories at once then from different angles: the girls vomited up, turned into air and, at the same time, behind it, our knowledge of another serial narrative, the procedural form of criminal law and order, still ongoing in televised reruns.

Notes

1. As a thought experiment, we can imagine capacious demands from a neoconservative perspective, like the right to pay zero taxes, but this would only ratchet up the existing inequalities of racial capitalism, rather than transform the underlying social system.
2. For more on race and reproductive justice, see Roberts, Ross and Solinger, Ross (2006 and 2017), and Spade.
3. See Wynter, Hartman, Weheliye, Naimou, Pinto, Jackson, Holloway, and Cacho.
4. See Spivak, Coundouriotis, Slaughter, Anker, Hesford, Parikh, Madhok, Dawes, Rizzuto, and Moore.
5. See Hunt for account of literary sympathy as social good. See Berlant for an early critique of this tendency.

Works Cited

Anker, Elizabeth S. *Fictions of Dignity: Embodying Human Rights in World Literature*. Cornell UP, 2012.
Arendt, Hannah. *The Origins of Totalitarianism*. Harcourt, 1968.
Arias, Arturo. "Authoring Ethnicized Subjects: Rigoberta Menhú and the Performative Production of the Subaltern Self." *PMLA*, vol. 116, no.1, 2001, pp. 75–88.
Berlant, Lauren. *The Queen of America Goes to Washington City: Essays on Sex and Citizenship*. Durham, NC: Duke University Press, 1997.
Beverly, John. *Testimonio: On the Politics of Truth*. U of Minnesota P, 2004.
Bolaño, Roberto. *2666*. Translated by Natasha Wimmer. Picador, 2004.
Brown, Wendy. *States of Injury: Power and Freedom in Late Modernity*. Princeton UP, 1995.
———. "Suffering the Paradoxes of Rights." *Left Legalism/Left Critique*. Edited by Wendy Brown and Janet Halley. Duke UP, 2002: 420–434.
Cacho, Lisa Marie. *Social Death: Racialized Rightlessness and the Criminalization of the Unprotected*. NYU Press, 2012.
Chu, Seo-Young. "A Refuge for Jae-In Doe: Fugues in the Key of English Major," *Entropy*, 2017.

Coundouriotis, Eleni. *Narrating Human Rights in Africa*. Routledge, 2020.

———. *The People's Right to the Novel: War Fiction in the Postcolony*. Fordham UP, 2014.

Dawes, James. *The Novel of Human Rights*. Harvard UP, 2018.

Grewal, Inderpal. *Transnational America: Feminisms, Diasporas, Neoliberalisms*. Durham: Duke University Press, 2005.

Gurba, Myriam. *Mean*. Coffee House Press, 2017.

Hartman, Saidiya V. *Scenes of Subjects: Terror, Slavery, and Self-Making in Nineteenth-Century America*. Oxford UP, 1997.

Hesford, Wendy S. *Human Rights Rhetorics: Human Rights Visions, Recognitions, Feminisms*. Duke UP, 2011.

Holloway, Karla F.C. *Legal Fictions: Constituting Race, Composing Literature*. Duke UP, 2014.

Hunt, Lynn. *Inventing Human Rights: A History*. Norton, 2008.

Jackson, Zakiyyah Iman. *Becoming Human: Matter and Meaning in an Antiblack World*. NYU Press, 2020.

Machado, Carmen Maria. *Her Body and Other Parties*. Graywolf, 2017.

Madhok, Sumi. *Vernacular Rights Cultures: The Politics of Origins, Human Rights, and Gendered Struggles for Justice*. Cambridge UP, 2021.

Moore, Alexandra Schultheis. *Vulnerability and Security in Human Rights Literature and Visual Culture*. Routledge, 2015.

Naimou, Angela. *Salvage Work: U.S. Caribbean Literatures amid the Debris of Legal Personhood*. Fordham UP, 2017.

Parikh, Crystal. editor. *The Cambridge Companion to Human Rights and Literature*. Cambridge UP, 2019.

———, *Writing Human Rights: The Political Imaginaries of Writers of Color*. U of Minnesota P, 2017.

Patterson, Orlando. *Slavery and Social Death*. Harvard UP, 1982.

Pinto, Samantha. *Infamous Bodies: Early Black Women's Celebrity and the Afterlives of Rights*. Duke UP, 2020.

Richards, Jill. *The Fury Archives: Female Citizenship, Human Rights, and the International Avant-Gardes*. Columbia UP, 2021.

Rizzuto, Nicole M. *Insurgent Testimonies: Witnessing Colonial Trauma in Modern and Anglophone Literature*. Fordham UP, 2015.

Roberts, Dorothy E. *Killing the Black Body: Race, Reproduction, and the Meaning of Liberty*. Vintage, 1997.

Ross, Loretta J. "The Color of Choice: White Supremacy and Reproductive Justice." *Color of Violence: the INCITE! Anthology*. Edited by INCITE! Women of Color Against Violence. South End Press, 2006, pp. 53–65.

———, editor. *Radical Reproductive Justice: Foundations, Practice, Theory, Critique*. Feminist Press, 2017.

Ross, Loretta J. and Rickie Solinger. *Reproductive Justice: An Introduction*. U of California P, 2017.

Shafer, Kay and Sidonie Smith. *Human Rights and Narrated Lives: The Ethics of Recognition*. Palgrave, 2004.

Slaughter, Joseph R. *Human Rights, Inc. The World Novel, Narrative Form, and International Law*. Fordham UP, 2007.

Spade, Dean. "Intersectional Resistance and Law Reform." *Signs: A Journal of Women in Culture and Society*, vol. 38, no. 4, 2013, pp. 1–25.

Spivak, Gayatri Chakravorty. "Righting Wrongs." *South Atlantic Quarterly*, vol. 103, no. 2–3, 2004, pp. 523–581.

———. "Use and Abuse of Human Rights" *boundary 2*, vol. 32, no.1, 2005, pp. 131–189.

Stonebridge, Lyndsey. *Placeless People: Writing, Rights, Refugees*. Oxford UP, 2018.

Weheliye, Alexander G. *Habeas Viscus: Racializing Assemblages, Biopolitics, and Black Feminist Theories of the Human*. Duke UP, 2014.

Williams, Patricia J. *The Alchemy of Race and Rights*. Harvard UP, 1991.

Wynter, Sylvia. "Unsettling the Coloniality of Being/Power/Truth/Freedom: Towards the Human, After Man, Its Overrepresentation – An Argument." *CR: The Centennial Review*, vol. 3, no. 3, 2003, pp. 257–337.

7
EMPIRES, DECOLONIZATION, AND THE CANON

Maryam Wasif Khan

The Western Canon in Our Times

This chapter comes in the wake of multiple debates around the discipline of classics and its broader legacies in both the Euro-American academy and Western societies. Contemporary scholars of the humanities and literary journalists, impelled above all by the intertwined questions and crises of race, intellectual thought, and politics, have often moved to identify classics and the Greco-Roman world it represents as one and the same with whiteness and racial privilege. This bold interrogation of a near-sacred discipline of the elite Euro-American academy has unsurprisingly resulted in a violent pushback from scholars and pundits who see intellectual work and civil society as somehow disconnected realms or, worse, believe that the culture written by the works that became the classics might serve as the balm to soothe its own ills. The beginnings of a decolonized curriculum in the Euro-American academy, then, are fraught with a strange nostalgia for imperialism itself.

For a comparatist trained within the elite academy, but whose practice lies outside of it, the classics and the body of works we still call the Western canon exercise a powerful pull: the canon exerts itself as a supreme literary prototype to the postcolonial reader, while also looming as a contested but obstinate subject, a reminder of the imperialism that shaped its Pakistani, Indian, Egyptian, Kenyan, British, and American readers. In states such as India or Pakistan, the very idea of the body of works that is called literature harkens back to the two and half centuries of English colonial rule that shaped and reshaped vernacular textual traditions and ideas of education. The colonial curriculum, "as early as the 1820s," as Saikat Majumdar reminds us, was "dominated" by the classics, a body of works that had shaped literary studies in England just a few decades earlier (11). Ironically, public and private curricula for English literature continue to celebrate and give pride of place to classical texts, be they the Homeric epics or Greek drama, so that English literature in the postcolonial academy continues to exist and thrive on the foundation of its self-declared origins in the classical world.[1] Even though literary studies in the postcolony continue to pay homage to the Western world and therefore grates upon scholars and students of empire and decolonization, it is both impossible and regressive to attempt to imagine literary worlds *without* these texts.

Instead, over the past few decades we have seen necessary ethical efforts that wrestle with the place and nature of inclusion that classical and canonical Western texts could and should have in a decolonizing world. It would not be an overstatement to say that these efforts begin, in fact, with Erich Auerbach's monumental *Mimesis: The Representation of Reality in Western Literature* (1953), a work that has traditionally been read as a celebration of canonical Western texts from Homer's *Odyssey* and the Hebrew Bible to Virginia Woolf's *To the Lighthouse* (1927). A great scholarly exposition of the Western tradition by an eminent Jewish-German intellectual, *Mimesis* is also a deeply felt literary tracing of the victory of National Socialist thought over the other, more esoteric impulses that are contained in Europe's extended literary history. Thus, as Edward Said observed in his essay "Secular Criticism," *Mimesis* is not "only a massive reaffirmation of the Western cultural tradition, but also a work built upon a critically important alienation from it" (*The World, the Text, and the Critic* 8). At the core of *Mimesis* is the struggle of a figure in exile to reconcile his great love and longing for that which has become instrumental in his expulsion. More specifically, as Aamir Mufti has elaborated in his reading of *Mimesis*, European civilization and its grand explicator, the Western canon, are "inherently unstable," because the tensions between Hellenic and Hebraic (as Auerbach himself writes about in the opening essay, "Odysseus' Scar") leave open the constant possibility of explosions and danger (230). This chapter, more explicitly than any other in the volume, explicates what Europe could become when its Hellenic (non-interpretive, legendary) elements persist and triumph over its Hebraic (interpretive, historical) impulses. The fascist tendencies that materialized as National Socialism in Germany of the 1930s, Auerbach suggests, take precedence when the Hellenic origins of the Western canon dominate over their equal partner, the Hebraic.

Despite his alienation from Europe and his recognition that this alienation emerged from Europe's own origins, Auerbach extends forth a mysterious appeal in the epilogue to *Mimesis*:

> Nothing remains but to find him—to find the reader that is. I hope that my study will reach its readers—both my friends of former years, if they are still alive, as well as all those from whom it was intended. And it may contribute to bringing together again those whose love for our western history has been serenely preserved.
>
> *(557)*

While much attention has gone on the part that precedes this strange plea—Auerbach's earlier reminder to critical readers of his conditions while in exile in Istanbul—this element of the conclusion also deserves our scrutiny. There is, on the one hand, an attempt on the part of the writer to reconnect with a past, with peoples, and with places that he knows are more than merely lost to him: they have in fact actively helped engineer his expulsion from the place he knows as home. His more urgent desire, however, is to unite those who jointly love and see themselves as part of a shared Western history. This desire orients itself toward the future, offering a set of inclusive possibilities for the texts of the Western canon in the world that emerged from the horrors of twentieth-century European fascisms and imperialisms. It is the readers of his book and the readers of the Western canon, whoever and wherever they may be, that must find and forge new forms of community based on their affiliations with Europe and its culture.

To ask for a conscious affiliation with European culture, let alone one motivated by a "love" for Western literature (to borrow Auerbach's emotive marker) seems more radical today than almost a century ago. Yet Auerbach was not the last scholar of our time to persist in his attachment to the body of works that appeared to mark him as peripheral, even foreign. Edward Said, himself a devoted reader of Auerbach, wrote about his own teaching career in one of his final works, *Humanism and Democratic Criticism*: "Despite my involvement in the struggle for Palestinian human rights, I have never taught anything but the Western humanities at Columbia, literature and music in particular, and I intend to go on doing so as long as I can" (5). Coming in the wake of influential works such as *Orientalism* (1978) and *Culture and Imperialism* (1993), *Humanism and Democratic Criticism* (2004) reflects on Said's efforts to rethink the American academy's commitment to the Western humanities. This work, like his earlier ones, relies on texts from the broader Western canon to make an argument against its historic dominance in the American academy. A reluctant lover of Western humanism, Said both reflects and extends upon what is at the heart of *Mimesis*: the conviction that the Western literary tradition, despite its centrality to the sins of "Eurocentrism and empire," could be both part of and be refashioned to participate in a broader, more democratic humanism that does not take Europe as it center.

The Origins of Humanism

While both Auerbach and Said speak to the broader tradition of Western humanism, an emerging set of scholars have recently been engaged in a series of important and wide-ranging efforts to rethink the idea of the classical world and its legacies. Notable among them is Donna Zuckerberg's *Eidolon*, a journal whose watchword was to make "the classics political and personal, feminist and fun," led to a new wave of accessible and equitable scholarship on the Greco-Roman world. Though *Eidolon* suspended publication of new materials in December 2020, its essays and Zuckerberg's book, *Not all Dead White Men: Classics and Misogyny in the Digital Age* (2016), forced scholars of the Western canon to reevaluate what classical texts had come to mean in the twenty-first century. Zuckerberg's essay, "How to Be a Good Classicist under a Bad Emperor," made especially clear how increasingly vulnerable an unreformed classics was to a rising Alt-Right in the United States. Above all, Zuckerberg showed that the recruitment of the discipline for a second wave of fascism was an imminent threat—unless, of course, classicists saved classics from itself. In making the classics resolutely and openly "political," Zuckerberg reiterates what scholars before and contemporary to her have already said: that the classics, like any other field of knowledge, is shaped by and wields power in the ways that it defines authority, morality, and space. If it is true that for movements such as the American Alt-Right, classics is a way to preserve the superiority of white maleness and its links to the Europe, then it is also true that for the humanist committed to a decolonized humanities, the classics must be reread and reimagined to include an account for a fuller and equitable history of the human.

Like Zuckerberg but emerging quite literally from the postcolony is the classicist, Daniel Padilla Peralta, who has unabashedly declared that classics as a discipline is "traditionally Euro-American in composition [and] propelled even to this day by a conviction of its centrality to 'Western civilization.'" As such, Padilla argues, the field has "made it really easy for the casual student—or the trained professional—to subscribe to facile narratives of static timeless white purity under assault from waves of immigrants." While Padilla's initial work as a classicist focused on the Roman Empire, he is now possibly the most influential voice within the discipline calling for an "explosion of the canon," a change in the very being of "classics," and "writing an entirely new story about antiquity and who we are today" (Poser). Padilla's clash with the very hand that feeds him—classics in the academy—has predictably been misread by conservative and even many liberal scholars in the field. Yet its fundamental (and fundamentally political) question is both urgent and deeply ethical: how do we—or should we— even study the origin of Western civilization given its centuries-long complicity in the exclusion and subjugation of non-white populations across the world?

Sites of Renewal: The Western Canon in the Peripheries

Indebted to the confrontations, admissions, and expansions that scholars from Auerbach to Padilla have made with respect to the sacred cultural ideals of the Euro-American academy, this chapter reimagines the place of the Western canon in the postcolonial academy, where literary scholarship is shaped entirely by its colonial foundations. It is continuous with the radical calls that each one of these scholars has made, aware that many postcolonial subjects and scholars remain marked by what Auerbach emotively marked as their "love" for the Western canon. Above all, it emerges out of a frank consciousness of the present moment in the postcolony—one that in states such as India and Pakistan is marked by rising fascisms that define themselves through religious-national terms. In our postcolonial present, rife with violence against minorities bolstered by state surveillance and urban securitization, I suggest that we quite literally invent new methods of close reading that are not exclusively contingent on the accepted historical contexts of a grand text, but rather upon on the place and time of the reader. This is neither a simple Euro- or American-centric exercise in reading world literature nor myopic presentism. Rather, it is an urgently ethical and political re-worlding of that which has for centuries remained the measure by which Euro-American intellectuals have categorized, organized, and ordered literature in parts of the world as disparate as India and Brazil. It is a simultaneous exercise in critique and empathy that emanates not from a socio-historical European ideal of what it may mean to be human; rather, the exercise comes from sites where the human has, for much of modernity, been produced as a secondary object-in-formation to be completed by a fully formed European counterpart. It offers, finally, ways to read canonical European texts that expand their meaning even as they question their authority.

This argument may at first present itself as a regression of sorts, a pernicious suggestion that once-colonized peoples whose aesthetic traditions have been indelibly lost to the forces of European modernity should once again succumb to the cultural hegemonies from which they have yet to properly disentangle themselves. Shouldn't we instead explore underrepresented vernacular traditions, authors, and aesthetic forms, rather than embark on a renewed act of affiliation that will privilege the already privileged by rereading that which has been read quite enough already, thank you? Should we not recall Said's own critique of notorious "core" curricula in the university humanities, which for decades have defined literary studies at institutions such as Columbia, Yale, Princeton, and the University of Chicago? "The practice of reading these wonderful books out of their historical contexts and at several removes from their original forms," Said writes, has in the past century idealized these works as foundational and singularly authoritative on the question of what it means to be human and civilized (*Humanism* 3). After all, this has historically meant that these texts have participated in and been recruited as members of broad ideological and nationalist processes through which people from the colonized world have been excluded from what it means to be European and, thus, from enjoying the status as masters and members of a great civilization and culture.

And yet I insist such a reaffiliation is not only possible, but desirable. Despite the deliberate cultural invention of certain figures as antagonistic, distinct, and incompatible with Europe and the West, scholars such as Auerbach and Said, differently exiled from Nazi Germany and from Palestine, persisted in their scholarly and personal attachments to Western literature. They were convinced that the problematic institution could nonetheless offer redemption where it long offered destruction, and at the heart of Auerbach's method stands a commitment to a "process of formulation and interpretation whose subject matter," he reminds his readers, is "our own self" (549). This is neither a Barthesian exercise in killing the author or histories of a text nor a simple-minded, supposed liberation of the reader from the hard work of interpretation. Rather, it offers a method of close reading that is radically inclusive, inviting the reader—he, she, or them, Jewish, German, Muslim, Indian, Pakistani, Kenyan, or white American—to engage in acts of interpretation that resist the universalizing maneuvers of canonical approaches. To do so is to allow for cultural behemoths such as the Western canon to yield unexpected meanings, to converse with and across space and time, and to offer empathetic possibilities that extend across the known and unknown spectrum of human experience. An exercise in exilic thinking, where the reader must separate from insular modern structures of nation and religion, this process can direct us toward a new humanism that relies not on the rejection of the past, or of the barbaric other, but on the possibilities that an empathetic encounter can engender.

"Now, goddess, child of Zeus, tell the old story for our modern times"—Homer[2]

To make this argument, I turn to Homer's *Iliad*, a foundational text of colonially sponsored university syllabi for English literature in Pakistani and Indian universities for two centuries. I argue that when we read a canonical, reified text such as the *Iliad* in and from a space devoid of the promissory oaths of cultural authority, it opens and adopts the more immediate concerns of the moment, and thus transforms from a culturally sacralized war epic to an offering of empathy, a code to speak of war in a moment of high censorship in the postcolonial Pakistani state where I write these lines now. Far from reinforcing the ideals of masculinity, honor, and uncompromised virtue for which it is often extolled, in this altered space and time it becomes a testimony to the fragility of narrative in a moment where forms of state fascism familiar to Auerbach are rising in multiple locales far from Germany, Italy, and Spain. This exercise broadly and aspirationally permits an anti-fascist humanism for our times, a departure from the traditional practice that once consolidated and confirmed that which was already known. A humanism for our times and our places, to borrow Said's notion, becomes "a means of questioning, upsetting, and reformulating so much of what is presented to us as commodified, packaged, uncontroversial, and uncritically coded certainties" (*Humanism* 28). Double-edged, it forces us to dislodge a text such as the *Iliad* from its pedestal of distinctively "western" cultural authority and thereby to speak to the crisis of human experiences that has historically been erased by and from the European imaginary. In contemporary Pakistan, the *Iliad* is a text about abjection and futility that nonetheless offers an opening, especially within the academy, to speak in a moment of deep and wide state censorship. Its concerns, far from epic, relocate us and are themselves relocated at the geographic and discursive peripheries of the nation-state.

"Muse, tell me," or, Speaking through an Epic[3]

A postcolonial state whose colonial government neatly gave way to an extended military dictatorship, albeit often partnered with a semblance of democracy, Pakistan has remained a site of imminent violence from the very moment of its founding in 1947. For Pakistanis who have come of age in the years since September 11, 2001, the scale and nature of state-sponsored violence has been uncomfortably intimate and has forged generations of young people who know little else. As the ally of two violent, bloody powers—the Taliban and the United States—Pakistan paid its dues through the lives of ordinary citizens, victims of terrorist attacks from state-sponsored drones in the sky and from non-state firepower on the ground. In contemporary Pakistan, life persists in a state of perpetual war where the battlefields are civilian public arenas as varied as parks, hospitals, and schools.

On December 16, 2014, six gunmen attacked a school in Peshawar, killing 156 middle- and high-school students, permanently injuring and disabling many of those who survived. This wasn't the first attack of its kind, though it may well have been the bloodiest. Malala Yousafzai had famously been shot a couple of years before; earlier in the year and less famously, a young man from a village in Khyber-Pakhtunwa named Aitezaz Hassan died while tackling a suicide bomber on the verge of invading his ramshackle school. Neither was this the last time. A year and a half later, 75 young parents and their children, mostly Christian, would die in a suicide blast at a popular park on Easter Sunday in Lahore, the second largest metropolis of Pakistan. On April 13, 2017, another young university student from the city of Mardan named Mashal Khan would be lynched by his fellow classmates for "blaspheming," synonymous in the Pakistani academy with the religious crime of asking questions, of expressing doubt, sometimes of loving poetry. In each case, the dead were labeled martyrs or *shahīd* by the Pakistani state (excepting, of course, the Christians and Mashal, whose lynched body was then tried for blasphemy).

With each blast and each death, the Pakistani state and its spokespeople both reignite the significance of war and enemies and reiterate their commitment to the destruction of India, to the terrorists who have been bred by the Pakistani state itself. Each generation is educated and re-educated to believe that Pakistan has won and will win every war it fights. Yet the greatest enemies of the state, it seems, are those who ask questions and narrate events in ways that seem to undermine official positions about Pakistan's endless wars and "un-Islamic" enemies. Thus, the question for humanists, journalists, and students (among others) is always: how do we speak of war and violence in a place and time where speech is disallowed? At historical junctures such as the one Pakistan finds itself in, the vernacular becomes a risky medium, susceptible to censorship on account of the possibilities it may offer in a space where critique and historiography have remained contained by the state. Instead, it is with no small irony that, by returning to seemingly reified literary territories and canonized forms of epic war in antiquity, we hope to find ourselves able to speak freely about violence that the postcolonial state commits, sanctions, and glorifies.

At our liberal bests, we would read the *Iliad* as a foundational text of the Western canon by applauding its metrics and aesthetics and analyzing its heroes, even as generations of new translators have attempted to revive and render an ancient language in the tongues of its constantly changing readership. We would then debate whether the *Iliad* is anti- or pro-war text and we might presently conclude that Homer offers us a condemnation of war. These are familiar interpretive exercises when war is a distant reality, an event that happened in times past or spaces unseen. When read during and in the space of war—as in the case of Pakistan, which maintained an extended alliance both with the United States' War on Terror, and with the Taliban and Al-Qaeda—the stakes are not "merely academic" when violence enters spaces in which private and public coalesce: schools and universities. In these sites of reading, war sits among its readers: in the beings of those who have lost family members from drone attacks; in the erect postures of security guards who point their guns as they guard high campus walls; in the perpetual fear that humanists, students, and teachers alike have of the state punishing or disappearing them for undertaking acts of critique; and in the form of armed violence, always imminent in the city we inhabit. The task of the critical reader is twofold: to read away from traditional readings of the *Iliad*, and to read against the greater state narrative that justifies decades of war.

To attempt to teach genre (epic), time (antiquity), tradition (Western), or meter (dactylic hexameter) in this time and place is to uphold a prescriptive ideal of the Western Canon: to borrow Edward Said's words, to present the canon as "marmoreally finished in itself, before which we need to bow down" (*Humanism* 26). The idea of a canon, or the Western Canon, to be specific, specifically Western canon falls apart when it travels beyond the Euro-American academy and its fragile outposts in the postcolonial world. That is to say, the scholarly apparatus upon which the canon stands, the reams of uncritical literary criticism that contain it, and the aesthetic mystique that floats around it, all appear incongruous and misplaced when we read the *Iliad* or *Inferno* in cities such as Lahore: a place where the freedoms to read, to imagine, and to critique are restricted to the slowly shrinking, imperiled space of the university in a time when we can no longer imagine a un-militarized society.

In Book 2 of the *Iliad*, "The Great Gathering of the Armies," the narrative shifts from its focus on the defining conflict between Agamemnon and Achilles to the swelling ranks of the Greek forces, "gathering now/as the huge flocks of winging birds, geese or cranes/or swans with their long lancing necks." At another moment, the armies are "crowding thick-and-fast/as the swarm of flies seething over the shepherds' stalls/in the first spring days when the buckets flood with milk" (Homer 114-115). From gathering geese, to swarming flies, the armies of the Achaeans appear, at first, to the narrator who attempts to describe them as familiar events of nature, a ritual of coming together, but these images soon fade to give way to what appears as a performed anxiety:

> Sing to me now, you Muses, who hold the halls of Olympus
> You are goddesses, you are everywhere, you know all things—
> all we hear is the distant ring of glory, we know nothing—
> Who were the captains of Achaea? Who were the kings?
> The mass of troops I could never tally, never name
> not even if I had ten tongues and ten mouths
> a tireless voice and the heart inside me bronze.
>
> (Homer 572)

In its classical contexts, we may appreciate this passage as a rhetorical celebration of the many thousands of Greek men who gathered to recover the lost honor of King Menelaus, "thrilling" to the battle call of their leader Agamemnon. It marks the grand scale of a war whose story is being told by a human, the narrator, who at certain points in the epic inserts himself as an "I," a lowly bard tasked with telling an extraordinary tale of gods and men. In the longer history of canonical Western narrators, the Homeric narrator inaugurates a tradition of summoning divinity to give truth to a fiction; to raise the epic genre from the level of the quotidian to the sacral; and to make the epic, as Mikhail Bakhtin has suggested, a genre of "firsts" and "bests," its narrative guided by the "profound piety" that the narrator holds for the past (13).

But when we shift the site of our reception and alter the pasts and presents of the reader from the Euro-American academy to a site where the state has sponsored a war against its own citizens, we are directed away from the rhetoric of nationalism and honor. The narrator's sudden inability to speak—he is at once paralyzed and at once rendered speechless—takes on a darker meaning. The idea of appealing to divinity for narrative strength and accuracy is motivated not by a desire to emphasize the grandeur of impending violence, but out of fear of the violence that may done to a narrator with a truth different from that of the state. In a shared moment for the narrator of the *Iliad* and the many varied narrators of war in Pakistan, the task of being a chronicler, a teller of events assumes a wholeness, a humanness that hitherto has not been required of narrative form, whether classical epic or journalistic op-ed. This is an army and a war that the narrator of the *Iliad*, his time, and its people have never seen. The task of faithful narration grows all the more important and looms impossibly, requiring perhaps "a heart of bronze," the metal of manual weapons and armor, to tell his story. Reading less like epic narrative and aligning more with scenes from a newsroom at the moment of the Peshawar school massacre, the fear of the *Iliad*'s narrator is best translated into the postcolonial present by Mohammad Hanif, the novelist and journalist:

> In the Karachi office where I work, we were scared of the TV screen, even though we had pressed the mute button. We had been terrified we'd hear the screams of children being slaughtered 1,000 miles away in Peshawar. But every time we looked at the TV, the numbers had gone up. Five minutes earlier it was 36. How did that become 107? A colleague paced up and down, making calls and feeding us the latest rumours: they were separating the older ones from the younger ones. As if the 11-year-olds were more innocent; as if that 15-year-old was really asking for it.

In Lahore or Karachi, cities no longer far from these conflicts, the idea, the image of "ten tongues and ten mouths, a tireless voice," and a "heart of bronze" offer what can best be described as a series of narrative possibilities, new ways to tell and hear of a war that has hitherto only been described in terms of martyrs and enemies of state. The rhetoric helplessness of the narrator in the *Iliad* translates into a buoyant call for other stories, other counts, other songs, a human effort to tell the costs of war, rather than a repeated echo of the "distant call of glory" that is always just out of reach, or that has taken place in a sacred time, the epic time (572).

In the epic that the state offers us, our forefathers—whether those who defend us from "internal threats," or those who fought for a separate state in 1947, or even the mythical Muslims who conquered India in the eighth century—sacrificed everything in the name of Pakistan. The epics of our founding are also epics of war. Our epic heroes range from Muhammad bin Qasim, the eighth-century Muslim general who invaded Sindh to save a group of fellow Muslims from the supposed wrath of a Hindu king, to Mahmud Ghazni, the eleventh-century Afghan warrior mythologized for his destruction of the idols of the vanquished, to men of the Pakistan army who defend Islam and their country against the somehow constant threat of Indian invasion. We must speak of such men with the "profound piety" that Bakhtin reminds us surrounds the epic and its subjects, never forgetting that Pakistan *is* the sacred ground upon which this epic was fought, even in the eighth century (17). We must live our lives, the state demands, but absolutely without "experiencing it, analyzing it, taking it apart, or penetrating it to its core" (Bakhtin 16).

Much like Hanif, the journalist who struggles to accept the numbers of the dead, the narrator of the *Iliad* appears during moments of deep crisis when we hear and read him in Lahore or in other parts of Pakistan. At some points, the Homeric narrator asks for multiple voices; at others, he declares his helplessness, his inability to tell it all, for the "strain is far too great." As Hector races toward his death, the narrator circumlocutes the impending tragedy, telling instead how Hector and Achilles pass "the lookout point," "the wild fig tree/tossed by the wind," describing how they run past the "washing-pools/scooped out in the hollow rocks and broad and smooth/where the wives of Troy and all their lovely daughters/would wash their glistening robes in the old days" (Homer 546). Briefly liberating himself from the darkness of his narrative duties by indulging in the comforts of an idyllic past, the narrator offers an alternative world to the one that he is bound to speak of—a world made unreal and impossible by the tragedies of the present. The summoning of this world is one manifestation of the presence of the multiple voices, the ten mouths and ten tongues that the narrator asks the Muses to bless him with, an attempt at telling it all. Despite the impossibility of a return to a past that knows only the beauty of the pastoral, it is the evocation of that same past that forces the readers/listeners to a place where war and violence were not quotidian.

The anxieties coded into the Homeric epic and its human narrator, then, direct us away from the idea of the epic as a national form or as a sacrosanct cultural paradigm, opening up for readers in contemporary Pakistan, the fragments of narrative that are born from the possibility of multiple voices. In our present, in Lahore, in Karachi, in Quetta, in Peshawar, in cities and towns that no one ever talks about, the epic of the state, the epic of our so-called bests and firsts, cracks under the weight of the ten mouths and ten tongues that its unrelenting, enforced truths have wrought into existence. The stories, songs, and accounts of war that come with the multiplicities of these myriad voices force us to rethink the weight of the epic and the sacralized identities that loom large in our literary and national canons. The openings and multiplicities of meanings a foreign, Western epic offers can direct the postcolonial humanist inward, away from an established national canon and toward a minor poetics. That is to say, a canonical Western text becomes an agent of subversion once read outside of and against the contexts the Euro-American academy has created for it.

A conscious repudiation of the state, of a national literary canon based on the fight for Muslim liberation from India, directs the Pakistani humanist to interrogate the glory of Pakistan's endless war against terror by turning to the spaces and languages of resistance. In particular, it asks us to privilege the bedraggled, grief-stricken, debased human above the ideal of the human that the Western canon has been so complicit in producing. A reading from postcolonial sites of war positions Priam, Chryses, Andromache, and Astyanax—bereaved fathers, enslaved wives, and orphaned children—as the central characters of the epic. Largely unspeaking, communicating through their bodies, through wails, bent knees, and prayer, figures such as Priam and Andromache reduce Achilles and Agamemnon to a mere rhetoric of might and masculinity. This re-centered reading of the Western epic by the postcolonial humanist also directs them to the seemingly unspeaking humans of the warring state. Curiously echoing the realms of multiple translation, away from a national Urdu canon that celebrates the state and its structure, war is not glory. In the Khyber-Pakhtunwa district, where the state imprisons those asking for an end to drone warfare and militarized checkpoints, the Pashtun voices of disfigured men, widowed women, and fatherless children sing "*Dā sanga āzādī dā*" (what kind of freedom is this), where "*bachiyān mu qatal kēgī, kurunā mē varanēgī, Pakhtūn pakē khvārēgē*" (our children are murdered, our homes are destroyed, and the Pashtun's fate is misery). In Balochi, the songs are not of mourning, but of the anger of ordinary men in a province whose resources power the rest of the country, while itself left to the mercy of neighboring Taliban fighters: "*mā bāghī, mā firārī, mā sarmachāren balōchan*" (I am a rebel, I am free, I fight for Baloch autonomy).[4]

In the postcolonial space, the Western, once-colonial, epic collapses, shedding its grand form to become one of several chronicles of citizens amidst a state-sponsored war. It is precisely its "Westernness" and canonicity that allow for it to access and become code for the costs of war that citizens, victims, scholars, and journalists cannot speak of under censorious regimes. Even as postcolonial humanists and scholars move to decolonize curricula through the recovery of vernacular narratives and an interrogation of the imperial legacies on literary studies, they must remain attuned to the possibilities of renewed methods of reading over the soothing ease of erasure.

Notes

1. See, for example, public university syllabi for English Literature at colonial and now government-run institutions such as Delhi University and Punjab University, Lahore.
2. Homer, *The Odyssey*. Translated by Emily Wilson (W.W. Norton, 2018), p. 105.
3. ibid.
4. I am grateful to Sara Saleem Khan and Sohaib Arif for translating and transliterating Pashto and Balochi anthems with me, and to Fatima Afzal for her first draft edits.

Works Cited

Auerbach, Erich. *Mimesis: The Representation of Reality in Western Literature*. Princeton UP, 2013.
Bakhtin, Mikhail Mikhaĭlovich. *The Dialogic Imagination: Four Essays*. U of Texas P, 1981.
Hanif, Mohammed. "By Targeting Schools, the Taliban Has Struck at the Heart of Pakistan." *The Guardian*, 18 Dec. 2014. https://www.theguardian.com/commentisfree/2014/dec/18/schools-taliban-pakistan-peshawar-massacre-education-mohammed.
Homer. *Iliad*. Translated by Robert Fagles. Penguin Press, 1992.
———. *The Odyssey*. Translated by Emily Wilson. W.W. Norton, 2018.
Majumdar, Saikat. "The Critic as Amateur." *New Literary History*, vol. 48, no. 1, 2017, pp. 1-25.
Mufti, Aamir R. *Forget English!*. Harvard UP, 2016.
Padilla Peralta, Dan-el. "Classics Beyond the Pale." *Eidolon*, 20 Feb. 2017, https://eidolon.pub/classics-beyond-the-pale-534bdbb3601b.
Poser, Rachel. "He Wants to Save the Classics from Whiteness." *The New York Times Magazine*, 2 Feb. 2021, https://www.nytimes.com/2021/02/02/magazine/classics-greece-rome-whiteness.html.
Said, Edward W. *Humanism and Democratic Criticism*. Columbia UP, 2004.
———. *The World, the Text, and the Critic*. Harvard UP, 1983.

PART II

Constituting the Polis

8
CITIZENSHIP AND ENSLAVEMENT

Elizabeth J. West

At the heart of politics is the matter of citizenship—the question of who belongs to a given community in possession of rights and obligated by duties—and, by extension, the matter of who is sanctioned into the body politic. Theoretically, members are entitled to participate in the formulation and interpretation of the collective ethics that ground the group's identity and normative behaviors. The shape and scope of that identity become wedded to sensibilities of right and wrong, which then buttress the body's notions of itself: its greatness, its worthiness, and its dividing lines of insiders and outsiders. In the United Kingdom colonies that would eventually become the United States, perhaps the most foundational opposition was between those who were ontologically "inside" as citizens and those who were ontologically "outside" as enslaved persons. This matter of polity was confirmed through some of the earliest settler era documents, foremost among them those legal or constitutional agreements that served as governing documents for the new British arrivals to the Americas. The pacts that established the governing body and rule for the earliest British settlements of Jamestown (1608), Plymouth (1620), and Massachusetts Bay (1628) would serve as models for the colonial settlements that followed. While these works were legal documents, formed out of the desire to maintain both economic and social order, they would later become interpreted through a lens of historiography that would also carry over to literature. Though not formally articulated as such, history as literature would become the nation's medium for propagation of its voice and its self-reflection. This relationship of history, politics, and literature in the making of the United States is one that rings loudly of the nation's intricate hand in the centuries arc of slaving.

As a matter of history and historiography, there are some facts that are established beyond dispute: Britain shipped over 3 million people from Africa to colonies in the Caribbean, North America, and South America. Perhaps half a million of those people died during the voyage, but truly vast fortunes that exist to this day were made by individuals and companies through the practice of treating human beings as disposable property. This centuries-long enterprise did not flourish simply by the will of those whose wealth was directly tied to its operations. Trans-Atlantic slaving was buttressed by an intricate relationship of key parts of which historiography, literature, and politics were central. This economic machine depended on the unending supply of people, and by the seventeenth century the diverse people and their descendants stolen from their native African homes were being constructed as a monolithic "race" sanctioned to labor for the advancement of white prosperity. This would be articulated in white interpretations of Biblical stories such as the curse of Ham or the banishment of Cain. In both cases, Africans were said to be descendants of these sinners who had been marked by God for all their generations to be denied his special providence. With the Bible as proclamation of African outsidership, rules would be installed to maintain what was said to be divinely sanctioned. History and literature could then be framed from this premise and fashioned into "enlightenment" reasoning. It would easily become a circular regenerative phenomenon: Blacks would be deemed natural outsiders because they were innately less than human, less than whites; rules and laws would be enacted to maintain this order, and writings would abound as fact and as fiction to ingrain this social ordering into policy.

Literature, then, has played and continues to play a central role in how the nation grapples with its hand in the atrocities of centuries-long enslavement of a population that it would later have to recognize as citizens. The foundational settler voices and their writings suggest the establishment of political entities guided by ideals and actions that represented and operated in the interest of the common good. If the body politic operates out of an agreed set of ethics or universal set of recognized and unquestionable principles, what has literature conveyed about the history and soul of this body? When considering enslavement as it is represented in American literature, the matter becomes necessarily more ambiguous. Through its deployment of speculative and imaginative modes routed through the instabilities of language, literature often engages the political in highly evocative ways. Certainly modern fictionalized histories such as Yaa Gyasi's *Homegoing* (2016), Toni Morrison's *Beloved* (1987), Octavia Butler's *Kindred* (1979), and Alex Haley's *Roots* (1976) exemplify this power of the literary. Through these literary histories the nation's narrative dissonance between its polities of goodness and its deep place in the enterprise of slaving is brought to the forefront.

A disturbing revelation of these contrasting literatures of enslaving is that the notion of the common good is often a veil for the reality of generational buy-in, commitment, or simply submission to a core set of conventions that get moralized as ethical. It then becomes evident that the set of beliefs and conventions that are markers of good/right or evil/wrong are not universal to humanity writ large any more than they are within the collective society. Predictably, tensions emerge when ethics are not mutually agreed upon and when all who reside within a shared space are not awarded shared rights and benefits. The natural consequence is dissent—whether passive or overt—and the intensity of that dissent will vary on the basis of the forces behind submission or coercion. When those who command submission also dictate the discourse, those who are coerced or forced become the silenced outsiders. This tension is evident in some of the earliest literatures of America, including the most sanctimonious literary works of America's earliest historical period.

Origin Stories and Original Citizens

In the academy we continue to generalize literary works as "creative" even when those works—such as biographies, memoirs, journals, and even essays—are presumed to be "factual" narratives that reflect on historical or political moments. This paradox is illustrated in one of the earliest published accounts of the British settlements in the United States, John Smith's *The Generall Historie of Virginia, New England, and the Summer Isles* (1624). While John Smith was a British citizen, his account of the establishment of the Jamestown settlement is readily found in contemporary anthologies of American literature and history. This immediate incongruence might understandably prompt the question of whether the text offers a "fact" of American history or a creative myth for an origins story of the nation. In the *Heath Anthology of American Literature*, the section editor does not frame the discussion of John Smith's text for its literary merit, but rather focuses on its importance in the history of the founding of Jamestown. To this end there is an emphasis on what the work tells us about political foundations of early American colonies. The editor emphasizes that what the text reveals is that with Smith as leader, the Jamestown settlement was one that teetered on the brink of disorder. With its "quarrelling colonists," their "competing interests," and the ever present threat of the native population, Smith responded by instituting "a policy of military discipline" (Winans 126). In this literary anthology, readers are directed to read the text not so much from a perspective of its creative import but rather for its importance in the history of the nation's early formation of political bodies and practices. The conventionally literary and the conventionally political are joined here, perhaps even with the suggestion that histories of political thought might stand in as art.

North of John Smith, in the territory the settlers later named New England, William Bradford would write an account that would as well be integrated into the origins narratives of the United States. Unlike their Southern counterparts, the early Northern British settlers would not become known for ushering in America's legacy of plantocracy; however, in both the north and the south, early British settlers and their economies quickly became tied to and even dependent on slaving and the trade of captured and enslaved Africans and African Americans. In his lengthy history, *Of Plymouth Plantation* (1620–1647), Bradford describes his part in the composition and signing of *The Mayflower Compact*. Lauded as one of America's first governing documents, *The Compact* acknowledged the British king as authority, but "bound the colony together in a 'Civil Body Politik' for the purpose of enacting and enforcing laws" (Conlin 36). A history of the British settlement that would be named Plymouth, William Bradford's *Of Plymouth Plantation* troubles the supposed distinction between "literary" and "political" documents. The history, or journal as it is also called, details the first decades of Plymouth Colony, including the settlers' initial encounters with the native people whom Bradford immediately casts as villans and outsiders. Although it is the settlers who have invaded the natives' homeland, Bradford assumes the voice of rightful inhabitant. This tone is set with his reduction of their human value to that of "savage barbarians," who would readily "fill... [the Puritans'] sides full of arrows" (76).

Bradford's work is commonly included in American literature anthologies that feature sections on early writings. Similarly, his work is regularly found in historical accounts where it serves as example of early lawmaking and government in the nation's history. While Bradford is conveying in the most clear and documented terms the British confiscation of native lands and the consequential removal or killing of Native Americans for British settlement, he is constructing the literary tradition of America's origins mythology. Early documents such as Bradford's would later morph into the mythology of exceptionalism—the claim that the supposedly universal democracy uniquely arising within the supposedly "New" world, but which rested on a practice of whites-only citizenship: economically, socially, and politically resting upon a foundation of enslavement, expropriation, and genocide of indigenous peoples that carries over into the twenty-first century.

Bradford's history of the Puritan settlers focuses on Native Americans as outsiders, but his instant characterization of the native people and their resources reflect how this construction of politics and ethics would become the play book for American slaving. By virtue of a politics oriented in his Puritan interpretation of Christianity, his mission and his people are divinely sanctioned. The native people, their land, and their resources become gifts from God to the Puritan elect—rather than Puritan theft of the rightful possessions of the Indians. Therefore when the Puritans scout the area and come across a stock of food the Indians have gathered in preparation for the winter ahead, Bradford describes how they helped themselves to the harvest: entering two of the dwellings where they "found" "sundry of their implements," the "corn and beans they brought away," to feed themselves in the winter days ahead (78). Lest readers see this as thievery, Bradford exclaims that this finding is a "special providence of God" (78). The elect are the citizenry, representing both a religious body and a body politic; they expect decency and generosity from the native people that they deem outsiders; and the rules that will determine their engagement within the group and with those outside rest in this simplistic paradigm. When you have been divinely chosen, you may operate justifiably under the premise that God has set before you all that you need to flourish. If it happens to be in the possession of entities outside your citizen body, then God allows that you should take what you need. This way of seeing the world would serve the colonial politics and narratives that justified confiscation and theft of Black people's rights to their bodies and the fruits of their labor.

When Bradford and the Pilgrim settlers signed the *Mayflower Compact*, which is referred to as one of the first governmental or constitutional documents of America, there was neither nation nor state called "America." They were signing a document that represented their own religious group and for their own interests. The Pilgrims, as Bradford notes in his history, considered themselves a special people with a special covenant with God. *Of Plymouth Plantation* makes clear that they have come to a new land to create a new world for themselves. As Bradford's animosity against the non-Puritans on the journey reveals, the settlers had also not yet conceived of their identity as white. The Pilgrims' vision was not a "melting pot" of geographically contiguous and legally united states: the *Mayflower Compact* was a union of bodies representing the interests of the Puritan elect. This very people, their binding document, and their historical origins story were rejected by the larger settler populations by the close of the seventeenth century. As Bradford notes in chapter XXIII, "Prosperity Weakens Community," by 1632 "the people of the plantation began to grow in their outward estates," their wealth grew, and "there was no longer any holding them together" (89). Despite this reality, however, the myth of these early settlers was adapted into narratives of the nation as government and people.

John Winthrop, Bradford's counterpart and governor of the second Puritan settlement, Massachusetts Bay Colony, was also central to the early mythology of exceptionalism. Winthrop's sermon "A Model of Christian Charity" exemplifies the delicate dance that allows for ideologies of racist hierarchies to coexist in the Puritan body politic. The reality of Winthrop's actions and his words demonstrate that, with the exception of the elect and whites that they had to engage for economic prosperity, the Puritans exercised with ease a theocratic politics founded on their interpretation of scripture. In allusion to the Biblical utopia that the Israelites anticipated after their exile from Egypt, Winthrop touted his exclusive society as "a city upon a hill" that would become the example for the world ("A Model of Christian Charity" 101). Delivered as a sermon in 1630 before Winthrop and fellow Puritan immigrants landed at the shores of Massachusetts Bay, it exemplified the myth of human hierarchies that fueled their presumptions of specialness before God; it would also, however, portend the morphing of this ideology into the United States that would take shape after the Revolutionary War. Winthrop maintained that God had created and ordered man in such a way that "in all times some must be rich some poor, some high and eminent in power and dignity; others mean and in subjection" ("A Model of Christian Charity" 91). Unsurprisingly, Winthrop was rich and powerful and held others in subjection, so his divine theory reflected the advantage he held. In the new land where the Pilgrims would reclaim home, this divine order would mark their society as a model for the world and they would be the new world Israelites. Confiscation of Indian lands and resources and the enslavement of Africans was not a contradiction in Winthrop's Puritan informed political ethos. All was part of God's divine structure and plan: as Winthrop noted, God made it so that there would always be rich and poor and the evil in that hierarchy only emerged when the divine order was threatened. This God-ordained structure is maintained so long as

> the rich and mighty should not eat up the poor, nor the poor and despised rise up against and shake off their yoke. Secondly, in the regenerate, in exercising His graces in them, as in the great ones, their love, mercy, gentleness, temperance etc., and in the poor and inferior sort, their faith, patience, obedience etc.
>
> *("A Model of Christian Charity" 91)*

The politics of manifest destiny, the political and theological ideology whereby settler colonialism wasn't just an opportunity but a divine mandate, are a clear outgrowth of Winthrop's vision that—somehow in this world of inequity—all will work together for a common good in which they would be bound not only by "conscience, but mere civil policy" (100). The result of the conformity that Winthrop called for in the beginning of his sermon is that collectively the elect of the Puritan society would "rejoice together, mourn together, labor and suffer together" in a divine society (101).

While one of the most iconic representations of enslaved people is the picture of Africans torn from their homelands and transported to the southern colonies, an early practice of slaving in the mythological "city upon a hill" was the exportation of young Indian captives to enslavement in the Caribbean in the aftermath of wars against the settlers. Correspondences between Winthrop and his enterprising brother-in-law, Emmanuel Downing, capture the spirit of this practice that would become a lucrative business for supplying unpaid laborers in New England (Hardesty 1). Indians and Africans were traded as commodities, and their humanity could be disregarded by virtue of their non-citizen status. Both had been marked in the early Puritan American imagination as savage outsiders. They were handled in any means that proved lucrative to the society of the elect. The Pequot War of 1638 was one of the most decisive victories for the settlers against the Indians, and illustrates the ease with which both Bradford and Winthrop could envision and articulate their desire to eliminate the Pequot in the name of the settler state.

In Chapter 28, "The Pequot War," Bradford describes the slaughter of the Indians in highly sensational details, rejoicing in the bloodletting and burning of Indian bodies: "It was a fearful sight to see them thus frying in the fire and the streams of blood quenching the same, and horrible was the stink and scent thereof; but the victory seemed a sweet sacrifice" (179). In his journal, John Winthrop also offered detailed accounts of the Pequot War, including not only details of the killings of the Indians but also the deportation and enslavement of those who were captured. Much like Bradford, he seemed to have quite an appetite for the details of tortured human flesh. He offered repeated accounts of Indian skin, scalps and heads that were delivered for show and count (221–228). In just a matter of one paragraph, for example, Winthrop reports the beheading of two Indians in a place that the settlers would then name "Sachem's Head" (226). He follows this description with a count of the slain and the fate of some of the captives: "We had now slain and taken, in all, about seven hundred. We sent fifteen of the boys and two women to Bermuda" (227–228). In his mention of the 17 Indians who had been deported to Bermuda, Winthrop did not mention that this delivery to Bermuda would include the opportunity to trade Indians for enslaved Africans, but this early practice would by the end of the century lead to a lucrative trade industry that was fueled by Puritan leaders (Hardesty 12). Bradford and Winthrop's origin narratives predate the founding of the United States, but again they reveal the literary beginnings of the nation's imagination of citizenship that was mired in the tortured flesh and blood and labor of non-citizens. In the next century, enslavement would emerge less as a duality of Indian and Black bodies and become synonymous with African/Black.

The early European settlers did not identify as "American," but a century later the colonial rebellion against the mother country borrowed heavily from Puritan settler tropes that were formed from the Puritan's version of their Christian informed body politic. By the time of the Mayflower's arrival and the signing of the Mayflower Compact, slaving had long been inaugurated in the Americas. The Spanish had led the way in the sixteenth century in the Caribbean and in the regions of what we today call the southern United States; if we consider the transaction that resulted in the delivery of more than 40 Africans to the shore of Jamestown in 1619, the origin of British slaving in North America is symbolized in that moment.[1] Racial categorization preceded the birth of trans-Atlantic slaving, accompanied by Western Enlightenment thinking and an emerging capitalist economy that required regenerative cheap labor; however, a paradigmatic black-white racial binary that naturalized black enslavement was easily inserted into the colonial discourses of a democratic ideal. Despite a history of ignoring the central place of blackness in the construction of U.S. identity and its literature, it was the nation's opposition to the presence of blackness "which shaped the body politic, the Constitution, and the entire history of the culture" (Morrison, *Playing in the Dark* 5). Embodied in the presence of the enslaved was the "not me" (Morrison, *Playing in the Dark* 38). Blacks represented the outsider—the not white, the not American, the not citizen—and an entire political imaginary was predicated upon the converse: whiteness represented legitimate membership in the sovereign American nation and state.

White politics were loudly seated in articulations of freedoms and human rights, but this political framework explicitly and aggressively denied political equality to Blacks. While we find evidence of early Black critiques of America's dissonant politics of democracy and its practice of slaving, scholarship and teachings on enslavement in the Atlantic world continue to be dominated by perspectives of the enslavers and the free white population. Despite this practice and the push in some sectors to silence challenges to narratives of white historical heroics, this tension is not a modern one. Indeed, enslaved and free Blacks were not without their own critiques of America's intersecting political rhetorics of democracy and its contradictory practice of slaving: "No slave society in the history of the world wrote more—or more thoughtfully—about its own enslavement" (Morrison, "The Site of Memory" 236). Blacks learned early the connection between democracy and politics in American national discourse, and before they would articulate in writing their skepticisms of these idealized declarations, they expressed their critiques through oral literary modes such as proverbs, work songs, spirituals, and folktales.

Within the Black community, Black literature has historically been a resource and resistance mechanism against oppression; because theirs was a shared experience of collective political alienation, African Americans shaped their own new world collective identity out of a necessity for self-preservation. For instance, early narratives and autobiographies provided a voice for the voiceless, as well as spaces for voicing Black resistance and solidarity. Before Black literature in the United States emerged into a written tradition, Black people sang, danced, and orated their narratives. For example, spirituals such as "Go Down Moses" and "Joshua Fit de Battle of Jericho" were not simply Black parroting of white Christianity. These songs were allegories of slaving in the new world where the evil pharoah was not in Egypt but in the big house on the plantation, and Jericho was not in the ancient Middle East but rather was the plantation and the slaving institution itself. Similarly, the early folk tale of the Flying Africans exemplifies the nonwritten tradition of African Americans that has resided alongside the written and long preceded modern iterations of the figure like Toni Morrison's *Song of Solomon* (1977). While the story may seem to outsiders a story of mass suicide, it survives in Black culture as a story of defiance: of blacks unwilling to endure enslavement, and acting as a collective body freeing themselves of both physical and spiritual bondage. Their self-inflicted physical death spoke a call for social justice, as the story revealed the barbarity of a system that, in the absence of justice, led people to depart this world and this life in hopes of finding that justice in the afterlife.

In the poetry of America's first published Black poet, Phillis Wheatley, we find early poetic calls for freedom that also allude to the humanity and desire for freedom of those enslaved. In the 1772 poem "To the Honourable William, Earl of Dartmouth" Wheatley is clearest in her poetic assertion of Black humanity and rights to citizenry. She first shows deference to the colonists' call for freedom from their tyrant mother country:

> No more, America, in mournful strain
> Of wrongs, and grievance unredress'd complain,
> No longer shalt thou dread the iron chain,
> Which wanton Tyranny with lawless hand
> Had made, and with it meant t' enslave the land.
>   (15–19)

In a sleight of hand, Wheatly follows by pondering whether the reader (who is white) might wonder how she, an African, might understand and desire freedom: "Should you, my lord, while you peruse my song, Wonder from whence my love of Freedom sprung" (20–21). In lines 22–31, she explains that she (like other Africans) came from a society where their freedom and their humanity were unquestioned. She makes clear that neither she nor the multitudes of Africans are "not-free" by nature but rather by the hands of men. It was only after she was "snatch'd from Afric's fancy'd happy seat" that she would be subject to "the iron chain" and "wanton Tyranny" (25). While she uses these terms to speak of the colonists' experience with what they deem the tyranny of their mother country, the poem makes clear that Wheatley's subjugation to outsider status and enslavement is delivered at the hands of the colonists.

Early Black writers imagined their rights to citizenship and understood the central mechanism employed by the powers that maintained denial of Black citizenship. As Bradford's and Winthrop's writings illustrate the city on the hill was built on a structure of hierarchy and domination. As scholar bell hooks explains, "A culture of domination demands of all its citizens self-negation. The more marginalized, the more intense the demand" (hooks 19). The establishment and preservation of a society built upon the presence of Blacks concurrent with the denial of their presence would require that Blacks also perform the fantasy. Whites imagined Blacks as the subjugated other who lacked "the ability to comprehend, to understand, to see the working of the powerful" (hooks 168). This was a performance that was often required of enslaved Blacks but in their own world, free of white oversight they were expressive of the faults they found in white fantasies of democracy that allowed for white only citizenship. In his 1797 Address to fellow Black Masons, Bostonian Prince Hall illustrates the rejection of a perjured notion of democracy available only to whites. He asserts that while the laws are against them in America, there is a model—i.e., Haiti—for Black citizenship and freedom. He does not call Haiti by name, but the allusion is clear as he speaks of a dawning quest for freedom by Africans in "the West-India islands" which foretells for "Boston and the world" that the wrongs of African enslavement and trafficking will eventually "fall, to rise no more" (164).

In his famous *Appeal* (1829), activist and fellow Bostonian David Walker was more direct, bold, and reproving of America and its sacred founding fathers. With the *Appeal's* lengthy subtitle, Walker makes clear that the citizenry of his imagination is a global African body politic, specifically "the Coloured Citizens of the World." In the "Preamble" that opens the manifesto of four articles, he makes clear that he is no respecter of America's manufactured myth of itself:

> I appeal to Heaven for my motive in writing—who knows that my object is, if possible, to awaken in the breasts of my afflicted, degraded and slumbering brethren, a spirit of inquiry and investigation respecting our miseries and wretchedness in this *Republican Land of Liberty!!!!!!*
>
> *(22)*

Openly mocking the authors of the nation's sacred constitution and its authors' hypocritical relation between white religiosity and democracy, Walker remains firm on his position of citizenry for Blacks of the United States. He was not singular in this regard, and clearly echoes Black AME Bishop Richard Allen, who in an 1827 article published in *Freedom's Journal* rejected white endorsed calls for free Blacks in the United States to immigrate to Africa (76–77). To fellow Blacks in the United States, Walker proclaims "America is more our country, than it is the whites—we have enriched it with our blood and tears" (84). Walker demands both that slavery be abolished and that Blacks be elevated to the status of citizen with all the rights and rewards therein.

In the nineteenth century, Black-authored critiques and reflections on the question of citizenship and enslavement would abound and expand into genres of fiction and slave narratives. While Frederick Douglass is more often noted for his open criticism of America's hypocritically curtailed democracy in his speech "What to the Slave is the Fourth of July" (1852), the theme is equally salient in his novella *The Heroic Slave* (1853). There, in his fictionalized account of real-life Black insurrectionist Madison Washington, Douglass raised the questions and emphasized the points posited in his 1852 speech. After he explains to his audience that the glorious occasion of which he has been invited to speak is one that excludes him, Douglass then allows himself to clarify the subject that is most imminent for him: "My subject, then fellow-citizens, is AMERICAN SLAVERY" (326). Asserting that for the enslaved in America the Fourth of July was merely a reminder of "the gross injustice and cruelty to which he is the constant victim" (328), he describes this national holiday as

> a thin veil to cover up crimes which would disgrace a nation of savages. There is not a nation of the earth guilty of practices more shocking and bloody than are the people of these United States at this very hour.
>
> *(328)*

This critique is echoed in the novella as the narrator considers the living hypocrisy of America's role in the internal slave trade, a point on which he expounds at great length in his 1852 speech ("The Heroic Slave" 60). He then notes that while Americans would deign as loathsome the "carrying away into captivity men, women, and children from the African coast," they in turn are "neither shocked nor disturbed by a similar traffic, carried on with the same motives and purposes, and characterized by even more odious peculiarities on the coast of our MODEL REPUBLIC" (60). It is this kind of third-person critique throughput the novella that can lead the reader to accept the recourse of violence to which Madison resorted in pursuit of his freedom. This connection, though, is not conveyed through Madison's articulation but rather through the recollection of one of the sailors aboard the ship at the time of the insurrection. He acknowledges that the impulse for Madison's actions was in fact "the principles of 1776" (68). The implication of the story's conclusion is that the rights of freedom, liberty, and citizenship awarded to whites are equally the rights of the enslaved.

Though the work does not appear to have met with reception from a significant readership in her own time, Harriet Wilson's 1859 biographical novel, *Our Nig*, was a scathing critique of the nation's misrepresented claims of democracy and citizenship. It was a work that did not exhibit the eloquent language of Douglass's 1852 Fourth of July speech, or the fire of David Walker's 1829 *Appeal*, but it matches the biting satirical wit of both authors. As with Walker, Wilson leads with a lengthy book title that divulges the key points to be interrogated in the pages to follow. While the novel focuses on the life of a young Black/biracial girl in the north, the title hints at the ambiguity of her status as free. The main title, "Our Nig," immediately suggests a status of Black and not free. The juxtaposition of the possessive noun, "our," and the shortened form of the derogatory and inflammatory racist N-word, "Nig," this title signals white possession and Black enslavement. Again, immediately it signals a story about the absence of freedom. The longer subtitle brings all into plain view: "or, Sketches from the Life of a Free Black, In a Two-Story White House, North, SHOWING THAT SLAVERY'S SHADOWS FALL EVEN THERE." The title tells readers that the protagonist is a Black person of free birth living in the free north in a white house (both of color and inhabitants), and given the allusion to enslavement in the main title and the ending of the subtitle, readers know before opening the book what they are about to hear. The story is then not surprising. The young protagonist, Frado, born from the union of a white woman and a free Black man, is delivered over into a household led by a white mistress who abuses her and deprives her of her freedom. It is slaving under the name of indenture, and the story unravels to show the marginal express of citizenship experienced by free Blacks in antebellum America. When Frado is abandoned and dropped off at the home of the Bellmonts and their white house, Mrs. Bellmont immediately envisions turning this situation into a future opportunity for an indentured child laborer ripe for exploiting (26). When Frado reaches adulthood, marries and becomes a mother left to fend for herself and child, she learns clearly that abolitionists may have frowned upon slavery in the south, but they ironically did not welcome Blacks into their spaces in the north (129). Wilson captured the state of citizen outsider that defined in general the tenuous place of free Blacks in the body politic of the nation's long era of enslavement.

The Emancipation Proclamation and the end of the Civil War would mark the conclusion of legalized enslavement in the United States. This would not, however, end the tainted legacy of "the city on the hill." In 1945, at the end of a world war putatively fought for the principled defense of universal freedom against foreign tyranny, Black U.S. writer Ralph Ellison described the persistent legacy of racialized political hypocrisy as

> a stave so deeply imbedded in the American *ethos* as to render America a nation of ethical schizophrenics. Believing truly in democracy on one side of their minds, they act on the other in violation of its most sacred principles; holding that all men are created equal, they treat thirteen million Americans as though they were not.
>
> (99)

This perversely paradoxical ethos of white-only citizenship qualifies as the nation's birthright, but hardly a remote and irrelevantly anachronistic one: it survives and thrives in the twenty-first century as the politics of anti-Blackness continues to unite a significant sector of white America.

The legacy of enslavement and its continued influence in America's conflicts around full and unequivocal citizenship continue to be explored in American literary works. The racialized relationship between literature and politics in former colonies (in the United States and elsewhere) and former colonizers in the United Kingdom may not enter the consciousness of most readers; if some legislators attempting to ban the teaching of literary and historical works that engage this legacy have their way, the number will only decrease. However, for a striking illustration of this interconnectedness one need only consider the selection of first term inaugural poets for the three democratic presidents since Jimmy Carter. In Bill Clinton's 1993 inauguration, African American author Maya Angelou composed and read the poem "On the Pulse of the Morning"; in 2009 African American author Elizabeth Alexander composed and read the poem "Praise Song for the Day" for Barack Obama's first inaugural ceremony; and for his 2021 presidential inaugural ceremony Joe Biden called on 22-year-old African American poet Amanda Gorman, who composed and delivered a stirring reading of her poem "The Hill We Climb."[2] All three poems scan the multiplicity of identities that constitute—at least in theory—the American body politic and suggest that to understand, to reconcile, and to find a way forward, Americans must see their collective identity through the realities of multihued multitudes instead of a singular mythical whiteness. Their call echoes Frederick Douglass's warning to his audience of white citizens in 1852 that to move the nation forward in the true spirit of liberty it must rid itself of slavery and its imprint, that "horrible reptile... coiled up in [their] nation's bosom" (332). It is telling that in the poem by the youngest in the country's history of inaugural poets, Gorman looked back to the legacy of enslavement to frame her vision of Biden's inaugural theme of "America United." Following the poem's opening allusion to loss at sea, "The loss we carry. A sea we must wade./We braved the belly of the beast" (lines 3–5), to the poet's description of her identity as "a skinny black girl descended from slaves" (lines 17–18), to the assertion that the future of the nation rests in its reconciliation of its past—its willingness to step into and repair the past (lines 52–54), Gorman is prompting America to reach within and free itself of the coiled serpent of racial exclusionism that leaves its citizenry in conflict.

Notes

1 For more on the significance of 1619 to literature in English, see Urvashi Chakravarty's chapter "On or about 1616 or 1619" in this volume.
2 As the controversy around the choice of translators for Gorman's poem suggest, the issue continues to be a global one; for more on this, see Roland Vegso's chapter "Translation" in this volume.

Works Cited

Alexander, Elizabeth. "Praise Song for the Day." 2009. https://www.poetryfoundation.org/poems/52141/praise-song-for-the-day

Angelou, Maya. "On the Pulse of the Morning." 1993. https://poets.org/poem/pulse-morning

Bradford, William. "Prosperity Weakens Community." *Of Plymouth Plantation*. 1620–47. *The Norton Anthology of American Literature, Shorter 8th Edition*. Edited by Nina Baym et al. WW Norton & Co., 2013, pp. 74–90.

———. "The Pequot War." *Of Plymouth Plantation*. 1620–47. *The Heath Anthology of American Literature Concise Edition*. Edited by Paul Lauter. Houghton Mifflin, 2004, pp. 178–179.

Conlin, Joseph R. *The American Past: A Survey of American History*. Second Edition. Harcourt Brace Jovanovich, 1987, 35–38.

Douglass, Frederick. "The Heroic Slave." 1853. *Three Classic African-American Novels*. Edited by William Andrews. Penguin Books, 2003, pp. 25–74.

———. "What to the Slave is the Fourth of July?" 1852. *Call & Response: The Riverside Anthology of the African American Literary Tradition*. Edited by Patricia Liggins Hill et al. Houghton Mifflin, 1998, pp. 320–335.

Ellison, Ralph. "Beating That Boy." *Shadow and Act*. Vintage International, 1995, pp. 95–101.

Gorman, Amanda. "The Hill We Climb." 2020. Printed in *The Hill*. https://thehill.com/homenews/news/535052-read-transcript-of-amanda-gormans-inaugural-poem/

Hall, Prince. *Charge delivered to the African Lodge, at Menotomy*. June 24, 1797. *Call & Response: The Riverside Anthology of the African American Literary Tradition*. Edited by Patricia Liggins Hill et al. Houghton Mifflin, 1998, pp. 164–168.

Hardesty, Jared Ross. *Black Lives, Native Lands, White Worlds: A History of Slavery in New England*. U of Massachusetts P, 2019. muse.jhu.edu/book/68186.

hooks, bell. *Black Looks: Race and Representation*. South End Press, 1992.

Morrison, Toni. *Playing in the Dark*. Vintage Books, 1993.

———. "The Site of Memory." *The Source of Self-Regard*. Knopf, 2019, pp. 233–245.

Walker, David. *David Walker's Appeal: To the Coloured Citizens of the World, but in particular, and very expressly, to those of the United States of America*. 1829. Introduction by James Turner. Black Classic Press, 1993.

Wheatley, Phillis. "To the Right Honourable William, Earl of Dartmouth, His Majesty's Principal Secretary of State for North America, &c." 1772?. *The Collected Works of Phillis Wheatley*. Edited by John Shields. Oxford UP, 1988, pp. 73–75.

Wilson, Harriet. *Our Nig*. 1859. Introduction by Henry Louis Gates, Jr. Vintage Books, 1983.

Winans, Amy. "John Smith." *The Heath Anthology of American Literature, Concise Edition*. Edited by Paul Lauter et al. Houghton Mifflin Co., 2004, pp. 125–126.

Winthrop, Jonathan. "A Model of Christian Charity." *The Norton Anthology of American Literature, Shorter 8th Edition*. Edited by Nina Baym et al. WW Norton & Co., 2013.

———. *Winthrop's Journal "History of New England" 1630–1649*. Vol. I. Edited by James Kendall Hosmer. Charles Scribner's Sons, 1908, pp. 221–230. https://marbleheadmuseum.org/wp-content/uploads/2021/01/pp-187-260-331Winthrop_s_Journal_History_of_New_Englan.pdf

9
HUMANS AND POSTHUMANS
Jennifer Rhee

Since at least early modernity, many thinkers have associated literature not only with people, not only with humans, but with humanism. Indeed, the title of one popular and literary anthology puts the two things together as a kind of identity: *Literature: The Human Experience* (Abcarian, 2019). Today, these associations are frequently mediated by artificial intelligence (AI) technologies. For example, companies routinely use algorithmic systems to make recommendations about what customers should read, watch, and purchase. AI systems are routinely deployed to make life-altering decisions about bank loans, policing, and judicial sentencing.[1] So-called "unmanned" drones are used by militaries to wage war remotely. Thus, the myriad aspects of human experience managed and influenced by intelligent machines fulfill many visions not of "the human," generally, but of "the posthuman," specifically, which imagines the synthesis of humans and intelligent machines. This speculative synthesis has taken many forms: celebratory fantasy (for example, dreams of uploading a person's consciousness into a computer); cautionary nightmares (dystopian visions of powerful technologies run amok); resigned yet hopeful reconfigurations of humans and intelligent machines (as in Donna Haraway's figure of the cyborg, which emerges not too innocently from "militarism and patriarchal capitalism" but also provides a site of subversive political potential [9]).

Despite the momentous shifts to people's lived experiences brought on by information technologies and AI, the posthuman does not herald the end of earlier conceptions of the human. Far from it. Instead, the posthuman is shaped by and extends specific conceptions of the human and the power relations that structure them. Today, as AI technologies continuously reveal the racialized and gendered logics that structure them and their normative visions of humanness, questions of which humans are included in these visions, which humans are excluded, and which histories and worldviews structure these technological figurations haunt posthuman discourses. This chapter turns to theorizations in criticism and in literature that take these questions seriously as they examine the intimacies between humans and intelligent machines figured by posthuman visions.

N. Katherine Hayles' *How We Became Posthuman: Virtual Bodies in Cybernetics, Literature, and Informatics* (1999) presented the posthuman not simply as a technological achievement or artistic genre or literary style, but as a "point of view" grounded in several positions. In one of those positions, information is prioritized over materiality, which presumes that information and materiality are in fact separable and that information is or can be immaterial. Additional positions central to the posthuman include the idea that human consciousness is epiphenomenal, rather than a grounding condition of lived experience, and that the human body is a kind of prosthesis that can be modified with technological enhancements. The most important posthuman position, according to Hayles, is the conceptual collapse of humans and intelligent machines: "In the posthuman," she writes, "there are no essential differences or absolute demarcations between bodily existence and computer simulation, cybernetic mechanism and biological organism, robot teleology and human goals" (3). These positions speak to the posthuman as a specific point of view or orientation toward information technologies, humans, and "the erasure of embodiment" (of information technologies and humans alike) as a key principle of the posthuman point of view (4).

This erasure of embodiment speaks to the centrality of a specific notion of the human—the liberal humanist subject—to the posthuman point of view. Hayles points to the importance of interrogating the human invoked by the posthuman: "just as the posthuman is increasingly necessary to understand what counts as human, so understanding the posthuman requires taking the human into account" (Afterword 137). In her examination of the posthuman, Hayles attends to the specificity of the human that is said to be transformed by the posthuman; she describes this human as "a historically specific construction" defined as the "liberal humanist subject" (2). This liberal humanist subject has historically been inscribed as "a white European male" and is "a conception that may have applied, at best, to that fraction of humanity who had the wealth, power, and leisure to conceptualize themselves as autonomous beings exercising their will through individual agency and choice" (286). In other words, the liberal humanist subject is a narrow, specific, and exclusionary subject position, despite its centrality in definitions of "the human" and in posthuman thought.

Thus, the posthuman is not a moment of rupture that leaves the liberal humanist subject behind, though the relationship between the posthuman and the liberal humanist subject has been complex. For example, Hayles describes how cybernetics research, an early and formative moment in posthuman thought, "imperil[ed]" the liberal humanist subject by reducing the human to disembodied information, despite individual cybernetic thinkers' attachments to this subject's centrality (84–112). Hayles is optimistic about the posthuman's potential to mark the waning—if not the end—of the concept of the human defined as the liberal humanist subject. However, to be imperiled is not to perish, as posthuman visions often extend liberal humanism in their conceptualization of embodiment as a mere representation of information or thought. Indeed, as Hayles observes, the liberal humanist subject and the posthuman share "the erasure of embodiment" as a dominant feature (4–5).

In *Bodies of Tomorrow: Technology, Subjectivity, Science Fiction* (2007), Sherryl Vint similarly highlights posthuman thought's attachment to fantasies of disembodiment. Not mincing words, she describes posthuman visions of disembodiment as "merely fantasies about transcending the material realm of social responsibility" (8). Linking these fantasies of technological disembodiment to liberal humanism's influence on posthuman visions, Vint also points to an emphasis on universality, another legacy of liberal humanism that structures the posthuman. This engagement with universality purports to reflect commonality in all humans but in actuality only reflects the highly specific subject position of those who were recognized as proper subjects by liberal humanism and by founding theories of liberal society (12).

Hayles concludes her study of the posthuman by gesturing to different versions of the posthuman, some of which merely extend the human qua liberal humanist subject while obscuring this subject's highly specific contours behind fantasies of disembodiment and universalism. Hayles describes these versions of the posthuman as "lethal" (286); they can obscure and displace other possible, and more hopeful, posthuman interactions with intelligent machines that are grounded in "embodied actuality" (287). In a later section, this chapter will attend to speculative fictions that reflect more hopeful posthuman possibilities. However, as Neda Atanasoski and Kalindi Vora's *Surrogate Humanity: Race, Robots, and the Politics of Technological Futures* (2019) details, in the decades since *How We Became Posthuman* was published, developments in AI have largely pursued the "lethal" posthuman visions that reproduce the human qua liberal subject and aspects of liberal humanism (13). Indeed, Atanasoski and Vora describe AI technologies' definition of the human as organized by "technoliberalism," which they define as

> the political alibi of present-day racial capitalism that posits humanity as an aspirational figuration in a relation to technological transformation, obscuring the uneven racial and gendered relations of labor, power, and social relations that underlie the contemporary conditions of capitalist production.
>
> *(4)*

In other words, technoliberalist ideologies deploy technology to extend and elevate the putatively universal liberal subject; they do so while obscuring the racialized and gendered power relations, exclusions, and oppressions on which the liberal subject depends not only for its claims to freedom but, indeed, for its very existence.

Building with Hayles, Vint, and Atansoski and Vora, this chapter turns to literary fictions that examine how various posthuman visions work to preserve the "human" as liberal subject and the racialized, gendered, and ableist power relations that produce this particular conception of the human, while also offering alternate posthuman visions that present more expansive visions of humanness. Thus, my chapter "tak[es] the human into account" by foregrounding the conceptions of the human that undergird the posthuman, from the narrow and exclusionary liberal subject masquerading as universal to more liberatory subject positions that foreground their specific situatedness and embodiments. In other words, the literary fictions, which depict the posthuman in the form of genetically engineered clones, artificial intelligence systems, and information technologies, contend with the conceptions of the human that organize posthuman visions; they also offer their own theorizations of how these technologies can extend "the human as a technology of differentiation and exclusion" while helping to imagine different reconfigurations of humans and intelligent machines that destabilize the exclusionary differentiations that have historically constituted the human (Rhee 38).

In the next section, I turn to fictional engagements with the posthuman that do not claim to move away from or beyond the human, but rather interrogate the specificity of the human that is purported to be left behind. I draw on fictions that attend to the history of the human and do not take this concept as given, inherent, or universal. Rather, these literary fictions take into account the history of the concept of the human and its specific embodiments in relation to race, gender, sexuality, class, and disability.

Moving Beyond the Posthuman

In N. K. Jemisin's short story "Emergency Skin" (2019), a small group of wealthy and powerful people, the Founders, who fled Earth after ravaging it for profit, left everyone else to die on the polluted planet and formed a colony on a planet in another solar system. The Founders took only those whom they thought were deserving (themselves), as well as a reserve of people to serve as laborers and servants for the elite Founders. The story begins centuries later when a soldier from the Founders' colony is sent on a mission to Earth to retrieve Hela cells, which the Founders require for their immortality. The soldier is implanted with an AI to guide him on his mission. The AI, the narrator of the story, introduces itself to the soldier as "a dynamic-matrix consensus intelligence encapsulating the ideals and blessed rationality of our Founders. We are implanted in your mind and will travel with you everywhere. We are your companion, and your conscience" (4). As the AI speaks directly into the soldier's mind, the reader does not have direct access to the soldier's speech; the reader only has access to what the AI says to the soldier and to the technologically translated speech of others the soldier encounters later in his journey. From the beginning, the story makes clear that the Founders' "ideals and blessed rationality" encapsulated by the AI are in fact the Founders' racist, misogynist, and ableist beliefs.

The Founder's space flight can be read as a representation of posthuman claims to move away from or beyond the human, despite how these claims maintain existing power relations that have structured exclusionary definitions of the human. Marked by the prefix "post," the term "posthuman" implies a movement away from the human. This movement is both temporal and spatial and suggests that the human is left behind, rendered obsolete, supplanted, or significantly modified. But what exactly is "the human" that is said to be rendered obsolete in posthuman visions? What are the specific contours that characterize this human? Zakiyyah Iman Jackson asks, what does it mean to call for going "beyond the human" when some humans are not included within the category of the human, and when certain notions of the human enable continued racial exclusions (215)? With this in mind, Jackson cautions that posthuman discourses invested in moving "beyond the human" risk reinstantiating the same erasures that continue to constitute exclusionary conceptions of the human such as the liberal humanist subject.

In addition to drawing attention to the specificity of the human inscribed in posthuman discourses, Jackson draws attention to the specificity of posthuman claims. Indeed, Jackson takes the posthuman as an occasion to examine the specificity of the human, as well as the positionalities from which posthuman claims emerge. Like the concept of the human that is purportedly rendered obsolete, these posthuman claims are also situated, racialized, gendered, and classed. "Calls to become 'post' or move 'beyond the human,'" Jackson writes, "too often presume that the originary locus of this call, its imprimatur, its appeal, requires no further examination or justification but mere execution of its rapidly routinizing imperative" (215). Jackson identifies the fact that posthuman discourses specifically ignore crucial theorizations of the human from black studies, which elucidates both the racialized construction of the human and the stakes of interrogating the concept of the human itself (216).

"Emergency Skin" locates the posthuman point of view in the Founders' racist, eugenic, misogynist, and ableist values and colonial and racial capitalist logics, as embodied in the AI's opening address to the soldier:

You are our instrument.
   Beautiful you. Everything that could be given to you to improve on the human design, you possess. Stronger muscles. Finer motor control. A mind unimpeded by the vagaries of organic dysfunction and bolstered by generations of high-intelligence breeding. Here is what you'll look like when your time comes. Note the noble brow, the classical patrician features, the lean musculature, the long penis and thighs. That hair color is called "blond."

(Jemisin)

By locating the posthuman call in these oppressive logics, "Emergency Skin" conceptualizes the posthuman as anything but universal, and instead as structured by discriminatory systems that understand the human as exclusively white, male, and without illness or disability. In its critique, the story incisively depicts a posthuman movement "beyond the human" that is, as Jackson theorized, situated in certain viewpoints and worldviews that reproduce the human as a racialized and gendered category of exclusion or dysselection, according to Sylvia Wynter, whose anticolonial thought analyzes the multiple Western conceptions of "the human."

Wynter identifies two dominant Western constructions that have shaped definitions of the human: Man1, the Renaissance figure of *homo politicus*, and Man2, the nineteenth-century figure of *homo oeconomicus* (Wynter). Man2 is associated with liberal monohumanism and its "overrepresentation as the being of being human itself" (Wynter and McKittrick 31). Given that the narrow and specific contours of this liberal monohumanist figure are too often taken to be the grounding criteria for being human, Wynter suggests thinking instead in terms of *"genres of being human"* to account for different modes of being human as well as the roles of discursive frameworks, narratives, and origin stories in shaping these conceptions and lived experiences of being human (31). Given the importance of narratives to Wynter's work, it is perhaps fitting that "Emergency Skin" does not just offer a critique of the human at the heart of the posthuman; the story also offers different narratives of being human that account for specificity and difference (rather than universality), as well as for care and collectivity.

These expansive modes of being human as critique of the posthuman are set up by the Founder's original flight from Earth (a metaphor for the posthuman movement away from the human), which positions those left on Earth—the purportedly unworthy—as the humans who were left behind or moved beyond. By way of this original metaphor, the story stages a confrontation between the posthuman and the exclusionary concept of the human around which it is organized, and other genres of being human that expand the definition of the human itself. In this way, the story engages a literary politics that critiques the human as a universal and natural category while offering a posthuman vision that does not reinscribe the human qua liberal humanist subject but rather identifies it as the ground for the posthuman itself.

Furthermore, the story insists on other modes of being human that invalidate the Founders' racist, misogynist, and ableist ideologies, as well as their false histories about Earth and the people who were left behind. These contradictions emerge when the soldier lands on Earth. He soon realizes that everything the Founders have told him about Earth is wrong. Earth is no longer a toxic, polluted wasteland; rather, it boasts lush greenery, ample rainfall, and the return of the polar icecaps. Perhaps most surprisingly, humans have survived and are thriving on this restored planet. As the soldier takes in this new world with wonder and curiosity, the AI continually espouses the Founders' values—anti-black racism, misogyny, ableism, and ageism—in response to the soldier's questions or expressions of awe.

Very quickly, the soldier finds out the truth: over the last few centuries, the people on Earth worked together to fix the world, to tend to each other and the planet, and to make the world hopsitable for everyone. They rejected the Founders' profit-driven ethos and greed and prioritized taking care of people rather than profiting off of them. This reversal allowed people and the planet to flourish, as well as the development of advanced technology that was unimaginable by the AI (and by extension, the Founders). This planetary repair was only possible because the Founders left the planet, taking their greed, racism, misogyny, and ableism with them. In fact, the event of the Founders' departure is known as "The Great

Leaving," and it marks the precise moment in history that led to the nurturing of a different society and future. In contrast to the dystopian posthuman visions that view posthuman synthesis as the cutting edge of the future (for example, in works such as *Neuromancer* and *The Matrix*), "Emergency Skin" offers a more utopian vision that positions the posthuman as antiquated and retrograde (embarrassingly so in the story).[2]

> For all these centuries, the Founders told us that the Earth died because of greed. That was true, but they lied about *whose* greed was to blame. Too many mouths to feed, they said, too many "useless" people... but we had more than enough food and housing for everyone. And the people they declared useless had plenty to offer – just not anything they cared about. The idea of doing something without immediate benefit, something that might only pay off in ten, twenty, or a hundred years, something that might benefit people they disliked, was anathema to the Founders. Even though that was precisely the kind of thinking that the world needed to survive.
>
> (Jemisin)

As the soldier spends more time on Earth, he begins to challenge the AI, who further entrenches itself in the Founders' values, thus further underscoring the connection between the posthuman and the Founders' beliefs:

> It is the guiding principle of our society. Rights belong only to those who earn them. [...] Only a few can have everything, don't you see? What these people believe isn't feasible. They want everything for *everyone*, and look at where it's gotten them! Half of them aren't even men. Almost none are fair of skin. They're burdened by the dysfunctional and deficient at every turn.

Throughout the story, the AI derisively refers to the humans on Earth as "inferior" and "primitive." However, it turns out that the Founders and their beliefs are viewed by people on Earth as antiquated, as relics of a distant past. When the soldier encounters people, he is met with their pity. To these people, he is not a threat, but, given his association with the Founders, a "quaint, harmless throwback."

As the story builds toward its conclusion, the soldier abandons his mission and remains on Earth; all the while, the AI still speaks to the soldier, attempting to get him back on mission or berating him for rejecting the Founders' beliefs. The soldier is provided with a home (everyone has access to shelter) that sits next door to the home of an elderly man. This man reveals that he's a fellow deserter from the Founder's colony—and not the only one, it turns out. As the soldier speaks with the neighbor (and as the AI vituperates him), the soldier becomes increasingly outraged at the Founders' lies and the societal injustices they presented as necessary and moral. Rather than remaining on Earth, the soldier decides to return to the colony and tell people the truth about the Founders. As is characteristic of Jemisin's fictions, hope and possibility do not reside in escape from injustice, but in working to "fix it" (Bereola). In the final moments of the story, the neighbor removes the implant that controls the AI, thus disconnecting the AI from the soldier's mind ("Can't start a revolution with the enemy shouting in your head, after all") (Jemisin). By removing the implant from the soldier, the story also removes the posthuman element and rejects the very specific and situated worldviews and concept of the human that structure it. Indeed, the story suggests that perhaps it is not the human that needs to be rendered obsolete or moved beyond, but the posthuman.

To highlight, rather than obscure, the posthuman's constitutive relation to the human, I propose considering "posthuman" as a compound word, not as a prefix affixed to a noun. In this reconfiguration, "post-" is not a prefix that suggests a movement beyond or a time after the human, but instead highlights the human as central to the posthuman, not as something rendered obsolete. Read as a compound word, "post" refers to an object that provides support to another object or structure; a post helps another object or structure persist. In this reading, the term does not invoke a movement away from the human amidst the development of information technologies; rather, "posthuman" conveys how information technologies can reflect an ongoing investment in maintaining and supporting a specific conception of the human. More specifically, through this grammatical reframing, "posthuman" refers to a phenomenon in which information technologies extend and further inscribe existing and exclusionary conceptions of the human. This reframing—as an invitation to "take the human into account"—holds open possibilities for engagements with the posthuman that work to destabilize the narrow concepts of the human often extended by information technologies and AI and by posthuman thought. Indeed, literature—itself an influential information technology—offers speculative engagements with the posthuman that do not just critique the posthuman but also offer more expansive possibilities for the human from within depictions of posthuman visions.

The depiction of cloning technologies in Kazuo Ishiguro's novel *Never Let Me Go* (2006) offers such a conception of the posthuman that interrogates the exclusionary vision of the human at work while challenging this vision's epistemological authority. Cloning technologies emerged from the field of biogenetics, which has been intertwined with computers and their ever-expanding data storage capacities and ever-quickening processing speeds. Thus, despite the lack of computational technologies in the fictional world (which is decidedly lo-fi), the novel can be read as offering a posthuman vision that is enabled by the development of information technologies and that is structured around the policing of a particular concept of the human. In the world of the novel, most fatal illnesses have been eradicated and many people's lifespans have been considerably extended due to advanced cloning technologies and cloned humans who exist only for the purpose of providing spare organs to non-cloned humans.

The novel focuses on three children who are part of the cloned human supply. Despite the dramatic circumstances that shape their lives, the novel focuses primarily on the children's friendships, romances, and poignant yet mundane concerns as they grow up together. The novel follows them briefly into adulthood, which marks the beginning of a series of operations to harvest their organs. Adulthood also marks the cloned humans' imminent deaths when these operations inevitably become too much for their bodies to endure. Kathy, the narrator, is 31 years old and is about to undergo her first operation. As a narrator, she is perceptive and contemplative as she moves from memory to memory about her life with her dear friends Ruth and Tommy. Each memory is told in significant detail, with Kathy's primary focus on the emotional lives of the three friends. With the novel's primary focus on the social dramas and powerful emotions experienced by three friends as told by Kathy, the cloned humans are, well, humanized. This humanization is in stark contrast to their dehumanization by society, including by the adults who were charged with their care. The novel's juxtaposition of the clones' complex interiorities with their artificially shortened lives and futures underscores the ableist conception of the human that structures the fictional world of the novel.

Rosemary Garland-Thomson analyzes how the world of *Never Let Me Go* reflects practices of eugenic worldbuilding that center a figure she names "the normate." The normate "embody[s] the form, function, behaviors, and appearances that conform to all of the culturally valued traits in the social systems of gender, race, class, sexuality, and ability" (135).[3] With its very narrow inscriptions of identity and embodiment, the normate represents the ideal subject that reflects the norms and values of a given society (135–136). For Garland-Thomson, *Never Let Me Go*

> comments on eugenic world building, I suggest, by making it seem surreal, disorienting, and thus newly apparent. This confusion of time and place and people asks questions that are central to disability ethics: What is disability? Who is disabled? Who is a normate? What is health? Who is healthy? Who are caregivers? Who are care receivers? Who serves whom? What is an open future? What is a quality life? What is a restricted life? What is freedom? What is self-determination? Perhaps most important, *Never Let Me Go* raises the central question of eugenics: Can disability be eliminated from the human condition? The answer *Never Let Me Go* gives us is no.
>
> *(136–137)*

Here, Garland-Thomson seamlessly moves from the defamiliarizing function of a particular literary style (surrealism) to the central issues guiding human decisions about what qualifies as moral action (ethics) to the fundamental questions that have long guided political theory (what and how are freedom and self-determination expanded or limited by particular forms of collective association). Garland-Thomson's reading of *Never Let Me Go* in relation to the question, "Can disability be eliminated from the human condition?" turns on the novel's insistence that cloned humans are just as human as non-cloned humans. In other words, her reading turns on the novel's simultaneous depiction and rejection of society's dehumanization of the cloned humans. In this way, the novel puts forth a posthuman vision in which futuristic medical science supports and protects a vision of the human that is shaped by eugenics and its histories, while also expanding the human beyond this specific repressive vision. Like "Emergency Skin," the novel both critiques the posthuman vision by highlighting the concept of the human it reinscribes, while insisting on "genres of being human" that have been excluded from this concept.

"Our Aim Is Not to Die" (2019), a speculative fiction short story authored by A. Merc Rustad, similarly offers a posthuman vision that underscores the posthuman's attachment to eugenic worldbuilding and its reinforcement of the human as an exclusionary category, while offering a more expansive and inclusive conception of the human through a speculative engagement with the posthuman. The story depicts a hyper-technologized surveillance society that polices and punishes anyone who does not conform to contours of the "Ideal Citizen," who is described as "white, male, straight" (28). The television program *The Ideal Citizen* makes clear who this ideal citizen is and what behaviors are permitted them: the program is "full of smiling white faces," with

> people jailed for not speaking correct English and therefore dubbed illegal. Neural reformatting therapy treated as a miracle. Only heterosexual relationships permitted. Once there was a self-described asexual character on an episode, but he turned out to be a serial killer and was issued a death sentence.
>
> *(32)*

The "Bureau of Genetic Purity" further underscores the eugenic contours of the ideal citizen. Meanwhile, surveillance is everywhere and inescapable. Every communication is monitored, posting approved messages on an approved social-media hub is mandatory, watching *The Ideal Citizen* is not optional, and everywhere signs announce: "YOU ARE BEING RECORDED FOR YOUR OWN SAFETY." There are strict rules about the "approved capitalization and punctuation" allowed in text messages (28). Any deviation from these rules would be considered suspicious and incur frightening repercussions.

The story follows Sua, who is neurodiverse, non-binary, and experiences this hi-tech eugenic surveillance society as an onslaught of intense anxiety in their body ("Panic scratches at their throat" [28], "Sua's fingers tremble" [38], "Their pulse races in their ears" [39]) and constant fears about the consequences if they are not able to perform the identity of an Ideal Citizen ("Sua is scared of everything" [32]). The story opens with Sua encountering the pairing of technology and oppressive regulation:

Sua's phone chimes with a notification:

> You are due for your mandatory Citizen Medical Evaluation in three days. Call your authorized health service center to schedule an appointment. Late responses will be fined and your record will show you are resistant to becoming an Ideal Citizen.
>
> *(27)*

Sua is immediately beset with fear:

> Sua stares at the full-screen decree, their hands shaking.
> This is bad. They didn't realize the biannual checkup was due so soon. That's not enough time to shape their profile and generate a baseline of neurotypical-approved behavior to fool the medical professionals.
> Shit.
> Sua can't risk being outed. They'll be expected to respond verbally to everything. Their flat inflection will be flagged. Lack of eye contact will be frowned upon. It'll all lead to the conclusion that Sua is wrong. Must be remade.
>
> *(27)*

Returning to Jackson's attention to the situatedness of posthuman visions, "Our Aim Is Not to Die" associates its vision of a hyper-technologized posthuman society with a repressive racist, homophobic, and ableist state and its terrifying consequences for people like Sua. In other words, in contrast to glorified fantasies of technological excess and giddy dreams of disembodiment, the story reframes the posthuman as embodied fear and anxiety when experienced from the perspective of someone not aligned with the forms of being that have access to and are protected by power. If Sua is deemed "wrong"—that is, not neurotypical—they will be subject to *"neural reformatting therapy,"* which is "the present's term for *lobotomy*" (28). Here, the posthuman is represented by the ubiquitous information technologies that monitor and surveil the population; this posthuman vision further inscribes a narrow and exclusionary vision of the human that is used to control people, including what they think and what they ignore: "An Ideal Citizen is never worried, because everything about the climate is *fine*, no cause for concern" (29). Sua is always worried, always scared, as they are constantly bombarded by technological reminders that they do not fit into the specific, normative definition of "the human" that organizes this society and its elevation of the Ideal Citizen.

Despite the story's undeniably dystopian posthuman vision, "Our Aim Is Not to Die" concludes by reflecting Hayles' hopes for a less "lethal" vision of the posthuman entanglement of human and intelligent machines, one that foregrounds embodiment in its individual specificities and differences and that is not invested in upholding the liberal humanist subject. The story moves toward its climax when Sua is introduced to the Purge, an app developed by a network of AIs working to liberate people like Sua who are surveilled, threatened, and punished for their difference from the Ideal Citizen. The Purge's plan for liberation relies on the very information technologies and networks used to surveil and oppress; the AIs also work in collaboration with people who risk their lives to realize a different world and future. This networked collective of humans and machines working together to overthrow the systems of oppression reconfigures the posthuman vision of the story. After learning about the Purge, Sua joins them. The story concludes just as the Purge's revolution begins, so the reader is left uncertain of whether it succeeds and what happens to Sua. However, for the first time in the story, Sua's body is not registering fear. Throughout the story, they are gripped by anxiety and have to remind themselves to breathe. In the final moments of the story, as the penultimate sentence describes, "Sua leans back against the wall and breathes" (47). As part of this alternate posthuman network, Sua sees hope and the possibility of a different world and, for a moment, does not have to remind themselves to breathe; they just do. The final line of the story reads, "Revolution has begun." The story's final two lines connect the possibility of revolution to Sua's breath, an embodied expression of hope and possibility. In doing so, the story grounds the posthuman in embodied actuality and an expansive conception of the human that rejects the model of the human defined by the Ideal Citizen and liberal humanism.

The literary fictions discussed in this chapter do not separate the posthuman from the human, nor do they take "the human" as a given or universal concept. Rather, they attend to the power relations, situatedness, and embodiments that shape their visions of the human and the posthuman amidst the significant cultural and political authority of information technologies and AI. In so doing, these texts critique certain visions of the posthuman—as well as the human—and offer alternate visions of being human in a posthuman world.

Notes

1. These AI systems extend historic racialized hierarchies and injustices, despite their claims of machinic objectivity. See Benjamin, (2019), Browne (2015), Buolamwini and Gebru (2018), Chun (2022), Noble (2018), and Scannell (2019).
2. For more on the politics of utopia and dystopia, see Deanna Kreisel's chapter "Utopia" in this volume.
3. The film adaptation's glaring whiteness underscores the intersection of ableism and racism in the film's eugenic logic.

Works Cited

Abcarian, Richard et al. editors. *Literature: The Human Experience*. 13th edition. MacMillan, 2019.
Atanasoski, Neda and Kalindi Vora. *Surrogate Humanity: Race, Robots, and the Politics of Technological Futures*. Duke UP, 2019.
Benjamin, Ruha. *Race after Technology: Abolitionist Tools for the New Jim Code*. Polity, 2019.
Bereola, Abigail. "A True Utopia: An Interview with N. K. Jemisin." *The Paris Review*. December 3, 2018. https://www.theparisreview.org/blog/2018/12/03/a-true-utopia-an-interview-with-n-k-jemisin/
Browne. Simone. *On the Surveillance of Blackness*. Duke UP, 2015.
Buolamwini, Joy and Timnit Gebru. "Gender Shades: Intersectional Accuracy Disparities in Commericial Gender Classification." *Proceedings of Machine Learning Research*, vol. 81, no. 1, 2018, pp. 1–15.
Chun, Wendy Hui Kyong. *Discriminating Data: Correlation, Neighborhoods, and the New Politics of Recognition*. MIT Press, 2021.

Garland-Thomson, Rosemary. "Eugenic World Building and Disability: The Strange World of Kazuo Ishiguro's *Never Let Me Go.*" *Journal of Medical Humanities*, vol. 38, 2017, pp. 133–143.

Haraway, Donna J. "A Cyborg Manifesto: Science, Technology, and Socialist-Feminism in the Late Twentieth Century." *Manifestly Haraway*. Duke UP, 2016, pp. 3–90.

Hayles, N. Katherine. *How We Became Posthuman: Virtual Bodies in Cybernetics, Literature, and Informatics.* U of Chicago P, 1999.

Ishiguro, Kazuo. *Never Let Me Go.* Vintage. 2006.

Jackson, Zakiyyah Iman. "Outer Worlds: The Persistence of Race in Movement 'Beyond the Human.'" *GLQ: A Journal of Lesbian and Gay Studies*, vol. 21, nos. 2–3, 2015, pp. 215–18.

Jemisin, N. K. "Emergency Skin." Amazon Original Stories, 2019.

Noble, Safiya. *Algorithms of Oppression: How Search Engines Reinforce Racism.* New York UP, 2018.

Rhee, Jennifer. "'A really weird and disturbing erasure of history': The Human, Futurity, and Facial Recognition Technology." *My Computer Was a Computer*. Edited by David Cecchetto, Noxious Sector Press, 2022, pp. 33–52.

Rustad, A. Merc. "Our Aim Is Not to Die." *A People's Future of the United States*. Edited by Victor LaValle and John Joseph Adams. One World, 2019, pp. 27–48.

Scannell, R. Joshua. "This Is Not *Minority Report*: Predictive Policing and Population Racism." *Captivating Technology: Race, Carceral Technoscience, and Liberatory Imagination in Everyday Life*. Edited by Ruha Benjamin. Duke UP, 2019, 108–113.

Vint, Sherryl. *Bodies of Tomorrow: Technology, Subjectivity, Science Fiction.* U of Toronto P, 2007.

Wynter, Sylvia. "Unsettling the Coloniality of Being/Power/Truth/Freedom: Towards the Human, After Man, Its Overrepresentation – An Argument." *CR: The New Centennial Review*, vol. 3, no. 3, 2003, pp. 257–337.

Wynter, Sylvia, and Katherine McKittrick. "Unparalleled Catastrophe for Our Species? Or, to Give Humanness a Different Future: Conversations." *Sylvia Wynter: On Being Human as Praxis*. Edited by Katherine McKittrick. Duke UP, 2015.

10
ANIMALS
Mario Ortiz Robles

Political Animals

Human beings, Aristotle famously argued, are "by nature" political animals. Nature, which, in his view, "does nothing in vain," has endowed humans with speech, a "gift" that allows us to formulate laws and moral concepts that deliver us from animal existence by giving rise to social structures (1253a 3–9; 29–39). The state, which for Aristotle is a "creation of nature," categorically excludes non-human animals, no matter how "gregarious," since, unlike humans, non-humans lack a sense of justice. The categorical distinction Aristotle makes between human and non-human animals on the basis of speech is only the first in a long conceptual itinerary in Western thought by means of which humans have sought to define themselves as animals that have the unique capacity to speak, cry, laugh, pray, lie, keep time, dream, wear clothes, and tell stories about other animals that behave like humans. This itinerary forms a thematic constant in the history of the West such that the very definition we give ourselves of ourselves, of what it is to be human, is premised on our not being like other animals. But if speech in Aristotle is the difference that structures all other differences, it is politics that makes possible the different material distinctions we install between humans and non-humans. Indeed, the exercise and practice of politics can be understood as the endeavor by means of which humans establish and police their difference from other animals. But what does it mean to police the categorical distinction that separates humans from other animals, especially in the face of mounting scientific evidence that there is in fact nothing "natural" about it?

We might begin by noting that the distinction between human and non-human animals is a moving border whose political efficacy is both conditioned and condoned by the ambiguity of the term "animal," which we employ to refer to the zoological other of the human as though a single word could encompass the vast multiplicity of the living. Jacques Derrida coined the awkward portmanteau "animot," a homonym of "animaux" ("animals" in French) that ends in "mot" ("word" in French), in order to draw attention to the fact that in using a single word to express zoological difference we not only curtail multiplicity but also that, in doing so, we employ this form of discursive violence to justify and sanction our dominance over non-human animals (41). The term "animot" thus points to a structural feature of the categorical distinction we have installed between human and non-human animals—namely, that the distinction is both figural (mot) and material (animaux)—and thus to the political logic that fortifies the borders that keep us apart. For even though we tend to think of animals as a generalized category, we also divide them into assortments whose referential status varies according to human criteria of proximity, objectivity, interest, utility, need, situation, and so on. These groupings are based on conceptual distinctions—wild vs. domesticated, pet vs. pest, edible vs. non-edible, laboring vs. non-laboring, etc.—but they are also established and enforced by means of cages, traps, fences, yokes, laboratory enclosures, abattoirs, and museum displays. By thus compartmentalizing our relation to non-human animals—by rendering literal the words we use to describe them—we erect walls within walls (animurs?) following a logic that oscillates between representational and material (or constative and performative) registers. Indeed, the slippage between sense and reference, or what I have called the figural and material instantiation of the human/animal distinction, is the condition of possibility of animal politics.

The effort to recognize animals as political agents has tended to revolve around the discourse of rights. We can trace the beginning of the modern animal rights movement in the West back to the publication in 1975 of Peter Singer's *Animal Liberation*, but, as his own argument makes clear, animal rights were already a matter of political and philosophical concern as far back as the eighteenth century. Jeremy Bentham, whom Singer quotes in the first chapter of his book, argued that the principle of moral equality ought to apply to members of other animal species since the distinction established between human and non-human animals on the basis of speech or reason, even if true, cannot be upheld when it comes to suffering: "The question is not, Can they *reason*? nor Can they *talk*? But, Can they *suffer*?" (qtd. in Singer, 7). In this famous passage, Bentham does not intend to erase differences obtaining among species but rather to establish the fact that, since humans and non-human animals alike possess the capacity for suffering, the amelioration of suffering ought to be the fundamental premise for equal moral consideration.

Bentham's utilitarian argument was a moral rather than a political argument, but a series of Parliamentary Acts passed over the course of the nineteenth century in Britain—the Act to Prevent the Cruel and Improper Treatment of Cattle of 1822 (also known as Martin's Act); the Cruelty to Animals Act of 1835, which was repealed and replaced in 1849, 1850, 1854, and 1876; and the Wild Animals in Captivity Act of 1900—established legal grounds for addressing the public outcry against the cruel treatment of animals. The passage of these laws, together with the vigilant efforts of organizations such as the Royal Society for the Prevention of Cruelty to Animals (RSPCA) and the Victoria Street Society, which militated against animal vivisection, gradually curbed common eighteenth-century practices such as animal baiting and staged animal fights and began to regulate invasive scientific procedures involving live animals. Anna Sewell's *Black Beauty* (1877), the best-selling fictional autobiography of a laboring horse, illustrates the need for, as well as the practical effects of, these parliamentary reforms by showing us how horses suffer at the hands of vain and unscrupulous humans but flourish under caring "masters," even as the very fact of their servitude remains unexamined. Endorsed by the RSPCA, Sewell's novel also points to the public's role in educating humans about the proper treatment of horses by staging scenes of instruction in which enlightened humans try to shame those humans who refuse to hear it from a horse's mouth into treating horses with dignity. Like other animal rights advocates, Sewell makes claims on behalf of horses with the aim of improving their lot, but she does not question the fact that horses, however treated, are almost entirely subordinated to human politics. Animal rights endow animals with some rights (the right, for instance, to be anesthetized during medical experiments) but not with the right to claim these rights, to paraphrase Hanna Arendt's famous description of statelessness.

For Singer, who, like Bentham, makes an argument grounded in utilitarian philosophy, the so-called rights of animals rest on the principle of equality insofar as equality maximizes happiness across the board. Singer argues that there is no moral justification for refusing to consider the suffering of a living being; equality requires that all suffering be considered equally. The gradual amelioration of animals' suffering by means of legal enforcement and social reform goes some way in addressing the principle of equality, but does not eradicate what, following Richard D. Ryder, he calls "speciesism," the view that some species are more worthy of moral consideration than others. Like racists and sexists, speciesists violate the principle of equality by allowing "the interests of their own species to override the greater interests of members of other species" (9). Singer suggests that, in order to avoid speciesism, we must follow the principle of minimizing suffering and give the same respect to the lives of animals that we give to the lives of those humans who have a mental level similar to that of at least certain animals. But if we wish to change the lives of animals we must not only change the way we treat animals; we must also engage in political action to grant them freedom and, with it, moral status.

Wild Animal Politics

To understand the politics of wild animals we must turn from philosophy to environmental studies, and from rights to wrongs, to examine some causes of catastrophic biodiversity loss. The politics of wild animal populations has perhaps nowhere been more visibly at play than in the US, where the modern environmental movement has made great strides in passing laws that protect a number of key species and their natural habitats. We can trace the emergence of the modern environmental movement back to two groundbreaking texts, each of which embodies a specific approach to wild animal politics.

The first text, Aldo Leopold's *A Sand County Almanac*, published in 1949, offers a conservationist's approach to wild animal politics by showing the complexity of ecological systems and the role humans have to play in both preserving natural habitats and managing human interactions with living environments. Forming part of the rich tradition of American nature writing—a tradition Lawrence Buell credits with transformative powers due to its attention to nature for its own sake—Leopold's work uses keen observation and personal experience to describe the natural world for its own sake, but also to draw our attention to the role humans have had in shaping it. In "Thinking Like a Mountain," one of the most celebrated fragments in the *Almanac*, Leopold urges us to view wolves from the perspective of the landscape they inhabit. Wolves have been, and indeed continue to be, hunted remorselessly, yet if you eliminate the wolves, the deer on which they prey will end up defoliating the trees, the trees will die, and the deer will have nothing left to eat. Similarly, the farmer who kills the wolves that prey on his herd will end up with a herd that, untrimmed by predators, will exceed its range. Leopold's "land ethic" proposes a sustainable relation between humans and non-humans in the face of erosion and overgrazing such that our failure to "think like a mountain," as Leopold wrote, will result in "dustbowls, and rivers washing the future into the sea" (132). The political impact of Leopold's text is hard to gauge, not least because the long-term, place-based ecological thinking he asked his readers to espouse tends to run aground on the short-sighted exigencies of industrial farming and extractive economies. Leopold's own impatience with bureaucracies and the glacial pace of environmental legislation, however, did not minimize the great lesson imparted by his text: understanding nature and its inhabitants can help us become better stewards of a landscape that is at once natural and historical.

The political impact of the second text, Rachel Carson's *Silent Spring*, is somewhat easier to quantify since it was widely cited in the late 1960s when the public outcry against the toxins and pollutants that were increasingly being released into the environment led to legislative action. Indeed, the publication of Carson's book in 1962 made visible to a wide public for the first time the deleterious effects that a number of synthetic pesticides developed during World War II and subsequently used to increase agricultural production had on the animal populations that were indirectly exposed to them. Carson, who had once worked for the Fish and Wildlife Service and had already written two best-selling books on marine ecosystems, gathered data from field reports, scientific studies, internal government documents, and personal accounts to make the case that DDT and other insecticides were not only counterproductive in that they failed to eradicate the insects they were meant to eradicate; they were also unexpectedly toxic, triggering massive die-offs among the fish, bird, and mammal populations that fed on the targeted insects. The "silent spring" of Carson's title, for instance, refers in part to the sudden disappearance of common songbirds, especially robins, in places where the authorities had used DDT to treat Dutch elm disease, which is caused by a fungus carried by the elm bark beetle as it bores into the trees. DDT may have killed the beetle, but this did not save the trees, which were already infected by the fungus, and, since it was indiscriminately applied, DDT made its way through the trophic pyramid, poisoning the worms that ingested the fumigated leaves and ultimately killing the robins that ate the worms.

The impact of Carson's book on the public's environmental conscience is hard to overestimate. The establishment of the Environmental Protection Agency in 1970 as well as many of the laws that passed under its aegis including the Clear Air Act (1970/77), the Clean Water Act (1972), the Endangered Species Act (1973), and the Federal Environmental Pesticide Control Act (1973), among others, can be traced back to Carson herself. This is not only because she actively lobbied congress but because her work drew attention to the "silent" effects of toxic chemicals on the environment and, indeed, to the silencing of these effects by the government's indiscriminate use of surplus insecticides.

While ecological advocacy has moved in different political directions since the publication of these two texts, many of the arguments we make today about the interdependence of human and non-human actors in nature owe some of their relevance and poignancy to their legacy. That so many today are justifiably focused on anthropogenic climate change and catastrophic biodiversity loss is in no small measure the result of the highly evocative work of pioneering environmentalists like Leopold and Carson. From the perspective of the debates surrounding the idea of the Anthropocene—that is, the somewhat belated acknowledgment that humans have had a geological impact on earth that renders moot the distinction between nature and culture—the work of Leopold and Carson may seem quaint in comparison. Yet, the fact that we are living "after nature," to use James Purdy's suggestive phrase, does not mean we must renounce the twin impulses that fueled their passionate engagement with the environment: love and fear. For Purdy, we have not lived up to a version of democracy that is "open to post-human encounters with the living world" (288) and that may yet temper its demands on a taxed planet through both fear of catastrophe and love as an extension of humanism beyond humans.[1]

But animal politics need not be understood exclusively through human efforts to right wrongs; the phrase "animal politics" can also refer to politics as practiced by non-human animals. Aristotle acknowledges that some animals are gregarious—in the etymological sense of tending toward a flock—and that some of these gregarious animals are social, with humans "partak[ing] of both characters." Moreover, some social creatures, such as bees and cranes, submit to "a ruler," while others, such as ants, "are subject to no rule." For Aristotle, this form of sociability is not necessarily political because, as we saw above, the practice of politics entails the use of speech, which is for him a uniquely human attribute. There is little doubt among biologists today, however, that social animals engage in practices whose aim is to distinguish friend from foe, configure the distribution of power within their societies, or act in concert to assert territorial and resource rights; that they engage, in other words, in what we would call politics in the human context. It is even possible to claim that animal politics, like human politics for Aristotle, is articulated through speech if we understand language use to include chemical, olfactory, visual, as well as vocal forms of communication.

The biologist E. O. Wilson is understandably reluctant to describe the social behavior of ants as political—their "social order is different from our own in almost every key respect" (Company 58–59), he notes—yet in detailing the remarkable social organization of ant colonies he uses terms borrowed from human political theory. Ants, Wilson notes, use battlefield tactics "whose sophistication is worthy of von Clausewitz" (Company 50); they engage in frequent territorial battles that may involve "kamikaze assaults by sterile workers" (Company 50–51); their nest is a "climate-controlled factory within a fortress" (Company 51); certain colonies employ an "intricate division of labor based on caste" (Company 56) that allows ants to create and maintain highly successful "agricultural states of imperial proportions" (Company 55); some colonies occupy vast territories that, "like the Roman empire at its peak" (Company 52), are connected by networks of trails; ants, in sum, have "seized control of a large part of the terrestrial environment" (Company 59) by virtue of their complex social activities. While Wilson insists that social behavior among ants is not "culturally transmitted" (Company 52) but rather driven by instinct and genes, it is not difficult to see that, whatever its origin, ant behavior is thoroughly political. Indeed, "Trailhead," Wilson's fictional account of a war waged between two ant colonies, may be read as an illustration of von Clausewitz's famous quip that war is the continuation of politics by other means. The possibility of a "Pax Formicana," Wilson wryly quips, is thwarted by the sudden assault of one colony upon the other followed by a fierce battle after which "the dead and the injured were collected and eaten by their conquerors" (Trailhead).

Wilson's description of ant politics is strikingly anthropomorphic. Yet to say that it is anthropomorphic is not to deny the validity of his account nor to minimize the fact that it results from painstaking scientific study carried over the course of an illustrious career; rather, it is to suggest, first, that our accounts of the natural world are inevitably anthropocentric, and, second and more important, that the anthropomorphic description of animal politics can help shape human politics with respect to animals. Anthropomorphism may well compromise scientific investigations of the natural world by clouding the interpretation of empirical observations by attributing human motives to forms of behavior that take place among non-human species, but to the extent that, as a figure of speech, anthropomorphism tends to aestheticize the comparison between humans and non-humans, it can also help us understand animal behavior in ways that may yet alter our own behavior toward animals. And even if the *anthropos* in anthropomorphism is taken as a given and the figure of the human becomes, as Barbara Johnson notes, the ground of comparison, the relation it articulates between humans and non-humans can establish a form of reciprocity found in similarity (237). In any case, we need not be scientists to accept in a general sense that dolphin pods, lion prides, bee hives, and a murmuration of starlings all practice forms of collective living that involve political calculation and that this calculation ought to be considered if we take seriously our commitments to a truly planetary politics.[2] Indeed, if used responsibly, anthropomorphism can help us imagine new social arrangements that move across differences not so as to eliminate them but as a means to find political accommodations in difference. In this sense, anthropomorphism becomes a crucial political device as we try to recalibrate our relation to animals under the catastrophic conditions afflicting our planet.

Yet, the history of anthropomorphism offers little encouragement in this regard. Animal fables from Aesop to La Fontaine tend to represent animals as though they were humans with the aim of imparting moral lessons on humans about human behavior; lessons, naturally, that do not generally make us reflect on our own behavior toward animals. The attributes fables use to personify specific animals—the cunning fox, the vain crow, the arrogant hare, the wise owl, and so on—are portrayed as "natural" but would under no circumstances pass ethological muster since they stand in for particular attributes of human nature. The record of anthropomorphism in modern literature is similarly mixed. On the one hand, anthropomorphic animals tend to be portrayed as literary rather than stock characters (Wile E. Coyote vs. the cunning fox, say) and, in keeping with their almost total generic relegation to children's literature, they are often rendered in pedomorphic terms with big eyes and infantile features that trigger what biologists call the "cute response" (see Serpell, 76). On the other hand, the anthropomorphic representation of animals is sometimes literalized to yield animalized characters that come to allegorize something like the "human condition" (think of Franz Kafka's "The Metamorphosis," George Orwell's *Animal Farm*, and Günther Grass's *The Rat*, among others). Even though both trends, what we might call the literarization and the literalization of anthropomorphism, tend to distance us from non-human animals by making them abstract, each follows a specific political logic with concrete material implications. Portraying animals as literary characters, especially through the aesthetic techniques of animation—what we might call the Disneyfication of animals—naturalizes the technological manipulation of animals by humans, while rendering humans as animals tends to make visible the dehumanization of humans who are subject to political oppression (anti-Semitism in Kafka, authoritarianism in Orwell, nuclear proliferation in Grass, etc.).

Like the ethologist before the puzzling behavior of a dreaming octopus, we seem to be left with an unexpected paradox: biologists, traditionally resistant to anthropomorphism, rely on anthropomorphism to describe the political lives of animals, while humanists, historical practitioners of anthropomorphism, fail to get past their humanism to engage the politics of animals. Put differently, the problem is that humanists seem ill-equipped to understand animal politics while scientists seem far removed from human politics. How, then, can we begin to understand human politics regarding animals from the perspective of animal politics? Using anthropomorphism to account for our relation to animals is inevitable since our ideas, as Mary Midgely puts it, "are made up of human elements and expressed in human terms" (128). When we talk about other animals, we are bound to describe them from an anthropocentric perspective, but this does not, for all that, prevent us from trying to understand them with attention and sympathy. The powers of observation of the scientist and the imagination of the humanist must be fruitfully paired in order to give animals their proper due and thus set the stage for a more inclusive, encompassing, and transformative sense of politics.

Sympathy and Imagination

It is instructive to consider two fictional scenes under this head. The first appears in J. M. Coetzee's *Lives of Animals*, which is composed of two lectures that were originally delivered by Coetzee as works of fiction. Centered on the character of Elizabeth Costello, a novelist who has been invited to a small college to deliver a lecture and run a seminar, the scene is structured around a classroom reading of Ted Hughes's poems "The Jaguar" and "Second Glance at a Jaguar." Costello argues that, unlike Rilke's "The Panther," Hughes's poems do not represent the idea of a jaguar, but rather portray "the" jaguar that is before him; the poems, that is, ask us to imagine what it would be like to inhabit the body of the jaguar. The poems, Costello insists, are the "record of an engagement" between the poet and the caged animal (51). Hughes's poems exemplify the exercise of what Costello calls the "sympathetic imagination," our capacity to imagine ourselves into the being of another—a capacity that has "no bounds" (35). The elaborate fictional framing of these lectures suggests that, just as Coetzee imagines himself into the lives of his characters, we too can imagine ourselves into the lives of animals in sympathy in a figural relay we might call personification without anthropomorphism.

The second scene is more explicitly political. It occurs near the end of Wes Anderson's *Fantastic Mr. Fox*, a stop-motion animated film that addresses the logic of anthropomorphic representation by following the adventures of a humanized fox who feels at odds with his suburban lifestyle because it suppresses his animality. He has no desire to live in the wild, but yearns instead to return to the life he once led as a cunning thief, a life of crime on the edges of human culture that he had promised to abandon when his wife revealed to him that she was pregnant. Seemingly driven by his predatory instincts, Foxy nevertheless begins to steal again from three neighboring poultry farms. Foxy's adventures are as exciting as they are gratuitous since he does not need to steal in order to survive. But they also threaten to upend his lifestyle when he becomes more successful than expected and the farmers get wind of his exploits. In response, the farmers, Boggis, Bunce, and Bean, vow to destroy him and, as their increasingly militaristic attacks drive him underground, Foxy and the other animals whose homes the farmers have destroyed begin to draw the battle lines. Foxy persuades the other animals to raid the farms while the farmers are busy trying to hunt them down by appealing to their wild animal instincts and specific natural abilities. The farmers try to flush them out of the town's sewers, but the animals stage a counteroffensive.

The political stakes involved in the animals' war against the farmers are poignantly articulated in one episode near the end of the film. After successfully rescuing his wife's nephew, who has been captured by the three farmers, Foxy, his son Ash, and their friend Kylie, an opossum, all find themselves on the open road. Spotting a black wolf by the side of the road, they stop the motorcycle on which they are riding in order to greet him. Foxy calls him by his Linnaean binomial, but the wolf does not respond, possibly, Foxy conjectures, because he speaks no Latin. It is only when Foxy, longing for an impossible existence in the wild, raises his fist in solidarity that the wolf, standing on a promontory just off the road, finally responds, raising his own fist. The image is reminiscent of the black power protest staged by Tommie Smith and John Carlos at the 1968 Mexico City Olympics when they raised their gloved fists during the medals ceremony. This gesture of solidarity between wild and semi-domesticated animals, occurring just before Fox and the other humanized animals living within the bounds of human civilization stage a successful coup, suggests that multispecies justice begins by a form of interspecies solidarity. Moreover, to the extent that Fox is a humanized animal who yearns to live like the wolf yet recognizes that he can no longer do so because humans have treated him as the animal that he no longer is, his actions—those of the proverbial fox in the chicken coop—can be seen as a form of protest against industrialized farming and the ever receding edge effects of human encroachment on the landscape.

If the traditional anthropomorphic representation of animals tends to bracket animal agency by construing animal characters as infantilized playthings or moral proxies for humans, these two scenes suggest themselves as expressions of anthropomorphism's political possibilities by representing politics from the animal's point of view and extending the idea of "person" beyond the species barrier. By reconfiguring the generic conventions we tend to associate with animal representation (fables, *contes moraux*, cartoons, children's stories, Romantic nature poetry, etc.), the works in which these scenes appear create the conditions of possibility for changing our perception of animals and of our relation to them. Put in these terms, anthropomorphism can help effect a shift in what Jacques Rancière calls the *partage du sensible*, the distribution (*partage* in French is both to share and to partition) of that which counts as sensible (as opposed to illegitimate, imperceptible, or insensible) in the political arena. For Rancière, the line dividing the sensible from the insensible, a line assiduously policed by the reigning social order, is a site of political struggle where the question of what counts as legitimate and illegitimate is determined by the reconfiguration of that which is given to sense perception (39). Politics is thus an aesthetic activity not because aesthetic works represent politics, and not because they purport to have a political impact, but rather because the use and meaning of words and images are always contested. Rancière specifically mentions sight and sound, but there is no reason why smell, tactility, trophallaxis, echolocation and the many other forms of communication that operate in the natural world cannot challenge the distribution of the sensible. Given our rather limited perceptual capabilities, anthropomorphism is the best, perhaps the only, means we have to disfigure the perceptual assumptions that configure animal politics as passive and thereby render sensible a new politics of equality.

So far I have been describing the political relation between human and non-human animals as a function of binaries: human/animal, us/them, rights/wrongs, friend/foe, sensible/insensible, etc. But what if we were to reject this view of politics for a more creatively disruptive account of multispecies assemblages based not on distinctions but on something like equality. To direct political action toward investing in what she calls "human and nonhuman naturalcultural flourishing," Donna Haraway offers a slogan: "Make Kin Not Babies!" While Haraway cautions that this slogan is dangerous and partial, she also insists that it is necessary and urgent (Clarke and Haraway 68). For Haraway, our present, to which she refers as the Chthulucene, is composed of "ongoing multispecies stories and practices of becoming-with" during precarious times in which the planet itself is at stake. Unlike concepts such as the Anthropocene and Capitalocene, which are anthropocentric "dramas" in which non-humans can only react, the Chthulucene features human and non-human actors whose order is "reknitted" such that "human beings are with and of the earth, and the biotic and abiotic powers of this earth are the main story" (55).

Though the term is derived from the name of a California spider, *Pimoa cthulhu*, named by biologist Gustavo Hormiga (whose last name, coincidentally, means "ant" in Spanish) after U.S. writer H. P. Lovecraft's cosmic diety Cthulhu, Haraway makes a point of changing the spelling (from cthulhu to chthulu) in order to distance herself from Lovercraft's "mysoginist racial-nightmare monster Cthulhu" (Trouble 101) and, in doing so, imagine a new name for rich multispecies flourishing. In her telling, the Chthulucene entangles "myriad temporalities and spatialities and myriad intra-active entities-in-assemblages—including the more-than-human, other-than-human, inhuman, and human-as-humus" (Trouble 101). Haraway's account of kinship as a form of multispecies entanglement is both a description of material practices and a political program urging us all to engage in new modes of living. Significantly, Haraway notes that these creative entanglements, as we see in her own writing, are to some degree aesthetic, not only because they require new modes of storytelling to account for them but because assemblages are brought about by something akin to a poetic act. Indeed, she borrows the term "sympoiesis" from environmentalist Beth Dempster to signal the role of creative collaboration across species and their inter- and intra-actions in favor of accounts that view both biological and cultural units as though engaged in competitive relations.

To acknowledge, if not quite privilege, the aesthetic in new political formations is not only to make the non-human sensible, in a process akin to Rancière's notion of the *partage du sensible*; it is also to make possible, to bring into being, new modes of relation that may yet save us from ourselves. When Ursula Heise suggests that elegy and tragedy, the genres we tend to employ to portray the catastrophic loss of biodiversity, need to be supplemented with new modes of storytelling that provide a more affirmative vision of the future, she is urging us to imagine extinction as a complex process of recalibration and reinvention by means of which we can more profitably engage with species loss as a cultural and well as "natural" phenomenon (13). Similarly, Thom van Dooren views extinction as the unraveling of intergenerational forms of life that have coexisted for a long time in entangled biocultural processes that we must take into account when we mourn for lost species (193). To the extent that mass extinction is the ultimate horizon of animal politics at the present time, we must effect a radical shift of perspective. The different philosophical arguments and aesthetic modes I have mentioned in this account of animal politics can help us move in this direction, but only if we accept that we are all co-implicated in the future of our planet; that we are all, in short, political animals.

Notes

1 For more on the political implications herein, see Jennifer Rhee's chapter "Humans and Posthumans" in this volume.
2 For more on the politics of "the planet," see Gerry Canavan's chapter "Planets" in this volume.

Works Cited

Aristotle. *The Complete Works of Aristotle*, edited by Jonathan Barnes. 2 vols. Princeton UP, 1984.
Buell, Lawrence. *The Environmental Imagination: Thoreau, Nature Writing, and the Formation of American Culture*. Harvard UP, 1995.
Carson, Rachel. *Silent Spring*. 1962. The Library of America, 2018.
Clarke, Adele E., and Donna Haraway, editors. *Making Kin Not Population*. Prickly Paradigm Press, 2018.
Coetzee, J. M. *The Lives of Animals*. Princeton UP, 1999.
Derrida, Jacques. *The Animal That Therefore I Am*. Edited by Marie-Louise Mallet. Translated by David Wills. Fordham UP, 2008.
Fantastic Mr. Fox. Directed by Wes Anderson, Twentieth Century Fox, 2009.
Haraway, Donna. *Staying with the Trouble: Making Kin in the Chthulucene*. Duke UP, 2016.
Heise, Ursula. *Imagining Extinction: The Cultural Meanings of Endangered Species*. U of Chicago P, 2016.
Johnson, Barbara. "Anthropomorphism in Lyric and Law." *The Barbara Johnson Reader*, edited by Melissa Feuerstein et al. Duke UP, 2014, pp. 235–261.
Leopold, Aldo. *A Sand County Almanac*. Oxford UP, 1949.
Midgely, Mary. *Animals and Why They Matter*. 1983. U of Georgia P, 1998.
Purdy, Jedediah. *After Nature: A Politics of the Anthropocene*. Harvard UP, 2015.
Rancière, Jacques. *The Politics of Aesthetics*, edited and translated by Gabriel Rockhill. Continuum, 2004.
Serpell, James. *In the Company of Animals: A Study of Human-Animal Relationships*. Cambridge UP, 1996.
Singer, Peter. *Animal Liberation*. 1975. Ecco Press, 2001.
Van Dooren, Thom. "Spectral Crows in Hawai'i: Conservation and the Work of Inheritance." *Extinction Studies: Stories of Time, Death, and Generations*, edited by Deborah Bird Rose et al. Columbia UP, 2017, pp. 187–216.
Wilson. E. O. "In the Company of Ants." *In Search of Nature*. Island Press, 1996.
———. "Trailhead." *The New Yorker*, Jan. 25, 2010 (online)

11
WORKERS
Benjamin Balthaser

Part I: The Work of *Capital* as Literature

Where does "the worker," understood not just as a character who works but as a member of a distinct, historically emergent class, first appear as a figure in literature? One might find possible, even necessary, answers in slave narratives, nineteenth-century realism, naturalism, proletarian literature, work songs, the IWW song book, or folk story-telling. Yet, given how many influential accounts of labor return to it, one text above all others seems central when thinking about working-class cultural representation, even if it is not conventionally understood as "literature": Karl Marx's first volume of *Capital*.

Unlike any other text about workers, *Capital* is the first grand historical and theoretical attempt to construe labor as a global imaginary, tied in specific historical ways to an economic system and to forms of political representation in locales ranging from the work houses of late feudal England to the slave plantations of the Americas and back to the factories of Manchester. As many scholars have noted, *Capital* is also a profoundly literary text: with its allusions to the novels of Balzac, Greek philosophy, the Bible, and Dante's *Inferno* and its frequently gothic and grotesque metaphors, it is a text distinguished by its penetrating analysis and also for its highly crafted structure and style. Yet too often, *Capital*'s literary qualities are not read as part of its complex task of working-class representation. William Clare Roberts' *Marx's Inferno* is perhaps the longest recent work to think about the literary structure and allusions in *Capital*, yet the idea that the question of style is also a form of working-class representation remains unaddressed. And indeed, scholars are partially correct when they often understand "the worker" in *Capital* as a kind of global abstraction: a uniform commodity bought and measured by time, dictated by the abstract and impersonal social relations of capitalism (Postone 129).

Cultural representations of the working classes are often caught between a central contradiction: on the one hand, labor is purchased by capital as a commodity and forced into a uniform and objective labor process. On the other hand, both this labor process and the workers themselves are anything but uniform, historically static, or evenly exploited across single regions and whole markets. The shifting modes of representation correspond with radical stylistic shifts in *Capital*, from an ironic mode of immanent critique to gritty realism of the final section where Marx describes how peasants, slaves, and indigenous people are wrested from their lands with sensational forms of violence. Rather than suggest that this is a contradiction solved temporally (capitalism will mature into formal wage labor), I suggest it is an inherent problem in the representation of labor through literature.

Asking how this contradiction manifests for proletarian novelists, I pose that Upton Sinclair's novel *The Jungle* (1906) attempts to imagine capitalism as a universal form of wage relations. As the formal beginning of proletarian literature in the U.S., *The Jungle* at once captures the horror of industrial production, and yet narrowly defines the working class as European-descended wage workers, racially and politically separating them from other workers, especially African Americans. Contrasting *The Jungle* with Richard Wright's most famous novel, *Native Son* (1940) begins with the very workers that Sinclair marginalizes. Set on the South Side of Chicago just before World War II, Wrights' Bigger Thomas is, as one critic describes, "lumpenproletariat," apolitical, violent, and unpredictable. He is also seen as having a powerful will to resist his own objectification and to insist on his own agency. The novel concludes much as Marx does, with an ambiguous vision of workers uniting across differences of race and region with no illusions about how difficult this may be to accomplish. Finally, Wright represents the working class as a contradiction: simultaneously an objective form of exploitative domination and a subjective entry point that cannot construct itself as a universal subject.

Labor as a commodity is perhaps the central story that Marx intends to tell in *Capital*. For Marx, capitalism is different from other forms of domination such as feudalism or slavery because the worker is dominated not by an embodied lord or master, but by the social abstraction of value itself. That is, what drives a worker on an assembly line, a peach orchard, or a delivery truck is not (only) the personal whim of a boss but the socially average labor time needed to produce a commodity or service: the manager and the worker alike are bound by the fastest, most efficient productive apparatus within the same market. Under capitalism the relationship between the boss and the employee is mediated by a wage: a worker "exchanges" their labor on a "market" for its "price" that is not determined by one capitalist, but rather by an entire system of commodity production. This price is not determined by one capitalist, but rather by an entire system of commodity production.

At the conclusion of *Capital*'s chapter 6, when we finally enter the "hidden abode of production" and meet our first worker, the portrait of the worker and the capitalist renders this abstraction as a concrete character: the capitalist as "money-owner" now "strides out in front," the possessor of "labor power now follows," and the image depicts the worker as a living commodity, like "someone who has brought their hide to market and expects only a tanning" (280). While this relationship is unequal, as Moishe Postone points out, the relationship is also "objective and non social" (154). That is, it is the capitalist who strides ahead while the worker follows. While it is a form of domination, it is mediated by the money the capitalist carries and the "hide" the worker sells. Unlike the coffle of enslaved people, it is the worker who seems to follow the capitalist willingly, even if in a relationship of subservience. In the same way that each commodity is merely the "congealed quantities of homogenous human labor," it seems that this abstract worker and abstract capitalist may follow each other across the globe, from work place to work place, factory to factory, office to office (Marx 128).

Like the dual quality of the commodity, however (whether toy, or cigarette, or hour of television), labor power is not only an abstraction: it has both a use-value and an exchange-value. On the one hand, labor is something produced for exchange on a market and is thus equivalent to all other commodities, and Marx famously bores generations of readers with his long lists of equivalencies: only under capitalism would ten pounds of linen be the equivalent to one shirt, or 1,000 pounds of coal to an ounce of gold distantly traded in the form of paper, and all of them with labor, where one worker from any part of the world is fungible with any other. Yet once the linen or coal or gold has left the sphere of exchange, their value once again lies in their usefulness, not their exchangeability. In the same way the worker's labor power is at once a commodity, bought by a capitalist to produce more value than what is paid, and yet at the same time is "living labor," awakening raw materials "from the dead" to make into use-values (Marx 289). Like the contradiction of the commodity, at once a use-value and exchange-value, at once made for need and yet only valued in the act of exchange, so the worker in the first ten chapters of *Capital* at once is concrete and universal, a living biological being and an object. Yet it is implied that the "living labor" at the point of production or reproduction still must fit into the iron law of value, the socially necessary labor time required to make any commodity. Indeed, this is the critique of capitalism leveled by disability activist and writer Sunny Taylor: because capitalism requires a homogenous worker to make products/services according to the law of value, so any difference is immediately excluded in the workplace, unless it can be seamlessly incorporated. Living labor has its living limits.

Yet for all the abstraction embedded in the commodification of labor, as *Capital* descends from the airy heights of political economy (the world free-market exchange) to lived reality (the factory floor), the style of the text and the assumed homogeneity of the worker both radically change. We are frequently introduced to the quotidian horrors of labor under capitalism, hunger, exhaustion, and overwork; we are introduced to workers' movements, legislative acts to limit the working day, and slavery and the relationship between African-descended slaves and the English working class. Gone is the high literary style of the first three chapters, with their metaphysical riddles, extended metaphors, and mathematical charts, along with the idea of a homogenous worker: the slave and the English factory worker are connected by a global system and yet also entirely divided, differentiated by law and custom in their concretization by a world market. The market is at once a unifying force, subjecting the globe to the law of value, and yet also produces radical unevenness and contingencies; it is a rupture with pre-capitalist history and its continuation.

Early in chapter 10 Marx devotes considerable time and space to, of all things, the adulteration of bread in London, the notable "discharge of abscesses, cobwebs, dead cockroaches and putrid German yeast, not to mention alum, sand and other agreeable mineral ingredients," matched in horror only by the lack of sleep and continuous labor of the bakers themselves (358–359). Capitalism did not change the quality of bread, only shortened the lives of its makers. And yet, as Marx lays out in chapters 1–3, in a world of market exchange one expects equivalents to trade for equivalents; if true, such grimly realistic journalistic detail should be superfluous. No market would sell good bread alongside bad for long; in the same way, no theory of labor value would have workers paid both above and below their value. Yet Marx spends pages detailing the way our very sustenance is destroyed under capitalism. It seems there is something about *Capital*'s descent from the heights of political economy that not only changes the relations of the market but also changes the style and subject of the text itself.

Crucially, Marx's introduction of race and slavery, nearly halfway through *Capital*, coincides with his discussion of capitalism's concrete effects on the human body and the products it consumes. Much as he introduces the broken body of the London baker in the nineteenth century, so Marx introduces the way in which capitalist production and the law of value have intensified the cruelty and violence of slavery. In a "natural system" (i.e., a system before capitalism begins to discipline time itself), Marx claims that "some security for human treatment" of slaves prevailed because the slave was not easily replaceable and the profits not great enough to endlessly purchase new human beings (377). "In Cuba," he writes, "whose revenues are reckoned by millions....we see in the servile class, the coarsest fare, and the absolute destruction of a portion of its numbers every year," where the complete destruction of thousands of slaves annually is factored into the value produced by sugar and coffee in the world market (377). While the exploitation of the baker and the potter in London and Manchester is connected by the same market that shortens the lives of slaves, it is clear in this chapter that a global law of value does not produce the same worker the world over. In the same way a person is stolen from Africa and their enslaved body is consumed by labor within a year, so a potter in London works 16-hour days. Capital's voracious need for value unites the system, yet due to the racialization of slavery (among other things), this universal abstraction of commodity production has an unevenly combined effect. With the abrupt change in literary style, from an immanent critique of professional economists such as Adam Smith and David Ricardo to the citation of newspaper reports and vivid descriptions of putrid bread, Marx seems to suggest that when one looks at capitalism, reality—or at least a kind of modern Realism—must intrude.

Thus, chapter 10 of *Capital* is marked with the constant evocation of unevenness and political contingency. From the first mention of communist labor organizing (in the International Working Men's Association's attempts to shorten the work-day) to the first Factory Acts that legislatively responded to such organizing, one sees the role of "state power" in both protecting English workers from dangerous overwork and forcing them to overwork; the "law of value" appears not only socially determined, but radically different across time, geography, and political landscape. Even the advent of the factory, Marx notes, originated not from conceiving the practice of free labor but rather in the coercive state power of the "House of Terror for paupers....brought into being a few years later" and "called a factory" (389). Thus, not unlike slavery, the prison house and the work house are part of a connected, dialogic, and yet entirely divergent whole.

One of Marx's finest dialectical lines, about the connection between the "free labor" under wages that cannot "in a white skin emancipate itself where it is branded in black skin," emphasizes how capitalism as a global system relies on differential modalities of exploitation and violence in order to continue the accumulation of capital (414). Labor "in a white skin" is intentionally an odd construction—the phrase denaturalizes "whiteness" not as something intrinsic to the worker or to labor, but rather race as a differential condition applied to both "free" and "branded" work under a single regime of exploitation and terror. And yet Marx continues to note that the relationship between workers around the globe is simultaneously connected, and yet never reducible to one another. The first "eight hour work laws" were fought immediately following the abolition of slavery, suggesting again that capitalism and its laws are as contingent as they are material: a change in one part of the world may help produce a different kind of change in another. This chapter is an amalgam of genres: from references to workers as "Cyclops" to labor reportage to graphs and charts about the length of the working day, the literary style not only reflects but the same unity in difference that Marx ascribes to capital (363). The sudden shift in genres at the very moment of representation suggests a tension in the very subject Marx hopes to capture: the structural shape of capital determined by value that produces a cacophony of varied and disarticulated subjects.

As Frederic Jameson argues, *Capital* is at tension with its own capacity to represent its subject: capital is "never visible as a totality" but "visible...only in its symptoms" (6).[1] In other words, one can only perceive capital and its circulation indirectly, through representations that themselves are only partial and refracted. And as Clare notes in *Marx's Inferno*,

Capital proposes two separate starting points for the origins of capitalism: in the circulation of commodities and in the primary accumulation of European peasant land, enslavement of Africans, and dispossession and ethnic cleansing of the indigenous peoples of the Americas (69, 400–401). This "montage" and "assemblage of distances," as Elena Vogman writes of *Capital*, rarely however consider how the "heterogenous style" of the text is also a complex representation of an uneven and highly racialized form of labor (90, 104–106). Like chapter 10, Marx's writings on surplus populations and the reserve army of labor in chapter 25 focus on those workers at the point of production but also at the ways even the unpaid, unemployed, and the never-employed are within the circuit of capital (783–785). "An abstract law of population only exists for plants and animals," Marx writes, for in the very particular valorization requirements of capitalism, the question of surplus population (those who can be imprisoned, sent to war, or killed) fluctuates wildly (784). And Marx's most dramatic departure from the orderly exchange of equivalents in his early chapters is his final description in section 8 of capital's origins, "dripping from head to toe, from every pore, with blood and dirt" (926). Completely outside the circulation of commodities, or the law of value, Marx describes colonial plunder predicated on violence and theft: "the entombing in the mines of the Americans," "the hunting of blackskins," and "bloody legislation against vagabondage," all rendered in linear and narrative realism rather than high immanent critique (915, 896). As John Bellamy Foster and Kevin Anderson have pointed out, slavery and colonialism were not passing concern's for Marx: they were central to his theory of capitalism and to his activism, realizing long before Western historians that slavery was a feature and not an aberration of industrial capitalism (Foster 99).

The inability to fully represent *Capital* as Jameson articulates, this "assemblage" and "montage" does not indicate a contradiction in the text but rather Marx's understanding that capitalism as a system is not uniform, nor is it expressed in the same way across the globe. Rather, capitalism comprises multiple and often contradictory modes of domination, exploitation, theft, and murder, from adulterated bread to the genocide of an entire continent. One way to think of the first chapters of *Capital* is as an argument with political economy: that even if the economy functioned as an exchange of equivalents on a fair market as leading classical economists such as Smith and Ricardo maintained, it would still be theft in the form of surplus value extracted from workers. And yet Marx reminds us every time we get up close and personal that the system is anything but a smooth circuit of equivalent exchange: from the factories designed with the literal floor plans of "Houses of Terror" to laws of value pulverizing Manchester workers in a decade and enslaved people in the Caribbean in a year, it is violence, slavery, murder, and theft written in "letters of blood and fire" (875).

"Profit is a form of appearances," Ann Cvetkovich reminds us (174), one long dissociative chain that both hides and reveals its sources of value. Realism collides with abstraction in the text, and they form a unity, even if they never really meet. The value congealed in the commodity as an abstraction is linked to the burning fields of the Americas, yet they seldom recognized each other and, indeed, would appear to be part of two separate systems, under particular and universal laws governance: the racialized slave, the migrant worker, the colonial subject, the free worker, and the commodity that traverses borders and languages. Understanding *Capital* as a literary text—perhaps even the ur-text of proletarian literature— we have to ask what these different modes of representation should tell us about how we represent labor to a reading public that includes workers. How are the abstraction and the concrete, the particular surplus population and the universal worker, to be represented in the same text as a complex, inextricable totality that cannot itself be fully grasped? *Capital* partially addresses this question through genre and style, as genre and style are means to both express and contain insights within their own formal rules. Perhaps this is how *Capital* acknowledges that its own subject is, following Jameson, only visible indirectly, partially, as an assemblage rather than a fixed totality.

Part II: Capital and the Literature of Workers

Working-class literature as a recognizable genre is fundamentally shaped by the contradictions articulated in *Capital*. The contradictions are legion and inextricable: between the worker as an abstract commodity and as embodied living labor; between workers as a necessary part of capital's valorization and as surplus population; between racialized workers within the same global commodity chain and yet subject to differentiated laws, forms of violence and citizenship status; between generic conventions that limit or expand a novel's capacity to capture the many various symptoms visible in Jameson's "unrepresentable totality." In what critics Bill V. Mullen and Michael Folsom have called the U.S.'s first proletarian novel, Upton Sinclair's *The Jungle* (1906) stands as one of the first North American texts to attempt to portray capitalism not only as a totalized system but from the point of view of its most exploited workers moving from production to consumption, from country to city, from politicians to foremen, from brothels to prisons.

Jack London called the novel the "Uncle Tom's Cabin of wage slavery," as central to the movement to abolish wage labor as Harriet Beecher Stowe's sentimental novel was to the abolitionist struggle a half-century earlier. The comparison is a telling one, and not only because Sinclair believed his novel produced the Pure Food and Drug Act rather than the proletarian revolution he was after: "I aimed at the public's heart, and by accident I hit it in the stomach" ("Life" 594). *Uncle Tom's Cabin* is most famous for its role in generating public support for the abolition of slavery and the Republican victory, but among many literary scholars, it is also known for its lack of African Americans collectively resisting slavery and its embrace of racist tropes in characterization. In this context, Tom's Christian sacrifice, from which the eponymous epithet stems, is read more often as passivity than passive resistance. And while Sinclair took great pains to make *The Jungle* free of the sentimentality that gave *Uncle Tom's Cabin* its affective power and has made it subject to criticism by modernist writers, the novel's very attempt to represent capitalism as a unitary system also limits its ability to understand how other forms of social domination are central to capitalism. Most notably, the treatment of Black workers stands in stark contrast to the novel's treatment of Eastern European immigrants. The protagonist, Jurgis Rudkus, is neither a paragon of virtue nor granted the rich interiority one would expect from a nineteenth-century realist novel; unlike the Black workers in the slaughterhouse, however, he is nonetheless depicted as a democratic subject, capable of comprehending his circumstances and acting to change them.

For white workers, *The Jungle* is exacting and clear-eyed about the mechanized ruthlessness of capitalist production and its relationship to the state. Jurgis, like a proletarian Job, loses everything in the novel; perhaps like Job, his sufferings are not redeemed but at least comprehended by his faith in socialism at the text's conclusion. Even so, the exploitation and brutality Jurgis experiences is methodical: Jurgis begins as a cheerful "cog in this marvelous machine" of the meat processing industry, greeting every challenging with the refrain, "I will work harder" (Sinclair 33, 22). The "pork making by applied mathematics" foreshadows Jurgis' own life: the "trusting" and "innocent" hogs are caught within the machinery of the slaughterhouse, and "all his protests, his screams, were nothing" to the machine that "cut his throat and watching him gasp out his life" (36–37). Sinclair employs the masculine pronoun "he" rather than the usual "it" when referring to animals to make the point more clearly, and like the animals he slaughters, Jurgis is caught within the levers of the cruelly indifferent machinery of industrial production and capitalist speculation. The "relentless and savage… lash of want" hung over Jurgis so that even his elderly father and his children were forced to work in the slaughterhouse (73). Experiencing his first "speed-up," which applied the force of a "thumb-screw" by "clock-work," Jurgis comes to understand that his cheerful insistence that he will "work harder" means nothing in the face of the law of value. Increasing the rate of exploitation decreased the number of workers the plant needed and subjected most of his family to industrial violence: Jurgis' son permanently injured his hand; Jurgis' father dies when the poison at his factory seeps into his boots; Jurgis and his wife Ona are both laid off as overproduction decreases the price of meat. "They had gotten the best out of him—they had worn him out, with their speeding up and their carelessness, and now they had thrown him away" is the novel's succinct commentary on capitalism (121). Like the abstract labor in each commodity that is "congealed," so too Jurgis is rendered, and enters the labor market like Marx's metonymic worker: with only his hide to sell and about to receive a tanning.

The rest of the novel's denouement moves like clock-work: Jurgis' wife is forced into prostitution; Jurgis is sent to prison attacking her trafficker; they lose their house; Ona dies in childbirth; Jurgis' sister eventually winds up in a brothel and Jurgis first tramps and then becomes a fixer for corrupt politicians. Jurgis' redemption, like much of the novel, barely records him as a full person, and when he joins the Socialist Party at the novel's conclusion, the text abandons him like the factory: the novel devolves into socialist speeches and slogans, and Jurgis vanishes into the background. Little interiority is granted to Jurgis or any of his family throughout the text, for his motives, his personality, are two-dimensional, responding to immediate need with simple thoughts and actions. Sinclair himself admitted that he began the book as journalism and initially had no characters, which perhaps helps explain why explanations of socialism, of unions, and of capitalism are granted to the omniscient narrator. Jurgis and his family are vehicles as their bodies are commodities in the text, serving a function and then discarded. Yet Jurgis is capable of understanding what befalls him: after resisting, he comes to be a passionate supporter of his union; he feels guilt and shame at working as a strike-breaker; he ultimately becomes a supporter and advocate of socialism. He is, in short, a political subject.

The African American workers, however, show up only as "stupid black negroes" and an "army of beasts" who arrive as strikebreakers. Where Jurgis is finally denied a rich interiority, the Black workers are denied even basic humanity and function only as a threat to union (256, 261). To be clear, the animus the text has for them is linked to their race, not only their role as "scabs" (those who undermine a labor action by replacing striking workers); while Jurgis' crossing of the picket line and other criminal acts are understood as moral failings, they are not dehumanizing ones. Unlike Jurgis, the "negroes, foreigners and criminals" who appear as non-union workers are represented as animals and automatons, a lesser category of human rather than part of capital's reserve army of labor to be mobilized when emergency calls.

While African Americans appear only briefly in *The Jungle*, Sinclair clearly does not view them primarily as members of the working class. Unlike Jurgis, they are not an intrinsic part of the production of value; unlike Marx who finds a dialectical unity between "labor in a white skin" that cannot be free "while in a black skin it is branded," African Americans in Sinclair's novel represent an external threat outside any potential for solidarity or collective action. African Americans haunt the peripheries of the novel less as a group dominated by capital structurally even if separated legally and socially; they are rather a kind of eugenic threat that industrialism will sink everyone to the animal state of blackness. One would never know from reading Sinclair that African American workers had been central to major labor actions such as the Pullman Strike of 1894 and would later be instrumental to a series of strikes after World War I and to the success of organized labor ranging from the Industrial Workers of the World (I.W.W.) to the Congress of Industrial Organizations (CIO).

Part III: Can the Lumpenproletariat Speak?

If *The Jungle* inaugurated proletarian literature in the U.S., then Richard Wright's *Native Son* may mark the genre's pinnacle and terminus as a coherent movement. In the same way the explosive cultural event of *The Jungle* coincided with the rise of the Socialist Party (SP) and the IWW with its largely European immigrant base, so *Native Son* emerged as a national event at the height of the Congress of Industrial Organizations (CIO) and Communist Party's (CPUSA) influence in the U.S., only a few short years before the onset of the Cold War's second red scare would mark the decline of both. *Native Son*, about a Black working-class anti-hero and the white daughter of his employer, marks not only changes in representations of class from the early twentieth century but, more importantly, changes in the ways class and race are understood. Unlike the SP, the CPUSA placed antiracism and anti-colonialism at the center of both their political analysis and their organizing.[2] As Hakim Adi framed it, the CP was the "era's sole international white-led movement...formally dedicated to a revolutionary transformation of the global political *and* racial order" (155). From the point of view of literary representation, this attention to the racialization of the working class in the U.S. allowed for a far more dialogic, uneven, and varied approach to what it means to be, to identify with, and to express working-class identity and politics.

As Nathaniel Mills argues in *Ragged Revolutionaries*, *Native Son*'s Bigger Thomas is "American literature's most representative lumpenproletarian character" (49). An ambiguous category in Marx's writings, the "lumpen" appear in *Capital* as "the reserve army of labor," as "surplus population," and the dispossessed "vagabond," structurally produced by capitalism and yet cast off by it simultaneously: in Jameson's terms, the lumpen are the most visible symptom of capitalism's willingness to violently dispose of the people who provide its wealth. In *Class Struggle in France* where Marx deploys the term, he imbues "lumpen" with far more moral and political judgment, noting that these cast-off "vagabonds" are the recruiting ground for "thieves and criminals," and cannot see their own class interest (50). Bigger Thomas, a working-class Black youth on Chicago's South Side, is both a "thief and criminal," and yet also someone who feels intensely his exclusion from all but the most menial and low-paying jobs. Thomas' eventual incorporation into the waged economy as the driver for a rich white family did not offer Thomas the sense of stability and purpose his social workers desired. Rather, his body is seized by his new white patrons with the same sense of violence and neglect as it was an object barred earlier from entry into such an economy. Jan and Mary's well-meaning abduction of Bigger for their tour of Chicago's South Side produces not solidarity, or sameness, but a feeling of traumatized anxiety and non-being for Bigger, the "No Man's Land" that "ensnared him in a tangle of deep shadows" (Wright 67, 72). That Thomas reacts violently and unpredictably to his incorporation into the wage economy is both a sign of the utter alienation that Marx describes and also possibly a sign of Thomas' agency, will, and drive to be a subject in his own narrative (446).

Unlike *The Jungle*, the task of *Native Son* is to present a character wholly on the margins of capitalist production with a powerful subjective voice, autonomously able to transform and self-reflect. As the communist organizer Jan apologizes to Thomas for his role in a white racist society even as he grieves the death of his partner at Thomas' hands, Jan's fervent belief in fairness and revolution offers Thomas his first glimpse at a truly intersubjective relationship: "suddenly this white man had come up to him," Bigger thinks, "flung aside the curtain, and walked into the room of his life" (289). Though Mary, Bessie, and Bigger are all murdered by the novel's end, Wright suggests how the uneven, broken assemblage of the working class may come to recognize their coincident interest. For Wright, Bigger is a potential revolutionary, someone who "conditioned as his organism is, will not become a…supporter of the status quo." At the novel's conclusion, Thomas rejects the elderly lawyer's explanation of his status as a victim and insists that his murders have meaning. Taken as a metaphor, one could echo C. L. R. James to observe that the Black (lumpen) proletariat is not simply oppressed but has a pivotal role to play in a revolutionary struggle.

As Wright argues in "Blueprint for Negro Writing" that the "Negro writer must create in his readers' minds a relationship between a Negro woman hoeing cotton in the South and the men who loll in swivel chairs in Wall Street and take the fruits of her toil." In many ways, Wright makes the argument *Capital* makes throughout, only instead of an English worker in a Manchester factory, the center of Wright's argument about the totality of the capitalist system is a black woman who likely does not even work for a steady wage. *Native Son*, like *Capital* itself, is a novel that both articulates capitalism as a global system of accumulation run by "men in buildings" (427) at great commanding heights above the city, and yet is experienced in the disorderly, violent confrontations between Jan, Bessie, Bigger, and Mary on Chicago's streets—an assemblage of disunified and yet connected parts, written in an often lurid and sensational style cross-cut by modernist montage and realist reportage. Ironically, it is the doomed figure of Mary who, as a stand-in for the Marxist intellectual who has only an abstract notion of capitalism, just "wants to see" how the racialized working classes live—and in her desire to traverse such boundaries, she ends up a victim of them (69).

The role of the novel to represent the working class is thus not to represent a unity, but rather to grasp all the ways in which the notion of "class" is both structural and not visible, an experience lived through the modalities of other identities, genders, races, and regions as much as through the wage relation itself. *Native Son* was of course not alone in this effort to represent the multiple modalities and subjectivities of proletarians under capital: Tillie Olsen's *Yonnondio*, Ann Petry's *The Street*, Carlos Bulosan's *America is in the Heart*, H. T. Tsiang's *And China Has Hands*, and Mike Gold's *Jews without Money* are but a few of the "red decade's" proletarian novels that focused as much on workers outside of the formal wage economy or the terrain of equal citizenship, from gendered social reproduction to small time gangsters to migrant farm workers, novels that are as varied as the working classes around the globe. Thus, unlike *The Jungle*, "the worker" cannot be simply represented by a singular, unified deracinated subject, no matter how brutalized and marginalized Jurgis may be. While capitalism may be a global system, its wage relations, conditions of exploitation, and means of reproduction are as subjective and contingent as the workers who express their desire for liberation.

Notes

1 See Benjamin Kohlmann's chapter "Symptoms" in this volume.
2 See the work of Mark Naison, Robin Kelley, and Barbara Foley.

Works Cited

Adi, Hakim. "The Negro Question: The Communist International and Black Liberation in the Interwar Years." *From Toussaint to Tupac: The Black International since the Age of Revolution*, edited by Michael O. West, William G. Martin, and Fanon Che Wilkins. U of North Carolina P, 2009, pp. 155–178.

Anderson, Kevin. *Marx at the Margins: On Nationalism, Ethnicity, and Non-Western Societies*. U of Chicago P, 2010.

Cvetkovich, Ann. *Mixed Feelings: Feminism, Mass Culture, and Victorian Sensationalism*. Rutgers UP, 1992.

Foley, Barbara. *Radical Representations: Politics and Form in U.S. Proletarian Fiction, 1929–1941*. Duke UP, 1993.

Folsom, Michael Brewster. "Upton Sinclair's Escape from *The Jungle*: The Narrative Strategy and Suppressed Conclusion of America's First Proletarian Novel." *Upton's Sinclair's Jungle*, edited by Harold Bloom. Chelsea House, 2001, pp. 21–48.

Foster, John Bellamy. "Marx and Slavery." *Monthly Review*, vol. 72, no. 3, July–August 2020, pp. 96–114.

James, C.L.R. "Revolutionary Answer to the Negro Question." *C.L.R. James and Revolutionary Marxism: Selected Writings of C.L.R. James*, edited by Scott McLemee and Paul Le Blanc. Prometheus Books, 2000, pp. 179–187.

Jameson, Fredric. *Representing Capital: A Reading of Volume One*. Verso Books, 2014.

Kelley, Robin D.G. "'This Ain't Ethiopia, But It'll Do: African-Americans and the Spanish Civil War." *Race Rebels: Culture, Politics and the Black Working Class*. The Free Press, 1994, pp. 123–158.

Kornbluh, Anna. "On Marx's Victorian Novel." *Mediations*, vol. 25, no.1, Fall 2010, pp. 15–38.

London, Jack. "What Jack London Says of The Jungle." *Chicago Socialist*, vol. 11 (1905), p. 25. Reprinted in *The Jungle: Norton Critical Edition*, edited by Clare Virginia Eby. W.W. Norton and Co, 2003, pp. 483–484.

Marx, Karl. *Capital: A Critique of Political Economy*. Translated by Ben Fowkes. Penguin Books, 1990.

———. *The Class Struggles in France, 1848–1850*. International Publishers, 1964.

Mills, Nathaniel. *Ragged Revolutionaries: The Lumpenproletariat and African American Marxism in Depression-Era Literature*. U of Massachusetts P, 2017.

Mullen, Bill V. "Proletarian Literature Reconsidered." *Oxford Encyclopedia of Literature Online*. April 2017. https://doi.org/10.1093/acrefore/9780190201098.013.236

Naison, Mark. *Communists in Harlem During the Great Depression*. U of Illinois P, 2004.

Postone, Moishe. *Time, Labor, and Social Domination: A Reinterpretation of Marx's Critical Theory*. Cambridge UP, 1993.

Roberts, William Clare. *Marx's Inferno: A Political Theory of Capital*. Princeton UP, 2017.

Shocket, Eric. "'Discovering Some New Race': Rebecca Harding Davis's 'Life in the Iron Mills' and the Literary Emergence of Working-Class Whiteness." *PMLA*, vol. 115, no. 1, pp. 46–59.

Sinclair, Upton. *The Jungle: Norton Critical Edition*. Edited by Clare Virginia Eby. W.W. Norton and Co., 2003.

———. "What Life Means to Me." *Cosmopolitan*, Oct. 1906, pp. 591–595.

Vogman, Elena. *Dance of Values: Sergei Eisenstein's 'Capital' Project*. Diaphanes, 2019.

Wald, Alan. *American Night: The Literary Left in the Era of the Cold War*. U of North Carolina P, 2012.

Wright, Richard. "Blueprint for Negro Writing." *Norton Anthology of African American Literature*. W.W. Norton and Co., 2014, pp. 125–132.

———. "How Bigger Was Born." *Native* Son. Harper Perennial, 2005, pp. 431–462.

———. *Native Son*. Harper Perennial, 2005.

12
DEBTORS
Robin Truth Goodman

In Hwang Dong-hyuk's 2021 South Korean TV mini-series *Squid Game*, the desperately indebted choose to participate in deadly children's games in which the final survivor would win a combined cash prize if their organs are not sold first. In each plotline, the affective relationships developed between the players turn macabre when they discover that the rules of the game will exploit those relationships as obstacles to winning the grand prize of debt cancellation. Meanwhile, masked rich investors hide in a glorious room of lounge chairs, feasts, and expensive liqueurs, entertained with laughter and jokes as they bid on the games they see through a screen. With the easy identification of its character types and the familiarity of the children's games like tug-of-war and marbles (to the death), the series dramatizes Annie McClanahan's observation that "debt is such a ubiquitous yet elusive social form that we can most clearly and carefully understand it by looking at how our culture has sought to represent it" (2).

Debt is very much like a promise made by a debtor. A promise, as Friedrich Nietzsche describes it, "ordain[s] a future in advance" (58). A debt anticipates and represents an unknown future, but does so in recognizable terms of known values. Though economic and financial values seem categorically different from literary values, debt bears a significant resemblance to literature because both involve imaginary moments made present through an interpretive social and symbolic framework. This framework tames uncertain futures with seemingly certain present calculation, making reality of the unreal while changing our relation to time by extending present time indefinitely. Debt, like promises in general, certainly can be said to bring to the surface the social tensions over who controls the constitution of the real through its representation. Commenting on Nietzsche, Maurizio Lazzarato adds, "The importance of the debt economy lies in the fact that it appropriates and exploits both chronological labor time and *action,* non-chronological time, time as choice, decision" (55). Where debt flattens value by capturing the future in the present, literary narrative can *thematize* temporal movement as it plays inside the tensions among interacting temporal frames.

A critical theory of debt would be misleading if it shared with debt the tendency to frame political decision-making narrowly in terms of economic rationality and market logic. Debt tends to contribute to a vision of human community and association as based on calculations of reciprocal exchange. Yet, the possibility that the value of human relations can be made into a comparable quantity is thoroughly social, based as it is on institutional frameworks and power struggles, or politics. Debt is social in that it reproduces subjectivities in line with a denser infiltration of capital into everyday life, consciousness, and culture. As Lazzarato elaborates: "You are free insofar as you assume the *way of life* (consumption, work, public spending, taxes, etc.) compatible with reimbursement" (31); a *way of life* that is based on inequality, power asymmetries, control, and command. Literature can help us understand the broader cultural and political milieu in which debt operates.

In the wake of the 2008 financial crash and the response by Occupy Wall Street, the politics of debt—national debt, international debt, housing debt, credit card debt, consumer debt, student debt, medical debt—was already a clear area of political engagement around which to organize. This was true despite the fact that debt was so clearly reliant on preexisting conditions of deep social inequalities.[1] As Andrew Ross noted at the time, "In societies like ours, which are heavily financialized, the struggle over debt is increasingly the frontline conflict – not because wage conflict is over (it never will be) but because debts, for most people, are the wages of the future" (23). Indeed, the 2008 debt crisis showed that different racial, ethnic, gender, and class populations were constructing their identities in response to the disparate effects of debt on identity.

In addition, debt was distributed along a moral axis, where, as Randy Martin noted, consumer debt in the United States would be seen as "signs of strength," elevating the economy, where "the debt of the third world, inert and immobile, was treated as bad" (28). The development and attachment of a moral valence to a financial practice was far from a twenty-first-century invention, as suggested by the title of David Graeber's *Debt: The First 5000 Years*. Graeber traces representations of money lenders as evil back to medieval Europe and, cross-culturally, to Hindu and Buddhist codes as well, connected to cultural practices like sacrifice as payment to the gods and retributive justice. In his timely anthropology of debt that became an international bestseller and exerted an influence on the Occupy Wall Street movement, Graeber investigates debt as co-evolving with the development of human society as a barter society.[2] The concept of debt arises, according to Graeber, in connection with the advent of money, which in turn results from the demise of community and the first call for traveling soldiers who needed to be paid in wages, or in some form of payment that could be used afar, outside of the directly local context. Graeber historicizes how debt intensified over time—as more of sociality was understood through depersonalization, abstraction, calculation, and violence—into a mechanism not only of theft but also of political and militaristic control: "Any system that reduces the world to numbers can only be held in place by weapons, whether these are swords and clubs, or, nowadays, 'smart bombs' from unmanned drones" (387). Indeed, much like the intertwined relationship between force and ideology, the relationship of debt to militarism and authoritarianism is more than coincidental and more than closely. As Juan González's characterized the Puerto Rican debt crisis (and which might equally apply to places as distant from one another as Greece and Haiti), debt has actually replaced the military as a colonizing force: "You no longer need foreign armies to control the population.... [Debt] has rendered historical concepts of national independence almost meaningless."

Much of the speculation described in nineteenth-century literary texts was based on false rumors and reporting and sometimes outright deception. People were persuaded to invest in projects that either did not exist or were severely overvalued, often needing to be backed by force. This was one reason why fortunes were so volatile. The beginning of the twenty-first century has proven to be a time of enormous financialization which parallels the end of the nineteenth century, the heyday of the British Empire when speculation was ripe and belief needed to be fashioned to make distant speculative projects seem valid when oftentimes nothing of value was there.

Realism and Imperial Capitalism

In a speech he delivered to Congress on March 19, 1937, Democratic Congressman Charles Binderup attributed a line to Henry Ford that equally described the United States of 2008: "It is well enough that the people of the nation do not understand our banking or monetary system for, if they did, I believe that there would be a revolution before tomorrow morning." In 2008 words were spinning around to talk about financial instruments like credit default swaps, derivatives, collateralized debt obligations, and mortgage-backed securities. Such words became mainstream almost overnight but it wasn't clear anyone really knew what they were talking about; the words circulated in reference to obscure instruments that themselves had no recognizable, agreed-upon set of meanings. In fact, these terms for debt indicate self-referential bundles of cut-up debt obligations, securities, and insurance bound together in "tranches" without logic, coherence, or oversight. Like floors in a tower where each level secures the level below, "tranches" were meant to balance out risk but, without standardized methods to determine risks, they were a combination of pieces of mortgages without possible evaluative assessment, as those involved in trading and evaluating them did not understand the criteria for grading them. The mortgage takers at the bottom end often had bad credit scores, low incomes, and no collateral; the instruments themselves depended on the continued flow of high returns that would cover up the insufficiencies at the bottom until the economy began to contract.

Like literature, debt has been formulated as a symbolic invention—money-value—cut-up and bound by an emptied-out symbolic term, a title, or genre. "Now a fairy tale was being reinvented before his eyes in the financial markets" (63), writes Michael Lewis, describing debt in *The Big Short: Inside the Doomsday Machine*. "The details were complicated" (156), he goes on, and what he means is that Triple-A bonds were bundled up in "tranches" (or layers) of subprime mortgages lent to people whose financial backgrounds had not been investigated but who were overleveraged. Indeed, Lewis tells the story of the financial crisis through vignettes of quirky characters who bet against the surging U.S. economy as they came to understand that these new financial products were baseless. As each chapter narrates a biography of a character who noticed the mortgage crisis because of their development and perspective, chance encounters, and even dialogue, the journalistic account *The Big Short* takes on many of the features of a suspense novel. Like poststructuralist understandings of infinitely if playfully deferred chains of signification with no final anchor for stable, reliable, linguistic value, these financial instruments were pure representations with nothing backing them but the faith of people who believed in stories they had been told. *The Big Short* is an example of where literary narrative, as Mathias Nilges illustrates, examines the temporality of finance in ways that parallel the instruments that finance has produced to understand its own operations, mediating between "monetary production and accumulation" (32) without passing through commodity/objects.

Literature has played a historical role in defining and teaching debt to the public. Realism in the novel developed in the nineteenth century alongside the standardization of such monetary instruments as paper currency, coins, balance sheets, stocks, and credit bills and shared with credit culture the need to produce a belief in something that, by definition, *is not there*. Mary Poovey points out that the fields of literature and economics once overlapped; in the nineteenth century the disciplines split, however, and literature became one of the devices to explain how property could acquire symbolic value, displacing landed property or things as conferring value. Literature then served pedagogically to explain how a thing could simultaneously not exist and yet be valuable, where "the reader must be willing to extend to these [financial] abstractions a variant of the belief that she would extend to a fictional character" (142). Where Marx discussed "fictional capital" as value in circulation but yet to be realized, Poovey analyzes how the representational structure of finance derives from imaginative techniques, a "fact/fiction continuum" (77) where what could be counted as "fact" "borrowed features from imaginative writing in order to give readers what no numbers could provide" (274). Indeed, as Anna Kornbluh elaborates, the contradictions of the credit economy were often portrayed as resolved in the realist novel's character development, through the birth of the psychological character: "Where fictious capital made the financial economy inexplicably complex," Kornbluh expounds,

> the psychic economy realized capital, domesticating the economy as the natural issue of interiority. [...] Where money might be useful evidence that the mind works in abstract ways, derivative abstractions like credit and stock required mental truisms for proof. [...] Psychology lent a ground to economic relations.
>
> *(39–43)*

Instabilities in the market were not only representationally funneled through character moods and troubles but also instantiated, as Audrey Jaffe notes, in the figure of the dark foreigner whose "admission to polite society threatens its [market society's] solid values" (78).

Such a novel is Anthony Trollope's 1871 *The Eustace Diamonds,* which tells of Lizzie Greystock who, like the dark foreigner, forces her way into society by "falsely"—according to the mores of that society—acquiring its attributes. Lizzie's father dies and leaves her in debt until she marries Sir Florian Eustace who, in turn, dies a year after the wedding, leaving her with their son and an ambiguous will. The Eustace family stakes claim on Sir Florian's estate, and the novel shows how the values and ownership of different properties depend on their narrative frames that are struggled over between the various relatives, lawyers, sentimental journalists, and gossipers. *The Eustace Diamonds* is a pedagogical novel that explains to the Victorian public how value can be created without referring to landed property or solid objects but rather to linguistic instruments like letters, laws, contracts, wills, and agreements. In particular, the diamonds are an invisible object, both there and not there like Lizzie Eustace herself, who feigns her own kidnapping. The necklace foregrounds types of property that depend on legalistic jargon and belief systems rather than inheritance or referentiality: "If a thing is a man's own," contemplates Lizzie, "he can give it away;—not a house, a farm, or a wood, or anything like that; but a thing he can carry with him—of course he can give it away" (94). But it is not so simple, as lawyers, politicians, and judges vie to label it as an heirloom, a chattel, a gift, or a piece of paraphernalia, whether her husband bequeathed it to her or whether it would revert to the family via her son, whose interests contradicted her own. The decisions about how to define these financial instruments mobilized power, class, and control to attribute moral weaknesses to the main character Lizzie Eustace as she sought to manage her debt: as Richard Dienst notes in his post-2008 analysis of the utopian literary tradition's rendering of debt, questions of obligation "might appear to be philosophical questions, but they often receive literary answers" (53). Lizzie's "fault" is exposing the property as fiction, showing how debt lets her fake her way into society, using the symbols of privilege against themselves and thereby confusing the rituals that uphold wealth and ruling-class authority.

The Eustace Diamonds also raises the question of the relationship between this ethereal object and the financialization of the British colonies. While Lizzie fakes her way into high society via her "fake" claims on the diamonds, her friends and enemies in Parliament argue over the fate of an Indian prince in Mysore in the wake of the 1857 Indian Mutiny. The Indian prince or Sawab wants to bequeath his rulership to his adopted son while the liberals in Parliament want to annex the region to control its trade, using the argument that adoption provides a fraudulent line of inheritance. The symbolization of debt (the diamonds) as negative value—as something Lizzie does not and really cannot have—allows the colonies to come into relation with the global system as negative value, as something the British are constantly at risk of losing or not ever having and which they hold only through its representation, which is what the parliamentary debates in the novel put into dispute. That is, the geopolitical system recognizes decolonized spaces only as negative identities, identities in debt, and identities like Lizzie's.

The financial dealings of pre-Victorian and Victorian characters are well known: just recall the various marriage plots in Jane Austen, the troubled family life in Charles Dickens' most debt-focused novel, *Little Dorrit* (1855–1957), or the corruption in Anthony Trollope's tome about the world financial system, *The Way We Live Now* (1875), to name but a few examples. Debt is linked in these works to the development of moral character. The early twenty-first century was another time where the obscurity of how financial instruments worked concurred with literary output that highlighted this epistemological obscurity as a literary device. This surge in finance-related literary narratives did not only include *The Big Short*—more famous after Adam McKay's 2015 film adaptation starring Christian Bale, Steve Carell, Ryan Gosling, and Brad Pitt, where the literariness of financial products was well on display: "In August, he wrote a proposal for a fund he called Milton's Opus" (53), describes Mike Burry, who worked his way into a career in off-beat finance and "esoteric insurance contracts" from a teenage obsession with comic books. ("The first question was always, 'What's Milton's Opus?' He'd say, '*Paradise Lost*,' but that usually just raised another question)" (53). The quirkiness of the characters directly corresponded to, and explained, the quirkiness of financial markets.

Also, for example, Teddy Wayne's 2010 novel *Kapitoil* narrated the reduction of life to financial algorithms. Karim Issar, an immigrant from Turkey in New York, discovers an algorithm that can control financial resources in the West by predicting fluctuations in oil futures as a result of world events and also could end disease in poor countries, and he wants to de-encrypt it for global access: like a literary symbol, the algorithmic equation travels between applications, taking on agentic, predictive, and tragic capacities and is struggled over. Jess Walter's 2009 *The Financial Lives of Poets* tells of Matthew Prior who quits working as a reporter to start a poetry website which launches him into debt that he responds to by selling pot. Kim Stanley Robinson's 2021 novel, *The Ministry for the Future*, relates about the post-World War II world economy constructed around debt as the condition for environmental planetary collapse partly because debt blocks imagining the future otherwise.

And the necessarily truncated list goes on: Gary Shteyngart's 2010 comic novel *Super Sad True Love Story*; Adam Haslett's 2010 bestseller *Union Atlantic*; John Lanchester's 2012 novel *Capital*, which follows the lives of houses on a London street into the twenty-first century as they gain and lose value; Margaret Atwood's 2007 review of debt in literature, *Payback: Debt and the Shadow Side of Wealth*; Mohsin Hamid's 2014 mock self-help *How to Get Filthy Rich in Rising Asia*; and Aravind Adiga's Booker Prize-winning 2008 novel *The White Tiger*, about the indebtedness of the ruling classes to their serving classes and the ensuing reprisals, made into an Oscar-nominated movie in 2021 by Ramin Bahrani. Debt in the twenty-first century had grown and continued to grow exponentially because both wages and public spending were in decline, so that workers had to borrow what should have been their fair share during a period of steady growth, with surplus being handed off to the owners, managers, investors, and CEOs. This situation created unprecedented class polarization. Though debt is seemingly financial, it is a cultural response to economic polarization. McClanahan usefully notes that the needs of the credit economy that literature answered—to make value *believable* in something *not there*—change at a moment like our present when the prevalence of debt has put belief in credit into question along with its realist representations now made more uncertain, liquid, limited, and fungible. The culture of debt, continues McClanahan, therefore incites literary and other cultural texts that exacerbate contradictions rather than resolving them, as, ostensibly, realism does (it is arguable, though, that realism was able to ensure the security in beliefs that McClanahan attributes to it).

Again, none of this is a product only of nineteenth-century realist literature. Twentieth-century modernist writers also recognized debt as a fiction in the interests of imperial power. In 1932, for example, the African American poet Langston Hughes wrote a newspaper polemic about the early twentieth-century crisis and military occupation of Haiti, explaining,

> You will discover that the Banque d'Haiti, with its Negro cashiers and tellers is really under control of the National City Bank of New York. You will become informed that all the money collected by the Haitian customs passes through the hands of an American comptroller.

In 1920, African American author and educator James Weldon Johnson wrote a four-part series of articles for *The Nation* in which he spotlighted the military invasion and occupation of Haiti as defending the interests of the National City Bank of New York which controlled the ports, the treasury, the issuance of bonds, and the importation and exportation of currency. Johnson writes,

> This Government forced the Haitian leaders to accept the promise of American aid and American supervision. With that American aid the Haitian Government defaulted its external and internal debt, an obligation, which under self-government the Haitians had scrupulously observed. And American supervision turned out to be a military tyranny supporting the program of economic exploitation.
>
> (38–39)

The "Third World-ization" of debt underlies the creation of national space as negative value that is demographically expansive and yet floating, invisible, and untethered.

And it is not just the genre of realism that engages these issues: notably, Kenyan Ngugi wa Thiong'o's 2006 novel *Wizard of the Crow* is a financial comedy of errors that dismantles the symbiosis between work and the productive machine as well as between economic activity and the local flourishing of its social context. It tells of Aburiria, a fictional "Third World" nation that is debt financing a large, useless reproduction of the multi-lingual Biblical Tower of Babel to commemorate the corrupt Ruler, to attract foreign investments, and—at least rhetorically—to create jobs. As soon as the Ruler and his cronies start negotiations with the Global Bank for the grand construction project of the Tower, the organic coherence of the territory, the state, the economy, and the literary all come apart simultaneously. The streets in the business zone are filled with "flies, worms, and the stench of rot" (36) caused by "mountains of uncollected garbage, the factories in the industrial area, or simply human sweat" (48). The novel opens in this dump, a space collecting negative or toxic value, when the protagonist, Kamiti (later to become the Wizard of the title), levitates like they hope the local economy will. When the Global Bank cancels the loan for the Tower, more and more workers line up in four directions from the Eldares Modern Construction and Real Estate sign that reads "*No Vacancy*," which is intended to send these workers away. The Ruler, now in New York begging bankers not to divest, becomes ill with an undiagnosable disease that causes him to swell preposterously and float to the ceiling when he discovers he is pregnant with Baby D., or small "d" democracy, as he watches the chaos of his own country through the TV: "It is natural for money to give birth to money" (660), reflects Kamiti, ironically. Ngugi's novel is a comical dystopia of the transience of a world made substanceless through financialization and literary translatability at the expense of localized democratic and creative sovereignty.

Symbolic Capitalism

Ngugi predicts how the empty symbols of power and growth are unsustainable within a financial system, depleting the local territory and miscarrying its nascent democracy. As Ericka Beckman has demonstrated, "novels highlight finance capital as an illusory and indeed fictive form of wealth" (97) (Latin American nations being her example), often linking imbalances in character to the irresolutions of financial economies: in Latin America, "the realist novel ultimately rests on foundations of credit and belief that are... shaky and illusory" (97). In a sense, though, *The Wizard of the Crow* also foreshadows a transition where literature is not only operating in a pedagogical mode to clarify characters' moral psychology by resolving finance's contradictions but also exposing such contradictions as unresolved and irresolvable. With the Tower of Babel at its center, Ngugi's novel also alludes to a neoliberalism where the economy is understood as expansive through language. The debt economy coincides with the rising dominance of symbolic capitalism: trade in symbolic products, an "immaterial" or "reproductive" economy of ideas, affects, sensations, narratives, brands, information, communication, experiences, relationships, and identity formations. This economic tendency is often informed by literary tendencies.

Christian Marazzi calls this "*semio-capital*," or "the semioticization of the social relations of production" (44), where "constant capital has become linguistic" (61). Marazzi elaborates, "in the New Economy *language* and communication are structurally and contemporaneously present throughout both the sphere of the production and distribution of goods and services and the sphere of finance" (14), and therefore the "putting to work of the language of social relations, the activation of productive cooperation beyond the factory gate, is the origin of the economy... of the communicative-relational cooperation of the workforce" (60). *Semio-capitalism*, the New Economy, targets workers' creativities and cognitive capacities as the machine of profit while turning those workers into non-salaried entrepreneurs at work on themselves, where aspects of life and subjectivity are financialized to be freed up for extraction. As Ivan Ascher adds, "with risk shifting onto the worker, the commitment of capitalists to the place of production receded, privatizing insurance and social functions of care like health care and retirement" (93). Debt is the mechanism through which subjectivities are controlled and reshaped as commodities within a field of commodities. "Debt" as a legal category, as a discourse blurring the putatively clear boundaries between "economics" and "politics" and "literature," marks the extension of an economy based on sign systems or communicational functions where the entire expanse of social and cultural life is ripened for profit extraction.

The great advance and increase of debt across contemporary sociality must be understood as part of transformations in the post-1970s economy. Gilles Deleuze and his followers have identified this as a time when the production of surplus became co-extensive with the entirety of social life—as a control society—rather than restricted to certain sites like factories. At the same time, the reproduction of subjects was increasingly absorbed into productive processes. This means that our thoughts, emotions, consciousness, experiences, and relationships, like the commodity, can be turned into money. This sprawling indebtedness has been linked to a centrality of communications as a target of capital growth. By the early 1990s, Jacques Derrida observed the overlap between the logic of debt and the structure of language: the "symbolic," he notes, "opens and constitutes the order of exchange and debt" (13); that is, the arbitrariness of signification—or the arbitrariness of the relationship between the referent and the thing referred to—parallels the arbitrariness of value. The difference between the supposedly positive (true) and negative value of money (or debt) is finally indeterminable, for all money is debt. This, for Derrida, links debt to literature: authority\authorship "is constituted by accreditation, both in the sense of legitimation as effect of belief or credulity, and of bank credit, of capitalized interest" (97) insofar as both debt and literary imagination create something out of nothing. Like debt, Derrida is saying, a literary text confers authority\authorship by creating the effect of belief in the system and its authority, interpreting or fixing value as negative or positive in a specific absence.

Derrida's analysis uses debt as a trope or example to explain symbolic economies through difference. He does not explain debt as a formation of power and governance. Others have identified the neoliberal economy itself as shaped by its integration within language, especially with its particular focus on the production of subjectivities. A tradition of Marxism has analyzed debt as spreading across the social fabric as communication has become a dominant mode of profit capture. Nicholas Thoburn, for example, reviews Marx's "Fragment on Machines" as it has been taken up by poststructuralist and autonomist thinkers to show that debt and finance in general are transforming the relations between work and profit by centralizing communications as capital itself. In the *Grundrisse*'s study on technology, Marx comes to two realizations: (1) that wealth depends less on labor time and more on the state of science and technology, which is dependent on individuals' artistic, scientific, and cultural attainments, including their use of free time; and (2) that workers themselves are inside the production process, so that their entire beings are co-extensive with the social body, not just in working time (Thoburn 81–82). According to autonomists like Antonio Negri and Mario Tronti, starting the analysis of capital from the position of workers does not explain why social antagonism is central whereas antagonism would be central if the analysis of capital started with an analysis of money as the mode of representation that makes inequality appear as equality. Following Marx and these autonomists, Thoburn calls this moment in capitalist development "real subsumption," the "general intellect," or the "social factory," where the worker becomes fully integrated into the temporality of the machine and its forms of cooperation and socialization and where language is primary as what expands capital logic into social space.

In fact, communication and its affects as "immaterial labor" become "central because it is the form of cooperation for the social whole" (Thoburn 86) as they have themselves become principle commodities. Thoburn does not go on, as some autonomists do, to prophesy the end of exploitation and work in the becoming-language of the economy as the worker's subjectivity becomes a continuous extension of the productive machine. Even in its "free time," the subject prepares itself for its further absorption into the productive code. To become commodities, the subject is, in this new milieu, a set of communicational competencies, skills, and capacities developed over a lifetime—or rather, a self-made but nonetheless indebted character/commodity in the enhancement of its social technology. As work time collapses into free time, as we are "freed" from the office by technology like phones that allow us to work everywhere from the dinner table to the bedroom, we spend our supposedly free time producing content to feed the machine. Thoburn does not directly mention debt as the control that sets the machine in motion, but we can recognize the structure: the subject is compelled to turn itself into a constant, fervent actor producing the promise of value in its future self by spending present time in "training, innovation, internal structures" (97) lest it fall into a deficit of capacity and lose its own value. Debt has become an entire way of life, a way of capturing the promise of the future in the everyday activities of the present; it has become so partly through language that prepares the malleable body for the production of value and the creation of meaning in the self, becoming the transparent expression of an appropriative subjectivity. If the transformation of the political citizen-subject into debtor-subject isn't complete, it seems well on its way.

Debt has now so saturated social space that almost nobody is beyond its grasp, and the only solution to its radical reshaping of subjective possibilities is debt cancellation. The intersections of literature and financial instruments have left traces in the historical record, partly because the function of literary language to produce something out of nothing but *belief* intersects with the logic of finance in general and with debt in particular. Literature therefore has sometimes taken on a pedagogical role in explaining the complexities of financialization and financial instruments. The coincidence between the logic of language and economy that late nineteenth-century writers observed recurs in the late twentieth century, visible inside depictions of power relations composed in the postcolony. In twenty-first-century neoliberalism, finance's disassociation from the commodity world and social contexts results from money's seeking profits by avoiding obstructions that would occur if productive momentum gets decelerated in objects, time delays, circulations, the reproductive lives of workers, or social welfare. This has led to an ever more intricate interweaving of the logic of money and language as they share de-realized, non-referential, fictional, and symbolic form. Language and communication have become greater sites of profit extraction as media capture productive space, affect is marketed, and socialization is technologized. In what Marx called "real subsumption" and what we call neoliberalism, where capital becomes coextensive with social space and socialization, "one *has to* express oneself," Thoburn explains. "[O]ne *has to* speak, communicate cooperate, and so forth and hence... a situation where every aspect of subjectivity... becomes productive of value" (99). One might wonder if literature, from within the social antagonism Antonio Negri describes as "what money is" (27), can still imagine social relations that, conflicting with their current form, may set the future free.

Notes

1 See Goodman, Robin. *Promissory Notes: On the Literary Conditions of Debt* (Lever Press, 2018).
2 For a critical account of Graeber's primitive utopianism, see Miranda Joseph. Joseph criticizes Graeber's positing of a utopian barter society focused on particularized relations between humans before the advent of debt society: "His story cannot account for the predatory attention to the particulars of borrowers *enabled* by the apparently depersonalized technologies of mortgage lending" (9). According to Joseph, this leads Graeber to imagine a sociality of exchange *before* the institution of state violence, as though exchange were the basis of *natural* human relations before violence, even as Marx's theory of "primitive accumulation" tells us that violence is what naturalizes exchange by taking away from the laborer everything but his ability to exchange his labor power.

Works Cited

Ascher, Ivan. *Portfolio Society: On the Capitalist Mode of Prediction*. Zone Books, 2016.
Beckman, Ericka. *Capital Fictions: The Literature of Latin America's Export Age*. U of Minnesota P, 2013.
Derrida, Jacques. *Giving Time: I. Counterfeit Money*. Translated by Peggy Kamuf. U of Chicago P, 1992.
Dienst, Richard. "Debt and Utopia." *The Politics of Debt: Essays and Interviews*, edited by Sjoerd van Tuinen and Arjen Kleinherenbrink. Zone Books, 2020.
González, Juan. "Juan González on How Puerto Rico's Economic 'Death Spiral' Is Tied to the Legacy of Colonialism." *Democracy Now!*, 26 November 2015. https://www.democracynow.org/2015/11/26/juan_gonzalez_on_how_puerto_ricos.
Goodman, Robin Truth. *Promissory Notes: On the Literary Conditions of Debt*. E-book, Lever Press, 2018, https://doi.org/10.3998/mpub.10209707.
Graeber, David. *Debt: The First 5,000 Years*. Melville House, 2011, 2012, 2014.
Hughes, Langston. "White Shadows in a Black Land." *Crisis*, vol. 39, May 1932, p. 157.
Jaffe, Audrey. *The Affective Life of the Average Man: The Victorian Novel and the Stock-Market Graph*. Ohio State UP, 2010.
Johnson, James Weldon. *Self-Determining Haiti: Four Articles Reprinted from The Nation Embodying a Report of an Investigation Made for the National Association for the Advancement of Colored People*. The Nation, 1920.
Joseph, Miranda. *Debt to Society: Accounting for Life Under Capitalism*. U of Minnesota P, 2014.
Kornbluh, Anna. *Realizing Capital: Financial and Psychic Economics in Victorian Form*. Fordham UP, 2014.
Lazzarato, Maurizio. *The Making of Indebted Man: An Essay on the Neoliberal Condition*. Translated by Joshua David Jordan. Semiotext(e), 2012.
Lewis, Michael. *The Big Short: Inside the Doomsday Machine*. W. W. Norton & Co., 2011, 2010.
Marazzi, Christian. *Capital and Language: From the New Economy to the War Economy*. Translated by Gregory Conti. Semiotext(e), 2008.
Martin, Randy. *An Empire of Indifference: American War and the Financial Logic of Risk Management*. Duke UP, 2007.
McClanahan, Annie. *Dead Pledges: Debt, Crisis, and Twenty-First Century Culture*. Stanford UP, 2017.
Negri, Antonio. *Marx Beyond Marx: Lessons on The Grundrisse*, edited by Fleming, Jim. Translated by Harry Cleaver, Michael Ryan, and Maurizio Viano. Autonomedia/Pluto, 1991.
Ngugi wa Thiong'o. *Wizard of the Crow*. Translated by Ngugi wa Thiong'o. Anchor Books, 2006.
Nietzsche, Friedrich. "Second Essay: 'Guilt,' 'Bad Conscience,' and the Like." *On the Genealogy of Morals and Ecce Homo*, edited and translated by Walter Kaufman. Vintage Books, 1967.
Nilges, Mathias. "Finance Capital and the Time of the Novel or, Money without Narrative Qualities." *Topia: Canadian Journal of Cultural Studies*, vol. 30–31, Fall 2013/Spring 2014, pp. 31–46.
Poovey, Mary. *Genres of the Credit Economy: Mediating Value in Eighteenth- and Nineteenth-Century-Britain*. U of Chicago P, 2008.
Ross, Andrew. "Mortgaging the Future: Student Debt in the Age of Austerity." *New Labor Forum*, vol. 22, no. 1, pp. 23–28.
Thoburn, Nicholas. *Deleuze, Marx and Politics*. Routledge, 2003.
Trollope, Anthony. *The Eustace Diamonds*. Rev. ed. Penguin Classics, 2004.

13
REFUGEES

Hadji Bakara

Is there a politics of the refugee?

Asking this question in the third decade of the twenty-first century might seem counterintuitive. The news cycle brings stories of a new clash of civilizations between the anti-refugee right and the pro-refugee left. When crowds assemble at airports with placards that welcome refugees or at borders with weapons to deter them, the political lines appear clearly drawn. But beyond the gesture of welcoming refugees in the abstract or declaring that in the deep past or distant future "we are all refugees," it's difficult to discern what a pro-refugee politics consists of and what visions of human community and of the future it upholds.[1] Locating such a politics is difficult because the "cause of the refugee" has often fallen short of acknowledging them as historical and political actors who participate in movements for social change (Haralambous 182). Instead, refugees have been treated as subjects of a universal responsibility to aid the needy and innocent stranger or, more recently, as the new universal subjects of biopolitical modernity (Agamben 118) or catastrophic futurity (Colebrook 120). Yet in treating refugees as subjects of universal ethics, as the harbingers of an emergent collective "we," or as fundamentally innocent and in need only of the recognition of a sympathetic public or a sovereign state, what we imagine as solidarity with refugees can shade into an act of denying them both a history and a politics.

Literature in English since the early twentieth century has variously expressed and suppressed a politics of the refugee. From the mid-century writing of Muriel Rukeyser, W. H. Auden, Arthur Koestler, Martha Gellhorn, and Hannah Arendt to postwar texts by Flannery O'Connor, John Berger, Joan Didion, or Russell Banks, or the contemporary fiction of Dave Eggers, Viet Thanh Nguyen, Vu Tran, Laila Lalami, Mohsin Hamid, and Omar El Akkad, we witness a series of opposing representations of refugees as both political actors and apolitical subjects. By political actors I mean participants in shaping the societies they enter and the futures they will inhabit. Consider, on this point, one of the most pointedly political statements ever made about refugees: Arendt's claim that refugees constitute a historical "vanguard," a political minority that will shape societies to come ("We Refugees" 274). And by apolitical subjects I mean supplicants to sympathy and moral feeling or the sovereignty of a receiving nation. Consider, on this point, the longstanding tendency to represent refugees as children, innocent of history and endlessly conformable to the cultures and societies that harbor them.

In narratives that consign refugees to the "history-without-history" of humanitarianism and the pursuit of "life" over "living" (Fassin 8), or practice what Jana Schmidt has called "innocencing" (297), or universalize refugees as symbols of a migratory dimension in all humans, literature in English is a largely depoliticizing force.[2] Yet an antisentimental tradition of refugee writing, texts that refuse the inevitability or desirability of the nation and national sovereignty, and works that depict refugees as participants in political struggles show that literature in English also comprises a rich archive of political thinking about refugees.[3]

Delving into the modern archive of political literature about refugees raises several key questions: what does a literary politics of the refugee look like? What are its commitments and propositions? How does it compare to other ways of representing refugees? These questions are taken up here in four sections: two brief surveys of the politics and antipolitics of refugees from World War I through the Cold War, and two textual "cases." Case one is Muriel Rukeyser's poem "Mediterranean" (1936/1938), which she began aboard a refugee ship fleeing the Spanish Civil War. Case two is John Berger's first novel, *A Painter of his Time* (1958), about a Hungarian refugee who flees refuge itself. In conclusion, I consider what writing by and about refugees can tell us about the irreducible horizon of all politics: the future.

Neither Sympathy nor Sovereignty: The 1930s and 1940s

"Exile is as old as Western civilization itself," writes Saskia Sassen (35). But the modern refugee—without nation or passport, and with nowhere to go—is the product of a "rather new history of Europe, a history that began with World War I" (77). The years around World War I saw the universal introduction of the passport, alongside political changes that radicalized "processes of exclusion" and "reshap[ed] subjecthood and citizenship....making it more difficult for individuals to be naturalized and easier for them to be denaturalized and rendered stateless" (Caglioti 146). These shifts within and between European empires and nation states marked "the beginning of the modern notion of the refugee 'crisis' as we have come to understand this term today" (Sassen 78).

In the decades following World War I, several mobile and left-leaning writers brought attention to this new phase in the history of political expulsions. Auden, Christopher Isherwood, Gellhorn, Koestler, and Rukeyser, among others, all wrote important works about the unfolding European crisis. Taken as a whole, their combined work does not comprise a distinct refugee politics. Unlike most Anglo-American writing of the later century, however, political causes and movements run deep in representations of the displaced in the 1930s and 1940s. Whereas postwar literature tends to raise refugees above politics, literature of this period often embeds them within the political movements of the time. In these works, refugees are represented as political actors because they are something more than refugees—bearers of commitments that shape the claims they make on the world and the futures they imagine for themselves and for others.

When Koestler popularized the term "scum of the earth" as an ironic sobriquet for refugees, for example, he was not describing stateless camp dwellers possessing only their "bare life" (although he was himself a stateless internee in France) but rather opponents of European fascism who followed their "rational conviction[s] regarding the best way to organize human welfare" (93). Not only for their ethnic identities but also for imagining a different kind of future society, Koestler and his fellow refugees had been condemned to death by the Nazis. Likewise, in Gellhorn's novel, *A Stricken Field*, about the German invasion of Czechoslovakia, the refugees who populate Prague's dilapidated hotels are often Jews but also communists, socialists, and syndicalists who continue to assemble and print their "party paper" for other "German and Austrian refugees" (54). These refugees forge ties with local laborers and union leaders, and they anticipate a future not merely of refuge but of new soil where they can participate in the creation of democratic societies (54, 59). In other words, before refugees were made the principal subjects of international humanitarianism they were often cast as actors in an unfolding story of political internationalism.

Yet acknowledging the movements to which refugees belonged is only one part of the story of their politicization. Recognizing that refugees carried their political commitments over borders did not stop writers from seeing that these same people embodied a new and unprecedented element in international politics—"migrant groups who, unlike their happier predecessors in the religious wars, were welcome nowhere and could be assimilated nowhere" (Arendt, *Origins* 267). The distinct condition of modern refugees posed problems of both political theory and practical language. Being a stateless writer in the 1940s, Koestler wrote, was not only to navigate a new political landscape but also to be an "innocent explorer of a new language-continent" (ix). The refugee's "placelessness," as Lyndsey Stonebridge has called it, was not a situation that could be overcome either by a return to national citizenship (which relied on the very principles of sovereignty that had excluded them in the first place) or by a future revolution that might liberate citizens from capitalist domination without securing a fundamental "right to have rights" (3). Refugees may have been active participants in the politics of their present, but those politics did not necessarily offer a path back to an equal place in the future world. The newness of modern "refugeedom" thus pushed the most astute observers of the time to think beyond the political movements and forms of the present (Gatrell 12).

Herein lies the distinct political thinking provoked by refugees in the literature of the 1930s and 1940s, elaborated in a gradual process of apprehending how refugees posed new challenges to the foundations of Western political order. At its core, this apprehension revealed the insufficiency of either sympathy or sovereignty to properly address the losses and condition of peoples cast out of the nation. This was important because sympathy and sovereignty had heretofore been the twinned dispensations of political modernity marshaled to resolve the loss of rights and humanity (Genguli 27). To apprehend that sympathy and sovereignty were inadequate, therefore, was not only to rethink the claims that refugees made upon a world of sovereign states but also to rethink the grounds of modernity and the postwar future through the figure of the refugee. The rejection of sympathy and sovereignty stands behind many of the most important works of the period written by stateless people themselves, including Arendt, Bertolt Brecht, Anna Seghers, and B. Traven.[4] Among those writers who were not refugees, though, perhaps the most powerful critique came from the American poet Muriel Rukeyser.

Case One: Muriel Rukeyser, "Mediterranean" (1936/1938)

In the summer of 1936, Rukeyser, only 23 at the time, was on assignment in Barcelona for the communist magazine *New Masses* when the Spanish Civil War broke out. Days into the conflict, Rukeyser fled Barcelona on a "ship five times our capacity in refugees" (*Life of Poetry* 3). On the overnight journey to France, she began to write her poem "Mediterranean." When the *New Masses* published an early version of "Mediterranean" in 1936, it was accompanied by two sets of artworks that situate the poem within the dual goals of sympathy and sovereignty. One page features lithographs of forlorn refugees, walking in loose fashion, eyes turned downward, and another of refugees marching in profile. These more recognizably humanitarian images were then paired with a woodcut of a Spanish Republican fighter, rifle in hand, striking a heroic, combative pose, with eyes turned upward. The Republican fighter, who appears last in the sequence, seems to help pull the refugees along, directing them (and us) upward, compelled forward toward a future horizon of justice represented by a Republican victory in the civil war. Framed by the aesthetics of the Popular Front, the refugees who Rukeyser documented in "Mediterranean" can appear subsumed within the greater battle to defeat fascism in Europe. But as Rukeyser's poem evolved, it became apparent that her sense of future justice for refugees was not coterminous with a Republican victory against fascism. Rather, Rukeyser imagines a future radically different from the one that arrived with allied Victory in World War II. Her writing thus reveals a move toward a distinct political thinking about refugees in the 1930s because it begins within Popular Front politics and aesthetics but then moves definitely beyond them.

Two aspects of "Mediterranean" are key to the poem's politics vis-à-vis the refugee. First, the poem's orientation and point of view, which eschews sympathy by occluding the "face-to-face encounter with the other," clashes with the humanitarian images printed alongside it in the *New Masses* (Nelson 10). Second, the poem's speculations about the postwar future imagine World War II as a coming battle against European sovereignty rather than for its restitution. At the outset of "Mediterranean," Rukeyser sets up a central point of view. Having set sail from Barcelona, the speaker and her fellow travelers gather "Here at the rail, foreign and refugee" (270). In this process of bringing all to the "rail" Rukeyser uses physical posture to figure a way of looking with rather than at refugees. For the duration of the journey the speaker and refugees are positioned alongside one another, facing a common but uncertain future. Consequently, the individuated faces of refugees are never described or made available to our gaze, thus refusing the most common way of achieving a sense of recognition, empathy, and intersubjectivity. Where we expect a supplicating visage, there is the closeness and figurative weight of the refugees "at my shoulder" (276). That we cannot literally recognize their faces physically grounds a larger claim about the complexity of forging solidarity with the refugees: they seek something more durable and substantive than sympathy and fellow feeling. By grounding her poem in this disposition of the side-by-side, Rukeyser proffers a durable political posture to her future readers: unsentimental yet engaged, impersonal yet committed, intimate without consolation, turned toward a common future rather than toward a suffering Other. The orientation lends phenomenological heft to a vision of solidarity as the forging of "concrete alliances with human beings who await not our recognition but our participation in their struggles" (Esmeir 1545).

But what is this struggle? If Rukeyser's occlusion of sympathy directs us toward a more enduring solidarity, then solidarity in what and for what? The obvious answer would be the Spanish Civil War, anti-fascism, and the cause of the Spanish Republic. Rather than sympathize with the refugees, join in the battle against fascism and restore the sovereignty and integrity of the Spanish Republic. The early version of "Mediterranean" published in *New Masses*—accompanied by the image of a Republican fighter—seems to accord with this reading. In an axiomatic scene toward the end of the poem, the speaker gleans Europe's descent into war from the removed position of the refugee ship's deck. In the 1936 version published in *New Masses*, Europe's fracturing is witnessed only once, in the first-person singular, in an italicized section that mimics diegetic speech:

> I saw Europe break apart
> and artifice or martyr's will
> cannot anneal this war, nor make

> the loud triumphant future start
> shouting from its tragic heart
>
> --
>
> past and historic peace wear thin;
> hypocrite sovereignties go down
> before this war the age must win.
>
> (276)

By "hypocrite sovereignties," Rukeyser presumably means to invoke nations that no longer protect their citizens and nations that expel and denationalize them. Refugees, in this sense, are those for whom sovereignty has become a hypocrisy. Inherited narratives of the twentieth century, however, tell us that the Allied victory in World War II resolved these hypocrisies by putting Europe's broken pieces back together in the form of strong, democratic, and sovereign nation states. And on first reading, Rukeyser's vision of the postwar future might seem to foreshadow this triumphalist narrative of sovereign restoration. If Europe's breaking had rendered sovereignty hypocritical, then its reconstruction would logically entail the reclamation of sovereignty's integrity. It's easy to assume, then, that when Rukeyser declares the need for victory in "this war" (the conflict in Spain but also the war to come), she envisions a victory for less hypocritical forms of sovereign power. And indeed, the poetic "I" here invokes both a witness aboard the ship and a tragic speaker who strives and ultimately fails to hold Europe together. The lines have a dimension of longing for a "loud triumphant future" with a Europe that is solid and sovereign once again.

Yet the later, 1938 version of "Mediterranean" is more speculative. That version was published in Rukeyser's landmark volume *U.S. 1* (1938). And in it, Rukeyser adds a vital new line in which Europe's breaking is witnessed again, this time in the first-person plural and present tense. The line added in the later versions of the poem is bolded below:

> Once the fanatic image shown,
> enemy to enemy,
> past and historic peace wear thin;
> **we see Europe break like stone,**
> hypocrite sovereignties go down
> before this war the age must win.
>
> (276)

The inclusion of this "we" that incorporates the refugees on the ship complicates what, in the 1936 version of the poem, appears as a spirited assertion of future sovereignty to be regained after "this war." Throughout the 1938 version, Rukeyser oscillates between the first- and third-person plural, texturing the distinction between "I" and "we" by giving each a different relationship to time and action. The "I" is generally reserved for witness and recollection and for the past perfect tense: "I saw the city, sun white flew on glass" (270); "I saw first of the faces going home into war" (271). By contrast, the plural is almost always conditional and subjunctive. "If we had not seen fighting,/if we had not looked there," "if we had stayed in our world/between the table and the desk/between the town and the suburb" (274). For Rukeyser, then, to be part of a "we" *with* refugees is to be moved into the realm of the subjunctive, ungrounded in language and hitched to uncertainty and potentiality. This too is the effect of the added line, "*we see Europe break like stone,*" which interrupts the logic of sovereign restitution at the level of both syntax and politics. The indicative present of the line makes the already complicated tense of the section even more tortuous and disjoins any teleological flow linking the fall and rise of European sovereignties. Moreover, it raises and reinforces a basic political fact: putting Europe's broken pieces back together into a solid and sovereign entity might be a solution to the crisis for a speaking "I" who is "foreign," but it is a catastrophe for a plural "we" that includes refugees, and for all future peoples seeking refuge—not least those on ships cast out into the Mediterranean. In the 1938 version, therefore, it's just as possible to imagine that victory in the coming war must lead to the vanquishing rather than the reconstruction of an indivisibly sovereign Europe.

Rukeyser, of course, was wrong about the aims of World War II. It was not a war to end or even curtail the primacy of national sovereignty. Yet she was correct in foreseeing that the political future of Europe would be determined by the ability or inability to create democracies where a "we" that includes refugees could take root. On the one hand, then, "Mediterranean" is a wartime poem that misjudged the political motives of the Popular Front and the Allies; on the other, however, it is a future-oriented text that saw clearly how European sovereignty was hypocritical to refugees, and that such hypocrisy could not be resolved with an expansion of sovereignty but with a political struggle to transform the very grounds of political membership and participation. In this way, the poem speaks to both the past and the future of refugee politics.

Seeking Refuge in the Cold War

The decades following World War II have been described as a "Golden Age" for refugees when institutional and political changes made acquiring both asylum and humanitarian relief far easier than the preceding decades (Cohen 150). In 1948, the Universal Declaration of Human Rights (UDHR) nominally recognized the right of everyone "to leave any country" (Article 13) and "to seek and enjoy in other countries asylum from persecution" (Article 14). Soon afterward in 1951, the Geneva Conventions recognized refugees—on a limited historical and geographic basis—as persons possessed of a "well founded fear of persecution on account of race, religion, nationality, membership in a particular social group, or political opinion." These new legal and institutional norms then combined with the Cold War "politicization of flight," so that people in Europe who "emigrated across the Iron Curtain had very good chances of being recognized and permanently taken in" (Ther 184). The acceptance of Hungarian refugees after the 1956 revolution and of Czechs following the 1968 Prague Spring gave the impression of an "open door" policy for peoples persecuted under communism. Outside of Europe, a growing humanitarian apparatus devoted to refugees (such as the United Nations and Works Agency for Palestine Refugee in the Near East or UNRWA) aimed to provide permanent aid and relief to refugees left outside the borders of nations and boundaries citizenship. Thus for a time, sovereignty (in the form of new nation states and Cold War policies of political asylum) and sympathy (in the form of humanitarian management) made the mid-twentieth century "refugee crisis" appear to recede into history.

With durable solutions imagined to be in place, the prospect of refugees demanding something more than the sympathy and sovereignty offered to them became even more difficult to comprehend. Once emplotted in a putatively functioning system of aid and recognition, refugees were tacitly divested of excess political desires and commitments, as their horizon of expectations was imagined merging with the institutions and dispensations of the new global order. And insofar as they were cast as seeking only the largesse of an existing system, asking nothing more than what we can give as moral subjects or generous citizens, refugees became increasingly represented both as fundamentally innocent and as sources of redemptive possibility for those who came to their aid.

Literature of the postwar decades often paints a picture of innocence and redemption too. Here, refugees call on us to be moral, contrite, generous, holy, or even to imagine ourselves as refugees ourselves. But they rarely challenge an abiding sense that it is refuge and care alone that refugees are seeking. In Flannery O'Connor's story "The Displaced Person" (1954), for example, the titular Polish refugee who meets a gruesome fate on a farm in the American South is repeatedly cast as a suffering innocent and Jesus figure. "Christ was just another DP," one character quips (201). Consequently, his mistreatment and death at the hands of nativist Americans is not represented as a contravention of his desires to create a future in the wake of catastrophe, but rather the inability of the benighted characters around him to recognize that a source of holy grace and redemption is among them. In O'Connor's universe, the refugee comes to redeem a world of citizens, yet they are simply too selfish and stupid to avail themselves of his grace.

By contrast, Joan Didion's *Democracy* (1975) follows a wealthy American protagonist (the wife of a senator and mistress of an arms dealer) who finds redemption by devoting herself solely to the care of refugees. *Democracy* begins shortly after World War II with the image of an American nuclear test in Bikini Atoll, and it ends in a refugee camp in Malaysia amidst the "boat people" crisis set off by the end of the Vietnam War. Inez Victor, the novel's tragic protagonist, atones for the crimes of the "American Century" by tending to the most basic needs of the victims of her country in the "dozen refugee camps around Kuala Lumpur" (201). "Although she still considered herself an American national (an odd locution, but there it is)," Didion writes of Inez, "she would be in Kuala Lumpur until the last refugee was dispatched." And "Since Kuala Lumpur is not likely to dispatch its last refugee in Inez's lifetime, I would guess she means to stay on" (202). Since there will always be refugees, Didion suggests, there will also be a social cause and source of redemption for compassionate Americans and for a compassionate United States, which could welcome refugees as recompense for wars started abroad.

Case Two: John Berger, *A Painter of His Time* (1958)

But what if the care of a good Samaritan and even the security of a new citizenship are not enough? What if refuges are not supplicants to existing political forms but hope instead to transform them? In 1956, the Hungarian Revolution led to a mass exodus of refugees across the Iron Curtain, helping consolidate the positive image of a postwar refugee as a person (really a European) fleeing communist persecution. Yet shortly afterward, John Berger published a novel—his first—that upends not only the Cold War narrative of flight from communist oppression but also the narrative arc of refugee flight more generally, as a journey from the insecurity of political tumult to the security of a receiving nation. Berger depicts a Hungarian refugee who flees refuge itself to return to the core of revolutionary violence and socialist worldmaking. In doing so, he wrote perhaps the most pointedly political British novel of refugee life of the mid-twentieth century. And the novel's central proposition—that refugees should not be seen as fleeing politics but as agents in ongoing political change—has a lasting lessons for our political present.

A Painter of His Time has two interwoven parts: the private thoughts of a refugee, and the narrative of a man who tries to make sense of those thoughts. On one side is the journal of Janos Lavin, a Hungarian refugee who flees Nazism during World War II. Janos, a staunch socialist and a onetime "political machine," settles in London and marries his aid worker, Diana (22). When they marry, one form of care transforms into another. Diana is an

Englishwoman from an affluent family who spends the 1930s immersed in "Spain, modern poetry, and the Left Book Club," and spends the war "helping Jews and Nazi Victims get out of Germany" (23). Diana thus marries Janos, in part, because he "was a refugee." But his identity as such has at least two contradictory levels that attract her. "Janos, a foreigner, had arrived from mainland Europe, where a world war had been fought, the first Socialist revolution achieved and Fascism unleashed—arrived from the mainland, without money, friends or language, in London" (24). Does Diana feel solidarity with Janos's struggles or sympathy for his losses? The answer to this question is undeterminable: like everything else in the text, Janos and Diana's bond is structured by a tension between political commitments, on the one hand, and the succor of care and security (humanitarian or romantic) on the other.

The prospect that love and security might staunch the wounds and dampen the impulses forged in struggles for liberation and socialism hangs over the narrative like the promise of a good night's sleep at the end of a long day of toil. Liberation and love, commitment and care, subtend one another. For a time, Diana and Janos achieve a restless happiness and security in the idea that love and stability are more important than justice and freedom. But then Janos disappears. The other part of the narrative is the account of Janos' friend, who discovers the refugee's journal shortly after he has departed, leaving both his country of refugee and his wife—both his physical and figurative homes—behind. Janos leaves a short note stating his intentions to return to Hungary and take part in the 1956 uprising against Soviet rule. "Now that I travel in the opposite direction, do not think ingratitude. Simply the man in me reasserts itself" (190).

The bifurcated perspective of the novel—part inside and part outside of Janos' consciousness—aids Berger in making a general point about a refugee's sense of the world and their place within it. From the outside, a refugee might seem to seek only refuge, safety, security, and, if they are lucky, love. They want nothing more than to be helped, as Diana does for Janos on so many levels. But in giving us the direct thoughts of Janos himself, Berger directs us toward other horizons. As Janos notes in his journal shortly before his disappearance, "life does not end with bread and medical supplies"; nor presumably with care and love (146). Beyond mere life and bodily security is the desire to continue living in history and—and this is where the point becomes irreducibly political—to continue making history, too. If achieving refuge eventually extinguishes the "great universal, human need to look forward," Janos writes, then what is imagined as a refugee's successful flight from danger threatens to "take the future away from a man." And to do, he wagers, would be "something worse than killing him" (18). The climax of Berger's novel, then, in which Janos flees refuge itself to return to the streets of Budapest, is also the revelation of a refugee's historical consciousness—his reclamation of the "great universal, human need to look forward" (18). Berger thus gives us an image of the refugee not as grateful guest but as inveterate insurgent.

But also as artist. Janos is a painter, and long passages of his journal record his deliberations over the composition of a few large, abstract paintings. These moments raise the possibility that art might afford a sufficient region for a refugee to endure or even to flourish. As such, they foreshadow a critical orthodoxy that crystalized during the Cold War, linking territorial expulsion, modernist alienation, and Cosmopolitan aesthetics (Stonebridge 9). Edward Said disapprovingly called this the idea of art as a "modest refuge" for the displaced: art offering an existence not in the world but outside of it, detached in such a way as to recuperate political exile as an aesthetic orientation (Said 172). These ideas echo through the London art world of the 1950s, where Janos is surrounded by people who preach aesthetic cosmopolitanism as if it were one more gesture of care for the refugees in their midst. A wealthy gallery owner who champions Janos' paintings says that "Art begins where we can dare to be detached" (32).

But as salvific as these ideas might be for a refugee artist, Janos disagrees. "Cosmopolitanism and formalism feed together," he later retorts in his journal, because each hopes to "wrench pictures out of their context, and—more important still—imagine that they have none" (139). Janos sees art as a direct response to historical conditions and an attempt to "improve the world" (144). And when art cannot do the trick, artists should find no indignity in picking up a "gun or a stone" (142). When Janos returns to Budapest—just days after his first successful gallery show in London—he flees both the physical refuge of England and the metaphorical refuge of art. By making Janos a revolutionary and an artist, Berger challenged two prevailing ideas about refugees: that they flee politics in hope only of finding care and security; and that they find refuge in the creation of art.

Conclusion: Refugee Futures

Is there a politics of the refugee?

Yes. And these politics are grounded in refugees' ability to share in the creation of collective futures. To be political is to participate in social and political change and reimagine the meaning of the future. For refugees to be political they must be recognized as agents in a fluid and shifting global order rather than supplicants to a stable and immutable one. Consequently, refugee politics often begin where we imagine the journey of refugees to end: at the moment they secure care, refuge, and even citizenship in a receiving nation. Consider, in closing, the proposition often put forward by a generation of Vietnamese-American refugee writers such Viet Thanh Nguyen, Vu Tran, Bao Phi, and Thi Bui. Even though they have all achieved American citizenship, they continue to self-identify specifically as refugees. Through this act of political and narrative self-fashioning, these writers are scrambling the norms of political chronometry that make the refugee always the past of the citizen, and the citizen always the future of the refugee. These authors thus denaturalize national citizenship as a definitive end for refugees, treating it instead as one of many contingent and provisional identities, subject to change and destabilization. On a fundamental level, this recasts what refugee narratives can mean: not linear and progressive narratives that move from instability to stability, but stories of ongoing and unexpected uncertainties that capture both the promise and peril of the future, where the forms of community and belonging are always yet to be decided.

Notes

1 See Caitlin Chandler, "We are all Refugees: A Conversation with Mohsin Hamid." *The Nation*, October 30, 2017.
2 The favoring of "life" over "living" is Didier Fassin's distinction; see Fassin, "Ethics of Survival: A Democratic Approach to the Politics of Life," 82–83. For novels that favor "life" itself, see Joan Didion *Democracy* (1984); for texts that practice "innocencing" see Flannery O'Connor, "The Displaced Person" (1952), Dave Eggers, *What Is the What* (2006), and Omar El Akkad, *What Strange Paradise* (2021); for novels that universalize refugees as representatives of humanity's migratory essence see Mohsin Hamid, *Exit West* (2017), and Russell Banks, *Continental Drift* (1985).
3 For patently unsentimental refugee writing see Hannah Arendt, "We Refugees," Arthur Koestler *The Scum of the Earth* (1941), Viet Thanh Nguyen, *The Refugees* (2017); for texts that refuse the inevitability of future citizenship see Muriel Rukeyser, "Mediterranean" (1936/1938), and Vu Tran, *Dragonfish* (2015); and for writing that depicts refugees as participants in political struggles, see Martha Gellhorn, *A Stricken Field* (1940), and John Berger, *A Painter of Our Time* (1958).
4 See Hadji Bakara, "Time, Sovereignty, and Refugee Writing." *PMLA* (May 2022).

Works Cited

Agamben, Giorgio. "We Refugees." *Symposium* 49, 1995, pp. 114–119.

Arendt, Hannah. *The Origins of Totalitarianism*. Schocken Books, 1951.

———. "We Refugees." *The Jewish Writings*. Edited by Jerome Kohn and Ron H. Feldman. Schocken Books, 2007, pp. 264–274.

Bakara, Hadji. "Time, Sovereignty, and Refugee Writing." *PMLA*, vol. 137, no. 3, May 2022.

Banks, Russell. *Continental Drift*. Harper Collins, 2011.

Berger, John. *A Painter of his Time*. Vintage, 1958.

Caglioti, Daniela L. "Subjects, Citizens, and Aliens in a Time of Upheaval: Naturalizing and Denaturalizing in Europe during the First World War." *Journal of Modern History*, vol. 89, September 2017, pp. 495–530.

Chandler, Caitlin. "We are all Refugees: A Conversation with Mohsin Hamid." *The Nation*, October 30, 2017. https://www.thenation.com/article/archive/we-are-all-refugees-a-conversation-with-mohsin-hamid/

Cohen, Daniel Gerard. *In War's Wake: Europe's Displaced Persons in the Postwar Order*. Oxford UP, 2012.

Colebrook, Claire. "Transcendental Migration: Taking Refuge From Climate Change." *Life Adrift: Climate Change, Migration, Critique*, edited by Andrew Baldwin and Giovanni Bettini. Rowan and Littlefield, 2017, pp. 115–128.

Didion, Joan. *Democracy*. Vintage, 1984.

Eggers, Dave. *What Is the What: The Autobiography of Valentino Achak Deng*. Hamish Hamilton, 2007.

El Akkad, Omar. *What Strange Paradise*. Knopf, 2021.

Esmeir, Samera. "On Making Dehumanization Possible." *PMLA*, vol. 121, no. 5, October 2006, pp. 1544–1552.

Fassin, Didier. "Ethics of Survival: A Democratic Approach to the Politics of Life." *Humanity: An International Journal of Human Rights, Humanitarianism, and Development*, Fall 2010, pp. 81–95.

———. *On Humanitarian Reason: A Moral History of the Present*. U of California P, 2010.

Ganguly, Debjani. *This Thing Called the World: The Contemporary Novel as Global Form*. Duke UP, 2016.

Gatrell, Peter. *The Making of the Modern Refugee*. Oxford UP, 2015.

Gellhorn, Martha. *A Stricken Field*. U of Chicago P, 1968.

Hamid, Mohsin. *Exit West: A Novel*. Penguin, 2018.

Haralambous, Chloe Howe, "The Cause of the Refugee." *Boundary 2*, vol. 47, no. 4, November 2020, pp. 181–198. https://doi.org/10.1215/01903659-8677887

Koestler, Arthur. *The Scum of the Earth*. Eland, 1941.

Nelson, Deborah. *Tough Enough: Arbus, Arendt, Didion, McCarthy, Sontag, Weil*. U of Chicago P, 2017.

Nguyen, Viet Thanh. *The Refugees*. Grove Press, 2017.

O'Connor, Flannery. "The Displaced Person." *The Complete Stories*. Farrar, Strauss, and Giroux, 1979, pp. 205–245.

Rukeyser, Muriel. *The Collected Poems of Muriel Rukeyser*. Edited by Janet E. Kaufman and Anne F. Herzog. U of Pittsburgh P, 2005.

———. *The Life of Poetry*. Wesleyan UP, 1996.

Said, Edward. *Reflections on Exile and Other Essays*. Granta, 2001.

Schmidt, Jana. "An Uncertain Movement: Bertolt Brecht's *Refugee Conversations*." *JNT: Journal of Narrative Theory*, vol. 50, no. 3, Fall 2020, pp. 297–320.

Stonebridge, Lyndsey. *Placeless People: Writing, Rights, and Refugees*. Oxford UP, 2018.

Ther, Philipp. *The Outsiders: Refugees in Europe Since 1492*. Princeton UP, 2019.

Tran, Vu. *Dragonfish*. W.W. Norton & Co., 2015.

United Nations. *Conventions and Protocols Relating to the Status of Refugees*. UNHCR Media Relations, 2007. https://www.unhcr.org/en-us/protection/basic/3b66c2aa10/convention-protocol-relating-status-refugees.html

14
NATIONS AND STATES

Jessie Reeder

The nation is a violent fiction. Both its violence and its fictionality necessitate the attention of literary scholars, so let us take each in turn, beginning with the latter.

Nations are fictions in two distinct but interrelated ways. In one sense of the word, they are fictions in the sense of *lies*, statements that intentionally misrepresent objective conditions of the world. That is, both the national border and the collective it supposedly contains are incoherent, inconsistent, shifting, and contingent abstractions that pretend to exist as fixed realities. Borders suggest a transhistorical fixity of identity in terms of and in relation to delineated and policed space, which simply does not exist (and whose nonexistence is only accentuated by the nation's most nationalist of moves, imperial expansion).[1] And the idea that borders surround a people who correspond to not only shared geography but also shared language, ethnicity, and culture is a fabrication that denies "the interweaving of linguistic frontiers, migrations, dynastic claims, conflicts over colonies, revolutions, wars of religion, and so on" (Balibar 337).

This internal non-unity was clear to Benjamin Disraeli in 1845, when he described England's rich and poor as

> [t]wo nations; between whom there is no intercourse and no sympathy; who are as ignorant of each other's habits, thoughts, and feelings, as if they were dwellers in different zones, or inhabitants of different planets; who are formed by a different breeding, are fed by a different food, are ordered by different manners, and are not governed by the same laws.
>
> *(68–69)*

It was clear to John Dos Passos in 1936, when failed protests against the execution of Sacco and Vanzetti led him to conclude: "all right we are two nations" (1157). And it is still clear to social scientists studying the profound racial inequity in the contemporary United States, which has also been called a divide between "two nations."[2] The supposed unity and coherence of the nation, then, is a fiction. As Etienne Balibar suggests, however, it is also a complete one, in which the globe is divided entirely into remainderless nations and every individual is produced as "*homo nationalis* from cradle to grave" (337, 345).

Because of this internal incoherence and non-identity with its borders, the nation's defining paradox is that it simultaneously defies representation and yet does not exist outside of representation. It is this paradox that led Benedict Anderson to define the nation as an *imagined* community, a collective with real sovereign power but whose unity is merely an idea produced primarily by shared media. This reveals the nation's fictionality in the second sense, that of *narrative*, because while Anderson refers to a nation's "imagined" identity, it might more accurately be called "authored." As Eric Hobsbawm notes, national culture consists of traditions and histories whose ancestral depth and continuity are pure invention, or what Balibar calls "a retrospective illusion" (338). Invention, or illusion, whichever you will, has a specifically diachronic structure, producing the narrative effects of origin and continuity and giving the nation linear, teleological narrative form. In disciplines as wide-ranging as philosophy, history, and literary studies, scholars have not only identified the nation as a narrative construct,[3] but they have even suggested that the Western post-Enlightenment belief in progress positioned the nation as history's endpoint, thereby establishing it as the telos of historical narrative as such (Koselleck 287).

What, then, of the "state" to which a nation nearly always is imagined to correspond? A state may be identified by "its ideology and collective sovereignty; its juridical and administrative rationality; its particular mode of regulating social conflicts, especially class conflicts; and its 'strategic' objective of managing its territorial resources and population to enhance its economic and military power" (Balibar 330–331). In brief, the state is the complex aggregate of institutions that regulate a nation's borders, people, and resources. However, as Zarena Aslami argues, the state, like the nation, is also a product of illusion, storytelling, and fantasy, a protagonist in its own right of the stories people tell themselves about their relationship to their polities.

In the twenty-first century nearly all states have nations—that is, states make use of a national fiction to produce a people who consider that state theirs. The reverse, however, is not true. The imperial consolidation of the globe into a relatively few nation-states left thousands of groups, especially indigenous ones, without a territorial home or recognized sovereignty, privileges that many of these groups still seek today; they are nations without states.[4] All over the world, there is a dramatic "mismatch between nationalities and the borders drawn by European colonial administrators generations ago" (Lind 26). Although the nation-state is the hegemonic sociopolitical form of our world, therefore, nations and states turn out to only rarely align. That misalignment in no way prevents the nation-state from being a critical heuristic for the problems of the current and coming decades: the formation and threatened fracturing of multinational entities like the European Union, the rise of right-wing fascist nationalism around the world, and the crisis of climate catastrophe as a supra-national threat to humanity worldwide are all phenomena that will both produce and impact international migration and that will both challenge and reinforce existing borders.

The violence of the national fiction, then, should be readily apparent, as modern nation-states' histories are written in the blood of imperialism: people have been slaughtered, resources stolen, and cultures forcibly altered in the name of drawing borders and creating in-groups with no ontological coherence. The production and policing of the world map as it appears today is a longstanding exercise in death, in which the narrative of nationhood is equally and complicity violent. Indeed, the story of national destiny can be understood as a technology that enables exclusion, hierarchy, erasure, eugenics, and racism. As Anderson puts it, the "conjuring-trick" of empires is the paradoxical process by which they impose themselves on the world, attempting to absorb the people and resources of foreign places, while simultaneously excluding those foreigners from membership (113)—a dual expansion and contraction that defines both nineteenth-century European imperialism and twenty-first-century U.S. migration policy. The horrifically paradoxical relationship between the

United States's liberatory narrative of national identity and its history of violence against minoritized people—a relationship many would like to see as a gap but which might be better understood as an alliance—has rarely been more poignantly put than when Frederick Douglass asked, "What, to the American slave, is your fourth of July?" To put it bluntly, the fictionality of the nation-state does not stop it killing people; rather it is the very fiction of national origin and belonging that enables what Foucault calls "the murderous function of the state" (256).[5] Indeed, close beneath the surface of every state's national narrative echo the cries of "blood and soil."

Literary scholars have, unsurprisingly, seen in the nation-state's complex interplay of culture, geography, and violence a profound relationship to literature. In ramified ways that are too numerous to explore here, the concept of the nation lies thickly entangled in a web of proliferating ideological relations—including citizenship, race, diaspora, war, biopolitics, governance, and more—all of which inform our approaches to texts. This is all the more true given the fact that the nation is itself a narrative, a text, authored and written and contested across borders and generations. Postcolonial scholars, perhaps most famously Homi K. Bhabha, have revealed the way that national narratives are written against the image of the other and thus simultaneously structure and expose the anxieties of imperial literature. In this vein, while themselves actively deconstructing the narratives of nationhood, literary scholars have tried to work out how literature may or may not perform the same function. They do so by asking pointed questions: What is the relationship between the narrative of a nation and the narratives of literature? Do literary texts buttress, occlude, or transgress the fictionality of the nation? Do they align or misalign with it? See outside of it, or take their cue from it? Some scholars (largely following Anderson) maintain that literature serves as the valet of national narrative by helping to define, reinforce, or reify the nation.[6] Others look to literature as a mechanism for estranging or questioning the nation, offering the hope that it might "remak[e] the nation…by distortion rather than bearing witness to it" (Aravamudan 22).

But despite literary scholars' awareness of the nation(-state)'s fictionality—its violent fictionality, no less—and regardless of whether we view literature as its accomplice or its antagonist, we have by and large continued to rely on nations and nation-states as structuring principles for our own discipline. First, fields frequently remain divided into nationalized "American" and "British" and "Anglophone" categories, at least within English departments. More important, scholars working in these fields still tend to use national borders (the very category their work often questions) as the metric for determining which texts properly fall under their purview. Wai Chee Dimock calls this "metonymic nationalism," arguing powerfully that time, space, and culture are not and never have been coterminous or co-constituting. By looking at the expansive scale of "deep time," Dimock shows that over the long durée, global and non-territorialized groups force us to recall the incoherence both of borders and of the wholeness they supposedly contain. The globe's division into discrete nation-states, after all, is merely a fictional overlay disguising the messy reality of thousands of exiled, competing, and intermingling groups living in spaces that are plurally occupied and colonially structured. Cultural production like literature, therefore, cannot correspond in one-to-one fashion with specific geographic boundaries at specific moments in time; it simply cannot be approached as an "epiphenomenon" of nations that are themselves contingent, permeable, and discontinuous categories (755). Literature, in this sense, is best viewed neither as reinforcing nor as challenging the nation, but as simply failing to align with it in the first place. And if this is the case, then the nation suddenly looks deeply inadequate—or even damaging—as a frame for literary study.

The influence of this insight has spread significantly in the last 20 years. Here, for a case study, I turn primarily to my own field, nineteenth-century anglophone literary studies,[7] a discipline in which scholars have increasingly noted the pitfalls of too heavily relying on the nation as a disciplinary frame. Tanya Agathocleous, for instance, argues that the realist novel does not only or primarily produce the national imaginary but also or rather "both the city and the globe as important alternative paradigms of human collectivity" (5). And Caroline Levine proposes that we might be able to shed our dependency on texts' "autochthonous" belonging if we replace our national heuristic with the concept of the network, a flexible form based on movement and connection instead of stasis and boundedness. Kate Flint even questions the term "Victorian" itself, pointing out its "unmistakabl[y] national, and nationalist, overtone" (230). Might we as Victorian scholars, Flint's provocation suggests, be guilty not only of assuming the existence of (and therefore replicating) artificial national boundaries? Worse, do we actually pay homage to these boundaries by continuing to rely on the time-space coincidence of Victorian England as the framing principle of our study? These are just a few examples of how some scholars are beginning to turn the long-standing critique of the nation inward, to investigate our own reliance on it as the unspoken organizing principle of our work—something Balibar urged historians to do 30 years ago. And yet, the call-to-arms, manifesto style of such arguments suggests they have yet to become widely accepted.

That is perhaps surprising, given that there have been some rather seismic disciplinary shifts away from the nation-state. Transatlantic methods, for instance, stormed into nineteenth-century studies, carving new space in journals, conferences, and job ads. Scholars like Paul Gilroy and Paul Giles have asked us to see that so-called "British" and "American" literatures were never compartmentalized entities reflective of discrete national contexts, but rather were mutually forged in a space as much defined by oceanic openness as by the fixedness of borders. Likewise, recent attention to cosmopolitanism has been a useful way to engage the tension between local and global imaginaries rather than national ones. U.S. literary studies has been profoundly and positively influenced by a move to "hemispheric" methods, which view "America" as a porous region rather than a bounded nation.[8] Other scholars have begun to focus on oceans, rather than land masses, as organizing principles of cultural and literary experience, a move that has arisen in tandem with increasing interest in transimperial studies.[9] And most recently, and urgently, Victorian studies has been called by scholars like Ryan Fong to fully transition our attention from imperial states to stateless nations—to indigenous and first peoples, to those displaced and destroyed by the nation-states upon which we have been accustomed to expend so much critical ink. These are promptings to fully "undiscipline" our field, to recognize its "marked resistance to centering racial logic," and to shed the habit of prioritizing the literature of those imperial authors whose work helped write the violent fictions of the nation-state (Chatterjee et. al. 370).

Following such anti-national methodological threads is the work of other chapters in this collection. We must remain here, at this liminal literary critical orientation toward the fiction of the nation(-state): partly oppositional, partly aware of the crucial shaping influence that the idea of nationhood continues to have on literature, and certainly still grappling with what a deconstruction of the nation-state might mean for our discipline. Transatlantic scholar Amanda Claybaugh argues that this partial positioning has an ironic component. Literary scholars eager to bring twenty-first century critical insights about transnationalism to bear on nineteenth-century literature have in fact failed to listen in the other direction—they have not heard the questions nineteenth-century literature was already asking about the primacy of the national border. As Claybaugh explains, transatlanticism is not simply a new(-ish) theoretical approach; the permeability of British and U.S. national cultures was a formative structure of the nineteenth century that fundamentally shaped the way people experienced the world. Moreover, in a further irony, our antecedents may have understood this better than we do, since we continue to isolate our scholarship into national partitions. "New fields," she argues, have not rid us of our "conventional habits," chief among which is "an unthinking resort to the nation as the organizing principle for both our scholarship and our teaching" (443). For Balibar, this concern is more granular than department structures, appearing in the very way we speak and write about modern nation-states. When we submit to the habit of speaking about "a 'Russian' or 'French' or 'Chinese'"—and here I would also suggest a "Victorian"—"social formation as though they were given in nature, what that means is that one has straightforwardly incorporated the postulate of the transhistorical existence of nations, turning them into the framework within which occurs the history of the modes of production" (334). Balibar had not yet seen the provocative work of transatlantic, hemispheric, or oceanic methods, but his call, as well as Claybaugh's, remains only partially heeded.

Simón Bolívar, the Nation-State, and Language

While a promising amount of work in literary studies has begun to question its own orientation toward and reliance upon the nation-state, one area that demands more urgent attention is the widespread assumption of a unity between nation, state, and language. By this I do not mean that scholars are unaware of the linguistic heterogeneity of nations, nor of the border-crossing influence of translation and multilingualism. From a methodological perspective, however, many scholars remain themselves unilingual and thus ill-equipped to grapple fully with the nonalignment of their fields with a single literary language. Just as Dimock asks us to uncouple the link we have passively made between nation and literature, scholars like Joselyn Almeida now call on us to effect similar cleavages between, for example, transatlantic literatures and the English language. Joseph Rezek points out the political implications of this false conflation, arguing that "[l]iterature in English is perhaps the most conservative mode within transatlantic studies" and that our focus on it "falsely universalizes not just one perspective within a multilingual Atlantic but often the most privileged" (793, 795).[10] The violent fiction of nationhood is once again something we must grapple with in relation to our own discipline, as we continue to do work that, even when our scholarship acknowledges the fiction of national borders, often continues to operate as though an identical map of language divisions is not just as illusory and just as violent.

Consider, then, a figure who exemplifies the proliferating fissures—social, political, literary, and linguistic—of the national concept and who, either in spite or because of this, goes little remarked in nineteenth-century "American" and "British" studies. His name is Simón Bolívar.

In many ways Bolívar is a perfect figure for thinking about the relationship between nations, texts, and languages in the nineteenth century, and not only because he is one of the few people in world history to have a nation-state named for him. He helps us see, first of all, the simultaneous fictionality of nations and their real impact in the world. As the leader and most famous figure of the Latin American wars of independence between 1810 and the 1820s, he quite literally authored a continent of new nations—he was the central figure as they rejected colonial rule, drew boundaries around themselves, wrote constitutions and national anthems, sought international recognition of their sovereignty, built their economic futures, and began to establish their sense of national identity. The impact of this simultaneous state-building and nation-building was both real and world-changing.

And yet, it was also a fiction. Panama, Bolivia, Venezuela, and the rest were built on Spanish imperial administrative zones, but they had no prior existential reality as discrete, coherent communities. As Matthew Brown argues, Latin American "nations were much more the consequence of the wars of independence than they were their cause" (110). The divisions between the new nations arbitrarily divided people who shared a language, a colonial history, and a trajectory of new self-definition. They also enclosed tremendous heterogeneity within themselves, including current and former enslaved people, various indigenous groups, European migrants, and the newly emerging category of the American Creole—many of whom supported revolution and many of whom supported Spain. Unity, in other words, had to be invented.

Bolívar used the concept of the nation to accomplish this. In his "Decreto de Guerra a Muerte" [Decree of War to the Death] issued against Spain in 1813, he declares that any Spaniards who remain loyal to Spain will face execution, while those who "join us in proclaiming the government of Venezuela will keep their rank and offices; in a word, Spaniards who render distinguished service to the state will be regarded and treated as Americans." Meanwhile, Americans (in the hemispheric sense), no matter where their loyalties lie, "may count on absolute immunity" and are promised: "you will live, even if you are guilty" (116). Addressing this declaration to "Venezuelans," Bolívar summons both the nation and "the state" into being as apparatuses of justice, defined against Spain, and possessing the administrative power to grant not only inclusion and exclusion but also life and death. Neither the nation nor the state to which he refers existed before the revolution (at this moment nascent and ongoing), and neither will exist if it fails. Thus conjured out of sheer collective will and the power of arms, the nation-state emerges embryonically, spectrally, and yet forcefully determinative. For in this crisis of revolt, the category that matters most to Bolívar turns out not to be loyalty but nationality: even those Venezuelans who work against the republican cause—the very cause of national emergence—nonetheless belong by birth to this very nation whose existence they reject. Spaniards, meanwhile, face a choice between two nationalities, and therefore between life and death, forced upon them by the emergence of new nations whose fictional and shifting borders are nonetheless as sharp as blades. The nation of Venezuela, here in its fragile infancy, already possesses the power to divide its people into those who deserve life and those who must die. The nation produces this biopower, and this biopower produces the nation, where neither had previously existed. In fact, one might argue, this emergence comes as much from the performative speech act of Bolívar's inclusionary/exclusionary "decree" (and therefore from the power of the text) as it does from the act of revolution itself.

The effort to liberate the new world, therefore, pointedly highlights the nation's violent fictionality as it emerges with arbitrary boundaries and yet very real power. Bolívar and his fellow American nation-builders saw clearly that the nation concept was an effective technology for converting internal division into shared identity. As he argued in the Jamaican *Royal Gazette* in 1815, internal factionalizing is a constitutive feature of nations:

> What free nation, ancient or modern, has not suffered dissension? Can you point to a history more turbulent than that of Athens—factions more sanguinary than those of Rome—civil wars of greater violence than those of England—or disturbances more dangerous than those of the United States of North America? Nevertheless, these are the four nations that honor mankind most by their virtues, their liberty, and their glory.
> (Bolívar, "To the Editor" 123)[11]

More than simply absorbing dissent into the idea of the nation, Bolívar further couches dissent as an index of a nation's freedom. Internal division thus marks not only the existence of a nation but also its virtue. This was an extremely useful idea for the revolutionaries, since the wars of independence had actually exacerbated internal divisions within the nations they produced.

As Mariselle Meléndez argues, Latin American elites saw a path to national unity via the creation of national history:

> [L]a revisión del pasado colonial en el siglo XIX, surge como producto del miedo a la fragmentación y el caos que habían originado las violentas luchas de la Independencia y a la necesidad de persuadir al lector/ciudadano de que tal fragmentación podría ser evitada por medio de la construcción de la historia nacional [The revision of the colonial past in the nineteenth century arises as a product of the fear of the fragmentation and chaos that had caused the violent independence struggles, and the need to persuade the reader/citizen that such fragmentation could be remedied through the construction of national history].
>
> (18, translation mine)

The language Meléndez uses—the "construction" of national history and the "revision" of the past—implies what was indeed true: that Latin American national histories were no different from any others in being authored narratives. In many cases these narratives were, in Hobsbawm's terms, little more than "invented traditions," as the Creole elites appropriated indigenous history to suggest that they were not in fact establishing new nations but rather reclaiming an ancient sovereignty (Florescano). Indigenous genocide in this way underwent a double erasure, at once receding into the fabled past of new nations and also disappearing as the source of Spanish infrastructure upon which those nations were built. This act of narrative violence had its biopolitical counterpart in the new nations' pursuit of white supremacist land dominance. In the name of joining the modern world order of nation-states, they courted European capital and immigration while also (and as a means of) displacing and slaughtering remaining indigenous populations. (This is a reminder that the violence of the nation-state is directed within as much as beyond its borders, and that its development is "intrinsically a ruling-class operation" [Williams 262)]). Scholars like Benedict Anderson and Timothy Brennan argue that the Latin American independence movements actually brought the concept of nationalism into existence for the rest of the Western world. If they did so, it was certainly a concept soaked in blood.

Simón Bolívar's writings—spanning genres including personal letters, public essays, and letters to the editor—therefore both exemplify the violent fiction of the nation-state and reveal it to us in new ways. Bolívar could be fiercely specific about American identity, but from the beginning he also conceived that identity as uniquely international. For one thing, the fact that he served as president of four different Latin American nations in successive terms reveals some of the region's political and cultural fluidity that the drawing of borders would seem to deny. For another, he dreamed for his entire career of uniting the Latin American nation-states into a pan-continental council that many have since called a conceptual anticipation of the United Nations. In this sense, his prematurity offers a keen reflection on how the nineteenth-century Atlantic world conceived of nations more conservatively:

> [T]he tragedy of Bolívar's international career was that even his formidable analytical ability and diplomatic skills could not secure Spanish America's entry into the Atlantic

world as a force to be reckoned with. He failed because his idea of Spanish American unity was premature. The nineteenth-century age of romantic liberalism favored national projects over international ones.

(Ewell 52)

But his vision of united nations was not only American. A professed anglophile, fluent in English as well as Spanish, who sought British military, cultural, and economic partnership throughout his life, Bolívar saw Britain as not merely an ally but a quasi-citizen of Latin American nations. Like his revolutionary colleagues Francisco de Miranda and Andrés Bello, he sought to make Britain co-author of their national projects. These men traveled to and studied in London and other European capitals, and they made models of European constitutions and institutions as they built the structures that would define Peru, Ecuador, Colombia, and the rest. Bolívar even believed that "[t]he British should be given rights of South American citizens" and have a seat at his pan-American council, a remarkable vision of international national belonging that, while it failed to materialize, did help pave the way for British informal empire in the new world (Lynch 214).

As I have suggested, then, Bolívar is a terrifically important figure for understanding the relationship between nations and states in the nineteenth century. And this is not merely a political history but a literary one. His "Jamaica Letter" is one of the most famous examples of the essay genre in Latin American history, a genre which itself "representó el espacio discursivo por excelencia donde el pasado colonial fue reformulado de variadas e inimaginables maneras [represented the discursive space *par excellence* where the colonial past was reformulated in varied and undreamed-of ways]" (Meléndez 17, translation mine). In it, he grapples publicly with the difficulty of defining the "we" of the new nations he was building, expressing the liminality of their hybrid European and indigenous origins, and articulating for one of the first times for an international audience the positionality of the American Creole as a voice of national identity/ies.[12] And yet, this important text remains quite marginal within British, American, and transatlantic nineteenth-century studies. One cannot help but wonder once again just how much the concept of the nation-state has impoverished our discipline and methods as literary scholars; its fictional structures define our fields so powerfully that even influential articulations of its emergence go overlooked. Latin America as a whole remains "off the map" of our scholarship, and its literatures are inaudible to our anglophone ears. And that is to say nothing of literatures from Africa and Asia, from indigenous peoples, or from even "canonical" authors like Dostoevsky whose texts are so often studied via translations into English. How fully can we understand the nation while this goes on?

Notes

1. For more, see Stoler, especially pp.137–138. See also Anne Mai Yee Jansen's chapter "Borders" in this volume.
2. See Hacker, for instance.
3. See for instance: Bhabha, Carr, Gellner, and Koselleck.
4. For more, see Chouinard.
5. Raymond Williams puts it slightly less pointedly when he says that although the forms of the nation-state are artificial, "the artificialities are functional" (260).
6. Or, as Fredric Jameson famously and controversially argued, allegorize it.
7. The fact that the anglophone nineteenth century is my own field is not the only reason for focusing on it; given that the nineteenth-century "West" was largely responsible for both the political structure of the nation-state and the rise of nationalist ideology, this period of history is a formative one for anyone interested in the relationship among literature, nations, and states.

8   See Levander and Levine, for instance.
9   For more on the imperial and environmental politics of maritime spaces, see Alison Maas's chapter "Oceans" in this volume.
10 For more see Reeder. See also Mufti for a similar critique of world literature.
11 I have in most cases cited English translations of Bolívar's work because this volume is being published in English and because it is beyond the scope of this short chapter to delve into readings in Spanish. However, it is part of my argument that the fullness of what we can learn from writers like Bolívar will only emerge when we push our methods beyond the analysis of literature in English.
12 For more, see Rivas Rojas.

Works Cited

Agathocleous, Tanya. *Urban Realism and the Cosmopolitan Imagination in the Nineteenth Century: Visible City, Invisible World*. Cambridge UP, 2011.
Almeida, Joselyn. *Reimagining the Transatlantic, 1780–1890*. Ashgate, 2011.
Anderson, Benedict. *Imagined Communities*. 1983. Verso, 2006.
Aravamudan, Srinivas. "In the Wake of the Novel: The Oriental Tale as National Allegory." *NOVEL: A Forum on Fiction*, vol. 33, no. 1, Autumn 1999, pp. 5–31.
Aslami, Zarena. *The Dream Life of Citizens: Late Victorian Novels and the Fantasy of the State*. Fordham UP, 2012.
Balibar, Etienne. "The Nation Form: History and Ideology." *Review (Fernand Braudel Center)*, vol. 13, no. 3, Summer 1990, pp. 329–361.
Bhabha, Homi K. "Introduction: Narrating the Nation." *Nation and Narration*, edited by Homi K. Bhabha. Routledge, 1990, pp. 1–7.
Bolívar, Simón. "Decree of War to the Death." In *El Libertador: Writings of Simón Bolívar*, edited by David Bushnell. Oxford UP, 2003, pp. 115–116.
———. "To the Editor, *The Royal Gazette*, Kingston, Jamaica." September 28, 1815. *Selected Writings of Bolívar*, vol. I. Compiled by Vicente Lecuna. Edited by Harold A. Bierck, Jr. Translated by Lewis Bertrand. The Colonial Press, 1951, pp. 122–125.
Brennan, Timothy. "The National Longing for Form." *Nation and Narration*, edited by Homi K. Bhabha. Routledge, 1990, pp. 44–70.
Brown, Matthew. *Adventuring through Spanish Colonies: Simón Bolívar, Foreign Mercenaries, and the Birth of New Nations*. Liverpool UP, 2006.
Carr, David. *Time, Narrative, and History*. Indiana UP, 1986.
Chatterjee, Ronjaunee, et al. "Introduction: Undisciplining Victorian Studies." *Victorian Studies*, vol. 62, no. 3, 2020, pp. 369–391.
Chouinard, Stéphanie. "Stateless Nations in a World of Nation States." *The Routledge Handbook of Ethnic Conflict*, 2nd ed., edited by Karl Cordell and Stefan Wolff. Routledge, 2016, pp. 54–66.
Claybaugh, Amanda. "New Fields, Conventional Habits, and the Legacy of Atlantic Double-Cross." *American Literary History*, vol. 20, no. 3, 2008, pp. 439–448.
Cussen, Antonio. *Bello and Bolívar: Poetry and Politics in the Spanish American Revolution*. Cambridge UP, 1992.
Dimock, Wai Chee. "Deep Time: American Literature and World History." *American Literary History*, vol. 13, no. 4, Winter, 2001, pp. 755–775.
Disraeli, Benjamin. *Sybil: Or, the Two Nations*. Bernhard Tauchnitz, 1845.
Dos Passos, John. *U.S.A.: The 42nd Parallel; 1919; The Big Money*. Library of America, 1996.
Ewell, Judith. "Bolívar's Atlantic World Diplomacy." *Simón Bolívar: Essays on the Life and Legacy of the Liberator*, edited by David Bushnell and Lester D. Langley. Rowman and Littlefield, 2008, pp. 35–54.
Flint, Kate. "Why 'Victorian'?: Response." *Victorian Studies*, vol. 47, no. 2, 2005, pp. 230–239.
Florescano, Enrique. *Memory, Myth, and Time in Mexico: From the Aztecs to Independence*. Translated by Albert G. Bork. U of Texas P, 1994.
Foucault, Michel. "Society Must Be Defended." *Lectures at the Collège de France, 1975–1976*. Picador, 2003.
Gellner, Ernest. *Nationalism*. New York UP, 1997.

Hacker, Andrew. *Two Nations: Black and White, Separate, Hostile, Unequal*. Scribner, 1992.

Hobsbawm, Eric. "Introduction: Inventing Traditions." *The Invention of Tradition*, edited by Eric Hobsbawm and Terence Ranger. Cambridge UP, 1983, pp. 1–14.

Jameson, Fredric. "Third-World Literature in the Era of Multinational Capitalism." *Social Text*, vol. 15, Autumn 1986, pp. 65–88.

Koselleck, Reinhart. *Futures Past: On the Semantics of Historical Time*. The MIT Press, 1985.

Levander, Caroline F., and Robert S. Levine. "Introduction: Essays beyond the Nation." *Hemispheric American Studies*, edited by Caroline F. Levander and Robert S. Levine. Rutgers UP, 2008, pp. 1–17.

Levine, Caroline. "From Nation to Network." *Victorian Studies*, vol. 55, no. 4, 2013, pp. 647–666.

Lind, Michael. "Revenge of the Nation-State." *The National Interest*, vol. 146, November/December 2016, pp. 18–27.

Lynch, John. "British Policy and Spanish America, 1783–1808." *Journal of Latin American Studies*, vol. 1, no. 1, 1969, pp. 1–30.

Meléndez, Mariselle. "Miedo, raza y nación: Bello, Lastarria y la revisión del pasado colonial." *Revista Chilena de Literatura*, vol. 52, April 1998, pp. 17–30.

Mignolo, Walter. *The Idea of Latin America*. Wiley, 2005.

Mufti, Amir. *Forget English! Orientalisms and World Literatures*. Harvard UP, 2016.

Reeder, Jessie. "Toward a Multilingual Victorian Transatlanticism." *Victorian Literature and Culture*, vol. 49, no. 1, 2021, pp. 171–195.

Rezek, Joseph. "What We Need from Transatlantic Studies." *American Literary History*, vol. 26, no. 4, 2014, pp. 791–803.

Rivas Rojas, Raquel. "Del criollismo al regionalismo: Enunciación y representación en el siglo XIX venezolano." *Latin American Research Review*, vol. 37, no. 3, 2002, pp. 101–128.

Stoler, Ann. "On Degrees of Imperial Sovereignty." *Public Culture*, vol. 18, no. 1, 2006, pp. 125–146.

Williams, Raymond. "The Culture of Nations." *Raymond Williams on Culture and Society: Essential Writings*, edited by Jim McGuigan. Sage, 2014, pp. 257–278.

PART III

Periods and Histories

# 15
ON OR ABOUT 1066

Mary Rambaran-Olm

While periodization encapsulates historical narratives into meaningful compartments that seamlessly transition from one episode to another, time and history are much messier and more difficult to categorize equitably. White, Western thinkers have framed dominant strands of periodization, most often with a colonial mindset that prevents today's students of history from understanding complex historical narratives in a more global sense. While frequently taught and learned as both natural and obvious, the framework of "the Middle Ages" itself is a construct emerging from and anchored in Western perspectives, which center European cultures as the foundation of human progress and civilization.[1] Kathleen Davis' work on periodization highlights how Eurocentrism (and British colonialism especially) has shaped world history and historiography, and how a more globalized understanding of "Middle Ages" operates in two conflicting ways.[2] A more global perspective of the Middle Ages attempts to see the world operating in unison while still anchoring time within a Eurocentric framework.

The crux of Western periodization, though, is that it operates as a white supremacist construct and forces students of history, which all of us are in one way or another, to view time in a clear, teleological line rather than as a disorienting labyrinth. The purpose of this singular and linear narrative is to highlight Western civilizations' "progress" and ascent to what is imagined to be the apex of civilization: not just the "best" of history but the culmination of History. The traditional division between "medieval" and "modern" has long served the interests of colonialist narratives, as imperialists openly justified colonization of other places and peoples by describing foreign lands as "medieval" or "uncivilized." In this tradition, everything outside of the Western narrative remains framed by and compared unfavorably to its Western counterpart. Essentially, and not simply when discussing literary or political or social history, we bring past human narratives into our present to make sense of history and time. Yet the difficulty of reinscribing the past into the present is that features of history most important to the ruling classes often become the only identifiable characteristics emphasized.

The year 1066 is perhaps one of the most recognizable dates in English history, as it describes the beginning of a new political, linguistic, and cultural era in England. The Norman Conquest of 1066 marks a pivotal point in England's Imperial narrative story: transitioning from the Germanic tribal migration and the establishment of a united kingdom on the British Isle to the Norman invasion, conquest, and cultural transformation of England.[3] Precisely because 1066 might be the only date many people recognize from the early English period, it is useful as an orientation point for examining how England was established, re-examining the terminology used to describe the early English period, and reflecting on how the era was reimagined for the political agenda of justifying colonialism. The period formerly referred to as the "Anglo-Saxon" period that preceded 1066 has been fraught with controversy in more recent years, even though scholars have spent decades debating what "Anglo-Saxon" means and whether it accurately represents historical reality.[4]

"Early England" and the Imperial Legacy of Colonialism

The dates that comprise the early English period are befuddled and contested, adding to the complicated character of defining the period neatly. Most scholars typically agree that the early English period begins in Britain with the end of Roman rule sometime in the fifth century, but there is no definitive agreement among early English scholars in various subfields (e.g., literary, historical, and material culture studies) about the start and end dates (Higham and Ryan 7–19).[5] Widely known in European history as the "Migration period" or the "Volkerwanderung" ("migration of peoples" in German), this established historical narrative describes migrants coming to Britain as Germanic tribes, most notably those known as the Angles, the Saxons, and the Jutes. The fifth-century Latin chronicle *Chronica Gallica a CCCCLII* is one of the earliest textual sources of this migration, and records the following for the year 441: "Britanniae usque ad hoc tempus variis cladibus eventibusque latae in dicionem Saxonum rediguntur" [The British provinces, which to this time had suffered many defeats and misfortunes, are reduced to Saxon rule] (Jones and Casey 393).[6] The eighth-century monk and historian Bede's (d. 735 CE) account in his *Historia Ecclesiastica*, written around 731 CE, gives a slightly later date of 449 for "advenerant autem de tribus Germaniae populis fortioribus, id est, Saxonibus, Anglis, Jutis" [Those who came over were from the three most powerful nations of Germany, the Saxons, Angles and Jutes] (35). Determining the exact year of the tribes' arrival is difficult, and it has been argued that sources like Bede's may have misinterpreted his own sparse sources to yield an unintentionally inaccurate date.[7] Another record of the migration comes from the sixth-century Briton and British monk, Gildas (500–570 CE), who describes a council of leaders in fifth-century Britain offering land to the Saxons.[8] This treaty stated that, in exchange for their armed aid in defending the Britons against attacks from the Picts and Scots, the Saxons would receive the south-eastern part of the island and food supplies.[9] Given that all of these sources were written at least 100 years after Germanic tribal migration, there is no certain way of determining which of these historical records, if any, renders an accurate start date for the period.

While early medieval literary sources cannot corroborate a precise date for the beginning of the early English period, archaeologists have adjusted Bede's date from the latter half to the earlier half of the fifth century.[10] Additional material evidence seems to bolster this archaeological assessment as several molecular analyses studies by archaeologists claim that varying population numbers of Germanic migrants were already established in southern and eastern Britain by 500 CE.[11] With such evidence of an earlier migration date, archaeologists emphasize that extensive Romano-British elements—including Roman cultural and political institutions—survived in early England for centuries after the fall of the Roman Empire. The energy spent in some scholarly pursuits to determine a clearly demarcated beginning of the period comes precisely from a desire to find the origins of modern England in order to create a sense of progress that can be juxtaposed with an "uncivilized" past. Time, history, and material evidence have been used as anchors to chart when the Angles and other tribes landed on the British Isle not from disinterested pursuit of some imaginary historical "truth," but to position England (and by extension Europe) as the apex of civilization and "modernity."[12]

Determining an approximate commencement for the early English period requires pooling unruly evidence from literary, historical, linguistic, and archaeological sources; so too establishing an end date to the period is neither straightforward nor without controversy. Over the course of the six centuries following the initial Germanic migration to Britain, and despite 200 years of Danish attacks between the ninth and tenth centuries, the idea of nationhood had developed among the people and political unity had been achieved. The general consensus for the period's end date is 1066 CE or the end of the eleventh century. To understand the culmination of events in 1066 that changed the trajectory of England and its literary and cultural milieu, we must turn our attention to the continent in the previous century. In 911, the Carolingian ruler Charles the Simple (879–929) allowed Vikings under the leadership of Rollo (later Rollo of Normandy) (b. 846) to settle in the north of France. As part of a treaty, the Norsemen were expected to provide military protection against coastal invaders in exchange for land. Within a century, this successfully assimilated settlement renounced paganism in lieu of Christianity, transformed their Norse dialect to Norman, intermarried, and became known as the "Northmen," from which the name "Normandy" derives. By 1002 in England, Æthelred II (968–1016) and his wife Emma of Normandy (d. 1052) had produced a son, Edward the Confessor (1003–1066), who was exiled in Normandy until he succeeded the English throne in 1042.

Edward's succession and reign led to increased Norman interest in English politics as the king relied heavily on his former home for military support, clerics, and Norman courtiers. His throne was observed with great interest not only by the Normans but by the Danes and nobles within his kingdom as well. In England, the rich and powerful aristocrat, the Earl of Wessex, Godwin (1001–1053), had benefited from the favor of the Danish king of England, Canute (994–1035). Godwin attempted to secure his family's link to the English throne by giving his daughter Edith of Wessex (c.1025–1075) to King Edward; however, a legitimate heir was never produced. After falling into a coma in late 1065 without declaring his successor, Edward died on January 5, 1066, leaving a vacuum of power as three men believed themselves the rightful heir to the English throne. Edward's immediate successor was the son of Godwin, Harold Godwinson (d. 1066). However, during Edward's earlier exile in Normandy, his friend duke William of Normandy (d. 1087) said that he was promised the English throne. The third contender for the English crown, Harald Hardrada (1015–1066), King of Norway, claimed a right of succession based on lineage connecting him to the former Danish king of England, Canute. After the Witan (the English council) awarded the throne to Godwinson, both William and Hardrada assembled armies and fleets to fight for the throne.

Hardrada's army first landed on the eastern shore of England in the late Summer of 1066 and advanced south, defeating local forces of earls, thanes, and fyrd in the vicinity of York. All the while, Godwinson prepared his army and remained informed of his enemies' advancement. By late September, Godwinson's army took the Vikings by surprise at the Battle of Stamford Bridge, where Hardrada and Godwinson's brother Tostig (d. 1066) were killed. On the heels of Godwinson's victory, Harold faced another battle in the south, as William of Normandy's fleet and army had arrived on the southern shores. Reminiscent of military tactical blunders that plagued previous English kings and military leaders, Harold's fateful decision to engage in battle without rest and replenishment of supplies disadvantaged his fatigued army.[13] On October 14 at Hastings, Harold's troops formed the famous Saxon "shield-wall" while occupying higher ground, which put the Saxon army at an early advantage. However, once the Normans retreated after a series of unsuccessful attacks, the Saxons broke formation, chasing the Normans, who gained the upper hand with their cavalry while on more level ground. The body count was high on the Saxon side, including the death of Godwinson, so demoralized troops eventually fled. William emerged as William the Conqueror, changing the trajectory of England when the Norman duke was crowned king of England in late 1066. That year in particular, therefore, remains critical for those reflecting on English history, reinscribing it as a turning point where English defeat by continental forces ended early English rulers in England.

Although 1066 is a pinnacle year for historians of England, the complete conquest of the kingdom took several more years. This prolonged transformation of the country demonstrates how political transitions frequently involve long process rather than instantaneous change, evolution more than revolution, and persistent unwillingness to let bygones to be bygones. Looking back to the shift from early English to Norman rule, the twelfth-century chronicler Orderic Vitalis (1075–ca. 1142 CE), himself the product of an Anglo-Norman marriage, wrote: "And so the English groaned aloud for their lost liberty and plotted ceaselessly to find some way of shaking off a yoke that was so intolerable and unaccustomed" (Chibnall 202–203). In the immediate aftermath of the Battle of Hastings, early English lords were replaced by Norman ones, and for several years, English resistance, rebellions, and plots to regain lost land transpired. Early English nobility were either exiled, absorbed into the ranks of the peasantry, or they fled to Scotland, Ireland, and Scandinavia. The Byzantine Empire and Varangian Guard attracted English mercenary soldiers (Heath 23). Old English remained the vernacular among peasants, although some learned Norman French to communicate with their rulers. For at least a century after the Norman Conquest, England had a tri-lingual situation: Old English was spoken among the common people (along with Welsh and Irish), Latin remained dominant for the Church, and Norman French was the language of administrators, the nobility, and the law courts.[14]

Linguistics and analyses of literary sources/literature have proven an invaluable method in determining periodization of the early English period. Although the Battle of Hastings used to be the definitive end of the early English period, some scholars have extended this date to follow a linguistic transition when coins, manuscripts, law codes, charters, and other records of Old English disappeared in favor of Anglo-Norman and eventually early Middle English ones. Although still a conveniently round number, by 1200 CE Old English had shifted enough in manuscripts for scholars to distinguish a change to early Middle English. Thus, the early English period is thought by some to encompass the time from roughly the early fifth century to the beginning of the twelfth century. Our compulsion to compartmentalize history shows how England, in particular, evolved from a handful of migrant tribes to an imperial superpower that controlled and dominated one-third of the world.

The openly racist idea that this "evolution" was both natural and just was never a fringe position dismissible as antiquated, archaic, unrepresentative, or uninfluential. British Prime Minister Winston Churchill (1874–1965), for example, espoused white supremacist views that relied on a mythologized past of England. In 1943, he stated that he despised people with "slit eyes and pig tails" and "hated" people from the Indian subcontinent who he claimed were "a beastly people with a beastly religion" (qtd. in Gopal 464). Further still, he claimed that he "did not really think that black people were as capable or as efficient as white people" (Blundell 109).[15] His views were so extreme at the time that even his US contemporaries recognized his racism. When US Vice President Henry Wallace contested Churchill's notion of "Anglo-Saxon" superiority, Churchill snapped back by asking why he should "be apologetic about Anglo-Saxon superiority" (Wallace 208). The underlying narrative is one of British imperialism rooted within a Christian context of time. Bede himself popularized the term *anno domini* by including it in his historical and political writings, and thus established links between a Christocentric worldview and English history.

What's in a Name?

Just as some scholars within early English studies continue to grapple with political questions around periodization, many scholars are grappling with the politics of terminology in the field which, until recently, was more commonly known as "Anglo-Saxon" studies. The claim was that the field's name reflected the people central in the early English historical narrative, but current questions about what qualifies as "Anglo-Saxon" and the term's complicated ties to British imperialism have caused contentious debates. The term "Anglo-Saxon studies" is still used in some English departments, particularly in the UK: Cambridge University, for example, still uses the acronym ASNC (Anglo-Saxon, Norse, and Celtic) for its early medieval center of learning. It is becoming increasingly clear, however, that the term "Anglo-Saxon" not only inadequately describes the people and period in early medieval England, but that its misuse by white supremacists today actually corresponds with its historically racist use.[16] While the collective noun "Anglo-Saxons" has long been associated with the early English people, some scholars have long argued that the term is inaccurate and should be discarded: indeed, the people in early England or *Englelond* did not actually call themselves "Anglo-Saxons" and the term only gained popularity in the eighteenth and nineteenth centuries as a means of connecting white people to their supposed origins.[17]

In the centuries following the Norman Conquest, the term "Anglo-Saxon" disappeared from the English lexicon with sporadic reappearances in Anglo-Latin throughout the rest of the medieval period. It was not until the sixteenth century, when English antiquarians and scholars began to collect early English manuscripts and compile dictionaries of Old English, that the term resurfaced. Between the seventeenth and nineteenth centuries, an English nationalizing agenda emerged; centered on creating the myth of an English "race," the success of the agenda was dependent upon appropriating and refashioning the past. Post-medieval English discourse was concerned with what it meant to be English, and the "Anglo-Saxons" served as convenient symbols of national liberty.[18] For English Reformers and Victorians, the period before 1066 provided a pseudo-origin myth story of national liberty in England that had been obscured by the Norman Conquest. English political and religious discourse sought origin stories to amplify a "pure" Englishness, which meant that glorification of the period before 1066 became a necessary weapon in linking racial purity to those seeking to conquer new lands in the name of England and later Great Britain.

Rather than accurately portray the early English people as separate tribes that migrated to the British Isle, the "Anglo-Saxon" myth links white people with an imagined heritage based on supposed indigeneity to Britain. This false account of the "Anglo-Saxons" as a "race" has played heavily in political discourse over the last 500 years, often reconstructed to include fictitious narratives that promote political messages of patriotism, imperialism, or racial superiority. Indeed, as the English language erased indigenous languages and swept across the globe along with English imperialism, the newly minted "Anglo-Saxon" myth served as historical, justificatory "proof" of supposed racial superiority. The language that emerged after 1066 was the language of conquerors on a scale unimaginable at the Battle of Hastings.

The study of race fascinated scientists and ethnographers throughout the eighteenth and nineteenth centuries, and equally, early twentieth-century early English scholars directly worked with scientific racism, including phrenology, in their scholarship.[19] Their anachronistic medievalism ignored a more factual image of "others" in England who had ties to the land, such as the Britons. Despite the long history of invasion and integration in England, English scholars sought to imagine a direct connection to the "Anglo-Saxon" past free from alien associations in order to cleanse English history of the "foreign" elements that constituted the English population. Today, far-right Identitarian groups seek to prove their superior ancestry by portraying the "Anglo-Saxons" in ways that both promote a very particular, very white version of both English identity and national sociopolitical progress.

During British (and later, American) imperialism and colonization, the racial meaning of "Anglo-Saxon" became the most dominant usage of the term. Rather than anodyne reference to pre-Conquest England, this white supremacist movement in Euro-America has used the term "Anglo-Saxon" to justify racial violence and colonial genocide for at least 200 years. The racial meaning throughout the English-speaking world has deepened and come to be associated crudely with whiteness. "Anglo-Saxon" has become a supremacist dog whistle reinforcing the idea of the "Anglo-Saxon" race as a supposedly indigenous group in England, suspiciously erasing the fact that the Angles and Saxons were "migrants." Year 1066 allows white supremacists to see the Normans as a "foreign" conquering force and periodization reinforces that. The term's association with whiteness has saturated lexicon to the point that it is misused in political discourse.[20]

The term's white nationalist connections in predominantly English-speaking countries extend beyond laypeople's vernacular and some scholars refuse to re-examine the accuracy of the term or its connections to whiteness today. Such refusal to understand the racist roots of the discipline and how the term inaccurately represents the early English demonstrates an insidious and obstinate ignorance within academic institutions. Scholars are slowly coming to understand the need to interrogate the use of this term, and many are keen to find terms that represent scholars, the field, and the early English more accurately. Although a significant task, medievalists, in particular, have precedents in updating terminology with the removal of "the Dark Ages" and "Aryan" from the scholarly lexicon.

In English history, 1066 is a significant date in terms of its cultural development but it also bears importance in terms of its use within the framework of colonialism, which unreflectively qualified as belonging among "us" or "them." Of course, Stuart Hall queried who the term "us" refers to in Western discourse and language, arguing that discourse around "us" continues to reflect "the language of the West... its practices and relations of power towards the Rest" (318). Until recently, the classifiers and guardians of historical periodization have been predominantly white males grounded in Classical and/or Christian learning at the very institutions made rich by centuries of imperialism. This poses another problem for the field of early English studies because for its entire history as a discipline, "us" in the field has often meant white, middle-class, cis-heterosexual people, with considerable investments and interests in maintaining a status quo that was established far more recently than they were and are willing to concede. Scholars in various disciplines interrogate terminology for accuracy, for genealogy, and for pragmatic functions; so too must literary historians and other scholars in the humanities challenge our perceptions, our nomenclature, and our use of periodization. Anchoring a systemic understanding of English history in dates like 1066 has served to familiarize and accustom people with the history of "the English" as an imperial superpower spreading the supposed virtues of white "civilization" at the point of the sword and into the hull of the slave ship.

This sort of association is applicable to Old English texts that are most often featured and taught. The Old English epic poem *Beowulf*, the religious dream-vision poem *Dream of the Rood*, King Alfred's "Preface to Gregory's Pastoral Care," Bede's *History of the English People*, and heroic poems like *Widsith* are commonly used as core texts in Old English literary and linguistics courses. There remains a danger in teaching these texts without acknowledging that they are often favorites of Anglo-American white nationalists, who perceive these records as heritage texts rooted in a valorously masculine, "Anglo-Saxon" culture. White supremacists have often connected these texts to their own identity. The field of early English studies has thus belatedly begun to consider its role in perpetuating false narratives of the past that have been weaponized by the far-right. This reckoning must include examining how the content and history of early England has been whitewashed and that the voices that both invented and continue to dominate the field have almost always been exclusively white.

Early English studies has long signaled that it is a field for white people and closed itself off from innovative ideas and research, which, in turn, has preserved an ethnonationalist view of English history. Nonetheless, important work showing how England emerged through the influence of "outsiders" continues to be published as scholars seek to reflect on how whiteness, itself a contingently historical rather than natural category, has directed the field and its content. It might be helpful for readers to understand Bede's *Historia* within the context of England's cultural heritage as one that benefited from borrowing from abroad. People like the late seventh/early eighth-century abbot Hadrian (born before 637–d. 710) from North Africa and Archbishop of Canterbury Theodore (602–690) born in Tarsus (modern Turkey) brought with them traditions from abroad that enriched ecclesiastical and secular learning in the English kingdom. This constant contact with the outside world, migrations, and the inward and outward flow of refugees and migrants allowed for a rich and diverse cultural heritage that was erased when later England mythologized its past in the service of colonization.

Looking Back, Pushing Forward

Until the past few decades, scholars were teaching Old English texts utilizing more traditional and conservative methods. Concentrating on heroic values or the pagan and Christian elements of texts like *Beowulf*, the *Rood* poem, and *Widsith*, and using Bede's *Historia* or Alfred's "Pastoral Care" to emphasize "Anglo-Saxon roots" has stifled the field's growth and allowed white supremacist narratives to fester both within and outside the field. The most traditional approaches to these Old English canonical texts often illustrate Christocentric themes interconnected with Germanic or pagan warrior culture. Part of the intrinsic value and richness of these texts lies in the fact that they were not produced in isolation or hermetically sealed insularity; thus, white nationalist claims that these texts are "home-grown" are equally as inaccurate as the term "Anglo-Saxon" is. New and exciting pedagogical readings of texts like *Beowulf* are emerging as scholars look for ways to distance themselves from the openly racist past of the field and correct inaccuracies of history and terminology that are fundamental rather than epiphenomenal to the discipline. A number of scholars have breathed new life into *Beowulf*ian scholarship, long hidebound by the legacy of scholars like J. R. R. Tolkien, by shifting focus away from analyses of Germanic heroic ideals and themes around Christian vs. pagan elements. In more recent years, otherness, queer themes, and more have been highlighted and analyzed throughout the poem making a body of Old English texts relevant and legible for more diverse, newer generations of readers.[21] Furthermore, in light of increasing awareness of indigeneity and colonization in scholarly and general discourse, scholars have begun to analyze how the poem's main antagonists, the monster Grendel and his mother, might be read as protectors of their land against settler invasions from the poem's hero Beowulf and his seafaring men.[22] Readings like these are important not only in terms of advancing scholarship but as reparative work undoing more than a century's worth of ethnonationalist scholarship.

In addition to new *Beowulf*ian readings, innovative analyses of similar texts beloved by white supremacists like the *Rood* poem, *Widsith*, and "Pastoral Care" are being examined through various queer studies and close examinations of gendered and sexualized language.[23] This new work assists in pushing back at heteronormative and whitewashed readings of Old English literature. Traditional readings have often promoted patriarchal, homophobic, and racist ones, so it is important that new insights undo and complicate these and other problematic readings. For instance, Edward Said highlighted how depictions of those outside the "West" had often been depicted as sexually deviant (190, 311–316). This has also been tied to nineteenth-century ethnonationalist depictions of the Normans who were viewed as sodomites. Scholars like Erik Wade have highlighted how 1066 was reimagined as a binary depicting "Anglo-Saxon" masculinity opposed to Norman sodomy ("Skeletons in the Closet" 285–290). Not only do readings such as these disrupt the traditional heteronormative perceptions of the period and its people, but also they collapse the conflation of ultra-masculinity and early English culture that many white nationalists value.

To have a better grasp of history, we must accept that history is often tangled, and includes unraveling interconnected stories from across lands, cultures, and languages. Eurocentrism has driven our understanding of the past, but if we seek to better understand 1066 or the early English period in a global context, we must interrogate why it matters and to whom. It is important to understand and acknowledge how the idea of the "Anglo-Saxon" race has been weaponized through Old English texts to justify openly white supremacist ideologies at the core of Anglo-American society. More work must continue that challenges traditional, heteronormative, patriarchal analyses of Old English literature, not only for the field's survival but because it allows us to see the political contours of these historical episodes, relationships, and archives more accurately and ethically.

Notes

1 F. Robinson discusses the construct of the "Middle Ages" as a term, concept, and period within the West in "Medieval, the Middle Ages."
2 See Davis, pp. 15–16, 103–131. Davis describes how "the standard narrative of periodization, and its contradictions belie the idea that medieval/modern periodization emerged simply through the 'consciousness of a new age' that established a relationship between the ancient and the modern at the expense of 'the Middle Ages.'" p. 30. I agree that the idea of periodization betrays what we describe as the "Middle Ages" as it is reductionist, restrictive and centers European history in a way that is not useful or helpful in a global perspective.
3 Problems with the term "Germanic" have also been highlighted by scholars. See Friedrich and Harland.
4 See Malone; Horsman; Cedric Robinson; Reynolds; Dockray-Miller, "Old English has a Serious Image Problem"; Miyashiro; Rambaran-Olm, M. "Misnaming the Medieval"; Wilton; Vernon; Ellard; Da Silva.
5 For further references that discuss the chronology and the period's start date, see Snyder; Jones; Morris, p. 154; Higham.
6 All translations mine unless otherwise stated.
7 John Kemble first argued that Bede's dating was inaccurate and noted that upon close examination of his system of dating "the more completely [Kemble] was convinced that the received accounts of

our migrations, *our* subsequent fortunes, and ultimate settlement, are devoid of historical truth in every detail." Notably Kemble's 1849 account emphasizes that he saw this piece of history as part of *his* history. This point about ownership of this episode in history has functioned as a gatekeeper rooted in whiteness which signals to students and scholars from marginalized communities that this field does not belong to them (1, 16).

8 Gildas dates the adventus Saxonum to 441 and states:

> then all the councilors, together with that proud tyrant Gurthrigern [Vortigern], the British king, were so blinded, that, as a protection to their country, they sealed its doom by inviting in among them (like wolves into the sheep-fold), the fierce and impious Saxons, a race hateful both to God and men, to repel the invasions of the northern nations.

9 Another date for the period is 428 first purported in Nennius' *Historia Brittonum*.
10 See Hills and Lucy.
11 See Härke; Hills and Lucy; Hedges; Oosthuizen.
12 See Green, esp. pp. 14–15.
13 Some examples of military blunders include King Alfred, who suffered a series of defeats which were not always due to being outnumbered or overpowered, particularly at the Battle of Ashdown in 871. The 991 Battle of Maldon, led by earl Byrhtnoth (c. 931–991), is a well-known early English defeat as a result of Byrhtnoth's ill-fated decision to allow his enemy to cross a causeway that had been successfully blocked. Æthelred II (c. 966–1016) was well known for attempting to quell repeated Danish attacks to no avail. Despite peace deals and tributes (dane-geld), Æthelred eventually ordered the massacre of Danes in England during the St. Brice Day's massacre of 1002. Æthelred eventually lost the throne to the Danes.
14 See Scahill.
15 See also Webb.
16 For a summary of past and current debates see Rambaran-Olm, M. and Erik Wade's "What's in a Name? The Past and Present Racism in 'Anglo-Saxon' Studies."
17 There is little evidence that the term appeared outside the tenth century or outside of Latinate texts, most of which are legal documents. In a nutshell, the first-person term for people in early England was most often *Englisc* or *Angli*. See Wilton, "What Do We Mean by Anglo-Saxon?"; Rambaran-Olm and Wade, "What's in a Name?"; See Malone, "Anglo-Saxon: A Semantic Study,"; Reynolds, "What do we mean by 'Anglo-Saxon' and 'Anglo-Saxons'?"; Da Silva, "The Uses of the 'Anglo-Saxon Past.'"
18 See Rambaran-Olm, M. "Medievalism and the 'Flayed-Dane' Myth: English Perspectives between the Seventeenth and Nineteenth Centuries."
19 See Rambaran-Olm and Wade, "What's in a Name?"
20 See Gabbatt. In 2019 Congressman Mike Kelly referred to himself as a "person of color" saying he was "white" and an "Anglo-Saxon" (Puckett). Former President Donald Trump remarked that a Hispanic advisor looked more like a "WASP" (an acronym for 'white, "Anglo-Saxon," protestant) than the president (Smith). In April 2021, a leaked document from the America First Caucus endorsed by US Congresswoman Marjorie Taylor Greene stated that the group wished to return to "Anglo-Saxon political traditions" (Time). In May 2022, Canadian conservative leadership candidate Pierre Polievere described his language as one using "simple Anglo-Saxon words" which was criticized for being a dog-whistle. At the time, he had been supporting notorious white supremacist Pat King who had mobilized a racist, anti-science movement in Canada and decried that there was a "depopulation of the Caucasian race, or the Anglo-Saxon" occurring in Canada in 2022 (CTV News).
21 For instance, see Wade, "Skeletons in the Closet: Erasing Queer and Trans Issues in Early Medieval Scholarship"; Price, "Potentiality and Possibility: An Overview of Beowulf and Queer Theory"; Dockray-Miller, "The Masculine Queen of *Beowulf*."
22 See Abram, "At Home in the Fens with the Grendelkin"; Taranu, C. "Men into Monsters: Troubling Race, Ethnicity, and Masculinity in Beowulf"; Miyashiro, A. "Homeland Insecurity: Biopolitics and Sovereign Violence in Beowulf."
23 See Dockray-Miller, "The Feminized Cross of *The Dream of the Rood*"; Chaganti "Vestigial Signs: Inscription, Performance, and *The Dream of the Rood*"; Clark, *Between Medieval Men: Male Friendship and Desire in Early Medieval English Literature* and "Old English Literature and Same-Sex Desire: An Overview"; Pavlinich, "Queer Authority in Old and Middle English Literature." Unpublished dissertation.

Works Cited

Abram, Christopher. "At Home in the Fens with the Grendelkin." *Dating Beowulf: Studies in Intimacy*, edited by D. C. Remein and E. Weaver. Manchester UP, 2020, pp. 120–44.

Bede, Ven. *Venerabilis Bedae Historia Ecclesiastica gentis Anglorum*. Caput XV. §36. Sumptibus Societatis, 1838.

Blundell, Michael. *A Love Affair with the Sun: A Memoir of Seventy Years in Kenya*. Kenway Publications, 1994.

Chaganti, Seeta. "Vestigial Signs: Inscription, Performance, and the Dream of the Rood." *PMLA*, vol. 125, no. 1, 2010, pp. 48–72.

Chibnall, Marjorie, editor and translator. *Historia Ecclesiastica*. Ecclesiastical History. Vols. II–IV. *Oxford Medieval Texts*. Clarendon Press, 1969–73.

Clark. David. *Between Medieval Men: Male Friendship and Desire in Early Medieval English Literature*. Oxford UP, 2009.

———. "Old English Literature and Same-Sex Desire: An Overview." *Literature Compass*, vol. 6, no. 3, 2009, pp. 573–584.

CTV News. "Poilievre Faces Backlash for comments on Jordan Peterson Podcast." *CTV News*. 18 May 2022. https://www.ctvnews.ca/politics/poilievre-faces-backlash-for-comments-on-jordan-peterson-podcast-1.5910090 Accessed July 23, 2022.

Da Silva, Renato Rodrigues. "The Uses of the 'Anglo-Saxon Past' between Revolutions, Imperialism and Racism," *Práticas da História* vol. 12, 2021, pp. 129–160.

Davis, K. *Periodization and Sovereignty*. U of Pennsylvania P, 2008.

Dockray-Miller, Mary. "The Feminized Cross of the Dream of the Rood." *Philological Quarterly*, vol. 76. no. 1, 1997, pp. 1–18.

———. "The Masculine Queen of Beowulf." *Women and Language*, vol. 21. no. 2, 1998, pp. 31–38.

———. "Old English has a Serious Image Problem." *JSTOR Daily* 3, May, 2017. https://daily.jstor.org/old-english-serious-image-problem/

Ellard, Donna-Beth. *Anglo-Saxon (ist) Pasts, postSaxon Futures*. Punctum Books, 2019.

Friedrich, Mattias, and James Harland. *Interrogating the 'Germanic': A Category and its Use in Late Antiquity and the Early Middle Ages*. De Gruyter, 2021.

Gabbatt, Adam. "Romney Campaign Rolls Back 'Anglo-Saxon' Comments Ahead of UK Visit." *The Guardian*, 25 Jul 2012. https://www.theguardian.com/world/2012/jul/25/mitt-romney-anglo-saxon-comments Accessed March 26, 2022.

Gildas. *De Excidio Britanniae* (Concerning the Ruin of Britain). Chapter 23. Translated and edited by J. A. Giles. *Six Old English Chronicles*. Henry G. Bohn, 1848.

Gopal, Sarvepalli. "Churchill and India." *Churchill*, edited by Robert Blake and Wm. Roger Louis. Clarendon Press, 1996, pp. 458–72.

Green, William A. "Periodization in European and World History." *Journal of World History*, vol. 3, no. 1, 1992, pp. 13–53.

Hall, Stuart. "The West and the Rest." *Formations of Modernity*, edited by S. Hall & B. Gieben. *Redwood Books*, 1992, pp. 275–332.

Härke, H, "Population Replacement or Acculturation? An Archaeological Perspective on Population and Migration in Post-Roman Britain." *The Celtic Englishes III. Anglistische Forschungen*, vol. 324, Winter, 2003, pp. 13–28.

Heath, Ian. *Byzantine Armies AD 1118–1461*, Osprey Publishing, 1995.

Hedges, Robert. "Anglo-Saxon Migration and the Molecular Evidence." *The Oxford Handbook of Anglo-Saxon Archaeology*, edited by H. Hamerow, D. A. Hinton, and S. Crawford. Oxford UP, 2011, pp. 81–3.

Higham, Nicholas J. "From sub-Roman Britain to Anglo-Saxon England: Debating the Insular Dark Ages." *History Compass*, vol. 2, no. 1, 2004. https://doi.org/10.1111/j.1478-0542.2004.00085.x Accessed November 3, 2021.

———, and Martin J. Ryan. *The Anglo-Saxon World*. Yale UP, 2013.

Hills, Catherine, and Sam Lucy. *Spong Hill IX: Chronology and Synthesis*. The McDonald Institute for Archaeological Research, 2013.

Horsman, Reginald. *Race and Manifest Destiny: The Origins of American Racial Anglo-Saxonism*. Harvard UP, 1981.

Jones, Michael E. *The End of Roman Britain*. Cornell UP, 1998.

———, and John Casey. "The Gallic Chronicle Restored: a Chronology for the Anglo-Saxon Invasions and the End of Roman Britain." *Britannia XIX*, November 1988.

Kemble, J. *The Saxons in England: A History of the English Commonwealth Till the Period of the Norman Conquest.* Longman, Brown, Green, and Longmans, 1849.

Malone, Kemp. "Anglo-Saxon: A Semantic Study." *The Review of English Studies*, vol 5, no. 18, 1929, pp. 173–185.

Miyashiro, A. "Decolonizing Anglo-Saxon Studies: A Response to ISAS in Honolulu." *The Middle*, 29, 2017, https://www.inthemedievalmiddle.com/2017/07/decolonizing-anglo-saxon-studies.html

———. "Homeland Insecurity: Biopolitics and Sovereign Violence in *Beowulf*." *Postmedieval*, vol. 11, no. 4, 2020, pp. 384–95.

Morris, J. "Dark Age Dates." *Britain and Rome: Essays Presented to Eric Birley on His Sixtieth Birthday*, edited by Michael G. Jarrett, Brian Dobson, and Eric Birley. T. Wilson, 1966.

Nennius. *Historia Brittonum* (History of the Britons). Translated by J. A. Giles. *Project Gutenberg.* Feb. 2006, https://www.gutenberg.org/files/1972/1972-h/1972-h.htm Accessed, March 12, 2021.

Oosthuizen, Susan. *The Emergence of the English.* Arc Humanities Press, 2019, p. 7ff.

Pavlinich, E.J. "Queer Authority in Old and Middle English Literature." Unpublished dissertation. University of South Florida, July 2019.

Price, B.A. "Potentiality and Possibility: An Overview of Beowulf and Queer Theory." *Neophilologus*, vol. 104, 2020, pp. 401–419.

Puckett, Lily. "Republican Congressman Defends Trump's Racism by Saying: 'I'm a person of colour… I'm white'". *The Independent*, 18 Jul 2019. https://www.independent.co.uk/news/world/americas/trump-mike-kelly-racism-person-of-color-white-gop-republican-a9009706.html Accessed March 26, 2022.

Rambaran-Olm, Mary. "Medievalism and the 'Flayed-Dane' Myth: English Perspectives between the Seventeenth and Nineteenth Centuries." *Flaying in the Pre-Modern World: Practice and Representation.* Edited by Larissa Tracy. D.S. Brewer, 2017, pp. 91–115.

———. "Misnaming the Medieval: Rejecting 'Anglo-Saxon' Studies." *History Workshop*, 2 November 2019, https://www.historyworkshop.org.uk/misnaming-the-medieval-rejecting-anglo-saxon-studies/

———, and Erik Wade. "What's in a Name? The Past and Present Racism in 'Anglo-Saxon' Studies." *Yearbook of English Studies: Old English to 1200*, vol. 52, 2022, pp. 135–153.

Reynolds, Susan. "What Do We Mean by 'Anglo-Saxon' and 'Anglo-Saxons'?" *Journal of British Studies*, vol. 24, no. 4, 1985, pp. 395–414.

Robinson, Cedric J. *Black Marxism: The Making of the Black Radical Tradition.* U of North Carolina P, 1983, 2000.

Robinson, Fred C. "Medieval, the Middle Ages." *Speculum*, vol. 59, no. 4, 1984, pp. 745–56.

Said, Edward. *Orientalism.* Penguin Books, 2003.

Scahill, John. "Trilingualism in Early Middle English Miscellanies: Languages and Literature." *The Yearbook of English Studies*, vol. 33, 2003, pp. 18–32.

Smith, David. "Trump Says Hispanic Adviser 'looks more like a Wasp than I do.'" *The Guardian*, 16 Sep 2019. https://www.theguardian.com/us-news/2019/sep/16/donald-trump-steve-cortes-hispanic-new-mexico-rally Accessed March 26, 2022.

Snyder, Christopher A. *The Britons.* Blackwell, 2003.

Taranu, Catalin. "Men into Monsters: Troubling Race, Ethnicity, and Masculinity in *Beowulf*." *Dating Beowulf: Studies in Intimacy*, edited by D. C. Remein and E. Weaver. Manchester UP, 2020, pp. 189–209.

Time Magazine. "Why the America First Caucus Is Wrong on Anglo-Saxon History." *Time.* https://time.com/5956149/real-history-anglo-saxon/ Accessed March 26, 2022.

Vernon, Matthew X. *The Black Middle Ages.* Palgrave, 2018.

Wade, Erik. "Skeletons in the Closet: Erasing Queer and Trans Issues in Early Medieval Scholarship." *ELH*, vol. 89, no. 2, 2022, pp. 281–316.

Wallace, Henry. *The Price of Vision: The Diary of Henry A. Wallace, 1942–1946.* Edited by John Morton Blum. Houghton Mifflin Company, 1973.

Webb, Clive. "Reluctant Partners: African Americans and the Origins of the Special Relationship." *Journal of Transatlantic Studies*, vol. 14, no. 4, 2016, pp. 350–364.

Wilton, D. "What Do We Mean by Anglo-Saxon? Pre-Conquest to the Present." *JEGP*, vol. 119, no. 4, 2020, pp. 425–456.

16
ON OR ABOUT 1400

Susan Nakley

Blame and the Snare of the Political

Art and politics belong together, which is convenient since they have been living and working together for millennia. Olive Senior (the Toronto-based Caribbean writer) evokes Aristotle (the ancient Mediterranean thinker largely lost to medieval Latinate circles but for Arabic transmission) when she observes,

> Literature is political because we, the creators of literature, are political animals; it is part of accepting our responsibility of being human, of being citizens of the world.... Nothing escapes the snare of the political, big P or small p – it is about the price of bread, the paycheck you bring home, how you interact with neighbours or whom you choose to romance. You can rebel against the latter or hew your own path, but your choice will be shaped by political concerns, and those have always included religion, race or ethnicity, sex and gender.

Senior expounds Aristotle's capacious approach to political science, attributing politics to human responsibility. She adds that politics intersects with writing where writing is literary: "Non-creative literature operates according to a conscious mandate. Creative literature does not. Fabrication by a journalist is regarded as betrayal. Fabrication is what a fiction writer does." Writing works as art exceeding entertainment when it resists our generic, cultural, personal, or other assumptions. Then, "literature" demonstrates its intellectual value with political currency: the capacity to renegotiate power's obscure dynamics.

Aristotelian philosophy catalyzed fourteenth-century Latinate intellectual culture across vernacular, national, regional, and generic boundaries, compelling thinkers like Dante Alighieri, Marsiglio of Padua, William of Ockham, Nicole Oresme, and Geoffrey Chaucer to treat politics as the teleological science of how power changes hands. This chapter regards politics similarly as "dynamic and negotiated human power," and approaches literature narrowly as creative "literary art." Then and now, literature collapses boundaries between intellectual agents to implicate individuals and produce political consequence by renegotiating responsibility (authority and guilt) through fissured boundaries. Politics is the negotiable part of human responsibility that instantiates power shifts as it draws writers and readers into an intellectually and ethically charged public sphere. Late medieval English language, literature, and politics consistently resort to "blame" as a rhetoric that marks their interdependence and their evolving mutual definition.

1400ish

Fourteenth-century English historical turbulence usually sparked a nuanced rhetoric of blame and always revealed human power's political limitations. Only divine power meant absolute sovereignty when Henry Bolingbroke deposed his cousin King Richard II in 1399, becoming the first English king in centuries whose mother tongue was English. Henry IV's ascent relied upon the Archbishop of Canterbury, Parliament, and the cousins' patrilineal descent from Edward III (whose own ascension followed his mother's 1327 deposition of his father Edward II), which typified the moment's political precarity. Throughout the era, coalitions of religious and civic leaders destabilized monarchial power without forsaking their foundational authorities. Ousters blamed individuals for youth, homosexuality, insanity, and more. Beyond the English Crown, the Western Papal Schism (1378–1417) exposed the Roman Catholic Church's own limits and political precarity when two or three rival popes claimed legitimacy. Blame circulated among papal patrons and cardinals, so English and French kings manipulated the schism to their advantages in the Hundred Years War (1337–1453). Meanwhile, a poll tax to subsidize England's war campaigns ignited the 1381 Rising, during which commoners eloquently employed English to blame clerical and aristocratic hierarchies for popular woes even as they swore allegiance to King Richard. However, the 1348–1350 bubonic plague was to blame for the labor shortage that had raised wages and hopes enough to spur the workers' revolt.

James Simpson's *Reform and Cultural Revolution* thesis subtends my approach to this moment. Simpson exposes the "English Renaissance" as a comprehensive revolution, wherein the Crown consolidated and centralized authority in an absolutist Anglican culture to secure stability, contain power, and constrict politics. Conversely, late Medieval English culture diversified its authorities in competing religious and civic institutions, making the medieval the more internally dynamic era. Relative decentralization gave political actors space to renegotiate spiritual, aristocratic, intellectual, and other power via a culture of rebellion and reform. Blame fine-tuned guilt and authority within the larger conceptual framework of responsibility without bulldozing foundations. Thus, blame emblematizes English political and literary culture around 1400, for it demonstrates how linguistic erudition challenges competing authorities without discounting their influence or forsaking their mutual relevance.

Harmonizing Steven Justice on the 1381 Rising and Seth Lehr on language, Noelle Phillips writes, "[i]t was not just peasant literacy that was insurgent... it was English itself" ("English Society"). Indeed, that vernacular swept in all directions to remake political cultures formerly beholden to Latin and French. English literature around 1400 pulsed with the dynamic political consequence that destabilized cultural hierarchies and reveled in the improvisational, unstandardized English alive before William Caxton founded England's first printing press at Westminster in 1476. Examining blame here clarifies the moment's distinctive political theory, its historical relevance, and blame's enduring ethical stakes. Blame may not seem immediately political, but it is a vernacular rhetoric that expanded access to power and responsibility. In the *Canterbury Tales*, blame mocks authorial intention's presumed autonomy and unsettles morality to enshrine vernacular literature as a public politics and dynamic power-sharing form of collaborative meaning-making. Blame demystifies the individual integrity that shame preserves in *Sir Gawain and the Green Knight*, insisting instead on ethical judgment and negotiable politics. In the *York Play of the Crucifixion*, Jesus's refusal to blame his crucifiers (due to their spiritual ignorance) absolves imperialism and mystifies the ethical onus of shared temporal knowledge. The following readings show how blame crafts concepts that render political literature humanistic culture's consummate medium.

Public Literature: Chaucerian Blame

Drafted between 1386 and 1400, Chaucer's *Canterbury Tales* is an estates satire critiquing class structures surrounded by a frame narrative, whose narrator introduces characters who themselves tell tales across genres in the tale cycle tradition. About 30 pilgrim-narrators of sundry class and gender positions meet in Southwark at Host Herry Bailey's Tabard Inn and bar; there they enter a storytelling contest enroute to England's national Cathedral. Technically representing the aristocracy, clergy, and working class, they nevertheless blur most categories. For example, the weathered Knight fights for his keep; the ostensibly queer Pardoner rakes in cash by preaching orthodoxies while claiming masculine heterosexuality; the Wife of Bath both inherits wealth when widowed and earns it by making cloth; the Reeve manages manorial laborers yet identifies as a peasant carpenter himself; the Miller and the Cook enjoy guzzling booze despite their humble stations (and the Cook being on pilgrimage only to feed upwardly mobile guildsmen). Blame diversifies like their class perspectives, promoting literature as public art that shapes culture and politics whoever wins the contest. The pilgrim-narrators blame their storytelling flaws on devotion to truth, their own short wits, their audience's inability to listen, their drunkenness, similar narrators who have defamed them, their learnedness, their ignorance, their audience who is not listening but reading and able to skip material, and more. Blame-shifting reveals a troublingly similar ambiguity of meaning in both politics and literary fiction just as it establishes English as the people's political language: a vernacular fit for making political and literary meaning collaboratively.

The Canterbury Tales democratizes narrative authority and erodes authorial intention by redistributing doubt and confidence through blame. The Middle English word *auctoritee* itself emblematizes my point. It means "written authority"—encompassing legal power, formal consent, the power of writing and literature itself, and power accessible to people through their own writing and literacy. Middle English embraces literature and politics closely with diction like *auctoritee*, which *The Canterbury Tales* uses 15 times. Zadie Smith concisely gleans Chaucerian *auctoritee*'s politics in describing Chaucer's "democratic principle," thus: "Chaucer wrote of the people and for them, never doubting that even the most rarefied religious, political and philosophical ideas could be conveyed in the language the people themselves speak" (xv). Chaucer's idiom radiates perpetual confidence in the democratic potential of English language through characters like the Wife of Bath, whom Smith's 2021 *Wife of Willesden* resurrects. Smith recognizes that by debating powerful ideas in vernacular language and in various gendered and embodied narrator voices, Chaucer's art "democratizes" access to power and authority for it trusts readers to interpret religious, intellectual, ethical, and political life. However, Chaucer accomplishes this expressly through authorial self-doubt and blame-shifting.

We remember the *Canterbury Tales* not because of Geoffrey Chaucer's self-assurance or archetypal narrative authority, but because it remembers us readers, writers, and thinkers to ourselves and to each other. The main narrator, dubbed Chaucer-the-Pilgrim, apologizes for his retelling's offensive language and mediates between other narrators and readers, but refuses blame by admitting that his own "wit is short" (746). Thus, the text sharply limits readers' expectations of narrative authority and energizes our self-reliance. Meanwhile, the Host serves drinks, launches a storytelling contest, and randomly chooses the Knight first. He then reinscribes class hierarchies by deliberately selecting the Monk next. The Miller interjects, threatening to narrate next himself or defect. So, Chaucer-the-Pilgrim downgrades the Miller's tale with blame: "*Blameth noght me if that ye chese amis/ The Millere is a cherl, ye knowe wel this/... Aviseth you, and putte me out of blame*"; "Blame not me if you choose amiss/The Miller is a churl, you know well this/... Think for yourself and put me out of blame" (3181–3182, 3185). Chaucer-the-Pilgrim insists on the *auctoritee* of readerly choice, knowledge, and moral judgment by categorically refusing blame. This would-be authoritative narrator dilutes guilt, responsibility, and authorial power. He doubts conventional authorship but entrusts an intellectually and politically attuned literary community with ethical deliberation. Blame proliferates alongside fellowship, for in denying autonomy and deflecting blame, our unreliable narrators invite fellows (including us readers) to share responsibility, ultimately democratizing intellectual authority as they vindicate themselves. Blame-shifting conjures active audiences: communities of readers, writers, thinkers, tellers—some fictional and all political agents—sharing *auctoritee* through the literary process.

Chaucerians like Alcuin Blamires and Michael Kuczynski have engaged morality and authorship with blame-shifting, pursuing Chaucer's political positions and even his own moral stature and metaethical dilemmas through analyses of blame. Noelle Phillips uniquely explicates the pivotal, underappreciated *Miller's Prologue* detail that shows how blame and conviviality render "Chaucer" but one narrator occupying authorial space. After interjecting but before being repudiated, the drunk Miller stipulates: "*that I misspeke... Wite it the ale of Southwerk*": "if I misspeak...Blame it on the ale of Southwark" (3139–3140). He blames the entire pilgrim fellowship, founded on Southwark conviviality (drinking together at the Tabard Inn) (750, 819–821). Blaming Southwark ale firmly enfolds all the pilgrims within their fellowship allegiances. Phillips notes that here the Miller's local ale imports democracy: his successful bid "to speak as an equal to" the Knight signifies an "exercise of power enabled by beer, the drink of the people" wherein he refuses to "relinquish the authorial space he has claimed" (*Craft Beer Culture and Modern Medievalism* 34). No one can stop the Miller from succeeding the Knight; and the Host's parting jab, "*thy wit is overcome*," only "energizes the tale" (3135, 34). In this vein, observe how Chaucer-the-Pilgrim-narrator's earlier confession (that his own "*wit is short*") also energizes readers, piquing our interest and compounding the intellectual weight and authority of readerly wit (746). Furthermore, the Middle English verb used here (*witen*, from Old English) means both to blame and to have certain knowledge without doubt (whereas *blamen* from Old French implies neither knowledge nor certainty).

Megan Cook does not tackle blame or doubt directly, but does illuminate the doubt and uncertainty embedded in Chaucer's authorial self-representation. Cook concentrates on two instances of Chaucerian fourth-wall breaking: the short poem *Adam Scriveyn*, which ostensibly scolds scribes for distorting authorial intention, and *Chaucer's Retraction*, the prose appendix to the *Canterbury Tales*, which retracts Chaucer's secular writings based on Chaucer's personal failures of wit. Cook demonstrates how Chaucer anxiously acknowledges the limits of "authorial control" alongside the reach of "readerly judgment" in "textual meaning-making" (46, 51). Meaning emerges beyond the mirage of authorial intention in a space of democratic *auctoritee*, authority derived from participation in a public literary process. We may seek "the idealized, uncorrupted text," authorial intention, the poet's genuine politics, or the man's moral measure, but we find that "[r]eaderly judgment, rooted in an act of reading over which the poet has no direct control, remains central to Chaucer's own understanding of the value of his work" (52, 51). Doubt belies fantasies of autonomous authorship, individual morality, and political intention throughout Chaucer's work.

Chaucer's Retraction features not an author with canonical intention, but a Christian soul begging the reader's mercy "on the grounds of his 'unkonnynge'" (inability, ignorance, lack of wit) (Cook 50). Whereas "Chaucer" eschews blame early in the *Canterbury Tales* because of his short wit, he accepts blame because of his ignorance in his *Retraction*. Everywhere he dramatically doubts his own intellect and apologizes for his limitations, thus energizing readerly intellect and language itself. Blame emerges as an intimate, if resentful, gesture of sharing authorial control in Chaucer's *oeuvre*. The text's obsession with blame politicizes our interdependence and supplants private authorial intention with public literary authority. It transforms readers into fellows and intellectual agents who are as responsible for literary and political meaning-making as any *auctoritee* or author.

Blame, Shame, and the Ethics of Politics in *SGGK*

Sir Gawain and the Green Knight (hereafter *SGGK*, ca. 1400) is a Christian response to the genre of Arthurian romance as well as romance's response to political "problems of factional breakdown and royal insouciance" (Allen 137). *SGGK* begins and ends with the diction of "blame" and "shame," which frame three exchange games that drive the plot. Analyzing this diction reveals discursive political meaning and suggests that shame is mainly a visceral reaction, while blame interpolates deliberation and negotiation to insist on culture's political nature. The poem's political discourse presents a magnificent paradox, wherein blame eclipses shame to subvert the morality, religion, and individual integrity that the culture seems to promote.

After a fantastical Green Knight startles King Arthur's Camelot at Christmastime, Sir Gawain crafts blame as a rhetorical mechanism that levies shame and honor and through which power changes hands, or not. "Shame" enters the text with the enormous, spectacularly adorned, green and golden knight. Challenging the court to a "Christmas game" (of dismemberment via a structured yet violent exchange of battle axe blows), he maintains that he's a peaceful knight and it's just a game. However, his derisive laughter erupts as he accuses the Round Table of cowardice. In her study of shame and its antithesis, honor, Stephanie Trigg explains that shame registers itself "powerfully on the body" in *SGGK*, where shaming is usually "a speech act" (128–133,129, 131). The Green Knight's speech act triggers Arthur's visceral shame: "*Þe blod schot for scham into his schyre face*"; "The blood shot for shame into his white face" (317). This shame appears as elemental to Arthur's being as his own flesh and blood.

Enter Gawain: allowing Arthur to pass the baton, deferring to all Camelot, volunteering to absorb blame, and resting his case upon shame's conditional nature, Gawain insists that blame is avoidable yet drives politics (ll. 341–360). He concludes, "*And if I carp not comlyly, let alle þis cort rych bout blame*": "And if I speak not appropriately, leave all this mighty court without blame" (360). The conditional clause styles speech as evanescent, revisable, but the following injunction confirms Camelot's might. Gawain wields speech powerfully, admits language is open to political interpretation, and customizes blame to intercept shame by disentangling blame from speech. If blame and its accusations of guilt are as negotiable as Gawain ventures, shame need not corrupt Camelot's established political power despite Arthur's visceral reaction. Gawain's rhetoric of blame harnesses a durative sense of politics: nobility, wealth, honor, the vicissitudes of cultural power accrued over time. Gawain consistently shadows shame with blame to resist Camelot's political liabilities but is unable to resist the challenge to decapitate the fantastic Green Knight. His head (conveniently) turns out to be re-attachable, which sets the plot in motion by requiring Gawain (inconveniently) to present his own neck for reciprocal whacking a year later.

Gawain mitigates Arthur's instinctual shame in part one, but part three rudely awakens Gawain to his own vulnerability. After decapitating the Green Knight in part one, Gawain seeks him in part two, and discovers Hautdesert, a strangely familiar chivalric court, on the way. Hautdesert's food is delicious; its guestroom is lush; Lady Bertilak is lovely; Lord Bertilak is gracious; the wine flows, and Gawain enters a second exchange game, despite the enigma of the first: that mysteriously re-attachable noggin. This time, Gawain must trade what he catches in the house for what Bertilak captures in the field. Each day, Bertilak hears mass, inhales breakfast, and hunts, while Gawain slumbers, awaits rendezvous with the Green Knight, and is hunted. Lady Bertilak wakes him by creeping into his bedchamber, "*and þe burne schamed,/And layde hym doun lystyly, and let as he slepte*": "and the man shamed,/And laid himself down carefully, and let it seem as if he slept" (1189–1190). Gawain buries shame in feigned sleep until he composes himself enough to converse with the Lady. She flirts with him, praising his legendary chivalry and implying that he could have his way with her, but he politely admires her husband to avoid infidelity. Gawain accepts one kiss for courtly etiquette's sake and exchanges it (without naming its source) that evening for venison caught by Bertilak. Shame swiftly asserts itself when Gawain is unsuspecting, yet he hides his shame.

Consent and willingness to accept blame help Gawain recover on day two. Lady Bertilak arrives and, after pleasantries, derides him for failing her chivalric courtesy tutorial. Eagerly Gawain marches ahead of shame, offering, "*If hit be sothe what ȝe breue, þe blame is myn awen*": "If it be true what you state, the blame is my own" (1488). Chivalry stipulates that he should have kissed her already, she ventures; but Gawain belies her appeal to manners, noting how guilty he would be if she refused a kiss. Thus, the profoundly political question of consent, which (then, as now) drives sexual and gender politics as well as the politics of sovereignty and government, cracks the brittle shell of Lady Bertilak's etiquette lesson. So, she invokes gender and class to argue that Gawain neither could nor should be refused, for he is "*stif innoghe to constrayne with strenkþe... any... so vilanous*": "stiff enough to compel with force... anybody... so vulgar" as to resist the social hierarchies that ordain Gawain's masculine, aristocratic dominance (1496–1497). Lady Bertilak advocates blaming sexual assault survivors and degrades the class status of those who resist sexual advances of knights like Gawain by citing vulgarity to reinforce traditional gender and class politics.

Championing power-sharing via consent, Gawain reframes the conversation around his community: "*Bot þrete is vnþryuande in þede þer I lende*"; "But threat is ignoble in the community where I live" (1499). He leverages "greater cultural authority" as "the acknowledged master of the courtly discourse in question" to elevate consent's role in legitimizing rule: sexual power immediately and governmental dominion, by extension (Trigg 130). In much late-medieval political theory, lack of consent delegitimizes not only affection but sovereignty, a fact that reveals how in this moment Gawain explicitly promotes politics as a fluid, limited, negotiated stream of power (Nakley 2017). He eludes shame, prioritizes consent, but conjures moral relativism, for he stops short of exacting mercy or disavowing conquest whenever it fails ethical engagement with the well-being of weaker parties. Still, Gawain insists that his culture prohibits threatening the proper power and agency of others, because that's not how knights of the Round Table (renowned for Arthur's reliance on counsel and consent) roll. Gawain escapes shame by considering his responsibility and blameworthiness, yet stresses consent as the ethical imperative that exposes moral objectivism's inadequacy. An exasperated Lady Bertilak finally hurls shame straight at him, accusing him of considering her insipid "*For schame!*" (1530). Aiming to level his honor and power, her "invocation of shame is powerless to affect the knight" and fails to "produce the bodily affect of shame"; it lands flatly as "an unsuccessful speech act... because it is not supported by a matching cultural authority," which Gawain retains (Trigg 130).

Lady Bertilak fails to shame Gawain by increasing tensions between chastity and courtly love. Day three, however, reprioritizes Gawain's signature values listed in part two: generosity, fellowship, chastity, courtliness, and mercy (652–654). The Lady's flirtation temporarily lifts chastity and courtly love above the rest. Fellowship reemerges here with the political and ethical consequence of neighborly love, which Emily Houlik-Ritchey establishes in the Middle English context by adeptly explicating the "semantic range" of the word *felawe* (112). The lady kisses him thrice, but when he refuses further intimacy she pivots to blame: "*Blame ȝe disserue,/ȝif ȝe luf not þat lyf þat ȝe lye nexte*"/"Blame you deserve,/If you love not that life next to whom you lie" (1779–1780). Widening the focus from chastity to human life's magnitude rather than invoking her gender, class, or other narrow identity, the Lady deems life itself deserving of love (Cohen 46). Identifying herself literally as the life beside Gawain, she conjures fundamental humanity rather than class, gender, or race. They are adjacent lives, fellows, neighbors: "simultaneously antagonistic and cooperative" (Houlik-Ritchey 113). The Lady (perhaps inadvertently) recalls that his repertoire includes fellowship, which threatens courtly love and aristocratic power with democratizing potential. She presses for his superlative romantic love, but he enacts neighborly love (1781, 1801–1809).

Although Lady Bertilak's erotic ploys fail, her rhetoric of blame reorients Gawain's responsibilities toward fellowship (the ethics and politics of interaction with our neighbors, as Senior would write). Gawain's love blossoms not as eros but as a Marxian political action in Michael Hardt and Antonio Negri's terms:

> that love is a process of the production of the common and the production of subjectivity....
> ...Love— in the production of affective networks, schemes of cooperation, and social subjectivities— is an economic power. Conceived in this way love is not, as it is often characterized, spontaneous or passive. It does not simply happen to us, as if it were an event that mystically arrives from elsewhere. It is instead an action, a biopolitical event, planned and realized in common.
>
> *(Hardt and Negri 180)*

Evading eros, Gawain engages in commerce that exceeds the obligations of market transactions. He realizes his love of fellowship and life itself by consenting to exchange games, and he participates in affective economies of power-sharing, cooperation, and calculation that produce new senses of the common. His agreements systematically cultivate shared chivalric subjectivity with the Green Knight and Bertilak. The Lady redirects this *modus vivendi:* living through horizontal fellowship economies.

Although contained within a palatial suite, Lady Bertilak and Sir Gawain's exchange illuminates a late medieval Marxian class politics wherein horizontal fellowship's democratizing potential intersects with the politics of gender and governmental sovereignty. Since they will not consummate their flirtation, she requests a *drury*, a "word, denoting both 'love' and 'token of love,' the thing and its sign" (*SGGK* 1507, 1517, 1805, 2033, 2449; Dinshaw 216). Gawain has no *drury*, so the Lady produces a ring with conspicuous market value. He refuses it, withholding the reciprocal consent that roots relationships through gift exchange in anthropological theory. So, she offers her own girdle, which holds relatively little market value yet obligates ambiguous reciprocity. She also discloses the gift's defensive "*costes þat knit ar þerinne*,"/"powers that are knitted therein": its ambiguously quantified conditions and qualities (1849). Only then does Gawain consent to keep it from her husband (1861, 1863). Gawain wittingly accepts a gift with "inalienable" value bound to embroidery—that women's class-crossing labor generates networks of "inalienable" cultural power "in the Marxian economic sense," which is true of all personified gifts, as Robert Epstein explains (5–8, 6, 7). Like blame and *auctoritee*, *drury* is a Middle English negotiation tactic with democratizing potential.

Drury incorporates interpretation in constructing cultural power and obliges ethics to legitimize powershifting and community-building. According to Carolyn Dinshaw, the *SGGK* poet systematically associates the *drury* with heterosexual sex and Christian knighthood, so it represents "not only that identity but also the threats to it" (Dinshaw, 218). The Lady's calculated bequest carries "potentially violent" excess, as Walter Wadiak argues (92). The value of its ambiguity or perhaps the "instability in the gift's meaning—a semantic excess"—equips it to unstick Gawain's political loyalties (96). Its interpretability renders this poem "an embodiment of a political economy, not just a salvific" market or any limited economy (92). This *drury* (gift of love or sex) duplicates Gawain's lesson on consent in kissing: legitimacy requires consent, mutuality, and reciprocity. If love happens to us spontaneously or passively, as Hardt and Negri suggest, it loses political legitimacy. *Drury*, love, and token "must be planned and realized in common" to establish social subjectivity (180). Gawain accepts the girdle because its embroidery purportedly protects the wearer from violence: because he loves life itself, he knowingly allies himself with its encoded costs. He deliberates and wittingly invests his loyalties in feminine artisanal power, accepting blame for costs that accrue within affective political networks like anthropological gift economies exceeding conventional market economies. Gawain accepts the *drury*, which requires reciprocity exceeding commerce's finite obligations.

Beyond the bedchamber, Gawain complicates his masculine chivalric subjectivity by keeping a token inalienable from feminine crafting and a secret that threatens his chivalric integrity. While the *drury* claims to protect against violence with folk magic, it debases his chivalric integrity because he has already promised to exchange winnings openly with Lord Bertilak. Gawain never considers honoring that promise, but trades just three kisses for Bertilak's fox pelt that evening. With the girdle secretly stashed, Gawain pretends his chief concern is that his winnings are "*pertly payed*": "openly rendered" (1941). He speaks to his second agreement but honors only the third, for he is "*lelly*" or faithfully concealing a bargain he made to protect his life (1863). Acting on his compact with the Lady obligates him to the "*costes*": powers, expenses, and other inalienable conditions that she knitted into that girdle (1849). Gawain can neither conceal nor reveal the *drury* without violating his chivalric honor. On day three he privately invests in feminine economies of power but publicly maintains fidelity to masculine knighthood. Gawain gains courage to satisfy his first agreement by breaking his second with a third that splits his political loyalties between patriarchal Christian knighthood and feminine folk magic.

In part four, Gawain faces shame, succeeds as a teacher yet fails as a student. Wrapped in the green girdle, he finds the Green Knight on foot with head attached. After two mock swipes prolonging Gawain's agony, the anticipated strike lands, draws blood, but only scars Gawain's skin superficially. After passively withstanding that requisite blow, he prepares to fight. The Green Knight, however, is a peaceful knight, and this is just a game. In fact, all three agreements equal one test, for he is Bertilak de Hautdesert in disguise: he and Lady Bertilak are testing Gawain collaboratively (under Morgan le Faye's supervision). Bertilak's two mock swipes requite the days when Gawain honors their pact. The true strike requites day three when Gawain conceals the girdle, which Bertilak recognizes as his own "*wede... weued*": "garment ...given" (or woven: *weuven* means to give and to weave) by his wife but belonging to both, styling this a gender-inclusive girdle (2358–2359). He then justifies the strike thus: Gawayn "*lakked a lyttel... lewte/... /Bot for ʒe lufed your lyf; þe lasse I yow blame*"; Gawain "lacked a little... loyalty/... /But because you loved your life; the less I you blame" (2366). Last year in Camelot Gawain invoked blame's negotiability to protect his court from shame's political liabilities. Now, Bertilak in costume echoes Gawain, declares him the most faultless man on earth, reckons the girdle's appeal, and negotiates blame to Gawain's advantage as if they were always allies (2363). Recognizing blame's subjectivity and the value judgment behind his deployment of blame, Bertilak ethically engages his objectives with the value of Gawain's life.

Where Gawain should feel pride, his body performs shame, belying that he taught the ethics and politics of blame to the Bertilaks. Gawain's mortification manifests as blushing until "*he schrank for schome þat þe schalk talked*": "he shrank for shame at the man's speech" (2372). Bertilak kindly tempers blame, citing Gawain's admirable if imperfect loyalty in an impossible situation; conversely, Gawain exaggerates blame to purge himself of shame for his association with feminine power: "In anger and shame he flings the girdle to the ground and curses all women as deceitful daughters of Eve" (Trigg 60). Blame and shame's fourth duet forces Gawain to admit feminine agency even as he blames women collectively (Heng 501). He admits fault himself only after he "*brayde broþely þe belt*": "flung fiercely the belt" but fails to jettison his shameful duplicitousness (2376).

Gawain returns from his quest, but reaching home seems impossible. His homecoming spiel renders blame more essential than the "*schame*" his blushing signals (2504). Gawain rebrands blame a reason "*for his vnleute*," or disloyalty, and a "*nirt*" or scar: a unique trauma marring his individual character and body rather than the linguistic technique he customized to subvert communal political trauma (2499, 2498). Although blame served well as an improvisational rhetoric for escaping shame, he now imagines it a fixed moral defect that captures him, inherent in his scar: "*þis blame I bere in my nek/... is þe token of vtrawþe þat I am tan inne*"; "this blame that I carry in my neck,/... is the token of treachery within which I am captured" (2506, 2508). But nobody buys that—not Arthur, not Camelot, not even the historical Edward III, whose Order of the Garter motto, "*HONY SOYT QUI MAL PENSE*": "SHAMED BE WHOEVER THINKS ILL," affixes to the romance, hinging shame on thought (2531). Gawain cannot retract the rhetoric of blame that has taught Camelot to think beyond shame; indeed, his peers gleefully mass-produce and wear matching green girdles of honor. The romance eclipses Gawain's individual moral trauma with an elite line of accessories celebrating him, his rhetoric of blame, and cross-gender fellowship. *SGGK* prefers ethical fellowship to individual morality yet circumscribes fellowship's democratizing potential within aristocracy.

Conclusion: Resurrecting Blame to Decolonize Jesus

Authorial intention is the stuff of modern myth. Neither Chaucer as author nor Gawain as eponymous hero can cancel the lessons their associated literature teaches. While Chaucer's *Retraction* extols Jesus's sovereign wit and judgment, *The York Play of the Crucifixion*'s Jesus underestimates temporal knowledge for he cannot revoke human sentience or ethical responsibility. Jesus declares that spiritual ignorance of his divine innocence absolves Roman soldiers of blame for crucifying him publicly alongside countless others. His conventional absolution, "Forgive them Father, '*What þei wirke, wotte þai noght*': 'What they work, know they naught,'" excuses Roman colonialism and state terror (261). Most significantly, Jesus's refusal to blame his crucifiers precisely because of spiritual ignorance obfuscates the ethical imperative of shared temporal knowledge that the Middle English poetics of blame in *The Canterbury Tales* and *SGGK* assiduously pursues. Jesus mystifies the human responsibility that attends political thought, intellectual life, and the ethics of labor driving "civic cycle" drama like the York Pinners Guild's *Crucifixion* (Rice and Pappano).

For two centuries beginning before 1376, English craft guilds (communities of lay Christian workers) produced Biblical drama in towns like York and Chester. Imagining Jews in their own land colonized by Romans, their pageants critique global religious and racial politics from a Northern English artisan perspective. They project a distinctly political voice that challenged church and state hierarchies without forsaking either. A prime example is the *York Crucifixion*'s meditation on blame in the Passion's iconic scene of torture, which typically depoliticizes and removes Christian salvation history from human history while blaming Jews to exonerate Rome. The York iteration amplifies work and pain to welcome political history back into the Passion.

I have argued that the *York Crucifixion*'s scrupulous return to the Passion's colonial provenance laments empire's expenditures by imbricating the politics of torture, work, and knowledge (Nakley 2015). Despite the conventional absolution's inclusion, the *York Crucifixion* is no conventional Passion Play. It repoliticizes the whitewashed legend via setting and excavates Christian imperial hegemonies to recall ancient Israel's buried colonial history. Crammed together on a tiny pageant wagon representing "*Calvarie*," the Latin name that transforms a Jerusalem hill into a state terror arena, five actors perform claustrophobic colonial intimacy (7). Four soldiers address each other as "*Knights*" asserting their Roman social and racial superiority over Jewish colonial criminals condemned to crucifixion. They injure and exhaust their own bodies by nailing Jesus's subaltern body to the Roman cross. The Pinners Guild play gives them the final word: "*Þis travayle here we tyne*"; "This labor here we waste" (300). Jesus's dereliction of blame invites politics to creep back into this dangerously definitive depoliticization. York's soldiers blame their own profligate brutality in the play's most honest line. Thus, they indict this colonial scene of torture as a waste of human work, pain, and skill. The *York Crucifixion*'s *mise-en-scene* revises the Passion's typical medieval glorification of pain by restaging the insidious imperial hegemonies that Roman public execution sustains alongside the ethical responsibility that Jesus undercuts.

The vernacular literature this chapter analyzes may defend authorial intention, promote individual morality, and lionize spiritual knowledge. However, the rhetoric of blame driving it contains the potential to democratize such concepts with ethical responsibility. The consequence for English language, literature, culture, and politics was perhaps never greater than on or about 1400.[1]

Note

1 I heartily thank Maija Birenbaum, Bob Epstein, Rick Godden, Erin Labbie, and Kate Norako, who read early drafts, batted around ideas, or recommended useful bibliography for this chapter.

Works Cited

Allen, Elizabeth. *Uncertain Refuge: Sanctuary in the Literature of Medieval England*. U of Pennsylvania P, 2021.

Blamires, Alcuin. "Chaucer the Reactionary: Ideology and the *General Prologue* to The *Canterbury Tales*." *The Review of English Studies*, vol. 51, no. 204, 2000, pp. 523–39.

Chaucer, Geoffrey. *Norton Chaucer*. Edited by David Lawton. W.W. Norton, 2019.

Cohen, Jeffery J. "The Love of Life: Reading Sir Gawain and the Green Knight Close to Home" *Premodern Ecologies in the Modern Literary Imagination*. Edited by Vin Nardizzi and Tiffany Jo Werth. U of Toronto P, 2019, pp. 25–58.

Cook, Megan. "'Here taketh the makere of this book his leve': The "Retraction" and Chaucer's Works in Tudor England. *Studies in Philology*, vol. 113, no. 1, 2016, pp. 32–54.

Dinshaw, Carolyn. "A Kiss Is Just a Kiss: Heterosexuality and Its Consolations in Sir Gawain and the Green Knight." *Diacritics*, vol. 24, no. 2/3, 1994, pp. 204–226.

Epstein, Robert. *Chaucer's Gifts*. U of Wales P, 2019.

Hardt, Michael, and Antonio Negri. *Commonwealth*. Harvard UP, 2011.

Heng, Geraldine. "Feminine Knots and the Other *Sir Gawain and the Green Knight*." *PMLA*, vol. 106, no. 3, 1991, pp. 500–514.

Houlik-Ritchey, Emily. "Love Thy Neighbor, Love Thy Fellow: Teaching Gower's Representation of the Unethical Jew." *Jews in Medieval England: Teaching Representations of the Other*. Edited by Miriamne Ara Krummel and Tison Pugh. Palgrave, 2017, pp. 101–115.

Kuczynski, Michael. "'Don't Blame Me': The Metaethics of a Chaucerian Apology." *The Chaucer Review*, vol. 37, no. 4, 2003, pp. 315–32.

Nakley, Susan. *Living in the Future: Sovereignty and Internationalism in the* Canterbury Tales. U of Michigan P, 2017.

———. "On the Unruly Power of Pain in Middle English Drama," *Literature and Medicine*, vol. 33, no. 2, 2015, pp. 302–325.

Pappano, Margaret, and Nicole Rice. *The Civic Cycles*. U of Notre Dame P, 2015.

Phillips, Noelle. *Craft Beer Culture and Modern Medievalism: Brewing Dissent*. ARC Humanities Press, 2019.

———. "English Society c. 1340–1400: Reform and Resistance." *The Open Access Companion to the Canterbury Tales*. Edited by Candace Barrington, Brantley Bryant, Richard H. Godden, Daniel T. Kline, and Myra Seaman. September, 2017. https://opencanterburytales.dsl.lsu.edu/refenglsociety/

Senior, Olive. "Literature is Political Because We Are Political Animals" *The Guardian,* April 29, 2013.

Simpson, James. *Reform and Cultural Revolution*. Oxford UP, 2002.

Sir Gawain and the Green Knight. Edited by Tolkien, J.R.R. Clarendon, 1925, 1967.

Smith, Zadie. *The Wife of Willesden*. Penguin Random House UK, 2021.

Trigg, Stephanie. *Shame and Honor: A Vulgar History of the Order of the Garter*. U of Pennsylvania P, 2012.

Wadiak, Walter. *Savage Economy: The Returns of Middle English Romance*. U of Notre Dame P, 2017.

York Play of the Crucifixion. Medieval Drama: An Anthology, edited by Greg Walker. Blackwell, 2000.

17
ON OR ABOUT 1616

Urvashi Chakravarty

Shakespeare, Race, and Exceptionalism

1616 looms large in English literary history and in our cultural memory. For early modernists, it immediately invokes the death of Shakespeare; for those who might be more iconoclastic (but only slightly so) it might recall the publication of Ben Jonson's First Folio, seven years before Shakespeare's was compiled and published by John Heminge and Henry Condell. 1616, then, is both a high watermark but also a liminal year, anticipating the moment in 1623 when Shakespeare's works would be gathered and published in the celebrated First Folio of his work. 1623 is a providential turning point, for without the First Folio, several of Shakespeare's works—among them, *The Tempest*, *Macbeth*, and *Julius Caesar*, arguably three of Shakespeare's most "political" plays—would not even be available to us, might simply be lost along with so many other early modern plays. When, in 2016, the Folger Shakespeare Library's copies of the First Folio went "on tour" across the United States as part of a celebration of "400 Years of Shakespeare," the tour was titled "First Folio! The Book That Gave Us Shakespeare."[1] Without 1623, that is, would we understand the significance that 1616 holds?

1616 is, moreover, a provocation. To think of 1616 is to think of the celebrated and entrenched notion of Englishness that Shakespeare presents and propounds. It is to revert to a moment of cultural legacy and legibility, to recall a touchstone of English literary production, and to invoke (even by the marker of his absence) the playwright and poet through whom we understand so much of early modern social and political life. Work abounds on Shakespeare's politics and his representation of politics, on the putative universalism and timelessness of his work, and on the political register of the evasive, erasing universalism such a tendency achieves.[2] There is a particular kind of politics that the inheritance of a Shakespeare tied to 1616 produces; those politics are both sustained and amplified at times such as 2016, when the quadricentenary of his death was widely celebrated. The First Folio's tour, for instance, and especially its rhetorical framing as "the book that gave us Shakespeare," raised important questions about who was imagined as its audience, and the politics of the inevitable impression that was created of *noblesse oblige*.[3] The very word "politics," we note, recalls its etymological association with the *polis*, the state—and who might be said to belong, and who is excluded. It places pressure on the question of the polity, and who constitutes it.[4] 2016 was, of course, also the year which saw the Brexit vote and the election of Trump; in its aftermath, therefore, some also took the opportunity to mark assonances with the contemporary political moment. In a celebrated production of *Richard II* by Adjoa Andoh and Lynette Linton at Shakespeare's Globe in 2019, for example, Adjoa Andoh led a cast consisting entirely of women of color; in interviews, Andoh noted that the play was scheduled to run "while we [Britain] Brexited"—that is, as Britain put into effect the decision reached in the 2016 Brexit vote.[5] As *Richard II*—a play centered around concerns of both nation and governance—was staged, Britain undertook the difficult process of leaving the European Union, making the poster for the production as well as its closing image—Andoh's face projected against the English flag, a flag explicitly, even ostentatiously, invoked on stage as the play closed—both strikingly powerful and poignant.[6]

Andoh and Linton's *Richard II* deliberately spoke to the contexts of colonialism, empire, and slavery on which British history and Shakespeare's legacy rest. To speak of 1616 is then also to speak of 2016, the sense of Shakespeare's timelessness, his exceptionalism, and the capacity of his works to speak to the present moment. It is now commonplace to refer to events as "Shakespearean," which seems to announce an ambitious or grandiose context. It is more common still to remark that Shakespeare speaks to the "human condition" writ large, as evidenced not only by the range of settings and contexts for productions of his plays but also by their global reach, and the work of adaptation, re-imagination, and remediation in rendering Shakespeare a truly global property, a playwright whose work translates to a range of cultures, contexts, and even languages. Yet to talk of Shakespeare's universal applicability or timelessness is itself a political act: one that purports to speak and seek community across nations and cultures and contexts but often acts in the interest of eliding difference and obscuring some of the most damaging aspects of Shakespeare's legacy—and that of early modern England.[7]

Shakespearean Politics

I begin, then, by asking: what do we mean when we talk about "*early modern* politics"? Certainly the sense of politics as "[t]he theory or practice of government or administration," specifically "[t]he science or study of government and the state" reaches back to the sixteenth century.[8] But early modern lexicons also emphasized the sense of the "craftie or cunning" that attaches to the "politique" (Cawdrey, sig. G5v). It is therefore worth emphasizing the sense of the "politic"—in both early modern and contemporary senses—that the idea of politics includes. This is a sense that Shakespeare frequently, and famously, invokes in his plays. In *The Taming of the Shrew*, for instance, the fortune-hunting husband Petruccio who must tame the willful Katherina addresses the audience in Act IV to explain his wife-taming stratagems: "Thus have I politicly begun my reign,/And 'tis my hope to end successfully" (4.1.169–170), he confides.[9] In this address, Petruccio clearly analogizes marital domain to monarchical authority, rehearsing the way in which domestic politics and national order are closely interwoven, but also, in speaking to the audience, underscores the sense that domestic control is a matter of public interest. Such a confluence also speaks to the theater as part of a larger political economy. Meanwhile, in *King Lear*, Goneril argues that "'Tis politic and safe to let him [Lear] keep/At point a hundred knights" (1.4.293–294), as she fears that "He may enguard his dotage with their powers/And hold our lives in mercy" (1.4.296–297). Here, a king's access to military might is keyed to the possibility of regaining political control, and speaks to the recent history wherein liveried retinues were increasingly prohibited from coming to court under the reigns of Henry VII and Henry VIII in order to mitigate against the risk of a threat to monarchical power. But Goneril's worry also situates the locus of those political tensions as the household. Early modern understandings of the household included servants and retainers; the machinations of political power that forged larger questions of sovereignty and succession were thus also often rooted in the family and the household.

To explore early modern politics, then, is also to examine the domestic sphere. As a series of scholars have noted, the early modern household was a microcosm of the state as a whole; disorder in the former threatened the collapse of the latter. But the late sixteenth and early seventeenth centuries were also marked by intense and widespread anxiety over the problem of succession, as Elizabeth I's lack of an heir threatened to return England to a state of civil disruption. The larger question of political order is therefore deeply bound up with succession, inheritance, and legacy, and in turn speaks to the afterlives of 1616: not as a historical landmark, but rather as a set of shared cultural and national investments and inheritances.

What do we mean, however, when we talk about *Shakespeare* and politics? The term "politics" has become in some contexts a pejorative, so to talk about "political Shakespeare" might refer to the ways in which Shakespeare addresses political systems or speaks to the current moment—but, just as often, it refers to the sense that current political concerns are being "read into" Shakespeare, that Shakespeare is "becoming" political. This tension might speak to the difficulty in deriving or assuming a common understanding of the political. And just as the notion of a "political" early modernity rests on the domestic as much as the civil or governmental, so I suggest the problem of early modern succession points to the larger ways in which the cultural and literary legacy of Shakespeare, and our inheritance of his work, comprises part of the way we must think about his political import.

Despite the fanfare around 1616, therefore, I have suggested that that date is always in political conversation with the events of 1623 and 2016. The symmetrical neatness of 1616 also invokes the commonly held belief that Shakespeare was born and died on the same day, 23rd April, or St. George's Day. This mirrored date means that not only does Shakespeare's death date always already evoke his birth, but it also doubly reinforces the sense that he is a—*the*—quintessentially English poet and cultural figure, just as St. George is both the patron saint of England and a symbol of English nationalism. To talk about 1616 is to invoke the close association of Shakespeare with St. George's Day, and simultaneously to ratify and reinforce it with each telling.

But the invocation of Englishness, of course, also compels us to consider the legacy of English imperialism. To invoke 1616 is also to recall 1600, the year which saw the establishment of the East India Company. The question of sixteenth- and seventeenth-century English colonial endeavors is one that has preoccupied a generation of early modernists, often in ways informed by their own political investments. Shakespeare's *The Tempest* has been the locus of much of this work, particularly around its resistance to mapping: is the island in Ireland, Bermuda, the Mediterranean, or the Atlantic world (Brotton; Hulme and Sherman; Greenblatt; and many others)? Whose island, indeed, is it (Prospero's, Caliban's, Sycorax's, Ariel's)? The question surrounding precisely where the island is located constitutes part of the colonial fantasy of imperialism, but also serves perhaps to supplant or elide other vectors of enquiry. After all, *The Tempest*'s travelers are returning from Africa, which remains the place of both mystery and possibility in the play. More recently, scholars have considered the longer history of chattel slavery and the triangular trade in relation to *The Tempest* (Chapman), a play that is also deeply implicated in questions of Native sovereignty and dispossession and which speaks to current scholarly directions in early modern critical indigenous studies (Sayet and Stevens; Yim).

Indeed, there are several dates around 1616 that trace the links between race, slavery, and colonialism. 1607 saw the establishment of the colony at Jamestown; in 1618, meanwhile,

James I issued a charter for the Guinea Company. And 1619 marks the year when the first enslaved Africans arrived in Virginia, as I will discuss further later in this chapter. Within this cluster of dates and events, how can we think of Shakespeare—or indeed of any early modern writer—without the influence of the colonial, imperial, and enslaving practices that were shaping the future of English history and politics at that moment?

Despite its limitations, therefore, 1616 is a particularly generative date to think with around this problem: on the one hand, Shakespeare has become the quintessential early modern writer, thanks in part to the outsized influence of the 1623 publication of the First Folio, as I have discussed, and recent and ongoing celebrations and commemorations. Yet precisely the legacy of genius and universality surrounding Shakespeare has come to authorize a kind of "white innocence," as it were. In 2013, researchers uncovered evidence that Shakespeare had been charged with tax evasion and hoarding grain during a famine, producing a widespread sense of shock; as one waggish newspaper headline read, "Bad Bard? Shakespeare profited from famine by hoarding grains." The reaction seemed to confirm the researchers' conclusion that "Shakespeare the grain-hoarder has been redacted from history so that Shakespeare the creative genius could be born."[10] The sense of a playwright who transcends economic and political machinations has taken such a powerful hold that to note the ways in which Shakespeare's works are themselves deeply implicated in constructing or continuing inequities of class, race, and gender is in some quarters considered "overly political." This, then, is the danger of a "universalism" that rests on the convenient occlusion of Shakespeare's complicity in systems of inequity; the fact that these discourses rely upon the assumption that the "problem" of race has been solved, that Shakespeare unifies us out of the material disparities of race, is especially dangerous (Erickson and Hall; Chakravarty "The Renaissance of Race").

The revelation of Shakespeare's grain hoarding, although incidental, is particularly interesting not only because it recovers for us a Shakespeare who was a businessman deeply invested in the political and economic strategies of his time, but because it speaks to the larger social and political conditions that precipitated this action, particularly the contexts of famine. And it reveals the depth of our own investment in a particular ideation of Shakespeare, and what it might reveal about our inheritance of 1616 and all it conveys. The context of famine sheds new light on a play such as *Coriolanus*, widely considered one of Shakespeare's most overtly "political" plays, which stages the human and political devastation of hunger; but it also relates to larger imperial and colonial pressures. As Kim F. Hall argues, in a play such as *The Merchant of Venice*, which stages the shifts of mercantile capitalism, Shakespeare represents the unnamed Moorish woman whom the clown Lancelet has impregnated in a way that gestures to the charge she will pose to the "commonwealth" ("Guess Who's Coming to Dinner?"). Although Lorenzo himself has married the Jewish woman Jessica, he accuses Lancelet not in terms of personal but rather political responsibility: "I shall answer that better to the commonwealth than you can the getting up of the negro's belly: the Moor is with child by you, Lancelet!" (3.5.32–34). Lorenzo's language pointedly situates the health of the "commonwealth," and the political economy of hunger, in direct relation to the larger structures of race and colonialism. But attending to the contexts of food production also anticipates the role that sugar production would play in England's role in the global economy of slavery, a role underscored by Richard Ligon's *A True and Exact History of the Island of Barbados* (1657), published just four decades after Shakespeare's death (Hall, "Culinary Spaces" 170). The connections between the political economy of hunger and famine, the political economy of the household and national order, and the incipient histories of race and slavery are thus tightly interwoven in salient, persistent ways that, as Hall demonstrates, have often been overlooked.

I have noted that news of Shakespeare's unpleasant grain-hoarding activities seemed to compromise popularly received notions of his exceptionalism, which were also implicated in the construction of an emphatically white Shakespeare. It is this exceptionalism, however, that also lies behind the "authorship question," which is in actual fact less a debate than a baseless hypothesis. While the question of "whether Shakespeare wrote his plays" is a frankly ludicrous one, there are real implications entailed by the question: the politics of Shakespeare's exceptionalism. As James Shapiro has explored, the "authorship question" places contemporary understandings of class, education, and status under scrutiny; most people who doubt Shakespeare's authorship do so on the basis that they believe Shakespeare possessed neither the education nor the status to present his plays. Wrapped up in an authorship question, therefore, is actually a compelling insight into the political preconceptions we bring to the early modern period.

The exceptionalism that the so-called "authorship question" engages resonates both within the reception of early modern literature today and within the framework of Shakespeare's cultural moment. Those of us who teach early modern literature often need to begin by contextualizing and qualifying the now outsized importance of Shakespeare's work, explaining the repertory organization of the early modern theater, the contexts for manuscript circulation and print publication, and the larger early modern literary conventions of imitation and adaptation from other classical and European forms and texts. We need to clarify that any engagement with early modern politics must be concerned with the threat of monarchical tyranny, a concern inherited from and negotiated through classical sources and mediated through contemporary political philosophy, as well as the relationship between the court, civic participation, and other forms of government; persuasion and counsel; and the significance of political strategy, often in the invocation of Machiavelli on the one hand or the Vice figure on the other (Armitage, Condren, and Fitzmaurice).[11]

Indeed, even as we often think of the late sixteenth and early seventeenth centuries as charting the rise of the popular commercial theater, the role of the public theater itself as a participant in early modern political economy is a vexed one; what are the implications of the theater as a space for the circulation and dissemination of political thought, as opposed (for instance) to manuscript poetry, or cheap print, or an earlier dramatic history of medieval mystery or cycle plays? Possible answers to this question are many and varied, but they urge us to consider the relationship between genre, text, and politics. We might consider, for instance, the politics of patronage that inform the circulation of verse—including, of course, Shakespeare's sonnets; or the problem of censorship that potentially circumscribed dramatic production. We might recall that some of the most popular of Shakespeare's works were his history plays, which were explicitly concerned with contemporary politics and monarchical legitimacy, but which turned politics into popular entertainment centuries before popular entertainers became politicians. The relationship between literature and politics, in other words, is a matter not merely of content but of form. Just consider the effects produced by the 1611 publication of the King James Version of the Bible, widely used to this day. After the religious turmoil of the sixteenth century—the Reformation and Henry VIII's break from the Church in Rome, the return to Catholicism under Mary I, and the reversion to Protestantism under Edward VI and, more permanently, Elizabeth I—the King James Version marks a turning point in the relationship between "politics," writ large, and the forms of early modern literary and cultural production.

1616/1619

I have suggested thus far that the date of 1616 is a provocative one that acts as a springboard for thinking about larger questions of national as well as global politics, and the longer and larger trajectory of colonialism and slavery. But to speak of 1616 is also to invoke—in tension or conversation—the powerful resonances of 1619, the year when enslaved African people were brought to Virginia.[12] In recent years, the 1619 Project has sought to illuminate the afterlives and legacies of that moment, locating in 1619 the roots of political and economic structures that continue to determine American life today. The 1619 Project comprehends the long arc of 1619's legacy, emphasizing that current political, economic, and social life in the United States is the result of those events of 1619; that the bedrock of America is American slavery, conceptual and material traces of which continue to inform and differentially affect the lived experiences of Black and white people. Indeed, in *The 1619 Project*—the extraordinary compilation of essays, commentary, and poetry created by Nikole Hannah-Jones—Jamelle Bouie's section on "Politics" begins by thinking about the language around electoral fraud and disenfranchisement in the 2016 US election (Hannah-Jones et al). The political effects of 1619, therefore, consist of a material disparity that is as naturalized as it is rendered invisible. To speak of 1616, therefore, is to traffic in some of those naturalized assumptions. For although 1616 and 1619 are proximate not only chronologically but in terms of their long afterlives, they also speak to different political and, more broadly, national senses. 1616 is a quintessentially English moment; 1619 is a foundationally American one. Yet these two histories are far more closely entangled than these easy formulations would have us believe.

These questions and entanglements, as I shall discuss, also speak to the political force of disciplinary conventions and disciplinary mechanisms. At this late date, these include the question of who is allowed to work in the academic field in the first place and who qualifies as an early modernist or a Shakespearean. This is a question with particular urgency for scholars of color, and in a trenchant piece addressing both the place of scholars of color within early modern studies and the study of race, Dennis Britton asks:

> I wonder, does everyone who writes on and researches Shakespeare get to be considered a "Shakespearean"? To what extent does "Shakespeare Studies," and all the power and prestige that is associated with the scholarly study of Shakespeare, fully embrace the study of race in and through Shakespeare? Does the scholarship on race in the early modern period, even when it is primarily on Shakespeare, get to be counted as Shakespeare scholarship?
> ("*Ain't She a Shakespearean*" 224; quoted also in Chakravarty, "The Renaissance of Race")

Britton's queries encapsulate some of the opportunities and tensions in the field of early modern studies: who is welcomed and allowed to work, what it means to work on race, where that study of race has focused.

The study of race in early modern literary studies has seen a renaissance of interest in recent years, as I discussed three years ago in a "state of the field" piece for *English Literary Renaissance* (Chakravarty, "The Renaissance of Race"). But the question of what race actually is persists and the older histories of the field linger. These are questions that are also inflected by disciplinary concerns and trends. For instance, as this chapter has itself reflected, Shakespeare retains outsized importance in early modern literary studies, but this is in part due to the politics of disciplinary formation as well as institutional practice. The diminishing number of secure, tenure-eligible academic positions can be seen in the effects on hiring lines. Fifteen or twenty years ago, it was fairly common to see advertisements for tenure-line early modernists with expertise in Shakespeare or Milton, poetry or drama, sixteenth- or seventeenth-century literature. Today, positions for scholars with expertise across all early modern English literatures and genres, and for scholars specializing in "premodern" (that is to say, medieval and early modern, sometimes pre-1800) literatures are much more common.

This institutional shrinkage both derives from and exacerbates curricular offerings. The politics of cultural capital perpetuates the conventional wisdom that courses on Shakespeare are likely to fill, whereas courses on Renaissance drama or poetry are less so (whether or not this is borne out by pedagogical experience). This also means that scholarship on early modern race, in literary and cultural contexts, has tended to cluster around Shakespeare, in part because such expertise in Shakespeare is necessary to have a job in academia. What would it mean, then, in terms of our understanding of the relationship between early modern politics and literature, or indeed in terms of the political futures of our discipline, to think about early modern literature without Shakespeare? Indeed, what would it mean to move away from a siloed focus on English early modern literary production altogether? The possibilities of transnational enquiry, as scholars such as Barbara Fuchs, Noémie Ndiaye, and Emily Weissbourd have argued, afford us new opportunities to reassess the political import and impact of early modern English literature, and, in particular, to complicate and thicken our understanding of racial formation in this period. In the last few years, too, there have increasingly been calls to move away from periodization markers, so that premodern job calls are now commonly seen in conjunction with an interest in critical race studies, gender or sexuality studies, or ecocriticism.

I want to conclude, therefore, by first considering the state of the field, and then engaging what "early modern race studies" has come to mean over the past generation or so of work. The first question that arises concerns the politics of periodization. As I have noted, period markers and designations (1616, 1619) are themselves politicized, carrying specific political effects. What does it mean, for instance, to think of the early modern period as the Renaissance—or not? In addition to suggesting the teleology of the modern, the term "early modern" perhaps reflects an investment in—or at least a nod to—contemporary political matters and concerns, whereas the "Renaissance" returns us to perhaps an older model of a flourishing period of art and letters, revivifying classical antiquity in service of new literary forms and endeavors. These different designations also speak to broader explorations of temporality, history, and historicity, and the significance of anachronism (de Grazia; Summit and Wallace). But the problem of periodization—the investment in 1616, or indeed 1619, or any other date—must also grapple with the racial politics of periodization. As Ayanna Thompson and I have argued elsewhere (Chakravarty and Thompson), these must include the periodization of race itself. The legacy of 1619 asks us to consider the genealogy of the conceptual and material construction of race, and the histories of our present moment in an originary moment of racial capitalism. Yet respondents to the 1619 Project also point out that 1619 was not, in fact, a founding moment in the history of chattel slavery, and warn us against reifying this important temporal marker (Guasco).

But the larger and more urgent question that 1619 raises pertains to the history of race. The work of periodization, certainly in English literature as a discipline, exerts a disciplining force on the study of race itself. When race is thought to begin in the eighteenth century, as part of a larger interest in scientific enquiry, it renders race a scientific, and implicitly biological, category (Chakravarty and Thompson) rather than a cultural one, and thereby elides the study of racial formation in earlier periods as a function as well as a crucial component of systems of power. For it is important to be clear about what race *is*: not an essential or inherent quality, but a form of power that is both protean and strategic. To think about racial formation, about race-making, is to think about its social, material, and, yes, political form and effects, to think about the structural operations of inequity.

A now established genealogy of scholarship on premodern race has done exactly that, including, notably, the landmark work *Things of Darkness* by Kim F. Hall (1995). Although this was not the first work to consider the implications of race in the early modern period (work by Eldred Jones and Anthony Barthelemy, for instance, had examined the representation of race and especially blackness in early modern literature), it was one of the first to employ what we now understand as a critical race studies perspective, explicitly acknowledging its investments in and intellectual engagement with Black feminism, in particular. The 1990s, indeed, saw major work on early modern race by Hendricks and Parker and Loomba in addition to Hall, even as, in the years that followed, studies of early modern race were accused of being "anachronistic," or overly presentist, or indeed overly political (a leveraging of "politics" again as pejorative rather than productive). As critics queried whether "race" existed in the premodern period (or indeed whether there were people of color at all in early modern England, a revealing conflation of the somatic markers of race with the structures of racial formation), work by Imtiaz Habib methodically and assiduously both recovered the records of early modern black people, and modeled for readers how to gloss and interpret the archival traces of racial formation. At the same time, scholars of premodern race were carefully thinking through the nexus of early modern race and performance (Thompson); race, gender, and sexuality (Little; MacDonald); race and religion (Britton, *Becoming Christian*; Loomba; Kaplan); race and language (Smith); and race and conduct (Akhimie). Scholars such as Jennifer Morgan, meanwhile, carefully and clearly theorized the legacy of 1619 by attending to the centrality of Black women's reproductive and physical labor in the contexts of chattel slavery (*Laboring Women*; "*Partus sequitur ventrem*"; *Reckoning with Slavery*).

In the past decade, there has been even more attention to the strategies by which race is made in the premodern period, but also to the intellectual and ethical resonances of such work. Margo Hendricks' coining of the term "premodern critical race studies" (PCRS) in 2019 was explicitly intended to draw attention to the political valences of this inquiry, and to place it in conversation with the lived experiences of people of color as well as the political stakes of thinking about race (thereby also refusing and reclaiming the pejorative associations of race as "political"). As Hendricks writes,

> My use of PCRS is strategic, intersectional, *and political*. It recognizes the capacity of the analytical gaze to define the premodern as a multiethnic system of competing sovereignties. PCRS not only insists on the "presence" of Black and Indigenous bodies that early modern white supremacy considered disposable, but also demands we focus on the sovereignty stripped from those bodies by settler colonialism.
> *("Coloring the Past, Considerations on Our Future: RaceB4Race" 379, emphasis mine)*

Hendricks' call for a "strategic, intersectional, and political" lens of course reflects an important strand of the history of scholarship on race from Hall onward, which continues to be taken up to think about the role of race and adaptation and appropriation; race and ecocriticism; race and transnational enquiry; and the relationship between critical race studies and critical indigenous studies. These conversations therefore attend to urgent and public-facing political questions, but this is certainly not the first time that early modern studies has demonstrated its commitment to the political implications of its work. We might think, for instance, of the cultural materialist approach of Dollimore and Sinfield; or the feminist and queer scholarship of the 1990s onward, although that work is perhaps also, as I discuss elsewhere, tacitly invested in an assumption of whiteness that lies at its core.

I want to conclude, therefore, by reflecting briefly on the politics of whiteness in early modern studies. The discourse of exceptionalism that is the legacy of 1616 is, as I have already suggested, deeply bound up with the work of whiteness and the construction of white innocence. In proposing this, I draw on the work of Francesca Royster, Kim F. Hall, and Arthur L. Little, Jr., among other scholars who have compellingly argued that we need to excavate and expose the racial formation of whiteness, to render it both denaturalized and visible. But as we do so, and especially as we consider the institutional and disciplinary pressures that both demand and inevitably depoliticize work on race, I want to caution against an impulse to render scholarship on race yet another form of white property. As we consider what it might mean to reflect on the legacy of 1619 in early modern studies, we should also remember the lesson therein: that however contested the date itself might be, 1619 registers a landmark moment in the cultivation of and complicity in white supremacy. As we excavate its legacy, we must remain alert to the temptation to convert it into another form of intellectual currency for material benefit, to render work on race into yet another weapon in the arsenal of white property.

Notes

1. For more information about this tour, see https://www.folger.edu/about-the-first-folio-tour.
2. See, for instance, Erickson and Hall's critique of "universality" as eliding the political urgency of race (Erickson and Hall 5).
3. See Santos for an analysis of the First Folio tour.
4. For more on the various roles that literature plays in matters of political inclusion and exclusion, see this volume's selection of chapters in "Constituting the Polis."
5. See https://www.shakespearesglobe.com/discover/blogs-and-features/2019/09/12/making-sense-of-history/.
6. As Jami Rogers puts it, "The Adjoa Andoh–Lynette Linton *Richard II* was a statement of ownership, not only of Shakespeare but of Britain in 2019" (Rogers 214).
7. For the literary and political relationship between early modern England and the US and UK of the twenty-first century, see John Garrison and Kyle Pivetti's chapter "Reforms and Revolutions" in this volume.
8. *Oxford English Dictionary*, s.v. "politics, *n*.", 2., 2. a.
9. All references to Shakespeare follow *The Norton Shakespeare* and are cited parenthetically in the text; references to *King Lear* are to the Combined Text in that edition.
10. See *USA Today*, 2nd April 2013. https://www.usatoday.com/story/news/world/2013/04/02/-shakespeare-businessman/2046699/.
11. Armitage, Condren, and Fitzmaurice argue in their Introduction to this edited collection that the volume redresses a significant lacuna by being the first book of its kind to place Shakespeare's work in conversation with political thought. In this assessment of previous scholarship, Shakespeare here again appears in a kind of exceptional light.
12. For more on the literary context and legacy of early colonial slavery, see Elizabeth J. West's chapter "Citizenship and Enslavement" in this volume.

Works Cited

Akhimie, Patricia. *Shakespeare and the Cultivation of Difference: Race and Conduct in the Early Modern World*. Routledge, 2018.

Armitage, David, Conal Condren, and Andrew Fitzmaurice, editors. *Shakespeare and Early Modern Political Thought*. Cambridge UP, 2009.

Britton, Dennis Austin. "Ain't She a Shakespearean: Truth, Giovanni, and Shakespeare." *Early Modern Black Diaspora Studies: A Critical Anthology*, edited by Cassander L. Smith, Nicholas R. Jones, and Miles P. Grier. Palgrave Macmillan, 2018, pp. 223–228.

———. *Becoming Christian: Race, Reformation, and Early Modern English Romance*. Fordham UP, 2014.

Brotton, Jerry. "'This Tunis, sir, was Carthage': Contesting Colonialism in *The Tempest*." *Post-Colonial Shakespeares*, edited by Ania Loomba and Martin Orkin. Routledge, 1998, pp. 23–42.

Cawdrey, Robert. *A Table Alphabeticall, or the English Expositor, Containing and Teaching the True Writing and Understanding of Hard Usuall English Words*. London, 1617.

Chakravarty, Urvashi. *Fictions of Consent: Slavery, Servitude, and Free Service in Early Modern England*. U of Pennsylvania P, 2022.

———. "The Renaissance of Race and the Future of Early Modern Race Studies." *English Literary Renaissance*, vol. 50, no. 1, Winter 2020, pp. 17–24.

———, and Ayanna Thompson. "Race and Periodization: Introduction." *New Literary History*, vol. 52, nos. 3/4, 2021, pp. v–xvi.

Chapman, Matthieu. "Red, White, and Black: Shakespeare's *The Tempest* and the Structuring of Racial Antagonisms in Early Modern England and the New World," *Theatre History Studies*, vol. 39, 2020, pp. 7–23.

de Grazia, Margreta. *Four Shakespearean Period Pieces*. U of Chicago P, 2021.

Dollimore, Jonathan, and Alan Sinfield, eds. *Political Shakespeare: New Essays in Cultural Materialism*. Cornell UP, 1985.

Erickson, Peter, and Kim F. Hall. "'A New Scholarly Song': Rereading Early Modern Race." *Shakespeare Quarterly*, vol. 67, no. 1, 2016, pp. 1–13.

Greenblatt, Stephen. *Shakespearean Negotiations: The Circulation of Social Energy in Renaissance England*. U of California P, 1988.

Guasco, Michael. "The Fallacy of 1619: Rethinking the History of Africans in Early America." *Black Perspectives*, September 4, 2017. https://www.aaihs.org/the-fallacy-of-1619-rethinking-the-history-of-africans-in-early-america/

Habib, Imtiaz. *Black Lives in the English Archives, 1500–1677: Imprints of the Invisible*. Routledge, 2008.

Hall, Kim F. "Culinary Spaces, Colonial Spaces: The Gendering of Sugar in the Seventeenth Century." *Feminist Readings of Early Modern Culture: Emerging Subjects*, edited by Valerie Traub, M. Lindsay Kaplan, and Dympna Callaghan. Cambridge UP, 1996, pp. 168–190.

———. "Guess Who's Coming to Dinner? Colonization and Miscegenation in *The Merchant of Venice*." *Renaissance Drama*, vol. 23, 1992, pp. 87–111.

———. *Things of Darkness: Economies of Race and Gender in Early Modern England*. Cornell UP, 1995.

Hannah-Jones, Nikole, Caitlin Roper, Ilena Silverman, and Jake Silverstein, eds. *The 1619 Project: A New Origin Story*. One World, 2021.

Hendricks, Margo. "Coloring the Past, Considerations on Our Future: RaceB4Race," *New Literary History*, vol. 52, nos. 3/4, 2021, pp. 365–384.

———. "Coloring the Past, Rewriting Our Future: RaceB4Race," RaceB4Race Symposium on "Race and Periodization," Folger Shakespeare Library, Washington DC, September 2019.

———, and Patricia Parker, eds. *Women, "Race," and Writing in the Early Modern Period*. Routledge, 1994.

Hulme, Peter, and William H. Sherman, eds. *"The Tempest" and its Travels*. U of Pennsylvania P, 2000.

Kaplan, M. Lindsay. "Jessica's Mother: Medieval Constructions of Jewish Race and Gender in *The Merchant of Venice*," *Shakespeare Quarterly*, vol. 58, no. 1, 2007, pp. 1–30.

Little, Arthur L., Jr., ed. *White People in Shakespeare: Essays on Race, Culture and the Elite*. Arden Shakespeare-Bloomsbury, 2023.

———. *Shakespeare Jungle Fever: National-Imperial Re-Visions of Race, Rape, and Sacrifice*. Stanford UP, 2000.

Loomba, Ania. *Shakespeare, Race, and Colonialism*. Oxford UP, 2002.

MacDonald, Joyce Green. *Women and Race in Early Modern Texts*. Cambridge UP, 2002.

Morgan, Jennifer L. *Laboring Women: Reproduction and Gender in New World Slavery*. U of Pennsylvania P, 2004.

———. "*Partus sequitur ventrem*: Law, Race, and Reproduction in Colonial Slavery," *Small Axe*, vol. 22, no. 1, 2018, pp. 1–17.

———. *Reckoning with Slavery: Gender, Kinship, and Capitalism in the Early Black Atlantic*. Duke UP, 2021.

Rogers, Jami. *British Black and Asian Shakespeareans: Integrating Shakespeare, 1966–2018*. Arden Shakespeare-Bloomsbury, 2022.

Royster, Francesca T. "White-limed Walls: Whiteness and Gothic Extremism in Shakespeare's *Titus Andronicus*," *Shakespeare Quarterly*, vol. 51, no. 4, 2000, pp. 432–455.

Santos, Kathryn Vomero. "¿Shakespeare para todos?" *Shakespeare Quarterly*, vol. 73, no. 1–2 (2022), pp. 49–75.

Sayet, Madeline and Scott Manning Stevens. *Anti-Racist Shakespeare: The Tempest*. Shakespeare and Race series, Shakespeare's Globe. 19 August 2021. https://www.youtube.com/watch?v=Rh8XKqgaSOc.

Shakespeare, William. *The Norton Shakespeare*, edited by Stephen Greenblatt (General Editor), 3rd edition. W. W. Norton, 2016.

Shapiro, James. *Contested Will: Who Wrote Shakespeare?* Simon & Schuster, 2010.

Smith, Ian. *Race and Rhetoric in the Renaissance: Barbarian Errors*. Palgrave Macmillan, 2009.

Summit, Jennifer, and David Wallace. "Rethinking Periodization," *Journal of Medieval and Early Modern Studies*, vol. 37, no. 3, 2007, pp. 447–451.

Thompson, Ayanna. *Passing Strange: Shakespeare, Race, and Contemporary America*. Oxford UP, 2011.

Yim, Laura Lehua. "Reading Hawaiian Shakespeare: Indigenous Residue Haunting Settler Colonial Racism." *Journal of American Studies*, vol. 54, no. 1, 2020, pp. 36–43.

18
ON OR ABOUT 1789

John Owen Havard

In *The Prelude*, William Wordsworth captures the heady experience of living through the 1790s. Describing his time in France at the start of that decade, Wordsworth recalls a scene he encountered when walking in the countryside with a politically idealistic friend:

> we chanced
> One day to meet a hunger-bitten girl
> Who crept along fitting her languid self
> Unto a heifer's motion—by a cord
> Tied to her arm, and picking thus from the lane
> Its sustenance, while the girl with her two hands
> Was busy knitting in a heartless mood
> Of solitude—and at the sight my friend
> In agitation said, "'Tis against that
> Which we are fighting"
>
> (IX.511–20)

When crowds stormed Paris's Bastille prison on July 14, 1789—amidst widespread hunger and food riots—they confronted an infamous symbol of tyranny and repression. "By their actions that day," Colin Jones writes,

> Parisians forced the king to confirm the creation of a single unitary 'national assembly,' and to allow the establishment of a constitutional monarchy grounded in principles to be laid out in the historic Declaration of the Rights of Man and the Citizen

later that year (2–3). The French Revolution saw ideals of political justice, equality, and freedom ring through the air. Revolutionaries like Wordsworth's friend could believe that poverty and inequality were not long for the world. "Bliss was it in that dawn to be alive," Wordsworth wrote, "but to be young was very heaven!" (*1805 Prelude*, X.692–693).

The political hope that breathes through this portion of Wordsworth's poetic autobiography did not last. Revolution descended into factionalism and tyranny. The streets ran red with blood from the guillotine. With the emergence of Napoleon as head of the French empire, the continent fell to military conflict and repressive authoritarianism. Revolutionary hopes radiated out across the world; in England, however, a conservative counter-revolution took hold, bolstered by politician Edmund Burke's fiery denunciation of the revolutionaries, whom he saw as anarchists. France had torn up its venerable past, Burke railed in his *Reflections on the Revolution in France* (1790), in exchange for an empty, lawless future—and England was in danger of doing the same. By contrast with the American Revolution (in which men had used their freedom to create something genuinely new) the French revolutionaries had, in the view of twentieth-century philosopher Hannah Arendt, pursued dangerously hollow ideals unmoored from shared reality. In the name of Jean-Jacques Rousseau's "general will" (*volonté générale*) they had given license to *le peuple*, a monstrous entity both capable of and disposed toward endless violence.

Year 1789 marks a watershed. Historical time had, in some sense, been reset. After France declared a new Republic in 1792, the new French calendar started over from Year One. Year 1789 also marks a rough break between a period when "the people" did not matter to politics and a new historical epoch, in which the demands of the crowd and desires of the common man became inescapable. In some respects, "politics" was redefined. For eighteenth-century men like Burke, politics had to do with an at-times tense accommodation between aristocratic elites and dutiful subjects, inherited constitutions, and more-or-less flexible norms (surrounded by the implicit or explicit threat of peasant revolt and laboring unrest). But the French Republic saw "the people of Paris" emerge as "a political actor in their own right" as groups previously "outside or on the fringes of public life" were "hailed as key elements within a 'popular movement' that expressed itself not simply through armed intervention" but through "political and ideological engagement within expanded parameters of democratic space, now inclusive of newspapers and pamphlets, public meetings and clubs" (Jones 3–4). Whether the ultimate outcome was revolutionary transformation or conservative containment, politics now revolved around what the people wanted their *polis* to be.

We should always be cautious about buying into narratives of inevitable and irreversible progress. Eighteenth-century political debate had already factored in vibrant popular energies, while earlier revolts, such as the English Civil War, included their own calls to level society. The nineteenth century, meanwhile, saw renewed guises of discipline and population control, from patrols of the factory floor to the policing of global colonies—mechanisms of social and individual control that were entirely of a piece, theorist of governance Michel Foucault argued, with the burgeoning "Age of Freedoms." The recognition of popular demands—like the success of "populist" politics—may also be double-edged. To say that the people were now crucial to politics does not tell us whether or how their demands were translated into meaningful change. Appeals to "the people," then and now, do not include everybody; such calls may have as much to do with enshrining a restrictive understanding of the political nation (and propping up the power of divisive and mendacious "populist" leaders) as with giving voice to all those included within its current and future borders. While crowds can claim strength in numbers they can also silence dissident voices. In addition to asking how literature imagines the *demos* and the political system invented in their name, we must continue to ask what demands get heard, which lives matter, and who gets to sing. We may start by asking who gets to feel—and whose feelings get to count.

Cut to the Feeling

The French Revolution created a lot of feelings. Wordsworth's friend pointed to the "hunger-bitten" girl leading—in fact, being led by—her heifer as an example of poverty and neglect.

But his gesture also registers the antagonism ("'Tis against *that*") behind his political commitments. As Jonathan Bate notes in his study *Radical Wordsworth*, he speaks in "agitation," a word that captures the animated emotional states that also shaped Wordsworth's poetry. Taken to a further extreme, scholars including Jon Mee and Steven Goldsmith have shown how affective enthusiasm and excess inspired William Blake's visionary scenes of interpersonal and political emancipation. The energies driving events in and beyond France were grounded in principled conviction and fervent emotion. Burke was himself a theorist of heightened feeling, known for his sometimes hysteria-laden performances in Parliament. The literature of this period calls our attention to still-relevant fault lines: between revolutionary fervor and tranquil contemplation, excitement for the future and attachment to the past. In politics, as in literature, the establishment and its middle-class enablers tried to keep demands for change at bay. But those calls—rattling at the gate, marked on the pulse of the common man, firing the bellies of visionaries and artists—could no longer be ignored.

Decades before the French Revolution, the Bastille prompted the traveling narrator of Laurence Sterne's *A Sentimental Journey* (1768) to criticize France's *ancien régime*. Sterne's book begins by rejecting English superiority: "—They order, said I, this matter better in France—" (3). Watching the chaos unfold in France later in the century, observers like Robert Southey would assert that they ordered matters "better in England." In contrast with this British common sense, Sterne had mobilized a newly free-spirited language of feeling and connection, in parallel with that forged by Jean-Jacques Rousseau and his continental followers. The vogue for displays of "sensibility"—understood as susceptibility to delicate feelings, especially those elicited by disadvantaged groups—acquired growing significance as the eighteenth century continued. Sympathy was increasingly seen as crucial to cementing social bonds. Adam Smith emphasized the regulative role of feeling. The "moral sentiments" permitted us to standardize our responses, in his account, by measuring them against those of an "impartial spectator." But as the decades went on, feeling would acquire new targets and intensities, with politically disruptive effects.

Thomas Jefferson admired the tender feeling dramatized in Sterne's novel, which saw its hero learn to be self-critical, for example, about rejecting a poor Catholic friar's request for charity. Although Jefferson was not self-critical when it came to his own callous, dismissive treatment of Black people, *A Sentimental Journey* had used an encounter with a caged bird to make emotive appeals against human bondage (and Sterne himself entered into a spirited exchange of letters on this topic with Black author Ignatius Sancho). Sensibility, sentiment, and the wider culture of feeling went on to play crucial roles in emerging demands to abolish slavery. As the century continued, enslaved and formerly enslaved persons would increasingly speak for themselves, employing sentiment-infused scenes to play on the sympathies of their imagined readers—with a view to turning them to action. Published in London in 1789, *The Interesting Narrative of the Life of Olaudah Equiano* was not concerned, politically, with the events unfolding in France, but with the inhumanity and barbaric violence of chattel slavery—what its author memorably refers to, in one searing passage, as the "*insanity*" of a system that allows bodies to be purchased and destroyed (125). When he preceded the *Interesting Narrative* with a dedication to the English parliament, Equiano cannily recognized that his voice as a Black author—weaving eloquence and outrage into his beguiling story of global travels and intersecting selves—might play a crucial role in political debate.

Amidst the fallout of events in France, the relationship between politics and feeling became turbocharged. Against a backdrop of popular unrest, radical organizing, threatened uprisings, and even fears of French invasion, properly managed sympathies and transgressive feelings became charged with meaning and urgency. England was overtaken by a wave of paranoia, creating a culture of surveillance and suspicion that viewed even private conversations as potentially treasonous (Barrell). Feeling was especially politicized in relation to sex and gender. Mary Wollstonecraft, a political theorist and philosopher, mounted attacks on inherited institutions, patriarchy, and the cultivation of female weakness. Her controversial personal life saw her pose as her American lover's husband while in Paris during the early 1790s—and travel to Scandinavia with his baby, as recorded in a breathtaking series of published letters. Wollstonecraft's movements were keenly scrutinized at a time when individual conduct and the honoring of tradition were viewed as crucial to social cohesion and political stability. *Sense and Sensibility*, Jane Austen's story of an impulsive, self-indulgent young girl and her prudent, self-denying older sister, was legible a conservative response to the fault lines of the revolutionary moment. In Austen's *Mansfield Park*, the characters perform a scandalous European play from the 1790s. When their overbearing father Sir Thomas unexpectedly returns home, the ensuing spectacle illustrates the dangers of unregulated, self-willed actions. At the same time, the association of Sir Thomas with outmoded patriarchal authority (and with the wealth generated by slave labor on his Antigua plantation) suggests that even Austen, a religious and political conservative, may have been challenging some aspects of the past, albeit in the name of quietist reform rather than radical transformation.

These intangible fears about sedition came together, in Ireland, with threatened invasion from France—and actual violence. The 1798 uprising of the United Irishmen took shape against a backdrop of European revolution and deep-rooted colonial oppression. These legacies were only superficially subdued, after the violence was quelled, with the creation of the United Kingdom of Great Britain and Ireland. The 1800 Act of Union gave rise to richly layered literary explorations of this new composite entity. In Maria Edgeworth's mock-family chronicle, *Castle Rackrent* (1800), an affectionately sentimentalized and comic portrait of Irish manners is coupled with more pointed reflections on the losses and challenges associated with assimilating Ireland into a larger geopolitical whole. In Sydney Owenson's *The Wild Irish Girl* (1806), an English-based landowner's encounter with a poor Irish laborer includes a tableau worthy of *A Sentimental Journey*. But while the confrontation with his distress elicits tender feeling from Owenson's visiting narrator, this scene—like that of the "hunger-bitten girl" and her animal in *The Prelude*—also carries an unmistakable political charge:

> He continued brushing an intrusive tear from his eye; and the next moment whistling a lively air, he advanced to his cow, talked to her in Irish, in a soothing tone, and presenting her such wild flowers and blades of grass as the scanty vegetation of the bog afforded, turned round to me with a smile of self satisfaction and said, "One can better suffer themselves a thousand times over than see one's poor dumb beast want: it is next, please your Honour, to seeing one's child in want—God help him who has witnessed both!"
>
> *(25)*

This poignant scene summons an Ireland of musical beauties and natural wildness. But this is also a scene of sharp-toothed poverty and deprivation. The man's devotion to his "poor dumb beast" recalls the sentimental excesses attributed to Sterne. Yet this familiar outpouring of feeling becomes complicated: the cow becomes a proxy for the peasant's "poor" children while attracting sympathy in its own right as a suffering creature, thus drawing a sharp contrast between this scene of abundant sympathies and the surrounding destitution. For Wordsworth, tying the "hunger-bitten girl" to the "heifer's motion" conveyed the grinding down and wearing out of bodies and lives. While similarly suffused by poverty and hunger, this scene from *The Wild Irish Girl* also presents an enlivened scene that claims the sympathies of the outside observer—including claims that come from animals, the "poor dumb beast[s]," themselves.

In the early nineteenth century, calls to protect the rights of animals saw debates among lawmakers that were infused with sentimental language. The legislative culmination of what Tobias Menely has called "the animal claim" even saw the quotation of Sterne in Parliament. Anti-slavery campaigning would ultimately result in the 1807 Abolition of the Slave Trade Act (although action to end slavery outright would drag on into the 1830s). Writers including the religious poet William Cowper—widely admired, not least by Austen—wrote works contributing to both these causes. But the convergence between sympathy for enslaved people and animals also raises disquieting questions about the alignment of paternalistic sympathies for "grateful slaves" and "lower creatures." In other contexts—as in Ireland, or the plantations of the West Indies—the unleashing of feeling could appear acutely threatening. Whether in sentimental scenes, Romantic poems, revolutionary fantasies, or conservative paranoia, feeling acquired further complexities as revolution and hopes of change gave way to the return of old regimes and new consolidations of power.

Mary Shelley's *Frankenstein*

Mary Shelley's *Frankenstein* (1818) occupies a complicated intersection. Shelley was the daughter of Wollstonecraft—who died shortly after her birth—and the radical philosopher William Godwin. Echoing ideals voiced during Wordsworth's blissful time in France, Godwin's *Enquiry Concerning Political Justice* (1793) elaborated a wholesale program for reform, grounded in man's "perfectibility," which would culminate in the end of all government. But Shelley belonged, with Lord Byron and her eventual husband Percy Shelley, to what has been called the "second generation" of Romantic authors, for whom these hopes had been tarnished by subsequent decades of disappointment. In *Frankenstein*—the product of a ghost-writing competition, when the three writers spent the summer of 1816 in Switzerland—we can see how a work not obviously tied to politics became colored by the initial excitement of 1789 and the disenchantment that followed. In the reception of Shelley's novel, we can, in turn, trace new conceptions of the "body politic" and the rumbling calls for change that continued to be heard even as hopes of revolution faded.

The story of a man who brings an intelligent new creature to life, *Frankenstein* fuses elements of Christian creation and classical myth together with a wholly original story of scientific (and science-fictional) experimentation. Victor Frankenstein's act of quasi-divine genesis echoes like a thunderclap through the novel. His creation—both the act and its outcome—has since become saturated with cultural, political, and philosophical significance. As a result, it can be challenging to differentiate Shelley's original novel from a myth-like story that has, as it were, taken on a life of its own. The geographic plotting of *Frankenstein* offers some moorings for a politically oriented interpretation. As Julia V. Douthwaite has demonstrated, calls to create a "new man" were a central feature of the French Revolution. The idyllic early childhood scenes of *Frankenstein* invoke Godwinian ideals about perfectible minds and natural benevolence, in scenes associated with Rousseau and republicanism. Together, these contexts infuse *Frankenstein* with the idealistic hopes of the 1790s—and may even nestle visions of utopia, like those advanced by Wordsworth and Godwin, within Shelley's novel (Soni 200–220).

Those hopes were, in fiction as in reality, short-lived. Victor's act of creation gives way to catastrophe. The barren scenes that increasingly overshadow the novel, from rain-lashed hillsides to burned-out villages, may recall scenes of post-Napoleonic devastation that

Shelley had witnessed first-hand and thereby point toward an allegorical reading in which revolutionary hopes end in ruin (Randel 465–469, 472). We may also see Victor's creation, more straightforwardly, as setting in motion an unstoppable chain of destruction that parallels certain features of the revolution. That very-human chain of unintended tragic consequences acquires further resonances as the book's geography shifts to Britain, Ireland, and the Americas, folding in archaic colonial legacies and hollow modern freedoms (Havard). Politicized interpretations of Shelley's "monster" gained legs, as it were, during Britain's nineteenth-century Age of Reform. At a time when most men (and all women) were denied the vote, the idea of expanded suffrage could be cast as a dangerous experiment, depicted in visual culture as a grotesque, overpowering monstrosity.

Shelley's narration of the creature's story has poignant significance of its own. Describing himself as a wretch, an outcast, and a slave, he shares features with other marginalized and subordinated groups. In his sentimental attachment to the family of cottagers he discovers soon after awakening to consciousness—themselves exiles from France—he forges possible lines of connection with these similarly unattached fellows. His subsequent vengeance when his affections are spurned may point to the ways that society creates its own monsters (as Percy Shelley, channeling Godwin, argued in his review). In his righteous anger, the creature also may suggest ties with actual enslaved persons. Shelley had read accounts of recent slave revolts; from its inception down to the present, readers have approached the creature's Promethean struggle against his creator and socially constructed "monstrosity" in terms of racial conflict, anti-Black prejudice, and the failures of abolition (Hickman; Matthew).

As Maureen McLane points out, Victor's refusal to help the creature propagate locates their antagonism in relation to debates about population growth (and the boundaries of the human "race"). That circles around feeling: "[b]oth Victor and the monster come to agree [that] sympathy will not cross the species barrier" (976). *Frankenstein* presents us with buried utopianism, incipient anti-democratic conservatism, and a trail of unintended destruction. The novel can be read as a "technophobic allegory" and "a critique of masculinist presumption" but also as "a critique of the anthropological and anthropomorphic foundations of the categories 'human' and 'humanities'" (McLane 961–962). A story of rejection and abjection, the novel also features unyielding antagonism and resistance. When it comes to the polyvalent political significance of what Shelley termed her "hideous progeny," the best cue may come in dialogue added to the screen version: "It's alive."

False Flags? The Rise and Fall of Political Hope

In May 1797, the Indian ruler Tipu Sultan hoisted the new French flag "to the sound of artillery and musketry." The assembled company "swore hatred of all kings, except Tipu Sultan, the Victorious, the Ally of the Republic of France, to make war on tyrants and to love toward the motherland" (Dalrymple 339). A few years earlier, the dazzling Black general Toussaint Louverture raised the French tricolor in Haiti, newly founded by emancipated people of color, to celebrate continued military victories (Hazareesingh 65). During the early decades of the nineteenth century in England, industrial protestors and reformist candidates wrapped themselves in the French flag to celebrate the Second French Revolution as they agitated for change nearer home. The 1830 overthrow of the restored Bourbon monarchy echoed, in turn, through the subsequent century, from the continent-wide revolutions of 1848 to the founding of the Paris commune.

Yet the legacy enshrined in the flag of the new French republic was a mixed one. In theory, the tricolor stood for the rejection of tyranny, in the name of revolutionary ideals. But as

Frankenstein lets us begin to see, the events set in motion in 1789 were a mixed bag: entailing war and bloodshed, continued repression and imperial expansion in addition to hopes of a freshly dawning age for mankind. The founding of Haiti saw formerly enslaved persons improvise new kinds of freedom. But within the wider world system (in which the West Indies were inescapably bound) revolutionary hopes gave way to strongman leadership and economic imperialism. In Europe, the wave of revolutions over subsequent decades shaped modern nations. But despotism reappeared in other guises, at home and abroad. India's Tipu Sultan was the "implacable and relentless enemy of an encroaching British Empire." But the flourish of revolution marked by his raising of the French flag was short-lived, as hundreds of millions came under effective European control.

Perhaps surprisingly, we find a guide to these developments in Lord Byron, celebrity poet and notorious bad boy. After scandalizing London society with his affairs, Byron exiled himself to Europe. In 1818, he embarked on a new poem: *Don Juan*. The story of the notorious Spanish seducer, subject of an opera by Mozart, might not seem like promising source material for a commentary on the political age. But while Byron would have great fun with Juan's misbegotten trail of seductions, his poem would end up with bigger fish to fry. "I want a hero," that poem began, with grandly epic (or mock-epic) ambition (I.1). But as Byron worked on his draft—incorporating lengthy digressions that would become one of the poem's hallmarks—he used this stated "want," at once a desire and an absence, to reflect on the political losses of recent decades.

After calling for "a hero," Byron introduced an encyclopedic catalogue of names, beginning with celebrated eighteenth-century military leaders and culminating with the 1815 victory of the Duke of Wellington over Napoleon at the Battle of Waterloo. Byron moved on to France, starting with Buonaparte and Dumourier ("in the Moniteur and Courier" [I.16]) and concluded his unspooling list ("Barnave, Brissot, Condorcet, Mirabeau..." [I.17]) with a flippant allusion to the many more men "of the military set" he might include, who were "[e]xceedingly remarkable at times,/But not at all adapted to my rhymes" (I.22–24). These stanzas—added, concertina-like, between the stanzas of the original draft—made a serious point. Byron pointed to the hardening of British power following decades of bloodshed and conquest (including under the boot of Wellington's brother, in British-controlled India). But just as telling are the names *not* included here. The poet was acutely aware of ongoing revolution and democratic mobilization, traveling to Greece at the onset of the War of Independence (where he lost his life) and naming his sailboat for Simón Bolívar, the "liberator" of Spanish America. But when he came to look back on the decades since 1789, Byron focused on militarism and conservative reaction.

In his poem "England in 1819," Percy Shelley wrote of an "old, mad, blind, despised, and dying King." When George III finally expired the following year, Byron's poem on the occasion painted his own bleak picture of war, repression, and ascendant "Toryism," mocking the king's passing with ironic calls of "God Save the King" (and having the late monarch meet Satan at the gates of Hell). In a later canto of *Don Juan*, he pointed to brewing currents of anti-monarchical unrest, at home and abroad:

> But never mind;—'God save the king!' and kings!
> For if *he* don't, I doubt if *men* will longer—
> I think I hear a little bird, who sings
> The people by and bye will be the stronger:
> The veriest jade will wince whose harness wrings

> So much into the raw as quite to wrong her
> Beyond the rules of posting,—and the Mob
> At last fall sick of imitating Job
>
> (VIII.393–400)

Byron (informed by "a little bird, who sings") foresaw the people gaining their voice here. The people, "sick of imitating" the much-afflicted Job of the Old Testament, appear here as a mistreated horse, whose harness "wrings" her flesh. Byron was, as a rule, skeptical about the "rabble." But rather than a dangerous, overgrown monstrosity, he cast the "Mob" here as a diminutive David taking on a giant Goliath, the renovated English state:

> At first it grumbles, then it swears, and then,
> Like David, flings smooth pebbles 'gainst a giant;
> At last it takes to weapons such as men
> Snatch when despair makes human hearts less pliant.
> Then comes 'the tug of war;'—'twill come again,
> I rather doubt; and I would fain say 'fie on 't,'
> If I had not perceived that revolution
> Alone can save the earth from hell's pollution
>
> (VIII. 400–407)

The speaker here would rather ("fain") spurn popular resistance, viewing growing mobilization from an aloof remove. The "tug of war" staged in the poet's mind cuts against the hardening of purpose described here: where the people grow defiant in their "despair," his heart, by implication, remains "pliant" in its sympathies. But the final couplet, closing the deal, makes clear where he falls: choosing a "revolution" over the noxious, corrupted "pollution" of a dying regime.

Don Juan appeared when radical and reformist politics in England were in the doldrums. Aside from the leech-like king, Percy Shelley turned his attention to recent violence enacted on the body, in both senses, of the people. In August, 1819, sword-wielding troops on horseback descended upon a crowd of pro-reform protestors, hacking and trampling several to death and injuring hundreds more. That event was termed the "Peterloo" massacre, a gruesome allusion to Waterloo: the military might Britain had shown over its foreign rivals, that moniker implied, had been turned, as militarized state violence, against its own subjects. In Percy Shelley's *Mask of Anarchy*, that violence occasions a renewed assertion of political agency. As with Byron's late writings, the poem was written from abroad. Shelley had vague hopes of contributing to an inspirational collection of poetic songs. The poem was not published for a decade, rendering it impractical as a timely contribution to political debate; Amanda Jo Goldstein has shown, however, the ways in which *The Mask of Anarchy* seeks to reimagine the very terms of political agency. In the figure of a vividly imagined, allegorical "Shape," Shelley presents a "changed image of political collectivity—even of 'the people'—massive, fragile, aggrieved, in armor, in pieces, love-crowned." The elusive poetic figures and complex materialist agencies imagined by Shelley's poem thereby capture "a change in the national atmosphere," a "political feeling" that Shelley elsewhere called "a sentiment of the necessity of change" (Goldstein 178). In acknowledgment of the actual political struggle and imaginative possibilities condensed in *The Mask of Anarchy*, Jeremy Corbyn's Labour Party took its slogan from Shelley's poem: "ye are many, they are few."

Wordsworth retreated into poetry following his revolutionary disappointment. Shelley viewed this as a great betrayal. "In honoured poverty thy voice did weave/Songs consecrate to truth and liberty," he wrote in his sonnet "To Wordsworth." In rehabilitating political failure as poetic insight, Wordsworth's mourning included the "loss" of himself—and left his followers to "grieve." But while Shelley (no stranger to poeticized self-indulgence) was lamenting, radicals and reformers were remobilizing. The violence of 1819 was taken up in popular memory as the inspiration for renewed reformist activity, and the potential energy with which that date was imbued in its moment came together with the painstaking, recursive work of political organization. Year 1832 marked a further milestone when, just two years after English radicals and industrial protesters wrapped themselves in the French flag, came passage of the Reform Act. The expansion of suffrage and redrawing of the electoral map marked an important progressive victory. But that ultimately limited legislation, along with the similarly imperfect 1833 Slavery Abolition Act, also marked the transition into a new age: when unruly masses faced down a renovated political elite against a backdrop of imperial expansion, free trade, and liberal governance.

Do You Hear the People Sing?

The contemporary events in France celebrated by English radicals in the lead up to Reform provide the backdrop to Victor Hugo's epic novel *Les Misérables* (1862). Nineteenth-century historical fiction made lines of political succession inseparable from narratives about progress, converting political change into social development. Like Dickens's *Oliver Twist* (1838), Hugo's novel also brings together a teeming canvas populated by orphans, factory owners, uncaring authorities, hypocritical institutions, a criminal underworld, and the police. *Les Misérables* squarely belongs to a new literary age, in which fictional forms took up social problems. And as with the story of Dickens's cherubic orphan, *Les Misérables* has lived on in popular culture in ways that mark a sharp break with Wordsworth's "hunger-bitten girl" or Hugo's poor Fantine: the English-language musical version has been running continuously in London's West End since 1985, while serial-killing investment banker Patrick Bateman is portrayed as a fan of *Les Misérables* in Bret Easton Ellis' *American Psycho* (1991). In the film adaptation of Ellis' controversial novel (2000), the reflection of the psychopathic Wall Street trader in the musical poster, which shows a forgotten orphan girl, makes a clear satirical point: the colors of the French flag make a chromatic connection with the legacies of 1789 and 1830, but in Margaret Thatcher and Ronald Reagan's world of 1980s inequality and excess, *Les Miz* has become capitalism-friendly kitsch.

From Brooklyn to Mumbai, wealth disparities have exploded in recent decades. The flashy consumerism satirized in *American Psycho* has given way to an ever-more sleek world of tech companies, cellular networks, and cryptocurrency, amidst the continued reshaping of the urban environment by gentrification. The face of the orphan girl on the poster in Patrick Bateman's bathroom now appears like even more of a cruel joke (one that finds a twisted mirror in the protagonist of Aravind Adiga's 2008 novel *White Tiger*, an Indian servant whose grimaced smile turns vengefully on his master). Yet *Les Misérables* also remains popular with the masses. As the musical has endured and adapted, through decades of exploding wealth and enforced austerity, its lines on hearing the people sing come to resonate with renewed force. When blasted by a massive chorus under an enormous tricolor flag, the musical (whether sung with a gruff Northern English accent or in Spanish or Korean) powerfully channels the hope that continues to imbue appeals to *le people*. When asked, centuries later, about the consequences of the French Revolution, one historian quipped that it was too soon to tell. But some things remain certain. After 1789, the drumbeat of change, felt on the pulse of the common man, could no longer be ignored.

Works Cited

Arendt, Hannah. *On Revolution*. 1963. Penguin, 2006.
Barrell, John. *The Spirit of Despotism: Invasions of Privacy in the 1790s*. Oxford UP, 2006.
Bate, Jonathan. *Radical Wordsworth*. Yale UP, 2020.
Byron, George Gordon, Lord. *Complete Poetical Works, Vol. 5: Don Juan*. Edited by Jerome J. McGann. Oxford UP, 1986.
Dalrymple, William. *The Anarchy: The East India Company, Corporate Violence, and the Pillage of an Empire*. Bloomsbury, 2019.
Douthwaite, Julia V. *The Frankenstein of 1790 and Other Lost Chapters from Revolutionary France*. U of Chicago P, 2012.
Equiano, Olaudah, 1745–1797. *The Interesting Narrative of the Life of Olaudah Equiano*. 1789. Broadview Press, 2004.
Goldsmith, Steven. *Blake's Agitation: Criticism and the Emotions*. Johns Hopkins UP, 2013.
Goldstein, Amanda Jo. *Sweet Science: Romantic Materialism and the New Logics of Life*. U of Chicago P, 2017.
Havard, John Owen. "What Freedom? *Frankenstein*, Anti-Occidentalism, and English Liberty." *Nineteenth-Century Literature*, vol. 74, no. 3, 2019, pp. 305–331.
Hazareesingh, Sudhir. *Black Spartacus: The Epic Life of Toussaint Louverture*. Macmillan, 2020.
Hickman, Jared. *Black Prometheus: Race and Radicalism in the Age of Atlantic Slavery*. Oxford UP, 2017.
Jones, Colin. *The Fall of Robespierre: 24 Hours in Revolutionary Paris*. Oxford UP, 2021.
Matthew, Patricia A. "A daemon whom I had myself created": Race, *Frankenstein*, and Monstering." *Frankenstein in Theory: A Critical Anatomy*, edited by Orrin N. C. Wang. Bloomsbury, 2020, pp. 173–183.
McLane, Maureen. "Literate Species: Populations, 'Humanities,' and *Frankenstein*." *ELH* 63 (1996), pp. 959–988.
Menely, Tobias. *The Animal Claim: Sensibility and the Creaturely Voice*. U of Chicago P, 2015.
Owenson, Sydney (Lady Morgan). *The Wild Irish Girl: A National Tale*. Oxford UP, 2008.
Randel, Fred V. "The Political Geography of Horror in Mary Shelley's *Frankenstein*." *ELH*, vol. 70, no. 2, 2003, pp. 465–491.
Soni, Vivasvan. "The Utopias of *Frankenstein*." *Frankenstein in Theory: A Critical Anatomy*, edited by Orrin N. C. Wang. Bloomsbury, 2020.
Sterne, Laurence. *A Sentimental Journey and Other Writings*. 1768. Edited by Ian Jack and Tim Parnell. Oxford UP, 2003.
Wordsworth, William. *The Prelude 1799, 1805, 1850*. Edited by M.H. Abrams and Stephen Gill. Norton, 1979.

19
ON OR ABOUT 1885
Padma Rangarajan

Following the so-called Age of Equipoise and Before the decadence of the *fin de siècle*, Britain in the 1880s was a period between periods, when Victorian mores were in the process of unraveling. A surge of violent Irish nationalism beginning in 1880 coincided with anarchism's spread from the continent to Britain. Thanks to Alfred Nobel's patent in 1876 for gelignite, terrorism's iconic mode—the detonation of bombs in urban areas—was inaugurated. Crucially, for this essay, the 1880s also saw the birth of "constructivist imperialism"; what E. H. H. Green has defined as a deliberate effort to encourage a "genuine imperial consciousness," that would counter the capricious, atomistic nature of extant imperial policy (353).

In the literary world, the interstitial nature of the 1880s was reflected in the fracturing of the dominant form of the triple-decker novel into more uncertain and supple narrative styles that presaged modernist transformations on the horizon. The advent of New Journalism, with its sensationalism and blurring of news and entertainment, was ideally suited to capitalizing on and refracting terrorism's performative spectacularity. In fiction, the response to terrorism was reflected in a new genre of so-called "dynamite novels" and stories, which wedded melodramatic invasion fantasies and elaborate terrorist plots to a distinctly Victorian gothicism. The majority of these dynamite novels tended to the propagandistic, and were generally uninterested in exploring the nuances of political violence. Correspondingly, although how terrorists committed acts of violence was a tremendous fascination—hence the coining of the new appellation, "dynamitard," by the press—their identities and political motivations were opacified. Newspapers and fictional accounts often conflated the far more prevalent problem of Fenian terrorism with relatively peaceful continental anarchism (Shpayer-Makov, 490). The purpose of this may have been to neutralize the real threat of terror, which was a tactic that, as David Simpson notes, Edmund Burke had employed almost a century before in *Reflections on the Revolution in France* (1790), which determinedly withheld from the Jacobin state the power of terror he had so eloquently described in his *Enquiry… on the Sublime* (171). Practically speaking, ideologically fuzzy continental anarchism was less complicated for British audiences than the question of Irish self-rule, a heated debate which had grown even more volatile following Charles Parnell's election as chairman of the Irish Home Rule group in Parliament in 1880. Historical phenomena do not slot neatly into decades-long boxes, but, in this case, the call for a self-conscious imperial ethos and its intersection with new technologies (of violence, of media) and with long-standing political grievances indicates a crucial moment of coalescence.

Terrorism studies has consistently associated modern terrorism with this period, the last decades of the nineteenth century, precisely because of the intersection of new ideologies with new technologies. But this focus on the newness and unprecedentedness of terrorism is a key component of what Simpson describes as "terror talk": that is, the displacement of critical understanding which, when deployed by the state, describes a condition of unique vulnerability demanding an equally unique deployment of reactive violence (x–xii). Here, I argue that literary responses to the explosion of political terror in Britain in the 1880s illuminate a crucial inflection point in a longer and often occluded history of engagements, real and fictional, with colonial violence.

The discourse of terrorism is itself a phenomenon of the nineteenth century; when over time the word, coined in 1794 as a denunciation of Jacobin terror, became slowly but steadily freighted with cultural and political baggage. While literature of terror may be old and ubiquitous, with a history in the West that stretches back to antiquity, literature of "terrorism" is a subtly different thing. When terror becomes explicitly politicized—when it takes on an ideological burden as terror*ism*—the aesthetic valence of terror shifts in tandem. Thereafter, we may argue that there exists a tension between terror as aesthetic and terrorism as the political deployment of an aesthetic mode. As Simpson queries, "The problem with using the word *terror* is that it is often unclear or ambiguous in both kind and degree: is it political or aesthetic, and in whose sense political and aesthetic?" (137).

When the French Revolution birthed "terrorism," it was understood as illegitimate violence perpetrated by the state. But this does not account for the word's transformation, over time, to its present understanding of something anti-state and often implicitly foreign. In Britain, for example, "terrorism" was almost immediately adopted to reference illegitimate state and anti-state violence. Only a few years after word is first used by the French press, we can find examples of both supporters of Irish nationalism and their opponents accusing the other side of terrorism.[1] Thereafter, "terrorism" in English mostly retained a Jacobinical flavor while slowly extending to other modes of political violence. This transformation was neither linear nor invariable, but circuitous and elusive, if ultimately relentless. Even approaching the middle of the century, "terrorism" had the flavor of an outlandish, linguistic novelty. In 1839, for example, a Chartist newspaper published a short satirical play in which the liberal statesman Lord Brougham is administered an emetic to make him vomit ridiculous, "Benthamite" phrases like "bug-like-semi-spuriousness," and "brandishing terrorists." As "terrorism" slowly worked its way into usage, other words and neologisms like "thug," "fanatic," and "incendiary" became crucial semantic synonyms for illegitimate, anti-state violence. Meanwhile, the fact that early instances of "terrorism"'s semantic creep reference Ireland is not mere happenstance; they are rather an indication of the extent to which imperialism is inextricable from any understanding of terrorism's evolving signification.

Terrorism and the Colony

Terrorism's impact on contemporary fiction was nearly simultaneous with the word's coining. In particular, the rise of gothic fiction was considered a direct result of the pervasive influence of the Revolution's violent excess. Joseph Crawford's *Gothic Fiction and the Invention of Terrorism* (2014) traces a bidirectional movement whereby, as the Revolution created the gothic, the gothic created the mythos of the Revolution. The anonymous author of a

1797 article on "Terrorist Novel Writing" bemoans a sudden uptick in novels featuring "old gloomy castles...spectres, apparitions, ghosts, and dead man's bones," sarcastically insisting, in a deliberate invocation of the 5 September 1793 Convention, that contemporary authors have "made *terror the order of the day*!" (227). This article isn't a lament of the politicization of fiction, but it clearly disapproves of the extent to which contemporary politics had been transmogrified into the aesthetic register of the gothic. "Terrorist novels" in the 1790s are not political novels strictly speaking, but novels that demonstrate the way in which the aesthetic of terror was now transformed in the aftermath of the Revolution.

Robert Maniquis observes that, given their sympathy for the suffering of the French people, "Robespierre and the Terror were ... repulsive but explainable" for many English writers in the 1790s (373). It is important to note, though, that the French Revolution, while considered an unprecedented historical rupture, was also used to contextualize change occurring globally and on a tremendous scale. In the same year that *terrorisme* entered the French lexicon, Edmund Burke identified a nefarious dyad of modernity, "Indianism and Jacobinism," to describe what he saw as the dawning of an unprecedented era of spectacular and illegitimate violence in which colonial rapacity and domestic revolution were conceptually and materially intertwined ("Correspondence," 553). Maniquis phrases the relationship in a slightly different way when he observes that the new aesthetic imagination occasioned by the Terror and the "moral voice of poetry" would be drowned "in a vast, imperial noise" in its infancy (373). Either way, the French Revolution and its new assertion of the role of violence in establishing popular sovereignty need to be considered in the context of the decisive expansion of imperial power premised on the sovereign right to violence.

In his essay "The Colony: Its Guilty Secret and its Accursed Share," Achille Mbembe identifies the two principal levers of colonization as "the administration of terror and the management of seduction [fantasy]...always spectacular and ceremonial" (32). Mbembe defines these as parallel tracks, but terrorism (both state-sponsored and anti-state) is equally the intersection of terror and fantasy, premised as it is on futurity and the possibility of utopia, or, as Mbembe notes in the colonial sphere, the attempt by the "colonial potentate" to "create an unsullied new world upon the debris of the one he first found there" (32). The act of utopic worldcreation as it intersects with the colony as the space of emergency reveals that colonial state terror is a future without an end. Very often, the colony as a space of exception turns emergency from a temporary measure into a condition of existence. We see this in colonial India in the 1830s, for example, when British administrators cited the unprecedented nature of *thagi* as a justification for the extraordinary legal overreach of the Anti-Thuggee Campaign.[2] The essential lawlessness of *thagi* was, ultimately, a microcosmic example of the general lawlessness of the subcontinent: because colonies were always on the brink of lapsing into ungovernability, they required a governance that extended beyond the space of the law. Thus, the laws enacted to quell *thagi* were transformed into an infinitely expandable series of laws targeting a broad array of criminalized native identities.

Colonial Terrorism in Fiction

In the decades immediately following the Jacobin Terror, we find a robust series of reflections on the ramifications of colonial terror produced by Irish writers. Again, it was in the Irish context that the word "terrorism" as a neologism in English began to unmoor from its Jacobin signification. In the wake of the Revolution, the English feared that Irish nationalists and Jacobins would find common cause, a fear that was amply borne out by the two attempts (first in 1796, then again in 1798) to land French soldiers on Irish soil to aid the United Irishmen in extirpating British troops. Ireland's long colonial history and its vexed status within Britain's expanding empire meant that even literature that dealt with contemporary politics almost inevitably drew on the longer history of the repressive anti-Catholic Penal Laws and the dispossession of Irish Catholics at the hands of the Anglo-Irish Ascendency class. One such novel is Sydney Owenson, Lady Morgan's *The O'Briens and the O'Flahertys* (1827), one of the earliest novels that I have been able to locate that not only uses but actively interrogates the concept of "terrorism."[3] The novel traces the (ultimately futile) attempts of a disinherited Irish patriot to spark a principled nationalist movement in Ireland. But, as the novel meticulously tracks, idealism is no match for the centuries of oppression that the novel registers as psychological, environmental, and architectural strata, resulting in the failure of the '98 Rebellion. Morgan's novel mocks the idea that terrorist acts are fundamentally anti-state, demonstrating instead how invocations of terrorism were used to obscure Ireland's long history of colonial trauma.

Morgan was a popular, if controversial, writer, and she was well known for writing novels that overtly critiqued state power; but even authors far less incendiary than Morgan took up the subject of Irish terror. Maria Edgeworth's short story "Limerick Gloves" (1814) is an early and inverse example of a sub-genre—terrorist ridicule literature—that would become more common in the last decades of the century. While these later fictions stressed the impotence or empty ideology of would-be terrorists, Edgeworth uses wry humor to address the automatic association of the Irish with illegitimate violence. She gently mocks the small-mindedness of a provincial English village and its people who assume, without pretext or evidence, that the resident Irish glover plans to blow up the local cathedral. By the story's conclusion, it is revealed that the only truly mendacious character in the village is not the Irish glover but a roaming "gypsy" (who is himself an Englishman in disguise and thus a double fraud), while the holes in the cathedral that led to the suspicion of terrorism are the result of local mismanagement and not sinister plots.

In the periodical press, "terrorism" largely retained its associations with Jacobinism until the 1830s, when it was regularly applied in reference to Irish nationalism and Catholicism. This shift is anticipated by Thomas Moore's *Memoirs of Captain Rock* (1824), which uses the Irish agrarian-insurgent Rockite Rebellion of the early 1820s—which was explicitly referenced by some English contemporaries as a "system of terror"—to construct a genealogical history of Ireland in which responsibility for violence falls squarely on the occupying British and the Anglo-Irish Ascendency. If, as Stephen Morton argues, colonial states of emergency mobilized "an army of tropes and narratives to…obfuscate the terror and violence of colonial sovereignty," Moore deploys the personal intimacy of memoir to shift the locus of terror back to the state (10).

As this brief sampling indicates, the ongoing question of Irish self-rule produced a correspondingly complex literary engagement with the relationship between illegitimate violence and colonial terror. Ireland, as a colony both exceptionally violent and ultimately vanquished, was often contrasted to Scotland, the colony that managed to both successfully resist English incursions and integrate into the colonial metropole.[4] It is something of a surprise, then, to find a clutch of novels written in the second and third decades of the century that revive the uncomfortable and seemingly long-settled history of Scottish resistance to English domination. These novels do not address what would seem like an easy (if only aurally) parallel to Jacobin terror—the 1745 Jacobite rebellion—but focus instead on the thornier history of the Covenanters (radical Scottish Presbyterians) and their persecution during the so-called "Killing Times" of the late seventeenth century. The Covenantors' vision of a triadic religious polity (God, monarch, covenanted) is markedly different from Jacobinism's secular, centralized popular sovereignty, but it's worth remembering Burke's warning in *Reflections on the Revolution in France* that the current radical spirit was producing a fanatical fervor not seen in England since "the days of our solemn league and covenant" (13). For Burke, the Killing Times are an awkward historical codicil to his reading of the Glorious Revolution as a proleptic refutation of the Terror and its violence.

The immediate cause for the sudden surge in Covenanting novels, however, was not Edmund Burke but the publication of Walter Scott's *Old Mortality* (1816). Echoing the model he established with *Waverley* (1814), *Old Mortality* traces its protagonist's initial affiliation with and ultimate rejection of rebellious, atavistic historical forces. Scott's Covenanters are ideological extremists, whose model of sovereignty is premised, as Amy Witherbee argues, on an older model of divine sovereignty that ties text to body (martyrdom), while Scott endorses a modern idea of sovereignty tied to land and constitution (362). Throughout the novel, Scott depicts Covenanting as a historical moment overwritten by the modern nation-state. Thus, the titular "Old Mortality" who occupies the novel's fictional paratext is the last caretaker of Covenanting martyrs' neglected graves.

But this history of radical religious rebellion was not as entombed as Scott supposed; not only did the novel spark a serious debate in the Scottish periodical press over the role of historical fiction, several authors also published novels critiquing Scott's historical vision (Ferris, 142). Scott had downplayed Scotland's colonial status in *Old Mortality*, but his responders did not. John Galt's *Ringhan Gilhaize* (1823), for example, bemoans the violent excesses of Covenanting history, but it also stresses the trauma of English colonial rapacity. In his fictional accounting of three generations of a Covenanting family, Galt threads a careful needle as he attempts to condemn the violence of the Covenanting rebellion but not its founding principles. The novel foregrounds British violence is the primary cause of the eponymous Ringan's devolution into an incendiary and assassin, and relentlessly tracks the dispossession that drives his madness. James Hogg's *The Brownie of Bodsbeck* (1818), which covers the end of the Killing Times, takes a different tack. Hogg's story of a family who assists an outlaw band of Covenanters relies on an explicitly antimodern recuperation of the fantastical: folktales, superstitions, and legend are all presented as alternatives to Enlightenment rationalism and the exceptional cruelty of the English state. The yoking together of political and religious motivations in these fictions is particularly noteworthy. Although Catholicism plays a crucial, if uneasy, role in the Irish fiction mentioned above (all penned Protestant authors), these Scottish novels squarely engage the question of religious fanaticism and its relationship to civil society, demonstrating how the two "are born together and grow up together, each one unthinkable without the other" ("Fanaticism and Enlightenment," 62).

The political implications of fanaticism take an important turn in a novel that was primarily responsible for introducing the word, "thug" into the English lexicon. Philip Meadows Taylor's wildly popular *Confessions of a Thug* (1839), in which a captured *thug* relates his life story to a colonial interrogator, offers a dialectical representation of holy terror. On the one hand, *thagi* is represented in the novel as embedded in India's systems of religion and caste, so that the British administration in India must act outside the bounds of the law to counter an ancient and engrained system. On the other hand, *thagi* is also described as a fraternal organization that supersedes barriers of religion and caste, serving as a kind of proto-national comradeship that was seen as the exclusive provenance of the West. *Thagi* is presented as an unstoppable force that necessitates a new and infinitely expandable rule of law. As Meadows's captured *thug* boasts to his confessor: "Thuggee, capable of exciting the mind so strongly, will not, cannot be annihilated!" an improbable boast that the novel itself ends up confirming (15).

Terrorism and Genre

It is worth noting that many of the fictions mentioned above do not fit tidily into the generic confines of the novel, but perch uneasily on its borders. Hogg's novels are more properly "national tales," a genre that was conceived as a recuperative medium for national cultures under threat of extinction from a colonizing modernity. Galt did not consider *Ringan Gailhaize* a novel at all, categorizing it instead as a "theoretical history" that eschewed romance in favor of probability (Duncan, 219). These qualified forms of the novel form an alternative literary genealogy that is occluded in traditional accounts of the rise of the novel. Srinivas Aravamudan argues that transcultural fictions in the eighteenth and early nineteenth centuries acted for the novel much in the way that the "Orient" and colonized spaces did for the metropole: as an aesthetic mode against which domestic realism could define and authenticate itself (8). Significantly, Aravamudan notes that genres like the oriental tale "serve a critical function in relation to the public culture of the Enlightenment and political modernity" (17), an initially puzzling assertion given the genre's association with ahistorical fantasy and fabular escapism. In fact, the oriental tale, a genre inspired by Antoine Galland's groundbreaking 1704 translation of *One Thousand and One Nights*, quickly developed a distinct mode of political and social critique.

Although coterminal with the rise of the novel, the oriental tale was, for some considerable time, the more popular of the two genres; as late as 1813, Byron would recommend that his friend, the poet Thomas Moore, "stick to the East" because "the North, South, and West, have all been exhausted" and "the public are orientalising" (101). And while the oriental tale, beginning with Montesquieu's *Lettres Persanes* (1721), established itself as a vehicle for witty social and political critique, by the time Byron published his own series of oriental tales beginning in 1813, this gentility was on the cusp of evolving into something more incendiary. In the dedicatory letter of his second tale, *The Corsair* (1814), Byron charged Moore with the task of developing Moore's as yet-unwritten eastern tale into a vehicle for exposing the traumas of British imperialism, a project Byron thought would augment the somewhat circuitous critique of imperialism embedded in his own, earlier oriental tale, *The Giaour* (1813).

The Corsair's dedication specifically encourages Moore to draw upon the East, as only there may "the wrongs of your own country, the magnificent and fiery spirit of her sons, the beauty and feeling of her daughters...be found," forging an aesthetic and political connection in which Ireland and the East become interchangeable (vi). With the publication of *Lalla Rookh* (1817) four years later, Moore took Byron's plan a step further, creating a double allegory whereby the East alternately represents the excesses of Jacobinism and the terror of English colonialism in Ireland, yoking together opposing forms of illegitimate state violence. But thanks to Moore's decision to veil its politics behind fantastic orientalist exotica, *Lalla Rookh* became a spectacular literary success despite, and not because of, its anticolonial message. Decades later, one can see the faded political and literary purchase of the oriental tale in a Victorian commentator's observation that, while an "under-current of political allegory, with constant reference to the woes of Ireland" is out of place in "an Oriental romance" like *Lalla Rookh*, such sentiment at least serves to heighten the text's "human interest" (Garnett, 19). Further, *Lalla Rookh*'s intertwining of Irish and Oriental histories is a potent example of Celtic Orientalism, a historical, cultural, and quasi-racial affiliation that was exploited by Irish and Indian nationalists beginning in the late nineteenth century, as well as by their detractors. When, in 1909, the nationalist Vinayak Savarkar was arrested after the assassination of William Curzon Wylie, the plot to free him was assisted by Irish republican revolutionaries. Inversely, the 1887 poem "A word with the Fenian brotherhood" accuses Fenians of appropriating an ancient and gallant Irish name for the purposes of cold-blooded assassination and suggests a substitution: "Fenians, forsooth! Renounce that honest name...'Thugs' would more fitly suit your claim to fame" (MacColl, 288).

Two Victorian Novels of Terror

The merging of Irish revolutionary action and Jacobinism under the shared sign of "terrorism" in the early nineteenth century is only one indication of the intimacy of nation and empire; this intimate entangling is one which, over the course of the nineteenth century and well into the twentieth, historians and cultural arbiters often strove to uncouple (Pocock, 50–51). The period witnessing the canonization of the realist novel, in other words, parallels the creation of distinct "English" and "imperial" histories.

The consequences of this sundering are evident in two distinct fictions about terrorism, both published in 1885: Henry James's *The Princess Casamassima* and Robert Louis Stevenson and Fanny Stevensons' *More New Arabian Nights: The Dynamiter*. *Casamassima* and *The Dynamiter* are important literary examples of the distancing tactic employed at least as early as Burke: both novels attempt to neutralize the threat of terror by demonstrating terrorism's impotency. As we will see, unlike their early nineteenth-century fictional predecessors, neither novel exhibits any interest in probing the possible motivations behind terrorism: James's anarchists and the Stevensons' Irish terrorists are equally ideologically lazy and unpersuasive. Also strikingly unlike the novels of the beginning of the century, in both *Casamassima* and *The Dynamiter*, terror's failure becomes intertwined with meditations on the nature of authorship, perhaps reflecting Mikhail Bakunin's argument that "the desire for destruction is at the same time a creative desire."[5] If, in the early nineteenth century, "terror novels" translated the turbulent politics of the period into an aesthetic mode, in these later "dynamite novels," authors and terrorists become secret sharers of the same creative impulse. From that starting point, however, the two texts take radically different approaches to the problem of Victorian terror.

Casamassima is a frustrated Bildungsroman, a novel in which its protagonist Hyacinth Robinson's discovery of himself and his origins is superimposed on two interconnected issues: his initial embrace (and ultimate rejection) of anarchism and his evolving awareness of the immutability of art. In his essay "The Art of Fiction," (1884) James had noted that fiction, responding to its older association with wickedness, based its new respectability on a self-awareness of its mere fictionality by catering to a narrow definition of taste and readerly desire. Contrarily, James argued for realism as a mode of artistic freedom that merged imaginative flexibility with the pursuit of high truth. The implied expectation of James's essay is that the author of fiction, a chronicler of real life like the historian or philosopher, has the potential to affect real change. In contrast to James's emphasis on seriousness in fiction, Stevenson stressed the importance of romance in satisfying the "nameless longings of the reader...and the ideal laws of the day-dream" ("A Gossip on Romance," 56). It is helpful to place both *Casamassima* and *The Dynamiter* in the context of this critical dialogue over the role of art and the artist because both texts establish a relationship between the productive imaginative work of the artist and the destructive imagination of the terrorist. Moreover, the debate over realism versus romance is reflected in the way in which form and genre play into these fictions' negotiations of terror.

Margaret Scanlan argues that *Casamassima*'s mode of realism reflects the "terror shared alike by novelist and revolutionary that, no matter how they plot, they will never change the world" (382). As a frustrated artist working in an outmoded form of craftmanship (bookbinding), Hyacinth's work is ultimately only reflective, the "pastrycook's window" through which he participates in generating aesthetic value. As I've already noted, James's novel pointedly ignores Irish terrorism, by far the most prevalent and sensational threat during the period of its composition; this is striking given James's choice to make his protagonist half-French as a gesture to his interest in the French Revolution and its continued, or possibly renewed, historical potency in a new era of political terror. Absent Fenians, Hyacinth is thrown in with a gaggle of uninspiring anarchists. Their philosophy is contrasted to Hyacinth's growing appreciation for "the monuments and treasures of art," which he prizes despite his awareness that they have been created through "the rapacities of the past" (396). The novel can find no productive way to merge art and revolution: one fundamentally thrives at the expense of the other. Unlike Owenson's *O'Briens and O'Flahertys*, which parallels the plight of the author to the plight of the revolutionary, *Casamassima* draws the two together only to illustrate their fundamental impasse. The novel is a bleak rejoinder to James's own argument for the novel's place in high culture.

If *Casamassima* narrates the affinity between realism as a genre of inevitable failure and terrorism's ultimate impotence, *The Dynamiter* takes a radically different approach to the entangled issues of authorship, form, and function. A collaboratively written, experimental series of interconnected tales, *The Dynamiter* employs an old form—the oriental tale—as a more flexible genre from which to consider the twinned problems of terrorism and authorship. The oriental tale's supple approach to fantasy allows the Stevensons to draw writer and terrorist together as participants in radical acts of imagination, with narrative ultimately triumphing.

The Dynamiter follows the escapades of three hapless amateur detectives, whose collective vow to pursue adventure results in all three inadvertently aiding a gang of equally inept dynamiters. Technologically incompetent and prone to melodramatic bloviations, the terrorists are nevertheless vivid storytellers, and the tales they tell to entrap the three detectives form the main portion of *The Dynamiter*, around which the frame narrative entwines. *The Dynamiter* is one of the earliest fictions to explicitly proffer humor as an antidote to terror, and an obvious inspiration for later stories like Oscar Wilde's *Lord Arthur Savile's Crime* (1887), in which anarchists rig up explosives in commonplace items like clocks for aesthetic pleasure, not politics.

Modernizing the supernatural elements characteristic of oriental tales, the Stevensons provide surprise detonations that shake buildings and explode in the Thames. *The Dynamiter*'s obvious connections to the *Nights* aside (the parallel between Scheherazade and Fanny as female narrators, the embedded tales, the phantasmagoria), there are elements unique to the oriental tale that are particularly pertinent to the Stevensons' project: its troubled political potency, its long tradition of satire, and its exploitation of authorial and translative obscurity. In fact, the veiled politics of *Lalla Rookh* are a useful, if ironic, foil for *The Dynamiter*; as a deeply allegorical critique of British colonialism in Ireland, *Lalla Rookh*'s orientalist decoration veils its political critique, whereas *The Dynamiter* plays with the oriental tale's latent political potential to undermine the efficacy of terror as praxis.

A review of *The Dynamiter* in the *Pall Mall Budget* exults that over the course of reading, the oriental phantasmagoria is so vivid that the Thames comes to have a "remarkable resemblance to the Tigris" (28). The Stevensons conjure this sense of transposition in the novel's telescoping opening sentence, which locates the narrative in "the city of encounters, the Bagdad of the West, and to be more precise, on the broad northern pavement of Leicester Square," folding a newly rejuvenated and urbane piece of London into the ancient cosmopolis (1). Throughout *The Dynamiters*, London is described as an urban maze that discombobulates its amateur detectives even as the terrorists' narrative net of stories is woven around them. Correspondingly, the shifting aspect of the opening sentence takes on more atavistic overtones when that same nebulous perspective affects the three amateur detectives as, over the course of their adventures, London is compared variously to the Yucatan and Africa. Deaglán Ó Donghaile describes the novel's blurring of identities and places as "imperial recoil," whereby "the alien culture of the colonised, so central to the appeal of the genre of the far-flung imperial romance, is transplanted directly onto the already orientalised streets of the metropolis," presenting the possibility of a "reversal of the until-now one-sided dialectic of imperial violence" (30). But after conjuring this threat, the Stevensons diffuse it via the terrorists' ideological and technological incompetence. Unlike *Lalla Rookh*'s careful veiling of imperial politics under ornate and allegorical style, the Stevensons use style to eschew the real politics of Irish nationalist violence by aligning it with the fantastical.

Both *Casamassima* and *The Dynamiter* end by quashing terrorism without any need for police intervention, or any response from the government. Rejecting anarchism but trapped by his vow to carry out an assassination, Hyacinth commits suicide. The *Dynamiter*'s terrorist cell likewise implodes: one member marries and one is so dogged by the terror that he inspires that he dies of it. Their leader, meanwhile, accidentally detonates himself while trying to read about his earlier exploits in the evening paper. Both texts retreat into the fantasy that anti-state terror is ultimately cannibalistic, rather than galvanizing or symbiotic. Together, they demonstrate how "terrorism" had, by the 1880s, completed an important turn in its lexical and conceptual evolution. Responding to, and sometimes actively driving, this change, colonial literature was crucial to this shift in signification, as "terrorism," once a moniker for a particular historical moment of violence, gradually morphed into a broad and problematically fluid signifier, a performative utterance that actively shapes its reality.

Notes

1 In 1798, English parliamentarians referred to the United Irishmen's "threats of terrorism." That same year, Irish supporters argued that "Terrorism cannot, or ought not to give permanent security to any Government." *Report on Lord Moira's motion for an address to the Lord Lieutenant...* (Dublin, 1798), 19. *Vindex to the Thane, to which is prefixed for the purpose of reference, Sir John Freke's address to the electors of the county of Cork* (Cork, 1798), 4.

2 *Thagi* or "thug" refers to a form of murder-robbery in the subcontinent. Two important studies on the legal overreach of the Anti-Thuggee Campaign are Radhika Singha's "'Providential' Circumstances: The Thuggee Campaign of the 1830s and Legal Innovation." *Modern Asian Studies*, vol. 27, no. 1 (1993): pp. 83–146 and Tom Lloyd's "'Thuggee' and the Margins of the State in Early Nineteenth-Century India," http://www.csas.ed.ac.uk/mutiny/confpapers/Lloyd-Paper.pdf, 5–6.

3 For more on Morgan's analysis of Ireland and terrorism see Padma Rangarajan, "'With a Knife at One's Throat': Irish Terrorism in *The O'Briens and the O'Flahertys*." *Nineteenth-Century Literature*, vol. 75, no.3 (2020): 294–317.

4 Archibald Alison's *Principles of Population* (1840) accuses the Irish peasantry of "incredible violence" and total incompetence (509).

5 Lionel Trilling cites this saying of Bakunin's in his analysis of *The Princess Casamassima* in *The Liberal Imagination* (70).

Works Cited

Aravamudan, Srinivas. *Enlightenment Orientalism: Resisting the Rise of the Novel*. University of Chicago Press, 2012.

Edmund Burke, *The Correspondence of Edmund Burke*, ed. Thomas W. Copeland, vii, University of Chicago Press and Cambridge University Press, 1976

———. *Reflections on the Revolution in France*. London: J. Dodsley, 1791.
Byron, Byron George Gordon. *The Corsair*. A.E. Miller, 1818.
———. *Letters and Journals. 1813–1814*. Edited by Leslie Alexis Marchand, iii, J. Murray, 1974.
Crawford, Joseph. *Gothic Fiction and the Invention of Terrorism: The Politics and Aesthetics of Fear in the Age of the Reign of Terror*. Bloomsbury, 2015.
Donghaile, Deaglán Ó. *Blasted Literature: Victorian Political Fiction and the Shock of Modernism*. Edinburgh University Press, 2018.
Duncan, Ian. "Fanaticism and Enlightenment in Confessions of a Justified Sinner." *James Hogg and the Literary Marketplace: Scottish Romanticism and the Working-Class Author*, edited by Holly Faith Nelson and Sharon Alker. Farnham: Ashgate, 2009, pp. 57–70.
———. "Stevenson and Fiction." *The Edinburgh Companion to Robert Louis Stevenson*, edited by Penny Fielding. Edinburgh: Edinburgh University Press, 2010.
Ferris, Ina. *The Achievement of Literary Authority: Gender, History, and the Waverley Novels*. Cornell University Press, 1991.
Galt, John. *The Autobiography of John Galt*. Vol. 2, Cochrane and M'Crone, 1883.
Green, E.H.H. "The Political Economy of Empire, 1880–1914." *The Oxford History of the British Empire: The Nineteenth Century*, edited by Andrew Porter. Oxford: Oxford University Press, 1999, pp. 347–368.
James, Henry. "The Art of Fiction." *Partial Portraits*. Macmillan: New York, 1899, pp. 375–408.
———. *The Princess Casamassima*. Penguin, 1987.
"Lord Brougham's Vomit" *Northern Liberator* 6 Jan. 1839 British Library Newspapers, link.gale.com/apps/doc/Y3201408302/BNCN?u=ucriverside&sid=bookmark-BNCN&xid=a09c148d. Accessed 24 Aug. 2021.
MacColl, Evan. *The Poetical Works of Evan MacColl*. Toronto: Hunter, Rose &Co., 1883
Maniquis, Robert M. "Holy Savagery and Wild Justice: English Romanticism and the Terror." *Studies in Romanticism*, vol. 28, no. 3, 1989, pp. 365–395.
Mbembe, Achille. "The Colony: Its Guilty Secret and Its Accursed Share." *Terror and the Postcolonial*, edited by Elleke Boehmer and Stephen Morton. Chichester: Wiley-Blackwell, 2015, pp. 27–54.
Moore, Thomas, and Richard Garnett. "Introduction." *Thomas Moore Anecdotes, Being Anecdotes, Bon-Mots, and Epigrams, from the "Journal" of Thomas Moore*, edited by Wilmot Harrison, Jarrold, London, 1899, pp. 7–34.
Morton, Stephen. *States of Emergency Colonialism, Literature and Law*. Liverpool University Press, 2014.
Pocock, J.G.A. "British History: A Plea for a New Subject." *Journal of Modern History*, vol. 47, no. iv, 1975, pp. 601–621.
Quincey, De Thomas. *On Murder*. Oxford University Press, 2009.
Rapoport, David. "Fear and Trembling: Terrorism in Three Religious Traditions." *The American Political Science Review*, vol. 78, no. 3, Sept. 1984, pp. 658–677.
Review of *The Dynamiter*. *The Pall Mall Budget*, vol. 33, May 15, 1885, pp. 27–28.
Scanlan, Margaret. "Terrorism and the Realistic Novel: Henry James and The Princess Casamassima." *Texas Studies in Literature and Language*, vol. 34, no. 3, 1992, pp. 380–402.
Shpayer-Makov, Haia. "Anarchism in British Public Opinion 1880–1914." *Victorian Studies*, vol. 31, no. 4, 1988, pp. 487–516.
Simpson, David. *States of Terror: History, Theory, Literature*. The University of Chicago Press, 2019.
Stevenson, Robert Louis. "A Gossip on Romance." *R.L. Stevenson on Fiction: An Anthology of Literary and Critical Essays*, edited by Glenda Norquay. Edinburgh: Edinburgh Univ. Press, 2009, pp. 51–64.
——— and Fanny Van de Grift Stevenson. *More New Arabian Nights: The Dynamiter*. New York: Henry Holt and Company, 1885.
Taylor, Philip Meadows. *Confessions of a Thug*. London: Oxford University Press, 1998.
"Terrorist Novel Writing." *Spirit of the Public Journals for 1797*, vol. 1, 1802, pp. 227–229.
"The Terrorist System of Novel Writing." *The Monthly Magazine, Or, British Register*, August, 1797. London: Printed for R. Phillips, pp. 102–104.
"Thugee in India, and Ribandism In Ireland, Compared." *The Dublin University Magazine*, vol. 15, 1840, pp. 50–64.
Trilling, Lionel. *The Liberal Imagination Essays on Literature and Society*. New York Review Books, 2008.
Witherbee, Amy. "Habeas Corpus: British Imaginations of Power in Walter Scott's 'Old Mortality.'" *New Literary History*, vol. 39, no. 2, 2008, pp. 355–367.

20
ON OR ABOUT 1914

Tanya Agathocleous

The most familiar narrative about modernism in Anglophone literary studies still goes like this: "on or about December 1910 but definitely and decisively by 1914, human character changed." Shattering Victorian ideological certainties, the war helped to usher in new representational strategies, including the fragmentation of linear narrative, perspective, and sentence structure. Modernism, according to this account, registered the physical and psychic damage done in the trenches to Woolf's Septimus Smith, Hemingways' Jake Barnes, and Wilfred Owen... but not the damage done everywhere else to everyone else.

Yet World War I (WWI) was not just an international war, it was an inter-imperial war that enlisted millions of imperial subjects: more than a million South Asians and an estimated 2 million Africans from the British empire alone served on the Western front, among many other British imperial subjects, including "Anglo and First Nation Canadians ...Newfoundlanders, Jamaicans, Australians, New Zealanders, Maoris, South Africans and Egyptians" (Jarboe 181). Correspondingly, literature that emerged from the war included not just that which registered the psychic fragmentation of (predominantly) white British and American men. Another discernible and vastly influential form of modernist literature was that designed to guard against the political fragmentation of empire that the war had helped to precipitate: the literature of propaganda.

In May 1917, at the height of WWI, four stories by Rudyard Kipling were published serially and contemporaneously in the U.S. newspaper the *Saturday Evening Post* and the British *Morning Post* under the heading "The Eyes of Asia." The stories read as letters from Indian soldiers to their families back home and are filled with descriptions of German depravity, wonder at the civilizational marvels of English and French life, and reassurances that the soldiers were being well-cared for. In other words, they read as propaganda for the war and for empire; which is in fact what they were, for Kipling had been encouraged to write them by British Intelligence.

In one of the stories, a Rajput soldier convalescing in Hampshire writes to a friend in India:

> Here I am held in the greatest kindness and honour imaginable by all whom I meet. Though I am useless as a child yet they are unwearied of me. The nurses...minister to

me as daughters to a father. They run after me and rebuke me if I do not wear a certain coat when it rains daily. I am like a dying tree in a garden of flowers.

(Kipling 22)

Another letter, written in the voice of a Muslim soldier in France to his mother, states:

this world abounds in marvels beyond belief. We in India are but stones compared to these people. They do not litigate among themselves; they speak truth at first answer; their weddings are not [performed] till both sides are at least eighteen, and no man has authority here to beat his wife.

(94)

Though the effusive loyalty to the Raj and veneration for Western culture that permeated Kipling's epistolary stories may seem manifestly disingenuous to us now, "The Eyes of Asia" series were based on actual soldiers' letters that the British government had collected via an elaborate and rigorous censorship process and made accessible to Kipling: the story of how he came to possess and overwrite these letters with his own versions is laid out in detail in the important work of Santanu Das and Gujendra Singh on South Asian soldiers in WWI.[1] While drawing on their work, this chapter seeks to frame "The Eyes of Asia" within the longer history of British rule in India in order to show how censorship and propaganda during WWI—and the particular ways they shaped Kipling's letters—were a natural outgrowth of imperial censorship and propaganda practices that had been in place since the late nineteenth century.[2] The fact that Kipling's use of soldiers' letters as war propaganda was directly connected to the censorship of actual soldiers' letters is not that surprising: censorship and propaganda tend to go hand in hand as tools of authoritarianism, with one suppressing information the other amplifying and actively distributing misinformation. But what the history of imperial censorship brings into relief is how the manipulation of speech during wartime was related to the racialization of the public sphere; as I will show in the next section, brown speech in India was criminalized via a law against disaffection, while white speech was not.

For those in power, the need to control flows of information across the empire to stem criticism of British rule was greatly enhanced during the war, as was the need to maintain racial and imperial hierarchies that were rapidly destabilizing. At the same time, however, the involvement of Indian soldiers in the war had proven to be materially and ideologically important to the maintenance of British global power, and was being used by nationalist leaders in India to amplify demands for self-government. The British government thus had to pull off the tricky juggling act of controlling the public sphere along racial lines by continuing to suppress anti-colonial dissent (via techniques such as the censorship of the letters traveling between Europe and India), while acknowledging the indispensable contribution of colonial soldiers to the war effort.

Kipling's brownface letters are a symptom of this juggling act for, while ventriloquized and carefully shaped to reflect imperial interests, they seemed to allow for the centering of Indian voices in mainstream metropolitan newspapers. The first story published in the *Saturday Evening Post*, illustrated by the well-known artist Harvey Dunn, took up the whole front page, and even though Kipling's name was listed under the title, it had the appearance of a breaking international news story, which added to its studied realism. But while Kipling's four-part act of ventriloquism was an ingenious work of propaganda, it wasn't a replicable one and its elaborate staging of colonial loyalty reflects the degree to which that loyalty increasingly had to be manufactured and the ways in which the uneven application of liberal norms across the empire inevitably compromised press freedoms in the metropole as well. Even fiction, always ideological, had become instrumentally shaped to the ends of war.

Kipling's sepoy letters mimicked Indian soldiers performing the role of mimic men, professing and enacting loyal subjecthood by avoiding overt critique and voicing affection for their rulers. Because they were censored and subsequently archived, thousands of Indian soldiers' letters are available to researchers today and some of them do closely resemble Kipling's fictional letters. But many do not, expressing instead fatigue, horror, and a sense of being sacrificed to save white soldiers, making it clear that Kipling cherry-picked and cobbled together aspects of the letters he had been given in order to paint a quaint, realistic-seeming picture of the loyal sepoy.

Of the many British writers enlisted to produce war propaganda, Kipling would have been especially comfortable with this role because he had helped to invent the mimic man a decade and a half earlier through his character Hurree Chunder Mukherjee in his novel *Kim*. Predictably, the sepoy stories have a Hurree-esque voice, complete with linguistic error, comical malapropisms, and wide-eyed naiveté. The punningly titled "A Private Account" differs in form from the others in that it is presented as colloquial dialogue between the addressees of a letter in India rather than formal prose by an author on the Front, and thus offers more opportunity for caricature. For instance, the mother whose son is reading to her from a letter is impressed by the fact that the French could apparently leave expensive clothing hanging in unsecured spaces because of their honesty: "That is the country for me! Dresses worth 200 rupees hanging on nails! Princesses all they must be" (57).

But Kipling's soldier-mimic had to be more serious than comic, so as to encourage his readers to believe in the authenticity of the war experiences recounted, and the pro-Allies and anti-German sentiment professed. Thus, one of the "letters" that appeared under the heading "A Retired Gentleman," written in the voice of an elderly sepoy convalescing at an English hospital, represents the Germans as follows:

> The nature of the enemy is to commit shame upon women and children and to defile the shrines of his own faith with his own dung. It is done by him as a drill…We did not know they were outcaste. Now it is established by the evidence of our senses. They attack on all fours running like apes.
>
> (7)

Here the allusion to the caste system and to empirical "evidence" augments the letter's authentic ring, which works to dehumanize the Germans while emphasizing the modesty of the British. "Their greatness is to make themselves very small," the Retired Gentleman writes, before humbly concluding "[w]e are not even children beside them" (16).[3] Another of the letters based its extensive arguments for why more Indians should enlist on the superiority of French culture: "No man molests any woman here" the soldier writes. Touting the war as a form of cultural tourism, he insists his compatriots come to the front as fast as possible to learn the French ways of life because "such opportunities will not occur again" (99).

Based on actual letters, Kipling's letters are charged with affection for their addressees, the beloved family back home. But he also saturates his letters with a rival affection for the colonizer so that they might counter affect pointed toward India—and the possibility of seditious disaffection—with a sense of imperial belonging. Thus, the Retired Gentleman writes that he has no desire to return home to India after his convalescence because of the loving care of British nurses and his many "friends among the English." Another letter, "The Fumes of the Heart," devotes several lines to the kindness of a French woman who treated its writer like a son and wept for him accordingly: "I had never believed such women existed in this Black Age," the imaginary soldier writes in awe (36).

The "Eyes of Asia" letters are filled with affection, then, not only for the relatives and friends back home to whom they are addressed but also for the soldiers' caretakers and other British and French people they encounter, such as the kind old woman. This is unsurprising, given the nature of letters to relatives and the frightening, disorienting context of war, and makes the letters seem all the more heartfelt and realistic. But the full significance of affect to the performance of colonial loyalty that the stories sought to promote is best understood in the context of late-nineteenth-century sedition law: specifically a law against disaffection that became part of the Indian Penal Code in 1870 and made affection for the government a mandate of colonial citizenship.

Imperial Censorship: Disaffection in India

In 1870, Section 124a was added to the Indian Penal Code in order to make "disaffection" the equivalent of sedition and punishable by censorship, fines, imprisonment, or transportation for life. The focus on affect rather than seditious statements was significant. In this newly vague form, sedition law could shape what could be said, how it could be said, and who could say it, while literalizing the metaphor of the colonial relationship as a filial or romantic one. Disaffection, lawmakers argued, meant hatred of the government and evidence of it, according to judges of sedition trials, were words—phrases, passages, and allegorical tales brimming with incendiary potential that could leak off the page and affect the populace, igniting political rebellion.

The law against disaffection in colonial India essentially created a bifurcated public sphere in which British speech was associated with reason and detachment and Indian speech with affect and atavism. Since Section 124a was designed to suppress discontent with colonial rule, it was applied predominantly to Indian rather than Anglo-English or British texts. As a result, the colonial public sphere was explicitly racialized, with white writing recognized as civil discourse and brown writing seen as prone to irrationality and incivility and thus subject to exile from the realm of free speech. Section 124a was first introduced into the Indian Penal Code (IPC) in 1870 by the governor-general's law administrator, James Fitzjames Stephen. Between its first use in the *Bangavasi* case trial in 1890 and independence in 1947, Section 124a made every kind of text the government could think of subject to suppression, including "poetry, song lyrics, fiction, drama, essays, gramophone records, posters, broadsheets, and even garments, such as dhotis," as well as woodcuts and engravings (Kamra 99).[4]

Stephen was a vociferous critic of John Stuart Mill's more tolerant version of liberalism, against which he launched a book-length critique, *Liberty, Equality, Fraternity*. As an advocate for the curtailment of freedoms such as that of the press in the interests of morality and stability, he saw the codification, simplification, and standardization of aspects of British law in the IPC as an opportunity to make law the foundation of sovereignty in the colony.[5] The streamlining of British law that took place in the shaping of Indian law is an instance of the way forms of modern governance not yet ironed out in the West were to be tested in the colonies. Stephen acknowledged as much when he declared that "to compare the Indian Penal Code to English criminal law is to compare cosmos with chaos" (cited in Hussain, 41). In this telling analogy, the colony is the space in which the dark matter of Western democracy would resolve into a modern world-system.

In their work on censorship, Raminder Kaur and William Mazzarella argue that rather than shutting down discourse, censorship law tends to proliferate it, not only by generating "discourses on normative modes of desiring, of acting, of being in the world" but also by drawing attention to transgression and routinizing it (5). "There seems to be something of a correlation," they note, "between the regulation of cultural production and the proliferation of provocative forms" (4). If 124a helped to proliferate transgression by outlawing it, it also contributed to the kinds of expression it sought to outlaw by generating a specific form of vicious cycle, wherein the law's racism and repression provoked dissidence, which then required the law to be expanded by an added emphasis on affect, which made it more racist because of the heightened pathologization of Indians via their association with negative affect, thus producing more dissidence, and so on.

The irony of the disaffection law, then, was that rather than effectively propping up colonial rule, it ended up contributing to the rise and eventual success of the Indian nationalist movement. First, by giving criticism of the government a distinct character—disaffection—it helped to give shape to a practice of resistance and turn anti-colonialism into an identity, as evidenced by Gandhi proudly calling himself a "disaffectionist" in his 1922 trial for sedition. Second, by associating anti-colonial critique with affect—the life-blood of nationalism, according to Benedict Anderson and many other influential theorists of the nation—the law enhanced critique's power.[6] The antidote to disaffection with the government was not affection for Britain but for India, at least according to nationalist rhetoric. As Sartre puts it in his introduction to Frantz Fanon's *The Wretched of the Earth*, "Their feeling for each other is the reverse of the hatred they feel for you" (22).

If the disaffection law was meant to coercively court affection for British rule by suggesting that the realm of intimacy was the proper grounds of national belonging, then it had exactly the opposite effect. For, as Partha Chatterjee has influentially demonstrated, it was the private sphere—the realm of feeling—that was imagined by Indians as the space of tradition, religion, and affective bonds: of Indian identity, in other words.[7] By officially making affect the cellular structure of political community in India, the disaffection law validated rather than inhibited the nationalist cause. Furthermore, censorship and other forms of colonial repression helped to create a melodramatic narrative of Indian victimization and heroic resistance in which the law against disaffection was easily cast as one of the chief villains (Kamra 124).

Section 124a was also crucial to the rise of nationalism because it epitomized the hypocrisy of liberal-imperial governance and the racial double standard embedded in the structure and practice of colonial law. As Amitav Ghosh has eloquently put it, "Race is the unstated term through which the gradualism of liberalism reconciles itself to the permanence of Empire" (152). Unstated as it might have been, it was very much noticed by Indians: in 1907, the nationalist leader Bal Gangadhar Tilak—who was tried for sedition on three separate occasions—noted that "The goddess of British Justice, though blind, is able to distinguish unmistakably black from white." Sedition law and its uses thus became "a powerful rhetorical tool to criticise and contest the legitimacy of the British colonial government and the violence upon which that government is based" (Morton 84). The prohibition of critique, in other words, became the very grounds for critique because it served as irrefutable evidence of what Ranajit Guha terms the "unBritish character of British rule" (57).

Wartime Censorship

Indian soldiers' letters were subject to particular scrutiny because of fears of seditious sentiments and inflammatory political materials reaching them from anti-colonial activists in India or from those that had fled to the continent, often moving from Britain to France to Germany and Switzerland in order to evade arrest. In one instance where the French police were surveilling Indian anti-colonialists on behalf of Britain, they arrested a member of an Indian revolutionary group carrying seditious literature which he planned to circulate among Indian soldiers (Brukenhaus 44). This event and others like it inspired an intricate surveillance system targeting soldiers' correspondence. Eventually, just as much attention was paid to letters sent by soldiers as to those received by them, since they could not only reveal sensitive information but demoralize potential recruits.

This transcontinental policing of Indian dissidents was the origin of the system whereby the Indian soldiers' letters that Kipling used when writing his "Eyes of Asia" stories ended up in the hands of British intelligence and then his (Das, *India, Empire, and First World War Culture* 187). These letters, and thousands of others like them, were subject to several layers of mediation and scrutiny. First, because many of the Indian soldiers serving on the front had joined the army to escape poverty and were illiterate, a large number of letters would have been dictated to scribes out loud (and were equally likely to be read out loud to family in India), impeding candor. By 1915, sepoys had become aware of the censorship to which their writing were subjected, providing further incentive to be circumspect or disingenuous. Letters sometimes alerted their readers to their own circumspection. One letter stated:

> What more can I write? There are orders against writing. Oh, my elder brother, by your favour I am well, and my life has been spared hitherto; but I am not certain for the future and have no hope of life.
>
> *(Dayal 72)*

Both these factors, then, encouraged self-censorship. The next layer of mediation involved actual censorship; letters were first read by officers within a given soldier's regiment and then sent to the Indian Base Post Office, which had a team of translators and censors that read letters to and from the soldiers on the front and sent reports on them back to Britain: these reports, filled with excerpts from letters and the entire contents of confiscated letters, were the raw material of Kipling's stories (Omissi 7).

Like many journalists and authors in India affected by the law against disaffection, then, soldiers altered their writing to accommodate the suspicious gaze of the censor, using conventional British phrases and stock characterizations of warfare to appear adequately loyal, as well as cryptic references, allegories, and poems to convey negative sentiments that might otherwise provoke redaction (Das 207). These tactics confounded British censors even as they were alert to them. One censor complained that it is "almost impossible…for any censorship of Oriental correspondence to be effective as a barrier. Orientals excel in the art of conveying information without saying anything definite" (Singh 66). A frequently cited example of coded language was the use of the term "black pepper" to refer to Indian soldiers and "red pepper" to refer to white soldiers, as in the following extract from a letter:

> The black pepper which has come from India has all been finished, so now the red pepper is being used. But the red pepper is little used and the black more. You understand everything so I need not write any further
>
> *(Ram 58)*

Wartime Propaganda

Though he didn't like to think of his writing as propaganda, much of Kipling's literary output during the war functioned this way in practice: for instance, he was allegedly responsible for the widely used term "Huns" to describe Germans (Kendall, fn. 238). But he also participated actively in official propaganda campaigns, producing poems, speeches, and articles aimed at British and imperial audiences, alongside letters and verse addressed specifically to Americans that urged them to support the Allies (Jain 105). In 1916, he stated in a letter to a friend that, while retaining copyright, he had allowed his writing to be used "as articles in newspapers or as pamphlets in propaganda work in all countries" ("Letter to Sir Douglas Brownrigg" 363). Copyright allowed Kipling to republish his stories and poems in collections—"The Eyes of Asia" stories were collected together in book form the same year they were serialized in newspapers. It is ironic, though fitting, that in the case of "The Eyes of Asia," Kipling was copyrighting words not entirely his own, for some of the passages in the stories were taken virtually verbatim from the soldiers' letters given to him by the government (Das 188). In other words, the soldiers' writing was taken from their letters home via censorship, then channeled into propaganda via Kipling, who eventually monetized them as well, in an efficient combination of cultural and material appropriation.

Whether or not Kipling was commissioned by the government to write the epistolary stories that made up "The Eyes of Asia" series is unclear, but they were at least the product of official encouragement, as they ensued from a meeting engineered by the Intelligence department between Kipling and the Director of Special Intelligence: a week after the meeting, the letters were forwarded to the author by a British official in the Indian Army (Das 187). The Intelligence department's solicitation of Kipling for this propagandistic task makes sense, given that he had become renowned for his stories and poems about soldiers, in which he made lavish use of what he called "Tommy's vernacular" (famous examples include the stories collected in *Soldier's Three* [1888] and *Plain Tales from the Hills* [1888] and the poems published as "Barrack-Room Ballads" in 1890). Referencing a range of working-class dialects, including Cockney and Irish ones, Kipling's use of the vernacular sought to capture the voice and spirit of the common Anglo-Indian soldier, who he believed had been hitherto misrepresented. Critics have suggested that his writing was so influential that his portraits of soldiers shaped their behavior and jargon so that they reflected his writing rather than vice versa (Gilmour 50). Between his shaping of the figure of Anglo-Indian soldier (whether fictional or real), his creation of Hurree's Indian English in *Kim*, and his renowned jingoism, Kipling was well situated to produce literary propaganda that, as a natural outgrowth of his interests and talents, was more likely to register as literature than propaganda.

In encouraging Kipling to write the stories, British intelligence hoped not only to counter potential discontent among Indian soldiers fighting in France, but also to combat the spread of international anti-colonialism in the United States, where the revolutionary Ghadar movement on the West Coast—like anti-colonialists on the Continent—was collaborating with Germany. Kipling's writing was thus designed to sell the war, and its value to the empire, to the American and British public simultaneously; the "Eyes of Asia" stories were serialized on both sides of the Atlantic a month after the United States officially entered the war.

Building on the "affection allegory" that underwrote the logic of the law against disaffection—the idea that Britain was beloved by her subjects—British propaganda celebrated the filial bonds and ties of loyalty that brought together different subjects from the larger colonies (Canada, India, Australia, and New Zealand) to serve the cause: posters and postcards displaying soldiers rallying to the aid of Britannia from these countries had captions such as "One King, One Flag, One Empire" and "Friends in Need are Friends Indeed."

In his poetry on the Second Boer War, Kipling had promoted the idea of imperial federation that bolstered these forms of propaganda by writing poems about friendship between British and colonial soldiers—but only soldiers from the settler colonies were included in his vision (Rudy 164–5). Similar racial hierarchies persisted during WWI, belying the kinship suggested by the propaganda materials and the martial ideal of "brothers in arms." Indian troops had not been allowed to fight in the Boer War because of the perceived threat to white supremacy of the spectacle of men of color fighting white men on behalf of other white men. But for political reasons, such as the need to solicit funds from Indian princes and to bolster loyalty to the Raj at a time when nationalism was on the rise, Indians were actively encouraged to enlist in the war and were the only British colonial non-white troops to fight in the front lines in France (others were allowed to serve only in more menial capacities) (Das 10).[8]

Yet the Indian soldiers who served in the war were already racially defined subdivisions of the larger Indian population. As Das notes,

> Both England and France divided their subject people into 'warlike' and 'non-warlike' races…from the late nineteenth century, the martial race theory formed the backbone of the military recruiting system in British India. A combination of Victorian social Darwinism and indigenous caste hierarchy, this theory emphasized that some 'races' from Nepal and the North Indian provinces – particularly Punjab – were inherently more 'manly' and warlike than men from other parts of India.
>
> (12)

As a result, most of the Indians who served in WWI were from these regions. Racial hierarchy was also reinforced by segregation; Indian and African soldiers lived separately from white soldiers and subject to more rigid control, especially when barracked or hospitalized in towns, because of fears of mutiny and—equally but differently threatening—miscegenation. One soldier, writing to India from "Kitchener's Indian Hospital" in Brighton, combined the admiration for European life seen in Kipling's soldiers' letters with guarded resentment about the restraints to which Indian soldiers were subject: "Brother," he wrote, "there is plenty to eat here and it is a land of fairies; but the supervision over us is very strict, and we are not allowed to go anywhere, and are hard pressed, and we do not like it" (Chinoy 82).

Kipling's epistolary stories were thus part of a larger trend in imperial war propaganda of using colonial soldiers as evidence of empire's success and cohesion. The bravery of Nepalese Gurkhas became a favorite topic for British and French newspapers, with *The Times* telling its readers, in one article, that the presence of Indian troops in France was itself a rebuttal of "all the foul slanders which have been circulated in the past years regarding British rule in India" (Jarboe 184). Propagandistic forms of visual culture—posters, photographs, and films—featuring colonial soldiers circulated widely, and were also used as educational material in schools, while thousands of copies of a book on the treatment of wounded Indian soldiers in Brighton's Royal Pavilion were printed and shipped to India, where the government distributed them as evidence of the care and respect the soldiers were garnering. All in all, Andrew Jarboe argues, even as the war drastically undermined the purchase of empire, "Wartime propaganda about colonial soldiers played a key part in extending the lease of European imperialism well into the twentieth century" (189).

Alternative Networks

While wartime censorship and propaganda helped to shore up empire's image, which had suffered substantially during and after the Boer War, its counterforce was anti-colonial revolutionary networks that spread across Europe, straddled the Atlantic, and connected Britain's colonial possessions. As Das puts it,

> It is now generally accepted that, while the world was dragged into war under the banner of vast European empires, the war also prepared the stage for the collapse of the imperial world order...The carnage of the Western Front prompted not just pity or opportunistic nationalism but a sense of metaphysical bewilderment across Asia and Africa at the destructive potential of the West, the supposed agents of the 'civilising mission'; the critique of the empire would now develop into a wholesale civilisational critique of Europe.
>
> *("Precarious Encounters" 143)*

This critique was not only visible in speeches and writing after the war but was prefigured in soldiers' letters different from, but contemporaneous to, the kind Kipling used for his stories. One soldier, clearly trying to discourage his addressee from enlisting, wrote:

> the state of things here is indescribable. There is a conflagration all round, and you must imagine it to be like a dry forest in a high wind in the hot weather, with abundance of dry grass and straw. No one can extinguish it but God himself--man can do nothing. What more can I write? You must carefully consider what I say.
>
> *(S. Singh 77)*

Others evoked apocalypse even more starkly: "Do not think that this is war. This is not war. It is the ending of the world" while another proclaimed "This war will bring us to the end of the world and no one knows how long it will last. The news in the papers is all lies" (H. Singh 104–5).

What these letters convey is neither the affection for European civilization we see in Kipling's stories, nor the disaffection that censors had been looking for in Indian writing since 1890, but wholesale despair, and a sense of the inadequacy of language to the task of describing it. The war not only helped to generate unruly affective bonds—international anti-colonialism, Pan-Islamism, and Pan-Asianism—but strained signification, in part because the policing of speech under empire made all of it suspect and potentially duplicitous: that of the colonizer as well as the colonized. At a point where censorship in India could no longer contain anti-colonial writings as they spread around the world, from Ghadar newspapers in America to letters written in the trenches of France, Kipling was forced to invent the loyal Indian wholesale and become his own mimic subject. For if the soldiers Kipling created in his letters resemble his babu character Hurree, Kipling himself, performing in brown-face to produce "authentic" accounts from the front, resembles the shape-shifting Kim, who passes as an Indian while performing espionage for the British.

The title given to Kipling's four fictional letters, "The Eyes of Asia," is reminiscent of travelogues of the period, such as Behramji Malabari's 1893 autobiographical work *An Indian Eye on English Life*, that sought to reverse the anthropological colonial gaze and decenter Western culture by subjecting it to the detached scrutiny of the colonial outsider. Kipling's "Eyes," however, suggests a mass rather than individuation and Asia, too, is undifferentiated in the title. This choice is noteworthy, given that the word would have signified differently in America—which had just passed an Immigration Act that barred immigration from the Asia-Pacific zone after years of Yellow Peril hysteria—than it did in Britain, where it would have been more readily connected with India. The "Asia" of Kipling's title thus functions as a globalizing word, linking together two different national contexts and activating multiple, sometimes conflicting, anxieties about race, empire, and their imbrication.[9] WWI, and the images, texts, and people it set into circulation, made signification messy, even as governments tried their best to control communication. Collapsing colony into metropole, the war disordered the colonial systems of meaning that it was being fought to preserve.

The focus on the eye in these titles seems meant to suggest the disembodied perspective of an eye in the sky, a phrase once evocative of a watchful god or an objective overview but now, in the twenty-first century, associated primarily with security cameras, satellites, and drones. Given these current-day militaristic connotations, it is fitting that Kipling's appropriative voice turns the disinterested gaze of the traveler into one of mass surveillance, trained on the very subjects it claimed to represent in an effort to curb their dissent. The "Eyes of Asia," Kipling's letters, were tools of the state and, from a contemporary perspective, they evoke not participant-observation but dismemberment: the body parts of soldiers drawn into a war that mobilized their labor and lives against their own interests.

Notes

1 See Das, *India, Empire and First World War Culture*, esp. pp. 186–192, and G. Singh.
2 For a robust overview of imperial propaganda, see MacKenzie; also see Melissa Dinsman's chapter "Art, Truth, and Propaganda" in this volume.
3 Gilmour notes that Kipling instructed newspaper editors not to capitalize "Hun" and refer to a German as "it" (117).
4 The *Bangavasi* trial is discussed at more length in my book, *Disaffected*.
5 See Stephen.
6 See, for example, Anderson, and Rorty's arguments for the need for patriotic pride vs. shame in progressive politics.
7 See Chatterjee.
8 See also Das, Maguire, and Steinbach, Introduction, *Colonial Encounters in a Time of Global Conflict, 1914–1918*.
9 I thank Marina Bilbija for her helpful suggestions on this chapter.

Works Cited

Agathocleous, Tanya. *Disaffected: Emotion, Sedition, and Colonial Law in the Anglosphere*. Cornell UP, 2021.
Anderson, Benedict. *Imagined Communities: Reflections on the Origins and Spread of Nationalism*. Verso, 1983.
Brückenhaus, Daniel. *Policing Transnational Protest: Liberal Imperialism and the Surveillance of Anticolonialists in Europe, 1905–1945*. Oxford UP, 2017.
Chatterjee, Partha. *Nationalist Thought and the Colonial World: A Derivative Discourse*. U of Minnesota P, 1993.
———. *The Nation and its Fragments: Colonial and Postcolonial Histories*. Princeton UP, 1993.
Das, Santanu. *India, Empire and First World War Culture: Writing, Images, and Songs*. Cambridge UP, 2018.
———. "Precarious Encounters: South Asia, the War, and Anti-colonial Cosmopolitanism." *Colonial Encounters in a Time of Global Conflict*, edited by Santanu Das, Anna Maguire, and Daniel Steinbach, pp. 125–148.
Das, Santanu, Anna Maguire, and Daniel Steinbach, editors. Introduction. *Colonial Encounters in a Time of Global Conflict, 1914–1918*. Routledge, 2022, pp. 4–15.
Dayal, Prabhu. "Letter to Subiya Ram." 25 June, 1915. *Indian Voices of the Great War: Soldiers' Letters, 1914–18*, edited by David E. Omissi. 1999. Springer, 2016.
Ghosh, Amitav and Dipesh Chakrabarty, "A Correspondence on Provincializing Europe." *Radical History Review*, vol. 83, Spring 2002, pp. 146–72.

Gilmour, David. *The Long Recessional: The Imperial Life of Rudyard Kipling*. Farrar, Straus and Giroux, 2002.

Guha, Ranajit. *Dominance without Hegemony*. Harvard UP, 1998.

Hussain, Nasser. *The Jurisprudence of Emergency: Colonialism and the Rule of Law*. The University of Michigan Press, 2003.

Jain, Anurag. "The Relationship between Ford, Kipling, Conan Doyle, Wells and British Propaganda of the First World War." Unpublished doctoral thesis, University of London, 2009.

Jarboe, Andrew. "Indian and African Soldiers in British, French and German Propaganda during the First World War." *World War I and Propaganda*, edited by Troy R.E. Paddock. Brill, 2014, pp. 181–196.

Kamra, Sukeshi. *The Indian Periodical Press and Nationalist Rhetoric*. Palgrave Macmillan, 2011.

Kaur, Raminder and William Mazzarella. "Between Sedition and Seduction: Thinking Censorship in South Asia." *Censorship in South Asia: Cultural Regulation from Sedition to Seduction*, edited by Kaur and Mazzarella. Indiana UP, 2009, pp.1–29.

Kendall, Tim, editor. *Poetry of the First World War: An Anthology*. Oxford UP, 2013.

Kipling, Rudyard. "Letter to Sir Douglas Brownrigg," 24 April 1916. *The Letters of Rudyard Kipling Vol. 4: 1911–19*, edited by Thomas Pinney. U of Iowa P, 1999.

———. *The Eyes of Asia*. Doubleday, Page and Co., 1918.

MacKenzie, John. *Propaganda and Empire: The Manipulation of British Public Opinion, 1880–1960*. Manchester UP, 1984.

Morton, Stephen. *States of Emergency: Colonialism, Literature and Law*. Liverpool UP, 2014

Omissi, David, editor. *Indian Voices of the Great War: Soldiers' Letters, 1914–18*. 1999. Springer, 2016.

Ram, Mansa. "Letter to Guard Rameshwar or Divisankar." April 1915. *Indian Voices of the Great War: Soldiers' Letters, 1914–18*, edited by David E. Omissi. 1999. Springer, 2016, pp. 58.

Rorty, Richard. *Achieving our Country: Leftist Thought in Twentieth-Century America*. Harvard UP, 1999.

Rudy, Jason. *Imagined Homelands: British Poetry in the Colonies*. Johns Hopkins UP, 2017.

Sartre, Jean-Paul. Introduction. *The Wretched of the Earth*, by Frantz Fanon. Grove Press, 1968.

Singh, Gajendra. *The Testimonies of Indian Soldiers and the Two World Wars: Between Self and Sepoy*. Bloomsbury Academic, 2014.

Singh, Hukam. "Letter to his wife." 2 October 1915. *Indian Voices of the Great War: Soldiers' Letters, 1914–18*, edited by David E. Omissi. 1999. Springer, 2016.

Singh, Sowar Sohan. "Letter to Jodh Singh." 10 July, 1915. *Indian Voices of the Great War: Soldiers' Letters, 1914–18*, edited by David E. Omissi. 1999. Springer, 2016.

Stephen, James Fitzjames. *Liberty, Equality, Fraternity*. Edited by Stuart D. Warner. Liberty Fund Press, 1993.

21
ON OR ABOUT 1945

Claire Seiler

Until very recently, literature in English of the late 1940s suffered from a strange critical underestimation. In contrast to the patent world-historical and geopolitical import of the years just after World War II, the period's literature seemed somehow lacking, or insufficiently engaged with its time. You could point to expressly political exceptions all day long. George Orwell's *1984* (1949), a dystopian narrative of near-future totalitarian governance, is the obvious exception among novels; Ezra Pound's *Pisan Cantos* (1948), the late opus of a canonical modernist who denounced liberal democracy while serving as a champion for the Italian fascist government and then as a prisoner of the US government, is the most notorious poetic counterexample; and John Hersey's *Hiroshima* (1946), a "nonfiction novel" (Nadel 53) bearing witness to the destruction wrought by the United States' first use of an atomic bomb, must be the most debated exception among works of reportage. But in addition to reiterating a narrow mini-canon and accepting dated notions of what counts as "political" writing, you'd end up proving the long unexamined rule that the literature of the late 1940s failed in some way to meet its moment. Or, as Malcolm Bradbury once summarized the critical consensus on the 1940s as a whole, "in Britain and elsewhere, [the decade] seems to mark a vacancy in recent cultural history," "a period of relative artistic silence" in the face of overwhelming historical upheaval (69). To which I say, in my most scholarly tone, "Nonsense."

To read widely across late-1940s literary and public culture—and the former was still plainly contiguous with the latter—is to witness the emergence of an entire vocabulary for the self-consciously historical atmosphere of the middle of the twentieth century. Across various political orientations and formal traditions, cultural registers and geographic locations, generations and institutions, writers in the Atlantic world at the middle of the twentieth century confronted "the pressure of history," as Jean-Paul Sartre described it in "The Situation of the Writer in 1947" (639);[1] writers understood their historical present to bear "the weight of primary noon," to borrow a potent phrase from Wallace Stevens's poem "The Motive for Metaphor" (1947). Surveying British fiction at midcentury, the novelist Elizabeth Bowen reflected that "a century halfway along its course may be considered due to declare maturity, to have reached culmination-point." By its middle, however, the twentieth century was in too much "disarray" for self-certain declarations. The century's "development," Bowen wrote, had "been in some directions so violently forced, in others so notably arrested as to seem hardly to be a development at all, or at least to be difficult to recognize if it is one"

DOI: 10.4324/9781003038009-25

(321). And in the Pittsburgh *Courier*, a major African American newspaper, columnist Marjorie McKenzie described "reading comments on the meaning of the mid-century in press and periodical[s] with extraordinary interest." She was not alone. "My own intensity about 1950," McKenzie found, "is a widely shared emotion" (19).

Atmospheric pressure, anticipatory feeling, diffuse uncertainty, liminality: this is the hazy vocabulary, conceptual and idiomatic, through which a range of midcentury literature addressed, contested, or otherwise evinced the weight of the middle of the twentieth century. It is not, however, the language of self-professed newness that writers of the late 1940s inherited from their high-modernist forebears. Nor is it the sort of language that the institutionalized practice of literary periodization typically registers. The discourse of periodization privileges the origins and ends of, and the "historical contrast" (Underwood 2) between, successive periods; midcentury literature confronted an intensely fraught historical and epochal middle. In this mismatch lies the root of the problem: when it comes to the late 1940s, the baseline practice for periodizing the literary twentieth century—splitting it in half roughly at its middle, around 1945—assumes and reinforces the reputed opacity of its middle.

Periodic Contortions

The earliest efforts to characterize the 1940s as a literary period warped critical perception of the decade from the start. A high-profile, highbrow *Partisan Review* symposium on "The State of American Writing, 1948," for example, framed the 1940s as a sorry answer to the "first postwar period": "It is the general opinion that, unlike the twenties, this is not a period of experiment in language and form" (855). The *Partisan* questionnaire began by asking respondents (all men) to identify "the new literary tendencies or figures, if any, that have emerged in the forties" and worried over more pressing questions about literature's address to politics, among them whether one ought to confront the "growing tension between Soviet Communism and the democratic countries" and whether "in our time, when the fate of culture as a whole is called into question, [...] the basic meaning of the literary effort stand[s] in need of reexamination" (855–856). Scaling up from the academic question of how to rate 1940s literature to existential threats to culture itself, the *Partisan* questionnaire exhibits a literary-historical agita endemic to the late 1940s. What remained intact through the subsequent exercise of literary periodization, however, was mostly a presumption of the measly literary output of the 1940s as incommensurate with the decade's manifest historical freight. Like the once-standard "perception that the incontrovertible historical and social importance of World War II was not reflected in the quality of its art and literature" (Woodward 7), the wan reputation of the later, "postwar" 1940s was more inherited than debated.

The long critical disinterest in late-1940s literature in English has very little to do with the actual literary production of those years and very much to do with institutionalized practices of literary periodization in general and of modernism and its sequelae in particular. Under either periodizing sun, twentieth-century literature in English still tends to be studied and taught as bifurcated at 1945, the year that marked the end of World War II "hostilities," as contemporary euphemists would have it. Consequently, the discipline maps Anglophone literary history of the twentieth century onto a martial-imperialist timeline (from WWI to interwar to WWII to Cold War, etc.) through which war is tacitly understood as synonymous with "history" and therefore determinative of literary phases. In the latter case, the names and dates of sequential and ostensibly discrete wars and wartimes do for the literary twentieth century what the names of English monarchs (e.g., Elizabeth,

Victoria) or European projects (e.g., enlightenment, industrialization) long did for the study of previous epochs and still do for some subfields of English-language literary studies. If, as whole, the practice of literary periodization rests on what Eric Hayot, adapting Arjun Appadurai (1996), calls "Eurochronology" and defines as "the forms of historical time privileged by modernity at large, which make it very hard to think past the basic structures that keep European patterns of development at the center of history" (Hayot 6), then the temporal elongation of literary modernism offers a case in point. Whether as a specific aesthetic project or a broad heuristic, "modernism" now reaches across the twentieth century and even into the twenty-first. This temporal expansion runs uneasily parallel to urgent efforts to decolonize the modernist canon and to decenter the Euro-American metropole in the geography of modernism, but is nonetheless homologous with a highly militarized account of twentieth-century history.[2]

Still, the bifurcation of twentieth-century literature in English around 1945 has proven remarkably durable, persisting on academic syllabi, curricula, and job descriptions despite many challenges to the practice of "tearing history, literary or otherwise, at the perforation of 1945" (Saint-Amour 27). Moreover, the institutionalized break aligns with a far broader cultural sense that 1945 marked a transformative watershed in world history. 1945 was indeed "a catastrophic year," one that "etch[ed] European" and global "cultural memory with [the] atomic bomb and what would later be termed the Holocaust." As literature can uniquely illuminate, however, 1945 is also "crude division" impressed upon "the complex fluidity of public events and private imagination" (Plain 1). When the sheer momentousness denoted by "1945" is yoked to the contrastive imperatives of literary periodization, the effect is to naturalize the notion that the literary late 1940s must be notable, if at all, for what periods or movements began or ended during those years. Put another way, the 1945 boundary entails pre-conceptualizing Anglophone literature of the late 1940s as significant for either enacting the exhausted conclusions or spotting the first glimmers of established if serially renovated literary periods: for witnessing, say, the dusk of modernism or the dawn of postmodernism, the decline of imperialist national literatures or the rise of anti-imperialist postcolonial ones, or the end of a literary era defined by two World Wars or the start of a period called "postwar" or "post-45" but marked by continuous military violence. These last two are functionally synonymous period categories for literary studies; in practice they mean something more like "post-1955" or "post-1960," stretch to contain the whole second half of the twentieth century, and thereby help sustain the 1940s as what George Hutchinson, writing of the US context, calls "the black hole" of twentieth-century literary history (2).

Alternate Period Vocabularies

Among its deleterious effects, then, the baseline pre-/post-1945 periodization of twentieth-century literature in English obscures the distinct sense of historicity that late-1940s literature articulates. Given the glaring exclusions that result from martial—or, as in post-45, tacitly martial—and other conventions of literary periodization that privilege Euro-American conceptions time and history, this might seem like small potatoes. But consider that the stubborn utility of the 1945 break in twentieth-century literary studies squares with the equally persistent fiction that WWII was "bound in time," and that wars that aren't thus bound neither rate as "real wars" nor necessitate civilian scrutiny of the motives, costs, or legal consequences of their prosecution (Dudziak 62). Already at midcentury, no thoughtful writer mistook the year 1945 for the unqualified end of the war. For one example, the Japanese novelist, critic, and translator Toyoshima Yoshio wrote through Allied censorship in

March 1948 of the rhetorical but not material end of the war in his occupied nation: "The war is over but peace is not here [...] For now the world has laid down its arms, but they have not been abandoned" (qtd. in Lucken 144).[3] For another, in the prefatory note to his non-fiction collection *Two Cheers for Democracy* (1951), the English novelist E. M. Forster characterized WWII as "the war which began for Great Britain in 1939, though earlier elsewhere, and which is still going on" (Forster xi). Or consider recent efforts finally to bring the literature of the 1940s into critical focus. One strategy for this work is to revalue the year of 1945 itself, whether in discrete projects (Hepburn, Gumbrecht) or in newish disciplinary formations.[4] Another gambit is to subvert the imperatives of the 1945 split by embracing as generative limits external, ostensibly arbitrary chronological units that are *not* 1945. The decade of the 1940s (Plain, Hutchinson), the single years of 1947 (Åsbrink) or 1948 (Gandhi and Nelson): these "tapered units" (Gandhi and Nelson 297) of world-historical time foster scholars' collective recovery of diverse national and transnational literatures and cultures of the early postwar.

A third way of recovering the lost energies (political and otherwise) of the literary late 1940s is to seek the looser, less rigid chrono-historical units and narratives that emerged internally to those years to describe the historical present, and that attained a complex salience in or for the period's literature. How did literary works of the late 1940s name, and express something of what it felt like to live through, the staggering initial aftermath of WWII before this loaded historical moment disappeared into the longer arcs of "post-45" or "postwar"? By what terms, figures, and patterns did the literary late-1940s conjure the overwhelming magnitude of their moment before its outcomes got plotted along the forward march of the retrospectively "clear and hard path of cold war history" (Gandhi and Nelson 286)? And how did writers conceive imaginatively of what was then called "the recent war" before it was subsumed into the operative myth of "the good war" so championed and cherished, especially but not exclusively by the United States, the United Kingdom, and Russia?

No single essay can answer these questions fully, of course. Yet even to pose them is to hold in critical suspension some of the disciplinary structures that have constricted study of the literary late 1940s; to pose such questions is thus to make room for features and patterns of the literary late 1940s that bespeak the period's deep, diffuse, and inescapably political awareness of its historical present but that tend to slip through the cracks between dominant literary-period categories. Put another way, if one understands the relative obscurity of late-1940s literature as emblematic of, rather than exceptional under, standard literary periodization and the persistence of the 1945 "break," then one might begin to revalue that literature by seeking out its production or complication of messier, less conspicuous, less disciplined or disciplinary periodic self-concepts. Among those once nimbler, now mostly lost or decontextualized terms are "midcentury," "the recent war," and "the age of anxiety." The precise origins of, or meanings that attached to, these terms in late-1940s literary and public cultures can help to reopen to critical apprehension the literary expressions or registers of the weight that bore on the late 1940s.

Feeling "Midcentury"

The arbitrariness of the midcentury mark was lost on no one. Yet on either side of 1950, and especially as the neat round date approached, the sheer fact of the midcentury measure occasioned a swell of epochal self-reflection, historical stocktaking, and affective projection. Across poems, novels, essays, letters to the editor, magazine special issues, scholarly monographs, literary anthologies, and newspaper columns, writers articulated the keenly felt pressure of history at midcentury. Beginning in the late 1940s, a self-reflexive "midcentury" discourse hitched the arithmetic middle of the twentieth century to pervasive feelings of uncertainty; it stressed not so much the novelty as the incomprehensibility of the historical present, and it evniced a profound sense of suspension amid vague but consequential onsets and outcomes (Seiler, *Midcentury Suspension* 13–25). Little wonder, then, that immediately upon the publication, in February 1947, of W. H. Auden's *The Age of Anxiety*, the poem's title rushed into transatlantic popular idiom and print culture, taken up as shorthand for the affective self-concept of the historical moment.

"Midcentury" discourse turned the self-conscious historicity of the present itself into something close to what the literary and cultural theorist Raymond Williams was, already in the early 1950s, beginning to conceptualize as a structure of feeling. In a little book called *Preface to Film* (1954), Williams wrote:

> While we may, in the study of a past period, separate out particular aspects of life, and treat them as if they were separate, it is obvious that this is only how they may be studied, not how they were experienced. We examine each element as a precipitate, but in the living experience of the time every element was in solution, an inseparable part of a complex whole. And it seems to be true, from the nature of art, that it is from such a totality that the artist draws; it is in art, primarily, that that effect of the totality, the dominant structure of feeling, is expressed and embodied.
>
> *(Williams 611)*

Williams's first inklings at midcentury of structures of feeling (and of his *Keywords* [1976)] have fallen "off the radar in film studies and cultural studies, as well as in examinations of [his] work" (MacKenzie 607). However surprising in those disciplinary contexts, that apparent neglect squares with the broader critical elision of the literary late 1940s. Reading Williams in concert with "midcentury" discourse reveals that the felt historicity of the early wake of WWII helped to motivate his hashing out of a conceptual vocabulary through which to value critically and to understand politically the aesthetic traces of "living experiences" At once participants in and creative analysts of that discourse, writers of the late 1940s reckoned with what it felt like to live in and through the incomprehensibly vast and still-pending global outcomes of what was then often called "the recent war."

The Late-1940s Currency of "The Recent War"

The phrase "the recent war" was so ubiquitous in midcentury English as almost to defy citation: it appeared everywhere from Winston Churchill's 1946 "Sinews of Peace" address (better known as the "iron curtain" speech) and the Geneva Conventions of 1949 to the drop heads of obituaries and wedding announcements for veterans of "the recent war." There's an alarmingly ephemeral imprecision at work in the shifting referent of "the recent war" over time. In its wide late-1940s usage, however, the phrase had a stable referent—WWII—and a temporal slipperiness that were illustratively, if tragically, metonymic of the midcentury moment. Hovering in time across past, future, and present, "the recent war" simultaneously inscribed earlier wars (WWI most obviously) and anticipated the "next" war, which in the late 1940s heralded the novel threat of nuclear annihilation; the phrase also registered continuing aspects of WWII left unresolved by surrenders or treaties and captured how proximate and pressing the war still felt. How could it have felt otherwise in the late 1940s?

Hence Toyoshima's and Forster's clarity about the murky conclusion to WWII opens onto a broader literary probing of the ethical, political, affective, and experiential outcomes of the recent war. For many English-language writers in Allied nations, this questioning meant extending into the aftermath of the recent war the urgent wartime project of wresting English itself back from its manipulation into the brash bombast, shady euphemism, and the "uncritical, exclusionary, and blinkered forms of patriotism that war tends to elicit" (MacKay 5). Writers thus carried forward conscientious wartime writers' objections to the political degradation of English itself, and sought to drag the language and its poetics back from what Cecil Day Lewis (1943) described as the obligation to "Defend the bad against the worse" ("Where Are the War Poets?"). Some young US poets, for example, channeled their resistance to the nation's prosecution of the war by coopting self-regarding American phraseology that justified gross injustice during wartime. In "Guilt by Heredity," an undated sonnet of her wartime incarceration, the Japanese American poet Toyo Suyemoto repurposes certain phrases and principles from the US Constitution and jurisprudence. "'Guilt by heredity' presumes enough/For accusation and the summary": so begins Suyemoto's rewriting of the presumption of innocence and her poetic protest not only of her imprisonment as a member of a "suspect race" but also of the contortions of law and legalese that enabled it (140). Gwendolyn Brooks's "Negro Hero (to suggest Dorie Miller)" (1945), a persona poem spoken by the African American Messman Third Class serving in the segregated US Navy at Pearl Harbor, sustains a dichotomy between "I" and "they," lodging in its pronominal grammar the racial hierarchy and violence that Miller endured in service of a democracy that denied him full citizenship. "I helped to save them, them and a part of their democracy," the imagined Miller reflects toward the end of the poem (45). The line resignifies the phrase "making the world safe for democracy" that President Woodrow Wilson famously used to champion US participation in WWI; it also registers, in its very pronouns—the active subject "I" versus the triplicate objects "them" and "their"—and diction ("a part of") the fundamental hypocrisy and partiality of an American "democracy" that violently excluded entire populations from political participation, equal opportunity and rights.

In the UK, Orwell's classic essay "Politics and the English Language" (1946) advanced a similar scrutiny of the English language itself after the recent war. Published in the British little magazine *Horizon* just shy of a year after V-E Day, the essay does not bask in the nominal peace. "Politics and the English Language" instead connects "the present political chaos" the world over to "a decay in language," and suggests that "one can probably bring about some improvement by starting at the verbal end." Accordingly, the essay fuses the dos-and-don'ts practicality of a style guide with the urgency of polemic. Orwell urges his readers to rid their speech of tired metaphors, windy verb phrases, "pretentious diction," meaningless jargon, and other habits he regards as rhetorically consistent with, and thus lazily complicit in, the manipulation of English into the sort of political bunk used to license and conceal violence. The point of "Politics and the English Language" is not simply to encourage readers toward better writing in Orwell's signature plain style; nor is the goal to perpetuate the exclusions ensconced in "standard English," which phrase Orwell encases in scare quotes. The stakes are much higher. "In our time," Orwell writes in a key passage,

> political speech and writing are largely the defence of the indefensible. Things like the continuance of British rule in India, the Russian purges and deportations, the dropping of the atom bombs on Japan, can indeed be defended, but only by arguments which are too brutal for most people to face, and which do not square with the professed aims of

political parties. Thus political language has to consist largely of euphemism, question-begging and sheer cloudy vagueness.

(Orwell)

With the noteworthy exceptions of the elision of the word *American* before, and the passive phrasing of, "the dropping of the atom bombs on Japan," this passage is vintage Orwell. On its not-too-distant dystopian horizon sits "Newspeak," the totalitarian language "designed not to extend but to *diminish* the range of thought" that Orwell would create in *1984* (268).

The passage and the essay are also in many ways vintage late 1940s. For one thing, as in Brooks's and Suyemoto's appropriations of democratic language, and in keeping with many more and less plainly political works by English-language writers of the early postwar period, the essay skewers the official cant wrapped around state violence perpetrated by the victors of the recent war. Orwell enumerates not crimes committed by an enemy often constructed as monstrously other—and, in the case of Allied representations of persons of Japanese descent, constructed as racially other—but rather by the Big Three Allied powers themselves. For another, in "Politics and the English Language," the world-historical weight of the present takes specific rhetorical shape as a list of political and military abuses, what Orwell in his dressed-down language terms indefensible "things." Itemizing the British Raj, Russian purges, and American uses of atomic bombs, Orwell's list of injustices and violence which must be confronted reads as a kind of small, self-critical linguistic corollary to the grand international legal discourse asserting global human rights and the international adjudication of war crimes after the recent war (Stonebridge, *The Judicial Imagination* and *Placeless People*).

The Original "Age of Anxiety"

Where Orwell sought a concrete language—and for Orwell in the 1940s, the word "language" was never far from "literature"—to account for the "things" he lists, many other English-language writers proffered litanies of horrors and crises that summoned the anxious mood of the late 1940s in recently victorious nations. Like the early postwar critique of political bunk, this enumerative strategy was not exactly new; Mark Greif observes that by the early 1940s in the United States, "intellectuals who identified themselves with world politics could recite a continuous list of crises leading up to World War II" (5). By the late 1940s, the list was longer, still ready for recitation, and newly primed for emotional projection. Any number of works in the admittedly narrow canon of midcentury liberal philosophy, political theory, or psychology—e.g., Arthur Schlesinger, Jr.'s *The Vital Center* (1949), Rollo May's *The Meaning of Anxiety* (1950)— rattle off the "crises" and the anxiety they provoke in the implicitly white citizens of liberal(ish) democracies. Meanwhile, the poem that did more than any other text to associate the early aftermath of the recent war with a pervasive feeling of anxiety, Auden's *Age of Anxiety*, opens with an obliquely parodic recitation of that very accustomed list. In the poem, the oft-enumerated crush of world history redounds to the benefit of a Manhattan dive bar: "When the historical process breaks down and armies organize [...] then it looks good to the bar business" (3).

Decades ago, the phrase "the age of anxiety" morphed into a cliché applicable to any nervous time; anxiety, or the more pathologized state of paranoid anxiety, is the structure of feeling most often imputed to the longer cold war. Auden's poem, which runs to a hundred-plus pages in (mostly) a pastiche of Old English alliterative verse, can be as much a grind as it is a wonder to read. All this conspires with the ho-hum image of the literary late 1940s to obscure how the poem evokes an aura of anxiety specific to the self-consciously "historical" mood of the late 1940s. It's all too easy to gloss over, in turn, how the poem registers uneasiness with restrictively individual and psychological understandings of anxiety, which can incline citizens toward isolation and security rather than collectivity and solidarity. In keeping with both the affect that organizes it and the temporal elasticity signified by "the recent war," *The Age of Anxiety* defies linear time and historical decorum. Most tellingly in this vein, the poem sustains both a wartime setting and a manifestly postwar consciousness—and conscience.

The whole work turns on four white strangers (two servicemen on leave, two civilians) hearing a radio broadcast of the war headlines; it captures the desensitizing effects of euphemism and cliché on combatants as on civilians ("We fought them off/but *paid a price*" one of the strangers thinks "dully" of a gunner killed in battle [12, my italics]). It carries formal and affective traces of Auden's service in the Morale Division of the United States Strategic Bombing Survey, for which outfit he spent the summer of 1945 interviewing German civilian survivors of air raids about their experiences (Seiler 2016). Most starkly, in a pair of sequential conclusions, the poem betrays its knowledge of, and broaches an emerging moral reckoning with, the two horrors that marked ends of the war in Germany and Japan: the fuller exposure of the Nazi death camps and the American atomic bombings of the Japanese cities of Hiroshima and Nagasaki. Written in prose, the second end of *The Age of Anxiety* finds one stranger riding a commuter train into the sunrise over a mostly empty city and all humankind's "self-destruction [...] as usual postponed" (108). Together, the hint of nuclear aubade and the adjective "postponed" gesture toward the chilling bureaucracy required to produce human-made atrocity or apocalypse. The ending in turn works backward across *The Age of Anxiety* to string together the poem's several descriptions of vistas or scenes that, silent and unpeopled, suggest obliteration and induce anxiety. While its title was subsequently taken to define the cold war, the poem itself conjures a collective experience of anxiety specific to the recent war as it seeped into the atmosphere of the late 1940s. This diffuse feeling of anxiety neither exempts the victors from moral culpability and political responsibility nor assuages the individual anxieties of the most privileged citizens of liberal democracies.

Against "The Good War"

Cultural-theoretical efforts to conceive of historical feeling at "midcentury," linguistic critiques of Allied violence perpetrated in "the recent war," the ambivalent coinage of "the age of anxiety": these exemplary projects of literary-historical self-conceptualization around 1947 finally participate in an undervalued and politically urgent aspect of late 1940s literature. Across genres and in real time, the literature of the late 1940s offered ample forms of resistance to the narrative patterns by which the victors—most durably and consequentially, the Americans—quickly began to turn "the recent war" into the self-exculpatory story of "the good war." As Marina MacKay suggests, "it would take a criminally perverse form of historical revisionism to suggest that World War II was anything other than a war that the Allies had to win"; it takes a complacently self-congratulatory form of historical mythologizing to swallow the "trans-historical simplifications of 'good against evil'" that adhere to the war and elide "the real experiences of the real people" everywhere who lived through it (MacKay, "Introduction" 3).

In the UK, WWII "is always just 'the war', colloquially, as if there had been no other" (MacKay, *Modernism* 1). Its public narrative privileges civilian stoicism, especially during the

Blitz, while its legacy—a European victory on the eve of the end of the British Empire—buttresses political arguments for British participation in subsequent wars. Meanwhile in the United States, the tenacity of the "good war" myth has contorted public culture, thwarted national development of historical self-awareness, misinformed military policy, and inflamed American militarism ever since. "The good war [...] served as prologue to three-quarters of a century of misbegotten ones," writes Elizabeth D. Samet, cannily using the language of literary form ("prologue") to underline the "sacral force" that the narrative of "the good war" exerts in US politics and culture (5). Principal tenets of "the good war" myth include the beliefs that the United States "went to war to liberate the world from fascism and tyranny" and that "World War II was a foreign tragedy with a happy American ending" (Samet 25–26). Roy Scranton identifies as a principal figure in the US "good war" story "the war trauma hero," by which he means the dominant representation of "the American veteran [as] sympathetic victim, rather than a perpetrator, of violence" (3). The "war trauma hero" is serially reproduced across interlocking political, psychological, and literary conventions, in part to deflect public scrutiny of the justification and conduct of American wars and, in literary terms, to elevate a reassuring kind of veteran story.

Among its many challenges to the "good war" myth, US literature of the late 1940s was both written by and replete with veterans of the recent war who did not fit this profile. One especially stark and ingenious exponent of novelistic critique of "the good war" myth is Dix Steele, the fighter-pilot veteran and serial rapist and murderer at the center of Dorothy B. Hughes's 1947 noir novel *In a Lonely Place*. His hypermasculine name so blunt as to achieve its own kind of subtlety, Dix Steele hates women. But his service in the war did not so much spark his murderous misogyny as afford him gendered cover for it. Steele enlisted in the first place not for patriotic reasons but out of a combination of obligation and F.O.M.O.: "It was the thing to do. And the Air Corps was the thing to do. [...] I didn't want to be left out of any excitement" (13). After the war, under the cover conferred by his whiteness, his fraudulent access to cash, and his veteran status, Dix cruises around L.A. unsuspected of his crimes—even by his wartime friend Nicolai Brub, a happily newlywed police detective.

In a Lonely Place systematically "reverses and upends [the] conventions" of hard-boiled fiction, the subgenre of crime fiction popularized in the United States in the 1930s and focused on "(mostly) cynical detectives, crooked cops, and tabloid murder" (Abbott 202). Rather than through a world-weary cop, Hughes focalizes her novel through the criminal, which narrative choice means that *In a Lonely Place* derives its suspense not from jaded authorities solving a mystery but from the depiction of the inner life of a serial killer. Instead of sidelining and ultimately punishing stock female characters, *In a Lonely Place* casts the *femme fatale* and the good-girl blonde—"her hair was the color of palest gold," Dix notes (11)—as the savviest observers in the book. The two women collaborate with one another to catch the killer. And rather than narrate a detective puzzling through the grisly details of a crime scene where a white woman (typically) has been killed, Hughes mostly refrains from narrating Steele's crimes. These and other subversions of earlier crime novels align, politically and ethically, with Hughes's novelistic defiance of the rapidly consolidating "good war" myth and of one of its hero types. The subversions sketch an analogy between Dix's attempt to gaslight the reader about his crimes against women and the national project of remaking the horrors of the recent war into the comforting story of the "good" one. Crucially, Hughes's novel perceives the extent to which the dominant US public narrative of the recent war both proceeded from gender and race privilege and would produce only more gendered and racial violence.

At midcentury, Hughes, Auden, Brooks, and many other writers objected to Manichean simplifications of their recent war. Today, state and non-state violence persists in predictably gendered and racialized ways and the "next" war is always already here. What can literary history and periodization have to do with such violence and the attendant rightward heave of contemporary political life? And what can the literature of the late 1940s, in particular, have to do with these? It's tempting to leap to grandiose claims. Instead and at the very least, one can state with certainty that midcentury literature constitutes a vital and diverse repository of efforts to write and live with integrity through a profoundly uncertain, threatening time. It's a repository of many voices and forms that collectively refused to give up, go silent, or settle for deceptive simplifications during a moment that bore a historical weight as inescapable as it was incalculable. One can also state that encountering literature of the late 1940s on and through its own self-reflexive historical terms aids substantively, not just meta-critically, in unsettling the habit of splitting the literary twentieth century at or around 1945. Though literary-critical debate about periodization fosters important disciplinary self-reflection, it's unlikely to turn critical attention to brief moments that periodization itself cemented in place as (at best) transitions between more important movements or as (at worst) dormant. The late 1940s, as I've suggested, are one such moment. Reading the literature of those years by its own lights thus finally argues for detaching twentieth-century literary periodization from its convenient alliance with the myth of self-justifying military violence consolidated around WWII and 1945. Destabilizing such myths wherever one encounters them can, one hopes, contribute to the project of advancing a moral and political vision of just democratic struggle.

Notes

1 *Partisan Review* published the first English translation of this essay in July 1948.
2 In 2008, the "new" modernist studies defined itself on a principle of "expansion" (Mao and Walkowitz 737); quickly thereafter the field became "characterized by intense self-scrutiny as well as unprecedented geographical, temporal, and cultural diffuseness" (James and Seshagiri 88).
3 I thank Alex Bates for his help in dating this quotation, which first appeared in the magazine *Shakai* (Society), March 1948.
4 The "Post45" collective, for example, initially distinguished itself from both academic modernism and the once relatively fixed and overwhelmingly white and male canon of 1980s–1990s US postmodernism ("About Post45").

Works Cited

"About Post45." *Post45*, 8 Nov. 2010, https://post45.org/about-post45/. Accessed 12 July 2022.
Appadurai, Arjun. *Modernity at Large: Cultural Dimensions of Globalization*. U of Minnesota P, 1996.
Åsbrink, Elisabeth. *1947: When Now Begins*. Translated by Fiona Graham, Other Press, 2018.
Auden, W. H. *The Age of Anxiety: A Baroque Eclogue*. Edited by Alan Jacobs, Princeton UP, 2011.
Berryman, John. Untitled response. "The State of American Writing, 1948." *Partisan Review*, August 1948, pp. 856–860.
Bowen, Elizabeth. "English Fiction at Mid-Century." *People, Places, Things: Essays by Elizabeth Bowen*, edited by Allan Hepburn, Edinburgh UP, 2008, pp. 321–324.
Bradbury, Malcolm. "'Closing Time in the Gardens': Or, What Happened to Writing in the 1940s." *No, Not Bloomsbury*, Columbia UP, 1988, pp. 67–86.
Brooks, Gwendolyn. "Negro Hero (to suggest Dorie Miller)." *Common Ground*, Summer 1945, pp. 44–45.
Churchill, Winston. "The Sinews of Peace." March 5, 1946. https://winstonchurchill.org/resources/-speeches/1946-1963-elder-statesman/the-sinews-of-peace/. Accessed 16 January 2023.
Day Lewis, Cecil. "Where Are the War Poets?" *Word Over All*, Jonathan Cape, 1943, p. 30.

Dimock, Wai Chee. "Aesthetics at the Limits of the Nation: Kant, Pound, and the *Saturday Review*." *American Literature*, vol. 76, no. 3, Sept. 2004, pp. 525–547.

Dudziak, Mary L. *Wartime: An Idea, Its History, Its Consequences*. Oxford UP, 2012.

Forster, E. M. *Two Cheers for Democracy*. Harcourt, 1979.

Gandhi, Leela, and Deborah L. Nelson. Editors' Introduction. *Around 1948: Interdisciplinary Approaches to Global Transformation*, special issue of *Critical Inquiry*, vol. 40, no. 4, Summer 2014, pp. 285–297.

Geneva Conventions of 12 August 1949. International Committee of the Red Cross. https://www.icrc.org/en/doc/assets/files/publications/icrc-002-0173.pdf. Accessed 20 July 2022.

Gumbrecht, Hans Ulrich. *After 1945: Latency as Origin of the Present*. Stanford UP, 2013.

Hepburn, Allan, editor. *Around 1945: Literature, Citizenship, Rights*. McGill-Queen's UP, 2016.

Hersey, John. "Hiroshima." *New Yorker*, Aug. 1946.

Hughes, Dorothy B. *In a Lonely Place*. New York Review Books, 2017.

Hutchinson, George. *Facing the Abyss: American Literature and Culture in the 1940s*. Columbia UP, 2018.

James, David and Urmila Seshagiri. "Metamodernism: Narratives of Continuity and Revolution." *PMLA*, vol. 129, no. 1, January 2014, pp. 87–100.

Leick, Karen. "Ezra Pound v. *The Saturday Review of Literature*." *Journal of Modern Literature*, vol. 25, no. 2, Winter 2001, pp. 19–37.

Lucken, Michael. *The Japanese and the War: Expectation, Perception, and the Shaping of Memory*. Translated by Karen Grimwade, Columbia UP, 2017.

Mao, Douglas and Rebecca L. Walkowitz. "The New Modernist Studies." *PMLA*, vol. 123, no 3, May 2008, pp. 737–748.

May, Rollo. *The Meaning of Anxiety*. Norton, 2015.

MacKay, Marina. Introduction. *The Cambridge Companion to the Literature of World War II*, Cambridge UP, 2009, pp. 1–9.

———. *Modernism and World War II*. Cambridge UP, 2007.

MacKenzie, Scott. *Film Manifestos and Global Cinema Cultures: A Critical Anthology*. U of California P, 2014.

McKenzie, Marjorie. "Views Journalists Squeezing Last Vestige of Historicity from Passing of Mid-Century." *Pittsburgh Courier*, 14 Jan 1950, p. 19.

Nadel, Alan. *Containment Culture: American Narratives, Postmodernism, and the Atomic Age*. Duke UP, 1996.

Orwell, George. *1984*. Random House, 2017.

———. "Politics and the English Language." 1946. https://www.orwellfoundation.com/the-orwell-foundation/orwell/essays-and-other-works/politics-and-the-english-language/. Accessed 20 July 2022.

Plain, Gill. *Literature of the 1940s: War, Postwar, and "Peace."* Edinburgh UP, 2015.

Pound, Ezra. *The Pisan Cantos*. Edited by Richard Sieburth, New Directions, 2003.

Saint-Amour, Paul K. *Tense Future: Modernism, Total War, Encyclopedic Form*. Oxford UP, 2015.

Samet, Elizabeth D. *Looking for the Good War: American Amnesia and the Violent Pursuit of Happiness*. Farrar, Straus and Giroux, 2021.

Sartre, Jean-Paul. "The Situation of the Writer in 1947." *Partisan Review*, translated by Bernard Frechtman, vol. 15, no. 6, June 1948, pp. 634–653.

Schlesinger, Jr., Arthur. *The Vital Center: The Politics of Freedom*. Routledge, 2017.

Seiler, Claire. "Auden and the Work of the Age of Anxiety." *Auden at Work*, edited by Bonnie Costello and Rachel Galvin, Palgrave Macmillan, pp. 250–274.

———. *Midcentury Suspension: Literature and Feeling in the Wake of World War II*. Columbia UP, 2020.

"The State of American Writing, 1948," *Partisan Review*, vol. 15, no. 8, August 1948, pp. 855–894.

Stevens, Wallace. "The Motive for Metaphor." *Selected Poems*, edited by John N. Serio, Knopf, 2011, p. 152.

Stonebridge, Lyndsey. *Placeless People: Writing, Rights, and Refugees*. Oxford UP, 2018.

———. *The Judicial Imagination: Writing after Nuremberg*. Edinburgh UP, 2011.

Suyemoto, Toyo. "Guilt by Heredity." *I Call to Remembrance: Toyo Suyemoto's Years of Internment*, edited by Susan B. Richardson, Rutgers UP, 2007, p. 140.

Underwood, Ted. *Why Literary Periods Mattered: Historical Contrast and the Prestige of English Studies*. Stanford UP, 2013.

Williams, Raymond. From *Preface to Film*. In MacKenzie, pp. 607–613.

Woodward, Guy. *Culture, Northern Ireland, and the Second World War*. Oxford UP, 2015.

22
ON OR ABOUT 1989
Ian Afflerbach

In 1989, a wall was torn down. For those millions living in Berlin, and in the two German states sprawling behind this split city, the wall was first and foremost a physical barrier, some 150 kilometers long, made of concrete, mesh, and barbed wire. But for them and millions more, the wall was also a symbol, an ideological barrier dividing two ways of life run by two political entities vying for control over much of the planet's people and resources. When demolition of the wall began on November 9—direct action expressing popular will before being sanctioned by the state—it did not simply signal the free movement of persons between East and West Germany: it signaled the end of the Cold War. Witnessing this symbolic conclusion to the century's last global political struggle, some Anglophone intellectuals began to prophesy the coming of a new international harmony, an era of individual freedom and commercial prosperity with no real boundaries, and all nations united under the shared political banner of liberal democracy.

Liberal Pluralism at the End of History

Francis Fukuyama crystallized this idyllic vision in an essay entitled "The End of History?" published with *The National Interest* in 1989 and later extended into his book *The End of History and the Last Man* (1992). By "history" Fukuyama did not mean written accounts of past events; rather, he argued that the victory of liberal democracy and free markets over communism, their last great rival, represented the end of History, "understood as a single, coherent, evolutionary process," as proposed by G. W. F. Hegel—or at least Alexandre Kojève's reading of Hegel (x). Liberty and equality were the twin principles toward which all nations would aspire in the future; "events" would continue to occur in the process, but "History" as a fundamental contest over political ideals was over. Sweeping both Karl Marx's materialist account of class struggle and John Dewey's vision of educated social action under this Hegelian rug, Fukuyama affirmed that industrial capitalism and liberal pluralism were "free from…internal contradictions" (xii). With wealth and security apparently assured through technological advances, he proposed that political life would now center upon what Hegel called the "recognition" of personal and group identities (2).

Fukuyama's "good news," quipped Jacques Derrida in *Specters of Marx* (1994), came at an opportune moment; but of course this was all just a "soothing confusion" (68), an idealistic daydream destined to be "haunted by what it excludes" (61). The U.S. and Europe remain wracked by economic inequality, sexism, racism, and other oppressions, hardly resembling "the perfection of the universal State" or of liberal democracy (63). Most of the globe, moreover, suffers from what Jacques Derrida calls the "ten plagues" of the "new world order": unemployment, homelessness and deportation, economic war, contradictions between protectionism and free trade, foreign debt and austerity, the arms trade, nuclear proliferation, inter-ethnic conflicts, corrupt or failed states, and unreliable international laws (81–83). To these one might well add religious conflict, terrorism, global health concerns, mass immigration, and a planetary environmental crisis of existential proportions.

Intellectuals today, in other words, must view Fukuyama's pronouncements about 1989 as hopelessly, even dangerously naïve. On that basis alone, however, it would be wrong to insist that his ideas represent a political perspective that was neatly antithetical to the presumptively radical work of cultural critics such as Derrida. Literary scholars in the last quarter of the twentieth century did exhibit far more skepticism about liberal democracy, far more awareness of the globe's manifold political crises, than Fukuyama or other neoconservative pundits. And yet the key concerns shaping Anglophone literary history in and around 1989—the discourse around postmodernism, the canon and culture wars, and, above all, the growing authority of a cultural politics rooted in identity, diversity, and recognition—all reflect an underlying reckoning with the same governing paradigm of liberal pluralism championed by *The End of History*. One might revisit the late 1980s to condemn, yet again, an emergent neoliberal world order that has all too obviously failed today. Instead, this chapter performs the less comfortable work of examining how preeminent issues in the theory and practice of literary studies have been shaped by that moment's doubts about any progressive metanarratives and its concomitant turn toward an eschatological pluralism. Tracing the profound set of cultural changes, and changing ideas about culture, in and around "1989," this chapter tacitly affirms that any inquiry into "literature and politics" involves foregrounding not just authorial commitments and identities but also the critical, pedagogical, and institutional practices that necessarily mediate between readers and writers.

The End of Literary History?

When David Perkins asked, *Is Literary History Possible?* (1992), he was not doubting whether scholars could or would produce more narratives about the past. "The question," he insisted, was rather "whether the discipline can be intellectually respectable" (12). During the nineteenth century, "literary history enjoyed popularity and unquestioned prestige" (1) by remaining committed to developmental narratives, which tracked "the unfolding of an idea, principle, or suprapersonal entity" (2). But in the twentieth century, critics had exposed "certain fundamental cruxes in the theory of literary history" (18). Against the objectivity imagined and desired by positivist historians, scholars now understood that representing the past inevitably requires selections, excisions, and a definite point of view. In *Metahistory* (1973), Hayden White showed how even the grand developmental narratives of nineteenth-century historians such as Michelet and Ranke were structured by metaphor, metonymy, synecdoche, and irony: governing tropes traditionally associated with the literary and rhetorical arts. "*Metahistory*," remarks F. R. Ankersmit, "transformed historical writing into literature" (9).

Without a historical referent prior to or outside of rhetoric, however, there could be no non-literary narratives about literature, no extrinsic standard to judge how literary history should be written. For an interpretation to appear meaningful, observes Perkins, there must rather be some degree of "social consensus" (16). In the U.S. and Britain, with many readers and writers increasingly aware of their pluralist political bodies, pursuing such a consensus decreasingly seemed either plausible or desirable. The different stories needed to address different group identities require "literary history" as a discipline to ramify into countless distinct but intertwined strands rather than offer a holistic, unifying narrative. The "'postmodern' *Columbia Literary History of the United States* (1987)," remarks Perkins, offers an object lesson in this shift, as it assembles its disparate essays without claim to "consecutiveness and coherence" (3). Perkins concludes that we can no longer "write literary history with intellectual conviction, but we must read it. The irony and paradox of this argument," he adds, "are themselves typical of our present moment in history" (17).

That moment, for better or worse, was in the 1980s and 1990s, often called "postmodern." In *The Postmodern Condition* (1984), Jean-François Lyotard famously defined this epoch as rooted in "an incredulity towards metanarratives" (xxiv), a pervasive doubt that science, theology, philosophy, or history could supply stable criteria to legitimate knowledge or validate interpretation. A rough sketch of this term's protean history remains a minimal imperative for understanding how "postmodernism" came to be not only a vital concept in literary discourse, but also a keyword in debates over the politics of culture—before fading into near oblivion by the twenty-first century. "Postmodern" was first deployed by Charles Olson, Irving Howe, Charles Jencks, and Ihab Hassan to describe various turns away from modernism in literature, architecture, and the visual arts; even through the 1970s, it largely remained confined to conversations in the avant-garde art world, led by critics like Rosalind Krauss, Douglass Crimp, and the journal *October*. "Between 1981 and 1984," however, potent theoretical arguments from Lyotard, Jean Baudrillard, Jürgen Habermas, Richard Rorty, and Fredric Jameson suddenly made postmodernism "an indispensable concept in theories of the contemporary" (Bertens 111). In their hands, explains Bertens, postmodernism also became "unavoidably political," and a veritable deluge of books and essays appeared from the mid- to late 1980s with some combination of "politics" and "postmodern" in the title, such as Linda Hutcheon's *The Politics of Postmodernism* (1989).

Anglophone academics, who had been eagerly devouring the continental or "French" theory of Derrida, Jacques Lacan, and Michel Foucault, fused the claims of these poststructuralist thinkers with the ambient notion of a new cultural epoch. In this "mature" phase, postmodernism became a stand-in term for a form of cultural politics, for seeing power as rooted not only in agential action or economic capital but also, crucially, in representations and discourse. Intellectuals, especially literary scholars, now aimed "to expose the politics that are at work in representations and to undo institutionalized hierarchies," and, through an "advocacy of difference, pluriformity, and multiplicity," to prioritize those who are 'Other' "from the point of view of the liberal humanist subject (white, male, heterosexual, and rational)" (Bertens 8). This new cultural politics resulted in a tremendous acceleration of conceptual claims about literature: pick up any journal issue from 1989, and it will likely be freckled with a half-dozen different critical theories. This enthusiastic mixing of ideas, however, also quickly led to a terminological haze. By the late 1980s, champions and detractors alike were deploying terms like "postmodernism," "poststructuralism," and "deconstruction" as generalized synonyms, flattening and confusing once markedly different concepts into political buzzwords.

The discourse around postmodernism—especially when wielded by activist intellectuals working within ethnic studies departments, women's and gender studies programs, and other theoretically informed yet practically minded efforts—undeniably helped stimulate an epochal turn in literary studies toward politically vital issues of representation, alterity, identity, and subject-formation, and the next section explores how these crucial concerns reshaped the literary canon. First, though, more must be said about the historiographic consequences of this intellectual movement. Whatever else it might mean, postmodernism clearly implies an end to the modern. If this only implied a shift in artistic styles, it would seem a simple enough distinction, if also potentially superficial. However, for those who follow Marx in identifying modernity with capitalism, there are serious problems with suggesting that—even after Pynchon, Foucault, and the VHS—we have somehow escaped the problems of the modern. Worsening levels of income inequality, continued exploitation of peripheries by urban centers, and emerging technologies dissolving traditional labor markets all testify that the problems posed by Marxism remain far from solved.

In "Postmodernism, or the Cultural Logic of Late Capitalism," (1984) Jameson attempted to square this linguistic circle by fusing the socio-cultural transformations of postmodernism to a Marxist periodization of "late capitalism," influenced by Ernst Mandel. Jameson and others have since revised his schema, notably adding "late modernism" as a term to describe modernism's endurance into the Cold War years, which scholars like Jed Esty have made into a growing branch of twentieth-century Anglophone literary studies. Nonetheless, there remains a salient conceptual problem in proposing that some novel cultural movement replaced modernism, which had precisely been defined by its transgressive novelty. The first two major studies of postmodern fiction, Brian McHale's *Postmodernist Fiction* (1987) and Linda Hutcheon's *A Poetics of Postmodernism* (1988), try to partition periods by emphasizing a metafictional turn, a newfound tension between textual representation and authorial reflexivity. Hutcheon's term "historiographic metafiction" helpfully names a pattern of toggling between self-reflexivity and historical references in Anglophone fiction; yet even in the 1960s and 1970s, such metafiction was perhaps more captivating and definitional to critics rather than to literary artists. To be sure, Thomas Pynchon, Samuel Beckett, John Barth, William Gaddis, Robert Coover, and the brothers Barthelme did enjoy a vogue. For most of them, however, that time passed relatively quickly, and not simply because of the notable homogeneity of these metafictional authors. As postmodernism became an overdetermined concept often used by champions and detractors alike to point in incompatible directions, critical enthusiasm for the term waned. More recently, critics have offered labels like "post-postmodernism" or "meta-modernism" to describe yet another, subsequent era, but these terms also illustrate how the fundamental temporal and conceptual problems posed by "modernity" remain unsettled.

In sum, discourse about "postmodernism" only briefly succeeded in establishing a new, stable period in Anglophone literary history. It did, however, fundamentally help transform the core critical assumptions of literary-historical practice. Identifying cultural representation as the preeminent site of political struggle, postmodernism made difference—race, gender, sexuality, ability, color, and creed—into what is perhaps *the* governing political value in English departments, while also helping tear down conventional, hierarchical assumptions about who has made literature and why it matters. By deconstructing the universal claims of (an implicitly white, heterosexual, male) liberal humanism, however, postmodernism also eroded the normative standards that had legitimated and organized literary study as an enterprise up to this point. Theorists like Derrida and Foucault, moreover, refused to offer any alternative normative values, as doing so would inevitably reinstate an oppressive and exclusionary logic within discourse and representations. Much as most historians now lacked one stable "History," literature departments came to reject the idea of any one shared "Literature." Instead, literary scholars implicitly and explicitly promoted a disciplinary pluralism by assembling a growing array of narratives about minor literatures, recovered and "recuperated" writers, popular cultures, professional ideologies, and institutional affiliations.

Literary History, as Perkins and Fukuyama might agree, remains impossible but necessary; its early hopes have ended, and yet it has never been more popular; we are all literary historians now, only no one seems to be describing or accounting for the same thing. The social currency required to legitimate these new narratives, however, still unmistakably lies in a cultural politics that promotes alterity, resistance, and transgression. Once stable periods like "modernism" have now expanded to include more and more authors, until they are scarcely recognizable to earlier generations. At the same time, scholars challenge familiar national boundaries with broader international, transnational, or global interpretive frameworks. Down come the old walls.

Recognition and Literary Pluralism

"Demands for 'recognition of difference,'" observes Nancy Fraser, represent the common link between "groups mobilized under the banners of nationality, ethnicity, 'race', gender, and sexuality" (68). In "From Redistribution to Recognition?" (1994), Fraser proposed that this politics of recognition signals a new "post-socialist" era, wherein

> group identity supplants class interest as the chief medium of political mobilization. In this account, cultural domination supplants—or becomes—exploitation as the fundamental injustice. And cultural recognition displaces socioeconomic redistribution as the remedy for injustice and the goal of political struggle.
>
> *(68)*

In his seminal essay, "The Politics of Recognition" (1992), Charles Taylor explains that social recognition provides a key mechanism for defining identity, and that misrecognition—through demeaning cultural representations, for instance—can damage an individual's self-conception, especially for those belonging to "minority or 'subaltern' groups" (1).

Ironically enough, Fukuyama anticipated this new politics of recognition, but what he foresaw as the result of liberal capitalism's blanketing peace and prosperity was instead installed into Western culture by thinkers challenging the very liberal universalism that Fukuyama had believed triumphant. The "politics of universalism," as Taylor puts it, had always been rooted in "difference-blind liberalism," which treats individuals only as abstract entities possessing equal rights; but this juridico-political framework has been put under growing pressure by the "politics of equal dignity," rooted in a pluralism that demands all cultures be treated with equal worth (62). Because culture, rather than class, provides the ground of this struggle, Taylor explains, the "main locus" of dispute between these two political visions has been "the world of education," and especially "university humanities departments, where demands are made to alter, enlarge, or scrap the 'canon' of accredited authors on the grounds that the ones presently favored consists almost entirely of 'dead white males'" (65).

The growing pluralism in literary studies between 1975 and 2000 was not simply an effect of this shift in political discourse, but also one of its chief causes. Radical feminist scholarship, for instance, clearly predated attention to terms like "postmodernism" or "culture wars," and this work helped spark a wider effort toward recovering the occluded history of women's experience; this remains true even if insufficient attention to race and more fluid conceptions of gender now make some of this scholarship's binaries appear rather dated. In

1979, for example, Sandra Gilbert and Susan Gubar published their revelatory study, *The Madwoman in the Attic*, which traced "a distinctively female literary tradition...approached and appreciated by many women readers and writers but which no one had yet defined in its entirety" (xvii). Six years later, Gilbert and Gubar co-edited *The Norton Anthology of Literature by Women* (1985), whose third edition today reaches from Marie de France to Jhumpa Lahiri. This effort at recovering a suppressed tradition of women writers was further supported by Mary Eagleton's *Feminist Literary Theory: A Reader* (1986) and Robyn Warhol and Diane Price Herndl's *Feminisms: An Anthology of Literary Theory and Criticism* (1991).

At the same time, this tradition was extending into the future through exciting new books like Margaret Atwood's novel, *The Handmaid's Tale* (1985), a dystopian feminist novel that received enormous acclaim, if also continual backlash from schools and parents, uncomfortable with its challenging depictions of religion and sexuality. Indeed, thanks to theoretical bombshells like Judith Butler's *Gender Trouble* (1990) and *Bodies That Matter* (1993), the mutual constitution of gender and sexuality emerged as a central literary question in these years. Eve Sedgwick's pioneering study in queer theory, *Epistemology of the Closet* (1990), opened the way for rereading Herman Melville, Henry James, and Marcel Proust for linguistic traces of a struggle over the boundaries of male sexuality. Meanwhile, queer writers received serious public recognition, such as Jeanette Winterson for *Oranges Are Not the Only Fruit* (1985), *The Passion* (1987), and *Sexing the Cherry* (1989), and Tony Kushner for his Tony- and Pulitzer-award winning *Angels in America: A Gay Fantasia on National Themes* (1991, 1993), which confronted the AIDS epidemic that had devastated gay communities during the 1980s.

Work in gender and sexuality studies exemplifies a growing critical desire at this time to read texts through overlapping and mutually constitutive forms of identity. In 1989, Kimberlé Williams Crenshaw provided this imperative with a lasting name: intersectionality. Crenshaw, a legal scholar and pioneer in Critical Race Theory, called on critics to approach identity not through a "single-axis framework" of race, class, or gender, but rather to see such political forces—in theory and in lived experience—as entangled determinants, and her call had far-reaching influence in literary studies (139). Black feminist writers assembled their own textual traditions, in works such as Alice Walker's "Looking for Zora" (1975) and *In Search of Our Mothers' Gardens* (1983), bell hooks' *Feminist Theory: From Margin to Center* (1984), Hazel Carby's *Reconstructing Womanhood* (1987), and Patricia Hill Collins' *Black Feminist Thought* (1990). Once again, this critical enterprise reflected exigent concerns among contemporary writers. Toni Morrison's *Beloved*, for instance, appeared in 1987 to sensational acclaim, and has since remained a perennial inclusion in lists of the most taught and most admired Anglophone fiction of the century. Drawing on the experience of escaped slave Margaret Garner, Morrison's novel exemplifies the "neo-slave narratives" first named by Bernard Bell in *The Afro-American Novel and Its Tradition* (1987). Written by a generation removed from any personal experience with slavery per se, these texts included Margaret Walker's *Jubilee* (1966), Ishmael Reed's *Flight to Canada* (1976), Alex Haley's *Roots*, Octavia Butler's *Kindred* (1979), and Alice Walker's *The Color Purple* (1982). Connecting a post-Civil Rights era, in which black Americans faced rapidly declining living standards, to a longer African-American literary tradition, neo-slave narratives pose urgent questions about historical memory, trauma, and the oft-overlooked struggles to sustain filial bonds under the conditions that Orlando Patterson has influentially called "social death."

This growing recognition of minority writers, however, also raised pressing questions about what James Baldwin once called "the burden of representation." For instance, when Frank Chin et al. released *The Big Aiiieeeee!* (1991), an expanded version of their 1974 anthology of Asian-American writers, it infamously opened with a polemic essay titled "Come All Ye Asian American Writers of the Real and the Fake." There Chin accuses Maxine Hong Kingston's *Woman Warrior* (1976) and Amy Tan's *The Joy Luck Club* (1989) of selling out to white readers, offering familiar and denigrating stereotypes of Asian-American identity. Chin's own conception of Asian-American literature, as countless critics subsequently pointed out, was fiercely restrictive: "non-Christian, nonfeminine, and nonimmigrant," summarizes Sau-ling Cynthia Wong, and limited to "three subgroups—Chinese, Japanese, and Filipino" (8). Resistant to any essentialist definition of ethnic identity, scholars in Asian-American studies began to call for a more flexible, capacious understanding of the field, as in Lisa Lowe's important essay "Heterogeneity, Hybridity, Multiplicity" (1991). Yet how to maintain the coherence of "Asian-American" given the term's growing hybridity remains one of the field's decisive questions.

Similar issues of recognition confront other minority literatures as well. Kenneth Lincoln's *Native American Renaissance* (1983) captured a growing tradition that included N. Scott Momaday's Pulitzer-Prize winning *House Made of Dawn* (1968), Leslie Marmon Silko's *Ceremony* (1977), and Louise Erdrich's *Love Medicine* (1984), which won the National Book Critics Circle Award. Some critics prefer "indigenous" to "Native American," even if each necessarily aggregates dozens of independent nations; others, like the controversial bestseller Sherman Alexie, continue using the historical "Indian." Some writers who have emerged from a larger Chicano/a movement identify as Chicanx or Chican@ to avoid a gender essentialism that some critics see as perpetuated by the cult of machismo. Sandra Cisneros was acclaimed for *The House on Mango Street* (1983) and *Woman Hollering Creek and Other Stories* (1991), as was Lorna Dee Cervantes' poetry book *Emplumada* (1981) and Gary Soto's memoir *Living Up the Street* (1985), each of which won the American Book Award. Gloria Anzaldúa's provocative book *Borderlands/La Frontera: The New Mestiza* (1987) synthesized her interests in autobiography, queer theory, colonialism, and indigeneity, offering one of the era's quintessential examples of intersectional thinking and writing.

Even as scholars grappled with nomenclature and intersectionality, however, the new literary pluralism also faced far more vitriolic criticism from conservative commentators. The diversification of Anglophone literature in the 1980s took place within a broader atmosphere of cultural and political reaction, culminating in the Reagan and Thatcher right-wing (counter-) "revolutions." A conflict of ideals, values, and goals was inevitable. Allan Bloom sparked widespread debate with his polemic book, *The Closing of the American Mind* (1987), which attacked the new pluralism of American education as a provincialism that would lead to what conservatives saw as dangerous moral relativism and loss of what they insisted were—or at least should be—shared cultural values. Bloom's book, either despite or because of its crusty invectives against rock music, sold a half a million copies while propelling the politics of recognition from humanities departments into national discourse and triggering waves of public replies. Contra literary pluralism, Bloom championed "the Canon": a singular, sacrosanct body of texts (by dead, white, male authors like Plato and Shakespeare) that could and should instruct students in putatively universal truths about human nature.

Harold Bloom, self-appointed guardian of *The Western Canon* (1994), joined the fracas with scholarly essays and editorial columns inveighing against the "School of Resentment," which he cast as replacing the solitary aesthetic pleasures of reading with a political agenda. Roger Kimball's *Tenured Radicals* (1990) further pinned these cultural crosshairs upon the backs of literary scholars, notably singling out Eve Sedgwick for her paper "Jane Austen and the Masturbating Girl" at the 1989 MLA convention. Finally, in 1991, James David Hunter provided a lasting name to this ideological conflict: *Culture Wars*. As antidemocratic, reductive, and frankly ignorant as many conservative arguments from this era might be, their outrage in the culture wars ironically and explicitly ratified the progressive claim that outraged them in the first place: that the contents of literature syllabi were a proper site of political contest, to be fought alongside disputes over abortion, gun control, and marriage equality. Worry about "The Canon" may have quieted down since the 1980s; as current attempts to ban the teaching of Critical Race Theory in public schools show, however, the cultural battle lines demarcated during these years remain an unmistakable feature of contemporary life.

Globalization and Its Discontents

In 1989, Salman Rushdie published *The Satanic Verses*, a novel whose controversially imaginative representation of Islam sparked an international political crisis and seemed to exemplify the concrete political challenges of literary pluralism. All 46 nations in the Organisation of the Islamic Conference banned the book, as did South Africa, Thailand, Venezuela, and, for a time, Canada (O'Neill 220). Book burnings were held in places like Bradford, England, where thousands of Muslims also protested against Rushdie and his publishers; bookstores around the world were firebombed; riots in India and Pakistan left many dead and more injured. Finally, on February 14, the Ayatollah Khomeini of Iran issued a fatwa, sentencing Rushdie and those who had aided him to death, and promising spiritual and financial rewards for their killers. The European Community removed its ambassadors to Iran in response, which led to Iran severing diplomatic relations with Britain. Rushdie and his wife went into hiding, where they remained for years.[1]

These events, observes Daniel O'Neill, raised profound questions about "what theoretical support for multiculturalism entailed in practice," such as whether free speech has limits, what constitutes libel or defamation, to what degree nations should make allowances for minority cultures, at home or abroad (220). Even as "Western" critics discussed the topic of blasphemy, notes Parekh Bhikhu, they revealed the scope of cultural difference: "blasphemy is uniquely Christian and has no analogue in Islam," he explains, whereas some Muslims rather invoked Rushdie's "apostasy, a unique Islamic concept" that means "turning back" on the faith (698). British Muslims, meanwhile, "were far more concerned with the harm done to their cultural identity" by Rushdie's flippant and derogatory portrayals of Islamic figures and doctrine (O'Neill 231). Defenders of a liberal pluralism rooted in respectful cultural recognition, such as Charles Taylor, Michael Walzer, and Will Kymlicka, all responded to these issues, and yet provided few answers. Taylor conceded that free speech always has some limit based on "general consensus" ("The Rushdie Controversy" 118) and suggested that "it is misguided to claim to identify culture-independent criteria of harm" (120). But if everyone seemed to recognize the fundamental incompatibility between secular freedom of speech and nation-states claiming jurisdiction over religious faith, no one knew how to proceed when conflicting values collided in practice. This contact was visible in threats against Rushdie's life in the U.K.; it was equally visible in the U.S. when the Catholic Church successfully convinced Congress to cut the National Endowment for the Arts' budget because of artworks considered obscenely disrespectful against Christianity. "We are going to have to live with this pluralism for some time," Taylor concluded, so "we are going to need some inspired adhoccery" or else it will be "a rough ride on our shrunken planet" (121–122).

The Rushdie affair came at the end of a decade in which British literature "had been invigorated" by global writers, who began receiving substantially more notice and acclaim after Rushdie won the Booker Prize for *Midnight's Children* (1981). In subsequent years the

Booker went to writers like Thomas Keneally (1982, Australia), J. M. Coetzee (1983, South Africa), and Keri Hulme (1985, New Zealand); as Richard Todd has shown, the prize was instrumental in cultivating commercial, critical, and popular interest in post-colonial fiction, rooted in "a new public awareness of Britain as a pluralist society" (83). Yet prizes like the Booker, which accord cultural recognition a lasting symbolic stature, once again raise questions about the relationship between majority and minority, or "center and periphery." Does bestowing a British award upon a post-colonial writer such as white South African Nadine Gordimer or Black Nigerian Ben Okri signal "genuine respect and recognition," wonders James English, or "mere symbolic philanthropy" or, still worse, a covert way to maintain "the old patterns of imperial control over symbolic economies and hence over cultural practice itself" (286)? To be sure, English explains, the Booker's pluralism produces regular waves of "frantic hand-wringing about the prize's commercialist logic, its corrosive effect on traditional British literary culture" (213). And these concerns are by no means confined to publishing epicenters like the U.S. and the U.K. In 1986, the Nobel Prize for Literature went to Wole Soyinka, the first writer of African heritage to win. At the same time, the Nobel committee clearly passed over Léopold Sédar Senghor, leader of the Négritude movement and former president of Senegal; to many critics, their choice looked less like the apolitical recognition of great art and more like elevating a post-colonial champion of free speech over a Black nationalist committed to African cultural traditions (English 300). Concerns like these came to drive the field of postcolonial studies, which assembled in these years around key texts like Edward Said's *Orientalism* (1978), Gayatri Chakravorty Spivak's "Can the Subaltern Speak?" (1988), and *The Empire Writes Back: Theory and Practice in Post-Colonial Literature* (1989), an anthology by Bill Ashcroft, Gareth Griffiths, and Helen Tiffin.

In his essay "1989 in the Shadow of 1945," Jürgen Habermas suggests that "globalization of every kind of interchange and communication," from literature to weaponry, has created "problems that can no longer be solved within the framework of the nation-state" (168). And yet, he says, the desire for "a common origin, language, and history, the sense of belonging to a people," endures (172). This tension between international pluralism and national identity has clearly come to structure the Anglophone literary field. In 1993, for instance, the "Booker of Bookers," recognizing the best novel to receive the prize over the last 25 years, went to *Midnight's Children*, a fantasy that explores India's independence; the Booker affirmed its post-colonial pluralism, in other words, by consecrating Indian nationalism as part of the ever-more capacious category "British fiction." Likewise, Gillian Roberts notes how interest in "Canadian literature" as a tradition was ironically sparked by Michael Ondatjee—an immigrant born in Sri Lanka—winning the Booker for *The English Patient* (1992), a novel that imagines a motley of exiles and refugees seeking solace from the horrors of WWII. What the 1990s would call "globalization" did not mean the end of literary nationalism, then, but rather an uneasy effort to enroll national identity—which both assumes and posits an ideal, exportable form in literary tradition—within larger networks of commercial and cultural exchange. Kazuo Ishiguro, born in Japan, won the Booker in 1989 for his brilliant psychological study of a genteel English butler, *The Remains of the Day*, which interrogates an atavistic national desire for pastoral calm and aristocratic hierarchy. As the butler reflects on his career, he gradually reveals that his venerated Lord Darlington helped legitimate fascist leaders in Germany and rightwing aristocrats in England. In this way, Ishiguro's novel asks whether even the most quaint and mannered of English traditions, such as the butler's unwavering commitment to dignity, might belong to the same history of violence that lay behind closed-door meetings between Conservative British Prime Minister Neville Chamberlain and Nazi German Foreign Minister Joachim von Ribbentrop. To believe in the dream of 1989, remarks Habermas, is to see the tyrannies of 1945 as but "a transitory anomaly," an aberrant eruption of oppressive violence (167). As global markets continue to erode social bonds and traditions, however, and pluralism fails to arbitrate among competing values, liberal democracies like the U.S. and Britain face a crisis in legitimacy, and reactionaries now try to regain control over these circumstances by calling for a return to nationalism predicated upon ethnic or religious unity.

Precisely because "1989" and the symbolic fall of the Berlin Wall pose what Habermas calls "a question of historical punctuation" about how we narrate the ongoing relationship between history, freedom, and the state, it is a question that must be returned to now, when some people cry for their leaders to build new walls (165). In 1987, Ronald Reagan famously cried "Mr. Gorbachev, tear down this wall!" Thirty years later, Reagan superfan President Donald Trump signed Executive Order 13767, authorizing a new wall to be built along the U.S.-Mexico border. From the executive branch down to popular media, the order's objectives were inextricable from xenophobic vitriol and delusional descriptions of the U.S. as a homogeneous nation-state threatened from without—and from within. Reactionary forces that extend far beyond any one politician's cult of personality have increasingly learned to mobilize the language of anti-discrimination as a means to combat recognition of historical injustice. Under the auspices of combatting "critical race theory," Oklahoma's governor signed a bill in 2021 preventing public schools from teaching basic facts about race and racism in American history; the bill explicitly refutes the notion that individuals bear shared responsibility, or should feel any shame or guilt, for actions committed based on racial distinctions.

Many literary scholars have long recognized that such critical engagements with historical oppression represent more than simply intellectual honesty: such engagements are also a key means to remedy contemporary injustice and promote cultural difference. Political praxis today cannot simply mean reading fiction in and around 1989 to inveigh against the all-too obvious lies and privilege behind such wanton denials. To grasp fully the fault lines that have opened up within contemporary cultural politics, literary scholars must be willing to step outside the comforts of ideology critique and historicize their own discipline with its shifting institutional and intellectual priorities. Only by understanding how "critical race theory" has come to signify an essential and elementary means of reckoning with the past for one portion of the population, but an invidious and anti-American radicalism for another, might the increasingly fractious political pluralism of our era continue to function under the auspices of what both sides proudly call "democracy." At least for now.

Note

1 For the political significance of fatal attacks on Rushdie's translators, see Roland Vegso's chapter "Translation" in this volume.

Works Cited

Ankersmit, F.R. *History and Tropology: The Rise and Fall of Metaphor*. U of California P, 1994.
Bell, Bernard. *The Afro-American Novel and Its Tradition*. U of Massachusetts P, 1987.
Bertens, Hans. *The Idea of the Postmodern: A History*. Routledge, 1995.
Crenshaw, Kimberlé. "Demarginalizing the Intersection of Race and Sex: A Black Feminist Critique of Antidiscrimination Doctrine, Feminist Theory and Antiracist Politics." *University of Chicago Legal Forum*, vol. 1989, no. 1, 1989, pp. 139–167.
English, James F. *The Economy of Prestige: Prizes, Awards, and the Circulation of Cultural Value*. Harvard UP, 2005.

Fraser, Nancy. "From Redistribution to Recognition? Dilemmas of Justice in a 'Post-Socialist' Age." *New Left Review*, vol. 212, 1995, pp. 68–93.

Fukuyama, Francis. *The End of History and the Last Man*. Avon Books, 1992.

Gilbert, Susan and Sandra Gubar. *The Madwoman in the Attic: The Woman Writer and the Nineteenth-Century Literary Imagination*. 1979. 2nd ed. Yale UP, 2000.

Habermas, Jürgen. "1989 in the Shadow of 1945: On the Normality of a Future Berlin Republic." *A Berlin Republic: Writings on Germany*. U of Nebraska P, 1997.

O'Neill, Daniel I. "Multicultural Liberals and the Rushdie Affair: A Critique of Kymlicka, Taylor, and Walzer," *Review of Politics*, vol. 61, no. 2, 1999, pp. 219–250.

Parekh, Bhikhu. "The Rushdie Affair: Research Agenda for Political Philosophy," *Political Studies*, vol. 38, no. 4, 1990, pp. 695–709.

Perkins, David. *Is Literary History Possible?* Johns Hopkins UP, 1992.

Roberts, Gillian. *Prizing Literature: The Celebration and Circulation of National Culture*. U of Toronto P, 2011.

Taylor, Charles. "The Politics of Recognition." *Multiculturalism: Examining the Politics of Recognition*, edited by Gutman, Amy, et al. Princeton UP, 1992, pp. 25–73.

———, "The Rushdie Controversy," *Public Culture*, vol. 2, no. 1, 1989, pp. 118–122.

Todd, Richard. *Consuming Fictions: The Booker Prize and Fiction in Britain Today*. Bloomsbury, 1996.

White, Hayden. *Metahistory: The Historical Imagination in Nineteenth-Century Europe*. Johns Hopkins UP, 1973.

Wong, Sau-ling Cynthia. *Reading Asian American Literature: From Necessity to Extravagance*. Princeton UP, 1993.

23
ON OR ABOUT NOW

Rachel Greenwald Smith

Like experiments in which monkeys were raised with mothers made of wire to see what happens to a creature who has only a cold simulacrum of maternal presence for comfort, so might we think of the political circumstances of the turn of the millennium as an experiment in what happens when a generation is raised to see political dissent as always possible but never effective. This chapter is about a period that began in 1989 and ended in 2016, during which the mainstream Left in the US underwent a profound depoliticization. I mark this period as 1989–2016, but I imagine it as a curve, one that begins in 1989 with the fall of the Berlin Wall and the end of a major geopolitical socialist alternative.[1] It ascends sharply in 1994 with the Clinton Crime Bill, one of the first pieces of evidence that the Clinton administration would firmly uphold the structural priorities of neoliberalism when it came to racial capitalism. The curve reaches its high point in 2002 when the Democratic Party nearly universally stood in support of the war in Afghanistan and patriotic nationalism more generally. The curve stays high throughout the 2000s, a decade during which efforts to protest the war in Iraq, including marches of millions of people, were largely erased by the center-left media. The curve begins its descent back into a stronger sense of political power on the left in 2011 with the Occupy movement. And it turns sharply downward in 2014 after the murder of Michael Brown and the rise of the Black Lives Matter movement. Politics resumes as a priority, even on the mainstream center-left, with a vengeance upon the election of Donald Trump in 2016.

When the story of our recent past is told this way, a two-decade period concentrated in the center period of 1994–2014 emerges as crucial to an understanding of the contemporary. We could call this period "the long 2000s." In literary studies, the aughts/noughties in general have garnered less critical attention than most other periods, perhaps because they were marked by such minimal political efficacy on the left. Amplifying this period and naming it as the apogee of our moment rather than leaving it aside as a silent gap, I want to suggest that the most influential period of our contemporary cultural moment occurred precisely when left political action seemed most stymied.

Given how much politics has dominated left consciousness since 2016, arguing that a depoliticized period should be central to our understanding of "the contemporary" may seem counterintuitive. But the resurgence of the political in the post-2016 moment is the result of something else that occurred during the 1989–2016 period, and that also had a mostly silent

DOI: 10.4324/9781003038009-27

ascendency during the long 2000s: the signal shift in political energy—accompanied by subsequent shifts in law and policy—from the left to the right. Indeed, political theorist Chantal Mouffe tells us that these two phenomena—the depoliticization of the left and the rise in political energy on the right—are causally related. As she explains, with the rise of third-way thinking in the US as well as in the UK and Europe during the late twentieth century, the left abandoned even nominally socialist-leaning policy goals, and it ceded what was once its major political claim: the rectification of the economic inequality driven by capitalism. The mainstream left touted itself increasingly as technocratic, as politically neutral. Meanwhile, the right became increasingly the repository of political passion, of partisan energy, and of an activist response to the status quo. Mouffe explains that

> in this increasingly "one-dimensional" world, in which any possibility of transformation of the relations of power has been erased, it is not surprising that right-wing populist parties are making significant inroads in several countries. In many cases, they are the only ones denouncing the "consensus at the centre" and trying to occupy the terrain of contestation deserted by the left.
>
> (7)

Thus, given that the political reality of our moment now, in 2022, is marked by the rise of the far right, we can see how our contemporary political condition is very much the outcome of the depoliticized climate of the early 2000s.

Despite the robust archive of conservative and even proto-fascist works of literature, ranging from the fiction of Ayn Rand to *The Turner Diaries* the speculative Christian apocalypses of the *Left Behind* series, the literary culture to which most scholars and critics in prestige venues attend is largely a liberal and left endeavor. Moreover, it is one most influenced by the center-left politics practiced by people in positions of racial and economic privilege. This was the demographic most associated with the abdication of a socialist critique in the Democratic Party during the long 2000s, largely because such an abdication served its class interests. The third-way notion that one could pursue social goals such as anti-racism, feminism, environmentalism, and LGBTQ+ rights while furthering free market capitalism suggested that there was no contradiction between defending class privilege and fighting for left social priorities. And, as I will argue, it is precisely this politics that we see animating elite literary culture and scholarship in the turn-of-the millennium period, a period that I will argue is still "about" now in two senses of the word. It is about now in the sense that the literary aesthetics and critical modalities that gained ground in that moment are still very much our current aesthetics and modalities. And it is about now in the sense that it is what now is actually about; it is the basis from which the chaos of now—of global pandemic, of planetary descent into climate crisis, of potential thermonuclear war, of looming famine, and of the continued rise of an anti-democratic, proto-fascistic far right—continues to draw.

The End of the Social Novel

Jonathan Franzen's 1996 essay, "Perchance to Dream" (republished under the more pugnacious title "Why Bother?" for Franzen's volume of essays, *How to Be Alone*), is one of several works written in the 1990s by fiction writers that would contribute to a chorus of laments for the lost possibilities of the politically relevant novel. In works ranging from David Foster Wallace's disquisition on irony, "E Unibus Pluram" (1993), to Percival Everett's biting satire on race and the publishing industry, *Erasure* (2000), a consensus would emerge among writers at the turn of the millennium: that from its institutions to its readership, literary culture no longer allowed for the social novel to do what it once was imagined to do—to map social hierarchies and classes, to describe the institutional mechanisms by which such classes were maintained, and to challenge readers to reimagine how society might be organized.

It's easy enough to read pieces such as "Perchance to Dream" as artifacts of a certain kind of entitled white masculinity (which, in Franzen's case, is an accurate interpretation); as neo-Luddite works of crankery about the rise of the digital (also accurate); and as restricted, in their interests and implications, to a more-or-less mainstream literary sphere. But placing them in the historical context of the depoliticization of the long 2000s, one can also see them as documents of that period, both as responses to a quickly depoliticizing left and as contributing to that ethos of depoliticization. I therefore turn to Franzen's essay as a case study to better understand what role literary culture played in the political climate of the period.

"Perchance to Dream" begins with Franzen's account of the publication of his first work, the sweeping chronicle of St. Louis political corruption *The Twenty-Seventh City* (1988). As he describes it, the publication of the novel brought him both celebrity and cash ("the money, the hype, the limo ride to a *Vogue* shoot") but the thing he hoped for most—that the novel would work as a form of political critique—failed to occur. He explains: "I'd intended to provoke; what I got instead was sixty reviews in a vacuum." Meanwhile, the praise and the significant advance for his next project were, as he understood them, merely "consolation for no longer mattering to the culture" (38).

Franzen reads this occurrence as indicating "the death of the social novel," something he allows had likely taken place long before the publication of *The Twenty-Seventh City*, but to which he had remained naïve until his novel failed to provoke a widespread political response. Along with his disappointment following the publication of *The Twenty-Seventh City* and his follow-up attempt at the social novel, *Strong Motion* (1992), Franzen cites anecdotes from major publications as evidence as to the novel's lack of political reach. From the vantage point of now, his complaints about literature's cultural irrelevance, a phenomenon he links to the dumbing down of periodicals, the rise of cable TV, and the distractions of digital technology read as ahistorical and snobbish rather than as strong evidence of literary culture's demise. Add to this all manner of racist accounts of the non-white, non-male "Tribal" literature that he sees as overtaking the serious work of literary fiction, and there are many reasons to believe that "Perchance to Dream" is a document of heterosexual-cisgender white male whining rather than any kind of substantive cultural critique.

But Franzen's account of how difficult *The Corrections* was to write is nevertheless instructive—and, I want to argue, paradigmatic—of the relationship between politics and literature during the period. Franzen writes that for some time he could not complete the novel because it was "getting bloated with issues." He explains:

> I'd already worked in contemporary pharmacology and TV and race and prison life and a dozen other vocabularies; how was I going to satirize Internet boosterism and the Dow Jones as well while leaving room for the complexities of character and locale?
>
> *(40)*

This supposed conflict—between the inclusion of social and political material on the one hand and character complexity and feeling on the other—is a trope that occurs in much of the writing on literature and politics of the period.

Indeed, the tension Franzen identifies between describing the social order and accounting for individual experience within that order has been the site of considerable analysis and debate within the tradition of Marxist aesthetics reaching back at least to the Frankfurt School.

This tension is the explicit ground of contestation in a series of critical interventions by Ernst Bloch, Georg Lukács, Bertolt Brecht, Walter Benjamin, and Theodor Adorno written during and after the rise of fascism and chronicled in the *Aesthetics and Politics* collection published by New Left Books (now Verso) in 1977 featuring a conclusion by Fredric Jameson. The debates chronicled in the collection are central to an understanding of politics and aesthetics today, not only because they offer an anchor in Frankfurt School aesthetics but because they did so for the very generation of late twentieth-century Marxist Formalists (most prominently Jameson himself) who would become the targets of the post-critical method wars of the early twenty-first century.

Take, for instance, Lukács's critique of a range of experimental movements "from Naturalism to Surrealism," that, he argues, "take reality exactly as it manifests itself to the writer and the characters he creates." In doing so, such works "both emotionally and intellectually... remain frozen in their own immediacy" and fail to reveal "the real factors that relate their experiences to the hidden social forces that produce them" (Lukács 36–37). For Lukács, the novel's political force can be found in social realism's ability to describe the totality of social relations including its mediations (33). The political work of the realist novelist, then, is to use the formal affordances of the social novel to "scrutiniz[e] all subjective experiences and measur[e] them against social reality."

Franzen may or may not have read Lukács, but his understanding of the role of the social novel as a form of political education has Lukácian valences. And yet, when he confronts the inevitable limits to this particular concept of literature's political relevance, he does not look for dialectical alternatives, and instead sees the failure of the social novel as a failure of political intervention in the novel as such. In so doing, he produces a binary opposition that in practice does not exist in realist fiction: one between the "social" novel and the "psychological" novel; the novel that engages with structures and the novel that engages with selves; the novel that concerns itself with big issues such as infrastructure, geopolitics, and the economy and the novel that concerns itself with personal issues such as relationships, families, and feelings; the novel that requires looking beyond the surface of everyday life and the novel that reports on the affects and sensations that constitute human experience.

As we will see, the antipathy toward political critique that evolved in literary scholarship during the turn of the twenty-first century also imagines that such an opposition exists and casts Marxist critics on the side of the former rather than the latter. And yet Lukács's categorical argument for the structural over the affective is an exception within *Aesthetics and Politics* in particular and the post-Frankfurt School Marxist tradition in general. From Bloch to Adorno, there is a robust tradition of inquiry into the relationship between subjective states and structural ones—between feeling and politics. And ironically it is Jameson himself who has offered the most thorough account of the entanglement of these two poles in his *Antinomies of Realism* (2013), which argues that the realist novel is always a site of tension and negotiation between mapping the world and illustrating what it feels like to live in it.

Franzen presents "Perchance to Dream" as an essay about the political relevance of fiction. The tone throughout the work is elegiac and nostalgic, wishing after a time when great novelists appeared on the cover of *Time* magazine (as he himself would over a decade later with the publication of *Freedom* [2010]). But the end of the essay reframes the problem, as "a conflict between my feeling that I should Address the Culture and Bring News to the Mainstream, and my desire to write about the things closest to me, to lose myself in the characters and locales I loved." The solution he finds to this dilemma is hardly dialectical, even though it is posited as such. "I'm amazed, now," he writes, that I'd felt such a crushing imperative to engage explicitly with all the forces impinging on the pleasure of reading and writing: as if, in peopling and arranging my own little alternate world, I could ignore the bigger social picture even if I wanted to.

(10)

The tone of the essay in its final paragraphs moves from sorrow and tension to relief, as the "crushing imperative" to write a politically significant work of fiction is lifted. In its place is the assurance that the work will inevitably carry socipolitical meaning: after all, one need not try to capture "the bigger social picture," because its presence would inevitably come through without an explicit political aim. Politics in literature is no longer a matter of intention, description, and critique by the end of the essay; it is a matter of capturing a general atmosphere, of affirming the supremacy of literary creation for its own sake, and the subordination of social meaning to individual pleasure.

Franzen's despair over the fate of the social novel anticipates James Wood's post-9/11 argument that "The Great American Social Novel" has hit a breaking point at the turn of the millennium. But Wood's concern, unlike Franzen's, is not the absence of the novel's aspiration to social and political relevance; it is its overabundance. "Lately, any young American writer of any ambition," he writes, has been manifesting an "effort to pin down an entire writhing culture, to be a great analyst of systems, crowds, paranoia, politics; to work on the biggest level possible." However, the consequence for fiction, he argues, is bad writing: "curiously arrested and very 'brilliant' books that know a thousand things but do not know a single human being." While Wood's diagnosis is different, his prescription echoes Franzen's. Wood pleas for the opposite of the social novel: "a space for the aesthetic, for the contemplative, for novels that tell us not 'how the world works' but 'how somebody felt about something.'" And he believes strongly that such a novel will be on the rise in the twenty-first century. He argues that it is inevitable that in the aftermath of 9/11 the social novel will collapse. "For who would dare to be knowledgeable about politics and society now?" he asks.

With hindsight, in the wake of Abu Ghraib, Guantanamo Bay, the torture memos, the war in Iraq, and 20+ years of killing in the Middle East, one might just as easily ask, "how could anyone dare to lack knowledge about politics and society in such times?" But Wood, as it turns out, was right. Novelists during the long 2000s did largely turn to the project of representing "how someone felt about something": joined by Franzen, whose *Corrections* was, among other things, a correction in the direction of consciousness and feeling, were Dave Eggers, Jonathan Safran Foer, Alison Bechdel, Cormac McCarthy, Chimamanda Adichie, Marjane Satrapi, Jennifer Egan, and many others whose writing during the long 2000s was focused on individual emotion as the primary index of social meaning. That many of these writers turned to autobiographical material to do so anticipated the turn to autofiction in the late 2010 and early 2020s, which only intensifies the formal insistence on the individual as the privileged location for putatively political meaning.

As this tendency developed, there were some noteworthy outliers, nonconformers who also anticipated trends in more recent work. Junot Diaz's *The Brief and Wondrous Life of Oscar Wao* (2007) turned away from Diaz's earlier work in literary minimalism toward a project concerned with both geopolitics and genre. Richard Powers's *The Echo Maker* (2008) is an inquiry into consciousness, but, in its focus on neuroscience and the estrangement between brain and self, calls into question the notion of individual feeling as something that can be trusted to guide us in social or political decisions. Colson Whitehead's *Apex Hides the Hurt* (2006) uses a combination of satire and Beckettian stripped-down prose in a refusal to flesh out the novel's central protagonist in the service of foregrounding a critique of post-racial thinking and late capitalism. George Saunders's work throughout the long 2000s including *Pastoralia* (2000) and *Tenth of December* (2013) applied an equally devastating and hilarious satirical perspective on global capitalism and its consequences. And Tom McCarthy's *Remainder* (2005) suggested that avant-gardism and capital-t Theory, two tendencies widely dismissed during the long 2000s, still lingered, if only in small pockets of literary culture.

Nevertheless, the broad trend in literary culture during the 2000s was away from the social novel, a form that had continued to exist, if in parodic form, in the late- and postmodernist experiments of the 1970s and 1980s, in the work of writers such as Margaret Atwood, Thomas Pynchon, and Toni Morrison. In short, many novelists, critics, and scholars alike spent the 2000s celebrating the decline of literature and literary criticism that aspired to political critique by describing and engaging the social on a structural level.

The End of Critique

Many recent accounts of the diminishment of literature as a site of political critique are, if unintentionally and unknowingly, Franzenian and Woodian. By this I mean they are largely celebratory of literary culture's turn away from politics, and see the representation of consciousness, an emphasis on feeling, and the claiming of aesthetic pleasure as antithetical to the novel of social commentary or political critique. Paradigmatic in this respect are two works: Stephen Best and Sharon Marcus's "Surface Reading: an Introduction" (2009) and Rita Felski's *The Limits of Critique* (2015). Whereas Franzen and Wood are interested in how literature gets written and consumed by readers, Best, Marcus, and Felski are interested in how literary scholars make arguments. Reading their work as similar in any respect to Franzen's and Wood's essays therefore might seem like a category error, as they are not interested in parsing trends within literary works; they are interested in looking at how scholars should approach literature of all periods. But in placing these works (as exemplary of the post-critical turn more broadly) next to Franzen and Wood (as exemplary of certain arguments made by writers and reviewers in the period), my interest is in looking at the post-critical turn historically, as an intellectual product of its time. As Patricia Stuelke notes in *The Ruse of Repair* it is crucial to remember that such trends in scholarship "[have] a history," one that, as she argues of the reparative turn, "is inextricable from the cultural and social forms of US imperialism and anti-imperialism in the late twentieth century" (9).

My aim therefore is emphatically not to relitigate the critique/post-critique argument.[2] I agree with Felski that the best forms of critique often incorporate elements of what she refers to as post-critical. And I agree with Best and Marcus that forms of what they call "surface reading"—deep description, digital approaches, and attentiveness to the material of the page and the book—offer useful methods in literary analysis. But it is also the case that the—at times surprisingly categorical—rejection of politics in these critical interventions participated in the left's depoliticization in our recent past, as they and other works like them collaborated to tell a story whose moral is that politics and the literary are incompatible. Novelists and scholars are not to blame for telling this story individually; the situation is and was broadly structural. Telling this story was a collective process across the left—in politics and literature alike—that justified an abdication of the political precisely because it felt impossible to engage it at the very moment when the political was most urgent. As Stuelke notes, "in the academy, reparative and postcritical readings often seem to arrive as relief and reprieve" from devastating political circumstances. And yet, she argues, it is crucial to "[press] on these senses of relief and reprieve" (9). I agree.

To understand what the post-critical project is interested in undoing, one must first return to the source of what Felski calls "critique": the body of critical theory insisting that politics and literature are intrinsically and inseparably entwined, that to interpret literature is not to impose a concept of the political onto art (as Felski would have it), but rather to understand how the work of art represents, responds to, and acts within its political context. This body of theory originates with the Frankfurt School and finds its most recent expression in the major inheritor of their tradition, Fredric Jameson, and those many scholars who draw from Jameson's methods.[3] Crucially, what the tradition of critique teaches is not what Best, Marcus, or Felski say it does. This is not a tradition that proceeds by "casting around for a hidden puppeteer who is pulling the strings" (Felski 6); Frankfurt School critics and their descendants quite emphatically reject the notion of a volitional "hidden puppeteer" and instead diagnose the social systems that inform the production of culture in variform ways. Furthermore, there is no need to "cast about" to find these things: despite the edifices of mystification and ideology, one ultimately kind of knows what social system one lives in. In the US, there has only ever been one answer to this question, and that answer is capitalism. The question that underlies genuine political disagreement is whether or not this system should be championed, propped up, barely restrained, or actively destroyed.

But Felski's description of critical method is also misleadingly inaccurate: "the belief that the 'social' aspects of literature... can be peeled away from its 'purely literary ones'" (11). No one would disagree with this statement more than Adorno, for whom form was the site of the political work of literature. Jameson inherited this belief from Adorno, and it has powered his work throughout his career. Indeed, when Felski writes that "works of art cannot help being social, sociable, connected, worldly, immanent—and yet they can also be felt, without contradiction, to be incandescent, extraordinary, sublime, utterly special," one can imagine Bloch, too, nodding along. After all, for Bloch the "incandescent, extraordinary, sublime" aspects of art were precisely the sites for the necessary work of utopian thinking within the apparent stranglehold of capitalism.

These contradictions are meant not to squabble with Felski but rather to suggest that it's neither the towering presence of the Frankfurt School nor the (imagined) hegemony of Jamesonian political criticism that motivates *The Limits of Critique* and other works of post-critical theory. Phrased differently, the goal of post-critique is not to convince critics to stop doing Marxist formalism, which has been a prominent "critical" method in literary studies since at least the 1980s, if not the 1930s. Nor is it, as Felski would describe her aims, to merely decentralize this method (given the rise of the New Historicism in the 1990s that had been accomplished by the arrival of the long 2000s). Rather, it is difficult to escape the sense that Felski et al.'s work is fundamentally a reaction against the feeling that literary scholars are responsible for attending to politics in the first place. Hence the conclusion that one need not attend to the social in order to register social features of artworks. What Felski seems to want is a release from duty; someone to grant permission to retreat from politics, to say "relax, you really don't need to focus on the political anymore."

This is put much more directly in the work of scholarship that initiated the "post-critical turn," Sharon Marcus and Stephen Best's introduction to their 2009 "surface reading" special issue of the journal *Representations*. The rejection of Jamesonian criticism the editors propose is driven by the observation that many contemporary literary scholars "seem to be relatively neutral about their objects of study, which they tend less to evaluate than to describe." In coining the term "surface reading," which refers to a variety of methods of literary scholarship including work in the digital humanities, sociological approaches to literature, descriptive criticism, and others that eschew a depth model of interpretation in favor of attending to aspects of the text that are readily available without probing beneath what a work of literature is doing outwardly, their aim is to affirm and give coherence to this tendency. Late in the essay, they take stock of the implications of surface reading for the project it proposes to replace: political critique. "To some ears this might sound like a desire to be free from having a political agenda that determines in advance how we interpret texts, and in some respects it is exactly that," they write (16).

This "desire to be free" has echoes of Felski's overarching description of critique as an obligation, as something that presses on scholars, constraining their abilities to do something else, something that has what she calls a different "mood." But, like Felski, Best and Marcus quickly move from the desire to be released from obligation to a normative claim about what literature does:

> We think, however, that a true openness to all the potentials made available by texts is also prerequisite to an attentiveness that does not reduce them to instrumental means to an end and is the best way to say anything accurate and true about them.
>
> *(ibid)*

What is "accurate and true" about literature turns out to be the belief that there are features of the text that are decidedly not political, that carry no political import, that emerge from no political context, and about which there is nothing political to say.

What the post-critical school wants to ask amounts to "where is and where should politics appear in literature?" A better question would be "how do we possibly identify and define and value something not political in literature?" Is it not political to focus on individual consciousness over structural determinations? Is it not a particular political disposition and practice to write poems about epiphanies while gardening, at the very moment when one's tax dollars are paying for arms of the state to engage in extralegal forms of torture? (Set aside for the moment the fact that the carceral state is already engaged in legal forms of torture in the forms of solitary confinement and other atrocities.) What, precisely, are the features of literature that one can only engage if one is somehow liberated: not liberated by politics, but liberated from the mandate to speak about politics?

I ask these questions even as I agree with the basic critique that Best, Marcus, and Felski hurl at political criticism: that it is easy to overblow the relationship between literary and scholarly radicalism and actual practices of radical politics. It is true that too many studies of literature (and here I include some of my own work) hold up a work of literature as inherently politically meaningful without articulating the means by which literary experience translates into political experience. It is, however, one thing to say that there is bad political criticism in the world and quite another thing to say that one should simply stop trying. When I read much of the work of the post-critical turn, I hear words that seem to me to be of utmost urgency today, words like "political," "radical," "revolutionary," and perhaps most of all "critical" as if it they should always be placed in air quotes. As if the very effort to imagine a relationship between literature and the political is naïve, silly, outdated, and overblown.

Politics and Literature Now

While much of the left—and even, for a moment, the center—recommitted to the necessity of political action in the wake of the 2016 presidential election, both the forms of aesthetic evaluation articulated by Franzen and Wood and the forms of literary methodology articulated by Best, Marcus, and Felski continue to drive much of contemporary literary culture. We are still very much in a moment of individual feeling and consciousness in fiction; we are still very much in a moment of post-critique (and its sister concepts: surface reading, but also object-oriented ontology and new materialism) in method.

Yet, as the long 2000s wane, we are beginning to see the emergence of some new attempts to think the political and literary together. In method, there has been a robust rise in sociological approaches to literary institutions. Many of the scholars involved in this turn, including Merve Emre, Laura McGrath, Dan Sinykin, and Mark McGurl, have allied themselves with versions of post-critique or surface reading, even as their work insists upon materially traceable relationships between literary culture and social and economic (if not explicitly political) forces. Likewise, work in critical digital humanities by scholars such as Juliana Spahr and Richard So demonstrates that a strategy of surface reading can be directly politically engaged by revealing in stark terms the intersections between race, class, and access to literary institutions.

Meanwhile, in literature, there has been a sharp turn to politics, with politically engaged writing claiming most of the spots in the coveted national and international prizes. It may not be surprising that some of the writers I mention above, writers who were experimenting with forms of social and political representation during the long 2000s, have been celebrated in the late 10s and early 20s. These include Whitehead, winner of the National Book Award for *Underground Railroad* in 2016 as well as the Pulitzer Prize in Fiction in both 2017 and 2020 for *Underground Railroad* and *The Nickel Boys* respectively; Powers, winner of the Pulitzer for *The Overstory* in 2019; and Saunders, winner of the Booker Prize for *Lincoln in the Bardo* in 2017. These authors were joined by a new group of distinctively political writers, including Jesmyn Ward, whose *Sing, Unburied, Sing* won the National Book Award in 2017; Viet Thanh Nguyen, whose *The Sympathizer* won the Pulitzer in 2016; and Paul Beatty, whose novel *The Sellout* won the Booker in 2016.

In addition to these prize winners, consider several other writers whose work is aimed directly at the question of how literature and politics are inextricably linked. These include Mohsin Hamid, Ali Smith, Ben Lerner, and Ottessa Moshfegh. Together, these writers not only strive to depict politics, but imagine new literary strategies attuned to the difficulties of representing the seemingly un-critique-able structures of global capitalism, structural racism, climate change denial, and the global rise in neo-fascism. Their strategies include new work with allegory (Hamid), genre (Whitehead and Ward), play with language as material (Saunders, Smith, and Lerner), critiques of the aesthetic for its complicity in depoliticization (Moshfegh), inquiries into the cognitive as well as political factors in radicalization (Powers), and satire (Nguyen and Beatty).

All of these authors use the many strategies of fiction to demonstrate (often metafictionally) the effort to bring the resources of art to bear on politics in ways that presses the question asked above: what would art radically segregated from the realm of the political even look like? In their work, they often expose how difficult a process of composing politically active art is and how doomed this process is to fail. But crucially, they do not do what the dominant literary critical and scholarly narratives of the long 2000s did: they do not make the mistake of confusing difficulty with impossibility. And perhaps most important, they do not console themselves into thinking that because something is hard, it isn't meant to be done.

Notes

1 See also Ian Afflerbach's chapter "On or about 1989" in this volume.
2 There has been much writing on the so-called "method wars" between the critical and post-critical "camps," and much of it oversimplifies the arguments of both sides of the debate. One

exception is David Kurnick's wonderful chapter "A Few Lies: Queer Theory and Our Method Melodramas," *ELH*, vol. 87, no. 2 (Summer 2000): pp. 349–374.

3 For more on this tradition, see Benjamin Kehlmann's chapter "Symptoms" in this volume.

Works Cited

Beatty, Paul. *The Sellout*. Farrar, Straus, and Giroux, 2015.

Best, Stephen and Sharon Marcus. "Surface Reading: An Introduction." *Representations*, vol. 108, no. 1, Fall 2009, pp. 1–21.

Diaz, Junot. *The Brief and Wondrous Life of Oscar Wao*. Riverhead Books, 2007.

Emre, Merve. *Paraliterary: The Making of Bad Readers in Postwar America*. U of Chicago P, 2017.Felski, Rita. *The Limits of Critique*. U of Chicago P, 2015.

Franzen, Jonathan. "Perchance to Dream: In the Age of Images, A Reason to Write Novels." *Harper's Magazine*, vol. 292, April 1996, pp. 35–54.

Lukács, Georg. "Realism in the Balance." Translated by Rodney Livingstone. In *Aesthetics and Politics*, prepared by Rodney Livingstone, Perry Anderson and Francis Mulhern. Translations edited by Ronald Taylor. Verso, 2007.

McCarthy, Tom. *Remainder*. Metronome Press, 2005; Vintage Books, 2007.

McGrath, Laura. "Literary Agency." *American Literary History*, vol. 33, no. 2, Summer 2021, pp. 350–370.

McGurl, Mark. *The Program Era*. Harvard UP, 2009.

Mouffe, Chantal. *The Democratic Paradox*. Verso, 2000.

Nguyen, Viet Thanh. *The Sympathizer*. Grove Press, 2015.

Powers, Richard. *The Echo Maker*. Farrar, Straus, and Giroux, 2006.

———. *The Overstory*. W. W. Norton & Company, 2018.

Saunders, George. *Lincoln in the Bardo*. Random House, 2017.

———. *Pastoralia*. Riverhead Books, 2000.

———. *Tenth of December*. Bloomsbury, 2013.

Sinykin, Dan and Edwin Roland. "Against Conglomeration: Nonprofit Publishing and American Literature After 1980." *Post45*, no. 7, 2021.

So, Richard. *Redlining Culture: A Data History of Racial Inequality and Postwar Fiction*. Columbia UP, 2020.

Spahr, Juliana and Stephanie Young. "The Program Era and the Mainly White Room." *After the Program Era: The Past, Present, and Future of Creative Writing in the University*, edited by Loren Glass. U of Iowa P, 2015, pp. 137–175.

Stuelke, Patricia. *The Ruse of Repair: US Neoliberal Empire and the Turn from Critique*. Duke UP, 2021.

Ward, Jesmyn. *Sing, Unburied, Sing*. Scribner, 2017.

Whitehead, Colson. *Apex Hides the Hurt*. Anchor Books, 2006.

———. *The Nickel Boys*. Knopf Doubleday Publishing Group, 2019.

———. *The Underground Railroad*. Knopf Doubleday Publishing Group, 2016.

Wood, James. "Tell Me How Does It Feel?" *The Guardian*, 5 October 2001.

PART IV

Media, Genre, Techne

24
SOUND AND PRINT
Anthony Reed

In a much-cited aphorism, Louis Zukofsky declared that poetry is an integral function whose lower limit is speech and whose upper limit is song. While Zukofsky thought of poetry "as an order of words" opposed to "the wordless art of music" (19), to grasp the interplay of sound and print it will be helpful to read this alongside Robin D. G. Kelley's more capacious understanding of poetry as "a revolt: a scream in the night, an emancipation of language and old ways of thinking" (10). Emancipating languages from old ways of thinking requires the creativity of all involved in the cultural act: those who write or play, those who read or listen, those who prepare the scene by teaching and caretaking.

For people denied formal literacy and whose every utterance was subject to surveillance, sound has had to function as coded signification. The category of "sound" therefore offers an alternative, parallel, or even counter-archive to print. To study sound is to map the formation of publics, counterpublics, and other alternative relations; whispers, moans, cries, shouts, and silences have often been key to transmitting impermissible messages to people who need to hear them. This chapter, then, is less concerned with practices of listening as process of encounter or relation, and still less with intramural or intercommunal practices of encoding and decoding sound practice. Instead, it addresses the mechanisms by which critics have come to routinely ascribe extra-semantic qualities to printed text, and to see printed text as supplement to sound. One could trace editorial decisions, such as printing blues and popular song lyrics alongside poetry. More generally, to situate and to think about the emergent ideal sound/print articulation—the sound text—in a broader historical context is to engage the larger racialized field that subtends it.

The term "field," echoing Stuart Hall, refers to the dynamic articulation of heterogeneous and contradictory elements shaped by historical and economic forces. "Racialization" is the process by which differences between people are mapped onto geospatial populations and figured as "natural"—biological and/or ontological—in order to prescribe and justify group-differentiated relations of domination and exploitation. Racializing claims often have a temporal character, and Johannes Fabian argues (and Sylvia Wynter and others have elaborated) that colonial rationality reproduces itself in large part by reinscribing the colonized periphery's geospatial remoteness from colonial centers into the temporal or developmental remoteness. "This process effectively denies that *objects* of anthropological study—the primitive Other and her cultural artifacts—can or do exist in the same time frame as the *subjects* of anthropology who produce legitimate knowledge about the Other." In the refined print/primal sound hierarchy, the modern both authors and authorizes the "primal" sounds the Other makes. This hierarchy allows sound to indicate an abstract human universality that simultaneously reduces soundmakers to appropriable resources whose particular Otherness excludes them from membership in the supposedly universal category of the human. This poses a vital question: how do our commonsense understandings of the "radical" or "alternative" sounds of historically marginalized groups—especially racial, sexual, and gendered Others—reinforce and reproduce racialization, and what resources might there be for thinking otherwise?

In a certain commonsense understanding that persists despite decades of critique, qualm, and qualification, "pure sound" is by definition ephemeral and unstable, whereas print is defined by stability, reproducibility, and permanence. Speech is held to be prior to and thus superior to written language, while written language is the sign of a more "advanced" social order. At least since the rise of technical sound recording in the nineteenth century, inscription—impression on paper, wax, tape, or in memory and binary code—stabilizes sound that, through processes to which inscription is complementary, is already itself expressive. Insofar as the sound/print distinction depends on and reifies racialized categories, critics must attend to the colonial logics that animate that distinction rather than simply inverting the hierarchy.

At least since the Romantic era, and especially in contemporary criticism, the poetic text has been a site for consummating and reconstituting a fundamental unity between sound and mute print, so that printed words bear the prior, unruly imprint of a more-than-words sound, a words-can't-tell-you sound. In his *Critique of Judgment* (1790), which seeks to think "the particular as contained under the Universal" (§IV, 17), Immanuel Kant, like Plato before him, separated the sensory pleasures associated with "isochronous vibrations" of musical tones from true aesthetic pleasure (55).[1] In Kant's account of aesthetic judgment, sensuous sound has too much particularity for it to meet the conditions of "the beautiful" that can serve as a "symbol of morality." About a decade later, responding to controversy surrounding his (and Samuel Taylor Coleridge's) refusal of traditionally "poetic" language in the *Lyrical Ballads* (1801), William Wordsworth argued for a necessary relationship between "the language really used by men," "elementary feelings," "the necessary character of rural occupations," and the "beautiful and permanent forms of nature" associated with rustic life (447). Tonal qualities insufficiently engaged the understanding for Kant and were therefore inessential. Wordsworth argued that the problem resulted from human institutions corrupting more fundamental relationships to nature. He therefore elevated sound and the culturally defined vibrational field that corresponds with it to a resource to be appropriated and abstracted into the basis for forms of life lost to modernity.

Who were Wordsworth's rustic men (and, presumably, at least some women)? They were of relatively low social status and excluded from affairs in the urban center—among those affairs would be legislative "politics" proper—and therefore, for Wordsworth, had a relatively less alienated relationship to nature and the world around them. They were idealized versions of the proletarianized rural workers then self-organizing as a class, whose forms of life were being subsumed to the relations of capitalist agricultural production. In other words, they were dispossessed, alienated from their initial relationships to the land; they were also imagined to be both spatially and temporally remote from the "developed" urban centers, which themselves were flush with revenue from the slave economies in the colonies.

Some "rustic men" would find their way to the Caribbean and soon join the plantation order there (Carby 273–289). Their romanticized poverty no doubt helped soothe the consciences and excite the imaginations of urban poets and readers who aspired to belong to an emergent middle class, while their supposed lack of development made them closer to humanity's putative source. Pointedly, the ability to abstract (imagined) vocalization from those to whom the speech should correspond, framed by the supposed higher order authenticity of the speech as indicative of a primordial humanness, legitimates and requires thinking of speech as already inscribed in and by history, of voice as a tool of inscription.[2] And this process stands at the very fountainhead of thinking about poets, poetry, and poetics.

Crucial to the present argument, Wordsworth transforms the *geospatial* remoteness of the "rustic men" from the metropolitan center into *temporal* remoteness. Throughout the "Preface" Wordsworth praises them as closer to an essential humanness lost or threatened by urban modernity, stopping at the threshold of figuring those men as bearers of a more fundamental national spirit. Their way of using language thus becomes an essential, *racializing* characteristic. To recover their distinct form of life, expressed in their language, amounts to a crudely racialized nationalism, especially when one considers them in relation to the expanding British Empire of which transatlantic slavery was a key component. The literary text's relatively stable unity heightens rather than resolves the fundamental contradiction between sound and print, and that contradiction is related to the underlying structure of the social body to which it corresponds and the formal conditions of existence or "forms of life" at play at a given moment. Print makes sound into a medium in Lisa Gitelman's sense: a socially realized structure of communication encompassing "both technological forms and their associated protocols, and where communication is a cultural practice, a ritualized collocation of different people on the same mental map, sharing or engaged with popular ontologies of representation" (7).

About half a century later, from a very different perspective, Frederick Douglass would take up a similar problematic. In his 1845 *Narrative*, Douglass famously writes that when he was enslaved and "within the circle," he could not "understand the deep meaning of those rude and apparently incoherent songs" (24).[3] His narrative here choreographs a process of understanding for white readers, who would likely have taken the songs as signs of savagery or contentment. Against that racist ideology, he stresses that "every tone was a testament against slavery" (185). Considered allegorically, within the terms of the *Narrative*'s broader meditations on freedom, Douglass's departure from Wordsworth's nationalist framing is clear. Douglass's slave community is self-knowing, a hermeneutic circle, intimate rather than remote, contemporary rather than atavistic. Douglass assigns himself the task of re-signifying—making new signs to encompass—their practice as metonymic of the slave community, while in the same gesture making himself synecdochic of that same community. If print figures the possibility of a new "circle"—new modes of circulation—and new ways of figuring the relationship between the particular and the universal, it also allows Douglass to re-appropriate the black sound text as a sign of contemporaneity and fundamentally political struggle. But there's more. Freedom, like meaning, is relational. The sonic autonomy of the enslaved compensates for an unrealized freedom that, in the rest of the *Narrative*, comes only through struggle.

Douglass's description underscores a persistent problem: aesthetic autonomy rooted in group practice does not necessarily translate into political freedom. Quite the opposite in this case, since the songs the enslaved sang were, in some quarters, proof of cultural backwardness for which slavery was cure, or at least not worse than their "natural" condition. The discrepancy between aesthetic autonomy and substantive freedom haunts much subsequent work that seeks to engage group-differentiated aesthetics. In response to his editor's request that he account for the "Sorrow Songs" whose graphic form—fragments of sheet music—silently accompanied the essays of *The Souls of Black Folk* (1903), W. E. B. Du Bois declared the "wild notes" of the enslaved "the only American music which welled up from black souls in the dark past" (536–537). Du Bois recapitulates Wordsworth's "rustic men" argument, positing a necessary relationship between the people who work the land and the land's "spirit." Their physical and cultural labor, Du Bois implicitly argues, gives them a claim to belonging and, importantly, a claim against exclusion. Again the slave song surrenders its singularity to become synecdoche (part of the black whole), but by rhetorical sleight of hand it also becomes, metonymically, "the singular spiritual heritage of the nation," and thus evidence of the centrality of African American culture to U.S. culture more broadly. This is a contributionist argument, later developed and advanced by James Weldon Johnson and others associated with the New Negro Renaissance, claiming that the production of group-defined art legible within the aesthetic codes of the captors should bring about the captives' full incorporation into the larger society. However, this argument required the young Du Bois to grant race a solidity logically prior to enslavement rather than, as he would in later writing, seeing race itself as historically produced and reinforced contingency.

Even as Du Bois made a case for the sorrow songs' timelessness, a media revolution—the emergence of the phonograph for home use—was pushing the sheet music he used to invoke it to the margins of sound reproduction. Electric sound recording participated in a more general reorganization of and reproduction of already existing aesthetics, the relation of sensory experience to a collective common sense undergirded by the colonial dynamics of proximity/distance and its "ontologies of representation." The popularization of the phonograph changed some of these arguments, notably making problematic the view of black sound as the autonomous production of a historically specific group because now others could plausibly produce it. A booming "race record" market thrived, with companies selling consumers on the idea that race had a sound and then competing to shape, in David Suisman's terms, "not only notions of what race *looked* like but ideas about what it *sounded* like too" (206). To cite one example, "coon songs," inspired by African American composer Ernest Hogan's wildly popular "All Coons Look Alike to Me," and other minstrelsy-adjacent norms of black performance—by musicians on either side of what Du Bois had termed the "color line"—accompany and aid the shift in the nature of listening experience from public to private and from "life" to experience increasingly mediated by mechanical reproduction (via player pianos, records, and eventually radio).

Poets, who since Wordsworth were accustomed to developing their craft around ideas of chthonic culture, quickly absorbed and contextualized these changes, with differences playing out along what Du Bois had called the "color line." Langston Hughes' turn to urban blues and jazz or Sterling Brown's emphasis on the folkways that produced the music are well known and have inspired a raft of scholarship attentive to blues or jazz elements in printed works. Despite differences of approach, African American music for both writers signaled group membership that authorized their representation of African Americans. Matters of black sound were even more complicated for those writers whose racial positioning precluded them from claims to synecdoche. In order for the invocation of technologically mediated racial sounding to be effective, poets such as Hart Crane had to maintain distance between their personas and their inspiration. Brian Reed compellingly analyzes Crane's repeatedly listening to Bert Williams 78s while composing his poems. But the medium, for Reed, overshadows the meaning of its content. Williams was a brilliant Afro-Bahamian comedian and vaudeville star who often performed in blackface, and the perspective from which he navigated the particulars of U.S. racecraft differed from Crane's; it is, however, unlikely that either Crane or Williams took blackness as just one element among others.

As a practice and sign complex, vaudeville served to refine and clarify social antagonisms by defining the realm of the popular in descriptive terms (e.g., what many people like) and evaluative terms (opposed to and therefore definitive of "high" culture). The cultural meanings attached to racialized sounds and the record players that reproduced them, it seems to me, provide necessary context for grappling with the modernist project and its legacies. To take one famous example, critics generally agree that nascent mass culture—of which black-identified ragtime is an important example—informed T. S. Eliot's early poetics. By the time of *The Waste Land* (1922), ragtime was enjoying a resurgence thanks largely to Irving Berlin, who like Bert Williams was an immigrant (Berlin was from Belarus, Williams was from the Bahamas). Berlin's negotiations of African American culture were key to his success as both American and modern. Berlin had taken it upon himself to reinvigorate Stephen Foster's vaudeville era minstrelsy (one song invites listeners "to hear the Swanee River played in ragtime"), and his 1911 hit "Alexander's Ragtime Band" capitalized on the continuing popularity of black-identified syncopations and harmonies. Eliot's reference to the "Shakespeherian rag" (referring to a similarly titled 1912 hit "The Shakespearian Rag") in *The Waste Land* mocks not only Berlin and poets inspired by him (e.g., Vachel Lindsay), but African American composers such as James Weldon Johnson, James Reese Europe, and others who sought to elevate ragtime to the status of "high" art—that is, to re-racialize it while retaining the hierarchy that relegated it to the margins.[4]

Du Bois' argument for the "Sorrow Songs" as a part of the development of a national "folk spirit" made the songs, but not the people who produced them, central to an idealized America. Making the Sorrow Songs metonymic of a distinct African American culture thus cleared the way for members of other marginalized groups to "refine" those black sounds in order to stage larger contests over the composition of the national popular, with the black people who originally produced them logically required to remain in their position in order for "refinement" to be legible. Zora Neale Hurston simply eliminated the broader national claim, and in so doing insisted that the black "folk" were the best arbiters of their own culture. Her 1934 "Spirituals and Neo-Spirituals" offers among the most influential accounts of a specifically black sound as "unceasing variations around a theme," a changing same (869). Hurston, however, insists on the in-person transmission of the sounds, and is relatively agnostic on the possibilities of print. "The nearest thing to a description one can reach," she writes, "is that they are Negro religious songs, sung by a group, and a group bent on expression of feelings and not on sound effects" (870). Isolated from regular contact with whites, this subaltern group becomes the "folk," representative of a nation within a nation. Although Hurston delineates distinctive formal features such as "jagged harmony," "dissonances," "shifting keys and broken time," and spontaneous arrangements that signify differently "within the circle," Hurston's primary aim is to claim "the songs of the people, as sung by them" against modernist "refinement" and the neo-spirituals' abstraction (read: commodification) of techniques (871). The coincident de-composition of traditional black communities amid the Great Migration and burgeoning "race record" markets made such an appeal to radical exteriority (to capital, to national projects) both necessary and increasingly difficult to imagine.

In the following decades, white avant-gardes would remain invested in using electronics to recuperate a "primal, original voicing" (Labelle 48) while also rejecting the so-called "tyranny of jazz" (quoted in Sukenick 221) of the contingently integrated postwar arts scenes. I have written extensively about the Black Arts era—best conceived as the specific ways black people related to a changing racial situation—elsewhere.[5] Here, I want to underscore the degree to which Hurston's semi-anthropological account of "the people" persists alongside anxieties about non-whites reducing cultural practice ratified by communal listening into techniques to be freely recontextualized and recirculated alongside the real thing. One sees such anxieties surface in contemporary "cultural appropriation" debates. In a Hurstonian mood, Amiri Baraka would argue that "features such as basic rhythmic, harmonic, and melodic devices were transplanted almost intact [from Africa during the transatlantic slave trade] rather than isolated songs, dances, or instruments" (28–29). However, "the *system* of African music is much more significant than the existence of a few isolated and finally superfluous features" (29, Baraka's emphasis). In a way redolent of Wordsworth's Romantic poetics, here Black sounds remain associated with "rustic men." Instead of belonging to or constituting a more or less passive archive, black sound actively mediates and becomes a medium of transformative energy—what Larry Neal described as "the modern equivalent of the ancient ritual energy" (81).

Neal, writing at the opposite end of the Great Migration from Hurston, responds at once to social division within black communities, internally differentiated by race, class, and region, and to related aesthetic transformations. One response was intensified Africanist research—that is, research into a black past outside of slavery—and through that the reappropriation of the signs of blackness/Africanness. Such research intensified in the 1950s and 1960s as decolonization efforts on the continent accelerated. Such research appealed to diasporans who were excluded from the state (except as subjects of its policing and carceral apparatuses). Simultaneously, the U.S. touted its official colorblindness throughout the Cold War to shore up its legitimacy as a global hegemon, even as it engaged in proxy wars to undermine sovereignty in Africa, the Caribbean, and Latin America. Though excluded as political actors from equal participation in the state apparatus, black people were imperial subjects; the music associated with them, thanks to State Department-sponsored "good will" tours, was rebranded as "American" without the guarantee of civil inclusion Du Bois had envisioned.

Ralph Ellison, the novelist and critic most famous for writing *Invisible Man* (1952), and his friend the critic Albert Murray are two notable post-WWII exponents of Du Boisian nationalism. Writing about bebop guitarist Charlie Christian, Ellison famously held that the "true jazz moment" plays out as a contest in which "each solo flight, or improvisation, represents ... a definition of his [the soloist's] identity as individual, as member of the collectivity and as a link in the chain of tradition" (267). For Ellison, the bebop revolution signaled an effective end of a tradition defined by an ideal unity of instrumentalists, singers, dancers (and drinkers), and a capitulation to certain markers of middle-class respectability (*Essays* xxvi). Ellison's valorization of this motley assortment of wayward souls undermines the metaphysical presumptions of the liberal order—predicated on the interactions of sovereign individuals and mediated by property—but his discomfort with bebop's anarchic elements, analogous to Kant's "isochronous vibrations," put him at odds with writers like Amiri Baraka and Larry Neal who valorize the same "folk." The tradeoff emerges as a minor political-aesthetic paradox. In this essay (and elsewhere), Ellison makes African American music (especially jazz and the blues) bear the imprint of a broader American spirit. In other words, Ellison here makes black aesthetic practice and social poetics ideally embody and express a liberal social form that has historically excluded black people. His claim for black inclusion and celebration avoids reifying the onto-biological claims of earlier critics. The music derives from the community's democratic forms, which exist in apposition if not opposition to the broader society's discourses and institutions of democracy. Simultaneously, though he valorizes the music as America, he does not seriously contend in this essay with the role ascriptive hierarchies of difference play in the historic and ongoing practices of the liberal-capitalist state.

The music is valorized, as alternative, to the extent to which the people who produce it are not, and for the same reason.

Ellison staked his position against a new generation of critics, like Neal and Baraka, who are best understood to be dialectically related rather than simply opposed to him; perhaps less a "unity of opposites" and rather the other side of what Ellison called his own "vindictively American" coin of identity (*Conversations* 65). What I above referred to as Africanist research, seeking continuities among communities across the diaspora, posited a different source of the African American sound text. The aim was to enable critics and their readers to imagine futures separate from those promised by the oppressive dominant culture, and to break down, in Larry Neal's words, "any concept of the artist that alienates him [or her] from his [or her] community" (28). Yet, given the forms of social division within black communities, and the rapid transformation of those communities (owing to immigration from within the U.S. and beyond), exactly where "the community" could be found became an open question. Later in the decade, critics such as Neal and Baraka and musicians such as Archie Shepp and Max Roach were increasingly compelled to work in university settings. If what was called the New Black Music innovated on one level by defining other standards of technical excellence, making it fit for university curricula required standardizing techniques. To pass muster with trustee boards and other institutional gatekeepers further required changing cultural conceptions so that, instead of being anarchic people's music, it became "America's classical music." That designation effectively alienated the culture from the people who produced it, inscribing it within structures of national belonging where the nation increasingly incorporates alternatives to itself. Africanist research—emerging in the era of domestic and international black freedom struggles—redefines "the people."

An adequate account of the black sound text in the 1960s and 1970s should account for the ways critics like Ellison, Neal, and Baraka sought to consolidate an increasingly heterogeneous field of incommensurate elements ("jazz") only contingently articulated into a whole, whether through concepts of tradition (Ellison) or community (Baraka and Neal). In the Civil Rights Era context, racially inflected charges that emergent musicians didn't "swing"—that is, lacked an intangible element of "soul" that belonged more to Du Bois's "black folk" than Hegelian "Spirit"—exemplify the tendency to make particular elements function as nodal points around which other elements could be hierarchically coordinated.

By the 1980s, with formally integrated institutions becoming officially antiracist and with black studies having gained a toehold within U.S. universities (and thus being subject to their professional and disciplinary standards), specifying African American particularity was an important task even as the grounds of that particularity grew more elusive and the lines that might have separated the "folk" from others grew blurrier. In a different register, formerly marginal pockets of autonomous "folk" culture, already thoroughly permeated by commodity culture, took on a different value when "celebrating diversity" became official policy. This is the context in which to read critical theory relating sound and print in the era, of which Houston A. Baker's *Blues, Ideology, and Afro-American Literature: A Vernacular Theory* (1984) remains exemplary. Baker defines "Afro-American culture [as] a complex, reflexive enterprise which finds its proper figuration in blues conceived as a matrix," that is, "a web of intersecting, crisscrossing impulses always in productive transit" (3). This framing allows Baker to avoid the traps of what he calls an "integrationist" impulse keen to redeem a "democratic-pluralistic" ideal of the American society to which black culture has been integral. It also helps him eschew a counter-nationalism whose reliance on an onto-biological account of race commits it to what Neal and others would later condemn as a merely intuitive and idealist version of blackness. Baker's desire "to gain a view of subtextual dimensions of Afro-American discourse" and thus making it into an intelligible text continues powerfully to inform African American cultural study (26). In different terms, the blues matrix specifies a relationship between a cultural form and its social ground, allowing the blues to be in effect critique: at once marking, transgressing, and reinforcing the internal boundaries of a social formation. Moreover, in making the blues a matrix (tantamount to Spirit), it is not subject to empirical verification. As he sidesteps problems of classification (i.e., specifying the essential elements of blues composition), he makes the distinction between forms of impression—sound recording or literature—moot. A Bessie Smith performance, a Sarah Webster Fabio poem, or Ralph Ellison's novel all have similar claims on the blues.

Perhaps the most lasting intervention, however, is Baker's emphasis on performance, which mediates the "antinomy" of "creativity and commerce" (9). Vernacular performance—which offers "interpretations of the experiencing of experience"—comes to inspire the reading and writing of literature; to both inspire and happen on the page, encouraging generations following him to look beyond the opposition (paraphrasing Brent Hayes Edwards) of text-as-structure and text-as-event (80). Indeed, Baker anticipates Fred Moten's more recent claim for black performance: "There occurs in such performances a revaluation or reconstruction of value, one disruptive of the oppositions of speech and writing, and spirit and matter" (Moten 14). Although they aren't perfectly synonymous, black performance bears a family resemblance to what Moten terms "phonic substance" and "phonic materiality," usually but not necessarily black. Engaging "the space between [James] Baldwin's texts and his audio-visual projection in/on film," Moten refers to "an erotics of distant receptivity" whose "phonic materiality" opens to us its own invagination, a libidinal drive toward ever greater unities of the sensual where materiality in its most general—which is to say substantive—sense is transmitted in the interstice between text and all it represents and can't represent and the audio-visual and all that it bears and cannot bear (191).

Focusing on the materiality of "sound" or the "phonic" grants it conceptual solidity that allows it to conceptually unite disparate particulars under a single sign. The ability to think the particular as contained under the general—Kant's notion of "the power of judgment"—is a cornerstone of the critical tradition in philosophy. Invoking the deconstructive concept-metaphor of "invagination"—moments of rupture within the general/particular dyad, effecting a reversal of part-whole relationships to allow, in Jacques Derrida's terms, "participation without belonging"—Moten upends the seemingly abstract universality that, at least sense Wordsworth, has had a racialized if not racist underpinning rooted in colonial cultural conceptions of space and difference. "Participation without belonging" accurately describes the position of black sound in the field of U.S. thinking about popular music, and (for Moten) within the text of philosophy insofar as blackness within this matrix is a name for the unruly, the incalculable, the extrinsic, the Other, without which, at the same time, the orderly and "universal" beauty of Western aesthetic ideals would not be thinkable.

Moten implicitly builds on accounts such as Stuart Hall's argument that "race works like a language" or the attention to "the dynamics of naming and valuation" that Hortense J. Spillers thinks via grammar and Sylvia Wynter thinks via sociopoetics (Hall 362; Spillers 208). Nonetheless, this way of thinking of sound inscribed and inscribing puts us in a familiar place: "every tone [is] a testament" to the present order's founding and ongoing violence. There is, however, one key difference: Moten's account offers to move us beyond the image of the sovereign individual and what Saidiya Hartman has called a "romance of resistance" (54). The idea of music not as accompanying or substituting for a text or code but actually qualifying as text or code becomes a necessary presupposition, and what Kant called "isochronous vibrations" reveal gaps in our supposedly collective understanding, the theoretically universal "common sense" that in fact was from its origins both strongly and racially particular.

Figuring black performance as always already resistant is a necessary correction to the idea of spontaneous folk aesthetics awaiting appropriation by sufficiently "civilized" listeners "outside the circle," whether those listeners were anthropologists in the 1910s or white patrons of Harlem jazz clubs in the 1930s. Moreover, I'm willing to accept the argument that blackness, as unassimilable difference, is at once (onto)logically prior to the epistemological and regulative norms that seek to contain it and that it is the (onto)logical counterpart—indeed, the constitutive outside—of the normative, rights-bearing liberal subject: "Man," now in his secular form. However, solving the sound/print relationship by making sound a kind of counterinscription risks losing sight of the concrete historical circumstances that shape the contested field within which sound accrues meaning. It makes it difficult to account for the ability to produce "black sounds" without the burdens of black bodies on stage, as the case of Irving Berlin, the mid-century emergence of rock and roll as the music of middle-class white youth, or contemporary debates around "cultural appropriation" demonstrate. Moten provides a powerful account of the racial subordinativities at work in critical theory, and at that remove he tends to think brilliantly with sounds rather than engage the sounds or their circulation directly.

I'll conclude by returning to the Zukofsky aphorism with which I began, now with a more explicit argument for the importance of tracking the sound/print by way of attention to communities rather than emphasis on tradition. To grasp the development of traditions of writing and sounding corresponding to the Black Radical Tradition as Moten outlines it (by way of Cedric Robinson), we would do well to think about the spaces and times of circulation and, invoking Hortense Spillers in a related context, "the habits of public discourse evolved by particular communities" (256). Angela Davis and Hazel Carby on blueswomen, or Paul Gilroy, Alexander Weheliye, and Tsitsi Ella Jaji on the musics of the African diaspora are examples of such an approach. These approaches attend to relations between vernacular musics, technology, and—crucially—the reshaping of national and extranational communities. But this means, drawing on Spillers again, attending to the ways poems, critical documents, and songs offer their distinct audiences "a community of texts and propositions," where "'community' seems to hold out the possibility of intervention, of inclusion" and, at any rate, does not predetermine the effect of a new articulation or performance (256–257).

Considered historically, sound and print are irreducibly intwined through the discourses that sustain them, with each at different moments serving as the other's supplement. Remembering that integral functions determine the size of irregular shapes, the area within which sound and print define and constitute each other remains contingent, and aurality—always on the threshold of meaning—is a way of framing their mutual implication and contamination—the becoming-song of language, the becoming-language of song—defines poetry. Although Zukofsky appears to be making a hierarchical claim, the relationship he describes is spatial. Integral functions calculate the dimensions of irregular shapes by theoretically filling them with regular shapes of ever diminishing area. One need not believe in some essential difference between speech and song, the sensuous and the sensible; the dividing line, as I've tried to demonstrate, involves acts of cultural power and the corresponding dis- and re-organization of a racialized field. Print media add an element of circulation across space and time, in specific historical conjunctures and ideological contexts. A study of the sound text should start there.

Notes

1. For an account of race in Kant's critique, see Hoffman.
2. I make this point by way of Nina Sun Eidsheim's *The Race of Sound*.
3. For more on the political stakes of belonging to nation in these historical circumstances, see Elizabeth J. West's chapter "Citizenship and Enslavement" in this volume.
4. For more on Eliot's relationship to "race records" see Michael North's landmark *The Dialect of Modernism*, which sees the minstrel show as one important "prototype" for Eliot's early experiments (85). See also Anita H. Patterson.
5. See *Soundworks*, chapter 1.

Works Cited

Baker, Houston A. Blues. *Ideology, and Afro-American Literature: A Vernacular Theory*. U of Chicago P, 1984.

Baraka, Amiri. *Blues People: Negro Music in White America*. Perennial, 2002.

Carby, Hazel V. *Imperial Intimacies: A Tale of Two Islands*. Verso, 2019.

Derrida, Jacques. "The Law of Genre," translated by Avital Ronnell. *Acts of Literature*, edited by Derek Attridge. Routledge, 1992.

Douglass, Frederick. *Narrative of the Life of Frederick Douglass, an American Slave*. 1845. Reprinted in *Autobiographies*, edited by Henry Louis Gates, Jr. Library of America, 1994.

Du Bois, W.E.B. *Writings*. Edited by Nathan Huggins. Library of America, 1986.

Edwards, Brent Hayes. *Epistrophies: Jazz and the Literary Imagination*. Harvard UP, 2017.

Eidsheim, Nina Sun. *The Race of Sound: Listening, Timbre, and Vocality in African American Music*. Duke UP, 2019.

Ellison, Ralph. *The Collected Essays of Ralph Ellison*.

———. *Conversations with Ralph Ellison*. Edited by Maryemma Graham and Amtrijit Singh. UP of Mississippi, 1996.

Fabian, Johannes. *Time and the Other: How Anthropology Makes Its Object*. 1983. Columbia UP, 2002.

Gitelman, Lisa. *Always Already New: Media, History, and the Data of Culture*. The MIT Press, 2008.

Hall, Stuart. "Race, the Floating Signifier." *Selected Writings on Race and Difference*, edited by Paul Gilroy and Ruth Wilson Gilmore. Duke UP, 2021.

Hartman, Saidiya. *Scenes of Subjection: Terror, Slavery, and Self-Making in Nineteenth-Century America*. Oxford UP, 1997.

Hoffman, John. "Kant's Aesthetic Categories: Race in the Critique of Judgment." *Diacritics*, vol. 44, no. 2, 2016, pp. 54–81.

Hurston, Zora Neale. "Spirituals and Neo-Spirituals," *Folklore, Memoirs, and Other Writings*, edited by Cheryl A. Wall. Library of America, 1995.

Kant, Immanuel. *Critique of Judgment*. Translated by James Creed Meredith. Oxford UP, 2007.

Kelley, Robin D.G. *Freedom Dreams: The Black Radical Imagination*. Beacon Press, 2002.

Labelle, Brandon. "Raw Orality." *Voice: Vocal Aesthetics in Digital Arts and Media*, edited by Norie Neumark, Ross Gibson, and Theo van Leeuwen. The MIT Press, 2010.

Moten, Fred. *In the Break: The Aesthetics of the Black Radical Tradition*. U of Minnesota P, 2003.

Neal, Larry. "The Black Arts Movement." *The Drama Review: TDR*, vol. 12, no. 4, Summer 1968, pp. 28–39.

———. "Writers Symposium," edited by Hoyt Fuller. *Negro Digest* 17, no. 3, January 1968.

North, Michael. *The Dialect of Modernism: Race, Language, and Twentieth Century Literature*. Oxford UP, 1998.

Patterson, Anita H. "Jazz, Realism and the Modernist Lyric: The Poetry of Langston Hughes." *MLQ: Modern Language Quarterly*, vol. 61, no.4, December 2000, pp. 651–682.

Reed, Anthony. *Soundworks: Race, Sound, and Poetry in Production*. Duke UP, 2021.

Spillers, Hortense. *Black, White, and In Color: Essays on American Literature and Culture*. U of Chicago P, 2003.

Suisman, David. *Selling Sounds: The Commercial Revolution in American Music*. Harvard UP, 2009.

Sukenick, Ronald. *Down and In: Life in the Underground*. William Morrow, 1987.

Zukovsky, Louis. "A Statement for Poetry." *Prepositions +: The Collected Critical Essays of Louis Zukofsky*. Wesleyan UP, 2001.

25
PHOTOGRAPHY, LITERATURE, AND TIME

Emily Hyde

Photography and literature tend to get in each other's way. One claims the particular, the other the universal. One proffers veracity, the other gladly trades in the fictive. But which is which? And when, under what circumstances, and in what contexts? These are very old debates, with their own histories and politics that persist into the twenty-first century. For example, in a substantial special issue from 2006, Karen Jacobs introduces the topic of literature and photography with a military metaphor, remarking that all the contributors can agree "that the co-presence of photographic and literary elements leads to their infiltration of one another's territories" (1). This metaphor is one W. J. T. Mitchell lamented in his groundbreaking *Iconology* (1986): "Why do we have this compulsion to conceive of the relation between words and images in political terms, as a struggle for territory, a contest of rival ideologies?" (43).

Contemporary practices of bringing photography and literature together have, however, become less oppositional; while this shift certainly stems from the ubiquity of digital cameras and concrete practices of taking and making photographic images, the current moment also reflects shifting theoretical perspectives and attachments. This account of the politics of literature and photography will focus on recent work, both creative and critical, to describe an ongoing transition from a politics of referentiality to a politics of time in the practice of photography and literature. A quick example from Teju Cole's *Blindspot* (2016), a hybrid of lyric essay, travel journal, and photograph album, at first seems to rehearse the timeworn antagonism between photographic image and literary text. *Blindspot* pairs Cole's writing and his photographs in a peripatetic meditation on vision and its limits (325). The writing is aphoristic and allusive, the photographs are highly patterned and sparsely populated. One page spread questions photography's ability to depict politics at all. It begins: "Photography is good at showing neither political detail nor political sweep." It cannot show discourse, contestation, or compromise. "Photography can show violence and its aftermath," Cole writes, "but politics is elsewhere, hard to compress into a rectangular frame" (212).

The text goes on to condemn photojournalism with unruffled certainty, and Cole pairs this text with a decidedly non-journalistic image (Figure 25.1). It is a tightly framed photograph of a cedar tree, taken in the Qadisha Valley in northern Lebanon. The trunk is fissured brown and gray, multiple limbs have been sawn off, and the bark has bulged to grow back over some of these cuts. The cedar is the national emblem of Lebanon, but the

DOI: 10.4324/9781003038009-30

Figure 25.1 From Teju Cole, *Blind Spot*, Penguin Random House; Teju Cole, Lebanon, 2017. Courtesy the artist

photograph is not merely a symbol of the nation; it also depicts actions and relations that themselves can be understood as political. The trunk fills the width of the vertical frame: this is an ancient tree. It has survived, and it also makes a claim of continuity upon the future. It bears the saw marks of lived experience, of human history, of both natural and social transformation. The political relations it depicts include witnessing, the disposition to act with care and to take responsibility, the infliction of violence, and the comingling of suffering and survival. Word and image discourse, contest each other, find compromise. The text may despair, but the photograph opens to the future: its photographic contingency is also historical, demanding that the viewer ask how this image, this tree, could be different, how their futures could or could not be otherwise. This is a politics of time that is not compressed into a rectangular frame but opens the viewer to the literary text and to possible futures outside that frame.

Focal Point

Rays of light, running in parallel, pass through a lens and converge on a focal point. But photography, literature, and politics are not so easily delineated nor so easily brought together. Even the most influential theorizations of photography such as Walter Benjamin's "Little History of Photography" (1931), Susan Sontag's *On Photography* (1977), and Roland Barthes's *Camera Lucida* (1980) are fragmented and essayistic texts, offering nothing like a systematic approach. However, as fields grow and critical interest shifts, practices change and points of convergence come into focus. The study of photography, for example, is no longer as firmly seated in art history as it once was, nor so dedicated to medium specificity and aesthetic legitimacy. Photography is now examined in the context of much wider media histories and visual cultures (Batchen and Gitelman 206).

While critics may still search for origins and ontologies, they also examine photographs' alterations and adaptations, their dissemination and circulation. Today, photography as a medium may encompass the digital manipulations of postphotography as well as what Joanna Zylinska's describes as nonhuman photography, or "imaging processes from which the human is absent" (7). Indexicality, that "imprint or transfer off the real" so specific to the truth claims conventionally associated with the medium of film photography (Krauss 110), recedes in contemporary theoretical debates but perhaps "reverses direction" to linger in our minds (Tietjen 378). That is, the index persists less as a trace of the real and more as a psychological undertow produced whenever a viewer encounters a photographic image, no matter how far that image might be from the original capture of light reflecting off subject.

Another shift in the study of photography starts with the psychology of viewing a photographic image. Critics examine the photograph as both material fact and affective encounter—it is a representation but also a lived experience. Considering how photographs are viewed often centers marginalized subjects (Brown and Phu 7), as in the work of Tina Campt and Nicole Fleetwood. Christina Sharpe describes sounding an "ordinary note of care" when encountering an image (132). Faced with a photograph of a young girl awaiting transport by ship after the 2010 earthquake in Haiti, for example, Sharpe asks: "what was I being called to by and with her look at me and mine at her?" (45). Both intimacy and action resonate in this question. Overall, theoretical responses to photography are shifting: from thinking about the photograph's referentiality and its ability to accurately represent the world to thinking about the photograph as a social object, one that not only represents but also creates (and sometimes inflicts) experience. In Marvin Heiferman's words, "Photographs don't only show us things, they *do* things" (16).

A pair of recent examples shows how the literary text looks past questions of the photograph's referentiality and indexicality—the idea that photographs are inextricably tied to the material world they represent—in order to create affective encounters with the photographic image. Claudia Rankine's *Citizen: An American Lyric* (2014) is a work of poetry and criticism interwoven with prose and visual images. The book meditates on race, injustice, and belonging in America, transforming everyday experiences of racism into poems and tennis matches into metaphors. The visual images range from screengrabs drawn straight from the daily news cycle to polished reproductions of contemporary artworks. Included among these images is a manipulated photograph. It is uncaptioned and sits in the lower half of an otherwise blank page. The credits at the end of the book read: "Hulton Archive/Title: Public Lynching/Date: August 30, 1930/Credit: Getty Images/(Image alteration with permission: John Lucas)" (165). Lucas, together with Rankine, removed the lynched bodies from the photograph, leaving the top third of the image an expanse of black and accentuating the white faces lit by a flash below. A spectacle of Black suffering no longer, Rankine and Lucas's photograph instead becomes an image of white complicity. This is a risky move, because the complicity it depicts encompasses all the spectators of this image, both in the frame and outside it. The white spectators in the image are there to see a lynching, but they have turned to look at the photographer—they know a photograph is being taken, and they are actively participating in its creation. They know themselves to be a part of this spectacle, and their look directly at the camera seems also to recognize future spectators of this photograph: are those spectators also complicit? Readers of *Citizen* will miss this question entirely if they do not read the photograph in the context of the literary text, which includes the routine list of image credits at the end of the book as well as Rankine's fairly opaque writing on the facing page: "…we are all caught hanging, the rope inside us, the tree inside us, its roots our limbs, a throat sliced through and when we open our mouth to speak, blossoms, o blossoms..." (90). Reading for the index, here, feels complicitous—one white spectator literally points (with his index finger) to the bodies as if he is directing, or authorizing, your viewing. Rankine and Lucas's 2014 photographic manipulations of the image demand more than reading for the light that flashed upon the scene of atrocity back in 1930.

In the transnational spaces of global Anglophone literature, photography also moves through history, functioning less as a specific reference to the past than as a social object in the present. In Mohsin Hamid's 2017 novel *Exit West*, two young refugees migrate across the globe.[1] It is a story both topical and magical, a fable populated with motorcycles, cell phones, and social media. Nadia chooses to wear conservative black robes not from religious belief, but as protection for a single woman. Similarly, she cloaks her online presence in usernames and avatars. In London, after the authorities turn the electricity off to the sections of the city filled with migrants, Nadia sits outdoors on some steps, across the street from troops with a tank, seeking cell service so she can check the news on her phone. She sees an image of a young woman in black robes sitting on the steps of a building, looking at her phone, across the street from troops with a tank. She is startled, wondering how she could "both read the news and be the news," and she looks for a nearby photographer with "the bizarre feeling of time bending all around her, as though she was from the past reading about the future, or from the future reading about the past" (157). She is deeply unsettled and feels split into two selves, simultaneously a spectator and a subject. The photograph Nadia sees online is not so much an indexical photographic representation (when she zooms in, it turns out not to be her) as it is a physical and affective experience of photography. Rather than feeling identified (as in "hey, that's me! I'm in the news, my story is being told"), she feels divided. Her identity is not entirely her own, it is also the object of surveillance; her robes are not entirely her own choice, but also a visible image of a global crisis over which she has no control. This is an encounter with a digital photograph that is also an affective experience of a globalized world.

One of these examples involves an actual photograph, reproduced on the page; the other is an ekphrastic reproduction of a fictional photograph. If the state of photography criticism is hard to summarize beyond a shift in critical attachments, the study of literature and photography is equally indeterminate. The literary image and the photographic image are both likenesses, but the literary image can be of a photograph, as in *Exit West*, and the photographic image comes to us enveloped in language, as in *Citizen*. How to name and describe the convergence of the literary text and the photographic image? Taxonomizing is an understandable impulse, but critique and interpretation tend to drop out of overly systematic approaches. Does one study photobooks, photo-textualities, photomediations, photo-embedded literature, or the photographic essay, just to unpack the "Ps"? (Parr and Badger; Bryant; Kuc and Zylinska; Pitts, and Mitchell). The lodestones here, in literatures in English, are just as equivocal: in the early 1900s Henry James worked with Alvin Langdon Coburn on photographic frontispieces for his New York Edition, but he insisted they express "no particular thing in the text" (James 333). After that apotheosis of ambiguity, it's hard to know how to categorize iconic works from later in the twentieth century, such as Virginia Woolf's *Orlando* (1928); James Agee and Walker Evans's *Let Us Now Praise Famous Men* and Richard Wright's *12 Million Black Voices* (both 1941); Wright Morris's *The Home Place* (1948); John Berger's critical and creative work, especially in the 1960s and 1970s; and the reception of the works of W. G. Sebald in the English-speaking world starting in the 1990s. Rather than classifying, scholars must articulate the semiotic and interpretive work that photography does in—or with, or to—the literary text. Is that work thematic? Does it provide historical context or verification of contested claims? Is photography a technique of seeing and describing the world that infiltrates the language of the text, or does literary language envelope and construe the image? Is the photograph an example of ekphrasis—is it a verbal representation of visual representation, in James Heffernan's pithy definition (3)? Or is it a material object, printed on the page? (Is it therefore also a commodity, with permissions secured and duly paid for?) Following shifts in both photography theory and contemporary literature, this chapter will settle on examining photography as a social practice that can include actual photographs as well as descriptions of photographs and photography. Photography qualifies as a "practice," because photographs do things that are "social"—the work the photograph does in the text is to bring subjects and spectators together. This social practice becomes political when photographic image and literary text reveal unequal distributions of power in the past, enact relations between subjects and spectators in the present, and demand acts of political imagination for the future.

The politics of locating the focal point of literature and photography in social practice shifts, as I began to argue about the photograph of the scarred cedar tree, from a politics of referentiality to a politics of time. In the first half of the twentieth century, the rise of the documentary movement and the genre of photojournalism dominated political photography—the photograph could document injustice, champion progressive reforms, report the horrors of war. In the main, this was a politics of photographic referentiality, though avant-garde photocollage and montage also served as mode of political critique. In the second half of the twentieth century, photography criticism became more hostile toward the medium, viewing the glut of photographs in our everyday lives as an ideological tool trapping us in an accelerating consumer culture driven by the mass media (see Linfield). Political critique of photographs meant exposing their constructed representations of the real rather than imaginatively exploring their representations of time. Whereas political analyses of time and temporality tend toward arguments about periodization, historical consciousness, and temporal structures like "progress" or "the end of history," I am interested in time as a basis for political critique of our global contemporary moment and, especially, in futurity as the operative mode of that critique.

Photography has, of course, long been viewed as a time-based medium: in a moment of nostalgia for the clicking, ticking mechanisms of early photography, Roland Barthes described cameras as "clocks for seeing" (15). But instead of looking backward, only to the past, thinking of photography as a social practice can also help us see our contemporary moment as a bringing together of times—colonial, postcolonial, national, neocolonial, psychic, spiritual, geological, planetary, and more (see Anderson, Chakrabarty, Fabian, Mbembe, and Osborne). Photographs can also "see" the future, in that they anticipate future viewers. Shawn Michelle Smith, in her writing on contemporary art and the unfinished work of racial justice, describes a "temporal oscillation" intrinsic to photography—the photograph is "always signifying in relation to a past and a present, and anticipating a future" (4). It is the anticipation of futurity that underpins the politics of time inherent to the practice of literature and photography today. Futurity is not inherently political, or useful, in and of itself—Jill Lepore lamented in 2017 over a rash of dystopian novels that, in writing their histories of the future, eschewed action. They "cannot imagine a better future, and [they don't] ask anyone to bother to make one" was her blunt conclusion. But in literary texts that invoke photography as a social practice, futurity is, in Paul Saint-Amour's words, "an orientation toward the oncoming" (367). It is open to the future and to the action necessary to create alternative futures. Power is distributed differently in time when photography serves as an active form of witnessing the past not merely to freeze and preserve it, but also to imagine alternate future possibilities.

Depth of Field

A photograph's depth of field refers to the area in focus, which gradually fades to blur at its limits. A number of theorists congregate, in no particular hierarchy, in the depths of the field I have identified as the photographic politics of time visible in contemporary literature. Each of them, in their own way, is interested in the "unfinished-ness" of photography (Drucker 28), but each has a different way of pushing back against the idea of a photograph as a closed representation of the past, a fixed piece of evidence, a mere illustration. Kaja Silverman admits that Walter Benjamin's "Little History of Photography" hovers behind all these debates, and she deliberately follows Benjamin rather than Barthes, who, in *Camera Lucida*, she argues, "both expresses and contributes to the political despair that afflicts so many of us today: our sense that the future is 'all used up'" (4). Because, as she explains, discussions of photographic indexicality "always focus on the past" (2), Silverman, along with other scholars of both photography and literature, like Laura Wexler and Marianne Hirsch, prefers approaches to photography that are less inexorably fixed in time. For example, Marianne Hirsch and Leo Spitzer read children's school photographs in "liquid time," a term indebted to the photographer Jeff Wall, to show how the futures envisioned in the past are still active and acquiring new meanings in the present (12–13). That they are viewing school photographs of children who did not survive Nazi ghettos, internment in camps for Japanese Americans, or boarding schools for Native children makes the political stakes of reading in liquid time all the more trenchant (see also Hayes and Gilburt). Another important recent example of multitemporal reading practices appears in Jennifer Bajorek's *Unfixed: Photography and Decolonial Imagination in West Africa* (2020). In this exploration of urban photographic practices in independence-era West Africa, Bajorek sees photography "expanding the existing spaces of political imagination" (9). Bajorek, along with other scholars of West African photography, sees the photographs that appear in her book as running "directly counter to conceptions of photography that elevate fixity, permanence, and capture over transformation, revision, and flux, and that find their apotheosis in positivist interpretations of the photographic index" (22). Reimagining and remaking their world, these photographs may not be able to rewrite the history of the independence era, but they do ensure "a future for the myriad imaginative acts and solidarities they engender" (264). In these theoretical approaches, photographs are open-ended acts of the imagination, and the politics of time they encourage is oriented toward imagining, identifying, and pursuing political alternatives to a future that is frequently presented as ineluctably fixed.

Ariella Azoulay is a theorist of politics and photography who is also a practitioner—or perhaps "participator" in photography is the better term. She is a curator, filmmaker, and manipulator of photographic images, recontextualizing them, folding them, tracing over them in pencil. Azoulay expands one's sense of what qualifies as "political" photography in her voluminous books *Potential History: Unlearning Imperialism* (2019); *Civil Imagination: The Political Ontology of Photography* (2012); and *The Civil Contract of Photography* (2008). In Azoulay's photographic reading practice, one doesn't simply look at a photograph so much as encounter it in a political space with other users of photography. Those users include the photographer, the photograph's subject, and its past, present, and future spectators, real and imagined, who meet in "a potential place that enables the act of photography to occur while the participants acknowledge that they are not alone in front of the other" (*Civil Contract* 129). In this space, there may be violence, there may be injustice, but there is no ownership, no outright control. It is a relational space, where no one is alone.

As a result, Azoulay thinks less about photographic representation and more about forms of citizenship and address—encountering a photograph, she starts by asking "Why are they looking at me?" (18). The temporal implications of this type of reading practice are ambitious: in the political space of the photograph, spectators are held accountable because they can always "reopen the image and renegotiate what it shows" (13). For example, Tamara Lanier has sued Harvard University to return daguerreotypes of her enslaved ancestors, Renty and Delia Taylor, infamously held by Harvard's Peabody Museum of Archeology and Ethnology. In an amicus brief submitted to the court hearing the case, Azoulay argues that the photograph is a social object rather than a piece of property. As such, it documents an unequal, unjust photographic encounter, and its participants—which would include Lanier as heir and descendent—should be heard outside the confines of laws governing the possession of property. "What is recorded in photographs is not yet over," Azoulay writes, "redress is possible, and justice can still be granted" ("Captive Photograph"). The photograph is dynamic in time and also, even more than a century after it was taken, it demands action from its users. This is an active form of photographic futurity, one that is similar to Claudia Rankine's photographic manipulations in *Citizen*.

The imaginative action demanded here is not without its risks or its skeptics. Patricia Hayes has argued that Azoulay depends too much on imagining the voices of the subjects of photographs, and on imagining that they are even willing to inhabit the same political space as herself and her readers. Writing from the perspective of South Africa, Hayes worries about "the quality of that political space. It is uneven and unequal" (188). This seems right, and yet Azoulay's strident political theory frames a photographic reading practice that is not entirely heterodox. We do intuit other users of a photograph, whenever we snap a picture. We do imagine future retrospection. And when we view a photograph, we can imagine alternative futures for its subjects. Bajorek is also skeptical of fully applying Azoulay's political theory to West African photographic archives, yet she too enacts a multitemporal photographic reading practice open to imagining otherwise: the ultimate aim of Bajorek's book is to "imagine or envision, through photography, the end of colonial modernity" (31). I see the political imagination activated by photography in all of these differing theories and methods as oriented toward the future through practice in the present.

In Practice

Practice may be the dialectical testing of theory, but it also has a temporal aspect—practice involves habit, repetition, the slow gain of proficiency. In what remains of this chapter, I'll focus on the politics of time developed in a combined work of South African literature and photography by the writer Ivan Vladislavić and the photographer David Goldblatt. *TJ/Double Negative* was published by the Italian firm Contrasto in 2010; it was also released by the South African publisher Umuzi in the same year. *TJ*, subtitled "Johannesburg Photographs 1948–2010," is a photobook. *Double Negative* is simply subtitled "A Novel." If you open either of these texts, you'll see that each is defined in relation to the boxed set: *TJ* is called the "visual component," while *Double Negative* is the "fictional element"—it's a paperback nestled inside a cardboard box sized to match Goldblatt's photobook. According to Vladislavić, the boxed set was made possible by Goldblatt's international reputation as an artist ("Ivan Vladislavić by Katie Kitamura"), and so to explore the politics of time in this work of literature and photography is to recognize that the slipcase that binds the two media together is the glossy emblem of the multinational publishing industry. Which is to say, the politics of time in *TJ/Double Negative* should be read in relation to the expansionary and accelerating temporal logic of the global art market.

Goldblatt is a renowned South African photographer. His work, made between 1948 and his death in 2018, is held in major collections worldwide, but he always stuck close to home, visiting and revisiting South African landscapes, cities, and people. He founded the Market Photo Workshop in Johannesburg in 1989 and is widely regarded as mentoring an entire generation of young photographers in South Africa. He collaborated with Nadine Gordimer for *On the Mines* (1973) and *Lifetimes Under Apartheid* (1986), and as he and Vladislavić discussed their collaboration, Goldblatt handed over a "set of rather grubby prints" he intended to include in *TJ*. Vladislavić knew he wanted to write a novel, not a commentary, and so he approached these photographs with "studied inattention," letting them sit on a shelf for a few years ("Double Exposure" 46). Vladislavić is an editor and a writer known for working with artists and visual images in, for example, his 2004 novel *The Exploded View*. He is also known for nonfiction, including *Portrait with Keys: The City of Johannesburg Unlocked* (2006). The novel Vladislavić produced in relation to Goldblatt's photographs, *Double Negative*, is narrated by Neville Lister, a college dropout who one day in the early 1980s tags along with a fictionalized version of Goldblatt named Saul Auerbach and witnesses him take two iconic photographs. Neville will go on to become a commercial photographer, calling himself "the frozen moment guy. I specialize in things falling, spilling, flying apart" (97–98). But he cannot escape Auerbach's images: they nestle inside his memory, both as moments in time and as experiences that continue to develop into the present.

While Goldblatt has said that on first reading *Double Negative* he didn't recognize himself or his photographic practice ("Double Exposure" 47), critics have often articulated how his photographs similarly manage to record the "pastness" of the past while also extending its meaning into the future. Nadine Gordimer once said "David's photographs have an unstated political significance that goes before and grows beyond the obvious images" (Weber). Alexandra Dodd opened what turned out to be Goldblatt's last interview with this question: "There is a strange prescience about your images—an almost predictive sense of how history might unfold. It seems that in the present-tense moment in which you take your photographs you have an innate sense of how they might be read or received in the future" (Goldblatt, *Last Interview* 7). The photographs collected in *TJ* exhibit this multitemporality: they preserve the past and yet also seem to unfold over time into the future. Goldblatt achieves this partly through circling back to the same locations through the years to photograph what has changed and what has persisted. For example, one 2003 color photograph captioned "The Docrats' lavatory" shows a two-story concrete ruin threaded with rebar (*TJ* 270). Goldblatt—who is known for his detailed captions—jumbles dates in this caption, explaining that this ruin was part of a home that proved too sturdy to be demolished in 1977 when the multiracial suburb of which it was a part was finally destroyed, long after it was proclaimed a White Group Area in 1956. "The Docrats' lavatory" refers back to the series of photographs Goldblatt took of this particular family in their home before 1977, but it also refers forward in time: he notes that "the structure stands to this day" in 2003 (*TJ* 270). Goldblatt is interested in the erasure of history, its persistence in the built environment, and in return: he kept his eye on this particular ruin for at least 30 years. Similarly, Vladislavić is known for his interest in urban space, especially in its structures of separation and order. Sarah Nuttall describes one of Vladislavić's "figures of the city" in a way that must also have applied to Goldblatt roaming Johannesburg with his camera: it is the figure of "the aging white man, a new minority figure, trying to remake a public self" (215). *TJ/Double Negative* seems primarily, then, to spatialize the entangled temporalities of contemporary Johannesburg from a particularly privileged perspective. Yet the unruliness of its combined media also sets forth a politics of time grounded in photography as a social practice and uprooted from simple dichotomies between fact and fiction.

For example, in the novel, one of the iconic photographs Neville watches Auerbach take is of Mrs. Ditton in her lounge. Neville narrates how the great photographer sets up the shot and then seems to wait for some imperceptible change, perhaps in the light, perhaps in Mrs. Ditton's composure. When the shutter finally clicks, time splits in two. Neville says that Mrs. Ditton now has two destinies: in one, she continues to sit in the chair in the present of a progressing, "real" time. In the other, "anticipating a paper-thin future, she floats free of the fat-thighed cushions and the sticky shadows, she levitates. It is there in the photograph, you have only to look," Neville insists (Vladislavić, *Double Negative* 86). This levitation becomes a curiously reversed reference to Walter Benjamin's famous angel of history when Neville goes on to muse that Mrs. Ditton's paper-thin destiny "was receding into the past, but with its face turned to the future" (86). This is not a messianic vision of Mrs. Ditton—Neville is a commercial photographer after all, a "frozen moment guy" specializing in imminent futures such as the red wine stain on the carpet, the sudden need for whatever product is being sold. From Neville's point of view, time may be caught and stilled in Auerbach's photograph, but photographs can also indicate that everything is about to change. Mrs. Ditton is not, then, frozen in time but instead faces multiple possible futures.

This model of photographic contingency plays out against another form of time in *TJ/Double Negative*. Both the fictional Auerbach and, by extension, the real Goldblatt seem to represent the orderly progression of historical time. In the last section of the novel, Neville petulantly envies Auerbach's continuity: "He had soldiered on, one photograph at a time, leaving behind an account of himself and his place in which one thing followed another, print after print. My own story was full of holes" (236). And indeed, while *TJ* is organized chronologically by decade, *Double Negative* is structured across three slices of time: the early 1980s, then the early 1990s at the end of apartheid, and finally 2009. But literary text and photographic oeuvre aren't so neatly opposed: Goldblatt's photographs in *TJ* do depict gaps in time, slight shifts, "holes" in what seems like an inevitable historical progression, and it is Neville's petulant remarks that make *TJ/Double Negative*'s politics of time visible.

Neville's self-consciousness draws the reader's attention to another photographer who appears twice in *TJ*, first as a frontispiece and second in a two-page spread (Figure 25.2).

Figure 25.2 David Goldblatt, Portrait photographer and client, Braamfontein, 1955, Vintage silver gelatin print. Courtesy the David Goldblatt Legacy Trust and Goodman Gallery

Described only as a "portrait photographer" from 1955 (17), he clearly works on the street, and in both shots he peers down into a handmade box camera—we never see his face. (Another of Goldblatt's photographs showing his face does exist, but it was not included in *TJ*.) How self-consciously did Goldblatt include the images of this Black portrait photographer in his photobook? Is Goldblatt identifying with him? Is he appropriating his labor? Is that why he appears in the frontispiece to the whole collection of Goldblatt's work? The portrait photographer appears again later in *TJ* in a diptych spread over two pages, the photographer and box camera on the left in balance with his client posing on the right. The grassy hill descends in a perfect arc across the gutter of the book, emphasizing continuity and insisting on instantaneity: this is one moment sliced in two, it seems to say. But the chair hiccups awkwardly between the two photographs. The chair on the right is in slightly closer range than the chair on the left—Goldblatt has moved his camera, or adjusted his lens, or adjusted his enlarger in the darkroom. This diptych is actually a depiction of contingency: the chair contradicts the continuous slope of time between the two photographs. There is a "hole" in time, to use Neville's phrasing. In this way, Goldblatt appears to back down from appropriating the work of the portrait photographer or the pose of his client. Instead, his diptych points to modes of vernacular photography outside his own practice: it points to another, unseen, image from 1955 and to the possible futures it might have encountered and might still be encountering.

Neville challenges Auerbach on this point about photographic contingency when they meet again in 2009. "There's such an air of necessity about your photos, as if it had to be these images and no others," he insists. "It might look inevitable, read backwards, but it could all have been different. Every portrait could have been of someone else; every house could have been the house next door" (234). The fictional Auerbach bats Neville's query aside with a comment about getting up every day and doing the work, just as the real Goldblatt didn't fully engage Alexandra Dodd's question about the "foreknowledge" immanent in his images (*The Last Interview* 7). In both cases, the uncertainty and contingency of photography is balanced out by the long, slow, accumulating practice of the photographer. This mixing of different forms of time emerges from the mixed media of *TJ/Double Negative* itself, which also brings together multiple users of photography, both real and fictional. Power is distributed among all these participants: Goldblatt and Vladislavić, Saul Auerbach and Neville Lister, the portrait photographer and his client in 1955 and the unknown viewers of that unseen portrait, as well as all the readers and viewers of this combined text. The politics of time here is historical, in that the past is witnessed and preserved. But it is also speculative: it imaginatively encompasses futures past, present, and to come. The social practice of photography in *TJ/Double Negative* relies on both fact and fiction, word and image, photographic referentiality and photographic contingency. Its politics are grounded in reality and are also full of potential.

Note

1 For a different reading of Hamid's *Exit West*, see Ameeth Vijay's chapter "Cities" in this volume.

Works Cited

Agee, James, and Walker Evans. *Let Us Now Praise Famous Men*. Houghton Mifflin, 2001.
Anderson, Benedict. *Imagined Communities*. Verso, 2006.
Azoulay, Ariella Aïsha. "The Captive Photograph." *Boston Review*, 23 Sept., 2021, https://bostonreview.net/articles/the-captive-photograph/.
———. *Civil Imagination: A Political Ontology of Photography*. Verso, 2012.
Barthes, Roland. *Camera Lucida*. Translated by Richard Howard. Hill and Wang, 2010.

Batchen, Geoffrey, and Lisa Gitelman. "Afterword: Media History and History of Photography in Parallel Lines." *Photography and Other Media in the Nineteenth Century*, edited by Nicoletta Leonardi and Simone Natale, Penn State UP, 2018.
Brown, Elspeth H., and Thy Phu, editors. *Feeling Photography*. Duke UP, 2014.
Bryant, Marsha, editor. *Photo-Textualities: Reading Photographs and Literature*. U of Delaware P, 1996.
Chakrabarty, Dipesh. *Provincializing Europe*. Princeton UP, 2007.
Cole, Teju. *Blind Spot*. Random House, 2016.
Drucker, Johanna. "Temporal Photography." *Philosophy of Photography*, vol. 1, no. 1, 2010, pp. 23–29.
Fabian, Johannes. *Time and the Other*. Columbia UP, 2014.
Goldblatt, David. *The Last Interview*. Interview by Alexandra Dodd and edited by Brenda Goldblatt. Steidl, 2019.
Goldblatt, David and Ivan Vladislavić. *TJ: Johannesburg Photographs 1948–2010 / Double Negative: A Novel*. Contrasto Books, 2010.
Hamid, Mohsin. *Exit West*. Riverhead Books, 2017.
Hayes, Patricia, "The Uneven Citizenry of Photography: Reading the "Political Ontology" of Photography from Southern Africa," *Cultural Critique*, vol. 89, 2015, pp. 173–93.
Hayes, Patricia, and Iona Gilburt. "Retakes in Liquid Time." *Kronos*, vol. 46, no. 1, 2020, pp. 10–28.
Heffernan, James. *Museum of Words: The Poetics of Ekphrasis from Homer to Ashbery*. U of Chicago P, 1993.
Heiferman, Marvin. "Photography Changes Everything." *Photography Changes Everything*, edited by Marvin Heiferman, Aperture, 2012, pp. 11–21.
Hirsch, Marianne and Leo Spitzer. *School Photos in Liquid Time*. U of Washington P, 2020.
Jacobs, Karen. "Visual Developments and Narrative Exposures." *English Language Notes*, vol. 44, no. 2, 2006, pp. 1–5.
James, Henry. *The Art of the Novel: Critical Prefaces*. Edited by Richard P. Blackmur, U of Chicago P, 2011.
Krauss, Rosalind E. *The Originality of the Avant-Garde and Other Modernist Myths*. MIT P, 1986.
Kuc, Kamila and Joanna Zylinska, editors. *Photomediations: A Reader*. Open Humanities P, 2016. http://openhumanitiespress.org/books/download/Kuc-Zylinska_2016_Photomediations-A-Reader.pdf.
Lepore, Jill. "A Golden Age for Dystopian Fiction." *The New Yorker*, June 5 & 12, 2017, https://www.newyorker.com/magazine/2017/06/05/a-golden-age-for-dystopian-fiction.
Linfield, Susie. *The Cruel Radiance: Photography and Political Violence*. U of Chicago P, 2010.
Mbembe, Achille. *On the Postcolony*. U of California P, 2001.
———. *Out of the Dark Night*. Columbia UP, 2021.
Mitchell, W.J.T. *Iconology: Image, Text, Ideology*. U of Chicago P, 1986.
———. *Picture Theory: Essays on Verbal and Visual Representation*. U of Chicago P, 1994.
Morris, Wright. *The Home Place*. U of Nebraska P, 1999.
Nuttall, Sarah. "Literary City." *Johannesburg: The Elusive Metropolis*, edited by Sarah Nuttall and Achille Mbembe. Duke UP, 2008, pp. 195–218.
Osborne, Peter. *Anywhere Or Not At All: Philosophy Of Contemporary Art*. Verso, 2013.
Parr, Martin, and Gerry Badger, editors. *The Photobook: A History, Vols I-III*. Phaidon, 2004, 2009, 2014.
Pitts, Terry. *Vertigo*. https://sebald.wordpress.com.
Rankine, Claudia. *Citizen: An American Lyric*. Graywolf Press, 2014.
Saint-Amour, Paul K. "The Literary Present." *ELH*, vol. 85, no. 2, 2018, pp. 367–392.
Sharpe, Christina. *In the Wake: On Blackness and Being*. Duke UP, 2016.
Silverman, Kaja. *The Miracle of Analogy or The History of Photography, Part 1*. Stanford UP, 2015.
Smith, Shawn Michelle. *Photographic Returns: Racial Justice and the Time of Photography*. Duke UP, 2020.
Vladislavić, Ivan. "Double Exposure." Interview by Marlene van Niekerk, *The British Journal of Photography*, vol. 5, 2011, pp. 44–49.
———. "Ivan Vladislavić by Katie Kitamura." *BOMB Magazine*, Mar 15, 2016, https://bombmagazine.org/articles/ivan-vladislavic/.
Weber, Donald. "Lens on Apartheid's Haunting Legacy." *The Forward*, May 5, 2010.
Woolf, Virginia. *Orlando: A Biography*. Harcourt, 2006.
Wright, Richard. *12 Million Black Voices: A Folk History of the Negro in the United States*. Echo Point Books and Media, 2019.
Zylinska, Joanna. *Nonhuman Photography*. MIT P, 2017.

26
ART, PROPAGANDA, AND TRUTH

Melissa Dinsman

On or about August, 1914

"Who's for the trench" and "Who'll earn the Empire's thanks"? These are two of the questions the poet and journalist Jessie Pope asks her readers in her 1915 poem "The Call" (38). The poem is structurally simple. With its ABAB rhyme scheme, "The Call" takes on a singsong rhythm that calls, like a siren, men into war service in order to earn the "thanks" of the British Empire. Pope's poem has two purposes: to entertain readers and to recruit soldiers. But does this goal of recruitment, a goal that replicates and serves state-sponsored propaganda, prevent Pope's poem from being categorized as literature with a capital L? In other words, is "The Call" literature or propaganda or both? As the chapter will show, it depends on who you ask.

One of the authors who tried to answer this question was Virginia Woolf. In her 1924 essay "Mr. Bennett and Mrs. Brown," Woolf provocatively claims that "on or about December, 1910, human character changed" and that this change impacted all aspects of human experience, including "religion, conduct, politics, and literature" (4). Woolf, often held up as a bastion of high modernist literature and an ivory tower inhabitant who hunkered down to write in the figurative seclusion of Bloomsbury, saw a shift in art, politics, and the relationship between them prior to World War I. But it is the war that solidified these supposed changes in human character and their cascading effects. Indeed, to turn Woolf's famous proclamation to other purposes: it was on or about August, 1914, that propaganda changed. With that change, the division between art and politics—a division that was always problematic at best—became not just a fantasy but entirely obsolete in the Anglo-American context.

At the war's outbreak, Britain found itself behind other European nations when it came to state-sponsored and scientifically organized propaganda. In an effort to boost morale, encourage enlistment, and maintain military secrecy, the British government passed the Defence of the Realm Act and established the War Propaganda Bureau, better known as "Wellington House." From its inception, Wellington House sought to blur the lines between art, propaganda, and truth. Author, journalist, and liberal politician Charles Masterman was appointed to run the new propaganda bureau. Almost immediately, he called upon his literary connections and friendships with Britain's best known authors, inviting them to Wellington House for a meeting by the end of which he "had mustered them, conscripted them almost, into government service" (Hynes 26).[1] The result of this meeting was a massive output of government-sanctioned writing explicitly for and about the war. World War I, therefore, shifted the way many authors approached politics in their writing. Politics was not a part of their lives separate from their writing. Nor was it simply enough for literature to represent and serve existing political interests or personal politics. Rather, in 1914, literature became institutionally "political"; and with the help of Masterman and Wellington House, institutional politics became literature.

Yet, while Masterman conscripted authors into literary war service, some writers, like Pope, Rudyard Kipling, and the Poet Laureate Robert Bridges, wrote poems out of their own sense of national duty. Although the term "War Poets" is often used to describe soldier-poets like Wilfred Owen, Siegfried Sassoon, and Robert Graves, each of whom captured the horrors of the trenches in their verse, newspaper readers often preferred patriotic and jingoistic "war poetry." Pope, for example, found great success publishing poems that encouraged conscription. Her poems, which included multiple references to World War I as a "game" or sport ("Who's for the Game?" and "Play the Game"), found a readership in the *Daily Mail* and in her three volumes of poems published between 1915 and 1916. Kipling, too, encouraged soldier conscription in his 1914 poem "For All We Have and Are":

> For all we have and are,
> For all our children's fate,
> Stand up and meet the war.
> The Hun is at the gate!
>
> (63)

Using the anti-German term "Hun," a staple throughout British propaganda of the time, Kipling writes of England defending "civilization" and the future of English children. (The health and safety of children living as subjects of the British Empire was, of course, of little concern.) Kipling urges an "iron sacrifice/Of body, will, and soul" and asks "Who stands if freedom fall?/Who dies if England live?" (64). The suggestion to young men was clear: to sacrifice oneself for England and for "freedom" (a freedom not available to those living under their brutal colonial rule) would ensure that one would continue to live, even in death, through the health of the nation.

Perhaps one of the most surprising authors to write patriotic (and often anti-German) propaganda on behalf of the British government was Ford Madox Hueffer, better known as Ford Madox Ford. Ford had spent considerable time in Germany, was proud of his German connections, and considered himself a cosmopolitan writer. Yet through his friendship with Masterman, and perhaps from a fear that his Germanness might hurt his literary career, Ford became a pro-British propagandist. In 1915, and at the behest of Masterman, Ford wrote *When Blood Is Their Argument*, a critique of German culture and intellectuals, and *Between St. Dennis and St. George*, an attack on pacifism and some of his fellow writers like G. B. Shaw (Tate 51). Although already in his 40s, Ford enlisted in 1915 and was sent to the Front in 1916. His experiences in the war would cause him to regret his complicity in writing pro-war propaganda and would stay with him for the remainder of his life, influencing the themes and politics of his later literary works.

The meaning of the word "propaganda" has evolved since its earliest recorded usage in the fifteenth century; however, as early as 1822, propaganda was defined as "the systemic dissemination of information, esp. in a biased or misleading way, in order to promote a political cause or point of view" (OED). With the onset of World War I, this "systemic dissemination" became state-sponsored and relied heavily on modern mass media to distribute this propaganda widely. Because of the government's increased role in disseminating propaganda to influence public opinion, the definition of propaganda in the eyes of the public was changed and, in many cases, had become something sinister and malicious. This led to scholarly interest in propaganda techniques and dissemination methods in the early twentieth century.

Edward Bernays was one of the first to write about this new "propaganda" in an attempt to remove its negative perception, although this would prove to be a fool's errand. In *Crystalizing Public Opinion* (1923), Bernays argues that propaganda is similar to public relations and its transformation was due in part to the rise of a mass electronic media ecology. Propaganda, Bernays claims, is essential to modern democratic societies:

> We are governed, our minds molded, our tastes formed, our ideas suggested, largely by men we have never heard of. This is a logical result of the way in which our democratic society is organized. Vast numbers of human beings must cooperate in this manner if they are to live together as a smoothly functioning society.
>
> *(37)*

Harold Lasswell, however, was not as optimistic as Bernays about the uses of propaganda. In his 1927 book on propaganda, Lasswell explicitly ties the term to its wartime usage. Like Bernays, Lasswell argues that mass media is essential for propaganda to work and that "Successful propaganda depends upon the adroit use of means under favourable conditions. A means is anything which the propagandist can manipulate" (185). From his position within the government, Masterman understood this well, and thus used both the media (newspapers, film, radio) and well-known authors to shape the narrative that best fit Britain's wartime needs. The result of this explosion of propaganda during World War I was the creation of the propaganda front, which formed a triad with the already existing military and economic fronts (Lasswell 214).

Bernays's and Lasswell's differing perceptions of propaganda and its uses help introduce some of the ethical issues with which Anglo-American authors of the 1930s and 1940s grappled. They also open up a series of thorny questions about the relationship between art, propaganda, and truth, including: what is at stake when describing particular forms of writing as propaganda, as politics, as resistance, or as mere information? Can we distinguish between "propaganda" and "art" by turning to authorial intention or by reader reception across time? If propaganda is by definition political, and "art" is conventionally distinguished from "propaganda," does that imply that art cannot be political? Perhaps unsurprisingly, clarity might depend upon the kind of consistent definitions that are rare when discussing both art and politics. What is clear, however, is that individual authors came to their own conclusions about the differences between what qualified as art and what would be reduced to the status of propaganda, even if their own writing blurred the line between the two.

Political Writing Is a Mule

By the beginning of World War II, the 1930s divisions between the political writing of the up-and-coming British poets (often referred to as the Auden group) and the old high modernist guard epitomized by Woolf and Eliot were hanging on by a thin thread. Now, with Francisco Franco's fascist victory in Spain, the Soviet Union's non-aggression pact with

Germany, and Britain's rapid transformation into a Home Front, where all economic, social, and cultural activities were conscripted into the war effort, the socialist politics of the Auden group found a less favorable public and literary reception. Likewise, the older generation of writers found that they couldn't escape personal politics in their writing and began to question if indeed they ever had.

For example, in a footnote to her 1938 anti-war and feminist essay *Three Guineas*, Woolf rails against politics in art, calling such political writing sterile:

> if we use art to propagate political opinion, we must force the artist to clip and cabin his gift to do us a cheap and passing service. Literature will suffer the same mutilation that the mule has suffered; and there will be no more horses.
>
> *(170)*

Although Woolf uses the term "political opinion" here, it seems clear that what she means is propaganda. Given that she is writing *Three Guineas* in the late 1930s, a time in which fascism and communism are on the rise throughout Europe, her argument against "political opinions" in writing seems to be an argument against dedicating writing to the organized institutional politics of the moment. This, she claims "clip[s]" or stifles the artist's ability, and the result is a piece of art that will not stand the test of time. Instead, she argues, writers should stay clear of politics (or propaganda) if they want their work to remain free (a "horse") and, one assumes due to the horse's fertility, influence future readers and artists.

This position, however, seems at best disingenuous, coming as it does in a note in one of Woolf's most overtly political tracts. As Woolf scholar Jane Marcus observes, "Virginia Woolf was no more certain of what the proper relations between art and propaganda should be than she was ready to dictate what exact proportions of 'truth of fact' and 'truth of fiction' would make a good biography" (266). In her footnote, Woolf seems to be airing her grievances more at the politics of newer writers than seriously reflecting on the theoretical or practical relationships between art, politics, and propaganda in her own work. Indeed, both *Three Guineas* and her final novel *Between the Acts* (1941) are not conventionally read as propaganda but are certainly understood to be political. Mia Spiro, for example, describes Woolf's later writings as "in conversation with European politics" and as using an "anti-Nazi aesthetic" (4). Thus, although Woolf's writing was not as overtly and purposely aligned with a specific political ideology, like the group of poets she sneeringly referred to as "W. H. Day Spender" (W. H. Auden, Cecil-Day Lewis, and Stephen Spender), her work was engaging with the politics of the day, even if those anti-war and feminist politics weren't well received. In fact, it may be that the poor reception of her political positions in *Three Guineas* kept her from thinking of her work either as political or as propaganda. Such a position begs the question as to whether a piece of art can usefully be considered propaganda if the position is not supported by a government, an organized political movement or party, established institutions, or the larger public.

For T. S. Eliot, the answer to this question was no. In his poem "A Note on War Poetry," Eliot claims that war poetry is "Not the expression of collective emotion/Imperfectly reflected in the daily papers" (237). The poetry that abounded in newspapers during World War I, like Pope's "The Call," fell under the category of "propaganda" for Eliot, not only because it was sanctioned by media outlets (and therefore the British government under wartime censorship) but also because it reflected the popular pro-war opinions of the British public. Pope and her ilk were propagandists. Sassoon and Owen were war poets. At the conclusion of Eliot's wartime poem, he states that poetry must be grounded in the individual's experience of "a situation" (237). Thus, war, as an experience, is worthy of poetry, but it is only the "private experience" of it that makes it art:

> But the abstract conception
> Of private experience at its greatest intensity
> Becoming universal, which we call "poetry,"
> May be affirmed in verse.
>
> (Eliot 238)

Politics, as a part of an individual's lived experience, therefore, was also the purview of the artist. Eliot seems to confirm this in a conversation with Woolf, in which he complained that "the young don't take art or politics seriously enough" and expressed his disappointment in Auden and Christopher Isherwood (Woolf, *Diary* 192). Woolf recorded this conversation in her diary on 19 December 1938 and its claim is as much a reflection of Eliot's position on politics in art as it is of Woolf's. There is, in this statement, a sense of the dividing line that existed between the political poets of the 1930s and Eliot and Woolf. However, Eliot's complaint also reflects his and Woolf's own sense that politics in literature should express the author's personal experiences and opinions, lest it cross the line over into propaganda for a specific ideology or nation. With the outbreak of the war in September 1939, however, Eliot would find that the dividing line between politics and propaganda in literature was more porous than he or Woolf might like to admit.

"All writing nowadays is propaganda"

Even Eliot's "A Note on War Poetry," which supports political art as separate from propaganda, blurs the line between the two. Eliot crafted this poem for the 1942 British literature collection *London Calling*, which was specifically targeted to American readers in order to bolster the wartime relationship between the two nations. *London Calling*, was commissioned by the Ministry of Information (MOI), Britain's propaganda department, and edited by Storm Jameson, who had warned about the dangerous rise of European fascism in her books. The title came from a BBC radio propaganda series targeted at occupied Europe, which started in 1941. Jameson, who thought of her writing as ethical and political as opposed to propagandistic, is not shy about the purpose of this collection in her introduction. Perhaps thinking of propaganda as "hidden" or "subversive," Jameson makes her intentions clear: the authors included in the volume are "writ[ing] for the glory of the Anglo-American friendship and the profit of the American U.S.O." (17). This gesture of "friendship" with America was in line with the goals of the British government and the MOI, which by 1942 was already imagining a postwar world in which America would emerge as a leader with Britain its closest ally.

And Jameson was far from the only author to work alongside the British government during World War II. Henry Green, for example, volunteered for the auxiliary fire service during the London bombings, Scottish novelist Muriel Spark worked for the Political Warfare Executive, spreading explicit (or "black") propaganda to occupied European countries, Graham Greene was posted in Sierra Leone by MI6, and numerous other writers lent their authorial talents to the Ministry of Information and the British Broadcasting Company. This included George Orwell, who in his 1941 essay "No, Not One" claims that "All writing nowadays in propaganda" (165).

Orwell was, of course, not the first person to claim that literature is propaganda. In "Criteria of Negro Art," a 1926 article written for *The Crisis*, W. E. B. Du Bois argues that "all Art is propaganda and ever must be" and that his own "writing had been used always for propaganda for gaining the right of black folk to love and enjoy" (103). Du Bois was co-founder of *The Crisis*, an official publication of the NAACP, and as such had a vision for what ideologies and politics the magazine should be expressing to its readers. One of the main goals was to challenge what Du Bois calls the "propaganda" of "the other [white] side" that sought to keep control of black representation by silencing black writers and artists. In his approach to publishing black writing, Du Bois openly declares his proselytizing intent: it is through literature that one can "tell the truth" and this "truth" (or "goodness" as Du Bois also calls it) is intended to "gain sympathy and human interest" (101). In this approach, Du Bois's understanding of propaganda as non-state sanctioned politics aligns more with the personal or oppositional politics of writers like Eliot and Woolf than with Orwell. By the early 1940s, however, Orwell was connecting propaganda with state-sponsored messaging, with which he had a complex, and at times combative, relationship.

Indeed, Orwell's position on art, propaganda, and truth is much more nuanced than his oft-quoted quip would suggest. His opinion on art and propaganda seems to shift throughout the war, during which he broadcast "white" propaganda (or "information") to India.[2] Before beginning his extended tenure at the BBC, this acceptance of literature as propaganda was consistent and reflected his own inclusion of politics in his 1930s writings. In a 1941 broadcast for the BBC's Overseas Service on "The Frontiers of Art and Propaganda," for example, Orwell offers a more nuanced version of the same claim. Speaking about literature in the decade prior to the war, Orwell states:

> It reminded us that propaganda in some form lurks in every book, that every work of art has a meaning and a purpose—a political, social and religious purpose—and that our aesthetic judgements are always coloured by our prejudices.
>
> *(126)*[3]

It is clear that what Orwell means by propaganda in this broadcast is akin to Du Bois's definition: it is political or social persuasion based on personal beliefs and not government machinery or ideologies. Of course, the irony here is that Orwell is broadcasting this position on propaganda and art on the Overseas Service during wartime, in which the main goal of the British government, and by extension the BBC, was to keep the colonies loyal to the crown.

It is worth noting that Orwell did not avoid the term "propaganda" in the early 1940s as Eliot, Woolf, and Jameson did, rather seeming to take the same view of propaganda as Bernays: the genre is more a matter of influence and persuasion than strict ontology, and that every author to some extent seeks to influence and persuade. This blurry demarcation between propaganda and persuasion leads to a more complicated understanding of the relationship between propaganda and art and their relationship to truth, or, as Orwell would come to call it at the BBC, "information." At the BBC, there was a distinction made between white and black propaganda:

> What the British government told the British people was regarded, in the terminology of the Political Warfare Executive, as 'white' propaganda: the necessary fostering and maintenance of the British people's innate will to win. What the German government

> told the British people was 'black' propaganda, intended to turn the public by devious means away from their natural patriotic inclinations.
>
> *(Nicholas 3)*

This was certainly Orwell's experience at the BBC, who noted repeatedly that the term "propaganda" was not used in reference to the BBC and was reserved for the Axis powers. This does not mean, however, that Orwell personally defined his work at the BBC in similar terms. In fact, Orwell's experiences at the BBC, under the watchful eyes and ears of the MOI, would partly inspire his postwar dystopian novel *1984*.

During their tenure at the BBC, Orwell and his literary friends were encouraged to think of their broadcasts for the Overseas Service and, more specifically, to India, as passing along "information" or sharing British culture. These broadcasts were, as Orwell and Indian writer and friend Mulk Raj Anand point out, not interested in overtly bellicose jingoism of the kind that had worked to boost enlistment in World War I. *Voice*, a six-part radio broadcast to India, covered a range of literary topics, including contemporary poetry, American literature, and representations of Christmas; it also presented literature from not only contemporary writers but also those from previous centuries.[4] The goal was, in part, to showcase British literary culture as a way to persuade the increasingly restive colony that Britain was worth defending.[5] For mid-century propaganda theorist Jacques Ellul, Orwell's use of literature is an example of how all-consuming propaganda is. As Ellul writes,

> propaganda will take over literature (present *and* past) and history, which must be rewritten according to propaganda's needs ... propaganda takes over the literature of the past, furnishing it with contexts and explanations designed to re-integrate it into the present.
>
> *(14)*

This is partially what Orwell does when he includes readings from writers like Keats, Milton, Shakespeare, and Dickens (authors who would be known in India) in his broadcasts and insists that their core values remain relevant to Britain today.

An example of this is the second *Voice* broadcast, in which Orwell, Anand, and literary critic William Empson debate whether there are "war poets" in World War II. Empson points out that there are a number of poets currently writing, which, by default, makes them war poets. But Orwell says there is a difference between writing during the war and writing a poem about war, whether for or against. And this is where Anand, the sole Indian voice on this broadcast, significantly notes that there isn't as much "jingoistic" poetry being written in this war in comparison to World War I (implying there is less state-sponsored propaganda in literature these days) and that "certainly we don't want anything jingoistic in 'Voice'" (suggesting that this broadcast to India is also not propaganda) (West 85). During the broadcast, no contemporary pro-war poetry is read, and Orwell struggles to think of anyone writing in favor of war. Anand replies meaningfully, as one who hopes to see India's independence in the near future, that "there is such a thing as recognising that war may be necessary, just as a surgical operation may be necessary. Even an operation which may leave you mutilated for life" (West 86–87).[6]

This is a position with which Orwell would come to agree. In his 1948 essay "Writers and Leviathan," in which he considers writers working under total state control, Orwell says,

> It is reasonable, for example, to be willing to fight in a war because one thinks the war ought to be won, and at the same time to refuse to write war propaganda. Sometimes, if a writer is honest, his writings and his political activities may actually contradict one another.
>
> (413)

Although he is referring to writers living under totalitarianism, it is easy to see how this statement also reflects his own struggles to maintain artistic independence during World War II. During his tenure at the BBC, Orwell broadcast core British values to Indian listeners in the hope of keeping Indians loyal to the crown for the duration of the war. But his broadcasts also included messages of resistance that propagate his own personal political goal that India would become free of British rule after the war's end.

"Resistance" was also how the Anglo-Irish writer Elizabeth Bowen defined war writing, specifically her own wartime fiction. As Bowen writes in her preface to her short story collection *Ivy Gripped the Steps*, "I wonder whether in a sense all wartime writing is not resistance writing?" (x). Like Orwell and Anand in *Voice*, Bowen makes the distinction between "wartime" and "war" stories, claiming that hers are "wartime" tales because "there are no accounts of war action even as I knew it—for instance, air raids." Instead, Bowen describes her wartime stories as

> studies of climate, war climate, and of the strange growths it raised. I see war (or should I say feel war?) more as a territory than as a page of history: of its impersonal active historic side I have, I find, not written.
>
> (viii)

It is true that the stories in *Ivy Gripped the Steps* focus largely on the domestic scene and introduce a general sense of unease caused by the "war climate." But these stories are also political and influenced by Bowen's work for the MOI, for which she traveled to Ireland and reported back on the Irish opinion of the war. So while her wartime stories may not be propaganda, they are a direct product of working for Britain's propaganda institution.

The same could also be said for John Lehmann, the sometimes poet and editor of *New Writing*. Although there was never an all-out censorship of writers in Britain during the war, as there was in Stalinist Russia or Nazi Germany, the MOI found a work-around, which included hiring writers and editors, like Lehmann, to work as a sort of go-between. Lehmann neither fully censored his writers in *New Writing* nor allowed anything to come to print that the MOI would find detrimental to their war aims. Even writers not employed by the British government found the politics of their work to be influenced not only by the MOI but also by their publication location. For example, Jan Struther's *Mrs. Miniver* series, which was published in the conservative London *Times*, focused on the domestic scene in the years leading up to the outbreak of war in Britain. The implicit politics of Mrs. Miniver's reactions to the war preparations matched those of the *Times*. Likewise, Mollie Panter-Downes, who wrote about the home front in her *London Letters* for the American magazine *The New Yorker*, had to make it past both the MOI censors and the *New Yorker* editorial staff, who strictly guarded the apolitical tone of the magazine. The letters between Mollie Panter-Downes and her editors show how the inclusion of politics and Britain's political agenda, both in Europe and in its imagined postwar relationship with America, was carefully crafted by Panter-Downes, the magazine, and the MOI. In this regard, her *London Letters* can be read as both an accurate snapshot of home front resistance *and* propaganda.[7]

A Modern "Truth"

In "Ode on a Grecian Urn," John Keats famously equates art and beauty with truth: "Beauty is truth, truth beauty,— that is all/Ye know on earth, and all ye need to know" (403). While this definition of truth may have satisfied in the Romantic era, modernist writers were not convinced that the truth of the world resided only in the beautiful nor that art could reveal it. Woolf, for example, challenges Keats' proclamation in *Mrs. Dalloway* (1925), in which she transforms "Ode on a Grecian Urn" for the post-World War I era and shows how the pastoral world Keats images has been lost. Septimus Smith, a veteran suffering from shell shock, remembers an early love, Miss Isabel Pole, who asks of Septimus, at the time a clerk with poetic ambitions, "Was he not like Keats?" (85). She encourages him to read Shakespeare and he immerses himself into the world of literature, writing her poems and thinking that his love for Miss Pole and his artistic pursuits "ha[d] flowered" (85). This belief in art and beauty as truth is swept away by the war, which "ploughed a hole in the geranium beds" (86). Postwar Septimus is no longer able to see beauty the way he once had, for now, after experiencing the horrors of trench warfare, "beauty was behind a pane of glass" (87): it was kept at a distance, obscured, no longer available to him.

For twentieth-century writers the definitions of art and truth, à la Keats, were undone by the brutal realities of war and state-sponsored propaganda campaigns that knowingly led young men to their deaths. Seemingly democratic nations told their citizens that they had access to "truth" and "knowledge," and through nationalistic propaganda they spoke about liberty and justice while carrying on with imperial cruelty and wartime slaughter. The belief that art and beauty equal truth was, as Septimus Smith comes to find, "ploughed" through and mown down just like men in the trenches and colonial subjects. Truth, if it existed, now resided in the ugly, the inhumane, and the lies. For Orwell, truth (like "liberty" and "justice") was an illusion. As he writes in "The Lion and the Unicorn" (1940), "In England such concepts as justice, liberty and objective truth are still believed in. They may be illusions, but they are powerful illusions" (63). Like Woolf and Orwell, modernist authors had no misapprehensions that there was some grand, overarching "truth" that they could reveal in their art. However, there was a remaining sense that art could reveal a personal, individual truth about an experience. In current colloquialisms, many of these authors believed they could speak "their truth" through their art. Even this, though, is a "powerful illusion," as this personal truth was always filtered through other sources and editorial voices.

During wartime, the stakes of writing a personal truth—a truth void of politics and propaganda—intensified and became all the more elusive. Artists disagreed on whether "true" art could include politics or whether during war all art was propaganda. For each author the answer was different and due largely to the individual's wartime experiences. What most Anglo-American writers agreed on, however, was that literature taken over by the state or state-sanctioned propaganda was a path that would lead to the strangling of truth and the destruction of art. While politics and propaganda were unavoidable, resistance was possible—resistance against war, the state, propaganda, fascism, communism, colonialism, and violence—as long as authors continued to write about their individual vision of the world they saw and the one they hoped to see.

Notes

1 Some of the 25 pillars of Edwardian literature who attended included: James Barrie, Arnold Bennett, G. K. Chesterton, Arthur Conan Doyle, John Galsworthy, Thomas Hardy, John Masefield, and H. G. Wells. Rudyard Kipling, who could not attend the meeting, also pledged his artistic services.

2 Orwell broadcast for the Indian Section of the BBC's Eastern Service from August 1941 to November 1943. During this time, he recruited a number of Anglo-American and colonial writers and scholars into the broadcasting house, including Mulk Raj Anand, T. S. Eliot, E. M. Forster, Una Marson, Herbert Read, Stevie Smith, and M. J. Tambimuttu.
3 Orwell presents a similar argument in a 1939 essay on Charles Dickens, where he writes that "All art is propaganda. […] On the other hand, not all propaganda is art" (448).
4 *Voice* was a monthly radio "poetry magazine" that was first broadcast on 11 August 1942 and ended on 29 December 1942. The point of this experimental on-air magazine in Orwell's own words was to "publish the work of the younger poets who have been handicapped by the paper shortage and whose work isn't so well known as it ought to be" (West 80).
5 Although it was ultimately discerned that Orwell's India broadcasts reached very few listeners and had minimal impact, they were part of a larger recruitment campaign in India that was ultimately successful. Paired with the devastating Bengal famine that drove people to seek the comparative food security of the colonial military, British propaganda, one that mirrored the colonial education used to produce civil servants in India, helped create a volunteer British Indian Army of more than 2.5 million.
6 For a closer analysis of the *Voice* broadcasts as propaganda, see Melissa Dinsman, *Modernism at the Microphone*.
7 For more on the propaganda in Struther's and Panter-Downes' writing, see: Melissa Dinsman, "Mrs. Miniver Builds the Home Front: Architecture and Household Objects as Wartime Propaganda," *Modernism/modernity Print Plus* 3.1 (Apr. 2018). https://modernismmodernity.org/articles/-mrs-miniver and Melissa Dinsman, "Marketing Masks and Makeup in Mollie Panter-Downes's 'Letter from London,'" *ELN*, 60.2 (Oct. 2022): 37-48.

Works Cited

Bernays, Edward. (1928) *Propaganda*. Introduction by Mark Crispin Miller. Ig Publishing, 2005.
Bowen, Elizabeth. "Preface." *Ivy Gripped the Steps*. Alfred A. Knopf, 1946, pp. vii–xiv.
Dinsman, Melissa. *Modernism at the Microphone: Radio, Propaganda, and Literary Aesthetics during World War II*. Bloomsbury Academic, 2015.
Du Bois, W.E.B. "Criteria of Negro Art." *Harlem Renaissance Reader*, edited by David Levering Lewis. Penguin, 1994, pp. 100–105.
Eliot, T.S. "A Note of War Poetry." *London Calling: A Salute to America*, edited by Storm Jameson. Harper & Brothers, 1942, pp. 237–238.
Ellul, Jacques. (1965) *Propaganda: The Formation of Men's Attitudes*. Vintage Books, 1973.
Hynes, Samuel. *A War Imagined: The First World War and English Culture*. Atheneum, 1991.
Jameson, Storm. "Introduction." *London Calling: A Salute to America*, edited by Storm Jameson. Harper & Brothers, 1942, pp. 1–17.
Keats, John. "Ode on a Grecian Urn." *The Oxford Book of English Verse*, edited by Christopher Ricks. Oxford UP, 1999, pp. 401–403.
Kipling, Rudyard. "For All We Have and Are." *World War One British Poets: Brooke, Owen, Sassoon, Rosenberg and Others*, edited by Candace Ward. Dover, 1997, pp. 63–64.
Lasswell, Harold D. (1927) *Propaganda Technique in the World War*. Martino Publishing, 2013.
Marcus, Jane. "'No More Horses': Virginia Woolf on Art and Propaganda." *Women's Studies*, vol. 4, nos. 2–3, 1977, pp. 265–289.
Nicholas, Siân. *The Echoes of War: Home Front Propaganda and the Wartime BBC, 1939–45*. Manchester UP, 1996.
Orwell, George. "Charles Dickens." *Essays Journalism & Letters Vol. 1: An Age Like This 1920–1940*, edited by Sonia Orwell and Ian Angus. Nonpareil Books, 1968, pp. 413–460.
———. "No, Not One." *Essays Journalism & Letters Vol. 2: My Country Right or Left 1940–1943*, edited by Sonia Orwell and Ian Angus. Nonpareil Books, 1968, pp. 56–109.
———. "The Frontiers of Art and Propaganda." *Essays Journalism & Letters Vol. 4: In Front of Your Nose 1945–1950*, edited by Sonia Orwell and Ian Angus. Nonpareil Books, 1968, pp. 407–414.
———. "The Lion and the Unicorn." *Essays Journalism & Letters Vol. 2: My Country Right or Left 1940–1943*, edited by Sonia Orwell and Ian Angus. Nonpareil Books, 1968, pp. 165–171.
———. "Writers and Leviathan." *Essays Journalism & Letters Vol. 2: My Country Right or Left 1940–1943*, edited by Sonia Orwell and Ian Angus. Nonpareil Books, 1968, pp. 123–127.

Pope, Jessie. "The Call." *Jessie Pope's War Poems*. Grant Richards Ltd, 1915.
"Propaganda." Oxford English Dictionary. June 2007. https://www-oed-com.york.ezproxy.cuny.edu/view/Entry/152605?rskey=Sa9H6n&result=1#eid
Spiro, Mia. *Anti-Nazi Modernism: The Challenge of Resistance in 1930s Fiction*. Northwestern UP, 2013.
Tate, Trudi. *Modernism, History and the First World War*. Manchester UP, 1998.
West, W.J., ed. *Orwell: The War Broadcasts*. Duckworth, 1985.
Woolf, Virginia. "Mr. Bennett and Mrs. Brown." The Hogarth Press, 1924. http://www.columbia.edu/~em36/MrBennettAndMrsBrown.pdf
———. *The Diary of Virginia Woolf: Volume Five 1936–1941*. Edited by Anne Olivier Bell and Andrew McNeillie. Harcourt Brace & Company, 1984.
———. *Mrs. Dalloway*. Harcourt, 1925.
———. *Three Guineas*. Harcourt, 1938.

27
CRITICISM
Thom Dancer

One of the first things an undergraduate literature student learns is that literature cannot be read apart from its contexts—social, political, economic, philosophical—and, therefore, that critical reading cannot help but be political reading. Of course, we know that from this fundamental conviction springs an extraordinary range of political criticisms with their own specific agendas, values, and objectives. The situation today is that while we readily understand criticism to be political (in some generalized sense), there remains a great deal of disagreement about the specific programs and principles political criticism ought to take, as well as the forms for criticism appropriate to them.

One way to approach the politics of criticism is from the perspective of what I call the "politics of method." This phrase describes the general assumption that practices of criticism themselves—the modes of analysis they favor, the kinds of knowledge acquisition they permit, the forms of reading subject they entail—are political in themselves even before they are put toward some specific political project. This chapter argues that the latter idea of the political, as a general understanding of criticism's engagement with the politicosocial character of the world, subtends and orients criticism toward more specific political programs of analysis. The emphasis of the discussion will be on how criticism's built-in political orientation gives shape and limits to the kinds of political work literary studies imagines criticism to be capable of doing. Today, literary studies is dominated by a particular politics of *critical* method, which either implies or assumes that critical reading and analysis are themselves acts of resistance against the status quo. This assumption, as we will see, shapes our disciplinary norms by determining what kinds of approaches to art and literature deserve to count as "critical" (and therefore valid) in the first place. Attending to the general politics of method reframes the history of literary criticism as one in which political values have always been present, rather than a history of progress from naïve, personal, apolitical criticism to a skeptical, impersonal political analysis. Moreover, doing so allows us to understand the recent return of formalist, evaluative, and other "old-fashioned" forms of criticism not as a conservative return to apolitical criticism but as the emergence of a new politics of method yearning for acceptance.

Focusing on a politics of method necessarily means that this chapter must pass over other possible approaches to the politics of criticism. It will neither catalog the different political criticisms in historical or taxonomical order, nor offer a comparative analysis of their relative merits. It will not pile on the well-known demerits of mid-century critics, even where such vilification is amply deserved: here's looking at you Southern Agrarians. It will definitely not be a critique of critique that asserts the one true path to politics is through such and such—and only such and such—method. In fact, just the opposite: the aim is to show that a healthy politics of criticism is characterized by competition between a range of different approaches for understanding criticism as engaged with our world, lives, and experience.

The Usual Story

One of the most common stories students and scholars of literature tell ourselves about the history of Anglo-American literary criticism is one about progress away from amateur evaluations of early and mid-century criticism and toward the mature, rigorous criticism we produce today. The common version of this story focuses on the establishment of criticism as an academic discipline in the twentieth-century university. It usually begins with modernist rejection of belles-lettres amateurism (T. S. Eliot is often the central figure) before moving to the important place that Practical and New Criticism played in securing literary studies departments in mid century universities. Focus on close reading as the central pedagogical practice in Archetypal, Practical, and New Criticism cemented English as a central humanist discipline in the middle decades of the twentieth century. This new security, however, permitted criticism to turn its eyes back on itself. Powerful currents in continental philosophy and British cultural studies challenged the dominance of decontextualized close reading, replacing it with a more self-reflective technique of critical reading and critique. Though this tale is ostensibly one that emphasizes criticism's progress toward methodological and disciplinary rigor, the introduction of ethico-political purpose to this method of criticism is no less essential.

This is a story in which criticism slowly, but inevitably, sheds itself of personal considerations found in acts of evaluation and judgment (even where those acts are concealed in a veneer of objectivity) to become a more impersonal analytic practice. As many historians of literary criticism have noted, the defining moment came about through a transformative self-critique, in which claims that criticism merely articulated natural, human, or universal values were revealed to be ideological expressions of domination and power. Indeed, the practice of critique itself becomes so central to the disciplinary imagination that critique and criticism become practically synonymous in the late twentieth and early twenty-first centuries. Critique's ever self-reflexive lens showed the ways in which those mid-century criticisms were engaged in a slight of hand by which the literary object (usually a poem) allowed the critic to project their own personal values as universal. New and Practical Criticism's focus on the work of art as detached from history and intention only appeared to offer a more objective grounding, but in actuality it facilitated an illicit normativity even while it was being disavowed. Of course, the claim that criticism did nothing more than express the humane values or moral sensibility found in the literature itself could not stand up to scrutiny. After all (and after Friedrich Niezsche, after John Dewey, after Michel Foucault, after Sianne Ngai, and so on) the values claimed as universal, aesthetic, or literary were, we found, deeply laced with power, privilege, capital, and distinction.

Criticism finally solves this problem by making the political elements of literature itself the object of study, thereby unifying social and political purpose with a method of rigorous analysis. I. A. Richards, F. R. Leavis, and Northrop Frye, the story goes, present a problem because they concealed an ethico-political "ought" under a veil of apparently natural values. The obvious solution, then, was to bypass the false trappings of aesthetic and humanistic values and proceed directly to more obviously political ones. Cultural criticism and critique secured the status of literature by seeing it as an expression of a deeper, more solid force than merely literary greatness: social conflict, economic history, political power. The story of literary criticism is one of progressively suturing methods rigorous enough for the modern university together with a relevant purpose to justify its wider social and cultural value. Critical reading, critique, and symptomatic reading, the modes that dominate criticism today, exemplify a powerful unity between method and purpose.

The point of telling this story is not to critique it (though admitted there is a lot to critique about it), nor to deeply contest it, to point out its exaggerations and unfair caricatures (though there are a lot of those too). Rather, rehearsing this "folk" history of literary criticism illustrates two assumptions that continue to operate in our disciplinary imagination. First, it makes clear how much is assumed about the ways in which the current state of method, criticism, and politics was formed in response to the mid-century paradigms that proceeded it. Second, and more crucially, it makes clear that the success that critique and symptomatic criticism enjoy today is the result of a particular unity of politics and methodology—the politics of critical method. Explaining the institutional power of "symptomatic criticism," Rónán McDonald says that with it literary studies found a powerful unity "offering both methodological rigor through hermeneutics and ethical seriousness through ideological critique" ("Critique and Anti-Critique" 307).[1] In disciplinary term, the success of this unity has rendered formalism, evaluative criticism, and other modes of aesthetic criticism *personae non gratae* in the halls of most universities. Against this powerful unity, other ways of encountering literature appear both apolitical and uncritical; any form of criticism that seeks to understand literature in terms of aesthetic experience, moral sensibility, or humane values cannot therefore help but appear hopelessly old-fashioned and politically naïve or worse.

Politics of Critical Method

Today, literary scholars are free to pursue a very wide range of politically inflected criticisms; for instance, *Literary Theory and Criticism: An Introduction* includes accounts of Early Marxist, Later Marxist, Postcolonial and Ethnic Studies, Critical Race Theory, Feminist Theory, Sexuality and Queer Theory, Disability Studies, and Environmental (Stevens). To be sure, these different styles of political criticism are often at odds with one another (or even themselves) as they argue for the best, most relevant, strategic, or efficacious politics to pursue. Yet, at the level of method, they share a common belief in the priority of analytical and critical reading. This belief that the central methods of professional literary studies must be at some level analytical and critical in turn informs a number of basic assumptions about the nature of the literary text, the text's relationship to the world, and the kinds of knowledge claims that can be made on literature's behalf. Michael Warner alerts us to the way that this commonly held "folk ideology of the profession" exercises enormous influence on the "self-conception of the discipline," especially how we justify our scholarly and pedagogical missions (14). Warner describes this self-conception as an "invisible norm" because it characterizes the assumptions that we make about what can count as a valid—that is, critical—encounter with the text before we actually engage in any techniques of interpretation (20). To approach a text critically and analytically is thus to assume that it is the kind of thing that will yield knowledge in response to this type of inquiry. It is at this almost invisible level that various political forms of criticism share a common methodological belief: that the job of the critic is to expose or reveal the hidden causes or forces wittingly or unwittingly recorded by the text.

These baseline assumptions are so ubiquitous, so common sense that they appear to be almost tautological requirements for doing criticism at all. What could be more obvious, Warner points out, than the idea that criticism must be critical? The critical appears to name something neutral to the act of reading without its own motivations, agendas, and values; in fact, this form of analysis sets conditions that necessarily include and exclude other normative practices of reading and interpretation. Moreover, the specific beliefs mobilized by the centrality of critical and analytical reading, namely an axiomatic faith in the power of knowingness itself, directly plug this method into a politics of resistance and revelation. As Toril Moi describes it, the very practice of critical reading therefore cannot help but participate in a political act "to undo an oppressive status quo, to raise our political consciousness" (33). This particular definition of politics combined with a strong methodological norm results in today's highly codified politics of method in literary studies (a "politics of critical method") with its regnant notion that critical analysis is automatically, perforce, and by definition engaged in a politics of revelation. For several decades, this specific politics of critical method gave any automatic justification and relevance to criticisms that engaged in critique and symptomatic reading, since "to engage in critique is to expose ideology and the workings of power, encourage resistance, and general contribute to social and political change" (Moi 31). The politics of critical method provides the foundations for all of the diverse political criticisms operating today precisely because it can be pointed at an almost unlimited number of structural causes and concealed powers.

There is a great deal of political and institutional utility in the politics of critical method, which accounts for its unprecedented success in Anglo-American literary studies over the last few decades. Among other things, the use value lies in the pragmatic fact that critics do not have to explain, let alone justify, the ostensibly political work of their critiques. Critics and students can simply announce "critique!" to mobilize a familiar, accepted conception of political resistance predicated upon the efficacy of exposure. However, the success of the politics of critical method has come at a price. As politically relevant work became the norm in literary studies, methods that did not meet the conditions of the political (as defined by critical method) meant that they could not be admitted to the disciplinary party. The politics of critical method entails a restrictive logic that, Moi believes, "leads to the idea that critics who refuse to accept a specific picture of the text and reading [of method] must be conservative or reactionary, whatever their actual political views may be" (33). Indeed, for all that the politics of method has enabled, it continues to rule out of bounds a whole range of methods that do not share the same settlement between political purpose and method.

For both Warner and Moi, the trouble with critical reading and critique is not that they are wrong or ineffective, but rather that they have become so dominant, so impeccable that it seems to define the very possibilities for doing criticism as such. Warner reminds us that "one of the deepest challenges posed by rival, uncritical frameworks of reading is recognizing that they are just that, rival frameworks" (33). Warner asks us to recognize that our assumptions about what constitutes "critical" reading are "historically and formally mediated," not just automatic or natural entailment of enlightenment reason (35). "We tend to assume," he writes, "that critical reading is just a name for any self-conscious practice of reading" (16). The idea that critical reading does not stand for anything itself but is just a procedure for exposing and therefore resisting any other normative claims gives it a kind of effective neutrality: it is political without having any politics of its own. This also, as Warner points out, is "why it seems so difficult for anyone to define or codify critical reading" (35). The politics of critical method tend, we might say, to operate below the level of conscious thought and practice. Part of the difficulty in elaborating these thoroughly common sense norms is that, in the very act of bringing them into consciousness, they seem to slip away. Thus, in order to provisionally give some actual, positive content to the politics of critical method, consider an example of criticism in action.

Politics of Critical Method in Action

Because the politics of critical method today shapes our understanding of the role of the reader, text, and world, the distribution of agency between critic and literature, and the kinds of knowledge production afforded by the literary experience, it might be best understood as an orientation that precedes any application of method or practice.[2] Because of this, it can be difficult to see in the final, polished versions of academic arguments. Perhaps counterintuitively, however, redirecting focus from scholarly examples to contemporary fiction reveals helpfully detailed descriptions of criticism in action; the fictionalized critic's approach to a work of art reveals those assumptions, thought patterns, and dispositional preferences that are occluded in the final published versions of scholarly work.

Perhaps the most useful of these works is Zadie Smith's satirical campus novel, *On Beauty* (2005). Smith's exaggerated portrait of Howard Belsey as a basic modern critic emphasizes the ways that methodological assumptions and political values mutually inform each other; moreover, Smith highlights the way that the specific politics of critical method too often lose track of important dimensions of aesthetic experience. Smith's representation of the politics of critical method usefully clarifies the ways that today's commonsense understanding of political criticism defines itself in contrast to what it marks as antecedent, uncritical, and naive ways of understanding literature. This contrast is most clear where Howard, a professor of art history, ruminates on Rembrandt's painting *The Staalmeesters*. The course of Howard's thoughts as he looks at the painting provides a mini-lesson in the history of criticism and the assumptions and values that subtend critical norms today.

The scene begins with Howard rehearsing the way that previous generations of art historians understood the painting. "The traditional art history," Howard thinks, understands this painting as a representation of the value of "cogitation" (383). Previous criticism tells us that "this is what *judgment* looks like: considered rational, benign judgment" (383). Traditional criticism understood art as providing "privileged insight into the human" that it was the work of the critic to express and pass on (252). The modern critic Howard, however, "rejects all these fatuous assumptions" as "nonsense and sentimental tradition" (383). Against this "pseudohistorical storytelling," Howard's criticism presents an entirely different analysis. "All we really see there," Howard says, "are six rich men sitting for their portrait" (384). Our desire to see the painting as a reflection of common aesthetic judgment is a fallacy because, Howard contends, aesthetic value, judgment, wisdom, "none of this is truly *in* the picture" (384). In "iconoclastic" defiance of tradition, Howard's criticism analytically bypasses the deceptions of aesthetics to reveal "an exercise in the depiction of economic power" (383–384). Howard's rejection of previous art history carefully frames the discipline as theoretically and politically naïve, offering wish fulfillment and fantasy in lieu of methodological rigor. Old criticism that seeks to understand art in terms of moral sensibility and aesthetic experience is mere "storytelling" and "sentimental tradition" that projects its values into the work of art. It attends to contingent values like personal values instead of the hard truths of power and material causes. Howard's rejection calls out older criticism for paradoxically being apolitical (in its efforts to understand art in terms of aesthetic experience) and simultaneously for having bad politics (insofar as "aesthetics" is "a rarefied language of exclusion" [155]).

Though clearly exaggerated, this fictional example helpfully brings into active perception what usually passes as automatic or natural. First, we see that between the two examples of criticism in the passage—traditional criticism and economic critique—the question of which is valid and which is not does not depend on any technical matter of method or reading. The choice between the two depends on a prior assumption about what counts as a real cause—humane judgment or economic power—since neither is more "truly in the painting" than the other. The two styles of criticism engage in different "modes of knowledge acquisition and even different ideas of what knowledge is," which in turn predetermines what kinds of things can serve as a real cause and which are pseudohistorical storytelling (McDonald, "Critique and Anti-Critique" 371). (In this case, economic exploitation is real while humane values are not.) Smith's depiction challenges the restrictiveness of Howard's critical method, especially its inability to deal with elements of aesthetic experience that cannot be reduced to expressions of power. Yet, here and throughout *On Beauty*, Smith juxtaposes different approaches to art to encourage her readers to recognize them as different but equally valid choices that produce different kinds of knowledge and experiences. She champions a diversification of thinking about art and literature such that it can include methods—the evaluative and the phenomenological—that were sent into abeyance with the exile of the New Criticism.

At this point, it is possible to identify several assumptions, implicit in and central to the specific politics of critical method, which shape the norms of literary criticism today; it is assumed that:

- the aesthetic, literary, and formal elements of the text are less real than its social and political contexts.
- the importance of the text lies in its expression of an extra-literary meaning, whether it be explicitly political, historical, social, or ethical.
- a "sense of solid knowledge acquisition" is cultivated through the enforcement of an attitude of critical distance; phrased differently, critical reading must distance itself from the phenomenological experience of reading.
- good criticism is situated in opposition to amateurism, uncritical, and old-fashioned modes of criticism, which cannot pass the bar of political meaning.
- knowingness itself leads automatically to radical or progressive political outcomes. To recognize, e.g., that *The Staalmeesters* is a depiction of economic exploitation is to resist and seek to overthrow such forms of exploitation.

This is the politics of critical method that cast critique, critical reading, and symptomatic reading as natural and necessary forms of criticism itself, while simultaneously ruling out formal, evaluative, and experiential criticisms as apolitical and uncritical. Yet the grip of this method on literary scholarship has begun to loosen in the last decades. Postcritical challenges to the sovereignty of critical reading and critique have themselves critiqued critique, revealing some of these normative assumptions and principles. However, a critique of critique still leaves in place the politics of critical method described above, since it operates in the same faith that exposure will necessarily produce resistance to the status quo of critical reading and critique. Since effectively expanding the kinds of criticism available to critics today requires the introduction of other conceptions of the politics of method, consider three examples of critics seeking to revive and reorient forms of criticism discouraged by the current politics of critical method. While they take up formalism, aesthetic judgment, and evaluative modes of criticism, these critics do so by articulating a new politics of method for them, jettisoning the bad faith and political disavowals that might have characterized earlier versions.

Rival Methods in Three Parts

Despite a growing number of scholars and novelists who follow Smith's work to introduce a greater range of methods into criticism, the many of kinds of critical approaches she champions remain "deeply, sinfully, unfashionable" (McDonald, *The Death of the Critic* 120). From a position of near total domination, formalist, evaluative, and individual forms of criticism have gone into "terminal decline" (Smith, "Read Better" 22).[3] Recently, though, these critical approaches have resurfaced. New Formalism, New Aestheticism, and defenses of evaluation, aesthetic education, and taste have returned to the scholarly conversation. Do these emerging criticisms signal a decline in the political justification for criticism? Do they signal a return to the public intellectual and *belles-lettres* elitism? Probably not. Despite the political outcry against a whole range of approaches that seek to be done with the politics of critique, it simply isn't the case that these new critical methods are apolitical. Indeed, many of these new modes of criticism frame their methodological interventions in explicitly political terms.

Part 1: Formalisms

Perhaps nowhere is a new politics of method more explicit than in new formalism, especially in Caroline Levine's *Forms*. Formalism has suffered a particularly tough fate in the history of literary criticism. Formalism remains strongly linked in the discipline's imagination with the New Criticism's focus on the "text-as-text, without befuddling the issue with any appeals to authorial intention (let alone biography), historical background, or reader response" (McDonald, *The Death of the Critic* 96). The fact that this focus camouflaged a politics of method whose aesthetic value of "unity" helped John Crowe Ransom et al. to purge American literature of women and other "undesirable" figures on putatively "objective" grounds is well known. However, even beyond this particular example, formalism became synonymous with an understanding of the literary work's value as divorced from context. In fact, Levine's first move in reviving formalism is to "dissolve" the "traditionally troubling gap between the form of the literary text and its content and context" (2). This gap has been perpetuated through the idea of form as "ideological artifice" that offers only fake consolation and prevents us from seeing actual reality (3). Smith makes a similar claim in *On Beauty* when she has Howard pompously declare that "prettiness is the mask that power wears" (155). While the politics of critical method asserts form as "epiphenomenal" responses to "social reality," Levine contends that social forms and aesthetic forms are both "real in their capacity to organize materials" and "*un*real in being artificial, contingent constraints" (14). Levine's formalism requests that we add to the list of causes that we might count as politically significant.

This version of formalism owns its politics, owns that it is immediately and inescapably political: "formal analysis turn out to be as valuable to understanding sociopolitical institutions as it is to reading literature" (Levine 2). Levine seeks a place for formalism in literary criticism on the grounds that it can also do political work, as long as we are willing to adjust our convictions about what counts as legitimately political: away from the idea "that ultimately, it is deep structural forces such as capitalism, nationalism, and racism that are the truly powerful shapers of our lives" (17). The word "truly" here recalls Howard's contention that it is only economic power that is "truly" in the painting; formalism's politics of method contests that "truly" by arguing that "social condition [are] organized not by single, powerful ideologies [as Howard wants to believe], but by numerous contending and colliding forms" (40). If the question of freedom is not determined by a choice between restrictive forms and perfect, formless freedom but between forms that hurt and forms that help, then formal analysis is an essential tool for practical politics. Formalism re-emerges at this moment less as a missing dimension of aesthetic experience than as a requirement for a politically engaged criticism capable of understanding the complex dynamics of contemporary life.

Part 2: Evaluative Criticisms

Michael Clune's *A Defense of Judgment* makes plain the ways that implicit definitions of politics tended to erect barriers to exclude other approaches. Clune touches on two major categories of objections to the "central role of judgment in professional practice" (2). One set of objections—that artistic judgments are expressions of opinions rather than knowledge, that they are subjective—involve the discipline's claim to some kind of scientific rigor, to justify itself as an academic discipline distinct from popular review and amateurism. The second set of objections revolve around the claim that artistic judgments focus on form and other features of art that do not register the relevant social, racial, ethical, gender, and economic contexts. Taken together we see how these two assumptions about why aesthetic judgments aren't good for the discipline reveal the synergy between methodological rigor and political relevance. Political purpose allowed criticism to marry a certain kind of tough-minded analysis with a "real world" relevance. As a result, judgment is discounted twice: not tough minded and therefore not political, and not political because not tough minded. Clune's defense seeks to rehabilitate judgment on these same grounds.

> At the outset, I want to highlight something about these objections that may not be obvious. They present as exemplifying the modern, rational skepticism of traditional practices. But in fact, each of these objections to expert artistic judgments depends on a concealed alternative vision.
>
> (2)

Here Clune offers an analysis of the assumptions on which criticism operates, exposing any claim to rational neutrality as actually if tacitly supporting political prejudice. Indeed, Clune claims that criticism's reduction of aesthetic value to simple cultural capital, even if well-meaning, has meant ceding the entire question of value to the market. Evaluative criticism practices an anti-market mode of judgment, and, therefore, automatically resists the drive of the market to determine all value. Far from being a surrender to capitalist logic, re-establishing value judgments and aesthetic education in criticism becomes the most politically savvy thing to do. "The fact that the resistance to judgment," Clune announces, "is historically bound up with commercial culture endows the defense of judgment with an unprecedented political salience." A return to judgment not only doesn't retreat from politics, it calls out the critical consensus's own blindness to a new political salience.

> To defend judgment today is not to express nostalgia for a regime before the consolidation of commercial culture. By carving out a space beyond the reach of market valuation, by defining a practice of valuing distinct from that of the market transaction, aesthetic education sets up a material barrier to market totalitarianism.
>
> (3–4)

Clune's defense of judgment is not, in fact or in value, substantially different from that of mid-century critics such as F. R. Leavis or I. A. Richards. All three of them make a claim for the value of aesthetic education on social grounds; that the world would be better if aesthetic education produced people who could resist the stifling effects of mechanistic and philistine market culture. Clune, however, connects his evaluative criticism to a specific politics of method that claims the efficacy of the method itself as a kind of resistance. Where for Leavis and Richards aesthetic education is ultimately about producing humans who conform in taste and values, Clune suggests that aesthetic education can produce "critical" humans capable of resisting the powerful forces of conformity circulating in contemporary life. As Clune defends it, evaluative criticism finally draws on a vision of politics as resistance that overlaps significantly with the political vision of both critique and symptomatic reading.

Nevertheless, as with formalism, one of the hurdles to accepting an evaluative politics of method consists in its open-endedness. Aesthetic education might produce readers who think for themselves, but as we know such freedom does not guarantee that such readers will support equality, peace, and the common good. For instance, Fred Moten and David Lloyd (in different works) show how the principles of freedom and subjectivity manifest in Kantian aesthetics both rely upon and lead to an anti-black and colonial concept of politics.[4]

Levine, like Clune, explains that forms can be put to all kinds of different work; thus, the political work of formal analysis, while automatically political, is not automatically revolutionary as erroneously assumed by practitioners of symptomatic and critical reading. Similarly, the capacities to resist market logic cultivated by an aesthetic education that includes evaluative criticism make no claim for a specific progressive, let alone radical, outcome. Both formalist and evaluative criticism present their politics of method as more relativistic than most current critics are comfortable with. But, perhaps it is time to grapple with the fact that whether criticism advances the causes of human flourishing and the common good depends not on anything inherent in method itself (whether that method is critique, formalism, experiential, or evaluative), but in its use in actual cases.

Part 3: Phenomenological Criticisms

The final example of a criticism that seeks to come in from the cold of the apolitical appears in methods that emphasize the experiential dimensions of reading—or at least do not seek to purge the personal and idiosyncratic from reading. Unlike formalism and evaluative criticism, there is no accepted label for these approaches, but McDonald usefully describes them as "phenomenological methods... geared towards capturing experiential events and attitudes" ("Critique and Anti-Critique" 370). Where formalism and evaluative criticism require only some expansion and reorientation of the symptomatic politics of critical method, phenomenological methods present a more severe break from those values. One of the few principles that have endured through the entire history of professional literary criticism (since its institutionalization in the university) has been the de-coupling of criticism from personal reading.[5] In order to prove its worth in a modern university context increasingly oriented toward verifiable facts and objective knowledge, academic criticism continually protested against the idea that it was a discipline of mere personal opinion. In doing so, it repeatedly invested in methods that produced "convergent knowledge" and "determinant causes" (370). The anchoring of literary significance in historical, social, and political context is a key part of this equation since it allowed the meaning of the text to be found in something more "solid" than aesthetic experience. Yet, a growing number of critics from a wide range of disciplines are attempting to reclaim on political grounds what Virginia Woolf called the necessity of the "idiosyncratic" (268).

One prominent example is Derek Attridge's efforts to reframe criticism as an event that remains faithful to the literary experience. Attridge argues for a criticism that attends to the

> reading as an event, for restraining the urge to leave the text, or rather the experience of the text behind (an urge that becomes especially powerful when we have to produce words about it), for opening oneself to the text's forays beyond the doxa.
>
> *("Against Allegory" 79)*

Where the current politics of method defines the value of criticism in terms of what it can tell us about other things—society, politics, history, power, ideology—Attridge makes his criticism attend to the value of the literary *qua* literary. "The value of criticism," he writes, "lies primarily in enhancing the reader's experience of what I term the work's singularity, alterity, and inventiveness" (*The Work of Literature* 10). McDonald explains the difficulties that such a criticism faces in the context of today's university: "this criticism is not about providing solutions, whether the detective work of symptomatic criticism or the factual explanations of scientific criticism, but rather about producing new meaning, about creating divergent values rather than convergent knowledge" (McDonald "Critique and Anti-Critique" 371). This challenge to the epistemological assumptions of professional criticism is significant, yet the emphasis on the production of new values also gestures toward a politics of method.

For Attridge, the encounter with singularity and alterity might "have intrinsic value in itself," but McDonald offers a more robust politics of method in its defense (Attridge, *The Work of Literature* 10). McDonald's defense hinges on the fact that the subjectivity is never actually, totally black-boxed from the world; thus, for critics "we cannot vault outside of our experience into objective or transcendent meanings, but there is a shared experience of a text, recognition, and communal participation between readers that criticism names or gestures toward" ("After Suspicion: Surface, Method, Value" 248). The politics of criticism consists in this "shared communal participation" in which new values are given form and negotiated. The politics of method for these phenomenological approaches consists in the belief that matters of valuation are themselves political (in so far as they are expressions of the kinds of common world we wish to inhabit with others). This is a very different idea of the politics of method since its political valances are creative, bringing into being what Hannah Arendt would call the novel, the wholly new rather than revealing something already there. Phenomenological approaches suggest exciting new ways of thinking about and defending the discipline of literary studies in a rapidly changing educational and cultural milieu. Yet, unlike formalism and evaluative criticism, they have yet to gain much of a foothold in the discipline.

Final Thought

Debates between critics about the relative merits of one politics of method over another, one form of desirable politics over another, one account of subjectivity and objectivity over others, will always be a part of literary studies. Indeed, a high degree of dissent about what it means to be properly political in one's criticism has usually been considered a signal of good disciplinary health—even a sign of healthy politics. Against the sense that critical method is in a period of crisis, expanding the sense of what politics actually means in the context of literary methods is a sure sign of vitality and hope for the future of criticism.

Notes

1 For more on this point, see Benjamin Kohlmann's chapter "Symptoms" and Rachel Greenwald Smith's chapter "On or about Now" in this volume.
2 Christopher Castiglia emphasizes the dispositions elements of critique and symptomatic reading in "Hope for Critique."
3 Note that ideas of form disappeared entirely, but rather they were seen not as revealing the harmonious unity of the poem but as expressions of deeper social, economic, or political causes.
4 In *Stolen Life*, Moten writes "The regulative discourse on the aesthetic that animates Kant's critical philosophy is inseparable from the question of race as a mode of conceptualizing and regulating human diversity, grounding and justifying inequality and exploitation" (2). See also David Lloyd, *Under Representation: The Racial Regime of Aesthetics* (Fordham UP, 2018).
5 For an account of how thoroughly even amateur readers were schooled in "political" methods of reading well before the rise of New Criticism, see Rachel Sagner Buurma and Laura Heffernan's chapter "Classrooms" in this volume.

Works Cited

Attridge, Derek. "Against Allegory: Waiting for the Barbarians, Life & Times of Michael K, and the Question of Literary Reading." *J.M. Coetzee and the Idea of the Public Intellectual*, edited by Jane Poyner, Ohio UP, 2006, pp. 63–81.
———. *The Work of Literature*. Oxford UP, 2015.
Castiglia, Christopher. "Hope for Critique?" *Critique and Postcritique*, edited by Rita Felski and Elizabeth S. Anker, Duke UP, 2017, pp. 211–229.
Clune, Michael W. *A Defense of Judgment*. U of Chicago P, 2021.
Levine, Caroline. *Forms: Whole, Rhythm, Hierarchy, Network*. Princeton UP, 2015.
McDonald, Ronan. "After Suspicion: Surface, Method, Value." *The Values of Literary Study: Critical Institutions, Scholarly Agendas*, Cambridge UP, 2015, pp. 235–248.
———. "Critique and Anti-Critique." *Textual Practice*, vol. 32, no. 3, 2018, p. 3650374. doi:10.1080/0950236X.2018.1442400.
———. *The Death of the Critic*. Continuum, 2007.
Moi, Toril. "'Nothing Is Hidden': From Confusion to Clarity; or, Wittgenstein on Critique." *Critique and Postcritique*, edited by Elizabeth S. Anker and Rita Felski, Duke UP, Apr. 2017, pp. 31–49.
Moten, Fred. *Stolen Life*. Duke UP, 2018.
Smith, Zadie. *On Beauty*. Penguin, 2005.
———. "Read Better." *The Guardian*, Jan. 2007, pp. 21–22.
Stevens, Anne H. *Literary Theory and Criticism: An Introduction*. Second Ed., Broadview, 2021.
Warner, Michael. "Uncritical Reading." *Polemic: Critical or Uncritical*. Routledge, 2004, pp. 13–38.
Woolf, Virginia. *The Second Common Reader*. Harcourt, 1986

28
DIGITAL PLATFORMS
J. D. Schnepf

Promptly at 8 pm Eastern Time on the evening of May 23, 2012, the *New Yorker* Fiction Department Twitter account (@NYerFiction) tweeted out the first lines of Jennifer Egan's short story, "Black Box." Leaping into action for an hour each night over the following ten nights, the account dispensed the story of a female national security agent in judiciously portioned, tweet-sized installments with the unwavering regularity of an automaton. Though the story would appear in print in the magazine's "Science Fiction Issue" the following week, the Pulitzer-Prize winning author of *A Visit From the Good Squad* (2010) claimed she wrote "Black Box" with the social media platform in mind: "This is not a new idea, of course, but it's a rich one—because of the intimacy of reaching people through their phones, and because of the odd poetry that can happen in a hundred and forty characters" (*New Yorker*).[1] Citing Egan as an example, literary scholar Aarthi Vadde has observed that "celebrated authors and esteemed arbiters of the literary have turned social media platforms into venues for formal experimentation" although the success of such experiments remains open to debate (39).

For professional and amateur authors alike, Twitter has established itself as a significant venue for the production and distribution of born-digital literature. Like other Web 2.0 platforms, Twitter facilitates online exchange and sharing of user-generated content. Founded in 2006, it has become one of the world's most trafficked social media platforms with active monthly users numbering in the hundreds of millions. Scholars of digital literature refer to stories published on the platform as "Twitterature" (Murray) or "Twitterfiction" (Thomas), while amateur Twitter authors often label their stories with hashtags including #twifi, #twitfic, #twitfiction, #twitlit, and #twitterstory to make them easy to find.[2] What makes for a popular story on the platform can be hard to predict. The viral success that author A'Ziah "Zola" King experienced with the publication of 2015's epic #TheStory, for example, stemmed in part from her responsiveness to readers; she found herself "riffing on the reactions of her followers who were responding in real time" (Kushner). In contrast, "Black Box" did not court reader engagement or use hashtags. It did not interact with other accounts or time its posts to correspond to the pace of the plot's unfolding action. And despite Egan's claim that the platform prompted literary experimentation, critics questioned whether the story took up Twitter's affordances in any meaningful way. "The general consensus post-publication centered around a missed opportunity to engage Twitter's real-time network of connections," one writer observed of the story's reception, "leaving critics to wonder, why tell this story through Twitter at all?" (Gutman 274).

While "Black Box" didn't take advantage of the usual array of features that shape the end-user's experience with the platform's graphic interface, it did draw on Twitter's rarely acknowledged networked connections to the US security state. Egan's story about a volunteer counterterrorism agent responds to how the post-9/11 US national security state's geopolitical interests merged with the volunteerism of feminized networked users. This merger is both thematized in the plot and experienced through the activity of reading Twitter literature on one's very own digital device. If it was difficult for some critics to see how "Black Box" maximized its particular medium, the story's significance to the study of platform literature lies in how it mediates the conjuncture of digital activities and national security operations at the level of narrative; ultimately, this conjuncture constitutes the contemporary condition of reading any work of digitally networked literature on a corporate platform.

Twitter's relationship to US national security might not be immediately apparent. To track this relation, this chapter revisits the political climate in the US in the wake of 9/11, when the Patriot Act expanded and reinvigorated the alliance between the federal security state and its telecommunications firms. As Mimi Thi Nguyen puts it, the Act's "sweeping measures of surveillance and incarceration target the racial stranger, the possible terrorist" perceived to be Muslim, North African, or Middle Eastern as part of a white nationalist fantasy of detection and detainment (134). At the same time, the Act established that this retrenchment of US imperial power would adhere to the technoliberal logic of "war as big data" (113), Tung-Hu Hui's evocative phrase for the figuration of national security conducted through an instantaneous and all-encompassing program of data surveillance. Social media platforms remain among those telecom companies that maintain robust partnerships with government agencies, optimizing surveillance of the public's electronic correspondence.

As a byproduct of this partnership, platform users are swept into the digital security fold, their online activity abstracted into securitized effects. Digital activity that is "[s]imultaneously voluntarily given and unwaged, enjoyed and exploited" (74) is what Tiziana Terranova has termed "free labour" (73). Scholars including Brooke Erin Duffy, Kylie Jarrett, and Lisa Nakamura have pursued the concept's intractably gendered dimensions: insofar as online activity is frequently affective, immaterial, and unremunerated, they argue, it is often feminized much like reproductive labor. For example, platforms regularly profit from the unpaid antiracist, feminist pedagogical labor that women of color and sexual minorities perform in digitally networked spaces to create safer online communities (Nakamura). However, feminized digital volunteerism does not necessarily work toward antiracist or feminist ends. For instance, Inderpal Grewal has written about Michelle Malkin and her fellow "warbloggers"—women whose online labor is consumed with concern for national security and homeland defense (126). This brand of "security mom" volunteerism works on behalf of white heteronormative femininity to shore up the settler colonial and imperial interests of the US security state. For Grewal, this gendered formation of the volunteer feminized security figure is born out of the US-led war on terror and twenty-first-century neoliberalism's enshrinement of privatization and human capital. Positioning the protagonist of "Black Box" as a surrogate for the online reader, Egan's story dwells on the role of the securitized, feminized digital media user who emerges here as the target of labor exploitation and data capture. These gendered considerations are significant given that, as Mark McGurl has asserted, the gendering of literary life continues apace in the digital age and that "literary reading as a whole is still significantly skewed toward women, as it has been for centuries" (18).

More broadly, "Black Box" prompts us to question how the geopolitical interests of the US security state, mediated through social media, ought to inform the way we study digitally networked literature that is hosted on and distributed across corporate platforms. From Amazon to Wattpad, leading scholars of contemporary digital literature foreground how a few internet companies have come to wield remarkable influence over contemporary literary life, structuring the conditions of online literary production and distribution.[3] Highlighting the capitalist imperatives that drive the culling of data to create user profiles, target online consumers, and generate advertising revenue (Brown), these studies pinpoint some of the literary and sociological forms that corporate platforms instantiate. For instance, McGurl observes that Amazon's Kindle Direct Publishing program has hastened the reconceptualization of all fiction as genre fiction while Sarah Brouillette notes that the self-publishing platform Wattpad invites "online sociality" while "mak[ing] its real money by using readership data to find out what content is the most popular and then optioning it for TV and film production." Without diminishing the significance of platform capitalism's impact on literature, we can draw on research in critical digital studies that identifies how domestic security agencies rely on user data to suggest that the militaristic and securitized political conditions shaping platform literature's production, dissemination, and reception should play a larger role in our study of it.[4] In what follows, this chapter first offers a brief history of Twitter as a geopolitical player in matters of US national security after 9/11. It then considers the implications of this arrangement for our understanding of platform literature by turning to Egan's story and drawing out how digital surveillance has become an everyday practice of counterinsurgency for Americans who read literature on corporate platforms. Finally, foregrounding the feminized user-reader, it considers what happens when the fantasy of data's immateriality confronts the embodied experience of reading online.

Twitter and Platform National Security

When one reads literature on a social media platform, the traditional literary role of the reader intersects with the Web 2.0 category of the social media user. This means that one's literary pleasures will be quantified—reduced, in other words, to the platform's corporate imperative to maximize the extraction of user data. Information about this reader-user (their age and location, say) or their readerly tendencies (the time of day they read, the number of tweets clicked in a serialized story, and the pace at which this happens) gets swept up in the culling of data and used for a variety of purposes. As scholars of digital and social media Daniel Trottier and Christian Fuchs explain, major platform infrastructures provide the conditions for the commercial surveillance of user data to co-exist with security and intelligence surveillance:

> Social media is predominantly a corporate-state-power phenomenon, a force field in itself, in which powerful corporate and state interest are present and meet, as evidenced by the existence of a surveillance-industrial complex (PRISM) that controls social media communication and is constituted by a collaboration of social media and Internet companies, secret service and private security companies (such as Booz Allen Hamilton, for which Edward Snowden worked before his revelations).

(34)

While the US government has a long history of collecting electronic information in partnership with US-based telecommunications corporations, such collaborations were reframed explicitly as counterterrorist measures in the days that followed September 11, 2001, when George W. Bush signed the Patriot Act into law. Among other things, the Act, which sought "to deter and punish terrorist acts in the United States and around the world, to enhance law enforcement investigatory tools, and for other purposes," included a series of provisions that gave legal justification for enhanced surveillance procedures (United States). In the years that followed, news of these government measures and the nature of private-public data-sharing arrangements would occasionally make national headlines. In 2005, for example, *The New York Times* reported that the National Security Agency (NSA) had conducted large-scale surveillance on internet communications and had obtained access to domestic and international communications, thanks to an alliance with telecommunications companies including AT&T ("NSA Timeline"). To protect the NSA's relationship with private companies the Bush Administration introduced a series of amendments that strengthened government surveillance programs by ensuring that those telecom companies providing user data were shielded from lawsuits, while continuing to erode privacy protections for internet users.[5]

However, for millions of Americans, the extent of these arrangements between internet companies and the state came into full view with Edward Snowden's disclosure of the NSA's PRISM program in June of 2013. Snowden—then a contractor working at the NSA—released classified government information revealing the existence of PRISM, a mass surveillance program targeting Americans' international communications via email, telephone calls, and social media. The program, initiated by the Bush Administration in 2007 under the supervision of the US Foreign Intelligence Surveillance Court (FISC), allows the NSA to request private user data from a broad collection of US-based tech firms without requiring search warrants. For the ACLU and other organizations that seek to defend civil liberties, the program plainly constituted a violation of the Fourth Amendment. PowerPoint slides among the leaked documents listed several prominent tech companies and platforms purportedly working in conjunction with PRISM, including Microsoft, Yahoo!, Google, Facebook, PalTalk, YouTube, Skype, AOL, and Apple (one ACLU National Security Project attorney stated in 2018 that the list "very likely includes an even broader set of companies" [Toomey]).

Twitter was notably missing from the list of PRISM-compliant internet companies. At the time, journalists speculated that the company's absence was likely due to two factors: first, unlike email, most forms of communication on Twitter are already publicly available for collection. Second, Twitter had a record of challenging what it characterized as "invalid government requests" from federal authorities compelling the company to divulge user information (Martin). Though such legal challenges would seem to suggest that Twitter maintains an adversarial relationship with the federal government when it comes to sharing user data, the platform has a robust history of working with the government to secure national interests in cases ranging from state-affiliated election manipulation to coordinated disinformation campaigns. In fact, as recently as 2018 the company has cited the evolving "geopolitical terrain worldwide" to justify its "partnering with civil society, government, our industry peers, and researchers" to root out what it termed "bad-faith actors" on the platform (Gadde and Roth).

Twitter also acknowledges that it complies with some of the requests it receives from federal national security organizations. This cooperation is an example of what legal scholar Elena Chachko calls the "platform-government nexus"—the "part-symbiotic, part-adversarial emerging platform-government relationship around core national security and geopolitical matters" (61). Twitter informs its users that while it "generally requires a search warrant to disclose any contents of communications" ("Twitter Transparency Report"), it also acknowledges that it occasionally suspends its commitment to Fourth Amendment protections: "Twitter may disclose content in the U.S. without receiving a search warrant in rare circumstances, in accordance with applicable law," the company states on its website ("Twitter Transparency Report"). These "rare circumstances" include "certain national security requests" in the form of National Security Letters (NSLs) as well as other orders that fall under the Foreign Intelligence Surveillance Act ("Twitter Transparency Report"). The ACLU has described NSLs as a "provision of the Patriot Act [that] radically expanded the FBI's authority to demand personal customer records from Internet Service Providers [and other companies] without prior court approval" ("National Security Letters"). Moreover, the full extent of Twitter's cooperation with the US government's counterterrorism mandate remains unclear in part because the platform is legally barred from disclosing the details of these arrangements. In 2014, the service provider announced that it was "prohibited from reporting on the actual scope of the surveillance of Twitter users by the U.S. government" ("Taking the Fight").[6] The company filed a federal lawsuit to remove government prohibitions; as of the writing of this chapter, however, Twitter is restricted from publishing national security request information the US government deems classified ("Twitter Transparency Report").[7]

Twitter also preemptively privatized many national security measures through self-imposed internal regulations. These measures included "proactive enforcement against terrorism and violent extremism, which requires independent monitoring and intelligence" (Chachko 83). To this end, the social media platform has built up its infrastructural capacity for surveillance by expanding the number of employees dedicated to issues of national security and acquiring new technologies that aid in the detection of "terrorist and violent extremist content online" (Chachko; "Addressing"). The platform's delivery of privatized national security also draws on its hundreds of millions of users whom it recruits to work toward this political objective. To encourage what it calls "User Reporting of Terrorist and Violent Extremist Content," the company even invites "users to report or flag inappropriate content, including terrorist and violent extremist content" that will in turn "allow the company to prioritize and act promptly upon notification of [such material]" ("Addressing"). In this way, Twitter proactively solicits its platform users to work as voluntary agents of the security state.

"Black Box" and Reading as Digital Counterterrorism

For the casual social media user, the breadth of Twitter's national security work in support of US empire is not front of mind. In fact, we ought to note the ease with which a powerful corporation's solicitation of users to perform volunteer counterinsurgency work slips from our awareness as we scroll, retweet, and read. How does our understanding of Twitter fiction—and the digital user who reads it—change when we center the platform's long-standing arrangements with US national security interests?

Consider the case of "Black Box"—a work of post-9/11 Twitter fiction that prompts such a consideration given its own thematic interest in counterterrorism work that is digitized, feminized, and voluntary. "Black Box" is the futuristic tale of an unnamed woman spy sent to the Mediterranean on behalf of the US government to infiltrate a criminal network and steal digital data. While much has been written about the short story, in what follows I draw out two aspects of the narrative that are relevant given its status as platform literature.[8] First, "Black Box"'s protagonist is a feminized digital laborer who assumes voluntary counterinsurgency work on behalf of the US surveillance state. Second, the protagonist is under constant surveillance by US security agents herself. Egan's decision to place the protagonist in the dual position of both an agent and target of state surveillance presents a complex and conflicted depiction of what is entailed in being a networked feminized user and reader of online fiction.

In interviews, Egan has disclosed that longtime readers will likely recognize the unnamed protagonist of "Black Box" as Lulu, a character from her novel *A Visit from the Goon Squad* (2010) ("'This is all artificial'"). In the final chapter of that novel, Lulu is at work in a music industry in the throes of a seismic transformation. "[P]aperless, deskless, commuteless, and theoretically omnipresent" (317), Lulu stands in for a new kind of worker. Endlessly adaptable and perpetually networked, Lulu's easy traffic in information blips and instant contact aligns with the neoliberal fantasy of market efficiency. This context is important to "Black Box" since Lulu's stint as an agent of counterterrorism effectively constitutes a form of unpaid gig work undertaken by American women who the story refers to as "beauties" (85).[9] As the story announces early on: "You will each perform this service only once, after which you will return to your lives" (85). From the start then we understand that success at state spy craft depends on a digital dexterity that Lulu—and any consumer with a smartphone— already possesses. In the sci-fi world of "Black Box," the digital worker's ability to meld with her technology is made literal: the assortment of digital apps she deploys—a microphone in her right ear canal, a data storage chip under her hairline, a record button in her fingertips, a camera in her left eye, and a "Universal Port" between her toes—are discreetly embedded in her body.[10]

Lulu's ostensibly private digital competence gets pressed into unpaid public service on behalf of the US security state. Here, it's useful to recall Inderpal Grewal's account of various feminist and feminized volunteerisms that emerge out of the twenty-first century's imperial wars. These include the "security mom" who "appears as conservative, white, and patriotic supporter of state security and the heterosexual, white family" (120) and the "security feminist" who "appears as a liberal, white, and patriotic feminist working for the state and military" (120). If Egan's 33-year-old protagonist is plucked from her almost parodically "normal" and normative life as a wife and information worker to be dropped into the high-stakes world of espionage, then this convergence of the basic mother-to-be and the militarized worker is reflected in the seemingly incongruous nature of many of the tweets. As a feminized family woman Lulu is reminded to focus on "giggles; bare legs; shyness" (85) and her conviction that this "service had to be undertaken before you had children" (87). As a security feminist, meanwhile, she recounts that her perilous work "will help thwart an attack in which thousands of American lives would have been lost" (96) and perhaps even "change the course of history" (85). We have seen how invisibly Twitter enables such an amalgamation for all of its users who perform this unpaid security work while leisurely scrolling their social media feeds. In such cases, the leisure activity of reading platform literature doubles as the counterinsurgent activity of monitoring tweets for "terrorist and violent extremist content" on behalf of the US security state ("Addressing").

It's significant too that, as a subject of the security state, Lulu is monitored herself: "Your whereabouts will never be a mystery; you will be visible at all times as a dot of light on the screens of those watching over you," the story affirms (89). Through an allusion to the satellite infrastructures of global positioning systems (GPS) that track Lulu as she performs her mission, the tweet speaks to the Twitter reader whose geographic positions might well be tracked digitally in the very process of reading. For, aside from users who voluntarily provide profile locations or geotag tweets, Twitter also constantly collects "the approximate location of the IP address you used to access Twitter" ("How to"). It's significant too that the missive beginning with GPS ends with the slippage from "watching you" and "watching over you"—a phrase that evokes the feminization of biopolitics in its merging of mass surveillance performed by national security agencies with privatized forms of care labor.

For Lulu, state surveillance is ultimately continuous with heteronormativity: "Imagining yourself as a dot of light on a screen is oddly reassuring," she notes. "Because your husband is a visionary in the realm of national security, he occasionally has access to that screen" (91). In this formulation, the violation of government surveillance is enveloped in the familiarity of the heteronormative couple so much so that the security subject is grateful to US agencies for tracking her. Lulu is a security subject who willingly offers herself up to the state for inspection, a phenomenon Rachel Hall has described as "feminine heterosexual acquiescence to the new surveillance technologies" (137). But Lulu's acquiescence to the demand for transparency is nowhere more apparent than in the "Field Instructions"—officially "a record of your mission and lessons for those who follow" (97) and harvested directly from her head by a futuristic technology capable of capturing a woman's interior monologue at the press of a hidden button.

Reembodying the Networked Reader

Whether Virginia Woolf's eponymous protagonist in *Mrs. Dalloway* or Molly Bloom in James Joyce's *Ulysses*, modernist fiction offers familiar portrayals of a woman's interiority, in which a woman's singular thoughts, private feelings, worries and pleasures find form in language attributed to internal monologue. This is not so with "Black Box," where the protagonist's networked status undermines even the possibility of private thought. As Egan affirms in an interview: "[...] with Lulu in 'Black Box' her thoughts are not even her own: they are, in some sense, owned by the state, the record of her work for them, and equally valuable whether she is alive or dead" ("This is all artificial" 12). These circumstances do away with the possibility that a woman's thoughts might be impervious to the acquisitive, extractive world of the surveillance-industrial complex in which they take shape. If Lulu must constantly "filter [her] observations and experience through the lens of their didactic value" (88), then the narrative's relentless second-person imperative mood abets the transformation of personal thought into useful instruction by addressing an implied "you." Indeed, if the imperative mood conveys the security feminist's pertinent guidance to civilian agents performing US counterterrorism operations, it also accords with "quasi-therapeutic discourses" assumed by the self-improving neoliberal subject and the familiar online idiom of self-help aimed at improving feminine conduct (Gill 156). The imperative's capacity to voice the discourses of military directive and social media's self-help culture makes it an apt mode of address to the vigilant feminized digital media user. Only once in the story does the imperative give way to the subjunctive mood: "For clearest results, mentally speak the thought, as if talking to yourself" (88). Here, the "as if" locates the possibility of "talking to yourself" in the realm of the desired but unattainable condition of being alone while under surveillance.

As "Black Box" intimates, Twitter fiction is inextricably bound up with the geopolitical alignments of the platform on which we encounter it. If Nakamura's digital laborers work toward an antiracist, antisexist networked future, then Egan's beauties present a circumscribed political vision of the feminized digital user-reader: isolated and denied a collective consciousness that might allow them to transform their conditions, they put their digital dexterity to work on behalf of heteronormative reproductive futurity and US imperialism. While "Black Box" will point out the subtle terror associated with the constraints that come with this form of exploited networked existence, the story nonetheless offers an unsettling allegory for the Twitter user who reads the story online. Egan makes this connection clear given that she imagines her Twitter story "reaching people through their phones" (*New Yorker*) while the story pinpoints "the handset" (94) as the key device for accessing one's digital data. In circulating the story on Twitter's social media platform, Egan tells a tale of securitized digital subjects to readers who become securitized digital subjects in the very act of reading. If we take "Black Box"'s tweets as the content of Lulu's "Field Instructions," the reader may well be "you"—that is, the civilian agent for whom the instructions are intended. Of course, for those who use Twitter regularly, the online activity of securitized digital readers working on behalf of US security interests looks utterly familiar and mundane. But channeled through the hyperbolic tropes of the science fiction spy thriller, the geopolitical ramifications of a social media user's everyday relation to the US security state are made starkly visible. In this way, Egan's turn to genre fiction clarifies the immense amount of volunteer online labor required to sustain the US security state's digital operations. In Egan's hands, those invisible acts of dutiful vigilance and transparency that securitized feminist and feminine subjects are asked to participate in every time they read platform literature move out from behind the computer screen. Reembodying the digital security worker through the citizen agent Lulu, Egan highlights her work as a form of active and physical participation in the political projects of US empire.

Reembodying the digital worker has other consequences too. What Hu has identified as the logic of "war as big data" depends on data harvesting—that is, the posthuman fantasy that abstract data is neatly separable from the material form of the human. And yet, as "Black Box" makes clear, this pernicious fantasy of "bodiless information" that N. Katherine Hayles once deftly described in *How We Became Posthuman* continues to rely on the hierarchal impositions of gendered embodiment to operate (1). The fact that Lulu is encouraged to dissociate from her body as it is repeatedly attacked and violated in the story only underscores the demand that women's embodiment must be erased to maintain the state and corporate fiction that digitized personal data circulates with seamless efficiency. The story's title is of course an oblique reference to the protagonist who, through her service, is reduced to little more than a vessel for the user data that has become so valuable to the US national security project. "[Y]our body will yield a crucial trove of information," she assures herself (97). But the title is also a reference to the networked reader who, in the course of reading "Black Box" on Twitter's platform, will "yield a crucial trove of information" herself.

Notes

1 In November 2017, Twitter changed its character limit from 140 characters to 280 characters.
2 See Project TwitLit's "TwitLit Data: Graphs." Since 2016, the most used hashtag to designate this literary form has been "twitterature."
3 See, for example, Brouillette's "Social Media Memoir and Platform Capitalism," McGurl's *Everything and Less: The Novel and the Age of Amazon*, and Vadde's "Amateur Creativity: Amateur Creativity: Contemporary Literature and the Digital Publishing Scene."
4 See, for example, Guzik's "Discrimination by Design: Predictive Data Mining as Security Practice in the United States' 'War on Terrorism'"; Hu's *A Prehistory of the Cloud*; and Trottier and Fuchs, "Theorising Social Media, Politics and the State."
5 These amendments include Foreign Intelligence Surveillance Act (FISA) of 2008—an amendment to the FISA of 1978. Among other things the amendment removed warrant requirements in certain cases and introduced a new Title that gave the government the authority to conduct surveillance on the electronic communications of non-US persons located abroad as well as US persons abroad with FISA Court notification. While individuals located within the United States could not be designated as an official target by government surveillance, they could be inadvertently surveilled in cases of incidental collection.

6. What the company does share are the number of National Security Letters ("NSLs") received which are no longer subject to non-disclosure orders ("NDOs")" ("Twitter Transparency Report 19"). The number of NSLs Twitter has received that are still subject to indefinite NDOs is unknown.
7. See the "Twitter Transparency Report 19" and "Twitter Inc. v. William P. Barr, Attorney General of the United States, et al.," for further details regarding the lawsuit.
8. For scholarship on Egan's "Black Box" see, for example, Gutman's "Cyborg Storytelling: Virtual Embodiment in Jennifer Egan's 'Black Box'"; Newman's "Your Body Is Our Black Box: Narrating Nations in Second-Person Fiction by Edna O'Brien and Jennifer Egan"; and Santini's "The Short Form Reshaped: Email, Blog, SMS, and the MSN in Twenty-First Century E-Pistolary Novels."
9. For reference purposes, direct quotes from "Black Box" cite page numbers from the story's print version.
10. For more on the shifting relationships between bodies and technology, see Jennifer Rhee's chapter "Humans and Posthumans" in this volume.

Works Cited

"Addressing the Abuse of Tech to Spread Terrorist and Extremist Content." *Twitter*. 15 May 2019. https://blog.twitter.com/en_us/topics/company/2019/addressing-the-abuse-of-tech-to-spread-terrorist-and-extremist-c. Accessed 9 February 2022.

Brouillette, Sarah. "Social Media Memoir and Platform Capitalism." *Chicago Review*, 19 November 2021. https://www.chicagoreview.org/social-media-memoir-and-platform-capitalism/. Accessed 9 February 2022.

Brown, Ian. "Social Media Surveillance." *The International Encyclopedia of Digital Communication and Society*, First Edition, edited by Robin Mansell and Peng Hwa Ang, 2015, pp. 1–7.

Chachko, Elena. "National Security by Platform." *Stanford Technology Law Review*, vol. 25, no. 1, 31 December 2021, pp. 55–140.

Duffy, Brooke Erin. *(Not) Getting Paid to Do What You Love: Gender, Social Media, and Aspirational Work*. Yale UP, 2017.

Egan, Jennifer. *A Visit From the Goon Squad*. Penguin Random House, 2010.

———. "Black Box." *New Yorker*, 4 & 11 June 2012, pp. 84–97.

———. "'This is all artificial': An Interview with Jennifer Egan." Interview by Zara Dinnen. *Post45*, 20 May 2016, https://post45.org/2016/05/this-is-all-artificial-an-interview-with-jennifer-egan/. Accessed 30 December 2021.

Gadde, Vijaya and Yoel Roth. "Enabling Further Research of Information Operations on Twitter." *Twitter Blog*. 17 October 2018. http://perma.cc/B4PC-HEZN.

Gill, Rosalind. "Postfeminist Media Culture: Elements of a Sensibility." *European Journal of Cultural Studies*, vol. 10, no. 2, 2007, pp. 147–166.

Grewal, Inderpal. *Saving the Security State: Exceptional Citizens in Twenty-First-Century America*. Duke UP, 2017.

Gutman, Jennifer. "Cyborg Storytelling: Virtual Embodiment in Jennifer Egan's 'Black Box.'" *Critique: Studies in Contemporary Fiction*, vol. 61, no. 3, January 2020, pp. 274–87.

Guzik, Keith. "Discrimination by Design: Predictive Data Mining as Security Practice in the United States' 'War on Terrorism.'" *Surveillance & Society*, vol. 7, no. 1, 2009, pp. 1–17.

Hall, Rachel. "Terror and the Female Grotesque: Introducing Full-Body Scanners to U.S. Airports." *Feminist Surveillance Studies*, edited by Rachel E. Dubrofsky and Shoshana Amielle Magnet. Duke UP, 2015, pp. 127–149.

Hayles, N. Katherine. *How We Became Posthuman: Virtual Bodies in Cybernetics, Literature, and Informatics*. U of Chicago P, 1999.

"How To Access Your Twitter Data." *Twitter*, https://help.twitter.com/en/managing-your-account/accessing-your-twitter-data. Accessed 7 February 2022.

Hu, Tung-Hui. *A Prehistory of the Cloud*, Cambridge, MIT Press, 2015.

Jarrett, Kylie. *Feminism, Labour and Digital Media: The Digital Housewife*. Routledge, 2016.

Kushner, David. "Zola Tells All: The Real Story Behind the Greatest Stripper Story Ever Tweeted." *Rolling Stone*, 17 November 2015, https://www.rollingstone.com/culture/news/zola-tells-all-the-real-story-behind-the-greatest-stripper-saga-ever-tweeted-20151117.

Lee, Timothy B. "Here's Everything We Know about PRISM to Date." *The Washington Post,* 12 June 2013, *http://www.washingtonpost.com/blogs/wonkblog/wp/2013/06/12/heres-everything-we-know-about-prism-to-date/.* Accessed 29 August 2021.

Martin, Scott. "Twitter Notably Absent from NSA PRISM List." *USA Today,* 7 June 2013, www.usatoday.com/story/tech/2013/06/07/nsa-prism-twitter/2401605/. Accessed 29 August 2021.

McGurl, Mark. *Everything and Less: The Novel and the Age of Amazon.* Verso, 2021.

Murray, Simone. "Charting the Digital Literary Sphere." *Contemporary Literature,* vol. 56, no. 2, Summer 2015, pp. 311–39.

Nakamura, Lisa. "The Unwanted Labour of Social Media: Women of Colour Call out Culture as Venture Community Management." *New Formations: A Journal of Culture/Theory/Politics,* vol. 86, 2015, pp. 106–112.

"National Security Letters." ACLU. https://www.aclu.org/other/national-security-letters. Accessed 1 January 2022.

Newman, Daniel Aureliano. "Your Body is Our Black Box: Narrating Nations In Second-Person Fiction by Edna O'Brien and Jennifer Egan." *Frontiers of Narrative Studies,* vol. 4, no. 1, 4 July 2018, pp. 42–65.

New Yorker, The. "Coming Soon: Jennifer Egan's 'Black Box.'" *The New Yorker,* 23 May 2012.

Nguyen, Mimi Thi. *The Gift of Freedom: War, Debt, and Other Refugee Passages,* Duke UP, 2012.

"NSA Timeline 1791–2015." *Electronic Frontier Foundation.* https://www.eff.org/nsa-spying/timeline. Accessed 1 January 2022.

Project TwitLit. "TwitLit Data: Graphs." Project Twitter Literature. https://twitlit.github.io/data.html. Accessed 4 January 2022.

Santini, Laura. "The Short Form Reshaped: Email, Blog, SMS, and the MSN in Twenty-First Century E-pistolary Novels." *Iperstoria –Testi Letterature Linguaggi,* issue 14, Fall/Winter 2019.

"Taking the Fight for #transparency to Court." *Twitter,* 7 October 2014. https://blog.twitter.com/en_us/a/2014/taking-the-fight-for-transparency-to-court. Accessed 28 November 2021.

Terranova, Tiziana. *Network Culture: Politics for the Information Age.* Pluto, 2004.

Thomas, Bronwen. "140 Characters in Search of a Story: Twitterfiction as an Emerging Narrative Form." *Analyzing Digital Fiction,* edited by Alice Bell, Astrid Ensslin, and Hans Kristian Rustad. Routledge, 2014, pp. 94–108.

Toomey, Patrick. "The NSA Continues to Violate Americans' Internet Privacy Rights." *ACLU,* 22 August 2018, www.aclu.org/blog/national-security/privacy-and-surveillance/nsa-continues-violate-americans-internet-privacy.

Trottier, Daniel, and Christian Fuchs. "Theorising Social Media, Politics and the State." *Social Media, Politics and the State: Protest, Revolutions, Riots, Crime and Policing in the Age of Facebook, Twitter and YouTube,* edited by Daniel Trottier and Christian Fuchs. New York: Routledge, 2015, pp. 3–38.

"Twitter Transparency Report: Report 19 (Jan–Jun 2021)." Twitter, 25 January 2022, https://transparency.twitter.com/en/reports/countries/us.html#2021-jan-jun

Twitter, Inc. v. William P. Barr, Attorney General of the United States, et al. Case no. 14-cv-4480-YGR. https://storage.courtlistener.com/recap/gov.uscourts.cand.281277/gov.uscourts.cand.281277.281.0.pdf

United States, Congress, House. *Uniting and Strengthening America by Providing Appropriate Tools Required to Intercept and Obstruct Terrorism (USA PATRIOT ACT).* Congress.gov, www.congress.gov/bill/107th-congress/house-bill/3162/text. 107th Congress, House Resolution 3162, passed 26 Oct. 2001.

Vadde, Aarthi. "Amateur Creativity: Contemporary Literature and the Digital Publishing Scene." *New Literary History,* vol. 48, no. 1, Winter 2017, pp. 27–51.

29
TRANSLATION
Roland Végső

Literature, Translation, Politics

The fact that discussions of literature sooner or later stumble across the question of translation appears to be quite self-evident. After all, literature is art made out of the raw materials of language. Thus, what has often been called in various Western traditions the "post-Babelian" confusion and plurality of languages constitutes the natural order (or disorder) of things from which works of literature periodically emerge. It is, therefore, not surprising that critical and theoretical discussions of literature often turn to translation to account for various aspects of literary expression and communication. For example, as Rebecca Walkowitz has recently argued, we could start with the basic observation that "[t]here is no literary history without translation. Never has been." (45) In fact, if there is plenty of empirical evidence to prove that there is no "history" of literature without translation, one might wonder if there could even be anything like "literature" without translation. Following the logic of this reversal of priorities, we would have to conclude that translation is not merely a secondary concern for so-called literary "masterpieces" whose putative greatness demands that they be shared with the highest possible number of readers from different national backgrounds. Rather, translation emerges here as something like a precondition for the constitution of literary tradition in general as part of a shared human cultural heritage.

What can we say about the politics of literature if we accept this priority of translation for literary production in general? If there is no literary history and, possibly, no literature in the first place without translation, we might have to start with the hypothesis that there is no meaningful way to address the politics of literature without accounting for translation. As we try to triangulate these three key terms (politics, literature, and translation), how far can or should we go to move translation from the margins to the very center of these discussions? Do we have to content ourselves with the observation that, under specific circumstances, translation plays some role in the politics of literature? Or is it possible to argue that translation occupies a crucial (maybe even structural) position as a mediating agent: in other words, can we suggest that translation takes place in a location where literature becomes "political" and politics becomes in some sense "literary"?

To do so, we might attend to the fact that once a literary work enters the "translation zone" (Apter, *Translation Zone* 3–11), it is by definition located in a political domain since the process of translation is impossible to describe without reference to a number of inherently political considerations. The matter of which texts are selected for translation into a given language, the matter of who gets to translate these texts, and the matter of the way these translations then enter broader systems of economic and social circulation all raise questions and express concerns that are fundamentally "political": by this, I mean precisely that these questions and concerns clearly demonstrate that the translation of literature involves larger collective and institutional infrastructures, which extend well beyond the domain of the individual. At the same time, when negotiations that we consider to be "political" in the more traditional sense (that is, in the sense that they involve some public deliberation concerning issues of legislation) explicitly involve problems of translation, we are—whether we like it or not—located squarely in the domain of the politics of language. In these moments, when political rhetoric itself becomes a problem of translation, a certain type of literariness surfaces at the heart of politics itself. Put plainly, ordinary language might imagine a fundamental distinction between the technical language of professional politicians and the literary language of political poetry, novels, or plays. Yet, the everyday experience of "translation" constantly reveals to us that this distinction is difficult to maintain with absolute clarity.

This situation, however, is further complicated by the fact that traditional perceptions of the "politics of literature" and the "politics of translation" can be quite at odds with each other. In fact, they often appear to have contrary values. While today it is largely accepted that works of literature cannot be grasped as purely aesthetic objects without some reference to historical (social and political) realities, the task of the translator is still often defined in emphatically apolitical terms. In fact, until relatively recently the "ethics of translation" was frequently defined in clearly anti-political terms. In this sense, the duty of the translator was to act as a transparent mediator: the politics of translation was reduced to neutrality. According to this tradition, a "good" translation is, first of all, an "accurate" and/or "faithful" reproduction of the original that assumes a political function only to the degree that the original work (as a piece of literature) fulfilled some kind of a political role. If translation had any political function, it was derivative in relation to the politics of the original work of literature. But the ethical duty of the translator was to be an impartial conduit, a mere bridge between two languages and two cultures. While over the years we got used to speaking about a "literature of engagement" (to use Jean-Paul Sartre's term, *littérature engagée*), to many the idea of an "activist translator" remained a contradiction in terms.

We could cite here Lawrence Venuti's by-now classic 1986 article "The Translator's Invisibility" (that became the foundation of his 1995 book with the same title) as a well-known example to illustrate how the supposed neutrality of translation was increasingly questioned by translators and scholars over the last few decades. Following Venuti's lead, we could argue that the expression "the politics of translation" can have at least two different yet necessarily related meanings: one socioeconomic, the other aesthetic in nature (Venuti 1986, 181). On the one hand, the politics of translation can be analyzed in relation to the material conditions that determine the lives of translators and govern the production, circulation, and reception of translated texts. For example, in this sense, the politics of translation consists of trying to increase the social visibility of processes of translation, doing so partially to oppose the economic exploitation and the unfavorable legal status of translators. However, the political dimension of translation can be analyzed on the level of the aesthetic, cultural, and social effects produced by translated texts. After all, acts of translation are always embedded in concrete historical and social contexts and, as a result, they contribute in various ways to the establishment, maintenance, and transformation of these historical situations. For Venuti, the socioeconomic exploitation of translation accounts for its low cultural status and is causally linked to the dominant aesthetics of "fluency" that continues to be the culturally reinforced industry standard. This is why Venuti argued in favor of translations that produce "foreignizing" effects in the target culture (without ever fully capturing the foreign as such) by going against dominant ideologies of translational fluency (Venuti 2018, xii–xix).

Globalization as World Literature

The timing of Venuti's argument is also worth reflecting upon. While the original article was published during the 1980s, the expanded monograph that grew out of it was a product of the 1990s, a decade that proved to be invigorating for the field of translation studies. After the end of the Cold War, the historical processes of "globalization" appeared to have reached a new phase with the establishment of what promised to be a fully unified global market. This historical development was reflected in the literary criticism of the 1990s, for example, through an increased interest in post-colonial criticism, a renewed attention to the question of cosmopolitanism, as well as the eventual resurfacing of the debates about world literature in the early years of the new millennium. In this new historical context, therefore, questions of translation were arguably becoming increasingly more visible in the critical literature. Not surprisingly, translation studies engaged a similar set of political questions (Niranjana; Robinson, *Translation and Empire*; Bassnett and Trivedi; Tymoczko and Gentzler). One aspect of this historical transformation was the politicization of translation studies that mostly manifested itself in the conflict between so-called "descriptive" and "prescriptive" theories of translation. While descriptive theories tended to model themselves on the discipline of linguistics (and, thus, aspired to imitate the natural sciences in their supposedly neutral descriptions of translation practices), the prescriptive approaches were often influenced by various strands of continental philosophy (and defined themselves in terms of ideology critique).

Confronting the realities of globalization unavoidably raised a number of important questions about the politics of culture and literature. Briefly consider a few statistics. According to the *Index Translationum* (the UNESCO database of books translated worldwide since 1932), English has been the most translated source language across the globe (outpacing French in the second place by almost six times as many books); yet English is not even among the top ten of the target languages of global book translations (a list that is led by German, once again with French in the second place). This imbalance is certainly worthy of some thought (Venuti 2018, 11). What can we make of this state of affairs, which suggests that the most translated language in the world itself appears to be quite unwelcoming toward translations? Following Robert Philippson, we could describe this historical situation in terms of a "linguistic imperialism": "The British empire has given way to the empire of English" (1).

In more general terms, we could follow Pascale Casanova's argument, which holds that languages are never simply "equal" and always enter relations of "domination" in relation to teach other (379). Casanova's conclusions, however, point toward an additional issue that has recently emerged as a major theoretical and political concern: "any language overly dependent on another is at risk of extinction, of dissolving, in a certain way, becoming gradually absorbed into the dominant language" (397). Of course, there is an already familiar general anxiety that the historical processes of globalization eventually will lead to diminished cultural diversity. In its most extreme form, however, these tendencies manifest themselves in the specific form of the extinction of languages. For example, based on the analysis of 6,511 spoken languages, a current estimate from 2021 holds that "[w]ithout intervention, language loss could triple within 40 years, with at least one language lost per month." A situation that could lead to "the loss of over 1,500 languages by the end of the century" (Brohman 2). In a similar vein, the UNESCO's *Atlas of the World's Languages in Danger* catalogues 2,646 endangered languages—out of which 228 have already gone extinct since 1950; 577 are currently critically endangered; 537 are severely endangered; 640 are definitely endangered; while 592 are vulnerable (http://www.unesco.org/languages-atlas/). A careful historical analysis of the specific languages that have either already died out or have become endangered over the last century could provide us a painful but necessary overview of the ultimate effects of globalization on human cultural diversity. But this approach also raises the important theoretical question of whether, in this broader political context, practices of translation function as means of conserving vulnerable cultures or, on the contrary, as tools of hastening their disappearance (through their integration into the databases of economically and technologically dominant cultures).

Thus, in this context, it becomes evident that the history of literature is to a large extent the history of the globalization of literary production as well. As Jacques Lezra has argued, translation can be treated as a political concept to the degree that it participates in this globalization in at least two senses: on the one hand, translation is one of the "instruments" that makes possible the "differential flow of peoples, labor, commodities, and capital among different regions" of the globe; on the other hand, translation in itself constitutes a form of "immaterial labor" that is fully inscribed in these flows (209–210). Arguably, then, the "translational" condition of global capital constitutes the historical background against which we should interpret the sudden rise of interest in the category of "world literature" beginning at the turn of the new millennium.

The teaching and consumption of world literature, however, immediately raises a number of practical questions: in fundamentally monolingual institutions (like the majority of K-12 and university classrooms in the USA), world literature could not exist without the necessary mediation of translations. While translation grants some access to cultural alterity, the enduring concern remains that translation simultaneously domesticates the unavoidable alterity of the original text. In her critique of the way "translation studies" and "world literature" were often coordinated in various critical discourses, Emily Apter describes this situation in the following terms: "Partnered, they would deliver still more: translation theory as *Weltliteratur* would challenge flaccid globalisms that paid lip service to alterity while doing little more than to buttress neoliberal 'big tent' syllabi taught in English" (*Against World Literature* 7–8).

But as Rebecca Walkowitz argues, the contemporary state of world literature might be best described in reference to texts that are "born-translated": "born-translated literature approaches translation as a medium and origin rather than as an afterthought. Translation is not secondary or incidental to these works. It is a condition of their production" (3–4). In other words, it is now increasingly the norm rather than the exception when literary works aimed at a wide international (if not explicitly global) readership are simultaneously published in several languages. This historical tendency, which to a certain degree undermines the very distinction between an original and a translation, clearly privileges literary works that display formal characteristics both inviting and anticipating further translations in the (hopefully) near future. From a literary point of view, of course, the crucial point here is that the formal constitution of literary works itself is determined in demonstrable ways by their opportunistic anticipation of their global circulation: circulation determines their production. Thus, translation is no longer a belated modification of a literary work's "afterlife" but part of the very constitution of literature in its actual present. And if translation is a precondition of literary production today, these "born-translated" works are no longer patiently awaiting the future realization of "world literature." They enact it in their very composition.

The Visibility of Translation

In this context, therefore, the crucial role of translation in the global circulation of literary works has become impossible to ignore: translation was finally becoming more visible. But as some scholars of translation have observed, the increased visibility of the translator might end up producing new opportunities as well as problems and conflicts for translators—some of them quite predictable, others less obvious (Maier 253). The politics of translation, in other words, cannot be conceived as a simple transition from a monolithic negative state of "invisibility" to an equally unified positive state of "visibility." Rather, this politics might have to be defined as the dynamic struggle of conflicting modes of visibility and invisibility. Just as translation was never absolutely invisible, full visibility in itself cannot be fetishized as the only utopian goal of an activist politics of translation. After all, as Michel Foucault famously observed, in the age of permanent surveillance, visibility can be a "trap" (200). At the same time, the question of what exactly should become more visible in these rearticulations of the cultural and political position of translation remains equally important: in addition to the actual person of the translator and the translated status of texts that we encounter in various institutional settings, the broader economic, social, political processes and networks of translations also need to become visible as inherently tied to the act of translation. The politics of translation might in the end consist of making the unavoidably collective and networked structure of translation visible in new ways.

Globalization has frequently been described as an enlightening increase in the availability of information, goods, and services to an increasing portion of a democratizing world population. Yet the increased visibility of translation illuminated a darker, less optimistically liberatory underside of globalization. Scholars of translation saw with increasing clarity that the processes of globalization also manifest themselves in the creation of a planetary market that is simultaneously unified and fractured by the proliferation of violent conflicts. Globalization, therefore, had two quite different faces: the global market and war that was paradoxically both global and civil.

The necessity of openly addressing the position of translators in these global conflict zones was clearly encoded in Apter's thesis: "The translation zone is a war zone" (*The Translation Zone* xi). As a result, scholars paid increasingly more attention to the role of interpreters and translators in historical conflicts like the wars in the former Yugoslavia (Stahuljak), the wars in Iraq and Afghanistan (Inghilleri), as well as in various peacekeeping missions or interactions with political refugees and asylum seekers (Baker 202). One of the immediate outcomes of these discussions was that the neutrality of acts of translation came into question. As Zrinka Stahuljak argued, commenting on the role of interpreters played in the 1991–1992 war in Croatia, "translation as mediation is always already an intervention" (403): "interpreter activism merely renders visible what is inherent in translation, that is, that interpreters, whether explicitly activist or not, do not occupy neutral, in-between positions, that they do not reside outside cultural or ideological systems" (393–394). The fact that the different participants in these conflicts do not see the act of translation as a neutral activity is clearly underlined by the fact that the USA on a number of occasions had to implement special measures to ensure the safety of interpreters and their families by evacuating them from their native countries—most recently, in response to the sudden withdrawal of US troops from Afghanistan (Donati).

Literary translation, however, is hardly ever such a hazardous enterprise—although it can be a potentially dangerous activity. In this regard, the best-known case remains the so-called "Rushdie Affair." In response to the publication of Salman Rushdie's novel *The Satanic Verses*, Ayatollah Khomeini (the Supreme Leader of Iran) issued a fatwa on February 14, 1989, ordering Muslims to kill Rushdie.[1] While Rushdie himself survived the ordeal, several of his translators became targets of violent attacks:

> in 1991 his Japanese translator, Hitoshi Igarashi, was stabbed to death and Ettore Cariolo, his Italian translator, was seriously stabbed and beaten. A deadly arson attack on a hotel in 1993 had as its chief target Aziz Nesin, Rushdie's Turkish translator.
>
> *(Beebee 301)*

In extreme situations like this, the politics of literature and translation assume highly visible forms that show that local acts of translation produce proliferating global effects in different cultural contexts in ways that are all but impossible to control.

More recently, the increased visibility of the person of the translator has given rise to a different set of public conversations that centers around the translator's body and lived identity in relation to the racial politics of global capitalism. As is clear, the linguistic imperialisms of globalization cannot be separated from the histories of racial capitalism. A case in point is the recent controversy concerning the translations of Amanda Gorman's poem *The Hill We Climb*. Gorman became an instant international celebrity when she was chosen to read her poetry at the inauguration of President Joe Biden on January 20, 2021. The publication rights for the poem were picked up by Penguin Random House (the book was eventually published in English in 2021 with Oprah Winfrey's foreword), and the poem was immediately set to be translated into more than a dozen languages (Bhanoo). Events began to unfold quickly when the Dutch publishing house Meulenhoff announced that Marieke Lucas Rijneveld (who won the 2020 International Booker Prize for their debut novel *The Discomfort of Evening*) was selected as the Dutch translator. The controversy was set off by an opinion piece authored by Janice Deul (a Surinamese-Dutch journalist and activist) in which Deul highlighted the fact that there is a "mismatch between the shared lived experiences of the black Gorman and the white Rijneveld" and called attention to Rijneveld's lack of experience as a translator (Kotze), finally raising the question why "Meulenhoff chose not to opt for a young, black, female, spoken-word artist" (Kotze). As a result of the ensuing controversy, Rijneveld withdrew from the project. Almost at the same time, the originally hired Catalan translator, Victor Obiols, was dropped by his publisher for similar reasons.

Interestingly, the most successful effort appears to have been by the German publishers, who decided to select a group of three translators rather than a single individual, thereby offering a different model for conceptualizing the politics of translation:

> In Germany, the translation trio was chosen long before controversies in other countries ensued. The team of three women included 33-year-old activist and author Kübra Gümüsay, whose book *Language and Being*, exploring the role of language in respectful communication, was a top-seller in Germany. Working with her was the Afro-German political scientist, journalist and author Hadija Haruna-Oelker, whose work includes research on migration and racism. Finally, poetry translation specialist Uda Strätling lent her talents. She has already translated works by African American author Teju Cole and poet-playwright Claudia Rankine, among others, into German.
>
> *("Amanda Gorman's Inauguration Poem Appears in German")*

A good part of the ensuing debate followed a limited number of predictable ideological lines. More productively, however, the international translation community engaged in sustained self-reflection on the intersectionality of socially and politically constructed lived experiences, as well as on the status of different types of "experiential knowledges" that are unavoidably mobilized in all acts of translation (Şebnem).

Translation in the Digital Age

Today, engaging the politics of translation and literature must acknowledge the almost total technological transformation of everyday life by contemporary capitalism. The increasing automation and digitalization of translation is forcing us to reconsider its contemporary fate in reference to rapidly transforming labor conditions, the changing landscape of copyright laws, the uneven distribution of digital access, decreasing availability of language instruction in schools and universities, as well as the increasing influence of AI in the general management of our social and private lives (Apter, *Translation Zone* 191–240; Baumgarten and Cornellà-Detrell; Railey; Vaidhyanathan). Our age is clearly marked by a strong sense of anxiety about the status and future of translation. In this spirit, Michael Cronin opened his 2013 book *Translation in the Digital Age* by registering a deep sense of "confusion":

> Is there a future for translators? In the age of Google Translate, is the human translator condemned to large-scale extinction, or to the quaint peripherality of the Sunday hobbyist? The demand for translation keeps growing apace in the contemporary world, but will humans continue to be asked to service this need, or will it be our machines that will do the bidding?
>
> (1)

Trying to avoid "the dual dangers of terminal pessimism and besotted optimism," Cronin argues that "our present age, which is often referred to as the information age with its corollary, the knowledge society, should more properly be termed the translation age" (3). The foundation of this potential generalization of the logic of translation is technological capitalism's increasing reliance on new structures of equivalence that presuppose the "convertibility" of all processes of production:

> the metamorphic or transformative effects of the convertible which are at the heart of the digital revolution that makes translation the most appropriate standpoint from which to view critically what happens to languages, societies, and cultures under a regime of advanced convertibility.
>
> (3)

For the time being, the extinction of the human translator is but an unrealized possibility. Yet some have already argued against translation as an ineffective tactic of engaging the contemporary flows of translational capitalism. For example, Kenneth Goldsmith claimed that the classic humanist praxis of "translation" is an outmoded technology that has been replaced by processes of "displacement": "Translation is quaint, a boutique pursuit from a lost world; displacement is brutal fact." Since globalization itself thrives on displacement (of human beings, of commodities, of language itself), Goldsmith argues that the binary logic of pure "appropriation" remains the only game in town: things either can be or cannot be appropriated. Translation remains, at best, a niche a commodity. In this new historical setting, according to Goldsmith, we have no choice and we have to live with the inherent contradictions produced by these technologically enhanced modes of appropriation: the traditional modes politics (left vs. right, progressive vs. reactionary) are displaced by the complicity between creative forms of displacement and contemporary capitalism's "colonizing imperative."

This anxiety about translation can be easily reframed in terms of the dynamic politics of visibility and invisibility. On the one hand, some predict a not-so-distant future where something akin to *Star Trek*'s invisible yet omnipresent "universal translator" device will be a reality.[2] In a situation like this, however, publicly inaccessible algorithms eliminate the need for human agency in translation as well as the human experience of translation. Translation being fully alienated from the human being, life would be experienced in invisibly monolingual terms (Lezra 217–218). On the other hand, as Christine Mitchell and Rita Raley have more recently argued, translation gains a "new visibility":

> Whether or not translation is a thing of the past—reduced to art form or artisanal practice in conditions of global reach and instant connectivity—it nevertheless gains new visibility as systems, protocols, and platforms for automated and crowdsourced translation, programming, and information exchange proliferate.

Of course, it is widely recognized that the technological mediation of translation is not something new in itself. Cronin himself takes the position that

> technology is not simply an accessory, an adjunct to translation, but that it has been central to the definition of translation activity in many different societies and in many different historical periods up to and including, of course, our own.
>
> (2)

Already in 2003, Douglas Robinson argued that "all translation in the world today is 'cyborg translation'—translation involving some significant interface between humans and machines" (369). At that point in time, well before the rise of Google Translate, Robinson predicted the dominance of computer-aided translation (CAT) in opposition to "strong" machine translation (MT) and old-fashioned human translation (HT): "What machine has ever translated without human aid, and what human translates any more without computer aid?" (369). As things stand today, the task of the translator is frequently reduced to mere "post-editing" (O'Thomas 287).

Just as the politics of photography must account for the fact that most people now carry cameras in their pockets, the contemporary politics of translation and literature must therefore be addressed in terms of these historical tendencies and new social realities driven by technology. For example, the rise of machine translation raised some very difficult questions about human agency itself. Thus, the rapid transformation of processes of translation by digital technologies also highlighted what Robinson called "the total act of translation" ("Cyborg Translation" 369). The inscription of processes of translation into the economic infrastructures of contemporary capitalism and the concomitant technological transformations of mechanisms of production and circulation necessitate a reconceptualization of translation in terms of a widely distributed or "disaggregated agency" (Robinson, "Cyborg Translation" 379). The idea of such a networked collective agency could, indeed, be seen as an "assault" on humanistic and individualistic ideologies of translation (Robinson, "Cyborg Translation" 380). Just as today there is no translator who eschews digital technologies, and who is therefore not also by definition a "cyborg" of sorts, we can also argue that there is no translator who translates alone. Translation has always been a collective process involving individual translators, professional organizations, physical and virtual professional forums and communities of translators, assistants, editors, publishers, etc. Yet the very concept of "agency" associated with this practice is currently undergoing significant transformations, which render this inherent collectivity increasingly more visible. As it turns out, translation creates networked communities in a number of different senses of the term.

The Politics of Translation

In the wake of these encounters with globalization and "technocapitalism" (Baumgarten and Cornellà-Detrell), one of the most remarkable and productive academic debates in translation theory of the last two decades focused on the status of the "untranslatable." This collective reflection on the inherent limits of translation assumed a new kind of urgency in this specific historical context precisely because it was clear from the start that the stakes were more than "just philosophical" in nature. The renewed interest in the question of the untranslatable was to a large extent ignited by the 2004 publication in French of *Vocabulaire européen des philosophies: Dictionnaire des intraduisibles*, edited by Barbara Cassin. The English language version of the book, edited by Emily Apter, Jacques Lezra, and Michael Wood, was published as *Dictionary of Untranslatables: A Philosophical Lexicon* in 2015. The discussions that followed quickly marked out a number of salient conflicting positions (Cassin, "The Energy of the Untranslatables"; Apter, *Against World Literature*; Walkowitz 29–42; Venuti, *Contra Instrumentalism* 41–82).

Whether despite or because of the conflicts, these passionate engagements with the concepts of "translatability" and "untranslatability" demonstrate what is at stake today: a conceptual and pragmatic tension between the theoretical possibility of translation, on the one hand, and the political necessity of translation, on the other. If we declare translation to be absolutely impossible, our politics might find itself reduced to either an uncomprehending hostility or an enthusiastic but fundamentally naively fetishistic celebration of alterity. If we assert the uncomplicated possibility of translation, our politics might end up being caught in the already familiar contradictions of false universalities. And if we claim to occupy an intermediary zone, in which translation is paradoxically both possible and impossible depending on the given context, we might end up feeling paralyzed by the seemingly endless proliferation of deliberations that render meaningful action increasingly less imaginable. To put it differently, what is significant about this debate is that it identifies a preliminary decision as the most fundamental political moment of translation. It suggests that we need to account for an historically specific, initial decision about what is translatable and what is untranslatable in a given context. This decision about translatability, made perhaps again and again in every specific situation, institutes the very "field" of translation in which actual acts of translation can take place according to the rules of the concrete "translation game" that these preliminary decisions put in motion in the first place.

The task that consistently anti-essentialist and non-instrumentalist definitions of translation have bequeathed to us today is the necessity of rethinking the very "ontology" of translation. To the question "what *is* translation?" we might have to answer that we do not quite know yet—for the simple reason that the history of translation has not been written yet. At the exact point where the politics of literature and translation meet today, therefore, the following question emerges: can the "globe" of globalization ever be translated into a meaningful "world" of shared experiences, and what roles do national or post-national or natural or invented languages play in that still-speculative process? Can the irreducible multiplicity of languages and cultures over the globe be articulated in an aesthetic totality that would frame this multiplicity as a world of partially successful (or failed) acts of communication? Literature becomes political when it lays claim on our globe through a forced confrontation with alterity that is impossible to conceptualize without acts of translation; politics becomes literary when it promises us a world that would be finally livable through successful acts of translation in spite of the violent antagonisms produced by these encounters with alterity.

Notes

1 For more on the Rushdie affair, see Ian Afflerbach's chapter "On or around 1989" in this volume.
2 The *Star Trek* franchise appears to have produced contradictory effects in relation to the cultural perception of translation. On the one hand, the fiction of the "universal translator" device embodies the utopian fantasy of the complete disappearance of translation from our cultural narratives. On the other hand, the *Star Trek* saga also gave rise to an enduring real-life interest in the fictional "Klingon" language. We could treat this latter phenomenon as a persistence of a "desire for translation" in face of the general tendency toward the total elimination of linguistic alterity.

Works Cited

Apter, Emily. *The Translation Zone: A New Comparative Literature*. Princeton UP, 2006.
———. *Against World Literature: On the Politics of Untranslatability*. Verso, 2013.
Baker, Mona. "Interpreters and Translators in the War Zone." *The Translator*, vol. 16, no. 2, 2010, pp. 197–222.
Bassnett, Susan, and Harish Trivedi, editors. *Post-Colonial Translation: Theory and Practice*. Routledge, 1999.
Baumgarten, Stefan, and Jordi Cornellà-Detrell. "Introduction: Translation in Times of Technocapitalism." *Target*, vol. 29, no. 2, 2017). Pp. 193–200.
Beebee, Thomas O. "Shoot the Transtraitor! The Translator as *Homo Sacer* in Fiction and Reality." *The Translator*, vol. 16, no. 2, 2010, pp. 295–313.
Bhanoo, Sindya. "Who Should Translate Amanda Gorman's Work? That Question Is Ricocheting around in the Translation Industry." *The Washington Post*, March 25, 2021: https://www.washingtonpost.com/entertainment/books/book-translations-gorman-controversy/2021/03/24/8ea3223e-8cd5-11eb-9423-04079921c915_story.html
Casanova, Pascale. "What Is a Dominant Language? Giacomo Leopardi: Theoretician of Linguistic Inequality." *New Literary History*, vol. 44, no. 3, Summer 2013, pp. 379–399.
Cassin, Barbara. "The Energy of the Untranslatables: Translation as a Paradigm for the Human Sciences." *Paragraph*, vol. 38, no. 2, July 2015, pp. 145–158.
Cassin, Barbara, Emily Apter, Jacques Lezra and Michael Wood, editors. *Dictionary of Untranslatables: A Philosophical Lexicon*. Princeton UP, 2015.
Cronin, Michael. *Translation in the Digital Age*. Routledge, 2013.
Donati, Jessica. "More Than 60,000 Interpreters, Visa Applicants Remain in Afghanistan." *The Wall Street Journal*, December 16, 2021. https://www.wsj.com/articles/more-than-60-000-interpreters-visa-applicants-remain-in-afghanistan-11639689706#:~:text=WASHINGTON%E2%80%94More%20than%2060%2C000%20Afghan,State%20Department%20official%20said%20Thursday.
Foucault, Michel. *Discipline and Punish: The Birth of the Prison*. Translated by Alan Sheridan. Vintage, 1995.
Gorman, Amanda. *The Hill We Climb: An Inaugural Poem for the Country*. Penguin, 2021.
Inghilleri, Moira. "The Ethical Task of the Translator in the Geo-Political Arena: From Iraq to Guantanamo Bay." *Translation Studies*, vol. 1, no. 2, 2008, pp. 212–223.
Kotze, Haidee. "Translation is the Canary in the Coalmine." *Medium,* March 15, 2021: https://haideekotze.medium.com/translation-is-the-canary-in-the-coalmine-c11c75a97660#:~:text=Translation%20is%20part%20and%20parcel,but%20also%20its%20imaginative%20possibility.
Lezra, Jacques. "Translation." *Political Concepts: A Critical Lexicon*. Edited by J. M. Bernstein. Fordham UP, 2018, pp. 208–231.

Meier, Carol. "The Translator's Visibility: The Rights and Responsibilities Thereof." *Translating and Interpreting Conflict,* edited by Myriam Salama-Carr. Rodopi, 2007, pp. 253–266.

Mitchell, Christine, and Rita Raley. "Translation-Machination." *Amodern* 8, January 2018: http://amodern.net/article/amodern-8-translation-machination/.

Niranjana, Tejaswini. *Siting Translation: History, Post-Structuralism and the Colonial Context.* U of California P, 1992.

O'Thomas, Mark. "*Humanum ex machina*: Translation in the Post-global, Posthuman World." *Target,* vol. 29, no. 2, 2017, pp. 284–300.

Phillipson, Robert. *Linguistic Imperialism.* Oxford UP, 1992.

Raley, Rita. "Machine Translation and Global English." *The Yale Journal of Criticism,* vol. 16, No. 2, 2003, pp. 291–313.

Robinson, Douglas. "Cyborg Translation." *Translation,* edited by Susan Petrilli. Rodopi, 2003, pp. 369–386.

———. *Translation and Empire: Post-Colonial Theories Explained.* St. Jerome, 1997.

Şebnem, Susa-Saraeva. "Representing Experiential Knowledge: Who May Translate Whom?" *Translation Studies,* vol. 14, no. 1, 2021, pp. 84–95.

Stahuljak, Zrinka. "War, Translation, Transnationalism. Interpreters In and Of the War (Croatia, 1991–1992)." *Critical Readings in Translation Studies,* edited by Mona Baker. Routledge, 2010, pp. 391–414.

Tymoczko, Maria, and Edwin Gentzler, editors. *Translation and Power.* U of Massachusetts P, 2002.

Vaidhyanathan, Siva. *Copyrights and Copywrongs: The Rise of Intellectual Property and How It Threatens Creativity,* NYU Press, 2001.

Venuti, Lawrence. *Contra Instrumentalism: A Translation Polemic.* U of Nebraska P, 2019.

———. "The Translator's Invisibility." *Criticism,* vol. 28, no. 2, Spring 1986, pp. 179–212.

———. *The Translator's Invisibility: A History of Translation.* Routledge, 2018.

Walkowitz, Rebecca. *Born Translated: The Contemporary Novel in an Age of World Literature.* Columbia UP, 2015.

30
COMICS

Daniel Worden

On January 10, 2022, the School Board in McMinn County, Tennessee voted to remove Art Spiegelman's *Maus* from its eighth-grade curriculum. The School Board's unanimous decision was picked up by news media in the United States and beyond, and 36 years after its first volume's publication as a book, *Maus* became a bestseller once again. Sophie Kasakove reported on the school board's decision and its aftermath in *The New York Times*:

> The McMinn County decision to ban "Maus" was widely interpreted as a rejection of or disregard for Holocaust education. The book, which portrays Jews as mice and Nazis as cats in recounting the author's father's imprisonment at Auschwitz, has been used in social studies classes across the country since the early 1990s, when it became the first graphic novel to win a Pulitzer Prize.
>
> But school board members cited more narrow concerns: several instances of "inappropriate words" — including "bitch" and "goddamn" — and an image of a partially nude woman.

The school board's objections to *Maus* seemed to so fully misunderstand the work as to be laughable. The particular panel that contains the word "bitch" and "an image of a partially nude woman" is even from an older comic that Art Spiegelman reprints as an artifact in *Maus*. "Prisoner on the Hell Planet" is drawn in a style even more reminiscent of German expressionism than the later *Maus*, and "Prisoner on the Hell Planet" is a more straightforward autobiographical or confessional comic than the mouse- and cat-themed narrative that surrounds it. Perhaps because this short interlude is more autobiographical, it signaled to McMinn County School Board member Mike Cochran that *Maus* was part of a curriculum "developed to normalize sexuality, normalize nudity and normalize vulgar language" (qtd. in Kasakove).

"Prisoner on the Hell Planet" begins with a title panel that includes both a family photograph and the artist's hand (Figure 30.1). This point of artist and reader identification—Spiegelman's hand parallels the comics reader's own hand holding the page—is duplicated in *Maus*, as Spiegelman draws his more simplified hand holding the older printed comic book, as well. Along with drawing his thumbs holding the family photograph and the comic book page, and thus asking the reader to identify with his perspective, Spiegelman is also the

DOI: 10.4324/9781003038009-35

Figure 30.1 Art Spiegelman, Illustration from *The Complete Maus: A Survivor's Tale* by Art Spiegelman, *Maus, Volume I* copyright © 1973, 1980, 1981, 1982, 1983, 1984, 1985, 1986 by Art Spiegelman. Used by permission of Pantheon Books, an imprint of the Knopf Doubleday Publishing Group, a division of Penguin Random House LLC. All rights reserved

main character in "Prisoner on the Hell Planet." He narrates from a psychological prison, dressed in a striped uniform. In the second panel, Spiegelman faces and addresses the reader directly: "In 1968 my mother killed herself....She left no note!" (100). On this page there are four versions of Art Spiegelman visible at once: at the ages of 10, 20, 24, and 36, and as a photographic subject, an artist, a character, and a comics reader. The reader sees Spiegelman in multiple ways on the page, and also sees these pages as Art Spiegelman, channeled as they are by his narration and his thumbs into his perspective. It's hard to imagine how this kind of layering, and the fully mediated sense of narrative time, memory, and trauma connoted by the artist's presence on the page, can be read as juvenile vulgarity or as pornography, let alone as unreflective realism. The discomfort generated by these layers of memory and history, by the destabilized self implied by Spiegelman's multiple incarnations, is surely and rightly troubling, but just as surely not troubling because of mild profanity and cartoon nudity.

Just as it is hard to imagine how *Maus* is a work of pornography, it is easy to see how *Maus* is a work of art. And in this chapter, I will develop different approaches to *Maus* that each get at something crucial to Spiegelman's book and to the importance that comics have in our culture today. Attempts to ban comics and to limit the kinds of comics that kids can read in schools and libraries have a historic precedent in the United States; like any artistic medium, comics art is fragile and can thrive or be squashed based on public opinion and the willingness of libraries and schools to purchase them. Today, comics should be valued for what they offer to students, teachers, children, young adults, full-grown adults, and more. Comics also need institutional support in the form of faculty teaching jobs, comics curricula, University Press book series that publish comics materials, and public arts funding for independent comics. One of the few decades-old canonical comics in literary history, *Maus* is a gateway for thinking about comics and all the medium offers in this moment. This is evident in the first thing one notices about *Maus*: its use of animals. And while moving from a plea to take comics seriously, straight over to funny animals might seem to be sabotage, it's actually one of the best ways to understand the historical importance of comics.

Funny Animal Comics

Animal caricature was widely practiced in the late nineteenth-century American press. Thomas Nast's Elephants and Donkeys became widely adopted as symbols for the Republican and Democratic parties; animal caricature was also common in political cartoons about Standard Oil, such as in Udo Keppler's illustration of the corporate monopoly as octopus. These more "serious" animal cartoons coexisted on turn-of-the-century American newsstands with comics, and as Leonard Rifas has noted, "funny animals appeared in newspaper comic strips just as that medium was becoming established" (n.p.). In 1913, one of the most celebrated "funny animal" newspaper comic strips would appear in William Randolph Heart's *New York Evening Journal*: now best known as *Krazy Kat*, it was created by George Herriman and would eventually inspire *Maus*'s Jewish mice and Nazi cats.

Herriman's *Krazy Kat* features a black cat named Krazy, and a white mouse named Ignatz. In most *Krazy Kat* comic strips, Krazy is in love with Ignatz, and Ignatz throws a brick at Krazy. The comic strip's simplistic premise and its elaborate execution—especially in its full-page Sunday comics—appealed to modernists in the early twentieth century, and while the formalist puzzle of Krazy and Ignatz seems to transcend politics, Herriman nonetheless weaves politics into the funny animal scenario. In the May 27, 1917 *Krazy Kat* comic, for example, Krazy and Ignatz engage in trench warfare (Figure 30.2). Published just over a month after the United States declared war on the German Empire, this comic doesn't so

Daniel Worden

Figure 30.2 George Herriman, "Krazy Kat," *Chicago Examiner* (May 27, 1917), 5.2. *Chicago Examiner* Digital Collection. Special Collections and Preservation Division, Chicago Public Library. http://digital.chipublib.org/digital/collection/examiner/id/96899

much critique war as it uses the imagery and actions of war to express a sense of love (weird as that may sound). In the comic, Officer Pup orders "Korporal 'Krazy Kat'" to investigate "something suspicious in trench number one." Twelve panels later, and after being hit by Ignatz's brick, Krazy returns, and Officer Pup asks if the suspicious figure is "a friend or a foe." Krazy responds, "Oh, I assure you 'Jenril,' it is positively a 'friend.'" One might expect funny animals to give us clear political allegories—as they do in a Thomas Nast editorial cartoon or a literary work like George Orwell's *Animal Farm*—but even in early newspaper comics, funny animals express complicated, artistic messages. In Krazy Kat, as in *Maus*, war's traumatic pairing of intimacy and violence inflects even the cycle of love and hate that is abstractly signified by the cat and the mouse comic strip.

Funny animals are also an expression of racist, segregationist America, as is apparent in Herriman's black-furred Krazy and German-named Ignatz. Comics studies scholar Rebecca Wanzo and biographer Michael Tisserand have analyzed how Herriman's own mixed-race heritage—not public information during his life as a cartoonist—inflected his comics about a black cat and a white mouse who were engaged in a never-ending, masochistic game of love and hate.[1] And as Nicholas Sammond and Philip Nel have shown in the cases of Walt Disney's Mickey Mouse and Dr. Seuss's The Cat in the Hat, funny animals naturalize racial caricature and popularize it as a seemingly universal, childish iconography. In *Maus* Volume II, Spiegelman acknowledges this racist history. The first chapter opens with Spiegelman's sketchbook. Comics editor, and Spiegelman's wife, Françoise Mouly approaches him and asks, "What are you doing?" (Figure 30.3) Spiegelman responds that he is "trying to figure out how to draw you... What kind of animal should I make you?" (171). Among his sketchbook options are a moose, a mouse, a bunny, a poodle, and a frog. The French frog, of course, plays on the common ethnonationalist slur, and Mouly insists on being a mouse, because if Spiegelman "is a mouse, I ought to be a mouse too. I converted, didn't I?" (171). Placed at the beginning of *Maus* Volume II (1991), published five years after Volume I first appeared in bookstores, this opening conversation serves to orient Spiegelman's controversial use of caricature as a weapon against racist essentialism. Mouly isn't a frog, but Americans are represented as golden retrievers and the Polish are still represented as pigs in Volume II.

The use of animal caricature in *Maus* is thus politically ambivalent. On the one hand, as is made clear in Volume II's epigraph (a mid-1930s German newspaper article exclaiming "Down with Mickey Mouse! Wear the Swastika Cross!"), Mickey Mouse and the joyful plasticity of cartoon art threaten the idealistic purity of white supremacists (164). On the other hand, animal caricatures are an expression of white supremacist culture, a mode of comic representation that dehumanizes others. Funny animals both express and condemn otherness, and Spiegelman's *Maus* does the same with its "converted" mice and its maintenance of ethnic stereotypes through frogs and pigs.

Spiegelman, then, doesn't so much appropriate funny animals, as just use them as artistic and political tools from comics history.

The Underground

Funny animal comics were plentiful during Spiegelman's own childhood, yet in the 1940s and early 1950s, more "adult" genres of comics circulated widely on American newsstands. Crime, horror, romance, war, and western comics were the subject of an earlier comics panic of the 1950s. As comics scholar Charles Hatfield notes of this period of early comic book controversy:

> Published commentary against comic books began as early as 1940. It surged again postwar, by which time the industry had shifted away from superheroes to a broader range of genres, including sensationalistic ones... These bred controversy. Sales of comic books grew even as a wave of moral panic, and attendant political and legal challenges, assailed the medium from 1947 to about 1950, prompting half-hearted industry attempts at self-moderation. This wave of distrust and fear, even revulsion, toward comic books recurred and spiked from 1952 to 1954, inspiring outcry from many sectors and in many forms: academic and professional articles and symposia; newspaper editorials; the drafting of statutes and resultant debates about constitutionality and freedom of speech; public burnings of comic books.
>
> *(Hatfield 32)*

Figure 30.3 Art Spiegelman, Illustration from *The Complete Maus: A Survivor's Tale* by Art Spiegelman, *Maus, Volume II* copyright © 1986, 1989, 1990, 1991 by Art Spiegelman. Used by permission of Pantheon Books, an imprint of the Knopf Doubleday Publishing Group, a division of Penguin Random House LLC. All rights reserved

In this period of comics history, often described as the "Golden Age" of American comics, one of the medium's influential publishers was EC Comics, a publisher of many renowned crime, horror, and war comics, as well as the humor comic *Mad*. After the implementation of the Comics Code in 1954, which effectively censored most American comic books, EC Comics and the artist Harvey Kurtzman converted *Mad* to a magazine format, a periodical form unrestricted by the new Comics Code Authority, and as Spiegelman wrote in a later autobiographical comic, "I studied *Mad* the way some kids studied the Talmud!" ("Portrait" n.p.). Spiegelman would even produce a *Mad*-inspired fanzine when he was in middle school, *Blasé* (1963–1964). Kurtzman's artistic references and ambitions had a clear influence on Spiegelman, and in 1978, the same year that Spiegelman began interviewing his father for *Maus*, Spiegelman started teaching at the School of Visual Arts in New York City alongside Harvey Kurtzman. In between *Blasé* and *Maus*, Spiegelman would become a part of underground comix—the field of independent comics published and distributed through record stores and head shops in the 1960s and 1970s.

A precursor to *Maus*, "Prisoner on the Hell Planet" is a comics story only four pages long that was first published in Spiegelman's underground comix series *Short Order Comix #1* in 1973, then collected in Spiegelman's 1978 book *Breakdowns*. Spiegelman includes it in *Maus* as a historical document in and of itself; like the tape recorders, notebooks, and photographs that populate the pages of *Maus*, Spiegelman's earlier work is reprinted in *Maus* as an artifact; framed by the very different line art that distinguishes the rest of the book, the story serves as evidence of Spiegelman's own grieving process and the ways in which the horrors of the Holocaust affected not only survivors like his mother, but also succeeding generations.

The "partially nude woman" that the McMinn County School Board objected to in January 2022 is Art Spiegelman's mother Anya, depicted nude in a bathtub where she has committed suicide (Figure 30.4). The word "bitch" articulates her son's anger at her death, but anger is not the only emotion expressed in this panel: "Menopausal Depression," "Hitler Did It!" and "Mommy!" are also there. The angry word "Bitch" is one of Art Spiegelman's many thoughts about his mother's suicide, a dialogic expression of a fractured consciousness, anxiously reaching for explanations. In her field-defining reading of *Maus* in 2006, comics studies scholar Hillary Chute wrote about this very panel:

> This frame, smaller than 2 inches by 2 inches, depicts several images from different time periods: Anja's dead body in the bathtub; a heap of anonymous dead bodies piled high underneath a brick wall painted with a swastika; Anja reading to the child Artie; Anja cutting her wrist, her tattooed number fully visible on her forearm; the young man Artie in mourning, wearing the same Auschwitz uniform he wears even as a child, happily listening to his mother read. "Prisoner," then, posits that Artie inherited the burden that the uniform represents, in a natural transfer of pain that wasn't consciously accepted or rejected but seamlessly assumed. He earned his stripes at birth.
>
> *(208)*

Where readers have understood the section of the book to offer a complicated set of reflections upon generational trauma and the difficulties—even impossibilities—of adequately or accurately representing the legacy of anti-Semitic atrocities, the McMinn County School Board saw salacious vulgarity in need of censorship.

Interviewed on CNN after the McMinn Country School Board's decision, Art Spiegelman responded to a question about the school board's objection to the panel containing the image of "a partially nude woman":

Figure 30.4 Art Spiegelman, illustration from *The Complete Maus: A Survivor's Tale* by Art Spiegelman, *Maus, Volume I* copyright © 1973, 1980, 1981, 1982, 1983, 1984, 1985, 1986 by Art Spiegelman. Used by permission of Pantheon Books, an imprint of the Knopf Doubleday Publishing Group, a division of Penguin Random House LLC. All rights reserved

You have to really want to get your sexual kicks by projecting on it. It seems like a crazy place to get them.... I think they're so myopic in their focus, and they're so afraid by what's implied in having to defend the decision to teach *Maus* as part of the curriculum, that it led to this kind of daffily myopic response. Daffiness would be easy. The problem, of course, is that it has the breath of autocracy and fascism about it, and it has a real problem with asking the parents to be on board to decide what is okay to teach the kids. The values are too far away from those I can recognize, to see how they got there. But I'm still trying to figure out, how could this be as limited as it is?

("Maus Author")

Objecting to one panel in a 206-page book seems like an over-reaction, especially since the nudity and vulgar language in that panel connect to suicide, mourning, and grief. Indeed, the school board's particular objections to *Maus* provide ideological cover for the larger project of censorship underway in the United States in the 2020s. As Kasakove described it in *The New York Times*:

> The fight over *Maus* is the latest flash point in a national wave of conservative challenges to reading material for young people in school libraries and classrooms. Dozens of bills aimed at banning the teaching of topics derided as "critical race theory" have been introduced in state legislatures across the country in recent years. Conservative groups have targeted books about race, gender and sexuality, with more than 300 book challenges reported last fall, according to the American Library Association, which called the number "unprecedented."
>
> *(Kasakove)*

In this larger context, the McMinn County School Board is metonymic of a conservative-led culture war in the United States, and *Maus* is merely one of many books (including many other comics) targeted by this censorship movement that is, as Spiegelman's invocation of authoritarianism and fascism suggests, driven as much by politics as by morality. The 1950s comics panic followed a similar logic, wherein moral outrage at violence and sex in comic books reflected a concern for children's well-being in general as well as 1950s cultural anxieties. As Charles Hatfield summarizes the 1954 Comics Code:

> The Code not only forbade explicit depictions of violence and sex and strong hints of danger and sensuality—thus putting a damper on crime, romance, and horror comics—but also espoused unambiguous moralism and obedience to official authority. In effect, it imposed a narrow, protectionist notion of childhood reading.
>
> *(Hatfield 33)*

In his 1954 book *Seduction of the Innocent: The Influence of Comic Books on Today's Youth*, the psychiatrist Fredric Wertham argued:

> comic books stimulate children sexually... In comic books over and over again, in pictures and text, and in the advertisements as well, attention is drawn to sexual characteristics and sexual actions. As one boy expressed it to me when I was discussing with a group what is good and bad in comics, "The sexism is bad in comics, but to tell you the truth, I like that most!"[2]
>
> *(175)*

Like the McMinn County School Board, Wertham would identify particular comics panels and illustrations as being particularly illustrative of comics' vulgarity. And like the McMinn County School Board, Wertham's art choices seem to undermine the seriousness of his claims. For example, in the image insert in *Seduction of the Innocent*, Wertham includes a panel and detail of a man's shoulder, with the following caption: "In ordinary comic books, there are pictures within pictures for children who know how to look." The detail emphasizes how the shading on a man's bare shoulder could be interpreted to be a female crotch with pubic hair; while comics work precisely through the complex interplay of verbal and visual information, details like this one strikingly exemplify the extent to which the visual component of comics, no matter how subtle or in need of advanced interpretive skills, stimulates a kind of anxiety over representation that not only ignores but denies the linguistic content of the medium that is both sequential and narrative.

Figure 30.5 Art Spiegelman, Illustration from *Breakdowns: Portrait of the Artist as a Young %@&*!* by Art Spiegelman, copyright © 1972, 1973, 1974, 1975, 1976, 1977, 2005, 2006, 2007, and 2008 by Art Spiegelman. Used by permission of Pantheon Books, an imprint of the Knopf Doubleday Publishing Group, a division of Penguin Random House LLC. All rights reserved

In the first version of "Maus," Spiegelman draws mice in a scene reminiscent of Margaret Bourke-White's well-known 1945 photograph of Buchenwald concentration camp survivors (Figure 30.5). A group of gaunt, sunken-eyed mice wear concentration camp uniforms and blankets, standing behind a tall barbed wire fence. An arrow points to one mouse with the caption "Poppa," and in the three-page comic, Poppa mouse tells his son Mickey mouse a bedtime story about "life in the old country during the war" (*Breakdowns*). The comic ends with Poppa recalling his journey to "Mauschwitz," and then tucking Mickey into bed. The ability to understand and interpret particular texts in longer cultural and historical genealogies profoundly changes the very meaning of the text, of course; what for McMinn County was the definitive image in *Maus* is, in actuality, merely one early rendition of that material, refined in the very book that includes it. Moving from the notoriously misogynistic and racist shapes often used by male underground cartoonists such as R. Crumb (whose "Fritz the Cat" character depicted cute animals both inflicting and suffering violence 20 years before *Maus*), Spiegelman adapts his style to suit his subject matter and thereby both invokes and repudiates the traditions of representation that themselves both reflect and contribute to pernicious, even deadly, understandings of classes of people.

Comics as Literary Art

Against conservative nostalgia for a 1950s America where comics were blessedly free from images and stories about political ideology, war, and genocide—and the attendant desire to Make Comics Great Again!—consider the work of Bernard Krigstein, who drew Golden Age comics and later taught at New York City's High School of Art and Design, where

Spiegelman would study cartooning. In 1955, Krigstein also published "Master Race," a somber comics story about a Holocaust survivor who seems to identify a Nazi officer on a New York City subway platform.[3] In panels that flash back to World War II, the narrator seems to relive history; in the final twist, the reader realizes that the narrator was the Nazi officer all along. Fleeing from someone who he believes to be a concentration camp survivor, the Nazi officer stumbles, falls in front a speeding train, and is killed in a chromophotographic illustration reminiscent of Marcel Duchamp's 1912 painting *Nude Descending a Staircase, No. 2*.

Duchamp's modernist masterpiece caused famous outrage when it debuted in 1913, and the controversies recently surrounding *Maus* serve as worthy reminder that art and indignation are familiar bedfellows. As Hillary Chute has argued, in addition to its visual bona fides, *Maus* also exhibits many "literary" qualities. In her reading of the work, Chute concludes:

> Epitomizing the possibilities of the new comics form, *Maus*, interlaced with different temporalities whose ontological weave it frames and questions through spatial aesthetics, rebuilds history through a potent combination of words and images that draws attention to the tenuous and fragile footing of the present.
>
> *(220)*

Maus's rebuilt history manifests the past into the present, as Chute demonstrates through a panel in *Maus* Volume II, in which "the bodies of four Jewish girls hanged in World War II dangle from trees in the Catskills as the Spiegelmans drive to the supermarket in 1979" (199–200). Like Krigstein's "Master Race," Spiegelman's representation of World War II brings the past into the present while calling into question the limits and affordances of representation in a way that is ubiquitous in "great" 1980s and 1990s literature. Don DeLillo's *White Noise* (1985), Toni Morrison's *Beloved* (1987), and Philip Roth's *Counterlife* (1986) all appeared around the same time as *Maus* Volume I; thus, Spiegelman's interest in mediated memory and fragmentary history places him within the broader movement of postmodernism in literature. As with its Pulitzer Prize and its appearance on the *New York Times* bestseller list, *Maus* accomplished a political feat within literary culture, by crossing the barrier between the "low" medium of comics and the "high" medium of literature, while also positioning itself as work of modernist art. In so doing, *Maus* overturned cultural hierarchies and became a classroom text.

Comics in the Classroom

Maus's ubiquity in the college classroom was confirmed by its inclusion in the *Norton Anthology of American Literature* in 2007 (the first for a comic), yet this boundary-breaking entrance was less of a novelty than a return to the longer history of comics and sequential art.[4] One of the creators of early comics, Rodolphe Töpffer, drew cartoons for his boarding school students, and later when he became a Professor of Literature at the University of Geneva, he would publish early comics works such as *Histoire de M. Vieux Bois* in 1837, translated into English in an 1842 American edition titled *The Adventures of Mr. Obadiah Oldbuck*. In his 1845 "Essay on Physiognomy," Töpffer explicitly states that his "picture-stories" could be effective educational tools:

> Other things being equal, the picture-story, with its unique advantages of brevity and, consequently, of clarity, would be much more effective than the written story, for two

reasons: it would make a more lively appeal to more people, and second, the fact is that in every argument the man who goes straight to the point gets the better of one who rambles.

(4)

Like Scott McCloud, who would label comics as "the invisible art" due to the medium's complex simplicity in 1993's *Understanding Comics*, Töpffer's nineteenth-century account of comics art also emphasizes the medium's ability to express complicated ideas in short, lucid stories that combine image and text. Contemporary comics educator Nick Sousanis has also emphasized the creative and critical thinking that comics facilitate, especially when students make comics in the classroom: "Comics let you say things you couldn't in another form and learn things about yourself along the way" (Sousanis 110).

In twentieth-century America, less interactive approaches to educational comics were very common, like Jack Patton and John Rosenfield, Jr.'s *Texas History Movies*, originally published as a newspaper comic strip in the *Dallas Morning News* from 1926 to 1928 and then published in a series of book editions widely used in Texas public schools. One of the most prominent advocates for comics as an art form and an early adopter of the term "graphic novel" to describe book-length comics, Will Eisner created educational comics both for the US Military, through the still-running *PS: Preventative Maintenance Monthly*, and in a number of other "public service" comics produced through his American Visuals Corporation. And while Eisner's comics were state-sponsored, underground comix offered decidedly less mainstream perspectives for students. Leonard Rifas's Educomics imprint carries education in its very name, and Rifas would publish an early translation of manga in English, Keiji Nakazawa's *Barefoot Gen*, originally translated as *Gen of Hiroshima* in 1980. Nakazawa's more autobiographical and shorter account of the Hiroshima bombing, translated as *I Saw It*, followed from Educomics in 1982. Nakazawa's autobiographical comic uses the exaggerated facial expressions and dynamic page layouts of manga, juxtaposing the childish exuberance of action-adventure comics with the realism of a war documentary. Translated into English as Spiegelman was working on the first volume of *Maus*, Nakazawa's comics, along with earlier visual books like Mine Okubo's 1946 *Citizen 13660*, an account of Japanese-American internment camps written and drawn by a camp resident, offered historically informed and experience-based accounts of World War II in image and text. *Maus* is, from this perspective, less of an anomaly than a part of a broader comics history: one that includes earlier works like "Master Race" and runs through graphic novels like Kiku Hughes' time-traveling *Displacement* (2020), about the forcible internment of Japanese-Americans in US concentration camps. Comics are an educational medium that directly engages politics in the most fundamental sense, and they have been from the start.

Today, comics artists have expanded the purview of comics representation, while retaining the experimental strategies and historical complexity evident in Spiegelman's work. Sonny Liew's 2015 graphic novel *The Art of Charlie Chan Hock Chye* uses the appropriative strategies of *Maus* to an even more fabulist degree. Liew's graphic novel focuses on the fictional Singaporean comics artist Charlie Chan Hock Chye, and his life story details an imaginary history of what comics could have been in Singapore, had the small nation nurtured its own comics culture. It also tells a story of Singaporean national identity, structured by struggles between nationalists and socialists, and underwritten by colonial wars, postcolonial movements, and ethnic hierarchies. Liew draws in different historical comics styles, adopting at times the style of Walt Kelly's funny animal comic *Pogo* (1948–1975), notable for its advocacy of civil rights and environmentalism through the animal residents of the Okefeokee Swamp, and at other times the style of EC war comics with their realistic human figures and somber irony. Liew's work uses the funny animal tactics of *Maus*, but in a broader context of comics history that places funny animals in a tradition of giant robots, urban superheroes, war stories, and memoir. Because comics comprise, subsume, and engage all of these genres, the medium has a unique purchase on representing history as both a series of events and a series of visual styles. Phrased differently, comics narratives highlight the enduringly temporal and aesthetic aspects of historical representation, and the best ones refuse to allow readers the luxury of dismissing the "past" as simply "past" (which perhaps suggests one reason why comics have been such frequent targets of political regulation by those who prefer their ethics and their histories to be not only simple but simplified). In its synthesis of visual styles, first-person narration, and history, comics like Liew's *The Art of Charlie Chan Hock Chye* convey both information and experience, an immersive sense of time and place.

While Spiegelman uses tropes from funny animal comics and modernist art, among other source material, the contemporary comics artist Emil Ferris makes comics that are both less refined and more art-historically inflected. Ferris's 2017 *My Favorite Thing Is Monsters* is drawn in ballpoint pen on what appears to be lined notebook paper, the format of the book intentionally resembling a teenager's composition notebook. Yet the ballpoint pen drawings in *My Favorite Things Is Monsters* are anything but absent-minded doodles. Instead, Ferris's masterful linework produces fictional monster magazine covers and also reproduces classic works of art from the Art Institute of Chicago and the Detroit Institute of the Arts. B-movie monsters and fine art paintings contribute to the graphic novel's coming-of-age story, in which teenager Karen Reyes explores a neighbor's suspicious death in the guise of a werewolf detective. Weaving movie monsters, art history, coming-of-age sexuality, and even a Holocaust narrative, Ferris's *My Favorite Things Is Monsters* demonstrates both *Maus*'s established tropes of the graphic novel format—its emphasis on coming-of-age stories, its focus on traumatic historical events, its appropriation of pop culture images—and a further extension of comics art into both fine art and outsider art.

One of the artistic genres that comics engage is the documentary. With a title that simultaneously evokes *Maus* and offers its readers an imperative verb, *March* (3 volumes, 2013–2016) documents the life of Civil Rights activist and US Congressman John Lewis. Drawn by Nate Powell and co-written by Andrew Aydin and John Lewis, *March* has become another staple of the classroom. Following the McMinn County School Board decision to remove *Maus* from its eighth-grade curriculum, *March* artist Nate Powell published a comic titled "Shelf It" on the political comics website *The Nib*. Powell details the work that went into *March* to ensure that it satisfied school standards and accurately represented history, and he then turns to what makes comics particularly fragile today. Powell writes (Figure 30.6):

> Comics do have a built-in weakness: creators and readers perpetually fight for the basic legitimacy of anything in comics form, against both decades-old stereotypes, dismissals, and today's attacks on their unique strengths in making other perspectives real and accessible. Comics are the most democratic mass storytelling medium.
>
> We always knew that *March*, by its choice of medium, carried this extra vulnerability in the face of racist policy-makers and history deniers. It's now part of an entire generation's means of learning the history of the Civil Rights movement. Challenges to these

Figure 30.6 Nate Powell, panels from "ShelfIt," *The Nib* (February 1, 2022). https://thenib.com/shelf-it/. Courtesy of the artist

and other comics – whether by bans or personal fears of retribution – are steps toward the larger goal of removing the history *itself* from classrooms.

In Powell's comic, history refers to both the actual history of Civil Rights struggles and the history of comics itself as a medium. I have tried to demonstrate in this chapter just how historical comics themselves are. Understanding history and politics today involves not just reading comics like *March* or *Maus* that educate students across the United States, but also understanding how comics have been a part of history and politics since the medium's emergence in the nineteenth century.

Comics are an integral part of American art, American history, and American literature. Yet today the medium is embattled once again, for precisely the same reasons that were used 70 years ago. In the 1950s, politicians and public intellectuals created a social panic about comics art while America was waging a Cold War and maintaining racial segregation as national policy. Today, school boards are removing comics from their curriculum while authoritarianism and fascism are on the rise domestically and abroad, and while young people face a world of increasing climate disaster, economic inequality, and failing social supports. With their combination of visual and verbal information, their undeniable appeal across age groups, and their ability to offer hyper-complex information in hyper-legible and entertaining ways, comics perhaps uniquely make these problems comprehensible even to those without advanced critical apparatus of the kind that is a prerequisite for the high-modernist and post-modernist fiction its authors often engage. As educators, it is our duty today to make space for comics and offer students particular experiences with and strategies for navigating the utterly unique information systems (comics) that used to be dismissed as mere juvenile diversions. This means that we must hire more full-time faculty to teach comics art and comics studies, we must design courses that teach comics as an artistic medium rather than a pop culture elective, and we must read and discuss the comics that force us to grapple with our histories. Only by understanding the complex histories that got us to where we are, can we hope to understand how to create a better future in word, image, and action.

Notes

1. See Wanzo, esp. chapter 1, and Tisserand.
2. For more on Wertham and the 1950s comics panic, see Beaty, Nyberg, and Tilley.
3. See Krigstein. For more on Krigstein and EC Comics, see Whitted.
4. For an account of *Maus*'s canonization, see Loman.

Works Cited

Ayres, Jackson, ed. "Comics and Modernism." *Journal of Modern Literature*, vol. 39, no. 2, Winter 2016, pp. 111–179.

Beaty, Bart. *Fredric Wertham and the Critique of Mass Culture*. UP of Mississippi, 2005.

Chute, Hillary. "'The Shadow of a Past Time': History and Graphic Representation in *Maus*." *Twentieth-Century Literature*, vol. 52, no. 2, Summer 2006.

Hatfield, Charles. "Comic Books." *Comics Studies: A Guidebook*. Edited by Charles Hatfield and Bart Beaty. New Brunswick: Rutgers UP, 2020, pp. 25–39.

Herriman, George. "Krazy Kat." *Chicago Examiner*, vol. 17, no. 47, May 27, 1917, p. 5.2. http://digital.chipublib.org/digital/collection/examiner/id/96899.

Kasakove, Sophie. "The Fight Over *Maus* Is Part of a Bigger Cultural Battle in Tennessee." *New York Times*, 4 March 2022. https://www.nytimes.com/2022/03/04/us/maus-banned-books-tennessee.html

Krigstein, Bernard. *Master Race and Other Stories*. Fantagraphics, 2018.

Loman, Andrew. "'That Mouse's Shadow': The Canonization of Art Spiegelman's *Maus*." *The Rise of the American Comics Artist: Creators and Contexts*, edited by Paul Williams and James Lyons UP of Mississippi, pp. 210–234.

"*Maus* Author Reacts to His Book Being Banned." *CNN*, 27 Jan. 2022. https://youtu.be/5BmjCDoIyV0.

Munson, Kim A., ed. *Comic Art in Museums*. UP of Mississippi, 2020.

Nel, Philip. *Was the Cat in the Hat Black?: The Hidden Racism of Children's Literature, and the Need for Diverse Books*. Oxford UP, 2017.

Nyberg, Amy Kiste. *The Seal of Approval: The Origins and History of the Comics Code*. UP of Mississippi, 1994.

Powell, Nate. "Shelf It." *The Nib*, February 1, 2022. https://thenib.com/shelf-it/

Rifas, Leonard. "Funny Animal Comics." *Encyclopedia of Comics and Graphic Novels*, vol. 1. Edited by M. Keith Booker. Greenwood P, 2010. Gale eBooks.

Sammond, Nicholas. *Birth of an Industry: Blackface Minstrelsy and the Rise of American Animation*. Duke UP, 2015.

Sousanis, Nick. "Thinking in Comics: All Hands-On in the Classroom." *With Great Power Comes Great Pedagogy: Teaching, Learning, and Comics*, edited by Susan E. Kirtley, Antero Garcia, and Peter E. Carlson. Jackson: UP of Mississippi, 2020. 92–116.

Spiegelman, Art. "Ballbuster: Bernard Krigstein's Life Between the Panels." *The New Yorker*, July 14, 2002. https://www.newyorker.com/magazine/2002/07/22/ballbuster.

———. "High Art Lowdown." *Artforum*, vol. 29, no. 4, Dec. 1990.

———. "Portrait of the Artist as a Young %@$*!." *Breakdowns: Portrait of the Artist as a Young %@$*!*. Pantheon, 2008.

———. *The Complete Maus*. Pantheon, 2011.

Tilley, Carol. "Seducing the Innocent: Fredric Wertham and the Falsifications that Helped Condemn Comics." *Information and Culture*, vol. 47, no. 4, 2012, pp. 383–413.

Tisserand, Michael. *Krazy: George Herriman, a Life in Black and White*. Norton, 2016.

Töpffer, Rodolphe. "Essay on Physiognomy." *Enter: the Comics: Rodolphe Töpffer's Essay on Physiognomy and The True Story of Monsieur Crépin*, edited and translated by E. Wiese. U of Nebraska P, 1965.

Wanzo, Rebecca. *The Content of Our Caricature: African American Comic Art and Political Belonging*. New York UP, 2020.

Wertham, Fredric. *Seduction of the Innocent: The Influence of Comic Books on Today's Youth*. Rinehart, 1954.

Whitted, Qiana. *EC Comics: Race, Shock, and Social Protest*. Rutgers UP, 2019.

PART V

Spaces

31
ARCHIVES
Megan Ward

The vexed concept of archival evidence raises a series of questions that reveal the archive as a political concept, space, and series of institutional practices. Whose lives have been preserved and under what terms? What kinds of stories do we want to tell about the past? What counts as proof when we tell those stories? Through these and other questions, scholars have demonstrated that archives themselves—the institutionalized long-term storage of documents and objects—and their use in studying the past have long encoded questions of authority, cultural memory, and state administration. Academic research of the twentieth and twenty-first centuries has considered archival evidence as fundamental to establishing historical truth while, at the same time, grappling with the ways that baseline puts limits on what histories are knowable. The politics of evidence are at the heart of the creation of archives, the determination of acceptable archival research methodologies, and the evaluation of published research.

Evidence is so fraught because of the power structures that govern its admission. As Rodney Carter puts it,

> The power of the archive is witnessed in the act of inclusion, but this is only one of its components. The power to exclude is a fundamental aspect of the archive. Inevitably, there are distortions, omissions, erasures, and silences in the archive.
>
> *(216)*

These silences originate from and perpetuate the white supremacy, class hierarchy, homophobia, misogyny, and other forms of oppression structurally encoded in the archive. Driven largely by humanities scholars of imperialism, slavery, and queer history, this political understanding of archival evidence has become foundational to archival research methods in the past two decades. Broadly known as the "archival turn," this work takes the archive itself as the object of study and critique rather than as a transparent source of information in order to see how the theory and practice of archival work have been shaped by political and ideological structures. Coined by anthropologist Ann Laura Stoler in 2002, the archival turn "rethink[s] of the materiality and imaginary of collections and what kinds of truth-claims lie in documentation" ("Colonial Archives" 94). At the same time, the profession of archival studies was making a similar turn, marked by the double issue of the journal *Archival Science* in 2002 on "Archives, Records, and Power," edited by Joan M. Schwartz and Terry Cook. The formulation "the archive," which is a product of the archival turn in the humanities and social sciences, can refer to a metaphorical body of texts as well as an extant archive. Archivists, however, typically refer to extant physical or digital "archives." This divergence has resulted in frustration from archivists who see their work being devalued, from the labor of constructing and maintaining archives or the scholarship that comes out of that community (see Caswell, *Urgent Archives* 15, and Eichorn). In this chapter, I engage with scholarship from both archivists and literary critics, referring to "the archive" and "archives" in accordance with their separate meanings. I use the term "collections" to refer to preserved groups of objects or documents, such as in a museum, that were part of the emerging discourse of institutional collections in the nineteenth century.

Bridging these disciplinary differences, an understanding of archival evidence as motivated by political authority has become foundational to archival research methods in the past two decades. Perhaps the most established text of the archival turn is Jacques Derrida's *Archive Fever* (1995), which understands the desire to collect and to conserve that is at once motivated and dissolved by the death drive. Derrida turns to Sigmund Freud to investigate the relationship between private and public memory, for "There is no political power without control of the archive, if not of memory" (Derrida 4). Or, as Saidiya Hartman influentially puts it, often in archival research "the arrangements of power occlude the very object that we desire to rescue" ("Venus" 14).

This chapter takes those arrangements as its starting point, attempting to both capture the salient methodological debates and also point toward future possibilities. The first section outlines the conceptual questions and approaches that thread through the period known as the archival turn. The structural authority of the archive drives contemporary research methods, which include attempts to subvert the archive's power through interpretation, to ameliorate it through expansive evidentiary practices, and to rebuke it by refusing to cover over the losses that entail. The next section takes up a series of related methodological developments, loosely grouped under the heading of speculation, that tackle the political problem of evidence by bringing in the methods of fiction. Speculative methods are often positioned in opposition to the traditional archive, which is a positioning that, I argue, ultimately restricts the efficacy of the speculative project. To begin unraveling that historical opposition, the final section examines briefly the mutual influences of the historical novel and the burgeoning archival standards of the nineteenth century in order to demonstrate the role that fiction has always played in the formation of archives. What emerges, I hope, is a sense of both the political stakes of archival evidence as well as the futures that may be found in the archive's past.

Archival Turns

At least since the 1990s, scholars have paid deep attention to and engaged in rigorous debates about the structures, processes, and effects of archival research. Questions of political agency, loss, and temporality recur across digital and physical archives and across methods for reading them. Early definitions of the archival turn were characterized by the archive's "grain," or the unspoken structures of authority that have governed what kinds of records have been preserved and who has agency within those records. Stoler, for example, describes reading "along the archival grain" as a way to break down the archive's seeming monolith, to expose its "granular rather than seamless structure." Doing so highlights the archive as a "field of force and will to power" rather than as a neutral repository for information and objects with self-evident value (*Along the Archival Grain* 48). The concept of grain has provided scholars of minoritized lives a way to interact critically with historical records. As Regina Kunzel puts it, "reading against the grain" is "perhaps the key methodological strategy of queer history, as it is for other histories of marginalization" (214). Scholars have also modified the practice, as when Marisa Fuentes reads "along the bias grain," a "methodology by which the archival record is stretched to accentuate the figures of enslaved women" rather than minimize them (153, note 16). In each of these cases, the grain of an archival record is a way of making visible the politics of its creation.

Archival recovery work has also attempted to correct the limitations of the official record. This work attempts to fill gaps and silences by looking for information around the edges of official records, incorporating non-documentary sources, and seeking out minor figures beyond the reach of official history. Jenny Sharpe gives more details on this process of expansion:

> an archive that traditionally designated government documents, public records, newspapers, pamphlets, private letters, and other papers housed in official repositories has been expanded to include oral histories, myths, folk tales, novels, poems, murals, paintings, dance, songs, music religious rituals, and other embodied forms.
>
> *(9)*

As early as 1925, when Arthur Schomburg published "The Negro Digs Up His Past," scholars and activists have sought to recover what has gone missing in the archive. Recovery work often considered itself scholar-activism, as its practitioners argue that correcting the historical record is foundational to working toward present and future equity.

More recently, however, recovery work has come under critique from scholars who argue that it doesn't go far enough to overturn the logic and politics of the archive. While acknowledging the value of archival recovery for "contesting legacies of racism and exclusion," Helton et al point out how that work undermines the power of insisting on the "archive as a site of irrevocable silence that reproduces the racial hierarchies intrinsic to its construction" (2). Working at the intersection of queer and Black studies, Stephen Best also notes the pressure that recovery work puts on scholars to resuscitate the past in order to give hope to the future. Too often, he claims, such efforts portray a difficulty distinguishing "the conditions of our own critical agency from the political agency of the enslaved" (85). Recovery work in the archive, this recent work suggests, may offer valuable evidence of hidden lives, but it also threatens to impose the researcher's anachronistic desires on their historical subjects.

More generally, the centrality of political agency to archival research has been called into question. Salvaging agency for historical subjects has long been seen as a way to combat their erasure in the official record, but recent scholars have questioned that goal as narrowly defined by a Eurocentric individualism that equates individual will with political freedom. Scholars have asked whether or not it is even possible to write the lives of historical subjects in terms of modern categories of identity, especially as they intersect with the researcher's own identity and desires. Valerie Traub, for instance, warns of the danger of falling into "the perception of the past as something we think primarily *in relation to ourselves* risks subordinating it under the planetary influence of our identifications and desires" (135). Other scholars such as Madhavi Menon, however, see such anachronistic thinking as essential to resisting heterotemporality: "desires," she argues, "always exceed identitarian categories" (2–3).

As these debates suggest, the work of archival recovery can be intensely personal, and affect theory has thus proven fruitful for exploring the embodied experience of work that can sometimes appear singularly intellectual.[1] In particular, scholars have drawn attention to the intractable sense of loss and impossibility at the heart of archival research, especially for marginalized subjects.[2] As Heather Love writes, "What happens in the archive is an encounter with historical violence, which includes both physical injury and the violence of obscurity, or annihilation from memory" (49). Stephen Best has labeled this "melancholy historicism" or the idea that "history consists in *taking possession* of such grievous experience and archival loss" (15). Best sees melancholy historicism stemming from over-identification, a condition where scholars are too bound "to the historical subjects about which they write" (17). Though he acknowledges that this approach has been "phenomenally intellectually generative," he urges a turn toward disidentification (17). Others such as Anjali Arondekar have critiqued melancholy historicism for its refusal of "alternative histories of emergence" ("In the Absence" 99). Despite these critiques, the emphasis on affect—especially on the embodied experience of loss—remains an important political stance for archival research, with scholars such as Jenny Sharpe still finding "creative potential in an engagement with archival loss" (9).

In the face of such questions of archival absence, some scholars have turned to digital technologies for both new research methods and new collections design. Interdisciplinary and often collaborative, guided by postcolonial and decolonial, feminist, and critical race theories, digital methods and collections originate in traditional libraries and archives, as well as history, literature, and other humanities departments. Data-driven methods of research via searchable databases were popularized decades ago but have since developed into ways of visualizing and connecting information that may have the potential to reframe the archive itself. In Lauren Klein's formulation, for example, new methods might offer ways of seeing archives not only as "a record of fixity or loss" but also as a "site of action" (141). This move toward action has the potential to resist the political structures that created such archival lacunae and move toward something like archival reparations.

Because each piece of information in a digital archive is both historically situated and potentially connected to all of the other information in the database structure, it may offer new ways to visualize the past, and thus to re-evaluate the centrality of loss to archival theory. Yann Ryan and Sebastian Ahnert's work on network analysis of early modern correspondence sets, for instance, reveals that results were surprisingly robust even when up to 60% of the data set was missing (84). Testing various kinds of loss (single letters, folio books, catalogues, entire years of correspondence), Ryan and Ahnert found that most type of analysis yielded strong results regardless of missing content. Though there are political and aesthetic reasons to center archival loss, this study suggests that absent evidence may not prevent empirical or "correct" results.

Of course, digital methods of archival research and design also raise their own political questions. Digital archives mediate among archivist, user, and artifacts, through use of databases and interfaces. As such, their design and structure are imbricated in the archive's political issues of cultural memory, authority, and institutionalization. Roopika Risam reminds us of the "vexing questions of authority, power, and legitimacy that are evoked in the rhetoric of technological development" that "challenge presumptions about 'good' universal design practices" (12). Open-access initiatives, for instance, stress the importance of making materials publicly available rather than hidden behind a paywall or restricted to those with physical access to a particular library or archive. And the presence of digital materials on the internet has certainly increased the use of once-difficult-to-find documents and, in doing so, increased representation in both scholarship and syllabi.

At the same time, making historically violent materials available may present a form of traumatic encounter and also raise critical issues of agency: beyond simple ownership, who should make decisions about access? Archivist Daniela Agostinho terms this the "archival encounter," seeking

> on the one hand to draw attention to the role of digitization in potentially unearthing the violent encounter of colonialism, and on the other hand to foreground the ethics and responsibility involved in encountering materials that [...] carry persistent power differentials and unresolved political demands that need to be heard.
>
> *(145)*

Changes in collection design have begun the work of responding to these issues. For example, the digital collections platform Mukurtu CMS (mukurtu.org) offers communities ways to control access to their cultural heritage resources, giving users varying levels of access. Initially developed for Indigenous groups in Australia, Mukurtu allows communities to protect valuable or vulnerable items to avoid reinscribing the violent use of information and co-opting of cultural heritage by colonial powers. Metadata is also structured differently to allow for multiple, even conflicting descriptors of a single item in order to tell overlapping stories and return more complex search results.[2] Mukurtu is just one example, of course. Digital methods continue to develop politically informed resources while also recognizing the digital archive's roots in the archive's politically charged silences—and in the places where it speaks.

Speculative Methods

Perhaps the boldest move in archival research methods has been to call into question the very notion of evidence, arguing that it always relies on a system that replicates hegemonic historicisms. Lessening our reliance on a too close "identification of historical subjects with archival objects," as David Squires puts it, opens up the alterity of historical subjects and addresses the recurrent questions of agency and loss so prevalent in methodological debates (598). To do this, many critics have positioned speculation as a necessary corrective to the archive's faulty empiricism, which overrepresents certain lives at the expense of others. Speculative methods differ by scholar and by discipline, but they share a sense of experimenting with the limits of what is knowable—both about the past and as a way to imagine possible presents and futures.[3] Because modern archival preservation in a Euro-American context typically depended upon a value system dictated by white, heteronormative hierarchies and linear concepts of time, imagination has been important for writing with and beyond the limitations of the available record. Saidiya Hartman's "critical fabulation," Michelle Caswell and Anne Gilliland's "imagined records," and Rebecca Olson's "responsible speculation" each offer different frameworks for speculating on archival evidence and its lack (Hartman, "Venus" 11; Caswell and Gilliland 55; Olson 298). Scholars work to resurrect past lives by speculating on missing evidence while still attending to historical credibility. Archivists Caswell and Gilliland argue that when communities can imagine evidence from the past, "it can provide a trajectory to the future" (49).

In this way, speculative methods sometimes share the futurist bent of recovery work, insisting on the importance of past knowledge for present and future equity. But speculation diverges from recovery work in its relationship to evidentiary standards. As David Kazanjian puts it, traditional archival research interprets archival sources in order to "answer the familiar questions of who did what, where, and when en route to forging an empirically grounded answer to the question of why they did what they did" (78). Instead, practitioners of speculative methods seek to tell not just untold stories but to imagine new modes of reading archival documents. They seek to go beyond reading against the grain to rethink the historical record in its entirety. For instance, Kazanjian reads nineteenth-century letters' formal and textual elements to constitute a theory of what can be written and preserved. Hartman seeks to capture interiority, to "inhabit the intimate dimensions" of the lives of young Black girls only recorded as social problems (*Wayward Lives*). Caswell and Gilliland propose that we look to "imagined-but-unavailable records" such as wished-for police bodycam footage as "fertile sources of personal and public affect" that have "political and social ends" (55).

Speculation also drives innovations in collection building, where the theoretical politics of archives and collections meet praxis. This can come from the affordances of digital technologies, as when Ryan Cordell proposes "speculative bibliographies" that would use algorithms to propose potential connections within the extant contents of an archive and "identify meaningful patterns for exploration" (521). Other information scholars draw from scholarship in the humanities to propose new methods entirely. Marisa Duarte and Miranda Belarde-Lewis, for instance, have argued for imagination as an important research methodology in building new kinds of classification systems that integrate Indigenous knowledges. Drawing from the theory and practice of Afrofuturism, librarian Bethany Nowviskie has called for what she terms "speculative collections," or digital collections that "*activate imaginations*—both their users' imaginations and those of the expert practitioners who craft and maintain them" (94). Nowviskie sees speculative collections as open-source, community-built platforms that position archival materials "not as statements about what was, but as toolsets and resources for *what could be*" (96). Archivist Michelle Caswell pulls that "what could be" closer to the present, pointing toward multiple models for maintaining archival records to reflect different knowledge systems (Indigenous, African diasporic, queer). She presses the urgency of archival "traces *in the now* for resistance and activism against oppressive power structures *in the present*" (38). In each case, these information professionals see collection building as a method for building on what is already established through tools and structures that encourage speculation.

That outlook differs from the humanities research on speculation, which often sees speculation as opposed to the empiricism of the archive, often framed as its "limits."[4] This position reflects the view developed during the archival turn that our institutional collections were built with a focus on empiricism that has limited forms of archival evidence ever since. The standard scholarly narrative is that "The belief in the sovereignty of reason and its potential to command nature fueled both the scientific enterprise of the time" and its concomitant forms of collecting. National archives and collections were part of the "right to rule which emerged as imperial in the militaristic and political sense" (Pearce et al xii). Over the course of the nineteenth century, archives became tied to nationhood, disciplinary methods of collecting emerged, and archivists and librarians professionalized.[5] This focus on empiricism and its ties to political modes of control has done valuable work. But it has also reified an idea of institutional collections' empiricism that is, I believe, holding us back from fully embracing speculative modes of archival research. Fearing that speculative methods may be dismissed as fictional—that such work on and against archives is solely imaginative and opposed to the empiricism of "real" archival evidence—misunderstands the intertwined history of novels and archives. Establishing that intertwined origin may, I hope, enable more speculative histories of marginalized subjects.

Writing Histories

The genre of the historical novel was foundational to changes in historiography during the nineteenth century. Taking as its setting a period from the past, the historical novel attempted to capture the social conditions and feeling of a past age through representative characters and realist detail. It shifted historians' investment toward the lives of ordinary people and asked how best to extrapolate from a few representative lives to groups and populations. This literary historical development provides context for nineteenth-century historian Thomas Macaulay's 1828 complaint that "those parts of the duty which properly belong to the historian have been appropriated by the historical novelist" (344). But those changes did not only happen through the craft of individuals novelists; they emerged through mutual entanglements among archives, natural history collections, and the writing of fiction. Together, we can see these forms shaping a new investment in origin and classification for both the historical novel and the archive. Though previous histories of collecting have identified collections' investment in origins and classification, those values have typically been attributed to a scientific interest in preserving a well-established "essential nature of things" (Pearce et al xii). But origin and classification were also perceived as subjective and inherently narrative concepts and practices, essential for telling stories about the past. Put plainly, the archive was never as far from fiction as we have come to believe.

Though it is commonly acknowledged that collecting practices influenced fiction, the opposite has yet to be explored, tending to focus on museum collecting rather than archives.[6] Barbara Foley argues that the historical novel emerged in the nineteenth century partially through "a new view of the historical process shaping the relation of character to event" (143). The novel understood historical events as coming from and inhering in individual lives, what an 1824 review of the "Historical-Novel" described as "the private passions of individuals" as opposed to an older way of thinking in terms of "general causes." This resulted in a new way of framing history: in the historical novel, the "most important general consequences are shown to have arisen from what may be accounted incidents of ordinary life" (446).

Similarly invested in questions of human origin over "general causes," provenance—a foundational principle of archival science—narrates where a document or object came into being and how it found its way into the archive. Specifically, the emergence of the principle of *respect des fonds* in France in 1841 stipulated that documents should be grouped and preserved by their originating entity, such as an individual, governmental organization, or corporation (Duchien 66). Previously, archivists grouped documents by subject (the "general causes" theory of history), but *fonds* hewed more closely to the logic of the historical novel, preserving and classifying documents according to their origins in ordinary life. Now, individual documents could be contextualized as part of their generating body; with the establishment of *fonds*, as archivist Michel Duchien puts it, the archival document "has therefore a *raison d'être* only to the extent that it belongs to a *whole*" (67, italics original). Many archivists criticize the principle of fonds because it can lead archivists to impose misleading order when trying to arrange records "to reflect the administrative structure of their creator and its activities," as Jennifer Douglas puts it (30). The order being created, she argues, is subjective. Yet, the idea that sequence is as much crafted as it is natural is central to the writing of history and has clear roots in the historical novel as much as in the development of specifically archival principles.

Both novels and collections simultaneously asked whether it was possible for an individual to represent a population accurately—what naturalist Richard Owen called the "true idea of the group"—in a question that emerged broadly across history and science (12). Studies of nineteenth-century collecting have emphasized institutional collections' emphasis on classification as a form of empiricism, but it was also a concept worked out through narrative, looking to individual characters and plot lines to explain the complex workings of historical change; this is clearly visible in the concept of "type," identified by Georg Lukács as a defining feature of the nineteenth-century historical novel. Lukács's sense of type differs from stock or flat characters; he sees type as the "synthesis between individual and the general so that the whole of humanity is somehow depicted through an individual character" (6). For Lukács, type is a way to accurately record historical change at a population level, condensed into the struggle of an individual.

Well before Lukács, Victorian reviewers were also thinking of classification as narrative. *The Saturday Review*, for instance, praised Charles Dickens for his ability to abstract from an eccentric individual to type. Riffing off the minor character Mr. Guppy from *Bleak House*, the reviewer writes that "If there is one Guppy, there must be many thousands previously undreamed of by social science" ("Fresh Types" 615). The implication is that to create a credible character, the novel draws on thousands of other examples that lie outside the text, which is a realist technique that both influenced and was influenced by the burgeoning classification systems of social science, natural history, archives, libraries, and museums. Here, the reviewer puns on the character's last name, Guppy, to make that connection even more explicit: Dickens

> dredged the lowest deeps, occasionally brought up a fish, not merely queer, but probably typical, a fair example of the hordes that range in silent and sunless abysses. More frequently his spoils, though undeniably odd, had the air of being unique and portentous creatures like those which are preserved in bottles on the shelves of museums.
>
> *("Fresh Types" 615)*

Through the function of character, the single specimen is preserved to tell a story, not only to illustrate a static concept.

That shift is reflected in the emerging professional standards in archives, as well. As the establishment of *fonds* made context important, archivists began redefining the process for describing collection content and, in this process, leaned toward the identification of type over individual descriptions. The foundational *Manual for the Arrangement and Description of Archives* (aka "the Dutch Manual") called for naming the collection's "dominant idea" rather than describing documents or clusters (Muller et al 101).[7] "The most detailed description of the contents of the documents," the Dutch Manual instructs, "cannot possibly give as clear a notion of their contents as a short description by a person who has grasped this dominant idea" (101). In addition, archivists Wendy Duff and Verne Harris point out that this description is inherently narrative: "description is always story telling – intertwining facts with narratives, observation with interpretation" (276). We can see the roots of that relationship in the Dutch Manual's comment that "it is not more possible to confine a whole inventory in the rigid form of a table than to give it the form of poetry" (106). Pointedly, the Dutch Manual wants us to understand that archival description has a genre and that genre is prose. Only through prose can an archivist express "the natural sequence of events" that led to the formation of the collection; to express it in other forms would warp that sequence (107). Explicating classification thus meant borrowing from the novelist's craft as much as the scientist's.

These examples are necessarily limited in scope, but I hope they may point the way toward more extensive research. Reconnecting archives to fiction and de-ossifying their relationship to the power-laden, history-haunted, putatively empirical fact potentially opens up new avenues for ameliorating the political problem of evidence. The archive's historical power structure remains intact, but its attachments to forms of evidence that perpetuate that power structure may still be open to change. And with them, we might further fuel the scholarship and collection development work already underway that seeks to represent marginalized lives, past, present, and future.

Notes

1. For a foundational example, see Cvetkovich.
2. For more on the principle's behind Mukurtu's collecting and access practices, see Christen and Anderson.
3. Speculative archival methods span disciplines, and can be theoretical, creative, and critical. In addition to the scholarly pieces cited in this chapter, art and creative nonfiction have also developed speculative methods. See, for example, Jenn Shapland's *My Autobiography of Carson McCullers* or "We Will Live to See These Things, or, Five Pictures of What May Come to Pass," by Julia Meltzer and David Thorne, who worked together under the name The Speculative Archive.
4. See, for instance, Hartman, *Wayward Lives* xiii. Burton opposes narrative to the false empiricism of the archive in *Archive Stories*. For a different reading on the idea of limits, see Arondekar, *For the Record*.
5. See Richards for an example of the relationship between archives and imperial control. See Eastwood for the history of archivists' professionalization.
6. See, for example, Black and McIsaac.
7. The Dutch Manual wasn't published until 1898, but archivists generally agree that it was, at that point, mostly solidifying archival practices that had emerged over the course of the nineteenth century, not inventing them. See Horsman et al.

Works Cited

Agostinho, Daniela. "Archival Encounters: Rethinking Access and Care in Digital Colonial Archives." *Archival Science* 19, 2019, pp. 141-65.
Arondekar, Anjali. For the Record: *On Sexuality and the Colonial Archive in India*, Duke University Press, 2009.
———. "In the Absence of Reliable Ghosts: Sexuality, Historiography, South Asia." *differences: A Journal of Feminist Cultural Studies*, vol. 25, no. 3, 2015, pp. 98-122.
Best, Stephen. *None Like Us: Blackness, Belonging, Aesthetic Life*. Duke UP, 2018.
Black, Barbara. On Exhibit: Victorians and their Museums, U of Virginia P, 2000.
Burton, Antoinette. "Introduction: Archiver Fever, Archive Stories." *Archive Stories: Facts, Fiction, and the Writing of History*, edited by Antoinette Burton, Duke UP, 2005, pp. 1 – 24,
Carter, Rodney. "Of Things Said and Unsaid: Power, Archival Silences, and the Power in Silence." *Archivaria* 61, 2006, pp. 215-33.
Caswell, Michelle and Anne Gilliland. "Records and Their Imaginaries: Imagining the Impossible, Making Possible the Imagined." *Archival Science*, vol. 16, no. 1, 2016, pp. 53-75.
Caswell, Michelle. *Urgent Archives: Enacting Liberatory Memory Work*. Routledge, 2021.
Christen, Kim and Jane Anderson. "Toward Slow Archives." *Archival Science* 19, 2019, pp. 87-116.
Cordell, Ryan. "Speculative Bibliography." *Anglia*, vol. 138, no. 3, 2020, pp. 519-31.
Cvetkovich, Ann. *An Archive of Feelings: Trauma, Sexuality, and Lesbian Public Cultures*. Duke UP, 2003.
Derrida, Jacques. *Archive Fever: A Freudian Impression*. Translated by Eric Prenowitz, U of Chicago Press, 1996.
Douglas, Jennifer. "Origins and Beyond: The Ongoing Evolution of Archival Ideas about Provenance." *Currents of Archival Thinking*, edited by Heather MacNeil and Terry Eastwood, Libraries Limited, 2017, pp. 25-52.
Duarte, Marisa Elena and Miranda Belarde-Lewis. "Imaging: Creating Spaces for Indigenous Ontologies." *Cataloging and Classification Quarterly* 53, 2015, pp. 677-702.
Duchien, Michel. "Theoretical Principles and Practical Problems of *Respect des fonds* in Archival Science." *Archivaria* 16, 1983, pp. 64-82.

Duff, Wendy M. and Verne Harris. "Stories and Names: Archival Description as Narrating Records and Constructing Meanings," *Archival Science* 2, 2002, pp. 263-85.

Eastwood, Terry. "A Contested Realm: The Nature of Archives and the Orientation of Archival Science." *Currents of Archival Thinking*, edited by Heather MacNeil and Terry Eastwood, Libraries Unlimited, 2017, pp. 3 – 24.

Eichhorn, Kate. *The Archival Turn in Feminism: Outrage in Order.* Temple UP, 2013.

Foley, Barbara. *Telling the Truth: The Theory and Practice of Documentary Fiction.* Cornell UP, 1986.

"Fresh Types of Character" *Saturday Review of Politics, Literature, Science, and Art*, Vol. 45, no. 1117, 18 May 1878, pp. 615-6.

Fuentes, Marisa. *Dispossessed Lives: Enslaved Women, Violence, and the Archive.* U of Penn Press, 2016.

Gilmore, Dehn. *The Victorian Novel and the Space of Art: Fictional Form on Display.* Cambridge UP, 2013.

Hartman, Saidiya V. *Wayward Lives, Beautiful Experiments: Intimate Histories of Social Upheaval.* W. W. Norton, 2019.

———. "Venus in Two Acts." *Small Axe* 26, 2008, pp. 1 – 14.

Helton, Laura, Justin Leroy, Max A. Mishler, Samantha Seeley, and Shauna Sweeney. "The Question of Recovery: An Introduction." *Social Text*, vol. 33, no. 4, 2015, pp. 1 – 18.

"Historical-Novel Writing." *Edinburgh Magazine and Literary Miscellany*, Vol. 14, April 1824, pp. 446-9.

Horsman, Peter, Eric Ketelaar, and Theo Thomassen. "New Respect for the Old Order: The Context of the Dutch Manual." *The American Archivist*, vol. 66, no. 2, 2003, pp. 249-70.

Kazanjian, David. "Scenes of Speculation." *Social Text*, vol. 33, no. 4, 2015, pp. 77-84.

Klein, Lauren. *An Archive of Taste: Race and Eating in the Early United States.* U of Minnesota P, 2020.

Kunzel, Regina. "Queering Archives: A Roundtable Discussion." *Radical History Review* 122, 2015, pp. 211-31.

Love, Heather. Feeling Backward: Loss and the Politics of Queer History. Harvard UP, 2007.

Lukács, György. *Studies in European Realism.* Translated by Edith Bone, Grosset and Dunlap, 1964.

Macaulay, Thomas Babington. "Hallam." *Edinburgh Review*, September 1828. Rpt. in *Critical, Historical, and Miscellaneous Essays*, vol. 1, Sheldon and Company, 1860, pp. 433-543.

McIsaac, Peter. *Museums of the Mind: German Modernity and the Dynamics of Collecting.* Penn State UP, 2007.

Menon, Madhvi. *Unhistorical Shakespeare: Queer Theory in Shakespearean Literature and Film*, Palgrave Macmillan, 2008.

Muller, S, J.A. Feith, and R. Fruin. *Manual for the Arrangement and Description of Archives*, translated by Arthur H. Leavitt, 1898, Society of American Archivists, 2003.

Nowviskie, Bethany. "Speculative Collections and the Emancipatory Library." *The Routledge International Handbook of New Digital Practices in Galleries, Libraries, Archives, Museums, and Heritage Sites*, edited by Hannah Lewi, Wally Smith, Dirk von Lehm, and Steven Cook, Routledge, 2020.

Olson, Rebecca. "The Continuing Adventures of *Blanchardyn and Eglantine*: Responsible Speculation about Early Fan Fiction." *PMLA*, vol. 134, no. 2, 2019, pp. 298-314.

Owen, Richard. *Of a National Museum of Natural History.* Saunders, Otley, & Co., 1862.

Pearce, Susan et al, "Introduction," *The Collector's Voice: Critical readings in the Practice of Collecting*, edited by Susan Pearce, Alexandra Bounia, and Paul Martin, vol. 2, Ashgate, 2000, xii – xxiv.

Risam, Roopika. *New Digital Worlds: Postcolonial Digital Humanities in Theory, Praxis, and Pedagogy.* Northwestern UP, 2018.

Richards, Thomas. *The Imperial Archive: Knowledge and the Fantasy of Empire.* Verso, 1993.

Ryan, Yann C. and Sebastian E. Ahnert. "The Measure of the Robustness of Correspondence Network Analysis in Early Modern Correspondence." *Cultural Analytics*, vol. 6, no. 3, 20221, 57-88.

Schomberg, Arthur. "The Negro Digs Up His Past." *The New Negro: Readings on Race, Representation, and African American Culture, 1892-1938*, edited by Henry Louis Gates, Jr., and Gene Andrew Jarrett, Princeton UP, 2007, pp. 326-9.

Shapland, Jenn. *The Autobiography of Carson McCullers*, Tin House, 2020.

Sharpe, Jenny. *Immaterial Archives: An African Diaspora Poetics of Loss.* Northwestern UP, 2020.

The Speculative Archive (Meltzer, Julia and David Thorne). "We Will Live to See These Things, or, Five Pictures of What May Come to Pass," 2007, Jack H. Skirball Screening Series, Los Angeles.

Squires, David. "Roger Casement's Queer Archive." *PMLA*, vol. 132, no. 3, 2017, pp. 596-612.

Stoler, Ann Laura. "Colonial Archives and the Arts of Governance." *Archival Science*, vol. 2, no. 1, 2002, pp. 87-109.

Stoler, Ann Laura, *Along the Archival Grain: Epistemic Anxieties and Colonial Common Sense*. Princeton UP, 2008.

Traub, Valerie. *Thinking Sex with the Early Moderns*. U of Penn P, 2016.

32
HOMES
Natalie Pollard

Ecopoetry from Greenland to the Marshall Islands

Since at least the late 1990s and early 2000s, the social sciences and humanities have witnessed a shift away from notions of home as a largely place-bound, static or permanent form. Home is no longer assumed to be nominally synonymous with house, homeland, or nation (Pugh 1040). Instead, it is often approached relationally: as a mobile, interconnected construct that is ever in flux (Bourriaud; Dépelteau). As Nadje Al-Ali and Khalid Koser write, "home" is perpetually created through "dynamic processes, involving the acts of imagining, creating, unmaking, changing, losing and moving 'homes'" (6). Although this emphasis on the relationality of home is customarily applied to human practices, it has continued to stimulate fruitful lines of investigation across disciplines, for example in unsettling binaries such as home-away, origin-exile, lost-new, and mainland-island (Ahmed; Biagini and Hoyle; Chandler and Pugh). Insofar as this chapter considers home as constituted through *ongoing and adaptive processes* (which I call acts of "homing"), I also read home relationally. However, "homing" specifically emphasises the interplay of diverse nonhuman participants ("actants") that modify one another and humans across time.[1] In this respect, it identifies more closely with contemporary literary and new materialist practices, which challenge the notion that humans are the sole or most significant planetary agents. As Timothy Morton argues in *Ecology without Nature*, part of that challenge lies in becoming "fully aware of how human beings are connected with other beings – animal, vegetable, or mineral," and—as we will see—it also involves alertness to the long-standing constitutive force of earth processes in homing (7).

This chapter focuses on global literary narratives that investigate twenty-first-century understandings of home in the light of anthropogenic climate change and ecosystemic disruption. It traces links between new materialist thinking and activist poetry that challenges humanist understandings of a planetary home (Bennett; Chen; Zylinska). Foregrounding the constitutive role of nonhuman processes in earth systems functioning, it shows how such scholarly and literary works attend to the deep time of geological processes, which predate and will outlast humans for near-unimaginable duration. Grappling with the sheer scale of the problem leaves most ordinary (and indeed many scholarly) readers struggling to conceptualise extreme temporal dispersion and far future anthropogenic effects: consider the fact that plutonium-239 (one of the main radioactive isotopes produced in nuclear reactions) has a half-life of 24,000 years, or the estimate that it will take 400,000 years for atmospheric CO_2

to return to pre-industrial levels. As Claire Colebrook observes, climate change "take[s] our environmental imagination beyond homely conceptions of the Earth" (190). This unhomely, even "uncanny," planetary timescale cannot be easily integrated into human temporal grasp. Drawing on Colebrook's questioning of "the notion that the earth is our place," this chapter investigates how contemporary activist literature punctures anthropocentric thinking, which Colebrook emphasises is "precisely what has blinded us to the ravages of our mode of life" and to the accelerating havoc this mode wreaks (190).

In an attempt at "unblinding," I consider a poetic collaboration authored by two environmental activists: Aka Niviâna from Kalaallit Nunaat (Greenland) and Kathy Jetñil-Kijiner from the Republic of the Marshall Islands. Their 2018 video poem *Rise: From One Island to Another* adopts site-specific methodologies which are attentive to homing in the context of anthropogenic ecological crisis, and which push at the limits of human-centred thinking (the entirety of *Rise* can be viewed by following the link in the endnote).[2] Jetñil-Kijiner and Niviâna's work offers an accessible and influential re-temporalising of environmental and political thinking, engaging audiences with deep time, exploring how soft power can influence policy on ecological and climate change, and challenging the humanist dimensions of earlier environmentalist practices. Re-configuring earlier colonial, national, and environmentalist models of understanding home, their poem highlights the impacts of climatic change and biospheric damage on the earth, on heterogeneous ways of living, and on interconnected local and global environments. *Rise* specifically focuses on ice cap melt, sea level rise, nuclear contamination, and ocean acidification. Rather than a stable location of human residence, the poem figures home as a collaborative process—the active relationality of which I emphasise with the verbal noun "homing"—and emphasises the worldmaking agencies of nonhuman co-inhabitants.

Rise was commissioned and disseminated by 350.org, an environmental activist organisation co-founded by Bill McKibben, and was featured as part of the global campaign "Rise for Climate." Jetñil-Kijiner and Niviâna were invited to accompany McKibben and glaciologist Jason Box to a melting glacier at the south of Greenland's ice sheet, where they would perform and record their video poem. McKibben's commission sought to harness poetry to communicate the social and environmental impacts of climate change to a global audience. Specifically, he wanted to illustrate the trans-hemispherical connections between Arctic melt and rising sea levels on low-lying Micronesian islands, and to emphasise a causal link with the long, cumulative effects of industrial capitalism. In the early sections of *Rise*, Jetñil-Kijiner and Niviâna take turns speaking, carefully locating their voices:

> I'm coming to you
> from the land my ancestors chose.
> Aelōn̄ Kein Ad,
> Marshall Islands,
> a country more sea than land.
>
> I welcome you to Kalaallit Nunaat,
> Greenland,
> the biggest island on earth.

Directed by filmmaker and photojournalist Dan Lin, the video poem intersperses images of Jetñil-Kijiner as a lone human form wading into water off the shores of Majuro—the capital of the Marshall Islands—with footage of Niviâna and Jetñil-Kijiner reciting their poem while standing back-to-back high up on Greenland's diminishing "Eagle Glacier." As "[o]ne poet watches her heritage turn to water; the other watches that same water sweep up the beaches of her country and into the houses of her friends. The destruction of one's homeland is the inevitable destruction of the other's," McKibben explains in the Guardian. Among his key aims was to share with the global community images of "Kathy Jetñil-Kijiner literally stand[ing] with two feet planted on the ice that will submerge her country," because he "wanted to have that image for the world of someone standing on top of the water that would drown their home when it melted" (McKibben 2018) (Figures 32.1 and 32.2).

On the one hand, these depictions of sea inundation and ice melt play into long-standing anthropocentric and colonial tropes of the vulnerability of "isolated" and "remote" island homes, and of islanders as disappearing frontline communities (Hayward 2012; Farbotko and Lazrus 2012; Chakrabarty 2012). The film's visual field portrays human protagonists dwarfed by immense aquascapes: ice sheet, glacial meltwaters, rising oceans. One might suggest these images help put *homo sapiens* in its place by de-accentuating its power and—like many forebears of literary Naturalism—emphasising the comparatively miniscule scale of the human species. Yet such well-intentioned footage also participates in a scopic regime that closely resembles what Elizabeth DeLoughrey has termed "salvage environmentalism," in which a fetishised Western focus on the so-called "ruins" of Indigenous culture in the Pacific

Figures 32.1 and 32.2 Video stills from *Rise*

Source: Kathy Jetñil-Kijiner and Aka Niviâna, *Rise: From One Island to Another* (2018), https://350.org/rise-from-one-island-to-another/#watch

"decouple[s] the Pacific Islander from modernity and suppress[es] the causal links between industrialized continents and sinking islands" (*Allegories* 32).[3]

On the other hand, contra this narrative, Jetñil-Kijiner's and Niviâna's spoken word performance critiques the very eco-colonial and humanist regime in which they participate, and which structures global climate change agendas such as 350.org. *Rise* might be thought of as what Anna Tsing calls a "contingent collaboration," in which local actions, storytellings, and inscriptions of knowledge are circumscribed by wider circuits of power that reach into and structure their expression (89). *Rise* is circumscribed by the power relations expressed by the invested constituencies that make its production and distribution possible, so that Jetñil-Kijiner's and Niviâna's critique issues from within the predicament they depict. Theirs is not an idealised view from nowhere. In their own words, the poem acts as

> [...] a reminder
> that life in all forms demands
> the same respect we all give to money
> that these issues affect each and every one of us
> None of us is immune

Speaking as part of this inclusive "we," *Rise* does not portray people and places as innocently removed from neoliberal functioning or from the effects of the global marketplace. As Jetñil-Kijiner and Niviâna unearth (indeed re-earth) ancient stories, their allusive poetic dialogue points to the ways in which modern Micronesian and Inuit understandings of planetary home have long been forced to negotiate global networks of exchange and land relations, which structure local agendas relating to security, sovereignty, and stewardship. One historical example is the utilisation of Greenland's ice sheet for the advancement of US "strategic defence" interests during the Cold War, which notably included Project Iceworm: a top-secret military programme that sought to house up to 600 ballistic nuclear missiles beneath Greenland's inland ice, where they would be close enough for the US to retaliate against key military and civilian targets in the Soviet Union in the event of nuclear war.[4]

Today's accelerated rate of melt threatens to expose the toxic legacy of this "nuclear waste/dumped/in our waters/on our ice" (*Rise*). Meanwhile, economic opportunities are also being uncovered by the thaw: new shipping routes and access to valuable oil, gas, and rare earth metals. Geology in this context is equally an academic discipline and a political tool for advancing the interests of Arctic-neighbouring states—amongst them the US, Norway, Iceland, Sweden, Russia, and Canada—by expanding their maritime borders.[5] Reading and viewing *Rise* raises questions about who will participate in opening Greenland's resource frontiers, and whether any "fair distribution" of the expected gains from these extractive is even possible given the apocalyptic conclusion to this rising action. Indeed, the idea of "fairly distributing" profits exemplifies a fatally narrow logic that itself must be radically reimagined.[6]

Comparably, when Jetñil-Kijiner talks of "bulldozed reefs, blasted sands" and "forcing land/from an ancient, rising sea," the poem points to the fundamental alteration of the Marshall Islands' atoll sediment regime by postwar modernisation and US military-scientific experimentation. These lines also draw attention to current reef-damaging climate "mitigation" plans to dredge Majuro lagoon in order to build elevated islands that can withstand rising sea levels—a process that would require assistance from partner nations including the US, Taiwan, and Japan in consultation with local governments, chiefs, and clan heads (Letman). "Dredging and reclaiming land, there's nothing new about that," climate scientist Chip Fletcher observed at a 2018 climate change conference held on the Marshall Islands: "it's environmentally damaging [...] [but] I would rather destroy some reef than see an entire culture go extinct" (ibid).

Responding to these extractive and anthropocentric earth logics—which do not and cannot acknowledge nonhuman acts of worldmaking such as those performed by coral cultures—Jetñil-Kijiner's and Niviâna's stories re-emphasise the powerful agencies of stone, reef, ice, and ocean in earthly homing. In so doing, the two poets exchange words and more: each presents the other with a foundational offering of stone and shell "from the land of my ancestors" and "from one island to another." Jetñil-Kijiner begins:

> Sister of ice and snow
> I'm coming to you
> from the land of my ancestors,
> from atolls, sunken volcanoes–undersea descent
> of sleeping giants
> [...]
> I bring with me these shells
> that I picked from the shores
> of Bikini atoll and Runit Dome
> [...]
> With these shells I bring a story of long ago

Niviâna responds:

> Sister of ocean and sand,
> I welcome you
> to the land of my ancestors
> [...]
> I hold these stones picked from the shores of Nuuk,
> the foundation of the land I call my home.
> [...]
> With these rocks I bring
> a story told countless times

These exchanges emphasise the participation of nonhuman agencies in forming "the land I call my home." Niviâna and Jetñil-Kijiner show how home is created in the present by phenomena whose manifestations are part of multimillion-year processes: the birth and demise of volcanoes, the (de)formation of ice sheets dating from the Pleistocene Period (from circa. 2.6 million to 11,700 years ago), the formation of circular atoll islands, the breakup of ancient decaying reef into coral rock by wind and water, and the production of crystalline rocks of the Precambrian Shield. This attention to zones of worldbuilding activity emphasises the striated ecohistorical frameworks of the late Holocene, which are entangled with the verbal exchange of story and myth: "With these rocks I bring/a story" and "Let me bring my home to yours" (*Rise*). Jetñil-Kijiner and Niviâna's gifts of stone as story—narrative as matter and vice versa—point to what Susan Naramore Maher calls "multiple histories of place, those cross-sectional stories of natural and human history as traced through eons and generations" (10).

To some extent, this poetic attention to nonhuman homing is reminiscent of geological accounts that read sedimentation as a living archive, in which the earth's strata are seen to possess stories accrued in them over time. "The mountains and fjords of Greenland preserve a record of nearly four billion years of Earth history," explains geologist Niels Henriksen: "a story of mountain building, volcanic eruptions, primitive life and ice ages." Metaphors of stone as story are key in Henriksen's account of Greenland's geology; he sees its mountains and its belts of metamorphosed sedimentary and igneous rock as ideal for geological studies rendered as literary studies "because the rocks, the structures that deform them and the details of the development of the rock complexes with time can be read like an open book."

However, geology is not neutral within the politics of colonisation. Its mapping and survey tools have played a significant role in identifying which lands are profitable for Western utilisation and occupation, especially through natural resource extraction. Kathryn Yusoff has articulated how extractive geologic processes and knowledge modes have sustained colonisation around the world, such as in economic evaluation of the "mineral kingdom," which disrupted Indigenous lifeways and knowledge systems in Minnesota (11–13). In Greenland, since the 1970s, targeted geophysical surveying studies were conducted to stimulate mineral exploration activities. These surveys contributed to the overall mapping of the country's geology as part of a collaboration between the Greenland Government and GEUS (the Geological Survey of Denmark and Greenland, located in the Danish Ministry of Climate, Energy and Utilities). Via the Mineral Resources Portal, exploration companies, scientists, and other interested parties can gain full access to data, reports, maps, and scientific background information about Greenland's geology. To read these recent lithic "stories" is to engage with histories of striated transnational power relations: the "open book" of stone reveals sedimented colonial violence and competing global interests.

Manuel De Landa has argued that attention to nonhuman forms of storytelling can stimulate less geologically and ecologically violent perspectives: "To view human history as unfolding immersed in this cauldron of nonorganic life is one way to eliminate notions of progress or unilineal development" (265). For De Landa, vast planetary flows (continental shift, lava, glacier flows) intersect with human meaning and action (history, poetry, story) in ways that undermine narratives that perpetuate the hegemonic dominance of *Anthropos*. And indeed, "stone is a catalyst for relation" rather than just inert matter to be used (Cohen 33). But if, as Jeffrey Jerome Cohen argues here, stone's powerful "techtonicity" is a medium "through which story [...] emerges," it is geologists who are trained to read these nonhuman stories of homing (33).

The performance of *Rise* issues a wider invitation. The poem urges non-scientific audiences to grasp stone's dynamic but immensely slow movement: to "read" its "fluidity." While "fluid stone" may seem oxymoronic, the video poem makes palpable the lithic vitality that produced Greenland and the Marshall Islands as they are known to date. Robert Frost may famously think of stone as only contingently dynamic when "frozen-ground-swell [...] spills the upper boulders" of a wall. In longer time frames, however, stone exists in constant metamorphoses, as erosion into sand and clay, and as lava and ash in volcanoes: "stone is fluid when viewed within its proper duration [...] of erosion and petrogenesis" (Cohen 34). Paleobiologist Jan Zalasiewicz has identified "the continually moving lithosphere" as a "sea of stone" which the continents are "carried atop" (*The Earth After Us* 48). His 2010 book observes how:

> a normal pebble's history carries us into abyssal depths of time; events in the Earth's ancient past: volcanic eruptions; the lives and deaths of extinct animals and plants; long-vanished oceans; and transformations deep underground [...] geologists reach deep into the Earth's past by forensic analysis of even the tiniest amounts of mineral matter. Many stories are crammed into each and every pebble around us.
>
> (*The Planet in a Pebble* i)

When Niviâna "offer[s] you these rocks, the foundation of my home," the act acknowledges her co-presence within the "storytelling" of land formation, alteration, and decomposition. The heterogeneous actants that comprise "my home" emerge through these invocations of "land of my ancestors" and the "story told countless times," as we criss-cross lithic and mythic, tectonic and ecological agencies. Homing is performed by ice, rock, coral, shell, and narrative: these are not its mere by-products. *Rise* thus points to how entities—such as glacier, bedrock, ocean, and reef—do things and shape the behaviour of humans and others in numberless ways. As such, the poem resists reducing the world's entities to vehicles of human intention. Stone and ice are not a blank slate for human stories and knowledge processes. *Rise* demands audiences read "the foundation of home" as constituted through a complex interplay of mobile earthly actants across near-unthinkable temporal scale:

> Sister of ocean and sand,
> I offer you these rocks, the foundation of my home.
> On our journey
> may the same unshakable foundation
> connect us,
> make us stronger [...]

However, as Niviâna utters these lines, the diminishing presence of the ice cap from which she speaks unsettles the poetic assertion of strength and "unshakable" foundation. It is a material reminder of the scale of geological harm. Although the glacier is not referred to directly in the spoken text, its presence and agency inform these utterances. It is the ground under the poets' feet as they speak. Its melting endurance acts both as a metaphor for ecosystemic change beyond human scale and as a real-world, precarious meeting place for these humans. The glacier is neither remote or unreachable, nor a symbol of the sublime otherness of the "natural" world. The changing Arctic ice sheet offers a material register of tangled anthropogenic and nonhuman agencies. This gigantic act of slow dissolution visually attunes audiences to the haunting forms and processes that unfold at divergent tempos, as the poets tap into ancient and modern stories of human-elemental activity and global interconnectivity.

With the shells Jetñil-Kijiner brings to Greenland from the Marshall Islands, we are offered further stories of lithic transformation:

> With these shells I bring a story of long ago
> two sisters frozen in time on the island of Ujae,
> one magically turned into stone
> the other who chose that life
> to be rooted by her sister's side.
> To this day, the two sisters
> can be seen by the edge of the reef,
> a lesson in permanence.

The story of the shells unsettles distinctions between stasis and animation, life and death, rootedness and fluidity, as well as deep temporal development and sudden transformation. Permanence here is not stillness, but almost unthinkably slow, unfolding motion. The human sisters whose lives are "turned into stone" are made to stand for an active principle: an ongoing story, ever being adapted, translated, retold as a changing "lesson" across time, language, and "vital material formations" (Bennett 5).

Vital materiality and hybridity are written into the bedrock of the Marshall Islands, which comprise over a thousand volcanic islands and islets. Twenty-nine of these are atolls (distinctive ring-shaped landforms enclosing a central lagoon). They were created from geologic processes working in tandem with living creatures over vast amounts of time. Although this is a story of land formation that begins abiotically—from the eruption of underwater volcanoes—its later protagonists are corals, which built a circular reef around each island, comprised of deposits of billions of their hard limestone exoskeletons (cemented through the living and dying of calcerous algae, oysters, echinoderms, and more). Studies of Marshall Island atolls estimate that their volcanic phases of development date as far back as 140–68 million years, with evidence of later reef formation and erosion during the mid-Holocene. These lithic formation narratives are plural and multispecies.

As Jetñil-Kijiner narrates her connection to reef, shell, and stone, lithic animation takes on human resonances:

> I offer you this shell
> and the story of the two sisters
> as testament
> as declaration
> that despite everything
> we will not leave.
> Instead
> we will choose stone.
> We will choose
> to be rooted in this reef
> forever.

Jaimey Hamilton Faris has observed that "the sisters become the stone of the island, and in so becoming, they cannot be washed away from it. They *are* aspects of the island" (83). But the affiliation with the island is also a recognition of cross-ontological alliance. The poets' "lesson in permanence" is also an illocutionary act: it brings into existence the state of affairs to which it refers. "We will not leave" is a "testament" and "declaration," as the pairs of sisters (mythic and contemporary) are connected through acknowledgement of becoming-island: "we will choose/to be rooted in this reef/forever." This is not as final a transformation as it seems. The poem acknowledges its human kinship with mutably permanent matter, chiefly with the ecology of reef development. The "sisters" become bonded with forms of ongoing vitality, both as the coral sustaining the reef and lithic alliance (with the limestone deposit that supports new coral reef growth).

"Corals are live buildings" write Carlos Jiménez and Covadonga Orejas:

> When living in the reef, their carbonate skeletons offer three-dimensional frameworks enabling coral polyps to emerge from the sea bottom and populate huge areas of the ocean. Even after death, the coral skeletons play an important ecological role as they can host assemblages of disparate species within their calcareous remains.
>
> (Jetñil)

The deep lagoons of Marshall Island atolls are unique as they provide huge areas of sheltered habitat conducive to coral growth and diverse communities of reef organisms.

In this sense, *Rise* figures its poets as reef, declaring their kinship with the animate island bedrock itself. In making such "kin"—to use Donna Haraway's "assembling sort of word" (164)—the poem envisages homing as assembling with reef. Poetic speech is assembled with the growth and decompositional cycles of coral, its atoll-forming, slow geologic accrual into the Marshall Islands, and its provision of homes ("live buildings") to diverse marine creatures. To "choose stone" is not to become inert matter, but to continue becoming part of reef-assemblage "forever": to offer a testament to the non/human inheritance of the myriad and ongoing animacies of the aquatic and lithic, living and non-living. The poem points to the shared investments (kinship/allyship) of trans-agential homing across deep time.

These alliances become palpable not least because the poets argue against the perspective that only human intentionality and activity counts. The illocutionary acts of *Rise* challenge the exceptionalism of the affluent global north that cannot

> […] see beyond
> SUV's, ac's, their pre-packaged convenience
> their oil-slicked dreams, beyond the belief
> that tomorrow will never happen, that this
> is merely an inconvenient truth.

The poets show and tell the forms and figures of ecosystemic change occasioned by explosive economic growth and the technological innovations that act as engines of accelerated earth-systemic alteration: "Can you see our glaciers groaning/with the weight of the world's heat?" If so, they continue, then "Let me show you the tide/that comes for us faster/than we'd like to admit." However, *Rise* also raises the question of how it is possible publicly to communicate these changes, when, as Curt Stager puts it, "a long view is not necessarily welcome to those who are preoccupied with events in the here and now" (2). Precisely because the immediate future of a consumerist lifestyle of "pre-packaged convenience" does not look rosy, widespread disavowal and denial is endemic: "tomorrow will never happen," "this/is merely an inconvenient truth." With its canny reference to former US Vice President Al Gore's 2006 documentary about climate change, the poem insists that even liberal Western environmental reform advocates remain fundamentally in "oil-slicked dreams" where consciousness slumbers on, eyes averted from the waking recognition that change is "coming for our homes/our lives." If even the dawn's changes will not be looked at, it is beyond difficult to make perceptible the "sustained influence of our actions today on the immensely distant future" (Stager 11–12).

"Resilience is currently propounded by neoliberal agencies and institutions, especially, as the fundamental property that people and individuals worldwide must possess in order to […] make the 'right choices' in development of sustainable responses to [environmental] threats and dangers" (Chandler and Reid 251). *Rise* resists environmentalist and ecopoetic impulses that seek to mitigate and manage anthropogenic biospheric alteration. Such practices have been criticised as an extension of humanist fantasies of problem fixing through intervention and governance, which sustain Western ethnocentrism. These approaches are often reliant, Chandler and Reid remind us, on neoliberal discourses that focus on "how individuals and communities can overcome vulnerabilities and learn to process information to become self-aware and to govern themselves more reflexively" (*Neoliberal Subject* 123). As DeLoughrey observes, these power discourses have helped to decouple island subjects and spaces from the history of modernity in order to justify their exploitation as "ahistorical" places ripe for Western socio-biological experimentation, nuclear colonialism, and extraction as "resource frontiers" (*Allegories* 190). Such aspirations have been aided through the discourses of development, local autonomy, conservation, and mitigation that enable rationalisation of the ecosystemic and human costs of extraction, experimentation, and resettlement.

Jetñil-Kijiner's and Niviâna's poem distances itself from ideals of sustainability and resilience. It gestures to how international speculators were attracted to the promises of underexploited resource frontiers in "remote" regions, such as Arctic gas, oil and rare earth reserves, or the utilisation of the Pacific Proving Grounds for military nuclear experimentation and bio-surveillance. Both Greenland and the Marshall Islands are in this sense interstitial zones:

shaped through processes of global appropriation that are tied into a capitalist history of slow violence that gives rise to biospheric crisis through radically disrupting longstanding activities of earthly homing.

> Can you see our glaciers groaning
> with the weight of the world's heat?
> I wait for you, here,
> on the land of my ancestors heart heavy with a thirst
> for solutions
> as I watch this land
> change
> while the World remains silent.
>
> Let me show you the tide
> that comes for us faster
> than we'd like to admit.
> Let me show you
> airports underwater
> bulldozed reefs, blasted sands
> and plans to build new atolls
> forcing land
> from an ancient, rising sea,
> forcing us to imagine
> turning ourselves to stone.
>
> Let me bring my home to yours.
> Let's watch as Miami, New York,
> Shanghai, Amsterdam, London,
> Rio de Janeiro, and Osaka
> try to breathe underwater.
> You think you have decades
> before your homes fall beneath tides?
>
> <div align="right">(<i>Rise</i>)</div>

To think with Morton, one might assert that a contemporary ecological poetry—capable of stimulating acknowledgement of the diverse actants engaged in planetary homing—would "transcend the elegiac mode" of environmental loss and nostalgia. Rather, such art would direct attention to the structural inequalities in twenty-first-century economic systems, sustained by geopolitical coordination, and their increasingly devastating effects. As such, *Rise* engages audiences with the repercussions of the intensified extractivist and expansionist strategies of global capitalism and with the new techno-scientific innovations that accompany (and that claim to futureproof) them.

Climatic and ecosystemic change is "spatially unbounded. It is everywhere and nowhere, hence not easily accessible to imaginations rooted in specific places" writes Sheila Jasanoff (237). For this reason, such changes are often visualised for Western audiences in terms of catastrophic sea-level rise, in which threatened low-lying islands stand metonymically for an imperilled earth. But "[r]epresenting climate change is challenging because it is a process that can be measured only by turning to deep geological time beyond the human and because like nuclear radiation greenhouse gases cannot be seen by the naked eye" (DeLoughrey,

Allegories 176). The distribution of images of melting glaciers or Pacific Islanders knee-deep in flood water offers a graspable, scalable imaginary for what Farbotko and Lazrus call "a Western crisis of nature" (383). These images, however, do not help people to understand themselves as participants in the production of climate change through accelerated capitalist circulation; nor do discourses of climate disaster—especially those visited upon "remote" islands—inspire the conditions for people's resistance within them. *Rise* refuses these popular narratives of loss and migration as the inevitable future for Arctic or European, North American or Pacific Island communities. Instead, it hands on to viewers the obligation to co-construct alternative plots: to continue the story of shared human-nonhuman futures in ways that propel us from spectatorship to participation, and from the protection of "our" homes to engagement with a planetary homing that is increasingly marked by radical disturbance and disorientation.

Rise refuses to offer a human-centred retrospective standpoint (it is not a coming-to-awareness narrative of ecological crisis or individual culpability), resilience through technological advancement, or improved eco-systems management. Instead, it invites audiences into alternative modalities of envisaging planetary dwelling, via engagement with the constitutive powers of nonhuman actants. This connects viewers with emergent cross-disciplinary ways of thinking-with-others, fostering attention to the complex interspecies and abiotic relationalities of earthly homing. Such literature stimulates a politics grounded in recognition of the planetary commons, fostering lexicons of mutuality and trans-agential intimacy with powerful elemental forces and forms that changeably constitute "home."

Notes

1 See Latour's use of the term "actants," *Politics of Nature*, 75.
2 Kathy Jetñil-Kijiner and Aka Niviâna, *Rise: From One Island to Another*, https://350.org/rise-from-one-island-to-another/#watch
3 See also DeLoughrey, "The Sea is Rising: Visualising Climate Change in the Pacific Islands" (185–197) and Rosaldo, "Imperialist Nostalgia" (107–122).
4 See Nielsen and Nielsen, who detail the document that brought Iceworm to light: the 1996 White Paper of the Danish Institute for International Studies, "Greenland during the Cold War: Danish and American security policy, 1945–1968" (255). Although the 1960 construction of Camp Century—a short-lived nuclear-powered US research base near Thule Air Base—had been agreed with the Danish government, Project Iceworm remained secret until 1996.
5 See Petrov. The potential for resource exploitation is connected to political and economic strategies that drive Greenland's ambitions for possible future independence from Denmark, or at least further self-determination.
6 The Intergovernmental Panel on Climate Change predicts that *non-Arctic* stakeholders are likely to benefit the most. The 2018 Utqiaġvik Declaration, adopted by the Inuit Circumpolar Council, states the need to support responsible mining policies and to utilize indigenous knowledge to advise these processes. See Lucht; Coggins, Ford, et al.

Works Cited

Ahmed, Sara. "Home and Away: Narratives of Migration and Estrangement." *International Journal of Cultural Studies*, vol. 2, no. 3, 1999, pp. 329–347.
Al-Ali, Nadje, and Khalid Koser, editors. *New Approaches to Migration? Transnational Communities and the Transformation of Home*. Routledge, 2002.
Bennett, Jane. *Vibrant Matter: A Political Ecology of Things*. Duke UP, 2010.
Biagini, Emilio, and B.S. Hoyle. *Insularity and Development: International Perspectives on Islands*. Pinter, 1999.
Bourriaud, Nicolas. *Relational Aesthetics*. Les Presses de Réel, 2002.
Chakrabarty, Dipesh, "Postcolonial Studies and the Challenge of Climate Change." *New Literary History*, vol. 43, no. 1, 2012, pp. 1–18.

Chandler, David, and Jonathan Pugh. "Islands of Relationality and Resilience: The Shifting Stakes of the Anthropocene." *Area,* vol. 52, no. 1, 2018, pp. 65–72.

Chandler, David, and Julian Reid. "'Being in Being': Contesting the Ontopolitics of Indigeneity." *The European Legacy,* vol. 23, no. 3, 2018, pp. 251–268.

———. *The Neoliberal Subject: Resilience, Adaptation and Vulnerability.* Rowman & Littlefield, 2016.

Chen, Mel Y. *Animacies: Biopolitics, Racial Mattering, and Queer Affect.* Duke UP, 2012.

Coggins, Shaugn, James Ford, et al. "Indigenous Peoples and Climate Justice in the Arctic." *SFS Georgetown Journal of International Affairs,* vol. 23, Feb. 2021. https://gjia.georgetown.edu/2021/02/23/indigenous-peoples-and-climate-justice-in-the-arctic/

Cohen, Jeffrey Jerome. *Stone: An Ecology of the Inhuman.* U of Minnesota P, 2015.

Colebrook, Claire. "Not Symbiosis, Not Now: Why Anthropogenic Change is not Really Human." *The Oxford Literary Review,* vol. 34, no. 2, 2012, pp. 185–209.

De Landa, Manuel. *A Thousand Years of Nonlinear History.* Zone, 1997.

DeLoughrey, Elizabeth M. *Allegories of the Anthropocene.* Duke UP, 2019.

———. "The Sea is Rising: Visualising Climate Change in the Pacific Islands." *Pacific Dynamics,* vol. 2, no. 2, Nov. 2018, pp. 185–197.

Dépelteau, François, editor. *The Palgrave Handbook of Relational Sociology.* Palgrave Macmillan, 2018.

Farbotko, Carol, and Heather Lazrus. "The First Climate Refugees? Contesting Global Narratives of Climate Change in Tuvalu." *Global Environmental Change,* vol. 22, no. 2, 2012, pp. 382–390.

Frost, Robert. "Mending Wall." 1914. https://www.poetryfoundation.org/poems/44266/mending-wall

Hamilton Faris, Jaimey. "Sisters of Ocean and Ice: On the Hydro-feminism of Kathy Jetñil-Kijiner and Aka Niviâna's *Rise: From One Island to Another.*" *Shima: The International Journal of Research into Island Cultures,* vol. 13, no. 2, 2019, pp. 76–99.

Haraway, Donna. "Anthropocene, Capitalocene, Plantationocene, Chthulucene: Making Kin." *Environmental Humanities,* vol. 6, no. 1, 2015, pp. 159–165.

Hayward, Peter. "Aquapelagos and Aquapelagic Assemblages." *Shima: The International Journal of Research into Island Cultures,* vol. 6, no. 1, 2012, pp. 1–11.

Henriksen, Niels. *Geological History of Greenland Four Billion Years of Earth Evolution.* Geological Survey of Denmark and Greenland (GEUS), 2008.

Jasanoff, Sheila. "A New Climate for Society." *Theory, Culture & Society,* vol. 27, nos. 2–3, 2010, pp. 233–253.

Jiménez, Carlos, and Covadonga Orejas. "The Builders of the Oceans – Part I: Corals From the Tropics to the Poles." *Marine Animal Forests,* edited by Sergio Rossi et al. Springer, 2017, pp. 627–655.

Latour, Bruno. *Politics of Nature: How to Bring the Sciences into Democracy.* Harvard UP, 2004.

Letman, Jon. "Rising Seas Give Island Nation a Stark Choice: Relocate or Elevate." *National Geographic,* 19 Nov. 2018. https://www.nationalgeographic.co.uk/environment-and-conservation/2018/11/rising-seas-give-island-nation-a-stark-choice-relocate-or-elevate

Lucht, Hans. "Chinese Investments in Greenland Raise US Concerns." *Danish Institute for International Studies Policy Brief,* 20 Nov. 2018. https://www.diis.dk/en/research/chinese-investments-in-greenland-raise-us-concerns

Maher, Susan Naramore. *Deep Map Country: Literary Cartography of the Great Plains.* U of Nebraska P, 2014.

McKibben, Bill. "High ice and hard truth: the poets taking on climate change." *The Guardian,* 12 Sep. 2018, https://www.theguardian.com/environment/2018/sep/12/high-ice-hard-truth-a-poetry-expedition-to-greenlands-melting-glaciers-bill-mckibben

Morton, Timothy. *Ecology without Nature.* Harvard UP, 2009.

Nielsen, Kristian H., and Henry Nielsen, *Camp Century: The Untold Story of America's Secret Arctic Military Base Under the Greenland Ice.* Columbia UP, 2021.

Petrov, Eugene. "Cover Story: Political Geology in the Arctic." *GEOExPro,* vol. 12, no. 1, 2015, pp. 20–25.

Povinelli, Elizabeth. *Geontologies: A Requiem for Late Liberalism.* Duke UP, 2016.

Pugh, Jonathan. "The Relational Turn in Island Geographies: Bringing Together Island, Sea and Ship Relations and the Case of the Landship." *Social & Cultural Geography,* vol. 17, no. 8, 2016, pp. 1040–1059.

Rosaldo, Renato. "Imperialist Nostalgia." *Representations,* vol. 26, Spring, 1989, pp. 107–122.

Stager, Curt. *Deep Future: The Next 100,000 Years of Life on Earth.* Thomas Dunne, 2011.

Tsing, Anna Lowenhaupt. *Friction: An Ethnography of Global Connection.* Princeton UP, 2005.

Yusoff, Kathryn. *A Billion Black Anthropocenes or None.* Minnesota UP, 2019.

Zalasiewicz, Jan. *The Earth After Us: What Legacy will Humans Leave in the Rocks?* Oxford UP, 2008.

———. *The Planet in a Pebble: A Journey into Earth's Deep History.* Oxford UP, 2010.

Zylinska, Joanna. *Minimal Ethics for the Anthropocene.* Open Humanities Press, 2014.

33
CITIES

Ameeth Vijay

Midway through Mohsin Hamid's 2017 novel *Exit West*, Nadia and Saeed, the protagonists, exit a portal from a refugee camp in Mykonos and arrive in a mansion in Kensington, London. Soon others arrive—refugees from all over the world—traveling through mysterious, looking-glass portals from the global South to the North. The novel tells us that

> all over London houses and parks and disused lots were being peopled in this way, some said by a million migrants, some said by twice that. It seemed the more empty a space in the city the more it attracted squatters, with unoccupied mansions in the borough of Kensington and Chelsea particularly hard-hit, their absentee owners often discovering the bad news too late to intervene.
>
> *(129)*

Through checkpoints and other security measures, London responds to the arrivants with methods of control. The city finally shuts off power to these wealthy neighborhoods, creating dark London: "from dark London," Hamid writes,

> Saeed and Nadia wondered what life must be like in light London, where they imagined people dined in elegant restaurants and rode in shiny black cabs, or at least went to work in offices and shops and were free to journey about as they pleased.
>
> *(146)*

Instead they are hemmed in through checkpoints guarded by riot police who work to enclose this occupied dark London, placing it under siege. Meanwhile, far-right nativist groups emerge to threaten the refugees. The latter, however, respond in turn, forming ad hoc communities of political resistance. Thus, we learn that

> something they could never have expected happened: other people gathered on the street, other dark- and medium- and even light-skinned people, bedraggled, like the people of the camps on Mykonos, and these people formed a crowd. They banged cooking pots with spoons and chanted in various languages and soon the police decided to withdraw.
>
> *(128)*

Exit West is speculative fiction of the near future that imagines how contemporary global politics might change if the world became connected through these magic portals, but it also shows how those politics are fundamentally intertwined with those of cities. Hamid's speculative "dark London," after all, emerges from the material conditions of the contemporary city: London, as an archetypical "global city" (Sassen) or "world city" (Massey), is a neo-imperial center for global finance, with its wealthy neighborhoods housing an elite class that is not only British but global—often-absentee owners who use urban real estate not only for its own amenities but also as one means to stash excess capital. Similarly, dark London only dramatizes the already-existing inequities that such a city reproduces, where uneven access to housing, infrastructure, secure employment, and identity documents reflect both class division and legacies of empire written into spaces of migration. In these actually existing urban spaces, however, much like in the dark London of the novel, migrants like Nadia and Saeed find moments of solidarity and alliance within and across communities of ethnicity, religion, and gender.

Hamid's figuration of dark London poses questions of how to situate "literature" as such in relation to other objects and areas of analysis: in this case, the political economy of global cities, the social and cultural dynamics of their development, the role of cities in reproducing culture, and the wider imaginary of the city—as a technology of modernization, a context for politics, or simply as the setting for everyday life. What is the relation, that is, between the materiality of the city and its social-political structures, the lived experiences and individual lifeworlds of its inhabitants, and the purposes, affordances, and effects of literary representation across a variety of forms and genres? In the abstract, it might not seem like the conceptual space of "the city" has anything in particular to say about these more general questions. However, the history of literary production in English shows that the space of the city has been deployed in ways that open onto the above questions and concerns, much like *Exit West* does in this instance. As a setting, it stages and dramatizes the politics of its historical and geographical context, and as such can serve as a vehicle for stories of wealth and poverty, of cosmopolitanism and segregation, of sexual freedom and violence. Further, as a site *par excellence* of modernity, the experience of the city both allows and invites experimentation in literary form to account for lives impacted by its speed, dynamism, and anonymity. Thus, the literary imagination of the city is necessarily caught up with its politics, defined here as the way that power, resistance, and conflict come to shape the different ways that space is experienced, apportioned, conceptualized, and expressed. Literature and other arts have often served to disclose the way that space, as opposed to being a neutral backdrop, is actively and continually produced and expresses uneven social relations. That is, literature can tell us something meaningful about what makes a city possible, from its daily regulation of movement to its orientation around economic production and its relationship to distant colonies or metropoles.

However, if we are inclined to ask how literature stages the politics of the city through different modes of literary expression (from locodescriptive poetry to social realism to modernism), we can just as easily ask how those politics are already deeply aestheticized and narrative in form and function. For example, the figuration of the city as the *polis* is essential to classical political thought; similarly, the city is where the aesthetic onslaught of consumer modernity enters everyday lived experience in ways more immediately familiar to us than the political gathering space of the Athenian agora. Engagement with the city is itself shaped by its aesthetic forms—the visuality of its skyline, the aural environment of its streets, the smells of its pollution, the narratives that emerge through fleeting encounters—in ways that all indicate something meaningfully particular about the structures of power and resistance in play. Literary criticism, then, does not need to take "literature" as its sole and primary object while placing it in tentative or necessary relation to some historical context or material reality. Instead, as a practice of reading focused on the interpretation of semiotic systems, criticism can also turn to the aesthetics of the built environment, including the way those aesthetics encode layers of politics and history, some preserved and some ruined.

Literatures of and about cities find ways to represent political contestation; moreover, in their concrete materiality and abstract futurity, cities are themselves composed through modes of narration and aesthetic production that are inherently political; that is, how the dynamics of power, resistance, and conflict affect and are affected by the experience of space. This volume argues in part that, in being so widely accepted, the relation between literature and politics can sometimes lack definition and specificity. Similarly, "cultural studies" can operate as a sort of umbrella term suggesting a relation between artistic production (in any mode) and something called "culture," while leaving the central terms and the types of relations vague so as to account for a wide variety of approaches. Accordingly, this chapter seeks to revisit and think through the available methods, possibilities, and limitations for placing aesthetics and politics within a common frame that is simultaneously urban and literary.

The City as an Object of Knowledge

Tracing the history of cultural studies as a field in his 1983 lectures, Stuart Hall notes the importance of literature and literary criticism in the work of key scholars. For example, Hall writes that the work of Richard Hoggart is "attempting to do the kind of analysis or reading of real social and cultural life that he would do on a poem or a novel," a method fundamentally "informed by the practice of close reading of texts" (8, 12). Likewise, Raymond Williams's work evolves into understanding "how literary and artistic productions can be thought in social and cultural terms, rather than in purely aesthetic and moral terms" (28). This is notable not because close reading or literary/aesthetic criticism should be a privileged mode of cultural analysis, and certainly not because there is an unproblematic canon of literary texts that might give us exemplary insight into the human condition; Hall and his contemporaries were in fact seeking to suspend such a Kantian framework for situating the aesthetic. Rather, it is to show what might now be a commonplace assumption, namely that "culture" can be understood as a more pervasive category that finds expression in historically and geographically situated repertoire of everyday practices and experiences. It is inherently political in the sense that "there is no way of describing economic life without reference to the cultural forms in which it is organised," and that the point of theory was to "break into experience, to open up to investigation the problematic nature that such political situations present to us in order to better understand what is going on and how to respond" (34, 2). A theorization of culture, in other words, is always connected to political praxis.

Hall and the figures he references, like Williams and E. P. Thompson, worked within but also sought to expand the traditional Marxist framework for understanding how power works and what resistance to and through that power might look like. Politics are fundamentally informed by the material conditions and circumstances in a given location and time period, but are also about the production of culture, of ways of inhabiting and relating to the world. Here they follow Antonio Gramsci in noting how cultural scripts form a kind of common sense, often working to replicate, perhaps unwittingly, structures of power and exploitation that eventually become known as an oppressive "hegemony." Likewise, through a (multi-disciplinary) analysis of how cultures are formed and reproduced, we might see how and where they might be subverted for the sake of political resistance. Marxist geographers extend these insights to our understanding and analysis of power dynamics in the city, the stakes of which include but also exceed the appropriation of resources. As David Harvey writes,

> the question of what kind of city we want cannot be divorced from the question of what kind of people we want to be, what kinds of social relations we seek, what relations to nature we cherish, what style of daily life we desire, what kinds of technologies we deem appropriate, what aesthetic values we hold. The right to the city is, therefore, far more than a right of individual access to the resources that the city embodies.
>
> *(4)*

All these vectors impact each other in ways that demand both materialist analysis and other practices of reading, thinking, and interpreting.

A city is not only an object in a particular space, existing at a particular time, but also an object of knowledge. Harvey and other geographers draw on theorists like Henri Lefebvre to think about how our existences and interactions with and within the city are mediated by a host of practices, discourses, and affects that all together work to produce the social meaning of a space. The everyday experience of, say, traversing a city might seem immediate and personal but in fact discloses the historicity of those spaces: their planning and development, their architectural and infrastructural utility and aesthetics, the way they are both the product and cause for political contestation, exclusions, and violences. This is true whether we are walking down Paris' grand avenues (the infamous result of Baron Haussmann's violent replanning of the nineteenth-century city), or stuck in traffic on Interstate Highway 5 in Los Angeles' Boyle Heights (a city, like many in the United States, where development of infrastructure worked to segregate), or passing by a slum in Mumbai. Indeed, it may also be true when we are reading a book or watching a film of any of those spaces, where we are also experiencing sites composed of and by social struggle. As Michel Foucault writes,

> we do not live in a kind of void, inside of which we could place individuals and things… we live inside a set of relations that delineates sites which are irreducible to one another and absolutely not superimposable on one another.
>
> *(3)*

Sedimented over time and sewn together through a vast array of subjects and experiences, the city presents itself not (just) as a unitary, idealized utopia but as a scrapbook collection of fragmented experiences and relations that, at their extreme, form what Foucault terms "heterotopia."

Representations of the city in literature or another medium operate as an aesthetic staging ground for exploring certain dynamics of subjectivity, community, and politics; it is also the case, however, that the city "itself" is composed of narratives and aesthetics as surely as it is made of concrete and brick. The rest of this chapter considers this mutual and open-ended dynamic through a variety of lenses. Most critically, we ought to ask how the changing of narrative perspective alters how the spaces of the city are experienced, and in doing so ask what kinds of social relations are established and privileged, on the one hand, and what relations and subjectivities are placed under pressure, or excluded, or even foreclosed, on the other.

The Politics of Modernization

One particular way that the city exists as an object of knowledge is as an epitome of modernity. We can think through the ways in which this happens through a combined analysis of its discursive and material production, including the tangible political effect of representations of the urban and the modern, on the one hand, and the aesthetics of the built environment, on the other. By the latter, I mean the way that a city is always experienced aesthetically, from its style of architecture and character of infrastructure to the makeup of its various communities. The former includes all of that ways that cities come to occupy a particular social imaginary, and the associations and expectations that attend to any urban space. It is not that one provides the "material reality" and the other its "discursive representation," but rather that both work in a dialogic way to make an urban environment legible and knowable.

The figuration of the city as "modern," for example, tracks the rapid urbanization of European metropolises in the nineteenth century, along with a host of contemporary and related developments: industrialization and the expansion of a capitalist base, new infrastructural and architectural technologies, the politics of liberalism and labor, consumerism, and the development of mass popular and national identities. This modernity emerges, at least in part, through its figuration. For example, the experience of anonymity in the crowd and the fleeting, everyday experiences of the city recall Edgar Allen Poe's "The Man of the Crowd" and its transfiguration in Charles Baudelaire's poetry and prose. Likewise, the Dickensian city brings to mind the inequality, poverty, and propriety of Victorian Britain. Perhaps most of all, we see the role of the artist in collecting and suturing together the alienated, fragmented experiences of modernity in literary epics of the everyday city such as Virginia Woolf's *Mrs. Dalloway* and James Joyce's *Ulysses* during the long literary movement that drew its name from the modernity that defined it: modernism.

Many of the more buoyant accounts of urban experience define its possibility along the contours of is cosmopolitan character. Here, for example, theorists of space like Michel de Certeau and Gaston Bachelard accentuate the phenomenological immersion of urban life and the pleasures to be found in its characteristically modern experience. Accounts of city life then, literary or otherwise, might give us insight into the heterogeneous lifeworlds to be found on urban streets; these accounts, in turn, coalesce into particular literary figures and tropes such as Baudelaire's wandering *flâneur*. The "modern" city (and the city as modern) is also understood as a particularly *cosmopolitan* space, that is one, if not composed of, at least hospitable to all manner of outsiders and amenable to identities and practices that would otherwise be repressed. This cosmopolitanism of the city would appear to index profound social changes, including increased possibilities for participation of women in political and social life, the liberation of urban transplants from what Marx called the "idiocy of rural life," and the possibility of visibility for queer sexual expression.

Yet, the focus on everyday experience places even these possibilities in tension, for it is not the case that the cosmopolitan, modern city suspends structures of power. Rather, this understanding presents the city as an object of knowledge and eventually assumes its position as the endpoint of modernization, when in fact urban modernity is deeply ideological and often reproduces existing hegemonies. Feminist and queer geographers and cultural critics have highlighted the particular ways that "modernity," as articulated by these figures of the urban, leaves out the experiences of differently marginalized subjects. On the one hand, the openness and anonymity of the city allows for the subversion of convention and the formation of alternative communities. On the other, geography, planning, and architecture operate from a perspective that has historically not registered an entire range of concerns about the safety of public spaces (for women and queer individuals, for example), the accessibility of those spaces (with regard to disability or the presence of information in multiple languages), and the differential ways they are surveyed and policed. Moreover, these critics have pointed out that geography has focused its analysis of labor on those professions and industries that are male dominated, at times leaving out an analysis of domestic labor or flexible, service work.

Beyond these materialist concerns, feminist criticism helps elucidate how the association of the city with modernity relies upon particularly gendered figures. As such, figures like the flâneur, composing painting and poetry from the fragments of the everyday, tend to universalize a particular, privileged perspective that is frequently coded and assumed to be both white and male. At the same time, the dangers of the nineteenth-century city could be summed up in the figure of the wayward woman, most notably the figure of the prostitute; as Leslie Kern writes, "women's bodies are still often seen as the source or sign of urban problems" (5; also see Walkowitz). Feminist criticism reveals that the city is a site of economic production and social reproduction, and that, as Doreen Massey argues, space and place are "constructed out of social relations" (*Space* 2). Thus, knowledge about and representations of bodies in cities are situated and relational rather than universal.

Together, this sort of work reveals how everyday experience is composed of and mediated by a dense politics of social relations. Being attentive to situated and relational knowledge helps bring into view who a city is for in ways that critically examine the many intersecting layers of identity and lived experience. For example, the gentrification of cities in North America makes use of particular bodies that present an image of an upwardly mobile "creative class," including those of middle-class white women and white gay men. The inclusion of these subjects, however marginalized, comes at the expense of working-class women and queer people of color into a structure of "meteronormativity." Critique through an orientation of queer people of color asks us to interrogate and re-conceptualize this imaginary of a "modern" city, and thus to consider those subjects that are displaced or otherwise absent in order to question the boundaries of the urban and reveal its intersections with larger geographies (Tongson 5).

"Modernity," therefore, is not simply a neutral state of existence, but is also an expression of power in material, ideological, and aesthetic forms. Thus, the above literary representations might be placed alongside this whole series of parallel forms that make up complex cultural objects of knowledge like "the city." Expanding the frame of analysis moves critique away from focusing on varying modes of representing the urban experience, or even the experience of a particular space in a particular time to consider how and why a space stages different kinds of politics. For example, as such an object of knowledge, the city might connect to its figuration as a bounded community, one classically formed through selective political representation. Similarly, the metropolis has been figured as a space of both utopian possibility and dystopian terror, both expressing various and conflicting attitudes and affects toward modernity. Thus, in the background of Hamid's dark London—both its emergent refugee communities and the police state that expands and devises new technologies and techniques to surveille and control those communities—are speculative imaginaries like William Morris's *News from Nowhere*, Edward Bellamy's *Looking Backward*, H. G. Wells' *The War of the Worlds*, and Aldous Huxley's *Brave New World*.

These figurations are all inextricably conjoined with the material and ideological construction of both modernity generally and the city particularly, and are so within the framework of hegemonic capitalisms and colonialisms. That is, "modernity" in all its various figurations works to express power and produce violence even as it frequently conceals the sources and effects of that powerful violence. As a supposed image of the future, the glittering, dynamic, cosmopolitan urban environment is counterposed with other spaces that are also putatively less modern, more static, and "traditional." Here, modernity is also the process of modernization, which takes as its object the Others of historical "progress." Progress refers to the ideology that human societies develop in a similar, predicable, linear fashion, and can be achieved through material and cultural "improvement." Though seemingly a neutral, universal good, progress is like modernity itself: an expression of a power dynamic. In this case, what is a utopian future city for some is in practice a dystopia for others. Thus, the political geography created by cities is not limited to them alone, but speak to larger structures of power and their temporalities. These relations of power are inscribed into spaces at all different scales.

The Social Contradictions of Urban Life

In the capitalist city, the conditions of extraction and exploitation and processes of destruction become naturalized by the ideology of modernization. Here, social heterogeneity becomes sorted into closed off and separate spaces: the slum or the inner city, on one hand, and the gated communities and wealthy enclaves, on the other. Within these spaces all sorts of harm—economic, social, and environmental—are unequally and inequitably distributed. The slum, as a concentration of informal construction and development, is marked by its precarity and ability to be modernized out of existence. As Mike Davis documents in *Planet of Slums*, impoverished urban areas are not merely expressions of politics interior to a given city, but rather express global patterns in capital allocation. Those common patterns reveal the similar precarity of large-scale urbanizations in Lagos, Johannesburg, and Cairo, for example, such that seemingly distant and different places with such different histories are revealed to be fundamentally interconnected.

Such spaces, with such high concentrations of formal and informal working-class labor, are always available for destruction and redevelopment in the name of progressive and redemptive modernization. That is not to say that this violence goes unopposed, and literature turns out to be especially capable of revealing these conceptual connections and also staging possible modes of resistance. For example, a scene in Chris Abani's *Graceland* presents a standoff between police trying to demolish a slum in Lagos and residents preventing them with a makeshift "barricade made of broken furniture, old care skeletons, poles, building debris, and other junk…there was no way a small vehicle could get past them, much less a bulldozer" (263). The ensuing scene is one of comedy, as the forces of development are, at least temporarily, routed by a community that comes together to preserve its home, however precarious it remains. This ad hoc assemblage of "junk" speaks to the politics of the "right to the city" and the way it is staged both in the built environment and in literature, and also reveals a fundamental irony in the ways that people can more successfully battle to remain within their precarity than to emerge from it. Slum clearance is usually represented from the perspective of planning and development, in which the slum is either a technical problem to be managed or an economic problem of space that is not efficiently capitalized. In both cases, the slum is not regarded as a problem resulting from capitalism but rather one to be solved through "improving" the area via redevelopment. However, as represented in *Graceland*, the residents of this slum are not faceless integers but the creators, members, and protectors of a community. In giving these characters a voice, Abani shows how the forces of development appear as the sudden, arbitrary, and violent erasure of spaces, of social relationships, and of lives that make the city possible.

The juxtaposition of economic extremes—the opulent and securitized wealth of gated communities on the one hand, the extreme poverty and precarity of global south slums on the other—can also negatively sensationalize political struggle and romanticize the informality of precarious spaces and lives. For example, we might consider the long history of the middle class practice of "slumming it," a slang term describing a vicarious, temporary exposure to the lives of the urban working poor that often results in sensationalized accounts and attempts at social philanthropy. Indeed, urban planning as a modern, technical practice emerges less from the wholesale destruction of urban spaces than through middle class movements and forms of knowledge which seek to modernize by "improving" areas of the city. Rather than simply being repressive, interventions like the late-nineteenth-century model villages and garden city movement, which would become influential for more comprehensive attempts at city planning, sought to use the built environment to improve and cultivate working-class subjects. This was, crucially, a deeply aesthetic approach, in which improvements to the environment could lead to the improvement of its populace.

For example, the "greening the city" movement—wherein a city was understood to need parks, natural amenities, individual gardens, even space to hang flower pots—stemmed simultaneously from a concern for urban sanitation and health, social amenity, and beautification. The nineteenth-century greening of the city resonates with the contemporary politics of urban planning and its aesthetics. The city is still a figure of futurity in the present day, but one that is imagined not just as consisting in towering steel skyscrapers and more efficient, complicated infrastructure, but also through discourses of sustainability and ecology; it is thought that the harm to the environment and health that the city produces might be solved through a technological fix, through better design and planning.

Similarly, the politics of class contestation do not often take the aesthetic form of the barricade made famous by the short-lived revolutionary actions on the streets of Paris in 1871 and 1968. More likely, we see these class politics in scenes of gentrification, a capacious and expanding understanding of the way neighborhoods become slowly captured by bourgeois interests. Defined by Ruth Glass as an individual middle-class practice of small-scale improvement, gentrification has been elaborated by Neil Smith, Loretta Lees, and others into a more general understanding of why particular "neglected" neighborhoods become targets for redevelopment and how that process operates through stages of change. In popular understanding, however, we come to recognize those processes through visible markers of change. This includes a changing demographic to a neighborhood and sense of displacement, in a way that, particularly in the United States, is an inherently racialized dynamic. It also includes the aesthetic markers of the new gentrified neighborhood, which might contain a host of class-specific amenities and businesses, from yoga studios to upscale coffee shops to increased green spaces that are also surveyed and policed in particular ways. In these conditions, the establishment of a particular kind of gallery might not be analytically essential to the "base" economic change happening in the city, but it is a space through which the multifarious politics of the city condense their meaning, and thus is liable to become as much a focal point of political contestation as a barricade. That is, changes in the built environment are political not only in their economic impact, but in how they alter the relationship of situated individuals to spaces around them. These aesthetics carry with them narratives about what a city should look like and, implicitly, who the city is for. A right to the city constitutes a right to its narratives and aesthetics, and vice versa.

The political economy of any given city is of course deeply entwined with the story of its genesis and development, and perforce functions within colonial and postcolonial history. In the hands of those who devise and benefit from state and interstate policies, the geopolitics of "modernity" continue to be represented and understood within a specific developmental logic: one which conjoins metropole and metropolis and pits them against the colonized periphery that was, by that account, to be understood not just as "primitive" but as not-yet modern. Colonization provided the means for urbanization in more concrete ways—literally—whether from the extractive enrichment of Europe and America through the transatlantic slave trade to the colonized world as a space of raw materials, cheap labor, and captive markets for industrial goods. Settler colonies appeared to Europeans as blank slates upon which the techniques and aesthetics of planning could be practiced. Colonial cities, meanwhile, were key sites of twentieth-century labor struggles and decolonization movements.

This history and its persistent if dynamic forms of colonialism in the present produces a curious legacy: that cities are not only segregated along lines of class but are fundamentally expressions of racial exclusion and racism. Yet literature turns out to be one mode of aesthetic politics that provides an alternative discourse to the official narratives of reform, renewal, regeneration, gentrification, and "progress" that is tied to initiatives that destroy particular parts of cities and consign countries to deep, expensive debt for the privilege. To return again to *Exit West*, the "dark" London of refugees brings to mind a series of racialized spaces, from immigrant enclaves to enforced racial segregation and apartheid. Even as the refugees in the novel inhabit the wealthiest neighborhoods and most luxurious housing in London, they have a particular relationship to the built environment. As Adrienne Brown writes in *The Black Skyscraper*, emblematic figures of urban modernity like the skyscraper are experienced differently by racial subjects even when they retain their capacity to imagine alternative futures.

Conclusion: Affectable Spaces and Subjects

To conclude, I return to the refugees of Hamid's dark London, a speculative, fictional space emerging from and adjoining the politics of the contemporary city, with its legacies of colonial and capitalist violence and gendered geographies. Nadia, Saeed, and the other characters find themselves in what Denise da Silva terms "affectable territory," spatially interior to the city but ethically and epistemologically exterior, a site of an internal border (as articulated by Étienne Balibar). The novel places them in the wealthiest parts of the city not by choice or coercion, however, but thanks to magical portals that have everywhere appeared. Hamid uses this inversion to think about what would happen if marginalized refugee subjects from the global South were suddenly transplanted into the center of the world city. That is, the novel understands that the space of the city not as abstract and homogenous, but rather as materially constituted through the social relations of its inhabitants.

The occupation of part of the city by refugees thus challenges a global hierarchy of identities constructed upon class, race, and nation and that have become congealed in urban property. It also, however, stages alternative possibilities for what kinds of communities might form in the wake of those capitalist, nationalist, and colonial modernities. This is imagined as utopian only in its mundanity, as groups of migrants alternatively assemble "themselves in suits and runs of their own kind, like with like, or rather superficially like with superficially like" and also come together in unlikely, inter-ethnic alliances (147). Thus, we learn that Nadia attends community meetings to discuss the living conditions of dark London, in which she and others

> conversed in a language that was built in large part from English, but not solely from English ... Also they spoke different variations of English, different Englishes, and so

when Nadia gave voice to an idea or opinion among them, she did not need to fear that her views could not be comprehended, for her English was like theirs, one among many.

(148)

There is perhaps a faith, here, in the fabled cosmopolitanism of the city, the way it continually presents encounters with difference; at the same time, this mixing of "different Englishes" is inherently political, a language less of appropriated multiculturalism and more of a strategic requirement for a refugee community to emerge and to resist the police state that envelops them.

At the same time, the built environment of the city tells other stories. Looking across the city from dark London, Nadia would perhaps be able to see the city's monuments to its imperial past, its brash neoliberal skyline, and perhaps the site of the 2012 Olympic Games, built on what was historically a site of slums, class rebellion, and migrant arrivals to the East End. Past the checkpoints and security enclosure that define and delimit the space of the novel's refugee city lies the space of modernity as defined by a globalized common sense. Here, development, as urban development, constellates processes that are both related and in tension. It takes as its object those spaces that are cast as anachronisms, out of time and disjunctive with the ever-receding horizon of a technological modernity. The aesthetics of this development are not incidental to but constitutive of the state's law-preserving violence even if, as an aesthetic, development can appear as immediate, natural, self-evident, and unrelated to political processes. This appearance naturalizes questions about ownership, about who counts as agential subjects of the city, and who inhabits literal and figurative affectable territory. The space of the city is itself composed of and produced through these social relationships, which is to say, through its politics.

Works Cited

Bachelard, Gaston. *The Poetics of Space*. Penguin, 2014.
Balibar, Étienne. *We, the People of Europe?: Reflections on Transnational Citizenship*. Princeton UP, 2009.
Baudelaire, Charles-Pierre. *The Painter of Modern Life*. Penguin UK, 2010.
Bellamy, Edward. *Looking Backward: From 2000 to 1887*. Applewood Books, 2000.
Benjamin, Walter. *Illuminations: Essays and Reflections*. HMH, 1968.
Brown, Adrienne. *The Black Skyscraper: Architecture and the Perception of Race*. Johns Hopkins UP, 2017.
Certeau, Michel de. *Practice of Everyday Life*. 1st edition, U of California P, 2011.
da Silva, Denise Ferreira. "No-Bodies: Law, Raciality and Violence." *Griffith Law Review*, vol. 18, no. 2, Jan. 2009, pp. 212–236. *Crossref*, https://doi.org/10.1080/10383441.2009.10854638.
Davis, Mike. *Planet of Slums*. Verso Books, 2007.
Dickens, Charles. *Oliver Twist*. Courier Corporation, 2002.
Foucault, Michel. "Of Other Spaces: Utopias and Heterotopias." *Architecture Culture 1943–1968*, edited by Joan Ockman, Rizzoli, 1967, pp. 419–426.
Glass, Ruth. *London: Aspects of Change*. MacGibbon & Kee, 1964.
Gramsci, Antonio. *Selections from the Prison Notebooks of Antonio Gramsci*. International Publishers, 1971.
Hall, Stuart. *Cultural Studies 1983: A Theoretical History*. Duke UP, 2016.
Hamid, Mohsin. *Exit West*. Riverhead Books, 2017.
Harvey, David. *Rebel Cities: From the Right to the City to the Urban Revolution by David Harvey*. 2nd edition. Verso, 2013.
Huxley, Aldous. *Brave New World*. Vintage, 2004.
Joyce, James. *Ulysses*. Vintage Books, 1986.
Kern, Leslie. *Feminist City: Claiming Space in a Man-Made World*. Verso Books, 2020.
Kureshi, Hanif. *The Buddha of Suburbia: Faber Modern Classics*. Main-Faber Modern Classics edition, Faber & Faber Fiction, 2015.
Lees, Loretta, et al. *Gentrification*. Routledge, 2008.

Lefebvre, Henri. *The Production of Space*. Translated by Donald Nicholson-Smith, 1st edition. Wiley-Blackwell, 1992.

Massey, Doreen. *Space, Place, and Gender*. U of Minnesota P, 1994.

———. *World City*. Polity Press, 2007.

Morris, William. *News from Nowhere and Other Writings*. New Ed edition, Penguin Classics, 1994.

Peeples, Scott. *The Man of the Crowd: Edgar Allan Poe and the City*. Princeton UP, 2020.

Rancière, Jacques. *Dissensus: On Politics and Aesthetics*. Bloomsbury Publishing, 2015.

Sassen, Saskia. *The Global City: New York, London, Tokyo*. Princeton UP, 2013.

Smith, Neil, and Peter Williams, editors. *Gentrification of the City*. Allen & Unwin, 1986.

Thompson, E. P. *The Making of the English Working Class*. Penguin Books, 2013.

Tongson, Karen. *Relocations: Queer Suburban Imaginaries*. NYU Press, 2011. JSTOR, *JSTOR*, https://www.jstor.org/stable/j.ctt9qfjnq.5.

Walkowitz, Judith R. *City of Dreadful Delight: Narratives of Sexual Danger in Late-Victorian London*. U of Chicago P, 2008.

Wells, Herbert George. *The War of the Worlds*. Baronet Book, 1996.

Williams, Raymond. *The Country And The City*. Random House, 2013.

Woolf, Virginia. *Mrs Dalloway*. Penguin Books Limited, 2000.

34
STREETS AND HIGHWAYS

Myka Tucker-Abramson and Sam Weselowski

The transformation of paving stones and carriages into barricades during the 1848 revolution in Paris. The destruction of the Vendôme column in the Paris Commune in 1871. The mass looting and burning of new durable commodities such as refrigerators in the 1965 urban uprisings across the US. The rearranging of street signs and other directional markers in Prague 1968 to block Soviet tanks. The occupation and blocking of freeways and public squares during Occupy, Black Lives Matter, and Idle No More, and the longer histories of Indigenous rail and road blockades across the US and Canada. Streets are the ground people walk on and the background to people's lives; they are built environments, entangled in long histories of settler colonial violence, that facilitate the flow of capital, containing within them raw materials and labour extracted at earlier moments. But they are also the sites that become the meeting points and materials of revolt.

The street is central to what Emily Fedoruk, drawing on Silvia Federici, identifies as urban spaces' role as a "prime mediator" of the "violent dispossessions" (68) that structure "the reproduction of colonial and capitalist social relations" both internationally and domestically (Federici 9). One way we can understand the street's mediating role is through the sensory, perceptive, and aesthetic experience of urban life: the shapes of buildings, the arrangements of space, the movement of traffic and bodies, all of which compose what Kanishka Goonewardena has termed the "urban sensorium" (47–48). But, as both Goonewardena and Fedoruk's turn to cultural forms (poems, novels, and films) suggests, literature and culture more generally are crucial to the construction, mediation, and renegotiation of urban sensoriums. No wonder, then, that the question of the meaning and status of not just the "city," but the seemingly more modest scale of the street, has become a central topic of focus in literary and cultural studies in recent years. To this effect, streets and highways have been taken up most seriously within three critical frameworks: experiential-positivist accounts that interrogate the meaning, experience, and temporality of specific urban transformations (e.g. industrial urbanization, urban renewal, slumification, gentrification, suburbanization, hinterlandization); the burgeoning field of literary infrastructuralisms; and accounts of capitalist logistics. These different approaches can be understood as forms of what Henri Lefebvre has termed "levels"—a term we will return to—which reveal the ways that the streets that populate, underpin, and shape literary texts also become sites through which literature can stake its political and aesthetic claims (*The Urban Revolution* 78).

DOI: 10.4324/9781003038009-40

To make this argument, we will examine Vancouver writer Mercedes Eng's debut poetry collection *Mercenary English* (2018), particularly the closing sequence, "autocartography," which is both literally and figuratively shaped by the street; the street is, in turn, wrought by the flows of capital, labour, and commodities in and out of Vancouver. "autocartography" circles around the gentrifying frontier of the Downtown Eastside (DTES), "Canada's poorest postal code" and a largely Indigenous neighbourhood (126). Eng deploys two textual forms in this sequence. First, the recurring poem "how it is" that maps and literally visualizes the buildings, storefronts, and empty lots that compose the four-block stretch of Hastings street (the neighbourhood's principal thoroughfare) between Main and Cambie in the years between 2007 and 2016. Indicated only by the blank space running down the middle of the page, Eng represents the street at the nexus of property developments, housing projects, public health institutions, and local shops such as "ginseng store," "craft beer place," and "meth clinic," which mark the battle over who the neighbourhood belongs to and serves (90). Second, Eng interleaves this spatial text with a series of lyrical poems that document her experience of sex work in and around the DTES during the 1990s; these poems move from the defined space of streets and alleyways across the Lower East Side to the highways that connect the mass incarceration and extraction sites in and around British Columbia and Alberta. This duet of "textual maps" and "logistical lyrics" (as we've termed them) braids together the impersonal structures of the street with the vocal subjectivities of the poem.

The years that these poems span were marked by intense struggle over the rapid and violent acceleration of gentrification of the DTES. This period of urban change centred on the redevelopment of the former department store Woodward's into a mixed-use space encompassing the art school of Simon Fraser University, high-end condos, shops and restaurants, and the "Goldcorp Centre for Performing Arts" (named after the notorious Canadian mining company Goldcorp); the period also saw the rise of the Indigenous Idle No More movement and the ultimately successful resistance of Wet'suwet'en and Gitxsan Nations against the proposed Enbridge Northern Gateway Pipeline. More broadly, Eng's poems are situated in the context of the large number of women, disproportionately Indigenous, who "were murdered and disappeared from the neighbourhood" (119). That many of the women were last seen engaging in outdoor sex work on the streets near the city's Port district, itself "intimately linked with the displacement of Indigenous peoples" (McCreary and Milligan 725), further highlights the relationship drawn out by Indigenous feminist scholars between the dispossession of Indigenous land and violence against Indigenous women (Nason; Simpson).

With its combination of street maps and road poems, "autocartography" examines how the ambient landscapes of urban life, physically shaped by capital accumulation, are subjectively experienced in the everyday. Eng's portrayal of the street illuminates the relationships between condo developments and oil sands, prisons and arts galleries, rural backwater and metropolis, sex work and extraction work, tent cities and luxury apartments, transnational pipelines and closed pawn shops. We also want to suggest, however, that Eng's "autocartography," not unlike what feminist geographer Cindi Katz has referred to as "countertopography," attempts to gain access to the street by critically turning to the history and meanings of the map itself. She thus performs what we might call a form of "battle mapping" in which different cartographic methods and modes of spatial representation—that of the Early Modern explorer, neocolonial real estate developer, and sex worker/luger-wielding "pirate," to use Eng's language—are placed in confrontation with one another (113). In sum, we propose that Eng's poetry not only illustrates what's at stake in paying critical attention to the streets and highways that undergird and appear in literary texts; the poetry also demands that such an engagement be carried out across the levels of the experiential, infrastructural, and logistical.

Levels in Concrete: Experience, Infrastructure, Logistics

The last decade has seen an explosion of articles and monographs that examine how literature grapples with the temporalities, histories, spatialities, and embodied experiences of (primarily Anglo-American) urban transformations, from the making of industrial cities to suburbanization, urban crisis, urban renewal, and gentrification. Building on Carlo Rotella's foundational *October Cities* (1998), works like Adrienne Brown's *The Black Skyscraper* (2017), Martin Dines' *The Literature of Suburban Change* (2020), Alice Levick's *Memory and the Built Environment in 20th-Century American Literature* (2021), and Thomas Heise's *The Gentrification Plot* (2021) have been particularly attuned to the central role that racial hierarchies, embedded in what Brown terms modes of "racial perception" (25), play in constructing "the city of feeling as much as it describes events in the cities of fact" (6), as Rotello neatly puts it. They have drawn literary studies' attention to space and built environment and, as Rotello explains, made clear the ways that urban spaces like streets are themselves "shaped by acts of imagination: redevelopment plans, speeches, newspaper stories, conversations, movies, music, novels, and poems create cities of feeling that help guide people in their encounters with the city of fact" (7). The focus of these books is on fixed or absolute spaces and scales, which is to say the fixed space of the city or the suburb, as opposed to ways in which the scales and spaces of the urban, exurban, suburban, rural are entwined and entangled.[1]

Alongside this focus, however, there has been a shift in literary studies that at once zooms in and out from the scales outlined above, through the examination of the seemingly innocuous infrastructures that shape our daily lives: from streets and highways, to the energy stations, water filtration plants, and pipes, cables, and pipelines that produce and deliver electricity, clean water, and internet to houses and institutions, as well as the ports and supply chains that provide the commodities of daily life. Michael Rubenstein, Bruce Robbins, and Sophia Beal note in their introduction to a special issue on "Infrastructuralism" that the very turn to infrastructure is responding to the issue that all is not working as it should: that climate crisis, privatization, and neglect mean that our life-sustaining infrastructures are themselves in crisis. As they put it baldly, "The recent interest in infrastructure by scholars in the humanities derives in some measure from the historical fact that […] 'water is being privatized'" (578). For them, this shift at once registers literature's own turn to the question of infrastructure, and calls for more works that might "defamiliarize our daily dependency on infrastructures and […] resensitize us to a host of urgent questions about access and ownership, rights and responsibilities" (585). Similarly, in her editor's column for *PMLA*, Patricia Yaeger argues that it's the fact of "quasi-colonized, overpopulated, densely inhabited cities" with "decaying or absent infrastructures," which necessitates that literary critics take up the "new intellectual apparatus" of infrastructure in order to understand the literatures coming from the peripheries (13).

The focus on infrastructures breaks down the artificial boundaries between cities, suburbs, exurbs, extraction sites, and sacrifice zones, by revealing the lineaments that connect the world. Here, streets and highways (alongside railways, pipelines, dams, prisons, etc.) aren't the abstract containers in which social life occurs, neutral means of moving or storing goods or services, or a natural backdrop for action; rather, they are themselves flashpoints of action that are connected to larger, global processes of neocolonialism, settler colonialism, and racialized-gendered violence.

And yet, as Lauren Berlant notes, the focus on infrastructures often belies an attachment to both infrastructure and the state itself as forces that can "manage the unevenness, ambivalence, violence, and ordinary contingency of contemporary existence" (394). Building on this point, Molly Geidel and Patricia Stuelke have warned that "the idea that infrastructure will save us, or help us achieve a vision of equality" that is often embedded in both the infrastructure humanities and what they refer to as "infrastructural-innovation realist" novels (e.g. Colson Whitehead's *The Underground Railway*, Mohsin Hamid's *Exit West*, and Namwali Serpell's *The Old Drift*) risks erasing the ways that such visions "for repairing or greening US infrastructure remains mired in capitalist logistics and unequal distributions of risk and exploitation" (123). The point here is not that infrastructures can't or shouldn't be repurposed towards liberatory ends; rather, these critics are pointing to the risk of fetishizing infrastructure itself as the force that can save us, or that can replace the work of confronting and dismantling persistent atrocities and depredations of settler-colonialism and racial capitalism.

Geidel and Stuelke's foregrounding of "capitalist logistics" suggests how concentrating on logistics, or the science of moving *stuff* (to use Deborah Cowen's shorthand), can address a broader horizon of sociospatial interconnectivity for which infrastructure is a single, albeit significant, part. Logistics both designates a set of activities and functions as a periodizing term. In the first instance, logistics names an organizational discipline and set of transportation and storage practices that superintends the movement of commodities, labour, energy, and capital across transnational supply chains. In contrast to the infrastructuralist emphasis on circulation's material apparatuses (e.g. ports, shipping containers, pipelines), the frame of logistics draws attention to how an ensemble of spaces unevenly embedded in the flows of global capital—from open pit mines to Foxconn factories, from oil tankers to the suburban kitchen—are organized to secure profit. Moreover, logistics doesn't simply refer to the pure movement of stuff through infrastructural spaces; rather, it underlines where stuff comes from and who is involved in its conveyance, attending as much to the physical sites of resource extraction and manufacturing as to the truckers, dockworkers, air traffic controllers, and delivery drivers that make logistics work. Consequently, the conceptual frame of logistics brings people, and particularly workers performing the labour of circulation, back into a picture that frequently omits or excludes them.

In the second instance, logistics is a periodizing term, which describes the increased importance of circulation to the global economy, following the post-1970s reorganization of global capital accumulation. In the wake of the Great Depression, the US government realized it had to regulate capitalism's excesses to maintain both domestic and international stability, and created a regulatory framework based on Keynesian principles to do so. These included the Bretton Woods system of international fixed exchange rates, underpinned by the US dollar; regular intervention into the economy based on an assumption of a manipulable trade-off between inflation and employment rates; and the management of relations between labour and capital. For 30 years these policies were effective, but in the 1970s they stopped working. Industrial productivity and economic growth in the capitalist core were upended by inflation and stagnation; the Bretton Woods monetary system collapsed; and anti-colonial, worker, and student insurgencies both domestically and internationally threatened American hegemony, which undergirded the global economy. In response, the US oversaw a reorganization of the global economy along neoliberal lines. Tax cuts, deregulation, privatization, the removal of subsidies and tariffs, and the divestment of social welfare programmes all served to remake the world for the benefit of profit and power. In this new business climate, manufacturing firms rapidly incorporated technological revolutions in information management, shipping and transport (e.g. containerization), and restored profitability by speeding up and expanding the global circulation of commodities (Toscano, "Logistics and Opposition"; Chua, "Logistics, Capitalist Circulation, Chokepoints"). In short, multinational corporations increasingly capitalized on moving rather than making stuff.

Increasing the speed of circulation also entailed enlarging the scope of circulation, and repurposing previously production-oriented landscapes, infrastructures, and life-worlds for new ends. Business firms developed new kinds of financial instruments and transportation strategies to penetrate hitherto inaccessible or weakly incorporated markets, resource landscapes, and labour pools, and policing and military practices were revolutionized and expanded to work in concert with international trade organizations like the International Monetary Fund to prevent worker organizing, regulatory laws, trade tariffs, or Indigenous or national claims to resources from disrupting the smooth movement of energy and workers (Chua, "Logistics"). The emergence of logistics in this period thereby becomes synonymous with, as Cowen emphasizes, the complete integration of "urban space into managed networks of goods circulation underpinning both trade and warfare" (193), increasingly blurring the line between the two. While some of these processes are new—as in the creation of entire logistics cities like Tsawwassen outside Vancouver, Basra in Iraq, or Antofagasta in Chile—they are rooted in the longer violent histories capital accumulation and urbanization. Logistics, as Fred Moten and Stefano Harney argue, "was founded in the Atlantic slave trade, founded against the Atlantic slave" (87), as well as in the processes of colonial dispossession, such as land clearances for railway lines and pipelines (Pasternak; Scott). To this end, logistics is not accidentally colonial; rather land dispossession, colonial violence, racialized forced labour, and imperialist wars are and have always been central to logistics' functioning.

We propose that literary representations of streets and highways can be likewise situated within logistics' expanded cartography, as an important base for both mapping the circulatory system of global capital and describing how that system shapes the particularities of place. At the same time, refocusing attention on logistics highlights the historical forces whereby literary works discover the political possibilities in and of the street. With reference to the circulation struggles organized by Occupy, Black Lives Matter, and Idle No More, Ruth Jennison and Julian Murphet argue that "[t]he resurrection of the mass action ... has created the possibility for spatial nearness between the poet and other bodies and voices. This resuturing of poet to street has revivified the question of what poetry can do" (15). By the same token, Eng's poetry addresses the street as semiosis, as both form and content at once hosting and representing a specific conjuncture of inner-city dislocation and political direct action by masses of people (as in the 2010 anti-Olympic tent city encampment in Vancouver, which drew attention to the growing problem of homelessness in Vancouver, exacerbated by Olympic-led downtown "beautification" and development projects). Here, logistics describes more than the efficiently, cheaply, and quickly delivered novel or Instant Pot or socks or phone from a factory city in China to your front door in Vancouver, New York, Toronto, or Cairo: it is instead a geographical constellation and historical force, bringing into relief both the representational dilemmas and conditions of aesthetic possibility for urban literatures.

One way we consider these levels of experience, infrastructure, and logistics is as instances of what Lefebvre identifies as three "levels" of a larger social totality: a "global level" aligned with both the state and global regimes like "neoliberalism"; a "mixed level" that he describes as the "specifically urban level" or the level of the "city"; and a private level," which he will refer to "everyday life" or what is more often now described today in terms of "social reproduction" (*The Urban Revolution* 78).[2] Within Lefebvre's schema, the street is of particular importance because it is both a site of production and also rooted in people's daily lives. The street, Lefebvre writes,

> represents the everyday in our social life [...] If anything is hidden, it tears it out from its darkness. It makes it public. It robs it of its privacy and drags it on to the stage of a spontaneous theatre, where the actors improvise a play which has no script. The street takes whatever is happening somewhere else, in secret, and makes it public. It changes its shape, and inserts it into the social text.
>
> *(Critique of Everyday Life 502)*

Central here is that the way that Lefebvre conceptualizes the street: not as belonging to the level of the urban, but as being made by other levels, and which render other levels visible. The street brings the private into the public, and takes what is happening elsewhere (e.g. rural resource extraction, commodity production in the periphery, colonial wars) and stresses its active role in the composition of urban social life. Following Lefebvre's lead, we suggest that literature's engagements with streets (and the houses and buildings located therein) becomes a key site through which literature negotiates, reimagines, and mediates its worlds.

"I call for new accurate maps": Textual Maps of the Street

Eng's work is exemplary in this regard, and "autocartography" opens with an introductory note on the practice of cartography: "it was "initially created for/mercenary pursuits/maps marked out/trade routes between Europe and the trading posts of the East/benefitting merchants who called for new accurate maps//I call for new accurate maps" (72). The opening demand frames the poems as offering just that accurate map through the entwining of its rhythmic, stanzaic lyric poems—"lean on the car door, have a chat/let him think he's brought the mac/be a bit sassy/so the cake'll lead him back" (77)—and the recurring map-index hybrid poems, "how it is." The first "how it is (November 2007)" reads:

MAIN	MAIN
Owl Drugs	The heart of the community
No-name money mart	The Roosevelt
Hotel Washington	Coastal Health Authority
Convenience store	The Regent
Empty building	Closed business
The Balmoral	Closed business
Pizza shop	Closed business
Porn store	Closed business
Insite (North America's 1st legal safe injection site)	The Blue Eagle
Vancouver Drug Store	The Brandiz
Empty lot	Closed business

Empty building (the old Smilin' Buddha where my dad saw Jimi Hendrix)	Convenience store
Art gallery	Convenience store
Subsidized housing project	COLUMBIA
COLUMBIA	Pigeon Park Savings
Pawn shop	Empty lot
	Convenience store

On the surface, "how it is" is an infrastructure poem that produces a "textual map" or street-level snapshot of the DTES. It adopts a range of identificatory registers, from the mundanely nondescript (closed business, porn shop, convenience store) to the emotionally charged and nostalgic, such as "the heart of the community"—the Carnegie Community Centre—and the former site of "the old Smilin' Buddha where my dad saw Jimi Hendrix" (74). The poem registers the visible juxtapositions that constitute Vancouver's paradigmatic urban environment: public parks beside pawn shops, hotels providing basic, transitory shelter beside an "empty building development" (75).

But the poem also provides the speaker's affective attachment to place. Eng positions this affective angle to "how it is" in contrast with another spatial map of these same city blocks, Stan Douglas' photographic project *Every Building on 100 West Hastings Street* (2002). In *Mercenary English*'s afterword, Eng talks about her encounter with Douglas' artwork during a writing course at SFU in 2017: "I wasn't impressed. There are no people in it, none of the low-income people that populate the area" (120). Her criticism (that Douglas erases Hastings street's residents) resonates with what Alberto Toscano describes as a dominant trend within the aesthetics of logistics, which is typified by images of "a depopulated landscape of megastructures" such as ports and factories that fetishize the "*modularity, abstraction,* [and] *indifference (or anaesthesia)*" of these sites ("The Mirror of Circulation"). For Eng, Douglas' photographs similarly portray Hastings street as an abstracted and fixed space able to grasp the outward signs of gentrification at a particular moment, but not how such spatial change is lived over time. By contrast, Eng's changing streetscapes are soaked in the ecologies, racial identities, and colonial relations of contemporary urbanization.

The poem "how it is" aims to socialize the built environment and urban geography of the downtown core by addressing the meaning individual sites hold for the DTES community and emphasizing the individual sensoriums and class conflicts that constitute a particular way of seeing infrastructure and social life. Eng produces a highly personalized account of Hastings that broadcasts her own intergenerational experience within the neighbourhood, for instance by labelling the "Downtown Eastside Residents Assoc." building as the place where "they helped my dad then me with housing" (75). She also foregrounds the broader, perhaps more fundamental class tensions embedded within such sites, as when she describes the "United We Can" building as the place where there are "poor people endeavouring every day to make money by cleaning up your environmentally-friendly water bottles" (75).

But the iterative structure of "how it is" also testifies to the temporal dynamics of urban change; the poem "mak[es] the shift visible not as a sweeping, immediate change," as Ryan Fitzpatrick contends, "but as a piece-by-piece process determined by relationships to property" (63). Five years later, "how it is (January 2012)" navigates a noticeably altered urban landscape:

MAIN	MAIN
Owl Drugs	The heart of the community
No-name money mart	The Roosevelt
Hotel Washington	Rest in peace AM & VS
Convenience store	The Regent
Empty building	Dev. app. no. DE414810
The Balmoral	Dev. app. no. DE414810
Pizza shop	Dev. app. no. DE414810
Porn store	Dev. app. no. DE414810
Insite	Dev. app. no. DE414810
Art gallery	The Brandiz
Community garden	Art gallery
Empty building (the old Smilin' Buddha where my dad saw Jimi Hendrix)	Convenience store
Art gallery	Convenience store
Subsidized housing project	COLUMBIA
COLUMBIA	Pigeon Park Savings
Convenience store	Empty lot
Closed pawn shop	Convenience store

The row of closed businesses west of the Regent from 2007 has now been assimilated into a single "dev. app. no. DE414810," including the Coastal Health Authority. Here we see Eng ventriloquize another imperialist cartographer, not the Early Modern mapmakers of colonial expansion but the urban planner and real estate developer who reimagines working-class urban space as a new wilderness, ripe to create a new neighbourhood more amenable to capital accumulation. The work of the developer-cartographer's dream is further born out in "how it is (November 2014)" in which the dev. App. No. DE 313810 has bloomed into "79 units of market housing/9 units of 'affordable housing/9 units at welfare-shelter rate," and further down the street, nestled between the "fancy furniture store" and "Money Mart," lies the developer's jewel SFU Woodward's/Goldcorp Centre for the Arts (100, 102).

MAIN	MAIN
Owl Drugs	The heart of the community
No-name money mart	The Roosevelt
Maple Hotel (PPP Canada SRO Initiative)	Rest in peace AM & VS
Convenience store	The Regent

Empty building	Dev. app. no. DE414810 approved
The Balmoral	79 units of market housing
Pizza shop	9 units of "affordable" housing
Porn store	9 units of welfare-shelter rate
Insite	Dev. app. no. DE414810 approved
Rest in peace Bud Osborn	
Art gallery	The Brandiz
Empty building (the old Smilin' Buddha where my dad saw Jimi Hendrix)	Convenience store
Art gallery	Convenience store
Community garden	
Subsidized housing project	COLUMBIA
COLUMBIA	Pigeon Park Savings
Convenience store	Empty lot
Closed pawn shop	Convenience store

Embedded within the poem, then, is a battle for the meaning of the city staged between the cartographic tools of the developer and the poet, and the ways of seeing baked within. In this view, "how it is" describes how Vancouver feels within a specific locale during a particular, gradually unfolding, historical conjuncture as it shapes the spatial, social, and affective relations of the inner-city.

"prison industrial complex explodes/but all the right people live": Logistical Lyrics

"autocartography" works through a double reversal. On the one hand, the seemingly impersonal infrastructural poems of "how it is" are ultimately revealed to be subjectively constructed, and arrayed within a larger war over the meaning of the urban infrastructures of the DTES. On the other hand, it is the interspersed lyric poems that ultimately draw into focus the sociospatial routes and logistical complexes that suture together the gentrifying downtown core with its carceral and extractive peripheries. Indeed, where the lyric poem is conventionally associated with the expression of emotional interiority, in "autocartography" this poetic form links personal history to the gentrification and displacement of Indigenous and other racialized populations from the DTES; moreover, it does so in tandem with the broader processes of mass incarceration, and continued land seizure for oil and gas extraction.

The lyric poems "low-track" and "schoolyard hooker" detail the daily routines of the "eastside hustle" performed by sex workers leaning up against the doors of potential customers, conducting negotiations over condom use, or buying heroin (77). Crucially, Eng reinserts the subject, the sex worker-turned-writer, into the infrastructural environment: "now my body of intellectual work/is about/the work/I did/with my body," Eng asserts in "post hooker micro.macro," "so I'm selling/with my body" (106). Lyric capture, as it attempts to crystallize personal testimony around a determinate historical moment, continues the work of "how it is" to populate the ostensibly abandoned DTES spaces. But, Eng also expands the scope of the lyric to contemplate how the "eastside hustle" is shaped by the urban's abrasions with global capital. Where the initial lyric poems of "autocartography" are set within the streets and alleys abutting Hastings street, "in dreams" hews closer to the highway system that shoots out from the DTES' urban infrastructures towards a much broader logistical archipelago of prisons and sites of resource extraction throughout western Canada and eventually the global market:

> the oil rigs me and my baby brother saw
> as we drove all over Alberta
> to visit our dad in correctional facilities
> that span the same provinces as the pipelines
> the institutions where you house the nation
> (98)

Eng's recollection of childhood visits to her incarcerated father participates in a tradition of the lyric confession par excellence, set against the equally overdetermined trope of the road narrative or automotive journey. But undercutting long-standing American (and to a lesser extent Canadian) depictions of the road as a space of freedom, expansion, individual development, and redemption, Eng posits the road as a space of incarceration set against a backdrop of petroleum extraction, one of the signature vistas of contemporary logistics. Insofar as "in dreams" supplies the autobiographical counterpart to Eng's cartographic writing, this poem is palpably bound up with the logistical landscapes of western Canada, where prisons—like the oil rigs and pipelines fanning out across Alberta and British Columbia—are another form of infrastructure that moves and contains surplus labour over space and time.

In turn, the poem troubles the desire for frictionless motion that typifies logistics, instead emphasizing the interplay of movement and enclosure: thus the imprisonment of her father involves shuttling across numerous penal institutions, "Matsqui, Mission, Mountain,/Drumheller, Bowden, BC Pen," which run parallel to the oil industry's arsenal of "extraction machineries" (99, 98). Taking the highway for its key mediating link, "in dreams" stresses the spatial nearness of tar sands and BC Pen to the DTES, entrenching childhood experience within the logistical routes that both seize and circulate people and petroleum. Eng thus ties "life on the streets" to a larger tableau of inextricably connected oil rigs, pipelines, prisons, cops, courthouses, residential schools, and government injunctions that forms what she calls the "truth and reconciliation industry" (97).[3] In doing so, Eng highlights how the implantation and concomitant synchronization of Canada's carceral system to its extractive economy is inseparable from what Heather Dorries, David Hugill, and Julie Tomiak term "settler colonial urbanism," by which they "draw attention to the ways that settler colonial dispossession and violence manifest in manifold ways in urban life."

With their nimble shifts in scale, Eng's logistical lyrics suffuse the experiential precision of poetic testimony with global capital's geographies of dispossession. As "in dreams" demonstrates, Eng perceives the highway not merely as an abstract space connecting rural sites, but rather as a fixture of her childhood and a mediating structure that rhymes spatially with petroleum pipelines. Eng's mixture of lyric capture and logistical landscape does not aspire to a kind of spatiotemporal immediacy that conjoins personal confession and extraction site, but rather considers the ways in which subjectivity is situated within and confronts settler colonial urbanism's interplay of enclosure and circulation.

Coda

The streets and highways of "autocartography" represent sites of contact between the unstable spaces of everyday life and the concrete instantiations of racial capitalism's extractive modes. Poems like "in dreams" trace the outer geographical limit for "how it is," where Eng's portrayal of metropolitan urban change appears textured by the lineaments of the petroleum industry and carceral state. Alternatively, the logistical landscapes of pipelines, prisons, and deforestation underpinning Eng's lyrics are baked into the financialized sensorias of the DTES, where the "hooker store (Model Express)" and SRO hotels are only a few doors down from the glitzy condo development/university campus boasting a mining company's name. In its toggling between and refiguring of foreground and backdrop, urban core and extractive periphery, and subject and setting, "autocartography" depicts streets and highways as distinct yet interrelated meeting points of capital accumulation and social experience. It highlights the importance of streets and highways as crucial junctures through which literature can turn towards the horizon of global capital, via the struggles over the making and meaning of everyday life. And it makes a case for the political potential of these poetic counter-mapping forms. The cycle ends where it begins, returning from the developer to the early modern cartographer, now dragged into the twenty-first century, while the lyric itself transforms into a battle cry. "this time/i'm a pirate/and your pathetic white ass is my booty/this time/i lead the ship," Eng writes,

> i make you and your sailors
> give me and my all-woman marauding crew pedicures
> while we storm the seas
> the best thing is
> you don't even see us coming
>
> (113, 114)

Notes

1 It is important to stress that this canon is primarily Anglo-American because there is a longstanding and rich body of work that has analysed how postcolonial literature has forefronted urban space's entanglements with global scales of colonial accumulation. See Anne McClintock's *Imperial Leather*, Andreas Huyssen's edited collection *Other Cities, Other Worlds: Urban Imaginaries in a Globalizing Age*, and Rashmi Varma's *The Postcolonial City and Its Subjects: London, Nairobi, Bombay*.
2 While it is tempting to read these levels as geographic or spatial scales (even defining M as the level of the urban), the reader does so at her own peril. As Goonewardena notes, in Lefebvre's account of the actual city, "all three 'levels' operate within it" (66). Instead, he suggests we read them as categories at the intersection of the social and the spatial, always in process, always requiring sustained mediation and renegotiation.
3 "Truth and Reconciliation" refers to a commission set up by the Canadian government in 2015 to document and repair the harms caused by colonial programmes, such as the residential schools. The process has been broadly criticized for treating colonialism as a past wrong that is concluded rather than as an ongoing process with persistent harms (Simpson 2011).

Works Cited

Berlant, Lauren. "The Commons: Infrastructures for Troubling Times." *Environment and Planning D: Society and Space*, vol. 34, no. 3, June 2016, pp. 393–419.

Chua, Charmaine. "Logistics." *The SAGE Handbook of Marxism*, edited by Beverly Best et al. SAGE Publications Ltd., 2022, pp. 1444–1462.

———. "Logistics, Capitalist Circulation, Chokepoints." *The Disorder of Things*, 9 Sept. 2014, https://thedisorderofthings.com/2014/09/09/logistics-capitalist-circulation-chokepoints/.

Coulthard, Glen Sean. *Red Skin, White Masks: Rejecting the Colonial Politics of Recognition*. U of Minnesota P, 2014.

Cowen, Deborah. *The Deadly Life of Logistics: Mapping Violence in Global Trade*. U of Minnesota P, 2014.

Dorries, Heather, et al. "Racial Capitalism and the Production of Settler Colonial Cities." *Geoforum*, Aug. 2019. *ScienceDirect*, https://doi.org/10.1016/j.geoforum.2019.07.016.

Eng, Mercedes. *Mercenary English: Poems*. Talonbooks, 2018.

Federici, Silvia. *Caliban and the Witch: Women, the Body and Primitive Accumulation*. Penguin UK, 2021.

Fedoruk, Emily. "'Never/Again': Reading the Qayqayt Nation and New Westminister in Public Poetry Installations." *A Feminist Urban Theory for Our Time: Rethinking Social Reproduction and the Urban*, edited by Linda Peake et al. John Wiley & Sons, 2021, pp. 66–91.

Geidel, Molly, and Patricia Stuelke. "Infrastructural-Innovation Realism in an Age of Collapse." *American Literary History*, vol. 33, no. 1, Feb. 2021, pp. 103–132, https://doi.org/10.1093/alh/ajaa039.

Goonewardena, Kanishka. "The Urban Sensorium: Space, Ideology and the Aestheticization of Politics." *Antipode*, vol. 37, no. 1, 2005, pp. 46–71.

Harney, Stefano, and Fred Moten. *The Undercommons: Fugitive Planning & Black Study*. Minor Compositions, 2013.

Huyssen, Andreas, editor. *Other Cities, Other Worlds : Urban Imaginaries in a Globalizing Age*. Duke UP, 2008.

Katz, Cindi. "Vagabond Capitalism and the Necessity of Social Reproduction." *Antipode*, vol. 33, no. 4, 2001, pp. 709–728.

Jennison, Ruth, and Julian Murphet. "Introduction." *Communism and Poetry: Writing Against Capital*, edited by Ruth Jennison and Julian Murphet, Palgrave, 2019, pp. 1–20.

Lefebvre, Henri. *Critique of Everyday Life: The Three-Volume Text*. Verso Books, 2014.

———. *The Urban Revolution*. U of Minnesota P, 2003.

McClintock, Anne. *Imperial Leather : Race, Gender, and Sexuality in the Colonial Contest*. Routledge, 1995.

McCreary, Tyler, and Richard Milligan. "The Limits of Liberal Recognition: Racial Capitalism, Settler Colonialism, and Environmental Governance in Vancouver and Atlanta." *Antipode*, vol. 53, no. 3, 2021, pp. 724–744. *Wiley Online Library*, https://doi.org/10.1111/anti.12465.

Nason, Dory. "We Hold Our Hands Up: On Indigenous Women's Love and Resistance." *Decolonization: Indigeneity, Education & Society*. Feb 12 2013. https://decolonization.wordpress.com/2013/02/12/we-hold-our-hands-up-on-Indigenous-womens-love-and-resistance/.

Pasternak, Shiri. "Occupy (Ed) Canada: The Political Economy of Indigenous Dispossession." *The Winter We Danced: Voices from the Past, the Future, and the Idle No More Movement*, edited by Kinonda-niimi Collective. ARP Books, 2014, pp. 40–44.

Rubenstein, Michael, et al. "Infrastructuralism: An Introduction." *MFS Modern Fiction Studies*, vol. 61, no. 4, 2015, pp. 575–586.

Scott, Cam. "Below the Barricades: On Infrastructure, Self-Determination, and Defense." *Viewpoint Magazine*, 11 Oct. 2021, https://viewpointmag.com/2021/10/11/below-the-barricades-on-infrastructure-self-determination-and-defense/.

Simpson, Leanne Betasamoke. *Dancing on our Turtle's Back*. ARP Books, 2011.

Toscano, Alberto. "Logistics and Opposition." *Mute*. Mute Publishing Limited, 9 Aug. 2011, https://www.metamute.org/editorial/articles/logistics-and-opposition.

———. "The Mirror of Circulation: Allan Sekula and the Logistical Image." *Society and Space*, 31 July 2018, https://www.societyandspace.org/articles/the-mirror-of-circulation-allan-sekula-and-the-logistical-image.

Varma, Rashmi. *The Postcolonial City and Its Subjects: London, Nairobi, Bombay*. Routledge, 2012.

Yaeger, Patricia. "Introduction: Dreaming of Infrastructure." *PMLA*, vol. 122, no. 1, Jan. 2007, pp. 9–26.

35
NATURE

Steven Swarbrick

Introduction: Inside Out

Raymond Williams observed that "Nature is perhaps the most complex word in the [English] language" (219) because its figurations range from hotly contested "human nature" to the personified "Mother Nature" who stands in putative opposition to "culture." More than three decades later, neither the meaning nor the political implications of that word have simplified. Amid the complexity, here are a few things ecological theory knows today about the politics of nature; or, in the judicious words of Eve Kosofsky Sedgwick and Adam Frank (after whose essay, "Shame in the Cybernetic Fold" this chapter is modeled), "here are a few broad assumptions that shape the heuristic habits and positing procedures" (93) of ecocriticism. These habits and procedures are not identified in ecocriticism as it appears locally in any one theory or text, but in ecocriticism as a global, planetary project spanning the humanities and posthumanities: a scholarly discipline comprising diverse premises and methodologies but largely intent on bridging the human and nonhuman as mutually entangled beings inextricable from nature. This is ecocriticism extending into interdisciplinary corners, including science and technology studies, the deep time of geology, evolutionary biology, and, increasingly, climatology and its racialized atmospheres; ecocriticism, that is, after major theoreticians have had their way and say: after Bruno Latour and Donna Haraway, after Gilles Deleuze and Félix Guattari, after Jacques Derrida, Karen Barad, and Timothy Morton, after Édouard Glissant and Christina Sharpe have posited relationships between "nature" and a word that is perhaps equally complex: "politics."

So, what does "ecocriticism" know about nature, literature, and politics?

1   We, literary critics and environmentalists, are not outside nature; according to ecocriticism, we are in nature. We are in nature as imbroglio (Latour), natureculture (Haraway), assemblage (Deleuze and Guattari), *différance* (Derrida), mesh (Morton, *Queer Ecology*), and web (Moore). To say otherwise is not only naive but dangerous. The danger can be summarized by René Descartes' mind-body dualism and the deleterious consequences that ecocriticism attributes to that illusory divide between mind and body and nature and culture: namely, gender oppression, racism, and extractive capitalism (Moore 2, 9). To say that we are thoroughly enmeshed with nature is thus to refuse an easy "outside"

DOI: 10.4324/9781003038009-41

2   Because we are fully entangled with the natures we write about, there is no "outside"—no remote, objective Archemedian point of observation or action—for us, no elsewhere to cast our toxic forms of waste ranging from petrochemicals to plastic bags to masculinity. The refusal of the outside sounds comforting at first, as if to say, "we are all in it together!" But the loss of an outside carries a negative twist. It means that we are everything we abject. As Stacy Alaimo argues, we are "trans-corporeal" beings; we wear pollutants in the flesh (2). This more sobering understanding of entanglement counts as another major inroad of ecocriticism to date; it rids us of the false comforts of pastoralism.

3   If we add (1) and (2) together, we arrive at a haunting proposition: with no outside to escape to and no elsewhere to cast our poisons, literary critics and ecologists can only mourn what Morton calls "ecology without nature." The upside is that ecocritics no longer have to look beyond the entanglements of nature and culture; the downside is that ecocritics no longer look beyond the entanglements of nature and culture. Instead of capital-N "Nature," ecocriticism now points to entanglement as a sort of liberatory, sort of queer, and utterly painful experience.[1] By expelling the outside as a humanist myth, ecocriticism gives itself a new problem: how to step outside and thus think outside its own ritual prescriptions.[2]

Despite Raymond Williams' clear-eyed reminder about the deep complexity of the word and concept of nature, the literature and politics of nature as represented in ecotheory of the past few decades has settled on a shared assumption: nature is an imaginary, romantic projection of industrial and late-industrial nostalgia happily overlooking the machine in the garden, and thus a highly problematic roadblock to properly political ecology.[3]

Bruno Latour says as much in *The Politics of Nature*, a manifesto of political ecology in the manner of Vladimir Lenin's "What is to be done?" but one fully aware of the exhaustion of manifestos and the avant-garde. In Latour's thinking, the political avant-garde relies dubiously on the outside as a space of critique. This outer space is, Latour argues, like a Möbius strip—or worse, a cul-de-sac of the imagination leading the ecocritic back to myth. In Latour's view, political ecology as it has hitherto been imagined is identical to Plato's "Allegory of the Cave": the philosopher or ecocritic divides nature (Plato's realm of Ideas) from culture (the cave of the imaginary) and puts undue importance on one side or the other: nature, the site of scientific objectivity, or culture, the site of the social construction of nature. Latour's update to the Platonic allegory is readily apparent in contemporary environmental activism: the rhetoric of environmental activist Greta Thunberg, for example, excoriates our cultural delusions and champions the truth claims of STEM (science, technology, engineering, and mathematics). As Thunberg told the U.S. Congress in 2019 and other activists repeat, "I don't want you to listen to me, I want you to listen to the scientists." Latour, for his part, seeks to mediate the divide between science and politics by attending to the entanglements (scientific, epistemological, and cultural) that political ecology tends to parse surreptitiously. The task Latour sets for political ecology, then, is not Plato's, but neither is it strictly speaking the environmentalist's: not to escape the cave of the imaginary into nature, but rather to get out of nature. Why?

Latour says that nature, like any fetishized commodity, is a collective fiction. Yes, it is real. Certainly, you can touch it, but only to a point. The nature we can see is fully mediated by relations that are scientific, epistemic, serial, and impossible to comprehend all at once; nature, in other words, is structured like a language. When we step out of the cave of the imaginary into the real, Latour argues, we step back into the realm of the imaginary because we miss the symbolic mediations that structure the reality before us. Hence, Latour writes,

> political ecology has nothing at all to do with 'nature'—that blend of Greek politics, French Cartesianism, and American parks. [...] [T]he belief that political ecology is interested in nature is the childhood illness of the field, keeping it in a state of impotence by preventing it from ever understanding its own practice.
>
> *(5)*

That "practice," Latour argues, is in essence democratic. The challenge of political ecology is not to insert nature into politics or politics into nature but to see the democracy of actions that compose a common world without reducing the world to one side of Plato's allegory: in or out.

Latour accepts the conundrum: nature is a cul de sac. Just when we think we have left the imaginary behind, we find ourselves standing in a fully fabricated nature park. Consequently, the democracy that Latour puts forth goes round and round to see what fruitful mediations and surprising encounters come into focus when we let go of nature. This only happens, Latour adds, when we sever the link between political ecology and nature, a nature conceived as "out there." Latour writes:

> While the ecology movements tell us that nature is rapidly invading politics, we shall have to imagine—most often aligning ourselves with these movements but sometimes against them—what a politics finally freed from the sword of Damocles we call nature might be like.
>
> *(1)*

To start down this road, he announces his intention "to show that political ecology, at least in its theories, has to let go of nature. Indeed, nature is the chief obstacle that has always hampered the development of public discourse" (9).

Of course, Latour is by no means the only voice in political ecology. The significant contributions by feminist, queer, Black, and Indigenous scholars to the literature and politics of nature cannot be collapsed into the pronouncements of a single French, white, male theorist. Nevertheless, Latour has had an outsized influence on ecocriticism in the humanities, environmental humanities, and adjacent fields such as science and technology studies, so his imperative "to let go of nature," which others have echoed, carries an understandable weight in the present context. Letting go of nature, the argument goes, is the first step toward democratizing the sciences, enmeshing the human and nonhuman, and letting go of nature's complementary fiction: white Cartesian Man, who has always preferred to stand outside nature looking in at nature's Others.[4]

Without a doubt, the democratization of Plato's cave carried out by Latour and others has transformed literary studies and gone a long way toward curing the political imagination of its "childhood illness": binary thinking. Nevertheless, this transformation itself is entangled with contradictions, for insisting on the inside of ecological entanglement logically entails an outside. Otherwise, why insist? It is undoubtedly a sign of maturity that ecological theory now says "no" to the pastoral imaginary by getting out of Nature and into political ecology. It is also true that these growing pains have resulted in a complex, hypermediated, posthuman network of symbolic actions and performatives. Yet the Latourian impulse (shared by eco-deconstruction and new materialism) forgets that the symbolic is not only incomplete, open to endless symbolization, but also self-external. When I say *this* plant, *this* animal, *this* actor-network, or *this* democracy, "this" can only appear absently, negatively, through a chain of signifiers that exceeds the here and now.

By rejecting one childish fantasy (Nature), Latour erects another fantasy no less imaginary than the Nature he hastens us to let go of. This contradiction on Latour's part reveals that the "outside" remains an animating force in the politics of nature, even when the politics of nature has shut the door on the outside and boarded all the windows. Curiously, although Latour and others posit our interwovenness with nature as a refusal of human exceptionalism, that very refusal ends up making the ecological subject master of its own house, where symbols work and speech acts perform without failure. The irony is that Latour's faith in symbolic action regresses to an imaginary position, one that takes the power of symbols at face value.

An ecocritical approach to the politics of nature begins with the assumption (shared by Latour) that the human being is not the sole arbiter of the world, but rather shares the ability to act and to represent with a wide range of nonhumans. This insight of political ecology is crucial in an age of biospheric feedback, when the wall separating human nature and ecology has collapsed. As Dipesh Chakrabarty argues in "The Climate of History: Four Theses," not only is the human part of natural history, but also most human freedoms hitherto imagined have been "energy-intensive" (208), because they depend on the ocean of extractable resources that Marxist ecologist Jason W. Moore calls "cheap natures" (17). The freedoms promised by capitalism are in direct conflict with sustaining life on Earth, Naomi Klein argues in *This Changes Everything: Capitalism vs. The Climate*. By emphasizing the critical point that nature is not a resource to be extracted and consumed for profit, ecocriticism gives the lie to fossil capitalism. It also points to a different history of the pastoral. This alternative history Williams calls "counter-pastoral" (Williams 1973), citing examples such as Ben Jonson's poem "To Penshurst," which challenge facile images of nature while highlighting the pastoral genre's dependency on entanglements of human and more-than-human actors to power the literary imagination. Counter-pastoral is a mode of literary and political critique that present-day eco-theorists revisit in the language of environmental toxicity (Stacy Alaimo) and extinction (Ursula Heise).

For a powerful and influential theoretical framework that can help diagnose the limits of currently existing ecocriticism and ecotheory, consider the Lacanian triptych of imaginary, symbolic, and Real. To drastically simplify Lacan's terms: the imaginary is what we see (it fills out vision); the symbolic is how we know (it structures perception); and the Real cuts into both, leaving the imaginary and the symbolic with an unknowable, unassimilable remainder—a hole.[5] With this triad in mind, consider the ways in which ecotheory has cured us of our "childhood illness" (the imaginary) and apprised environmentalists of the structuring role of mediation (the symbolic), but has utterly failed to account for the pre-symbolic void that Lacan called the Real. More than just a key term for psychoanalysis and Marxian accounts of history, here we may read "the Real" as the Lacanian defense of the outside and its resistance to symbolization.

Looking at the politics of nature from inside out with Latour, we run into contradiction: the "inside" of ecological entanglement must border itself off from the "outside"—not the "outside" that Latour rebuffs (i.e., "Nature out there") but the outside that Lacan insists is already here, corroding our symbolic system. What I would like to do now is reverse the argument by reading from the outside in. As we shall see, the outside is not what stalls the politics of nature (*pace* Latour); the outside is what keeps our minds, and thus our politics, fixed on future horizons.

The Call of the Outside: Or, Reading Like a Dog

Jack London's naturalist novel *The Call of the Wild* (1903) begins with a seemingly uncomplicated, factual observation that "Buck did not read the newspapers" (3). Since the protagonist of the novel is famously a dog who is abused and then trained out of his ultimately indomitable "natural" instincts, one might, like Buck, skip the invitation to read London's statement closely. The reader's mind is here split between the supposedly omniscient, Archemedian "God view" of the third-person narrative voice and the imputed, subjective, first-person perspective of the protagonist. One can read the words on the page, and yet, bucking the idea that what they express are—finally—the mental capacities of a dog (a dog possessed not only of consciousness—"he would have known"—but also self-consciousness—"for himself"), see little of note. London's brief observation, "Buck did not," nonetheless leaves the question of Buck's capacity for mindedness, let alone his capacity for narrative, tantalizingly suspended.

One of ecocriticism's major contributions to literary criticism is its attunement to capacities of mind and language that had hitherto seemed the sole prerogative of humans. Thanks to influential ecocritical texts like Cary Wolfe's *What Is Posthumanism?*, Derrida's *The Animal That Therefore I Am*, Laurie Shannon's *The Accommodated Animal*, and Tobias Menely's *The Animal Claim*, we can now read human capacities for mind and language as an evolutionary outcrop of nonhuman nature. We read and write, these critics argue, thanks to the countless nonhuman actors that ecocriticism brings to our attention. Read in this light, London's suspension of readerly expectation has less to do with one's inability to countenance an animal mind like Buck's and more to do with the difficulty of conceiving a mind that seems simultaneously inside and outside a narrative of human development. Poised at the start of what looks to be a progressive narrative of self-discovery ("Into the Primitive"), Buck's animality short-circuits the presumption that a narrative of self-discovery is necessarily an exclusively human activity.[6] It also calls into question the presumption that the telos of any such narrative is, finally, either a singular Cartesian mind or a node of political or evolutionary "progress."

Buck's capacity for mind appears in the novel as an emergent property of the relations—indeed, the opacity of the relations—between dogs, humans, the narrator, and reader. By treating mind as a relational property, London's novel suggests that there is value in thinking of mind as both singular and multiple, as an entity that is *differentiable* (to use Sedgwick and Frank's phrase) and *alien* to stories of self-origination. The experience of reading London's novel—that of being of two minds about the protagonist Buck—is of a piece with demands placed on a theory of mind for thinking mind as relational and indeed opaque. As Jacques Rancière avers in his theory of politics, the capacity to be "wrong" is not other to politics, though post-Enlightenment politics frames itself as an education and fight against ignorance. The capacity to be wrong, Rancière argues, is crucial to democracy, that is, to the dissensus that disrupts the normal flow of things and gives rise to a political order based on disagreement. For Rancière, disagreement or "noise" is essential to democracy, just as, for Sedgwick and Frank's cybernetic model, noise is vital to the disruption and realignment of any machine. Buck's reading is the noise in the ecological machinery. Buck teaches us to buck our critical reading habits. He confronts us not with the real—but the Real.

For instance, if the disorientation wrought by the opening sentence of London's novel has to do with the unlikely attribution of mind to the first-person perspective of a dog, note the uncanny merger of the first and third person in the following:

> Finally an idea came to him. He would return and see how his own teammates were making out. To his astonishment, they had disappeared. Again he wandered about through the great camp, looking for them, and again he returned. Were they in the tent? No, that could not be, else he would not have been driven out. Then where could they possibly be?
>
> *(15)*

Here the circular pattern of wandering and returning embodied in Buck's peripatetic movement is doubled by the recursive pattern of question and answer, which Buck and the narrator engage in through free-indirect discourse. The word "wander" enjoys a rich history in the English literary canon, from Chaucer's pilgrims to Milton's Adam and Eve who "hand in hand with wandering steps and slow,/Through Eden took their solitary way" (*Paradise Lost* 12.648–649). For London, the word serves less as a trope of self-discovery wherein the mind improves by correcting its path and more as a way of getting lost, of drifting. As the scene of Buck's wandering unfolds, we come to another free-indirect interrogative—"So that was the way they did it, eh?"—this time with the self-reflexive satisfaction of having learned what the narrator (or is it still Buck? And on what grounds would a reader decide?) laconically refers to as "another lesson" (15).

And yet, more startling than the wandering of mind or minds through London's free-indirect discourse is Buck's capacity for memory and past and present synthesis and, hence, for self-narration. In the following passage, we witness in Buck's fear response the Lamarckian principle that ontogeny and phylogeny operate together to produce layered temporalities of learning, memory, and instinctive response. These temporalities are not easily told apart. Here is Buck:

> It was a token that he was harking back through his own life to the lives of his forebears; for he was a civilized dog, an unduly civilized dog, and of his own experience knew no trap and so could not of himself fear it. The muscles of his whole body contracted spasmodically and instinctively, the hair on his neck and shoulders stood on end, and with a ferocious snarl he bounded straight up into the blinding day…. Ere he landed on his feet, he saw the white camp spread out before him and knew where he was and remembered all that had passed from the time he went for a stroll with Manuel to the hole he had dug for himself the night before.
>
> *(15)*

Perhaps what is most familiar about the passage is the tensioned opposition between an atavistic "nature" and an unstable condition of being "civilized." Perhaps what seems most alien is its refusal to delineate clearly or even at all between the muscles of Buck's body, their spasmodic contraction, and the more serene remembrance of the events leading up to the present moment of the novel. A few pages later, the narrator will describe Buck's employment by saying that "his development (or retrogression) was rapid," and it seems that such a double movement could also be applied to the way mind is unfolded in the above passage (18). Both progressive and retroactive, Buck's mental narrative extends beyond the mere affordances of memory or language or even self-knowledge into muscles, hair, neck, and shoulders.

We see further evidence of the linkage between mind and stimulus in the paragraph whose first sentence begins, "Irresistible impulses seized him" (65). Here we are returned to a scene fixated upon the idea of Buck reading, only this time, unlike with the newspapers, Buck is "listening to the subdued and sleepy murmurs of the forest, reading signs and sounds as man may read a book, and seeking for the mysterious something that called—called, waking or sleeping, at all times, for him to come" (65). Here the undecided status of Buck's mind, whether he is awake or asleep or somewhere in-between, would seem to fit nicely with the theory of mind advanced by London's contemporary, the American psychologist and pragmatist philosopher William James. Mind, for James, is always in flux.

In his essay "What Is an Emotion?" James describes this general flux in affective terms as

> a wave of bodily disturbance of some kind [that] accompanies the perception of the interesting sights or sounds, or the passage of the exciting train of ideas. Surprise, curiosity, rapture, fear, anger, lust, greed, and the like, become then the names of the mental states with which the person is possessed.
>
> *(189)*

What differentiates James's theory of psychic possession from the scene of reading in London's novel is the latter's emphasis on the call, that is, on "the mysterious something" that sets Buck (and us) adrift. Buck is alert to this call before knowing its source: "One night he sprang from sleep with a start, eager-eyed, nostrils quivering and scenting, his mane bristling in recurrent waves" (65). Buck's possession by this call signals a relation, but a relation to what remains enigmatic: a voice and nothing more. James describes this pre-individual relation as an aspect of the neural networks linking living organisms. He writes:

> the nervous system of every living thing is but a bundle of predispositions to react in particular ways upon the contact of particular features of the environment. As surely as the hermit-crab's abdomen presupposes the existence of empty whelk-shells somewhere to be found, so surely do the hound's olfactories imply the existence ... of deer's or foxes' feet.
>
> *(190)*

The "mysterious something" that possesses Buck is part of this greater network that links abdomen, shell, nose, and feet. James calls this network "a hyphen between determinate arrangements of matter" (190). What it communicates, however, is not simply the arrangement of fully individuated selves but more precisely the "hyphen" from which these networked selves emerge.

Conclusion: Outside In

To call this hyphenated way of being a theory of mind may transgress the limits of good sense. I would be lying if I said that was not partly my goal. To call this hyphenated way of being a "politics" might transgress political theory but that is precisely what Latour does when he deems it the very pith of ecological politics. After all, the hyphen is not an exit to nature; as both the highly educated Latour and the fiercely instinctive Buck imagine it, the hyphen is already fully immersed in nature, inextricably and ineluctably bound and connected within a thicket of ecological relations.

And yet, Buck answers to a call that Latour cannot answer. Because Latour so emphasizes the mediating relations of democratic practice, practices that narrativize nature and thus make it a material and symbolic object, he fails to mind and thus misses the gap: "the mysterious something" that Buck hears and that pierces the symbolic fabric. For Latour and other post-nature theorists, there is no "outside" to answer, only the inside of symbolic networks. Nevertheless, this "inside" repeats the very enclosure that Latour warns against. Demanding that we exit Nature, which we can all agree is illusory (a combination of Cartesianism, Romanticism, and American parks), Latour forgets that the hyphen is also an exit: a bridge to the outside. *Not* the outside of the American nature park, but the radical outside that parasites and perturbs our relations. In other words, it is perfectly possible, as environmental philosopher Frédéric Neyrat argues, to be immersed in a field of intelligible relations and still, like Buck, feel the call of the wild. Neyrat calls this hyphenated way of being a trajectory and wagers that we are all (this "all" includes nonhumans) "trajects" rather than subjects: trajectories without fixed coordinates. Neyrat follows the existentialists Jean-Paul Sartre and Simone de Beauvoir in this regard. Their politics rests on the ex- or exit from being to nothing.

Although this chapter has focused on the potential of psychoanalytic and existentialist frameworks to reconfigure what ecologist Gregory Bateson called "the ecology of mind," referring to our physical and mental imbrications with nature, other non-psychoanalytic critics like Jack Halberstam arrive at a similar point about the wild. Halberstam acknowledges that wildness as a concept is inextricable from colonial and racist histories of violence against Native and Black peoples. London's novel undoubtedly reenacts that violence by deploying a racist imaginary in which the dog's proximity to "nature" is aligned with the presumed proximity of people whose supposed "savagery" was noble and also in need of so-called "improvement": the word "Buck," after all, is simultaneously the name given to male deer and rabbits and also a racist epithet used to refer to Indigenous and African American men alike. Halberstam argues, however, that the word "wild" exceeds, indeed, skews and escapes oppressive representational systems. The wild in Halberstam's thinking is erotically and semiotically untamed. Thus, Halberstam "offer[s] another account of wildness within which it functions as a form of disorder that will not submit to rule, a mode of unknowing, a resistant ontology, and a fantasy of life beyond the human" (8).

Lacan calls this wild outside the Real. Although the Lacanian Real is by definition unthinkable, one way to conceive it is as a permanent noise or fault in a symbolic system. "Post-nature" theorists like Latour and others are thus quite right to insist on the iterative mediation of politics, which narrativize nature and thus remove it from a stable essence. However, this dyadic notion—symbolic plus imaginary—forgets or perhaps represses an important third element: the Real, the noise that conditions and corrodes sense. Lacan insists on this crucial third, as do I, because without it the democracy of social actions would become just as totalizing, just as imaginary, as Plato's cave.

Sensing something beyond the cave of the imaginary, sensing something beyond symbolic construction, Buck answers to a wildly enigmatic call. Surely, this call pulls Buck into a thicket of relations. Equally so, it pulls Buck and reader into a seductive encounter with the Real of nature, precisely that which is strange and error-filled (to harken back to Sedgwick and Frank's cybernetic language) in our ecological relations. I call this mode of encounter a seduction based on simple etymology: to seduce, the *Oxford English Dictionary* tells us, is to lead aside or astray. The essence of seduction, then, is that it causes one to drift.

I have drifted throughout this chapter from the current axioms of ecocriticism to a close reading of Jack London's literate hound to show the seductions, the "errancy," inherent in nature's call. This call is wildly enigmatic and does not tend predictably toward the democratic, as Latour wishes. For ecological politics to get real, as Latour and others insist it should, it is not enough to say, exit the cave of the imaginary. Following Buck's wandering steps, we will need to exit the cave of social construction too. For the outside is calling. Throughout human history, it is there. Literary critic Julian Yates likens nature to a series of unanswered calls. "There may, after all, be as many as twelve thousand years' worth of dropped or blocked calls from other forms of life, depending on how you care to date the beginning of the Holocene and of agricultural practices" (21–22).

The politics of nature rests on answering these dropped or blocked calls that now ring loudly in the form of melting ice caps, debilitating heat, sea level rise, ocean acidification, pandemic, species extinction, and desertification. Events that once seemed the stuff of science fiction now constitute our everyday reality, and they are only getting worse and more frequent, fueled by fossil capitalism's war against the planet. Ecocriticism bars our wish to return to naïve Nature and grapples with the histories of coloniality (Gosh) and racial capitalism (Yusoff) that got us in this mess.

Yet it also invites speculation about the many wild and disorderly forms of the outside that remain and resist exploitation (Tsing). Buck is one figure of that resistance. His name personifies refusal (i.e., bucking the system) and his way of reading nature uncovers the wildness that Halberstam sees overflowing dominant systems. Although Buck is never outside those systems, he answers to something beyond their control. Ecocriticism urges us to do likewise. It is an urgent call to act and to buck the systems accelerating environmental crisis. It is time we answered.

Notes

1. Morton splits the difference (*Queer Ecology*). They argue that the queerness of ecology derives from the fact that it repeats the loss of nature—a nature we never really had to begin with.
2. On this point, see Giraud and Neyrat, respectively. Giraud problematizes ecological doxa by pointing to the sites of negativity in ecocriticism's web. Likewise, Neyrat develops a radical existentialism attuned to the outside of ecological thought.
3. I derive this counter-pastoral phrase, the machine in the garden, from Leo Marx's timely study.
4. See Wynter.
5. For a canonical account of the Lacanian politics of the Real, see Žižek. For a lucid summary of Lacan's three orders, imaginary, symbolic, and Real, see McGowan.
6. For more on a politics of nonhuman and human animal relations, see Mario Ortiz-Robles' chapter "Animals" in this volume.

Works Cited

Alaimo, Stacy. *Bodily Natures: Science, Environment, and the Material Self*. Indiana UP, 2010.
Barad, Karen. *Meeting the Universe Halfway: Quantum Physics and the Entanglement of Matter and Meaning*. Duke UP, 2007.
Bateson, Gregory. *Steps to an Ecology of Mind*. U of Chicago P, 2000.
Beauvoir, Simone de. *The Second Sex*. Translated by Constance Borde and Sheila Malovany-Chevallier. Vintage Books, 2011.
Chakrabarty, Dipesh. "The Climate of History: Four Theses." *Critical Inquiry*, vol. 35, pp. 197–222.
Deleuze, Gilles, and Félix Guattari. *A Thousand Plateaus: Capitalism and Schizophrenia*. Translated by Brian Massumi. U of Minnesota P, 1987.
Derrida, Jacques. *The Animal That Therefore I Am*. Translated by David Wills. Fordham UP, 2008.
Ghosh, Amitav. *The Nutmeg's Curse: Parables for a Planet in Crisis*. U of Chicago P, 2021.
Giraud, Eva Haifa. *What Comes After Entanglement? Activism, Anthropocentrism, and an Ethics of Exclusion*. Duke University Press, 2019.

Glissant, Édouard. *Poetics of Relation*. Translated by Betsy Wing. U of Michigan P, 1997.Halberstam, Jack. *Wild Things: The Disorder of Desire*. Duke UP, 2020.
Haraway, Donna J. *The Companion Species Manifesto: Dogs, People, and Significant Otherness*. Prickly Paradigm Press, 2003.
Heise, Ursula K. *Imagining Extinction: The Cultural Meanings of Endangered Species*. U of Chicago P, 2016.
James, William. "What Is an Emotion?" *Mind*, vol. 9, no. 34, 1884, pp. 188–205.
Klein, Naomi. *This Changes Everything: Capitalism vs. The Climate*. Simon and Schuster, 2014.
Lacan, Jacques. *The Seminar of Jacques Lacan, Book XI: The Four Fundamental Concepts of Psychoanalysis*. Edited by Jacques-Alain Miller. Translated by Alan Sheridan. Norton, 1998.
Latour, Bruno. *Politics of Nature: How to Bring the Sciences into Democracy*. Translated by Catherine Porter. Harvard UP, 2004.
London, Jack. *The Call of the Wild, White Fang, and To Build a Fire*. The Modern Library, 1998.
Marx, Leo. *The Machine in the Garden: Technology and the Pastoral Ideal in America*. Oxford UP, 2000.
McGowan, Todd. *The Real Gaze: Film Theory After Lacan*. State University of New York P, 2007.
Menely, Tobias. *The Animal Claim: Sensibility and the Creaturely Voice*. U of Chicago P, 2015.
Moore, Jason W. *Capitalism in the Web of Life: Ecology and the Accumulation of Capital*. Verso, 2015.
Morton, Timothy. *Ecology without Nature: Rethinking Environmental Aesthetics*. Harvard UP, 2007.
———. *Hyperobjects: Philosophy and Ecology After the End of the World*. U of Minnesota P, 2013.
———. "Queer Ecology." *PMLA*, vol. 125, no. 2, 2010, pp. 273–282.
Neyrat, Frédéric. *Atopias: Manifesto for a Radical Existentialism*. Translated by Walt Hunter and Lindsay Turner. Fordham UP, 2018.
Rancière, Jacques. *Disagreement: Politics and Philosophy*. U of Minnesota P, 1999.
Sartre, Jean-Paul. *Existentialism is a Humanism*. Translated by Carol Macomber. Yale UP, 2007.
Sedgwick, Eve Kosofsky. "Shame in the Cybernetic Fold: Reading Silvan Tomkins (Written with Adam Frank)." *Touching Feeling: Affect, Pedagogy, Performativity*. Duke UP, 2003, pp. 93–121.
Shannon, Laurie. *The Accommodated Animal: Cosmopolity in Shakespearean Locales*. U of Chicago P, 2013.
Sharpe, Christina. *In the Wake: On Blackness and Being*. Duke UP, 2016.
Thunberg, Greta. "'Listen to the scientists': Greta Thunberg Urges Congress to Take Action." *The Guardian*, September 18, 2019, https://www.theguardian.com/us-news/2019/sep/18/greta-thunberg-testimony-congress-climate-change-action.
Tsing, Anna Lowenhaupt. *The Mushroom at the End of the World: On the Possibility of Life in Capitalist Ruins*. Princeton UP, 2015.
Williams, Raymond. *The Country and the City*. Oxford UP, 1973.
———. *Keywords: A Vocabulary of Culture and Society*. Revised edition. Oxford UP, 1985.
Wolfe, Cary. *What Is Posthumanism?* U of Minnesota P, 2009.
Wynter, Silvia. "Unsettling the Coloniality of Being/Power/Truth/Freedom: Towards the Human, After Man, Its Overrepresentation—An Argument." *CR: The New Centennial Review*, vol 3, no. 3, 2003, pp. 257–337.
Yates, Julian. *Of Sheep, Oranges, and Yeast: A Multispecies Impression*. U of Minnesota P, 2017.
Yusoff, Kathryn. *A Billion Black Anthropocenes or None*. U of Minnesota P, 2018.
Žižek, Slavoj. *The Sublime Object of Ideology*. Verso, 2008.

36
OCEANS
Alison Maas

From Plato's *Republic* and Sophocles' *Antigone* to contemporary imaginings, the ship stands as a venerable figure for conceptualizing the social makeup, hierarchical structure, and affective dynamics of political bodies from the Greek city-state to the modern nation-state. But if the figure of democracy was born upon a ship and should be brought upon a ship to wanting shores, this metaphor suggests a far deeper principle: politics is unthinkable without oceans and oceans unthinkable without politics.[1] Oceanic spaces are foundational in the emergence and expansion of European colonialism, capitalism, imperialism, and attendant forms of racialized and gendered violence. Yet oceans also resist most forms of human habitation and their dark depths obscure many forms of human perception and comprehension. Oceans thus have long floated through literary imagination and history, making their seemingly abstract and often unreachable fluid spaces accessible through metaphor, allegory, narrative, and poetics. If there are persistent tensions between conventional "literary" and "political" spaces, oceans shape and are shaped by political thought and action and can also dispel, resist, or complicate the political. Finally, oceans in literature might suggest a way to navigate these ongoing tensions.

Like the sea itself, the rise of oceanic humanities scholarship has been fluid, uneven, and at times contradictory in thinking about the intersection of politics and space. A key moment in establishing the field came with the 1982 UN Convention on the Law of the Seas (UNCLOS). As the UN's Division for Ocean Affairs and the Law of the Sea defines the convention, UNCLOS "lays down a comprehensive regime of law and order in the world's oceans and seas establishing rules governing all uses of the oceans and their resources." The treaty partitioned the sea into "exclusive economic zones" (EEZs), which extend 200 nautical miles from a nation's coast and grant control over that area's territory and its resources. If the treaty's vision and language was outwardly tidy, actually mapping and establishing sovereignty over the ocean has been an absolute mess. Neither coasts nor oceans can be equally divided into parts of 200 nautical miles, and as such many supposedly "sovereign" exclusive economic zones collide or overlap and inevitably produce the kind of conflict they proclaim to avoid.

Scholars in the humanities have reckoned with EEZs and other designations that treat the sea as "blank space." Elizabeth DeLoughrey, for example, has shown how defining the sea as a blank "aqua nullius" assisted in its territorialization, commodification, colonial mapping, the rise of nationalism, and masculine sociality for national ownership (*Routes and Roots*).

Against this history and regardless of differences, humanities scholarship shared a vested interest in re-establishing the ocean as a site of movement, materiality, historicity, sociality, and alien nature in order to repopulate its putatively "blank space." As we have come to see, problems arising from divvying up the constantly shifting, ecologically diverse, and inherently uncontrollable environment of the ocean only amplify with anthropogenic climate change. As the National Oceanic and Atmospheric Administration explains, EEZs grant coastal states rights for "exploring, exploiting, conserving and managing natural resources, whether living or nonliving." In the current climate crisis, this deadly paradox where states have the right to exploit and also to conserve natural marine resources emblematizes the near-impossible modern alignment of economic, political, and environmental agendas.

Irus Braverman and Elizabeth R. Johnson recently observed that "blue legalities are not of one ocean, nor of one law; instead, they are made up of the multiple and messy registers through which we engage the seas" (*Blue* 4). Indeed, any effort to delimit the ocean, its politics, and literary reactions counteracts the core drive of ocean humanities to embrace the unfamiliar messiness of the sea. In what follows, consider three different spaces on, within, or adjacent to the ocean that exemplify a long and tangled—but by no means exhaustive—history of attempts to chart the boundless space of seas and their politics.

The Blue Humanities, Oceanic Studies, and Critical Ocean Studies

Historian John Gillis defines what scholars refer to as the "blue humanities" at its absolute widest as "a shift in attention from land to sea" ("Blue Humanities"). Other scholars have similarly taken up the call to embark into and submerge beneath the wide planetary oceans to embrace challenges and possibilities introduced by its vast immensity, unfathomable depths, and undiscovered creatures. A move out to sea and away from both continents and nations defines the general parameters of the blue humanities, oceanic studies, and critical ocean studies.

Much of this scholarly development can be traced back to history's late 1980s–early 2000s maritime turn and its interdisciplinary discussions about "Atlantic history." At the forefront of these turns were scholars Paul Gilroy, Ian Baucom, and perhaps most notably Marcus Rediker. Rediker in his Marxist *Between the Devil and the Deep Blue Sea* (1987) traces the life and labor of common Anglo-American sailors in the eighteenth century to highlight their centrality in the rise of capitalism, initiation of wage labor, and burgeoning international working class. A foundational text that focuses on a convergence of race, culture, and politics, Gilroy's *The Black Atlantic* (1993) theorizes a black Atlantic culture that can historically be understood as modern, and which goes beyond ethnicity and nationality in producing "black cultural forms which are both modem and modernist" (73). Finally, Baucom's influential book *Specters of the Atlantic* (2005) returns to the 1781 massacre by drowning of 132 enslaved peoples aboard the slave ship *Zong*; he argues that the "event and its representations are central not only to the trans-Atlantic slave trade and the political and cultural archives of the black Atlantic but to the history of modern capital, ethics, and time consciousness" (31).[2] These texts represent a hard counter to the image of an empty sea devoid of its own history, politics, culture, and sociality that would eventually be systematized by UNCLOS. Instead, they demonstrate the Atlantic Ocean's core position in the very production of modernity and its myriad forms.

As "Atlantic history" increasingly influenced multiple humanities disciplines, scholars began to fill in the limitations and gaps that follow the creation of any new field. Despite the fact that the ocean features heavily in Atlantic history's arguments, it still remains in many respects a space of crossing—a "where" or "upon which" modernity arose. In response, Steve Mentz wrote a formative text within the blue humanities, "Toward a Blue Cultural Studies" (2009), which introduced a "blue cultural studies" distinguished by methods he differentiates from trends in New Historicist and "Atlantic" scholarship: "This new maritime perspective does not view the oceans simply as bodies to be crossed," Mentz writes, "but as subjects in themselves" (997). Considering oceans not merely as the spaces of cultural production but as themselves culturally produced, Mentz draws attention back to the ever-transforming ways in which peoples engage with the sea. The rise of ocean-oriented works sparked a move within literary studies to consider the role of the sea in literature and literary criticism, most clearly set forth in the 2010 *PMLA* "Theories and Methodologies" ocean-themed cluster.[3] In the issue, Hester Blum calls for a practice of oceanic studies that addresses the work of oceanic literature and "the material conditions and praxis of the maritime world, one that draws from the epistemological structures provided by the lives and writings of those for whom the sea was simultaneously workplace, home, passage, penitentiary, and promise" ("Oceanic Studies" 670).

Dubbed the "oceanic turn" or "blue turn," these scholars initiated a proliferation of ocean-based study and numerous new terms that came to frame the ever-expanding field of study: "new thalassology," "terraqueous globe," "terraqueous planet," "anthropocene at sea," and "wet ontology," to name a few.[4] Because the turn began with a focus on the Atlantic Ocean, however, subsequent scholars have critiqued the blue humanities for its potential Eurocentricity. In response, Alice Te Punga Somerville foregrounds perspectives of those in Oceania who didn't need a blue turn. Te Punga Somerville unravels the Atlantic centrality in ocean studies, its recent spotlighting of "marginal oceans to gain a broader view," and alternately proposes that

> Ocean Studies might be better understood as if it were itself an ocean: without a singular starting point or origin; endlessly circulating. Not beyond genealogy, because nothing is, but possessed of a genealogy that is impossibly and beautifully wide.
> *("Oceans Come From" 28)*

This brings us finally to the spatial turn, critical ocean studies, and blue environmental humanities. The spatial turn emerged around the same time as "Atlantic history" from the work of notable figures in the social sciences, primarily geographers David Harvey and Doreen Massey, to take on the concept of empty and abstract space and place. Political geographer Philip Steinberg brought this newfound inspection of space into the realm of the sea with his *The Social Construction of the Sea*. Instead of focusing on a particular ocean, Steinberg, along with Kimberly Peters, in their later articles, set forth a theory of "wet ontologies" that engages the planetary ocean's churning movement and volumic placelessness "within which politics is practised and territory is produced" and stresses that "we must continually rethink the borders that we apply to various materialities and their physical states" ("Wet ontologies" 259). Environmental humanities embraced wet ontologies and wet materiality to destabilize terrestrial bias and focalize the ocean's nature without placing limits to its alien depths. As Elizabeth DeLoughrey notes of this tension, the ocean is often figured as nonhuman and uninhabitable but nonetheless remains "domesticated, militarized, touristed, exoticized, and rendered anthropomorphic" ("Submerged Bodies" 133). DeLoughrey argues that the field "critical ocean studies" more widely encompasses "submarine immersions, multispecies others, feminist and Indigenous epistemologies, wet ontologies, and the acidification of an Anthropocene ocean" ("Critical Ocean" 22). Many critical ocean studies scholars have continued to submerge into the sea's material, historical, cultural, embodied, human, and nonhuman waters to refill that once emptied, putatively blank space.

Ship of State

Authors in a wide-reaching literary genealogy both within and outside the Western canon draw on the space of the ship to figure as allegory, metaphor, or symbol. DeLoughrey observes that while early Atlantic theorists often positioned the ship as a "fluid and nonhegemonic space, an alternative to the conservative nation-state," we must also be "reminded of a tradition of depicting the ship as the republic that dates back to Plato's *Phaedrus*" (*Roots* 77). As Herman Melville writes in *White Jacket*, "a ship is a bit of terra firm cut off from the main; it is a state in itself; and the captain is its king" (371). Resonating with but departing from Plato's "ship of state," Melville's bounded boat signifies an appendage of the nation-state enacting its will upon the seas while constructing its own unique hierarchies.

At other times "the ship" comes to represent a world, an island, or an enclosed ecosystem. For example, Melville allegorizes the ship in chapter 8 of *Moby Dick* to comment on religion, writing that "Yes, the world's a ship on its passage out, and not a voyage complete; and the pulpit is its prow" (45). The first round of traditional maritime literary studies thus set its sights almost exclusively on the maritime vessel, its voyage across seas, and its social makeup of owners, captain, and crew. In doing so, politics at sea was framed in relation to the state's conflicting landedness, transportable ideologies, or imagined communities. Bert Bender's text on American sea fiction from *Moby Dick* to the present organizes around the idea of brother sailors (both crew and authors) writing that "the social and political possibilities are integral with the potential ideal or religious significance of brotherhood in American sea fiction" (*Sea-Brothers* 12). Moving away from categorizing sea fiction, Robert Foulke looks to the sea voyage narrative as a more expansive and encompassing literary genre, noting that "another frequent and natural pattern for voyage narratives is the anatomy of society, in which the small world of the ship serves as a microcosm of civilization as a whole" (*Sea Voyage* 11). John Peck examines American and British maritime fiction as reflective of national identity, life, and history, distinguishing that "in some novels the ship is a mini-state where such questions about the moral condition of society can be studied in a microcosm" but that "more commonly the gap between the regime of the ship and the management of shore-based life is a reflection of competing impulses and social thinking" (*Maritime Fiction* 5).

These early studies of maritime fiction concentrated almost entirely on male writers, especially those most well known in the Western literary canon. Cesare Casarino connects Melville, Marx, and Conrad to ground his argument that the nineteenth-century sea narrative created a "laboratory" for representing and resisting the "crisis of modernity" (*Modernity at Sea*). Bringing about a new era of "maritime" literary studies, Margaret Cohen demonstrated the pre-eminent position nautical spaces hold in the very rise of the novel form by observing multiple oceanic spaces and their chronotopes, or literary representations of space and time. For example, drawing on the same *White Jacket* quotation, Cohen writes that "[w]hen a novel passes through the chronotope of the ship, its portrayal of the ship's hierarchical society is revealing of its politics" (664). These politics are largely stable, as Cohen argues that in Jane Austen's *Persuasion* the naval ship "epitomizes a harmonious domestic universe, where all are snug in their social place" (664). Unique to Cohen's formula, however, is its departure from portraying the ship as a "microcosm" of nation but instead offering sailors the promise of emancipation from the nation-state's oppressive rule. However, Hester Blum explains that although nautical life granted certain freedoms,

> sailors seldom received the benefits of national identification: they were subjected to near-absolute rule of captains; lived under threats of press gangs, piracy, and the slave trade; and toiled in an environment that prohibited the common practices of wage labor.
>
> *("Oceanic Studies" 672)*

So, while "the ship" surely served the governing forces of capitalism and nationalism and contained its own autocratic hierarchies, it also allowed for thinking against the grain of capital and the nation. After all, revolution and mutiny were born aboard the ship.

In perhaps one of the most powerful convergences of literary criticism, politics, and the ocean, Marxist theorist C. L. R. James wrote *Mariners, Renegades & Castaway*, an in-depth study on *Moby Dick*, while under detention on Ellis Island. For James, the Pequod can be seen as an allegory for cold-war era America, where the corporate manager Captain Ahab oversees his factory crew of workers. As the book bridges the two time periods: "Equality is an illusion [...] Men are inevitably divided into brigades and battalions, with captains at their head" (74). James wrote *Mariners* in an attempt to gain political purchase to stall a forced deportation from the United States. Literally suspended in the middle of the ocean and internally exiled from the nation due to his political views, James's personal experience and the conditions under which he wrote the text reflect the afterlives of colonialism and slavery, postcolonialism and racial prejudice.

Indeed, the ship of state carried not only crew and captains across the Atlantic but also enslaved African persons. The slave ship and the Middle Passage were sites of sweeping violence, torture, exile, murder, dehumanization, and unending horrors. Scholars in black studies, critical race studies, critical theory, and feminist studies in particular have returned to these sites to analyze atrocities committed during the Middle Passage, to track its ongoing impact, and in many cases to try to regain some of the innumerable losses suffered. For example, the ocean and vessel play a key role in Hortense Spillers' "Mama's Baby, Papa's Maybe" as the place of forced gender and kinship unmaking, and murder of the cultural subject's body turned flesh. Spillers writes:

> Those African persons in "Middle Passage" were literally suspended in the "oceanic" [...] removed from the indigenous land and culture, and not-yet "American" either, these captive persons, without names that their captors would recognize, were in movement across the Atlantic, but they were also nowhere at all.
>
> *(72)*

Christina Sharpe explores the metaphorical and material afterlife of the slave ship, theoretically locating "ongoing" Black being in the wake, the ship, the hold, and the weather. Sharpe writes that "Racism, the engine that drives the ship of state's national and imperial projects [...] cuts through all of our lives and deaths inside and outside the nation, in the wake of its purposeful flow" (3, 16). One major way scholars have countered the erasures of this purposeful flow is by imaginatively and materially submerging into the sea to account for lives stolen and bodies drowned.

Undersea Crossings

Derek Walcott's famous poem "The Sea Is History" (1979) opens with questions and answers: "Where are your monuments, your battles, martyrs? / Where is your tribal memory? Sirs, / in that grey vault. The sea. The sea / has locked them up. The sea is History" (137). Unlike the blank space over which history unfolded, Walcott declares that the sea not only has a history but actually is History. A second wave of critical ocean studies known as the "(sub)oceanic turn" draws heavily on this as it dives under the waves to reckon with locality and history, subjectivity and multi-speciation, materialism and anthropogenic climate change. Importantly, the turn addresses an underlying assumption of antecedent scholarship: that critical study of seas began in the geopolitical climate of the second half of the twentieth century. Instead, the (sub)oceanic turn tracks much of its study from the geopolitical, colonial, and postcolonial history of the Caribbean and Pacific. Barbadian poet and academic Kamau Brathwaite, for example, evoked the ocean's tidal rhythm to rework the Western dialectic to a "tidalectic, like our grandmother's—our nanna's—action, like the movement of the ocean she's walking on, coming from one continent/continuum, touching another, and then receding ('reading') from the island(s) into the perhaps creative chaos of the(ir) future" (34). Thinking of transoceanic movement through the tidal flow of kin, Brathwaite offers a counter to the colonial and imperially constructed narrative of history to answer his question, "What is the origin of the Caribbean?"

Martinique writer, poet, philosopher, and literary critic Édouard Glissant in *Poetics of Relation* imagines the slave ship as an open boat where "Experience of the abyss lies inside and outside the abyss. The torment of those who never escaped it: straight from the belly of the slave ship into the violet belly of the ocean depths they went" (7). Both Braithwaite and Glissant root their historical and political, theoretic and poetic visions in a submarine aesthetic that seeks to undo the imposed bounds of the slave ship's hull. DeLoughrey, as the first to articulate the (sub)oceanic turn, explicates both poets' influence on conceptualizing oceanic place by explaining how "in the Caribbean the enormity of the transoceanic history of slavery and indenture has created an aesthetics that imaginatively populates the sea in an act of regional historiography and ancestral memory" ("Submarine Futures" 35). As opposed to representations of the ship revealing or depicting a floating opera of politics, such repopulating required artistic modes of submersion. If politics is understood as the individual and collective activities associated not only with government but with those activities that affect public and private lives through exercising state and non-state power (including but not limited to various relations among individuals, the distribution of resources, the terms in which individual identities relate to collective identities, etc.), then the political power of the ship necessarily resides in the realm of the oceanic, the suboceanic, and the aesthetic. Refiguring and re-representing oceanic depths offers a source of active opposition that is illegible to state structures yet paradoxically made visible through different art forms.

Scholars like Stefan Helmreich and Melody Jue have plunged terrestrial theory and practice beneath the water—not to drown them but to consider how our broader conceptions of what it means to act "politically" (as individuals and collectives) have a mediated relationship to an oceanic imaginary that is appropriated into the metaphors of ordinary land-based language. Spotlighting the 2018 US election and its evocation of a Democratic "blue wave," for example, Helmreich argues that

> when social transformations are described as waves, we should ask questions about causality, and about what mix of form and material is being invoked. Who or what produces such waves, physical and affective? Are waves formed by large-scale historical structures, frameworks that overdetermine social action? Or are they, rather, expressions

of collective agencies—networks?—fracturing previously stable structures and finding until now unrealized materializations?

("Wave Theory" 318)

Meanwhile, Melody Jue and Rafico Ruiz consider "saturation" as a "material heuristic" that directs the vocabulary scholars use to speak about phenomena and which is informed by material and environmental characteristics. As Jue and Ruiz observe, saturation begins with water and invokes a "material imaginary where the elements are not a neutral background, but lively forces that shape culture, politics, and communication" (*Saturation* 1). Taking into account an elemental and water-soaked condition of mediation provides important framing for contemporary environmental activism, where elements shape politics but are also politically informed in their uneven effect or harm to certain populations. On the flipside, from the unstable, fluid, and material condition of water arises new possibilities of collective thinking beyond a terrestrial standpoint. For instance, what political relation emerges when we consider homogeneity not as the elimination of difference but instead as the evenly cooperative mixing of salt and water in seawater?

Anthropogenic climate change has also brought about new forms of "submarine aesthetics" and political possibilities. This submarine aesthetic asks us to de-center the human subject and imagine the human as a species in relation with nonhuman others, joined in our susceptibility to climate change; this task is challenging not least because of the seemingly sublime spatial and temporal scales of Anthropocene oceans and their unique environmental threats of pollution, plastics, and acidification. Projecting oceans into the future entails its own problems, as Stacy Alaimo recounts:

> The Anthropocene seas will be paradoxical, anachronistic zones of terribly compressed temporality where, it is feared, the future will move backwards, into a time when the oceans were devoid of whales, dolphins, fish, coral reefs, and a multitude of other species, but jellyfish (and algae) proliferated.
>
> *("Anthropocene Sea" 158)*

Trouble arises as the human timescale of political action runs counter to the devolving Anthropocene seas, and yet the future of both depends on their flows aligning.

With difficulties in conveying the sea's scale and temporality are creative prospects for thinking collectivity, relationality, and political engagement. For instance, Alexis Pauline Gumbs powerfully meditates on marine life and asserts that marine mammals are siblings, ancestors, and teachers. Gumbs states: "I identify *as* a mammal. I identify as a Black woman ascending with and shaped by a whole group of people who were transubstantiated into property and kidnapped across the ocean." Gumbs continues:

> And since I can't help but notice how marine mammals are queer, fierce, protective of each other, complex, shaped by conflict, and struggling to survive the extractive and militarized context our species has imposes on the ocean and ourselves, this work is accountable to the movements that are boldly seeking to transform the meaning of life on the planet right now.
>
> *("Introduction")*

Current phenomena such as erosion, sea level rise, pollution, toxicity, washed-up plastics, and even mass whale beaching represent some of the most significant manifestations of oceanic susceptibility during our current climate crisis. Unsurprisingly, many environmental activists and their resistance movements work from literature, seas and seascapes to demand collective action. Gumbs qualifies that this text is meant to remain a meditation that opens conceptual space for wondering and questioning together in a way that either is or will become political in a form of environmental activism.

The Coastal Zone

At seashores, all those possibilities, restrictions, politics, and literary re-imaginings complicate as oceans collide with land. The many names for "coast"—shore, beach, seaside, waterside, littoral—underscore the definitional haziness of the place where land meets sea, and this has long been the case. In *The Wealth of Nations* (1776), Adam Smith describes how intertidal kelp affects the rent of land, noting that

> [k]elp is a species of sea-weed, which, when burnt, yields an alkaline salt, useful for making glass, soap, and for several other purposes [...] was never augmented by human industry. The landlord, however, whose estate is bounded by a kelp shore of this kind, demands a rent for it as much as for his corn fields.
>
> *(161)*

Implicitly, Smith picks up on a contradiction underlying the modernization and industrialization of coastal areas—defining, incorporating, and ordering a disorderly sea that is simultaneously discernible in its relationship to land.

Coasts are deeply anthropocentric, habitable, engineered, and removed from the deep sea's mysterious nonhuman lifeforms. While typically understood as the terminus of land, coasts also represent the peripheral edges of the sea, and the concept of "coast" accordingly stands both in the foreground and at the edges of oceanic politics. For instance, Liam Campling and Alejandro Colás distinguish the tension between land and sea in their survey on the "maritime factor" of capitalist development, writing: "Our terraqueous predicament – simply meaning 'consisting of land and water' – has from the beginning forced different land-based societies to reckon with the bountiful but potentially ferocious energy of the liquid vastness that covers seven-tenths of the planet" (*Capitalism and Sea* 3). In the realm of Smith's early political economic theory, the intertidal zone resisted forms of commodification, undermined production, and complicated the rent of land. As such, coasts have remained throughout the development of empire, colonialism, and modern capitalism, a place complexly incorporated and yet crucial to furthering the interests of all of the above.

Thus, critics in the ocean humanities have recently begun to inspect the ways in which coasts and coastal issues nestle within the field and yet stand on their own across disciplines. For example, the coastal turn in maritime history came full swing when John Gillis, one of the first to name and define the field of blue humanities, published his influential *The Human Shore: Seacoasts in History*. Gillis follows the history of seaborne civilization, empire, and power from the Phoenicians to the Greeks and the Norse, to northwestern Europe, then the Dutch and British, and finally the United States. As he puts it: "Today, the last of the great thalassocracies, the United States, still uses its island bases and coastal enclaves to secure its economic and political interests around the world" (4). Scholars in literary studies and American studies picked up this thread and its contextualization in their critical engagement on geopolitical positioning of islands, now primarily explored through archipelagic studies. One such archipelagic studies scholar, Brian Russell Roberts, stresses that tension arises from the economic and political positioning of coasts and islands and argues that the United States is an "ocean nation" composed of "borderwaters" which continues to prosecute a violent "seagoing manifest destiny" (*Borderwaters* 7) that seems as deleterious to the health of democracy as it is to the health of oceans.[5]

Oceans of Resistance

Today, that mighty ship of state sails over ocean corals bleaching and dying. From a literary perspective, what can be done? In "Way Beyond the Lifeboat," Kyle Whyte demonstrates a relation between "colonialism, capitalism, industrialization and climate injustice" through an allegory of vessels that begins with the imperative to "Imagine a world of many vessels floating in a pool of waters under a sky" (15). Whyte thus employs the conventionally literary devices of imagination and allegory not just as objects of scholarship but as the means of practicing scholarship, and scholars and artists alike have wielded their critical and literary works to stress the relevance of arguments or to urge political action. Karin Amimoto Ingersoll surfs through a Kānaka Maoli seascape to resist the Western and colonial tradition of an ocean/land binary and offers "a counter politics to the colonial narrative that has determined Hawaiʻi to be a fixed geographic land with the sea as a mere boundary" (*Waves* 19). Alternate modes of scholarship and environmental justice movements employ poetry, prose, and other multi-media artworks to appeal to differing affective registers in the general populace and to galvanize pressure on governing political bodies.[6]

Oceans cover 70% of earth's surface and have contributed to the formation and dissolution of cultures, nations, economies, geographies, geologic features, and much more. For generations, oceans were falsely conceived of as a blank space upon which national, international, and political power struggles played out; bounds and restrictions externally imposed upon the sea continually failed. Yet out of that failure emerges alternative forms of gathering, acts of recovery, and a politics of resistance to destruction that draws strength directly from the ocean's immense natural power and rhetorical power. Oceans are distinct in helping humans to conceive of politics and political action because they produce a common space and public community unlike any other and yet indissolubly connected to every other. As we enter a new era of heightened ecological disaster wrought by anthropogenic climate change, oceanic spaces will occupy the global political stage with their ever-developing number of threats. The lives of human and nonhuman creatures alike will literally depend upon human response to these threats, continuing a venerable literary and historical tradition wherein oceans and politics are inextricably bound as subjects and objects. In fact, the mighty ship of state no longer sails only past the reefs but straight for them, heading toward catastrophic wreckage. What will we citizens of the ocean do to stop it?

Notes

1 Currently, scholars and critics generally agree on this point, but it has not always been so. Many ocean studies scholars begin their work with a counter to Carl Schmitt's 1950 statement: "On the waves, there is nothing but waves" (as quoted in *Blue Legalities* 1). Theorist and filmmaker Allan Sekula examines the ocean as the "forgotten space" of twenty-first-century global capitalism and containerized shipping (see *The Forgotten Space*).
2 M. NourbeSe Philip has published and performed *Zong!*, a deeply important book length poem, which excavates and recovers the missing archive of this mass murder. It's described as: "*A haunting lifeline between archive and memory, law and poetry*" (https://www.nourbese.com/poetry/zong-3/).
3 See Mentz for "new thalassology"; see Cohen for "terraqueous globe"; see Blum for "terraqueous planet"; see Alaimo for "anthropocene at sea"; see Steinberg and Peterson for "wet ongology."

4 See Yaeger, *PMLA*.
5 For more on the relationship between land, sea, and island politics under climate change, see Natalie Pollard's essay "Homes" in this volume. For geopolitics in Oceania, see Epeli Hauʻofa "Our Sea of Islands."
6 See Kathy Jetñil-Kijiner and Aka Niviâna's poem "Rise."

Works Cited

Alaimo, Stacy. "The Anthropocene at Sea: Temporality, Paradox, Compression." *The Routledge Companion to the Environmental Humanities*, edited by Ursula K. Heise, Jon Christensen, and Michelle Niemann, Routledge, 2017, pp. 153–161.

Baucom, Ian. *Specters of the Atlantic: Finance Capital, Slavery, and the Philosophy of History*. Duke UP, 2005.

Bender, Bert. *Sea-Brothers: The Tradition of American Sea Fiction from Moby-Dick to the Present*. U of Pennsylvania P, 2015.

Blum, Hester. "The Prospect of Oceanic Studies." *PMLA/Publications of the Modern Language Association of America*, vol. 125, no. 3, May 2010, pp. 670–77. doi: 10.1632/pmla.2010.125.3.670.

———. "Terraqueous Planet: The Case for Oceanic Studies." *The Planetary Turn: Relationality and Geoaesthetics in the Twenty-First Century*, edited by A. J. Elias and C. Moraru, Northwestern UP, 2015, pp. 25–37.

Brathwaite, Kamau, and Nathaniel Mackey. *ConVERSations with Nathaniel Mackey: An Evening with Nate Mackey & Kamau Brathwaite*. We Press, 1999.

Braverman, Irus, and Elizabeth R. Johnson, editors. *Blue Legalities: The Life and Laws of the Sea*. Duke UP, 2020.

Campling, Liam, and Alejandro Colas. *Capitalism and The Sea: The Maritime Factor in the Making of the Modern World*. Verso Books, 2021.

Casarino, Cesare. *Modernity at Sea: Melville, Marx, Conrad in Crisis*. U of Minnesota P, 2002.

Cohen, Margaret. "The Chronotopes of the Sea." *The Novel, Volume 2: Forms and Themes*, edited by Franco Moretti, Princeton UP, 2006, pp. 647–66.

———. "Literary Studies on the Terraqueous Globe." *PMLA/Publications of the Modern Language Association of America*, vol. 125, no. 3, 2010, pp. 657–62.

DeLoughrey, Elizabeth. *Routes and Roots: Navigating Caribbean and Pacific Island Literatures*. University of Hawaiʻi Press, 2007.

———. "Submarine Futures of the Anthropocene." *Comparative Literature*, vol. 69, no. 1, March 2017, pp. 32–44. doi: 10.1215/00104124–3794589.

———. "Toward a Critical Ocean Studies for the Anthropocene." *English Language Notes*, vol. 57, no. 1, April 2019, pp. 21–36. doi: 10.1215/00138282–7309655.

DeLoughrey, Elizabeth, and Tatiana Flores. "Submerged Bodies." *Environmental Humanities*, vol. 12, no. 1, May 2020, pp. 132–66. doi: 10.1215/22011919-8142242.

Division for Ocean Affairs and the Law of the Sea, Office of Legal Affairs, United Nations. "United Nations Convention on the Law of the Sea of 10 December 1982: Overview and full text." *Oceans & Law of the Sea, United Nations*, 11 Feb. 2022. https://www.un.org/depts/los/convention_agreements/convention_overview_convention.htm

Forgotten Space. Directed by Allan Sekula and Noël Burch, documentary film, Frank van Reemst & Joost Verheij Doc. Eye Film, 2012.

Foulke, Robert. *Sea Voyage Narrative*. Routledge, 2002.

Gillis, John R. "The Blue Humanities." *Humanities*, vol. 34, no. 3, May/June 2013. https://www.neh.gov/humanities/2013/mayjune/feature/the-blue-humanities

———. *The Human Shore: Seacoasts in History*. U of Chicago P, 2012.

Gilroy, Paul. *The Black Atlantic: Modernity and Double Consciousness*. Harvard UP, 2000.

Glissant, Édouard, and Betsy Wing. *Poetics of Relation*. U of Michigan P, 1997.

Gumbs, Alexis Pauline. *Undrowned: Black Feminist Lessons from Marine Mammals*. AK Press, 2020.

Hauʻofa, Epeli. "Our Sea of Islands." *A New Oceania: Rediscovering Our Sea of Islands*, edited by Eric Waddell, Vijay Naidu, and Epeli Hauʻofa. Univ. of the South Pacific, BeakeHouse, 1993, pp. 2–16.

Helmreich, Stefan, et al. *Sounding the Limits of Life: Essays in the Anthropology of Biology and Beyond*. Princeton UP, 2015.

———. "Wave Theory ~ Social Theory." *Public Culture*, vol. 32, no. 2, May 2020, pp. 287–326. doi: 10.1215/08992363-8090094.

Ingersoll, Karin A. *Waves of Knowing: A Seascape Epistemology*. Duke UP, 2016.

James, C. L. R. *Mariners, Renegades, and Castaways: The Story of Herman Melville and the World We Live In*. UP of New England, 2001.

Jetñil-Kijiner, Kathy and Aka Niviâna. "Rise: From One Island to Another." *360.org*, 2018. https://350.org/rise-from-one-island-to-another/

Jue, Melody and Rafico Ruiz, editors. *Saturation: An Elemental Politics*. Duke UP, 2021.

Melville, Herman, and Tom Quirk. *Moby-Dick, or, The Whale*. Penguin Books, 2003.

———. *White Jacket*. Library of America, 1983.

Mentz, Steve. "Toward a Blue Cultural Studies: The Sea, Maritime Culture, and Early Modern English Literature." *Literature Compass*, vol. 6, no. 5, Sept. 2009, pp. 997–1013. doi: 10.1111/j.1741-4113.2009.00655.x.

National Oceanic and Atmospheric Administration. "What Is the EEZ?" *National Ocean Service website*, 15 Feb. 2022. https://oceanservice.noaa.gov/facts/eez.html

Peck, John. *Maritime Fiction: Sailors and the Sea in British and American Novels, 1719–1917*. Palgrave, 2001.

Philip, M. NourbeSe *Zong!* Wesleyan UP, 2008.

Rediker, Marcus. *Between the Devil and the Deep Blue Sea: Merchant Seamen, Pirates, and the Anglo-American Maritime World, 1700–1750*. Cambridge UP, 1987.

Roberts, Brian Russell. *Borderwaters: Amid the Archipelagic States of America*. Duke University Press, 2021.

Sharpe, Christina Elizabeth. *In the Wake: On Blackness and Being*. Duke UP, 2016.

Smith, Adam. *An Inquiry into the Nature and Causes of the Wealth of Nations*. Edited by R.H. Campbell and A.S. Skinner, Liberty Press, 1981.

Somerville, Alice Te Punga. "Where Oceans Come From." *Comparative Literature*, vol. 69, no. 1, March 2017, pp. 25–31.

Spillers, Hortense J. "Mama's Baby, Papa's Maybe: An American Grammar Book." *Diacritics*, vol. 17, no. 2, 1987, pp. 65–81. doi: 10.2307/464747.

Steinberg, Philip E. *The Social Construction of the Ocean*. Cambridge UP, 2001.

Steinberg, Philip, and Kimberley Peters. "Wet Ontologies, Fluid Spaces: Giving Depth to Volume through Oceanic Thinking." *Environment and Planning D: Society and Space*, vol. 33, no. 2, April 2015, pp. 247–64. doi: 10.1068/d14148p.

Walcott, Derek. "The Sea is History." *Selected Poems*, edited by Edward Baugh. Farrar, Straus and Giroux, 2007, pp. 137–140.

Whyte, Kyle Powys. "Way Beyond the Lifeboat: An Indigenous Allegory for Climate Justice." *Climate Futures: Re-Imagining Global Climate Justice,* edited by Kum-Kum Bhavnani et al. Zed Books, 2019, pp. 11–20.

Yaeger, Patricia, editor. *PMLA* ("Oceanic Studies" special issue). vol. 125, no. 3, May 2010.

37
BORDERS
Anne Mai Yee Jansen

"The *Muro* is the iron wall that separates us from the US side. It ends where the ocean waves begin to form," Ernesto Cisneros writes. "See there. That's the Pacific. Same water on both sides of the wall" (188). This passage in his young adult novel *Efrén Divided* offers a typical representation of the U.S.-Mexico border, with all its attendant politics. Similar depictions of this familiar fixture are typical to border theory, which is inherently interested in studying border politics. As such, in this discussion of borders I use the term politics to describe the complex national (both inter- and intra-) power dynamics that arise from and around geopolitical borders and the spaces they intend to delineate. Correspondingly, I use the term geopolitics to refer to the relationship between politics and geography that forms the heart of the political landscape where borders are concerned. After all, a border signifies limits: "it keeps people in and out of an area; it marks the ending of a safe zone and the beginning of an unsafe zone. To confront a border and, more so, to cross a border presumes great risk" (Morales 23). In other words, a border's primary function is to confine and demarcate different spaces, and to traverse a border is a dangerous act.

But what exactly are borders? Borders are geopolitical constructs—lines drawn on paper maps across time as part of the history of colonialism. They are boundaries, imagined and built and policed to delimit spatial geographies of power. In her overview of borderlands, Nicole Guidotti-Hernández advances the notion that borders "are fictions of material consequence" that mark territorial limits and "signal the essence of power relations" (21). From this description, the tricky nature of borders becomes clear: they are at once imaginary and real. Also, significantly, they delineate not only territorial boundaries but also (especially) power. As such, borders can take many forms: spatial, temporal, invisible, social, psychological. To study borders is to study geopolitics, cultural studies, history, economics, identity, linguistics, and more; border studies has an expressed interest in studying and crossing borders, which is reflected in the disciplinary border crossings that have come to characterize the field (Naples 507). To put it succinctly, "Different borders and borderlands are different" (Johnson and Michaelsen 32). And, of course, the interconnected disciplinary frames that have developed in border studies (literary or otherwise) have resulted in a rich and, perhaps, overwhelming body of scholarship (Naples 508). Where, then, does one begin?

At one beginning, perhaps, since there is no singular beginning.

As a scholar of both literary studies and U.S. ethnic studies, the most obvious beginning is Gloria Anzaldúa's groundbreaking 1987 hybrid work of cultural criticism, poetry, and memoir entitled *Borderlands/La Frontera: The New Mestiza*, which has shaped much of the landscape of contemporary border studies. Anzaldúa brings together perspectives from Chicana, queer, feminist, and postcolonial theories in her investigation of the cultural, linguistic, personal, and overarching impacts of the border. In the decades since its publication, *Borderlands/La Frontera* has inspired a body of scholarship that interrogates "how gender, sex, violence, power, color, and race combine and collide in the region we call the borderlands" (Perales 170). Given Anzaldúa's monumental impact on border studies, I have elected to begin with her description of borders and borderlands:

> The U.S.-Mexican border *es una herida abierta* where the Third World grates against the first and bleeds. And before a scab forms it hemorrhages again, the lifeblood of two worlds merging to form a third country—a border culture. Borders are set up to define the places that are safe and unsafe, to distinguish *us* from *them*. A border is a dividing line, a narrow strip along a steep edge. A borderland is a vague and undetermined place created by the emotional residue of an unnatural boundary. It is in a constant state of transition. The prohibited and forbidden are its inhabitants [...] those who cross over, pass over, or go through the confines of the 'normal.'
>
> *(Anzaldúa 25)*

Immediately, Anzaldúa establishes two crucial ideas: first, the border is a site of trauma; second, the borderland is a cultural space. While these ideas have grown almost commonplace in the contemporary scholarship on borders, they are worth dwelling on—not in the least because of their foundational significance to border studies as a critical field.

For Anzaldúa, the border is born of and gives birth to trauma as the bleeding wound of contact between Mexico and the United States. Interestingly, in the above description Anzaldúa envisions the border itself as "a dividing line, a narrow strip along a steep edge" at the same time that she argues that what rises out of this open wound—unable to heal because of the continued chafing between two nations—is the "lifeblood" that births the "third country" of the borderland. Put another way, the border itself may be a razor-thin line but the resultant borderlands that it produces are robust communities that transcend borders.

In addition to this influential conceptualization of the U.S.-Mexico border, Anzaldúa offers language as a form of empowerment. She points to the need for a linguistic mode that reflects the cultural realities of the borderland: a language which those in/of the borderlands "can connect their identity to, one capable of communicating the realities and values true to themselves—a language with terms that are neither *español ni inglés*, but both" (77). Why the need for a borderland language? Because borderlands are not just physical but cultural spaces. As such, the need for adequate means of cultural production is crucial, especially since borderlands are, by definition, in the peripheries of hegemony.

The scholarship on borders and borderlands (border/lands) that followed in the decade after the publication of *La Frontera* demonstrated the great potential of border theory. The proliferation of ideas was such that only four years later, the editors of *Criticism in the Borderlands* made clear their aim to "remap the borderlands of theory and theorists" (Calderón, et al. 7). Such theories include Mary Louise Pratt's idea of "contact zones" as "social spaces where cultures meet, clash, and grapple with each other, often in contexts of highly asymmetrical relations of power" which builds on the idea of borderlands to think about the intersections of language, communication, and culture (34–37). In a similar vein, José Saldívar argues that what he calls "Chicano border narratives" from the latter half of the twentieth century replace hackneyed racist border narratives, thereby creating space for "a revitalized Chicano present and future" (178). In other words, the narratives Saldívar examines offer alternative perspectives to the flattening racist narratives about Chicanes and the borderlands. Contemporaneously, in *Border Writing: The Multidimensional Text*, D. Emily Hicks articulates an understanding of border writing as "writing that disrupts the one-way flow of information" in cultural production through which the United States controls global images of itself and other nations (xxvii). Hicks further contends that border writing depicts "a kind of realism that approaches the experience of border crossers, those who live in a bilingual, bicultural, biconceptual reality" (xxv). For Hicks, then, border writing is about difference—both emphasizing it and breaking it down. These apparently contradictory impulses are part of the Janus-faced nature of Hicks' approach to border literature: it requires "a model that will allow us to look in two directions simultaneously" (xxviii–xxix). Like Saldívar's claims about Chicano border narratives and Pratt's theories of language and community, Hicks' claims demonstrate an inherent tension in the simultaneous centering and decentering of dominant narratives.

Re-Bordering

This tension is evident in David E. Johnson and Scott Michaelsen's provocative claim that the "'border' in border studies remains the problem" (15). For them, the continued preoccupation with the border and all that it engenders reinforces the very systems of exclusion and difference that border studies purportedly seeks to undermine. In essence, the nature of borders as geopolitical constructs tied to imaginaries of power means that focusing too much on borders and the lands that surround them risks further entrenching the exclusionary, discriminatory, and harmful dynamics that are tied up in the construction and maintenance of borders. This line of reasoning lies at the heart of the innumerable theoretical constructs that imagine the border in terms other than a line, but here I will use Cisneros' portrayal of the U.S.-Mexico border to highlight three distinct ways of understanding borders that generate possibilities of critical inquiry.

In *Efrén Divided*, U.S.-born middle schooler Efrén has been struggling to keep it together after his mother's sudden deportation. In hopes of helping reunite his family, he convinces his undocumented father to allow him (as a U.S. citizen) to cross the border into Tijuana and deliver money to his mother so she can pay a coyote to help her cross back into the United States. During his time in Tijuana, Efrén finds himself momentarily on the beach where the following scene ensues:

> [F]amilies of every size lined the rusted iron beams, many in folding beach chairs. [...] Efrén's eyes searched the many faces along the fence. They came in all sorts. From babies to elderly folk with walkers—all different, beautiful shades of brown. Efrén began walking alongside the iron barrier. There were as many smiles as there were tears. A woman leaned into the space between the beams. She poked her arm through. [...] Less than ten feet away was a mother and daughter [...] resting their foreheads against the other, each with their eyes closed, tears flowing.
>
> *(Cisneros 191–192)*

Different theoretical understandings of borders will lead to different interpretations of the rich details on offer here. For example, a reading that focuses on the border as a dividing line, as per Johnson and Michaelsen's critique, would focus on details such as the description of the "iron barrier" and the many mentions of tears. In this reading, the border separates, causing a rupture between families. In essence, it traumatically divides them.

However, a refiguring of the border might lead one to focus instead on the failure of the border to effectively divide. To this end, Mark Salter proposes that instead of the line, the border be theorized as "the suture—as a process of knitting together the inside and the outside" resulting in a scar (734). For Salter, the paradigm of border-as-suture emphasizes coming together even as it acknowledges the violence of the border/lands. Such a reading of Cisneros' text might focus on the woman who leans "into the space between the beams" and pokes her arm through the permeable barrier of the iron fence. Despite its manifestation in iron, the border is porous and thus unsuccessful at dividing the people and spaces it is intended to separate. This failure to divide embodies Salter's configuration of the border as containing a unifying impulse. Because, for Salter, borders "knit the world together, but also knit us as subjects into the bordered world" (736), the border is a site of violence and empire even as human adaptability turns Anzaldúa's open wound into a scar. In effect, healing becomes a possibility even as the trauma (scar) of the border remains.

While Salter transforms Anzaldúa's open wound into a (healing) suture, others have inverted the conventional paradigm. Rather than viewing the border as a solid—albeit razor-thin—line, Norma Alarcón suggests the border be understood in terms of an empty space: "the interstice, discontinuity, or gap is precisely a site of textual production" (357). She points to the ways women of color and other marginalized groups are relegated to gaps in the narrative (356), conceiving of the border as a wide void rather than a thin division. Or, as Johnson argues in his exploration of language and translation in border literature, the border is not a place and because it "does not exist as such, [it] is always and only the limit of decision" (159). Put another way, the border itself holds no meaning, but instead marks the edge of identity and nation as reflected by the other side of the border. Returning to Cisneros' text, such an interpretation might then guide readers to focus on the purgatory-like space that surrounds the border. It is populated by "families of every size," people of "all sorts," and brown people ranging in age from "babies to elderly folk." Here, the border is not a location at all but a meaningless line—a spatial gap between nations where families meet despite the "rusted iron beams" that aim to separate them. Additionally, it is a narrative gap that Cisneros has filled with a story that differs from the dominant narrative: life continues despite the border, which fails to hold any meaning outside of what lies on either side of it.

In both of these readings, the border (however reconfigured) continues to be *a* border, singular. But many scholars have suggested that it might be more productive to think in terms of border*s*, plural. For instance, Chris Rumford argues that if "the aim is to re-frame borders as cultural encounters rather than simply mechanisms of division" then we must first move beyond "the underlying assumption of consensus" in which all parties recognize borders as divisive (889). Once we move away from an understanding of borders as agreed upon and mutually impactful, we can move toward a "multiperspectival border studies" that acknowledges invisible borders and the fact "that some borders exist for some people and not others" (894). In this vein, Alejandro Morales conceives of the borderlands (specifically the Southern California borderlands) in terms of Foucault's concept of a "heterotopia," explaining that literal and figurative borders are everywhere, creating a landscape of multiple and overlapping displacements (23). In Rumford's and Morales' configurations of the border/lands, the multiplication of borders—internal and external, spatial and imaginary, temporal and psychological—might lead to a focus on still other details in Cisneros' passage. Why are there "folding beach chairs" and babies and walkers here? Why are there young and old, all in "beautiful shades of brown"? These are the vestiges of Southern California beach recreation with an iron wall running down the middle of the beach. By rendering weekend beachgoing activities alongside border-divided families, Cisneros creates a space in which the border loses its meaning. It is a dividing line that cannot prevent families from connecting across it, and its delineation of separate spaces seems arbitrary and nonsensical. Additionally, these observations about the beach are rendered through a protagonist who is multiply determined: U.S. citizen, bewildered tourist, newly orphaned child, coming-of-age man, and curious observer all rolled into one. This protagonist not only observes the multiple borders at work here, but does so in a manner that embodies Morales' borderlands heterotopia.

Obviously, these are not the only ways to theorize borders. However, these theories demonstrate that the border is a flexible and evolving theoretical construct. By focusing on the portion of the U.S.-Mexico border where the wall disappears into the Pacific (itself simultaneously part of and separate from the border), Cisneros examines the limits of borders—the ways lines imagined across the landscape falter when they encounter real geographies and real people. Different border paradigms offer different possibilities for understanding literature. If, as discussed above, border studies as a field is invested in moving beyond intellectual theories, then border studies as a subfield in literary studies is necessarily invested in moving beyond the page. Put another way, literary border studies often keeps one eye on the text and the other eye on the sociopolitical landscape out of which the text arises.

A foundational premise of literary border studies is that the study of literature has the potential to shape how we think about geopolitical border/lands in meaningful ways. Regardless of how we conceive of the border itself, Alejandro Lugo argues that "the border region and border theory can erode the hegemony of the privileged center by denationalizing and deterritorializing the nation/state and culture theory" (45). This hegemonic erosion is central to the aims of literary border studies. Theorizing borders in literature creates space for "denationalizing and deterritorializing" intellectual and cultural production. As Guidotti-Hernández points out, border geographies and their resultant violence and racism are "not just a fiction on the page but in fact the cleaner version of lived and embodied experiences" (24). In essence, art reflects lived experiences and, in the case of literature about border/lands and their attendant violence and racism, theory must aim to move beyond the sanitized halls of academia and into the real world.

Beyond the Borders of Border Theory

This investment in politics is sometimes bound by the limitations of the field. With this in mind, it is worth noting that "the U.S.-Mexico border is 'the' border in Latina/o studies, despite the fact that the very same border is more primary to Chicana/o studies" (Guidotti-Hernández 23). In fact, Claudia Sadowski-Smith warns that the centrality of the U.S.-Mexico border "threatens to characterize processes of migration, enforcement, and racialization at this boundary as unique," thereby replicating "the very notion of US exceptionalism that an interest in the border geography was originally meant to challenge" (277).

Fortunately, many scholars use this specific border as a symbolic line that has relevance beyond Chicane studies, illustrating the portability and broad applicability of border/land theories. For example, Stephen Hong Sohn has engaged border theory in combination with Asian Americanist critique to demonstrate the ways border studies can be used in what he calls a "relational identity politics" that extends beyond a focus on the U.S.-Mexico borderlands (175). In a similar vein, Johnnella E. Butler points out that the United States is a "borderlands that maintains policed yet unmarked color-lines implicit in our actions and our folkways" and that border studies and ethnic studies (beginning with W. E. B. DuBois' treatment of the color line) together are productive theoretical fields that can help us think about race today. Beyond the confines of the United States, border theory extends into Central and South America, the Caribbean, Europe, and beyond. Border studies is global. Étienne Balibar's essay "Europe as Borderland" is a prominent example of the ways border studies—given its attendant preoccupations with citizenship, power, and sovereignty—is relevant to other geographical regions. Balibar asserts that territories in the political system "which has become associated with the 'European model' of the nation-states and the international law governing their relations [...] are not only associated with the 'invention' of the border, but also inseparable from the institution of power as *sovereignty*" (192). This is just one example (albeit a very influential one) of the global scope of border studies, which is malleable precisely because it often conceives of borders not only in terms of geopolitics but also in terms of "the sorts of 'soft' borders produced within broadly liberal discourse: benevolent nationalisms, cultural essentialisms, multiculturalisms, and the like" (Johnson and Michaelsen 1).

Regardless of location, the border is a cartographic tool that writes the imagined reaches of one group's power across the landscape. By their very nature, then, borders are politics written onto the earth and water. While this chapter focuses on land borders, one must recognize that oceans, rivers, and other waterways can be understood as borders and have become increasingly popular sites of inquiry in recent border studies (Guidotti-Hernández 22). Whatever the type of border, recall that in her work Anzaldúa ultimately turns to language. Specifically, there is something about language that is essential for theorizing, imagining, and enacting change in the border/lands. The importance of language is tied to linguistic difference, certainly, but the centrality of language to her is also about the power of words to shape worldviews; from a different angle, linguistic emphasis is about the multifaceted potential of the idea of the border and the power of words to (re)shape that border in the popular imaginary.

Part of the power of the border (as a theoretical construct) is tied to the performative nature of the border. Put simply, "All borders are performative: they must be created and given meaning through their delimitation and transgression" (Salter 734). For example, in their essay on expanding critical border studies, Noel Parker and Nick Vaughan-Williams write that airport security and customs practices illustrate how borders "are continually performed into being through rituals" so that reconceptualizing borders as performances "injects movement, dynamism, and fluidity into the study of what are otherwise often taken to be static entities" (729). In this understanding of borders, it is not the physical border that matters, but instead the performance of power, nation, and division that takes place around perceived or imagined borders which is truly impactful. If borders require such performances to inscribe them on the landscape, then literature—as a kind of artistic performance—has the potential to reinscribe them. For border studies scholars, many of whom are "activist scholars" that "argue for the importance of praxis to enhance the links between experience, political struggle, and theoretical analysis" (Naples 510), the importance of language is tied to an approach to the study of literature that understands the text as an expression of embodied experiences.

Of course, Anzaldúa is not the only one who recognizes the crucial role of language in the borderlands. Alarcón underscores the nationalistic impulse to "prepossess" the land "at the literary, legendary, historical, ideological, critical, or theoretical level—producing in material and imaginary terms 'authentic' and 'inauthentic,' 'legal' and 'illegal' subjects" (360). In other words, all manner of storytelling is employed in the project of reimagining border/lands to bring them into alignment with nationalistic narratives. With this in mind, it is especially important to think about the role of language and story in relation to borders. To that end, Pratt focuses on the way that self-representation can function as both a "selective collaboration with and appropriation of" colonizing constructions, thereby interrupting the logic of colonialism (35). Another way of looking at the situation is that the problem of borders is a problem of stories. Borders are stories power tells about itself, and literature offers a method of re-storying. More than simply retelling or telling otherwise, literature opens up possibilities for creating a wholly different narrative.

Even as the border offers nearly limitless possibilities for thinking about literature, it also has its limitations. Russ Castronovo advocates for a rethinking of border studies' optimism about border texts, pointing out that while the border may offer itself as a "discursive strategy capable of deconstructing ossified structures like patriarchy or the nation," it also has the potential to be used for the "counterpurpose of solidifying and extending racial and national boundaries" (196). Furthermore, Castronovo argues that the border, as a space regulated by the nation, is also used for nationalistic imaginings so that as "the site of difference, the border becomes strategic in promoting the desire for sameness" (197). The employment of borders for nationalistic imaginings of homogeneity underscores the need to attend to the specific kinds of border/lands drawn across the landscape through settler colonialism.

Border Theory and Indigenous Studies

Any discussion of Indigenous spaces and settler-colonial borders makes clear the need for an understanding of borders that moves beyond the image of the line. For example, the United States is a nation-state forged through multiple shifting borders that sought to map, remap, and map again the territory described by the name "United States." Studying U.S. history makes clear the ever-shifting borders of U.S. geopolitics (both internal and external), especially as they impacted populations of color. The Mason-Dixon line, for instance, had tremendous consequences concerning institutionalized slavery. The Louisiana Purchase and the Treaty of Guadalupe Hidalgo both remapped U.S. borders across Indigenous territories, such that huge swaths of sovereign land were claimed by the westward-expanding settler-colonial nation-state. The Indian Removal Act, the Dawes Act of 1887, and the Indian Relocation Act of 1956 all dictated reconfigurations of Indigenous peoples, lands, and sovereignty while the 1898 Treaty of Paris extended the borders of the U.S. nation-state beyond the continental land mass of North America. In essence, the history of the United States (and many other settler-colonial nation-states) is a history of ever-changing borders that seek to relegate and confine Indigenous populations to designated areas in order for the settler-colonial project to succeed.

With regard to Native peoples and nations, these shifting border histories complicate theories that focus on the more static U.S.-Mexico border. The relative fixity of the U.S.-Mexico border since the late nineteenth century has resulted in a fairly definable borderland space. Conversely, the continued sovereignty and presence of Native nations that exist within the same geospatial terrain the United States occupies and bleed across lines intended to demarcate supposedly impermeable national boundaries between Canada and Mexico—especially given histories of removal, assimilation, and termination—disrupts settler colonial border imaginaries.

In light of these histories, Métis writer Cherie Dimaline's horror novel *Empire of Wild* demonstrates the rich possibilities of bringing Indigenous studies into conversation with border theory. The novel's protagonist, Joan, has been searching for her disappeared husband, Victor, for nearly a year when she stumbles across him preaching in a revival tent in a nearby Walmart parking lot. Joan and her family (and the larger community in Arcand) are described as "halfbreeds" with French, First Nations, and Métis roots who were "brought from another place" and multiply dislocated by histories of colonialism (1–3). Because of their positionality, Joan and her family are framed in terms of liminality: both Indigenous and without status cards (which would signal federal recognition of their Indigeneity), with land but not on a reserve. Significantly, during his lifetime Joan's father had painstakingly purchased "small parcels of land on his traditional territory" for his wife and children (71). Over the course of the novel, Joan discovers that Victor is in the process of turning into a rogarou: a werewolf-adjacent creature which Dimaline describes as "a dog, a man, a wolf" that a person can turn into by being attacked by one, mistreating women, or betraying their people (4, 69). His suggestion that Joan sell the 26 acres of land her father acquired for her is the event that triggers his transformation.

Empire of Wild uses Victor's rogarou to interrogate histories of dispossession and border/lands within the context of contemporary settler colonialism. When readers encounter Victor in the novel, he is relegated to brief chapters wherein he is seen endlessly wandering a parcel of woods described as a "twenty-six-acre cell" that Victor reflects "was and [...] wasn't" Joan's land as his rogarou counterpart slowly hunts him (42, 258). When Victor asks the rogarou where he is, it responds that he is "'wherever the betrayal happened'" (258). Significantly, then, the lands that are and are not Joan's lands become a contested site in which Victor must come to terms with his act of betrayal. Their transformation into a "cell" signals the fraught nature of land within the settler-colonial context, especially with regard to restricted movement. The importance of "free communities and the free exchange of people between those communities" to George Manuel (Secwépemc) and coauthor Michael Posluns' concept of the Fourth World is reflected in Victor's confinement (12). The Fourth World is a decolonizing mapping strategy that erases the geopolitical significance of hegemonic boundaries. The 26-acre cell is the antithesis of Manuel's Fourth World: borne of settler-colonial temptation and individualistic greed, this nonporous zone has no borders and no opportunity for freedom of movement or Indigenous self-determination. Deprived of mobility, Victor is at the mercy of the rogarou hunting him with the intention of wearing his skin and assuming his identity. Only when Victor is able to reestablish his connection with Joan is he able to transcend borders and escape his rogarou.

The rogarou itself is a border/lands creature. In *Empire of Wild*, the rogarou has its roots in both Métis tradition and French mythology. Additionally, it is a creature (between human and animal) that literally embodies the kind of liminality defining the border/lands. Significantly, Victor's transformation to rogarou is tied to the land: it is triggered by developers' offer of a "shit ton of money—life-changing money" if he agrees to sell the land Joan's father gave to her (72). Put another way, Victor's transition from human to monster is directly linked to the prospect of surrendering Indigenous lands. As Jeffrey Cohen argues in his foundational treatise on monster studies, monsters are "disturbing hybrids whose externally incoherent bodies resist attempts to include them in any systemic structuration" (6). In other words, the monster's body is "difference made flesh," always in-between—human/creature, living/dead—so that it exists in that space between borders (7). Dimaline's rogarou arises from tensions between settler land developers and the Indigenous community so that its "externally incoherent" body refuses to be bound by the "systemic structuration" of settler colonialism. Victor is an Indigenous man, the face of an evangelical Christian missionary group, and a lost soul trapped in an alternate space where his rogarou hunts him. His multiply determined monstrous body—a border/lands body that refuses categorization—offers a critique of settler-colonial systems concerning Indigeneity and dispossession.

Through the portrayal of mining as a dispossessing endeavor, Dimaline's novel interrogates the multiple temporal and spatial borders that overlay the North American landscape. These borders are inherently linked to mapping as a geospatial manifestation of colonial and imperial impulses. As a white miner tells Joan,

> 'Those traditional Indians, they put up the biggest fight. They can stall work for years. But when the missions come through? [...] They're too busy praying to protest. [...] Mission tents are an important part of mining, of any project, really—mining, forestry, pipelines'.
>
> (Dimaline *220*)

The fact that religion takes the form of "missions," complete with an "old-timey revival tent" that seems like a weapon "from a dead civilization," blurs the temporal borders so that histories of missionization and dispossession rip into the fabric of contemporary reality (27). Importantly, these missions function to map settler-colonial resource extraction across Native lands, eroding the borders of Indigenous sovereignty. In their book *Border as Method, or, the Multiplication of Labor*, Sandro Mezzadra and Brett Neilson underscore that mapping "was a key tool of colonial domination" which used "cartographic tools constructed on the model of the sovereign state" to redraw Indigenous spaces (15). Concerning Indigenous North American peoples specifically, Mishuana Goeman (Tonawanda Seneca) points to the use of state-sponsored mapmaking expeditions and advocates for an understanding of "mapping as a means of discourse that mapped an imperial imaginary" (18, 20). For Dimaline's characters, the colonial mapping process employs Christianity to chip away at land and water rights and encroach on Indigenous land holdings.

While Dimaline's novel revolves primarily around the rural community in Arcand, an Indigenous framework for understanding the landscape in its totality also holds significant import for the field of border studies. With this in mind, Kevin Bruyneel's concept of the "third space of sovereignty" names the ways that Native nations "straddle the temporal and spatial boundaries of American politics, exposing the incoherence of these boundaries as they seek to secure and expand their tribal sovereign expression" (xv). In this configuration, the borders between Native lands and the settler-colonial nation-state become ever-changing and vast encompassing entities rather than fixed lines. Additionally, the continued presence of Native peoples within the geopolitical borders of the settler-colonial nation-state problematizes settler spatiality. Similarly, Laura Furlan's reconfiguration of metropolitan centers in *Indigenous Cities: Urban Indian Fiction and the Histories of Relocation* boldly proclaims that "all US cities are Indigenous cities; that each city has a long and complex Indigenous and settler colonial history; that the city functions as a 'contact zone'" (12). Her exploration of contemporary urban Indian literature performs its own kind of (re)mapping in which she proposes a rethinking of the "boundaries of national identity for modern tribal peoples, especially those who live away from their ancestral homelands" and "the imperial borders of the reservation" (Furlan 9). The reminder that "all US cities are Indigenous cities" and reservations are defined by "imperial borders" frames urban centers and reservations alike in terms of borders, sovereignty, and empire.

Inescapable Borders

Within this context, North American literary border studies must be attentive to the (re)locations of Indigenous peoples and the innumerable colonial maps that were historically and are contemporarily overlaid across the North American geopolitical landscape. Literature, according to Goeman, is a generative decolonial mode "precisely because the 'real' of settler colonial society is built on the violent erasures of alternative modes of mapping and geographic understanding" (2). In other words, literature is a powerful tool for reimagining the landscape and its border/lands. In a similar vein, Sonia Saldívar-Hull posits that hegemony has a specific idea of what theory looks like so that Chicana feminists "have to look in nontraditional places for our theories" (206). The same might be said for literature. Perhaps concerningly, the same might even be said about the literature(s) of the border/lands. While works like *Efrén Divided* offer explicit portrayals of the border/lands, a literary work need not depict literal border/lands in order to be examined through the lens of border theory. For instance, writers like Cherie Dimaline offer texts rife with cultural critiques of border/lands. After all, as Roger Luckhurst posits, monsters "rear up" in the border/lands, as sites of structural inequality (277–278). This renders borders, their attendant monsters, and border theory broadly applicable, since "borderlands are everywhere and nowhere, and can impact the subject at any time" (Guidotti-Hernández 23). Once you think in terms of border/lands, you will find that the border is inescapable.

Works Cited

Alarcón, Norma. "Anzaldúa's *Frontera*: Inscribing Gynetics." *Chicana Feminisms: A Critical Reader*, edited by Gabriela F. Arredondo, et al. Duke UP, 2003, pp. 354–369.

Anzaldúa, Gloria. *Borderlands/La Frontera: The New Mestiza*, 4th edition. Aunt Lute, 2012.

Balibar, Etienne. "Europe as Borderland." *Environment and Planning D: Society and Space*, vol. 27, no. 2, 2009, pp. 190–215.

Bruyneel, Kevin. *The Third Space of Sovereignty: The Postcolonial Politics of U.S.-Indigenous Relations*. U of Minnesota P, 2007.

Butler, Johnnella E. "Introduction: Color-Line to Borderlands." *Color-Line to Borderlands: The Matrix of American Ethnic Studies*, edited by Johnnella E. Butler. U of Washington P, 2001, pp. xi–xxvi.

Calderón, Héctor, et al. "Editors' Introduction: Criticism in the Borderlands." *Criticism in the Borderlands: Studies in Chicano Literature, Culture, and Ideology*, edited by Héctor Calderón, et al. Duke UP, 1991, pp. 1–7.

Castronovo, Russ. "Compromised Narratives Along the Border: The Mason-Dixon Line, Resistance, and Hegemony." *Border Theory: The Limits of Cultural Politics*, edited by Scott Michaelsen and David E. Johnson. U of Minnesota P, 1997, pp. 195–220.

Cisneros, Ernesto. *Efrén Divided*. HarperCollins, 2020.

Cohen, Jeffrey Jerome. "Monster Culture (Seven Theses)." *Monster Theory: Reading Culture*. Edited by Jeffrey Jerome Cohen. U of Minnesota P, 1996.

Dimaline, Cherie. *Empire of Wild*. William Morrow-HarperCollins, 2019.

Furlan, Laura M. *Indigenous Cities: Urban Indian Fiction and the Histories of Relocation*. U of Nebraska P, 2017.

Goeman, Mishuana. *Mark My Words: Native Women Mapping Our Nations*. U of Minnesota P, 2013.

Guidotti-Hernández, Nicole M. "Borderlands." *Keywords in Latina/o Studies*, edited by Deborah R. Vargas, Nancy Raquel Mirabal, and Lawrence La Fountain-Stokes. New York UP, 2017, pp. 21–24.

Hicks, D. Emily. *Border Writing: The Multidimensional Text*. U of Minnesota P, 1991.

Johnson, David E. "The Time of Translation: The Border of American Literature." *Border Theory: The Limits of Cultural Politics*, edited by Scott Michaelsen and David E. Johnson. U of Minnesota P, 1997, pp. 129–165.

Johnson, David E. and Scott Michaelsen. "Border Secrets: An Introduction." *Border Theory: The Limits of Cultural Politics*, edited by Scott Michaelsen and David E. Johnson. U of Minnesota P, 1997, pp. 1–39.

Luckhurst, Roger. "After Monster Theory?: Gareth Edwards's *Monsters*." *Science Fiction Film and Television*, vol. 13, no. 2, 2020, pp. 269–290.

Lugo, Alejandro. "Reflections on Border Theory, Culture, and the Nation." *Border Theory: The Limits of Cultural Politics*, edited by Scott Michaelsen and David E. Johnson. U of Minnesota P, 1997, pp. 43–67.

Manuel, George and Michael Posluns. *The Fourth World: An Indian Reality*. 1974. U of Minnesota P, 2019.
Mezzadra, Sandro and Brett Neilson. *Border as Method, or, the Multiplication of Labor*. Duke UP, 2013.
Morales, Alejandro. "Dynamic Identities in Heterotopia." *Bilingual Review/La Revista Bilingüe*, vol. 20, no. 3, 1995, pp. 14–27.
Naples, Nancy. "Borderlands Studies and Border Theory: Linking Activism and Scholarship for Social Justice." *Sociology Compass*, vol. 4, no. 7, 2010, pp. 505–518.
Parker, Noel and Nick Vaughan-Williams. "Critical Border Studies: Broadening and Deepening the 'Lines in the Sand' Agenda." *Geopolitics*, vol. 17, no. 4, 2012, pp. 727–733.
Perales, Monica. "On *Borderlands/La Frontera*: Gloria Anzaldúa and Twenty-Five Years of Research on Gender in the Borderlands." *Journal of Women's History*, vol. 25, no. 4, 2013, pp. 163–173.
Pratt, Mary Louise. "Arts of the Contact Zone." *Profession*, vol. 91, 1991, pp. 33–40.
Rumford, Chris. "Towards a Multiperspectival Study of Borders." *Geopolitics*, vol. 17, no. 4, 2012, pp. 887–902.
Sadowski-Smith, Claudia. "Introduction: Comparative Border Studies." *Comparative American Studies*, vol. 9, no. 4, 2011, pp. 273–287.
Saldívar, José David. "Chicano Border Narratives as Cultural Critique." *Criticism in the Borderlands: Studies in Chicano Literature, Culture, and Ideology*, edited by Héctor Calderón, et al. Duke UP, 1991, pp. 167–180.
Saldívar-Hull, Sonia. "Feminism on the Border: From Gender Politics to Geopolitics." *Criticism in the Borderlands: Studies in Chicano Literature, Culture, and Ideology*, edited by Héctor Calderón, et al. Duke UP, 1991, pp. 203–220.
Salter, Mark B. "Theory of the/: The Suture and Critical Border Studies." *Geopolitics*, vol. 17, no. 4, 2012, pp. 734–755.
Sohn, Stephen Hong. "Minor Character, Minority Orientalisms, and the Borderlands of Asian America." *Cultural Critique*, 2012, vol. 82, pp. 151–185.

38

PLANETS

Gerry Canavan

In 1902, British imperialist Cecil Rhodes issued a lament that has become common currency in the study of science fiction and empire. "The world is nearly all parceled out," he wrote,

> and what there is left of it, is being divided up, conquered and colonized. To think of these stars that you see overhead at night, these vast worlds which we can never reach. I would annex the planets if I could; I often think of that. It makes me sad to see them so clear and yet so far.
>
> *(qtd. in Csicsery-Ronay 234)*

While the inhabitants of those planets are fortunate to have escaped Rhodes' brutality, key questions remain. How did planets—once seen as just "wandering stars"—become reimagined as a space for potential habitation? How did their vast distance from Earth and their fundamental, irreducible inhospitality to Earth life become so quickly transmogrified from an impenetrable barrier to a temporary obstacle to be overcome through technological ingenuity, bravery, and gumption? Today, as the ecstatic proclamations of tech billionaires like Jeff Bezos and Elon Musk would have it, the human colonization of other planets is not just a historical inevitability but a moral necessity, a heroic bid to immortalize the "light of consciousness" (Oremus n.p.)—this, despite the fact that permanent colonization of outer space by human beings is likely physically and biologically impossible.

This fantastic science fictional notion has become a major political force outside the genre, enshrining one possible "destiny" for the human race that continues to dominate visions of the future in the Global North. Against this logic of expansion stands the environmentalist understanding of the Earth as a planetary totality on which human beings evolved to thrive and whose biome is threatened by the ongoing ecologically destructive activities of the industrial nations. In this reading there is simply no alternative to the Earth for humans, who will likely never live off the planet for any prolonged length of time or in any substantial numbers, and whose planetary home is in the process of being destroyed by the unchecked excesses of capitalist technomodernity. These two parallel modes echo in what Gayatri Chakravorty Spivak has posited as "the planetary," an anti-imperial theoretical alternative to "the global": "The 'global' notion," she writes, "allows us to think that we can aim to control globality. The planet is in the species of alterity, belonging to another system; and yet we inhabit it, on loan" (291). They also converge in the grimly fiery slogan that is ubiquitous in climate change activism: "there is no Planet B," so we must take better care of this one.

Early Planets

The planets have a long history of idiomatically registering a mode of radical difference, which changes into imagining the planets as similar enough spaces to inhabit. The *Oxford English Dictionary* notes, for instance, Washington Irving's 1824 "peep into another planet" as well as James Smith's 1840 bewilderment in *Comic Miscellany:* "I wonder what planet some people come from" (OED n.p.) By the twentieth century this sort of usage would be ubiquitous. Fantasies about other planets and the life forms that might inhabit them would become a way of imagining alterity, often in quite political or philosophical terms; the space travelers in our science fictions travel to other planets to find Utopia, or hell, or both at once, from Soviet author Alexander Bogdanov's *Red Star* (1908) to Ursula K. Le Guin's *The Dispossessed* (1972). A grimmer mode of difference marked by extrasolar bodies is specific to wartime, especially after the advent of trench, tank, and air war in the global conflicts of the twentieth century so utterly destroyed land- and cityscapes as to be unrecognizable as terrestrial spaces. While J. R. R. Tolkien refigured No Man's Land in World War I as the ruined swamps and blasted landscapes of the fantasy kingdom of Mordor, the traumatized narrator of Kurt Vonnegut's *Slaughterhouse Five* (1969), Billy Pilgrim, rendered his experience surviving the firebombing of Dresden instead as the poisonous argon atmosphere of the faraway planet Tralfamadore (whose imaginary inhabitants neither suffer nor care as humans do, because they exist outside both time and memory). In all three of these modes—idiomatic, political-philosophical, and imagistic—the idea of a planet as a space of difference shifts subtly from one that is fundamentally unreachable by human minds to one that is potentially graspable by them. The figure of the planet thus shifts to a space that might be already occupied by intelligent life, and/or one where humans might one day settle.

These are old stories. "A True Story," written by the Greek satirist Lucian around 160 C.E., is often cited as the first known work to include travel to other planets. Its madcap tour of literary and mythological tropes includes an accidental trip to the Moon and a peace treaty between the inhabitants of the Moon and the Sun, who are warring over their attempts to colonize the Morning Star (now known as the planet Venus). "A True Story" may well be the first science fictional narrative ever written, though Lucian's contemporaries had also imagined such travel; this includes Antonius Diogenes, whose "The Wonders Beyond Thule" is often understood to be one of the texts that Lucian was parodying. In *The Cambridge History of Science Fiction*, Ryan Vu links Lucian's text to Plutarch, whose "On the Face in the Moon" was one of the first known texts to imagine a potentially habitable lunar space, with "a detailed description of its surface and the argument that life on the Moon is no less plausible than life in the ocean (populating it, as per tradition, with 'daemons,' or human souls)" (16). *Somnium* (1608), by the German astronomer Johannes Kepler, is widely considered to be the first text to take the idea of living on the Moon seriously—i.e., science fictionally—outside the realm of parody or folk tale; the novel not only contains detailed descriptions of the Moon's geography and topology and of the sorts of beings that might live there, but also imagines what became an archetypal science-fictional image: the Earth as seen from space. Similar stories about traveling to the Moon would follow later in the seventeenth century, among them Francis Godwin's *The Man in the Moone* (1638) and Cyrano de Bergerac's *The Other World or the States and Empires of the Moon* (1638), comprising a modern tradition of fictional lunar voyages that would come true in 1969.

Perhaps the most influential Mars novel of all time, H. G. Wells's 1898 *War of the Worlds*, inverts this extraplanetary paradigm and reinforces the melancholy attending Copernicus's removal of both Earth and humanity from the center of the universe. Indeed, Wells begins chapter one of the novel with an epigram from Kepler: "But who shall dwell in these worlds if they be inhabited?.../Are we or they Lords of the World?.../And how are all things made for man?—") (3). Wells expressly borrows the proposition from the "nebular hypothesis": the idea that, because Mars formed first as a planetary body, its inhabitants would live almost as if in Earth's future with a head start on natural and social evolution. In a judo-like reversal, however, Wells further postulates that this historical progression would turn Martians into the exact same sort of remorseless brutal colonizers the British had become. Thus, as "the secular cooling that must someday overtake our planet" wreaks havoc with the Martians' way of life, they look "sunward" toward Earth with a mixture of climatological terror and imperialist greed:

> And looking across space with instruments, and intelligences such as we have scarcely dreamed of, they see, at its nearest distance only 35,000,000 of miles sunward of them, a morning star of hope, our own warmer planet, green with vegetation and grey with water, with a cloudy atmosphere eloquent of fertility, with glimpses through its drifting cloud wisps of broad stretches of populous country and narrow, navy-crowded seas.

Wells's human narrator sympathizes with the Martians, noting that they might not see dispossessing us of our planet as a crime; invading us from our own future, humans would seem "to them at least as alien and lowly as are the monkeys and lemurs to us" (4–5). Even if they did recognize us as equals, Wells suggests, they would still wage the sort of exterminationist war that Europe and the United States had waged against so many others. From numerous possible examples, he refers specifically to the Tasmanians, "entirely swept out of existence in a war of extermination waged by European immigrants, in the space of fifty years. Are we such apostles of mercy as to complain if the Martians warred in the same spirit?" (4–5).

Indeed, one of the last gestures of the novel—after the Martians have been defeated, not by human artifice or trickery but by a bacterial infection native to Earth to which they had no immunity—the narrator speculates that someday human beings will have to invade Venus when Earth turns cool and inhospitable:

> If the Martians can reach Venus, there is no reason to suppose that the thing is impossible for men, and when the slow cooling of the sun makes this earth uninhabitable, as at last it must do, it may be that the thread of life that has begun here will have streamed out and caught our sister planet within its toils.
>
> *(163)*

War of the Worlds is a pointedly anti-colonial text, predicated on a critique of imperial violence and the horrible thought that someday somebody might do to London what London has already done to everyone else. Nevertheless, colonization—including the extraplanetary sort—becomes the necessary and unquestioned prerequisite for the continued survival of the human species as such.

Twentieth-Century Visions

While anti-colonial alien invasion stories like *War of the Worlds* remain a vital subgenre in the field, note how many of the unauthorized and fan sequels to *War of the Worlds* imagine a more triumphant humanity taking the fight to the Martians on Mars. The politics of these narratives typically rely on a logic of Manifest Destiny that shades into a kind of Terran exceptionalism, imagining a triumphant human species (led, of course, by the United States) that spreads itself across the solar system, the larger galaxy, and beyond. Perhaps the most notable of these is Garrett P. Serviss's *Edison's Conquest of Mars* (1898), in which Thomas Edison himself develops flying machines that can reach Mars and also disintegrator rays to eradicate the Martian population once the humans arrive. In Edgar Rice Burroughs's "Barsoom" series of stories and novels (1912–1943), the imperial encounter between Europe and the rest of the planet is again transplanted to Mars. There, through ingenuity and physical superiority, Burroughs's Great White Hero John Carter encounters and subdues monstrous green- and red-skinned "savages" on the surface of Mars (and also anticipates the adventures of Burroughs's other famous Great White Hero, Tarzan). One remarkable short story from a 1932 issue of *Wonder Stories*, "In Martian Depths" by Henrik Dahl Juve, goes further than even Burroughs in its transplanting of the imperial "frontier" to Mars; Juve reframes the American claim of its Manifest Destiny to an immutable law of nature that recasts the westward march of empire as an inescapable historical progression: "Those in the west conquer those immediately to the east. Those in the west continue to advance while those left behind merely settle down and live" (321). Having reached the earthly limits of the frontier in California, the logic goes, the progression of civilization/empire must sustain itself by moving even more westward still—westward to Mars! Truly, as Eric Michael Rogin once put it: "Where history fails, science fiction steps in, projecting onto the future the terms on which the United States can redemptively recover its past" (26). Or, as Istvan Csiscery-Ronay put it: "imperialism promises the stars; sf delivers" (234).

Other formulations of outer space were more apocalyptic in character but entail the same core internal logic framing necessary imperial expansion as the only alternative to civilizational and/or species death. A brief craze in the early science fiction pulps concerned the destruction of the supposed fifth planet from the sun, commonly called Bodia or Bode's Planet, which became the asteroid belt; in his indexing of the pulp magazines, *Science Fiction: The Early Years*, Everett F. Bleiler lists dozens of stories about the notion. *When Worlds Collide* (1933), by Edwin Balmer and Philip Wylie, imagined two rogue planets, Bronson Alpha and Bronson Beta, entering the solar system and threatening Earth with annihilation; a tiny number of humans are able to escape on arks to survive on the habitable Bronson Beta as it finds a stable orbit around the sun, a situation depicted in the sequel, *After Worlds Collide* (1934). Balmer and Wylie's novel has sometimes been thought of as anticipation of, and possible inspiration for, a young Kal-El's flight from a doomed Krypton in *Action Comics* #1 (1938). Such stories remain influential today; they are the Ur-text for the claim that humanity must settle other planets if it hopes to achieve "species immortality," and not be forever at risk of extinction due to asteroid strike, anthropogenic or nonanthropogenic climate change, nuclear war, or some other planetary disaster.[1]

Science has come to understand why expanding into the cosmos is either improbable or impossible: the vast distances involved, the inability to travel at sufficiently fast speeds to make it worthwhile, and the radical inhospitality of such places to Earth life if getting there were even possible seem to be insuperable barriers to fulfilling the fantasies of colonizing Mars and elsewhere. Yet the notion that the future of the human race entails expansion into the cosmos, whether in triumph or in a desperate flight from danger, has become a kind of shorthand for the expansionist, inflationary future, not only in science fiction but in the wider sphere of imperialist-capitalist self-conception of nation-states ranging from the United States to the United Kingdom and across Europe. This idea ultimately has become what, following Donald A. Wolheim, is frequently called the "consensus future" of the twentieth century: the sense, as Soviet rocket scientist Konstantin E. Tsiolkovsky put it, that "Earth is the cradle of humanity, but one cannot remain in the cradle forever" (qtd. in "Konstantin E. Tsiolkovsky" n.p.).[2]

Wollheim's idea of the "consensus future" is ubiquitously visible throughout the work of so-called "Big Three" writers of the 1930s–1950s Golden Age (Robert A. Heinlein, Arthur C. Clarke, and Isaac Asimov); the theme also pervades the work of 1960s and 1970s authors like Philip K. Dick, Ursula K. Le Guin, Samuel R. Delany, George Lucas, and others. Indeed, the theme is so dominant that, for much of the history of science fiction, the only major counter-subgenre to space opera was nuclear holocaust. The single text that perhaps best embodies the theme of interplanetary politics is *Star Trek*, whose original series (1966–1969) launched a host of transmedia extensions and spinoffs that continue to this day: more than five separate *Trek* series premiered in the past five years alone. *Star Trek*'s vision of the human race unifying in a utopian planetary collective before working together to colonize the stars to create an intergalactic "Federation of Planets" is one of the most popular and nakedly optimistic presentations of humanity's future, where the mastery of both political organization and technology is deployed with rigorous democratic and humanistic ethics rather than unbridled rapacious authoritarianism. In *Star Trek*, humanity lives in a post-capitalist, post-scarcity economy facilitated by matter replicators; planetary terraforming is so advanced that basically every human colony the *Enterprise* encounters has the paradisal feel of a Southern California summer (before the fires took over). The colonists on these other planets don't typically need to wear special gear while living in protective domes, and don't face hardships more dire than those in an ordinary vacation resort; when problems arise, the Federation flagship is there to help with advice, medicine, and photon torpedoes. The show short-circuits the preexisting generic connection between extraplanetary exploration and imperialism through the Federation's "Prime Directive": an absolute ethical imperative that prohibits Starfleet from interfering with populated worlds until the inhabitants develop star-traveling technology letting them join the community of planets as equals. Like *A Canticle for Leibowitz*, *Star Trek* also manages to bridge the consensus future of galactic empire with its extinctive negation, nuclear war; the utopian Federation only arises after World War III has destroyed twenty-first civilization, a dyspeptic element of the series backstory that the show's creators rarely emphasize.

Of course, many episodes of *Star Trek* explore lacunae, edge cases, and reversals of its largely optimistic vision of humanity's future. Overall, however, *Star Trek* serves as a kind of permission structure for the fantasy that humanity will someday spread to the rest of the universe, not as imperial conquerors but as peacefully benevolent scientists, diplomats, and explorers. The idea of such a galactic republic managing the affairs of a humanity safely and happily strewn about the cosmos is so attractive that resistance is futile; to be against space exploration seems to oppose futurity itself. This is surely not unique to *Star Trek*, as evidenced by films such as *Things to Come* (1936). Directed by William-Cameron-Menzies and adapted for the screen by H. G. Wells from his novel *The Shape of Things to Come* (1933), the film concludes with a strident call to colonize outer space that quickly becomes universally compulsory. Indeed, for Menzies and Wells's characters, the idea that human beings might do anything else (e.g., build a cozy utopia for themselves here on Earth) becomes a sort of antihuman political nihilism that must be opposed at any cost:

> Raymond Passworthy: Oh, God, is there never to be any age of happiness? Is there never to be any rest?
> Oswald Cabal: Rest enough for the individual man. Too much and too soon, and we call it death. But for Man, no rest and no ending. He must go on, conquest beyond

conquest. First this little planet and its winds and ways. And then all the laws of mind and matter that restrain him. Then the planets about him... and at last, out across immensity to the stars. And when he has conquered all the deeps of Space, and all the mysteries of Time, still he will be beginning.

Raymond Passworthy: But we're such little creatures. Poor humanity's so fragile, so weak. Little... little animals.

Oswald Cabal: Little animals. And if we're no more than animals, then we must snatch each little scrap of happiness, and live and suffer and pass, mattering no more than all the other animals do or have done. It is this, or that—all the Universe or nothingness! Which shall it be, Passworthy? Which shall it be?

In such moments, the stakes of a humanity that lives and dies on a single planet become quasi-theological; our ability to "annex the planets" is not just a matter of joy or sadness but an existentially final cosmic judgment on the superhistorical import of the species. When Copernicus discovered that the Earth revolves around the Sun, rather than the other way around, he may have bitterly removed the specialness of the human species, but in colonizing the universe we might reclaim that special status.

Octavia E. Butler's terrifyingly prescient pair of novels from the 1990s—*The Parable of the Sower* (1993) and *Parable of the Talents* (1998)—make this implicit connection between science fiction and theology literal. Speculatively narrating a 2020s America disintegrating in the face of economic, political, and climate emergency while turning viciously theocratic and neofascist, Butler's teenaged protagonist Lauren Oya Olamina creates the "Earthseed" religion. Based on the core proposition that it is the "Destiny" of the human race to "take root among the stars" (68), the novels suggest that Olamina's invented faith may reflect a serious error in judgment. The duology begins with the death of one of the first astronauts on Mars and ends with the launch of the first Earthseed colony ship, chillingly named the *Christopher Columbus* (Butler *Talents* 445).[3] Other characters in the novels, echoing a Black political critique of the space program dating back to Gil Scott-Heron's "Whitey on the Moon" (1970), frequently ask Olamina how she can devote so much time and energy to something so obviously fruitless as colonizing space when there are people suffering here on Earth. These are excellent questions posed by people living precarious and threatened lives, but have yet to dim the dream of the Federation's interplanetary mission "to seek out new life" in the popular imagination.

Revisionist Planetology

The novels of Kim Stanley Robinson, from the "Mars trilogy" (1992, 1993, 1996) through *The Ministry for the Future* (2020), offer one register for changes in how contemporary readers of science fiction understand what it might actually be like to live on other planets. Earlier science fictions were typically gestural in what terraforming would actually entail; *Star Trek*'s ships colonize planets with breathable atmospheres, drinkable water, and comestible florae and faunae. The planets in *Star Wars* host multiple mostly humanoid species, all originating from wildly different evolutionary contexts and planetary environments and all able to flourish on the surface of multiple planets with technology that is recognizably but not magically more advanced than our own. The Mars trilogy is ultimately quite optimistic about the prospects of human settlement of Mars in ways that Robinson has walked back in later works and interviews. Yet they also show what a tremendously difficult, generational engineering project would be needed to achieve even partial continuous habitation of another world.

And even that partial success would occur on a planet that is close enough to the Earth that a Martian colony could remain partially dependent on the home planet.

Robinson's Mars novels are focused on the First Hundred, an elite team mostly compromised of international scientists who are the first permanent human inhabitants of Mars. During their initial interplanetary voyage, the colonists realize (through the pointed interventions of a character loosely modeled on the Russian anarchist Mikhail Bakunin) that they will be radically independent from earthly political institutions and can form entirely new social relations. The idea that other planets might revolt against or even supplant Earth is an old one in science fiction; in particular Robinson seems to draw from Robert A. Heinlein's *The Moon Is a Harsh Mistress* (1966), where the Loonies living on the Moon realize that anyone living above another planet's gravity well has the power to launch nearly free but incredibly destructive asteroid weapons at their enemies, creating a radically new sort of arms race and the preconditions for an unprecedented degree of political revolution and social transformation. The deeply philosophical socialists who dominate the First Hundred do not go quite to this place, at least not right away—but later books in the series do depict a revolutionary war for Martian independence, with many of the First Hundred joining the side of the rebels.

The key debate in the series, however, is more scientific in nature, drawing on contemporaneous debates within NASA about the status of Mars. Does Mars have a right to exist independent of human influence and settlement? The question has a certain sort of obvious political valence if it were to turn out Mars had native life, but some within NASA believed even a fully lifeless Mars had status that needed to be respected.[4] Within the terms of the book, all the First Hundred are colonizers who fiercely debate the extent to which Mars should be bent to human will; some (the "Green Martians") believe the planet should be terraformed to maximal acclimation to Earth life, while others (the "Red Martians") believe that human transformation of the planet should be as limited as possible to allow some areas to retain their original character. The novels are dialogic, and never exactly "solve" the issue; the last book in the series seeks to find a productive union between the two camps rather than allowing one to triumph over the other, symbolized by a love affair between the two sides' most devoted spokespeople. This romanticization of compromise and consensus registers a larger turn away from political conflict in the post-Reagan, post-Cold-War moment of end-of-history neoliberalism; it should not escape our notice that the final revolutionary intervention that saves Robinson's Martian utopia at the end of the trilogy is a group of scientists giving a press conference, a proposition that seems ludicrously Pollyanish from the perspective of the dour 2010s or apocalyptic 2020s.

Robinson's later works frequently return to the terms of the Mars trilogy, typically remixing the plots of those novels to ends that are more suspiciously pessimistic about techno-utopian endings, and increasingly see a necessary role for political violence over reasoned debate. Novels like *Galileo's Dream* (2009), *2312* (2012), or *Aurora* (2015) deconstruct and deflate the fantasy that humans might find greener pastures away from Earth: the trip to other planets are impossibly long and miserable and the destinations are filled with disease, hardship, and catastrophic weather, and refuse to flatter the consensus future of interplanetary colonization science fiction fans frequently feel personally invested in.

Robinson's public interviews and his most recent non-fiction book, *The High Sierra: A Love Story* (2022), echo these later novels' sense that Earth is the single best place humans will ever know; they register his personal skepticism about the prospects for outer space colonization and are situated in the long deflationary arc (beginning in the 1970s) regarding the prospect of humans settling the cosmos. In the 1990s, many science fiction classics were released in revised editions that pushed the date of the story further into the future and thus preserved the fantasy's viability. Most, however, were left with the original dates in a bizarrely retro epigraph for a "future that failed." Among other speculative milestones, we have passed the dates of *2001: A Space Odyssey* and *2010: The Year We Make Contact* and long overshot the scheduled timeline for *Blade Runner* the novel (which took place in 1992) and the film (which depicted an equally dystopian 2019). Instead, the last manned mission to the Moon was in 1972, with no significant material progress toward Mars, the asteroid belt, the outer planets, or beyond since then. "Sorry, but it's true," says Robinson's narrator in *2312*, anticipating the grim disaster of the *Aurora* mission that would follow in the later book.

> It has to be said: the stars exist beyond human time, beyond human reach. We live in this little pearl of warmth surrounding our star; outside it lies a vastness beyond comprehension. The solar system is our one and only home.
>
> *(330)*

While Robinson retains some optimism about settlement of the local solar system (and *pace* the tech billionaires), perhaps, he insists it is Earth and Earth alone that is ultimately our species' one and only home.[5] Earth is the one planet where we evolved and live alongside other species; the one place that for now has ample air and water in the right concentration and at the right temperature for survival; and the one place we are currently destroying through unchecked capitalism and its anti-ecological way of life, an accelerating planetary catastrophe that has been called the Sixth Mass Extinction.

Conclusion: Thinking like a Planet

It has become habitual to think of the Earth in planetary terms, especially after the birth of outer space and satellite photography gave us visual access to the planet as a totality. Cosmopolitan political movements across the twentieth and twenty-first centuries, especially on the political left, have frequently evoked the notion of a single human race existing on a single planet to argue against the basic dominant form of the nation state. The environmentalist movement in particular has made many appeals to the notion that "we are all in this together" living "on this pale blue dot." And thus J. Baird Callicott extends Aldo Leopold's land ethic to a call to "think like a planet," a Whole Earth ethic that recognizes and acts in service of multiple globally interconnected ecosystems.[6] There are of course good reasons to use this sort of language; the environmental movement has helped raise awareness about the interconnected global flows of organic and nonorganic material that have been destabilized by human activity and highlighted the urgency of protecting the Earth if, indeed, there is no Planet B. There are also good reasons to be skeptical of calls to imagine the Earth as single and as singular, precisely insofar as that understanding obscures the primary drivers of environmental catastrophe (the richer, whiter, colonizing nations of the Global North) from those who are most likely to suffer its most immediate and most extreme effects (the poorer, Blacker and Browner, colonized nations of the Global South).

In the 1940s, physicist Enrico Fermi famously proposed the idea that if nonhuman life existed on other planets, we should already have seen some direct or indirect sign of it. The urgency of the environmental crisis, and the inability of political institutions to address it, has led to a newly proposed solution to "Fermi's Paradox." Perhaps civilization—not just human civilization, but all organized sociality as such—is simply and ineluctably doomed to undercut its own prerequisites for survival before it ever achieves that "consensus future" represented by freewheeling galactic empire; if that is true, perhaps we don't see traces of extraterrestrial life because every civilization completely consumes its home planet and dies off before it can colonize the universe. Why then, the logic asks, should the human race be any different?

Planetary thinking in this moment, especially in science fiction, is thus responding to a new and abiding pessimism about the prospects of a human species that once imagined that it was both able and destined to populate the universe. Margaret Atwood wrote a short-short story titled "Time Capsule Found on the Dead Planet" during the 2009 Copenhagen climate talks. The story imagines that someday alien life forms will find the ruins of our lives amid a decimated, murdered Earth and addresses them:

> 5. You who have come here from some distant world, to this dry lakeshore and this cairn, and to this cylinder of brass, in which on the last day of all our recorded days I place our final words:
> Pray for us, who once, too, thought we could fly.

I have suggested elsewhere that the "consensus future" has thus given way, in our time, to a sort of "consensus apocalypse." But attempts to imagine a more optimistic, non-extinctive future for the planet (whether or not human beings themselves survive) frequently evoke the logic of planetary unity rather than planetary eulogy as part of their imagined response to the climate catastrophe.

The works of Chinese science fiction author Liu Cixin, one of the first major Chinese authors to see wide readership in translation in the West, are a paradigmatic example. In his novella "The Wandering Earth" (2000s) which was later adapted to China's first major transnational science fiction film release, human beings must devote themselves to a generational project of physically moving the Earth away from a self-destructing Sun in order to protect life. With massive "Earth Engines" (3) altering its orbit, the Earth is launched into the interstellar void with human and animal life moving underground for what will be centuries of travel—a grim underground existence, reminiscent of life in nuclear fallout shelters, will be humanity's only hope to survive. N. K. Jemisin's Broken Earth Trilogy (2015–2017), the first trilogy ever to win back-to-back-to-back Hugo Awards, elaborates on a similar imaginary: on a future Earth ravaged by human activity and failed technoscientific innovation, a massive empire straddling a planetary supercontinent tries to keep ecological disaster at bay by exploiting the psychokinetic powers of mutant humans called orogenes. Here, though, the answer is not stability but revolution: the heroes of Jemisin's trilogy decide that the only true path for the future is transformation of the planet, beginning with the most powerful orogene, who uses his power in the opening pages of the novel to break the world and usher in something utterly new.

In *The Ministry for the Future*, Robinson likewise imagines a planetary totality struggling to find its path between a failed present and multiple possible futures. This global community, however, does not operate under any sort of formal governmental structure but is instead the cacophonous, chaotic union of a huge number of actors with different motives and tactics. The Ministry of the title is a special committee of the United Nations tasked to advocate on behalf of future generations after a climate-change-supercharged heat wave strikes India. The book sees the Ministry and its allies trying every possible tactic to save the future of the planet for human beings: legal reforms, ecologically based cryptocurrency, energy innovation, geoengineering, ecoterrorism, and the coerced "rewilding" of much of the Earth's surface. In the end, our heroes retire, the next generation of Ministry bureaucrats takes over, and the unfinished, multi-generational work of saving the planet goes on. In this novel, at least, Robinson does not even mention colonizing outer space; whatever future there is for humanity, it is on this planet alone.

Notes

1 This claim in turn leads to the growing philosophical movement called "longtermism," which argues that we should value the hypothetical extension of human life into the galaxy at large and the trillions of people who will supposedly one day live in that context, over and above the needs of anyone actually currently alive today. See Torres, "Against Longtermism."
2 Wollheim uses the somewhat more opaque term "consensus cosmogeny" in his book *The Universe Makers: Science Fiction Today*.
3 Butler's planned sequels for the series, never completed, would have followed the colonists to the extrasolar planets, where (in every draft!) they find the conditions on the other world alienating, difficult, and miserable, and find themselves hopelessly planetsick for Earth. See my *Octavia E. Butler*.
4 See, for instance, Christopher McKay's "Does Mars Have Rights: An Approach to the Environmental Ethics of Planetary Engineering."
5 For an account of an ecological and ecopoetic politics based on earth, see Natalie Pollard's essay "Homes" in this volume.
6 For more on Leopold and cross-species political ethics in the face of climate apocalypse, see Mario Ortiz-Robles' chapter "Animals" in this volume.

Works Cited

Amis, Kingsley. *New Maps of Hell,* reprint. Arno Press, 1975 (1960).
Atwood, Margaret E. "Time Capsule Found on the Dead Planet." *The Guardian*, 25 September 2009, https://www.theguardian.com/books/2009/sep/26/margaret-atwood-mini-science-fiction.
Butler, Octavia E. *Parable of the Sower.* Four Walls Eight Windows, 1993.
———. *Parable of the Talents.* Seven Stories Press, 1998.
Callicott, J. Baird. *Thinking Like a Planet: The Land Ethic and the Earth Ethic.* Oxford University Press, 2013.
Canavan, Gerry. *Octavia E. Butler.* University of Illinois Press, 2016.Csicsery-Ronay, Istvan. "Science Fiction and Empire." *Science Fiction Studies,* vol. 30, no. 2, 2003, pp. 231–245.
Juve, Henrik Dahl. "In Martian Depths." *Wonder Stories,* September 1932, pp. 320–339.
Kennedy, John F. "John F. Kennedy Moon Speech - Rice Stadium." NASA.gov, n.d., https://er.jsc.nasa.gov/seh/ricetalk.htm.
"Konstantin E. Tsiolkovsky." NASA.gov, n.d., https://www.nasa.gov/audience/foreducators/rocketry/home/konstantin-tsiolkovsky.html.
Liu, Cixin. "The Wandering Earth." *The Wandering Earth,* translated by Ken Liu et al. Head of Zeus, 2017, pp. 3–47.
McKay, Christopher, "Does Mars Have Rights: An Approach to the Environmental Ethics of Planetary Engineering." *Moral Expertise: Studies in Practical and Professional Ethics*, edited by Don Macniven. Routledge, 1990, pp. 184–197.
Oremus, Will. "Elon Musk and Tech's 'Great Man' Fallacy." *The Washington Post*, 27 April 2022, https://www.washingtonpost.com/technology/2022/04/27/jack-dorsey-elon-musk-singular-solution/.
"Planet." *Oxford English Dictionary,* n.d., https://www.oed.com/view/Entry/145058.
Robinson, Kim Stanley. *2312,* Orbit Books, 2012.
Rogin, Eric Michael. *Independence Day,* BFI Modern Classics, 1998.
Spivak, Gayatri Chakravorty. "Planetarity." *Paragraph,* vol. 38, no. 2 ("Translation and the Untranslatable"), July 2015, pp. 290–292
"The 'Canali' and the First Martians. NASA.gov, n.d., http://nasa.gov/audience/forstudents/postsecondary/features/F_Canali_and_First_Martians.html.

Torres, Phil. "Against Longtermism." *Aeon*, 19 October 2021, https://aeon.co/essays/why-longtermism-is-the-worlds-most-dangerous-secular-credo.
Vu, Ryan. "Science Fiction before Science Fiction: Ancient, Medieval, and Early Modern SF." *The Cambridge History of Science Fiction,* edited by Gerry Canavan and Eric Carl Link, Cambridge University Press, 2019, pp. 13–34.
Wells, H.G. *War of the Worlds,* reprint, Bantam Books, 1988 (1898).
Wollheim, Donald A. *The Universe Makers: Science Fiction Today,* Harper and Row, 1971.

39
UTOPIA
Deanna K. Kreisel

Utopia is a slippery concept. At first blush, it seems fairly obvious what we mean by the term: a theoretical ideal society and/or a literary work that describes such a society. Yet it is difficult to capture all the permutations of utopia in a single definition. Is it best understood as a genre, a mode, a style, a political project, or a structure of feeling? Contributing to the difficulty of defining utopia is the fact that arguments over its proper role and function sometimes take place in the "real world" outside of literature: in schemes of social reform, the planning of intentional communities, and other acts of political practice. Utopianism also has a psychological valence: the term is often used to refer to a type of impulse, need, or drive that some believe is inherent in the human psyche. Is fantasizing about ideal worlds hard-wired in the human brain? Or, at the very least, is it a strongly internalized cultural imperative whose sheer pervasiveness requires an explanation?

To complicate matters further, utopia is perhaps unique among literary genres in inspiring a robust theoretical conversation that often draws explicit connections between the literary and the political. Furthermore, for utopia the persistent question about how representation relates to praxis is particularly fraught and raises a series of questions: to what extent do we need to consider the political uses of utopia and the existence of real-world utopian experiments in order to understand and describe the form of the utopian novel? How do we account for parallel (and divergent) developments of utopia in different cultural contexts, in different languages, and in different literary traditions? How do we do so without artificially separating the literary, the pragmatic, and the theoretical? Finally, after all these centuries, where is utopia today?

Utopia's Beginnings

Thomas More coined the word "utopia" in his 1516 text of the same name, yet of course he invented neither the concept nor the genre. Western literary representations of ideal societies that predate *Utopia* include Plato's *Republic*, Hesiod's Golden Age, the island of the Phaeacians in Homer's *Odyssey*, the medieval Land of Cockaigne, and even the Biblical Garden of Eden. More's *Utopia*, however, not only gave the genre (and concept) an enduring name; it also codified the generic elements that subsequent authors have mostly honored: an ideal society, a traveler-narrator, a guide who explains the society's structure and rules, a return to the homeland, an audience waiting to hear the tale. Both the ideal society and the genre itself are governed by a rigid set of rules. Perhaps most important, the description of utopia contains a buried (or not-so-buried) critique of the traveler/author/reader's own country or society: through comparison to an ideal social organization, the flaws of the author's culture are laid bare. In the case of More's text these comparisons are more or less direct—the traveler Raphael Hythloday is given to pronouncements such as "your sheep... swallow up people: they lay waste and depopulate fields, dwellings and towns" (33)—but as we'll see later in this chapter, many subsequent utopias and dystopias have relied on satire to drive their critical points home.

The island of Utopia is located vaguely in the New World somewhere (the intradiegetic character of Thomas More conveniently forgets to ask Hythloday "in what part of that new world Utopia may be found" [13]). As Fredric Jameson points out, utopia as genre is, from its outset, "enabled by geographical exploration and the resultant travel narratives" that depict "tribal societies and their well-nigh Utopian dignity" (18). Thus from its very beginnings, utopia was a genre—and perhaps a political construct—inseparable from colonialist and racist ideologies. The tradition among More's Utopians is that their founder Utopus, "who gave his name to the island by conquest," later "raised its brutish and uncultivated inhabitants to such a level of civilization and humanity that they now outshine virtually all other nations" (57–58). The suggestion is that even this process of "civilization" was made possible by the shipwreck of a group of Romans and Egyptians who brought with them skills and techniques "developed for the improvement of life" (54). Apparently it was impossible for More to imagine a group of indigenous Americans developing a just and rational society *sui generis*.

The relationship between colonial conquest and utopian literature is fascinatingly complex. More's Utopians practice colonization as a means of population control; when their own island becomes too crowded, they establish a colony on the mainland, "wherever the native population has redundant and untilled land" (68), and forcibly conquer anyone who resists the implementation of their laws. The Utopians "view it as an entirely just cause for war when those who possess a territory leave it idle and unproductive, denying use and possession to others who, by the law of nature, ought to be fed by it" (69). This is arguably the earliest articulation of the principle of *terra nullius*—the idea that "waste" land cannot be owned and is thus legally subject to seizure—which underwrote colonial land grabs throughout the age of exploration (and beyond). John Locke is often credited with the development of the principle; his contribution was the idea that because it is a divine injunction to improve land, anyone who "in obedience to this command of God, subdued, tilled and sowed any part of [the earth], thereby annexed to it something that was his property, which another had no title to, nor could without injury take from him" (Locke Section 32). Legal historian Richard Tuck points out that Locke was influenced in this formulation by the writings of the Dutch political theorist Hugo Grotius (1583–1645), who was in turn influenced by the Anglo-Italian jurist and "Father of International Law" Alberico Gentili (1552–1608), who "often cited with enthusiasm" the passages from *Utopia* to which I have alluded (Tuck 49). Thus, the justification for appropriating "uncultivated" lands from indigenous peoples moved from imaginative literature to political principle to real-world practice.

More's island nation followed many more politically progressive practices, however, that became standard elements of future utopias—both fictional and real-world. As the character Thomas More acknowledges of the Utopians, the "linchpin of their entire social order [is] their life in common without any use of money" (122). Jameson notes that "More's initial utopian gesture—the abolition of money and property—runs through the Utopian tradition like a red thread, now aggressively affirmed on the surface, now tacitly presupposed in milder forms or disguises" (20). As we shall see, it was the embrace of communism from the earliest iterations of utopia that made the genre attractive to nineteenth-century socialist reformers, as well as to Marxist theorists from the nineteenth century onward. It is one of the paradoxes of utopia that a literary genre dedicated to describing idealized, perhaps impossible worlds—the word itself does mean "no place," after all—has from its beginnings been so entangled with real-world praxis.

Of the few dozen literary utopias written in English during the three centuries following More's inaugural text, Margaret Cavendish's imaginary ethnography *The Description of a New World, Called the Blazing World* (1666) is currently the most canonical example. It describes the adventures of a young aristocratic woman who travels to a parallel world, adjacent to the North Pole, inhabited by rational animal-human hybrid creatures who live in total harmony. Although Jonathan Swift's *Gulliver's Travels* (1726) is predominantly a satire, its final section describing the idealized Land of the Houyhnhnms has strongly utopian elements. Both texts avoid describing the "Utopian dignity" of indigenous peoples by populating their ideal worlds with humanoid animals. They do, however, enshrine other key components of early literary utopia: the abolition of private property and money, and the location of their ideal worlds in a physically separate space accessible through (arduous) travel. Not until the cusp of the nineteenth century would utopianist authors begin to locate their imaginary worlds in the future.

The Nineteenth Century

The development of progressive political ideas during the Enlightenment wrought a change in utopia. As Fátima Vieira argues, "By projecting the ideal society in the future, the utopian discourse enunciated a logic of causalities that presupposed that certain actions (namely those of a political nature) might afford the changes that were necessary in order to make the imagined society come true" (10). *Utopia* or *eutopia* ("no place" or "good place") ceded to *euchronia* ("good era") as authors shifted from critiquing their own societies through satirical comparison toward imagining what real-world alternatives could look like. Utopian discourse, including literary utopias, took on the prescriptive flavor of a blueprint—the description of a social organization that might, and should, happen in the future.

The nineteenth century was a period of extraordinary efflorescence for utopias: while there were about 70 English-language utopias written between 1516 and 1800, the nineteenth century saw the publication of over 400 utopian novels in English, fully half of which were published between 1887 (when Edward Bellamy's hugely influential novel *Looking Backward* appeared) and 1895 (Sargent 276, 278). Bellamy's novel and William Morris's response in *News from Nowhere* (1890) not only sparked a craze for utopia-writing that lasted over a decade; they specifically jump-started a vogue for prescriptive utopias set in the future. The two authors' utopian "blueprints" form the ends of a spectrum. While Bellamy envisions an idyllic America in the year 2000 whose just and equitable society is enabled by technological development and the gradual consolidation of capital in huge monopolies eventually taken over by the state, Morris sketches a future neo-feudal pastoral idyll in which human beings live in harmony with nature, dwell in small communal units, and labor by hand.

Most utopias written in the 1890s deliberately positioned themselves in one or the other of these "camps"—both of which, it is important to note, were predicated on communal property relations and the solution of the "labor problem" through collectivity, very much in the spirit of More's ur-text. Indeed, part of the reason for the boom in literary utopias during this period was the growth of socialism, in the form of both revolutionary Marxism and other "gradualist" socialist movements such as Fabianism and Great Britain's Independent Labour Party. Both agrarian and techno literary utopianists are thus responding (and contributing) to the growth of real-world political movements and events.

This was also the decade, however, that saw a mini-boom in dystopian novels that openly critiqued the traditional communist basis of utopia. As Gregory Claeys has discussed at length, the anti-socialist utopia typically depicts a revolution that turns into a dictatorship (xii). Often such novels warn of compulsory labor or detail eugenicist schemes of population control and species "improvement" through enforced selective breeding. The ideal society of Anthony Trollope's *The Fixed Period* (1882), for example, depends on a scheme of voluntary euthanasia for everyone at the age of 68. Walter Besant's *The Inner House* (1888), on the other hand, describes a population-stable society controlled by elite scientists who have discovered an elixir of immortality; all its citizens live in a passionless stupor and must wait for someone to die by accident before anyone is allowed to reproduce.

Not all the novels of this period that depict state-sponsored eugenics can be characterized as dystopian, however; eugenics itself (as deplorable and evil as we now understand it to be) contained strongly utopian elements in its earliest incarnations. Francis Galton (1822–1911), who coined the term "eugenics" in 1883, responded to anxieties about the "degeneration" of the human species—supposedly caused by depleted physical strength due to urban living and lack of manual labor among the upper classes—by trumpeting the capacity of selective interbreeding of the "gifted" to bring about a "higher" type of human being. While most utopias, including More's own, imagine the physical improvement of human beings in some form—usually through the application of healthful labor, outdoor weather, better food, and even selective marriage—it isn't until the 1890s that eugenicist and socialist thought began to overlap in the realm of utopia.

Many prominent British socialists openly espoused eugenicist ideas. In his 1905 novel *A Modern Utopia*, H. G. Wells, who was a committed Fabian, depicts an ideal society ruled by a class of physically and mentally superior beings known as *samurai*, whom the narrator explicitly likens to the guardians in Plato's *Republic*. More chillingly, in his pamphlet *The Decline in the Birth-Rate* (1907), Sidney Webb (a driving force behind the Fabian Society) complained that in

> Great Britain at this moment ... children are being freely born to the Irish Catholics and the Polish, Russian and German Jews, on the one hand, and to the thriftless and irresponsible—largely the casual laborers and the other denizens of the one-roomed tenements of our great cities—on the other.

(16–17)

It is one thing to note that early eugenicist thinking contained a utopian element—the dream of a better society—and quite another to notice that utopia itself is deeply, perhaps inextricably, entangled with eugenicist schemes and ideals. As the political philosopher Bertrand de Jouvenel wrote in his 1946 treatise *On Power*:

> Take a look ... at the way in which the master builders of Paradises, the Platos, the Mores, the Campanellas, set about it. They get rid of the clashes by getting rid of the differences ... . These dreams are, one and all, of tyrannies, of straiter, heavier, more oppressive tyrannies than any that history has yet shown us.

(133)

Yet critiques of utopia did not have to await the twentieth century, the rise of fascism, and the aftermath of two world wars. Marx himself famously denigrated contemporary "utopian socialists" for different reasons—for engaging in "fantastic" schemes, "standing apart from the contest" in an attempt to "deaden the class struggle" and to "reconcile the class antagonisms" (Marx and Engels 255–256). According to Marx, the followers of Owen, Fourier, and Saint-Simon are distracted from the revolution by their continued fixation on the "experimental realization of their social Utopias, of founding isolated '*phalanstères*,' of establishing 'Home Colonies,' of setting up a 'Little Icaria'... and to realise all these castles in the air, they are compelled to appeal to the feelings and purses of the bourgeois" (256).

For most theorists writing in the wake of Marx, the construction of detailed blueprints for a specific future society has been seen, at best, as a distraction from the immediate and pressing tasks of social change and, at worst, as an ideological, compensatory sop akin to religion. As the historian and scholar of utopia Ruth Levitas argues, however, the "real dispute between Marx and Engels and the utopian socialists is not about the merit of goals or of images of the future but about the process of transformation" (41). In other words, the Marxists and so-called "utopian socialists" debated primarily the *means* by which a workers' paradise will be effected: through an actual revolution, or through "an appeal to all classes on the basis of reason and justice" (60).

A deeper difference between the two "sides" is the extent to which they see the description of blueprints for utopia—including in literary texts—to be inherently transformative or a dangerous distraction from the pragmatic business of revolution. (As we shall see, the question of the psychological function of utopia becomes a particularly lively one for the Marxist theorists of the early twentieth century.) That said (and *pace* Marx himself), the conflict between Marxism and "utopian socialism" should not be overstated. Levitas argues that it is less stark than it appears, noting that "an outline of the principal features of communist society can be pieced together from the writings of Marx and Engels," who can thus be seen as indulging in their own blueprint-making (46). As Roger Paden notes, Marx and Engels incorporated a number of specific elements cribbed from British and French utopian thinkers in their own descriptions of the post-revolutionary workers' paradise. More importantly, they

> took from the Utopian socialists a specific conception of what it was to be a politically engaged Utopian thinker.... Utopianism, in this view, is a political project involving the description of an ideal society to be used both as a goal to guide social reform and as a normative standard to critically evaluate existing societies.
>
> (69–70)

Morris's *News from Nowhere*, the most influential and widely read utopia by a British socialist author, elegantly fudges the question of how the new social organization is to be effected. In chapters entitled "How the Change Came" and "The Beginning of the New Life," the historian Old Hammond describes to William Guest, the Victorian time traveler-narrator who has found himself mysteriously transported to an ideal future England, how their utopian society came about. Morris includes both gradualist elements—the influence of newspapers, the formation of powerful unions—and revolutionary elements—a massacre in Trafalgar Square and brutal police and military crackdowns—in his imaginary account of "how the change came."

However it envisions the transformation coming about, the nineteenth-century literary utopia still retains a laser-eyed focus on problems of labor and distribution, often sketching ideal social organizations in which labor is undertaken freely, without official remuneration, and in return everyone is supported by a centralized economy administered by the state. Usually money as such does not exist. The keen student of the century's utopias will notice, however, that the literary imagination often falters when it comes to envisioning true social equality. The women of Bellamy's *Looking Backward*, despite their separate-but-equal industrial army, are still considered "ornaments" who leave the men to their cigars after dinner, while a rigid gendered division of labor (men in the fields, women in the house) still pertains in *News from Nowhere*. Neither novel has anything at all to say about race relations.

More subtly, many authors fail to perceive how their ideal societies are propped up by the same problematic institutions as their real-life ones. As Dr. Leete, the twentieth-century utopian "explainer" in *Looking Backward*, proudly explains to his guest from the nineteenth century, money no longer exists in their ideal society: "A credit corresponding to his share of the annual product of the nation is given to every citizen ... and a credit card issued him with which he procures at the public storehouses ... whatever he desires." Each credit card, moreover, "is issued for a certain number of dollars," which serve "as algebraical symbols for comparing the values of products with one another" (51). That is, for all of Bellamy's powers of imagination, he seems incapable of imagining a society without money.

While this insight is perhaps an unfair quibble, we see deeper economic problems at work in Morris's Nowhere. As Old Hammond explains to Guest:

> [I]n the last age of civilisation men had got into a vicious circle in the matter of production of wares. They had reached wonderful facility of production, and in order to make the most of that facility they had gradually created (or allowed to grow, rather) a most elaborate system of buying and selling, which has been called the World-Market; and that World-Market, once set a-going, forced them to go on making more and more of these wares.
>
> *(80)*

Yet as we soon learn, the new anxiety in this utopia is that instead of a surplus of consumable objects there will be a surplus of laboring bodies: Nowhereians worry that the supply of pleasant labor will dry up. Thus, emigration becomes an integral part of the new economic organization:

> Those lands which were once the colonies of Great Britain, for instance, and especially America—that part of it, above all, which was once the United States—are now and will be for a long while a great resource to us .... [F]or nearly a hundred years the people of the northern parts of America have been engaged in gradually making a dwelling-place out of a stinking dust-heap; and there is still a great deal to do.
>
> *(84–85)*

Even in a world with abundant sustenance for all, a new scarcity is imagined; emigration becomes a necessary prop to the system, just as colonial markets were necessary to maintain adequate economic demand for products and goods. While most Victorian literary utopias are activated by deep skepticism about nineteenth-century capitalism's optimistic discourse of simultaneous infinite growth and self-contained sustainability, their critique of capital often results in depictions of a future society that is unable to escape the same contradictions as the one from which it sprung.

The Twentieth Century and Beyond

The twentieth century saw two crucial developments in utopia. First, the concept was taken up by Marxist philosophers associated with the Frankfurt School—perhaps ironically, given Marx's own antipathy to the term—and given serious consideration as both a political force and a psychological drive. Second, literary utopia seemed to disappear, muscled out by a wave of dystopias and utopia-dystopia hybrids—novels depicting worlds that think of themselves as utopian, but which readers are clearly meant to revile and condemn. Indeed, both trends could be seen as continuing to dominate utopian discourse up to the present moment—but as we shall see in the final section of this chapter, there is perhaps a bit of hope left when it comes to literary utopia, a little bit of energy left for imagining and describing ideal worlds, even if it is found in unlikely places.

The writings of the Marxist philosopher Ernst Bloch, particularly his multi-volume treatise *The Principle of Hope* (1954–1959), have been enormously influential on later utopian theorists. Bloch's crucial contribution is his description of the "utopian impulse," a general orientation toward utopian hope that spills over from the political and literary realms. For Bloch, the utopian impulse manifests in either concrete or abstract forms. The former, which he also calls "anticipatory" utopia, refers to reality-directed schemas of social reform such as intentional communities and revolutionary praxis. The latter, abstract or "compensatory" utopia, refers to personal wishes and daydreams and can be found in an array of cultural formations such as music, architecture, popular culture, myths, daydreams, and medicine. The former are social and the latter are selfish; the former are (or can be) properly Marxist while the latter are essentially ideological.

Yet Bloch is careful not to draw artificial or untenable distinctions. The distinction between concrete and abstract utopia is one of function rather than form; both kinds of impulse can be found in different kinds of cultural production. For Bloch, "hope" is a central term; indeed, it forms part of the title of his magnum opus. There is a core of political energy to be harnessed in even the most selfish, rubbishy dreams of a better future; the trick is to precipitate a nugget of concrete utopia from the dross of compensatory, abstract longings. For Bloch, what remains is "an unfinished forward dream" that "can only be discredited by the bourgeoisie—this seriously deserves the name utopia" (157).

Bloch expends a lot of space attempting to distinguish concrete from abstract utopia, wheat from chaff, yet there is an unsatisfyingly circular feel to his analysis: concrete utopia is what survives after the passing of the ephemeral trappings of particular wishes, yet this perdurable "cultural surplus" is by definition concrete utopia. As Fredric Jameson waggishly notes,

> There is here at work the same hermeneutic paradox Freud confronted when, searching for precursors of his dream analysis, he finally identified one obscure aboriginal tribe for whom all dreams had sexual meanings—except for overtly sexual dreams as such, which meant something else.
>
> (3)

Yet as Ruth Levitas points out, it is ultimately unimportant that the criteria are obscure by which concrete utopia is distinguished from abstract utopia. Bloch's project is fundamentally to rehabilitate utopia "within Marxism as a neglected Marxist category" (107).

In the end, Bloch was successful—if we measure success by the extent to which utopia has been taken seriously as a category by Marxist and other leftist critics in the twentieth and twenty-first centuries. Jameson, the most prominent such critic, sidesteps the hermeneutic problems in Bloch's original schema by reinscribing abstract-vs.-concrete utopia as a question of form: "the properly Utopian program or realization will involve a commitment to closure (and thereby to totality)" (4). It is the "very impress of the form and category of totality which is virtually by definition lacking in the multiple forms invested by Bloch's Utopian impulse" (5). The totalization of closure is a key feature of utopia beginning with More's island, which has been terraformed by the colonial conquerors: they "caused a channel fifteen miles wide to be excavated at that end of the peninsula joined to the mainland, so surrounding it with the sea" (58). We can see a commitment to closure in nearly all (dare one say "all"?) literary utopias ever since: either geographical separation (islands, hollow earths, Hyperborean poles, extraterrestrial colonies) or temporal separation (ideal civilizations—usually also geographically enclosed—that exist in the future or the past).

The work of Herbert Marcuse, a psychoanalytic-Marxist critic and member of the Frankfurt School, potentially points another way beyond the impasse between liberatory and ideological views of utopian impulse. For Marcuse, the psychoanalytic reality principle contains first a necessary element—the control of anarchic selfishness in the process of socialization—and second a "surplus" element, whose function is to ensure dominance and hierarchy (*Eros & Civilization* 35ff.). Different modes of production are associated with different modes of domination and thus different modes of repression; Marcuse names the particular form that surplus repression takes under advanced capitalism the "performance principle," and does so "in order to emphasize that under its rule society is stratified according to the competitive economic performances of its members" (*Eros & Civilization* 44). The performance principle has several crucial features:

1 It renders labor pervasive and all-encompassing for "Work has now become *general*" (*Eros & Civilization* 45).
2 It necessitates the repression of Eros: "repressive desublimation" sanctions and allows certain performances of libido that are channeled by and contained by the system of domination (*One-Dimensional Man* 59ff.).
3 It tragically curtails the realm of human freedom:

> the free space which the individual has at his disposal for his psychic processes has been greatly narrowed down; it is no longer possible for something like an individual psyche with its own demands and decisions to develop; the space is occupied by public, social forces.
>
> (*Five Lectures* 14)

Utopias are entirely about imagined alternatives, and Marcuse elaborates how difficult it is for subjects of modern capitalism to imagine an alternative to a social organization governed by the performance principle. In the last pages of the "Phantasy and Utopia" chapter of *Eros and Civilization*, Marcuse works through the implications of an imagined—that is, utopian—"non-repressive reality principle" (*Eros & Civilization* 155). Because our current social organization is characterized by (unnecessary) anxiety over scarcity and the inculcation of false desires, it easily co-opts any attempts to "improv[e] or supplement[] the present existence by more contemplation, more leisure" (*Eros & Civilization* 157). A utopian non-repressive reality principle would require nothing less than a complete reorganization of the psyche, an alteration in "the balance between Eros and Thanatos," a reactivation of "tabooed realms of gratification," and the pacification of "the conservative tendencies of the instincts" (*Eros & Civilization* 158).

Eros, or the pleasure principle, is the source of the utopian desire for a better world. While it is constantly struggling against forces of surplus repression, Marcuse envisions a world in which a non-repressive reality principle allows for the sublimation of Eros into non-alienated labor, labor that occasions true satisfaction and joy. One of the ways this process can be effected is through imagination and the arts, what Marcuse terms "the aesthetic dimension":

> Imagination envisions the reconciliation of the individual with the whole, of desire with realization, of happiness with reason. While this harmony has been removed into utopia by the established reality principle, phantasy insists that it must and can become real, that behind the illusion lies *knowledge*. The truths of imagination are first realized when phantasy itself takes form, when it creates a universe of perception and comprehension.... This occurs in *art*.
>
> (*Eros & Civilization* 143–144)

This is especially true, we might add, in one particular form of art: the imaginative utopia.

The crucial twentieth-century development in the domain of literary utopia was its near disappearance. The first dystopias appeared, as we have seen, as critical responses to the boom of late-Victorian utopian novels, and the two modes co-existed for a decade or so before dystopia gained the upper hand. The novels of H. G. Wells at the turn of the century, particularly *When the Sleeper Wakes* (1899) and *A Modern Utopia* (1905), inaugurated a powerful vision of utopia gone awry through the betrayal of revolutionary ideals. Yet as the title of the latter suggests, it is not entirely clear to what extent Wells is predicting, excoriating, or endorsing various authoritarian elements of the societies he depicts. Wells was committed (or perhaps reconciled) to the necessity of a world-state in order to effect social reform, but his literary visions of such worlds shimmer between utopia and dystopia, refusing to resolve definitively into one or the other.

Wells arguably brought forward contradictory elements in utopia—totalitarianism, uniformity, repression, eugenics—latent in the genre all along that were picked up and developed by the authors of dystopias in the years following the world wars. The most influential of such novels were Aldous Huxley's *Brave New World* (1932), George Orwell's *1984* (1949), and Anthony Burgess's *A Clockwork Orange* (1962). All three depict future worlds characterized by state brutality and a compliant populace, and concern themselves primarily with the problem of free will under a repressive regime. Utopia secured by authoritarianism was a central—perhaps the central—theme of dystopian novels throughout much of the twentieth century. Margaret Atwood's *The Handmaid's Tale* (1985), for example, one of the most important dystopias of the century, imagines a future theonomic American society in which women are subjugated to a patriarchal political order that brutally represses their freedom using Christian scriptures as the basis for secular law. At the time of its publication—indeed, at the time of the writing of the first draft of this chapter—such a society seemed a far-fetched thought experiment; with the recent Supreme Court decision overturning *Roe v. Wade*, the United States has moved dramatically closer to the repressive dystopia that Atwood envisioned. (Please visit www.safeabortionwomensright.org for ways to help safeguard reproductive freedoms around the world.)

If there is a general theme to dystopias from the latter decades of the twentieth century until today, it would be civilizational collapse rather than the growth of Stalinist authoritarianism. Often such collapse is brought about by environmental catastrophe in the form of uncontrolled climate change, pandemic, nuclear war, or other ecological disaster, and the societies (which are not always civilizations) that follow are just as often chaotic as they are totalizing and repressive. Notable examples include *Snow Crash* by Neal Stephenson (1992), *The Children of Men* by P. D. James (1992), *Parable of the Sower* by Octavia Butler (1993), *The Road* by Cormac McCarthy (2006), *The Windup Girl* by Paolo Bacigalupi (2009), the MaddAddam trilogy by Margaret Atwood (2003–2012), and the Hunger Games trilogy of young adult novels by Suzanne Collins (2008–2010).

Some of the novels on the above list skirt the blurred and contested boundary with science fiction—as do the handful of recent novels that can be characterized as proper utopias. Fredric Jameson's enormously influential critical work *Archaeologies of the Future: The Desire Called Utopia and Other Science Fictions* (2005) traces the long entanglement of the two literary modes. Classifying science fiction is a notoriously tricky and thankless task, but a rough-and-ready definition would include narratives that depict space exploration and extraterrestrial civilizations, advanced science and technology, and/or time travel. Ursula K. LeGuin's *The Dispossessed* (1974) and Marge Piercy's *Woman on the Edge of Time* (1976) are examples of important science fiction novels that are also utopias in the traditional sense. Many of the science fiction novels of Kim Stanley Robinson imagine future worlds that are utopian in their basic outlines. Robinson has recently provided an influential definition of utopia as "a positive course in history ... the best possible given where we are, given our technological base" (Nolan 65). His recent novel *The Ministry for the Future* (2020), published after the interview in which this definition was proposed, imagines a near-future world that has responded in useful ways to catastrophic climate events; it could be characterized more accurately as technocratic speculative fiction than science fiction per se. Another notable locus for literary utopianism is Africanfuturism. According to Nigerian author Nnedi Okorafor (*Lagoon*, 2014), who coined the term,

> Africanfuturism is concerned with visions of the future, is interested in technology, leaves the earth, skews optimistic, is centered on and predominantly written by people of African descent (black people) and it is rooted first and foremost in Africa. It's less concerned with 'what could have been' and more concerned with 'what is and can/will be'.
>
> *(Okorafor)*

It is undeniable that literary utopias are thin on the ground at the moment, and have been for over a hundred years. It is something of a commonplace to note that after the horrors of the twentieth century—which show few signs of abating in the twenty-first—the distaste for optimistic visions of the future makes perfect sense. And yet, if not now, when? The writing, reading, and analyzing of literary utopias seems more important than ever, as the urgency of imagining other modes of social organization becomes increasingly apparent. The alternative is worse.

Works Cited

Bastos da Silva, Jorge. "Introduction: Revis(It)Ing the Rationales of Utopianism." *The Epistemology of Utopia: Rhetoric, Theory, and Imagination.* Cambridge Scholars Publishing, 2013, pp. 1–6.

Beaumont, Matthew. *Utopia Ltd.: Ideologies of Social Dreaming in England 1870–1900.* Brill, 2005.

Bellamy, Edward. *Looking Backward 2000–1887.* Edited by Matthew Beaumont. Reissued, Oxford UP, 2009.

Bloch, Ernst. *The Principle of Hope.* Translated by Neville Plaice et al. MIT Press, 1986.

Claeys, Gregory. "General Introduction: The Reshaping of the Utopian Genre in Britain, c. 1870–1900." *Late Victorian Utopias: A Prospectus*, vol. 1, Pickering & Chatto, 2009, pp. ix–xiii.

———, editor. *Modern British Utopias, c. 1700–1850*. 8 vols, Pickering and Chatto, 1997.

———. "The Origins of Dystopia: Wells, Huxley and Orwell." *The Cambridge Companion to Utopian Literature*, edited by Gregory Claeys. 1st edition. Cambridge UP, 2010, pp. 107–132.

Claeys, Gregory, and Lyman Tower Sargent, editors. *The Utopia Reader*. New York UP, 1999.

Fitting, Peter. "Utopia, Dystopia and Science Fiction." *The Cambridge Companion to Utopian Literature*, edited by Gregory Claeys. 1st edition. Cambridge UP, 2010, pp. 135–153.

Frase, Peter. *Four Futures: Visions of the World After Capitalism*. Verso, 2016.

Gordin, Michael D., Helen Tilley, and Gyan Prakash, editors. *Utopia/Dystopia: Conditions of Historical Possibility*. Princeton UP, 2010.

Jameson, Fredric, and Slavoj Žižek. *An American Utopia*. Verso, 2016.

———. *Archaeologies of the Future: The Desire Called Utopia and Other Science Fictions*. Verso, 2005.

Kumar, Krishan. *Utopianism*. U of Minnesota P, 1991.

Levitas, Ruth. *The Concept of Utopia*. Peter Lang, 2011.

———. *Utopia as Method: The Imaginary Reconstitution of Society*. Palgrave Macmillan, 2013.

Locke, John. "Economic Writings and Two Treatises of Government." *Of Government: Book 2*, vol. 4, Rivington, 1824, http://www.nlnrac.org/earlymodern/locke/documents/second-treatise.

Marcuse, Herbert. *Eros and Civilization: A Philosophical Inquiry Into Freud*. Beacon Press, 1966.

———. *Five Lectures: Psychoanalysis, Politics, and Utopia*. Beacon Press, 1970.

———. *One-Dimensional Man: Studies in the Ideology of Advanced Industrial Society*. Routledge & Kegan Paul, 1964.

Marx, Karl, and Friedrich Engels. *The Communist Manifesto*. Penguin Books, 2002.

More, Thomas. *Utopia*. Translated by Dominic Baker-Smith, Penguin Books, 2012.

Morris, William. *News From Nowhere, or, An Epoch of Rest*. Edited by David Leopold, Oxford World's Classics, 2003.

Nolan, Val, editor. "'Utopia Is a Way of Saying We Could Do Better': Iain M. Banks and Kim Stanley Robinson in Conversation." *Foundation: The International Review of Science Fiction*, vol. 119, Feb. 2015, pp. 65–76.

Okorafor, Nnedi. "Africanfuturism Defined." *Nnedi's Wahala Zone Blog*, 19 Oct. 2019, http://nnedi.blogspot.com/2019/10/africanfuturism-defined.html.

Paden, Roger. "Marx's Critique of the Utopian Socialists." *Utopian Studies*, vol. 13, no. 2, 2002, pp. 67–91.

Roemer, Kenneth M. "Paradise Transformed: Varieties of Nineteenth-Century Utopias." *The Cambridge Companion to Utopian Literature*, edited by Gregory Claeys, 1st edition. Cambridge UP, 2010, pp. 79–106.

Sargent, Lyman Tower. "Themes in Utopian Fiction in English before Wells." *Science Fiction Studies*, vol. 3, no. 3, 1976, pp. 275–282.

———. "Utopia Matters! The Importance of Utopianism and Utopian Scholarship." *Utopian Studies*, vol. 32, no. 3, Nov. 2021, pp. 453–477.

———. *Utopianism: A Very Short Introduction*. Oxford UP, 2010.

Stableford, Brian. "Ecology and Dystopia." *The Cambridge Companion to Utopian Literature*, edited by Gregory Claeys, 1st edition. Cambridge UP, 2010, pp. 259–281.

Stewart, Janet. "'Breaking the Power of the Past over the Present': Psychology, Utopianism, and the Frankfurt School." *Utopian Studies*, vol. 18, no. 1, Jan. 2007, pp. 21–42.

Tuck, Richard. *The Rights of War and Peace: Political Thought and the International Order From Grotius to Kant*. Oxford UP, 1999.

Vieira, Fátima. "The Concept of Utopia." *The Cambridge Companion to Utopian Literature*, edited by Gregory Claeys. Cambridge UP, 2010, pp. 3–17.

Webb, Sidney. *The Decline in the Birth-Rate*. The Fabian Society, 1907, https://jstor.org/stable/10.2307/community.29886679.

Wells, Herbert G. *The Time Machine*. Edited by Nicholas Ruddick. Broadview Press, 2001.

40
CLASSROOMS

Laura Heffernan and Rachel Sagner Buurma

Politics and the Classroom Imaginary

The figure of the classroom nearly always serves as the staging ground for debates over the role of politics in higher education, and perennial right-wing attacks on higher education often pitch their battles on the imaginary field of the classroom. Though conservative ideology has come to pervade university board of managers' meetings, its consistent strategy has been to gin up outrage over what goes on within the walls of the undergraduate classroom. In the United States, this was true during anti-Communist Red Scares, in the book-banning era of President Ronald Reagan, in William Bennett's and Allan Bloom's "Canon Wars," and in the professor "watch lists" after the attacks of September 11, 2001; we see it now in the witch hunts around Critical Race Theory. Campaigns like these tend to figure the classroom as both too opaque and yet too familiar—an uncanny place positioned perilously close to students' inmost selves and too far beyond the grasp of parents, politicians, and markets. From recent state legislative bills giving students the right to record their professors and the *Wall Street Journal*'s surveys of course offerings to state laws requiring that course syllabi be openly available on the internet, conservative politicians and commentators have stirred controversy over what happens in school classrooms in the service of subjecting them to ever more surveillance and regulation.

The literature classroom has been a special focus of these public controversies, since English as a discipline has always had a special and complicated relationship with (though by no means a monopoly on) character formation and the development of students' moral and political imagination.[1] Yet attempts to face down right-wing accusations that English classes are occasions for indoctrination—such as Michael Berube's *What's Liberal about the Liberal Arts* (2006)—make little headway. For the classroom, in such debates, is really only a pretext.

Adjacent and somewhat connected to these public and political controversies over English class, debates within literary studies over the place of politics in our disciplinary methods often take place in the space of the classroom. When we are thinking and writing about disciplinary methods or disciplinary boundaries or the value of literary study, we do so most often with reference to classroom teaching rather than research and scholarship; setting these scenes of method struggle in classrooms seems to raise the stakes. Proponents of new methods stage their efficacy with classroom vignettes or evaluate them based on their classroom utility, often by imagining students who are underserved by existing methods. In perhaps the most famous example, Cleanth Brooks opens *The Well Wrought Urn* by conjuring a classroom of undergraduate students who are encountering Wordsworth's Westminster Bridge sonnet for the first time. As Brooks tells it, his students have a nascent sense of what's valuable about Wordsworth's poem, but they require a professor to usher them through the poem closely (rather than lecture about the context of Wordsworth's era) in order to elucidate the value of the poem, and in order to reveal the value of reading poetry more generally. Like Brooks, literary scholars regularly imagine the classroom as the place where we display our core disciplinary methods and reveal the value of literary study to an audience of undergraduate students, whom we imagine as a metonym for the larger general public despite the fact that college and university classrooms vary wildly in the extent to which they demographically resemble the societies in which they operate.

Yet for all that imagined and imaginary classrooms regularly appear in our pedagogical "meta-discourses" (writing about what we do or should do or could do), there is much less practical accounting of what has actually happened in English classes over the past century or so. When the MLA received a grant from the Mellon Foundation in 1998 to expand the MLA international bibliography to include scholarship on teaching literature, it became apparent that literary scholars have not produced much formal scholarship on their pedagogy. Indeed, John Guillory noted at the time "how thin in conceptual terms this scholarship remains by comparison with that produced in the fields of rhetoric and language" (165).[2]

Of course, individual scholars do often write about particular classes that they teach. In just one issue of *Profession* (2008), for example, we find Rita Felski describing changes she made to her literary theory course at UVA; Nancy K. Miller's remembrances of a course on feminist criticism she co-taught with Carolyn Heilbrun at Columbia in the mid-1980s; Geoffrey Galt Harpham's account of "Reading Conrad with America's Soldiers" at the Air Force Academy; and Marjorie Garber reporting on the 2007 Shakespeare course she taught in Harvard's Division of Continuing Studies. Such individual reflections are sometimes offered as bellwethers of disciplinary shifts, and other times as exemplary of the value of literary pedagogy (see Garber or Harpham), especially for non-traditional students. But such writing rarely coheres into an overarching historical narrative about what and how we have taught, particularly at the wide range of institutions of higher education that house most literature classrooms. The result of what Guillory calls this "occlusion" of pedagogy in literary study is that we cede our historical sense of our discipline's teaching—and thus of the place of politics within it—to meta-discourse. Furthermore, such meta-discourses overwhelmingly associate English classrooms of the past with our discipline's supposedly foundational methods of close reading, and imagine these methods as tied to an equally foundational apoliticism of the kind represented by both American and British New Criticism.

Yet when we turn to evidence of past literature classrooms, we find that teachers and students have discussed politics, literature, and the politics of literature in all kinds of English courses throughout the twentieth century. As we describe below, since at least the late nineteenth century, students have learned to read literary texts for gaps and silences; they have learned to think about how the author's class position affects their representations of the world; and they have considered how the history of literary forms and genres relates to the commercial aspect of literature (learning, for example, to think about the history of the novel as part of the history of bourgeois culture, and to think about the novel's modern fracturing as a mark of that culture's decline). And throughout the twentieth century, students have learned sociological approaches to skimming and classifying contemporary literary texts, inventorying the ideological bent of those texts' contents in order to track the countries they represented and how they represented them.

How English Became Apolitical

We might easily miss this long history of political and politicized readings of literature if we turn only to archives from classrooms at institutions like Harvard and Cambridge. Yet even a shallow dip into past literature courses at a wider range of institutions serving more diverse groups of students shows us just how consistently literature and politics have been studied together, even in introductory and survey classes for undergraduates. Histories of the discipline erase this past, instead telling a story in which the study of literature was apolitical from its antiquarian-historicist origins to Cambridge close reading to mid-century American New Criticism. In this story, literary study only became political in the late 1960s, when student-led protest movements erupted in the United States and the United Kingdom, resulting in the formation of new programs in ethnic studies and women's studies. These, along with international student movements and anti-colonial revolutions, came to inform the scholarship and theory of career academics in the 1970s, 1980s, and 1990s writing within and about Black studies, Native American Studies, Chicano studies, Asian-American studies, feminist criticism, cultural studies, film theory, post-structuralism, Marxist criticism, queer theory, and New Historicism.

For critics working within women's studies and ethnic studies during these decades, the politics of literature was directly connected to the radical political movements of the 1960s. As Hortense Spillers explains,

> The passage of Civil Rights legislation in 1964, voting rights in 1965, women's rights and title IX in 1972—all contributed to the erection of the academy, especially in branches of the human sciences, as we know it today. If we extract 1968, 1969, from this spate of years, this is what we see: on both sides of the Atlantic, youth movements in the streets of all over the world created a watershed moment that, in turn, forced the academy to absorb it as its *visible* other, as what is political motion one moment becomes not even in the next a *new curricular object*.
>
> *(Spillers, "Critical Theory in Times of Crisis," 2020)*

Spillers marks the late 1960s and early 1970s as moments of decisive change, when "what is political motion one moment" becomes a "*new curricular object*" instantly. Although the first undergraduate degree program in Black studies wouldn't emerge in the United Kingdom until 2017, the years 1969–1972 saw the rapid and widespread institutionalization of liberatory study at a variety of public and private universities and colleges in the United States. New programs in Black studies and women's studies were founded seemingly overnight, with curricula that centered conversations about civil rights and sexual politics, patriarchy, and racial caste. The years following the five-month student strike by the Third World Liberation Front at San Francisco State University saw the formation of ethnic studies programs and colleges, and the National Association for Ethnic Studies (NAES) in 1972. The mid-1970s also saw the formation of "Third World Literature" programs, like the one that Sylvia Wynter was hired to lead at UCSD in 1974, as well as programs in Native American and La Raza studies.

With new programs came new curricula and new courses. As Andy Hines describes, Judith Fetterly's *The Resisting Reader* (1975) builds upon her 1971 "Images of Women in American Literature" course at the University of Pennsylvania, in which she asked her students to interpret the gendered ideologies underpinning representations of women in canonical nineteenth- and twentieth-century fiction. J. Saunders Redding and Clarence Mondale structured the interdisciplinary American Civilization course they taught at George Washington University's Am Civ program by a series of "basic cultural antimonies or polarities by which we [Americans] define ourselves to ourselves"; each week featured a combination of literary, sociological, and historical texts, while the culminating antimony, "Black-White," drew almost entirely on literary selections, assigning multiple pieces from groundbreaking literature anthology *The Negro Caravan* as well as Redding's own higher education novel *Stranger and Alone* (Buurma and Heffernan 245–46 n60). And as Danica Savonick has described, when Adrienne Rich taught in CUNY's SEEK program in the late 1960s, her classes included "topics ranging from the history of plantations, slavery, and sharecropping to the definitions of metaphor, dialect, vernacular, and jargon" (308) and "sought to enact an 'undoing' and 'detoxification' [of the literary canon] by instead finding texts that students could relate to" (310).

While we could likely trace precursors to such courses, particularly within earlier courses taught by those faculty working in historically Black or regional colleges or colonial colleges who were often hired into these new programs, what was distinct in this moment was the tightly felt connection between these university courses and social and institutional change. Despite similarities to politically situated readings of literature in earlier decades, modes of reading power, patriarchy, race, caste, and colonialism through literary study in the late 1960s and early 1970s felt deeply connected to institutional change in higher education. Waves of student activism connected what happened in classrooms to what happened on the streets, where students—often with the help of faculty members—set up their own classrooms outside the universities. Black studies and women's studies courses brought new attention to the injustice of the double exclusion of Black and female writers from syllabi and of Black and female teachers from the university classroom. For practitioners in these new disciplinary formations, study of work by Black and woman writers and the expansion of opportunities for Black and female professors within the university were both inextricably related and a central part of the movement.

The 1970s and 1980s also saw the rise of critical "revolutions" that were less apparently tied to university politics and institutional change. This was despite the fact that these movements were also critical of enlightenment thought and disciplinary knowledge in tandem with student-led protests and political activism. For example, Jonathan Culler prefaced his *Structuralist Poetics* (written as a doctoral dissertation at Oxford in 1968–1969) with recollections of the "structuralist revolution" happening in France in those same years (vii). Terry Eagleton's retrospective 2006 reflection on his 1976 *Criticism and Ideology* remembered writing in the context of both the achievements of the changes and movements of the 1960s and the immanent conservative turn of the 1980s. And Fredric Jameson's *Marxism and Form: Twentieth Century Dialectical Theories of Literature* positioned itself as a sophisticated dialectical form of Marxist literary criticism quite different from both the American Marxist criticism of the 1930s with its "relatively untheoretical, essentially didactic nature, destined more for use in the night school than the graduate seminar" (ix) and then-current "political liberalism, empiricism, and logical positivism" (x) of American philosophy and literary criticism. Writing in a poststructuralist-informed Marxist vein in the 1970s, all these critics implicitly claimed that English professors had been prevented from studying anything but literature, and required to study literature a way that was formalist and apolitical or covertly liberal.[3] Rather than connecting themselves directly to contemporary movements for institutional change, they pitched themselves against the seemingly apolitical forms of literary study that preceded them.

Thus, by the 1980s and 1990s, the idea that earlier forms and methods of literary study (especially in the United States) had been primarily apolitical and formalist was firmly established as part of literary study's central narrative of its own history. Practitioners and observers of the New Historicism in (mostly) American English departments understood that the New Historicist focus on the analysis of power at play within a wide-ranging set of literary and cultural texts had "struck down the doctrine of noninterference that forbade humanists to intrude on questions of politics, power, indeed on all matters that deeply affect people's practical lives" (Veeser ix). As H. Aram Veeser influentially noted, to practice New Historicism was thus to take up a political position, even if the specifics of that politics varied wildly. For some, the New Historicism's anti-canonical mood and claim to bring the personal into the professional by challenging "the norm of disembodied objectivity to which humanists have increasingly aspired" sparked conservative ire; meanwhile, Marxists and cultural materialists accused the New Historicism of betraying its avowed leftist commitments by adopting a casual attitude toward historical fact and a friendliness toward poststructuralism (Veeser x).[4] And even as critics celebrated or denounced New Historicism's dominance, the "Canon Wars" of the 1990s falsely cemented the widespread sense that, for better or worse, engaging literature for politics rather than aesthetics was somehow a new phenomenon.[5]

The Longer History of Politics in the Literature Classroom

The advent of explicitly and self-consciously political literary criticism in the latter decades of the twentieth century thus produced—through its critique of an apolitical formalism—the now widely accepted sense that Anglo-American New Criticism was both foundational and ubiquitous. In fact, neither assertion is true. Students and teachers have discussed the politics of literature in classrooms since at least the nineteenth century. In the early 1890s, for example, "extension" (i.e., non-regularly matriculated) students in upstate New York took a 16-week course on the Fireside Poets. Absent other evidence, we might well expect that these students undertook a simple appreciation of poems by Henry Wadsworth Longfellow, John Greenleaf Whittier, and James Russell Lowell, when in fact the course offered a masterclass in what is now denounced as "suspicious reading." For example, the class read Lowell's *Biglow Papers*, using the "date of the poem, 1844" to "unlock the history" behind the text: not just "history" generally, but the history of the "Mexican war," which Lowell regarded as an atrocious attempt to extend slavery (Gannett 82).

For the students and tutor of this 1890s Fireside poets course, the political leanings of Longfellow, Whittier, and Lowell could be gleaned from careful contextualizations and close readings of their poems, and used in turn as a metric of literary judgment. The class took some comfort, for example, in Lowell's abolitionist tendencies, noting that "The keen insight, the ardor for truth and national honor, the scorn for political cowardice which these [Biglow] papers showed, struck home to the heart of every true citizen" (Gannett 81). At the same time, the class questioned whether Lowell's anti-slavery sentiment might be more self-serving then empathetic; the course syllabus indicates that they opened discussion with the question, "Does he see slavery most vividly from the standpoint of the slave who suffers from it, or the statesman who sees his country disgraced by it?" (Gannett 82). A final question, with directions for further research, asks students to consider the difference between those fighting in the Civil War and those making poetry about it: "Did Lowell suffer personal losses in the War of the Rebellion? (See Biglow Papers, 2d Series, No. X Also Memoriae Positum)" (Gannett 82). Having finished with Lowell, the class turned next to Longfellow, carrying with them scrutiny of authors' motives and a sense of disappointment: "His poems of Anti-Slavery,—so strong, but why so few, and all so early? Was it from a love of Peace, stronger than a hatred of Oppression?" (Gannett 25).

Working-class girls taking an English literature course through Bryn Mawr's extension program exercised an even greater level of suspicion toward classics of English literature. A 1924 seminar promised to study "literature in connection with social conditions and larger social movements" (Hader 54). To prepare for this work, the girls first read John Harvey Robinson's *Mind in the Making*, which included a chapter on "Rationalization." "Rationalizing," Robinson explains, "is the self-exculpation which occurs when we feel ourselves, or our group, accused of misapprehension or error" (44). Robinson draws his examples from the English canon:

> Milton wrote his treatise on divorce as a result of his troubles with his seventeen-year-old wife, and when he was accused of being the leading spirit in a new sect, the Divorcers, he wrote his noble *Areopagitica* to prove his right to say what he thought fit, and incidentally to establish the advantage of a free press in the promotion of Truth.
>
> *(45)*

Likewise, "Tennyson in beginning his 'Maud' could not forget his chagrin over losing his patrimony years before as the result of an unhappy investment in the Patent Decorative Carving Company" (Robinson 46). Armed with this education in critical reading that connected literature not just to the author's life but to their psychological responses to the social problems and movements in which they were embroiled, the girls proceeded to study how nineteenth-century English literature was shaped by "democratic and industrial movements of the day," and wrapped up their study by reading Ibsen's *A Doll's House* (Hader 56).

Anti-bourgeois, materialist, and Marxist analysis was a staple of Rise of the Novel courses during these early twentieth-century years. Many courses pronounced the novel to be a dying form; a ladies' club in South Carolina in 1920 regarded the novel as "deteriorating" after having "held a sort of literary primacy for nearly two centuries" (Wauchope 3). Like the students at Bryn Mawr, the South Carolina students also finished their course with Ibsen's *A Doll's House*—here sounding the death knell not only for bourgeois culture but also for its most characteristic literary form. Likewise, a 1920s History of the Novel course at Labour College considered "the *novel* [form]" as the "great contribution of the Bourgeoisie to Literature:" but one that was dying now that "bourgeois society was in decay" after the "Militant-Imperialist Phase of Capitalism" (Hader 65). This class aimed "to apply the principles of Historical Materialism to the Study of Literature, and to show by actual examples how the economic and social conditions of various periods influenced the creative literary work of its writers" (Hader 65). They briefly considered early Elizabethan attempts at novels, but noted that the form was only "triumphant after the Revolution of 1688"; they compared Scott's "ideals of feudalism" to Dickens's "post-Industrial revolution outlook" (Hader 65). The class ended by assessing the extent to which contemporary novels might align with the values of organized labor. Reading Wells, Bennett, Conrad, and Ibsen, they examined "present day tendencies in literature." They noted that although "most notable artists are critical of, and hostile to, bourgeois ideals," these writers were "not yet actually proletarian in spirit" (Hader 65).

The 1920s also saw the rise of courses in which students surveyed literary texts for indications of cultural anxieties over immigration and race and class or identified formal features of literary texts as products of a changing publishing industry. In 1922, a women's club in Chapel Hill, North Carolina gathered to study "Contemporary Literature" by reading as much as possible that had been published in 1921–1922, including poetry, short stories, drama, and novels. They read a slew of "best of 1921" anthologies for fiction and drama and poetry; in addition to these, they read Booth Tarkington's 1921 novel *Alice Adams* alongside several "best sellers of the past two years"; they read tons of contemporary magazine criticism and short stories; they read the contents of Harriet Monroe's *New Poetry* anthology—including poems by H. D., Frost, and Eliot. The rationale for the course admitted that not all of the course reading would be good, but that by giving up expectations of literary value they could cast a wider net and so capture "a record of contemporary life—of our interests, emotions, and means of expression" (Royster 4). In week three, the class read all of the plays by foreign dramatists in their *Best Plays of 1920–21* anthology (ed. Burns Mantle) in order to discuss how the "varied make-up" of the US population had changed the American stage in recent years (Royster 10). In week six, they coded each short story in their set of anthologies to note the stories' "geographic location," the "variety of racial characters" depicted, and the "social rank of the characters" (Royster 14). The noted whether authors were "humanizing…persons of lower orders" by "attempt[ing] to understand their hopes and fears" or simply "using them …for contrast" or "for humourous purposes" (Royster 16). Whatever else they were doing, and no matter how narrowly one defines "politics," neither teachers nor students were engaged in the disinterested appraisal of literary text simply for the pleasures they produced and the tradition of great, formal wonders they exemplified.

Students studying at historically Black colleges and universities read an "opened" canon throughout the twentieth century. At Hampton Institute in the 1940s, for example, the English Department described their core American Literature course as "a survey of American prose and poetry beginning with the most important present day Negro writers and going back to the most effective writers of the Colonial period" (*Hampton Bulletin*, May 1941, 64–65; qtd. in Buurma and Heffernan 112). "Until relatively recent times, writing by both black and white Americans had little to do with aesthetics either as philosophy or in practice," read one such syllabus at Hampton, taught regularly by J. Saunders Redding (Redding, English 364: The Negro in American Literature; qtd. in Buurma and Heffernan 20). For Redding's students, that is, literature was always political. Reading lists represented the work of Black and white writers in equal measure to accurately reflect their importance to American culture, and professors directed students' attention to the materiality of canon formation and the politics of literacy itself.

These are just a handful of examples of the many ways that early English classrooms housed methods of politicized reading and teaching; for too long we have mistakenly imagined that these methods and dispositions first appeared on the scene of literary study in the 1970s and 1980s. As with later peers, however, these students of the 1890s and 1900s, 1910s, 1920s and 1930s saw texts as attempts to "rationalize" hidden agendas; they self-consciously read mass literature alongside high literature; they analyzed how authors' class position and racial background influenced their representation of characters; they considered entire genres like the realist novel as the products of a particular social class and expressive of its (sometimes hidden) wishes and desires and perspectives; they read, especially in historically Black colleges and universities, Black writers alongside white writers in American Literature, and discussed literacy itself as a tool of political power. These examples gesture toward the longer histories of reading practices only lately associated with the advent of ideology critique associated with French Marxists like Louis Althusser, or sociological Marxism, or the formation of ethnic studies programs. As Sonia Posmentier argues in relation to the Black studies narrative in particular:

> Narratives of literary canonization often credit—or blame— activist student movements of the 1960s with shifting how we read: from the close reading that emphasized the

coherence and agency of individual texts to a focus on history, biography, theory, or the instability of subjectivity. Many posit black studies as a late-twentieth-century challenge from the margins to a semi-coherent genealogy of a modern Anglo-American literary criticism centered on practices of textual—especially poetic—interpretation. But "race" was not a challenge to literary study that emerged sui generis with the institutionalization of black studies as a discipline…interpretive reading practices focusing on textual aesthetics are rooted in earlier twentieth-century questions about racial ontology and racial history.

(58)

Pointedly, as Posmentier demonstrates in "Lyric Reading in the Black Ethnographic Archive," the idea that modern Anglo-American literary criticism constitutes a "semi-coherent genealogy" centered on poetic interpretation is itself false.

The courses we have described were not institutionally and disciplinarily marginal (as Jameson imagines the Marxist literary "night school" to be), but were taught by instructors with foundational ties to research universities and research journals. The contemporary literature course at Chapel Hill, for example, was taught by James Finch Royster, who had just trained under early modern philologist John Manly at Chicago and was helping to start the English department at the University of North Carolina. In a few years' time, Royster would take over the editorship of *Modern Philology*. George Armstrong Wauchope, who taught the drama course to the South Carolina Women's Club, had earned a PhD from Washington and Lee in 1889; he taught at the University of Virginia and the University of Iowa before coming to the Department of Language and Literature at the University of Southern California in 1898. Other courses were taught by instructors with links to the University of Pennsylvania in the United States, and to the University of London, Bedford College, and the University of Reading in the United Kingdom. After teaching for three decades in historically Black colleges in the south, J. Saunders Redding went on to teach in the new American Studies Program at George Washington University and at Cornell University, among others.

Across these decades, such practitioners were not united by meta-discursive calls to politicize the study of literature, nor did they author manifestos or method statements. Compared to the larger body of meta-discursive texts that promote close reading and aesthetic education as core to the discipline, these teachers of literature rarely discussed their methods in print. They did not identify as a movement or present their methods as an innovation. But the records that remain—just a small sampling of what was surely a much larger body of teaching materials—indicate a long and steady history of approaching literature in classrooms with an eye to the politics of texts, authors, generic forms, and classroom study itself.

The Scene Today

As the "Canon Wars" of the 1980s and 1990s petered out, the early years of the new millennium saw scholars advocating for a more modest "sense of political realism about the revolutionary capacities of both texts and critics" (Best and Marcus 15–16). Where Gerald Graff once called for a "teaching the conflicts" approach that would recognize and reflect upon the disputes within literary study that "have remained unresolved, unacknowledged, and assumed to be outside the proper sphere of literary education," scholars and critics of late have attempted to resolve conflict by turning from theory to method (15). Rita Felski describes this shift as a shift from the macrolevel to the microlevel of intellectual argument, a move from big pictures - theories of sexuality, postmodernism, power-discourse relations - to reflections on how those pictures are translated into the working assumptions and routines of particular disciplinary fields.

(115)

This recent turn from "theory to method" (Felski) or from "knowledge to method" (Collier) registers a sense of exhaustion as it tries to conclude a conversation about how literary study might entail a specific politics (and vice-versa) by imagining method as a value-free, flexible toolkit: "trusting the student to use the tools we offer as he or she sees fit," as Patrick Collier puts it in *Teaching Literature in the Real World: A Practical Guide* (7).

It suggests that the politicized schools of the 1970s, 1980s, and 1990s had attenuated into a tired set of rote reading methods or mechanical gestures or professional habits—a "regime of class-gender-race as lenses for literary study" (Collier 8). The turn also conveys the sense that political interpretation has gone "too far" and that, while once powerful in the hands of a handful of skilled practitioners, open political criticism has become dangerous in clumsier hands.

As David Kurnick suggests, however, these recent essays on method may offer us "not new ways to interpret texts but new ways to feel about ourselves when we do" (351). Methodologists respond to the "diminished standing of the humanities in general and of literary criticism in particular" by suggesting that "the blame for that loss of prestige lies not on external factors but on the failure of other scholars—aggressive critique-mongers, depth-obsessed symptomhunters, paranoid pattern-makers—to appreciate literature properly" (Kurnick 351). They imaginatively transform, that is, a political issue originating outside the discipline into one that can be worked out within the discipline.

And once again, like the conservative outrage over dirty politics supposedly invading previously pristine classrooms in 1968, more recent fantasies of how to fix an errant discipline crucially rely on an idea that is demonstrably untrue: that the political interpretation of literature was but a blip in a longer history of apolitical literary study to which we should easily and profitably return. For if we pay attention to the everyday practices of literary study in actual classrooms, it is clear that the study of literature has always been attended by politics.

Political interpretations of literature in the classroom have been a steady and central part of the discipline of literary study for more than a hundred years—one of the core ways in which we help students to see how literature "matters to students' lives—to their experiences, beliefs, and identities," as Patricia A. Matthew and Jonathan Greenberg put it in "The Ideology of the Mermaid" (231). We should incorporate this living history into our own disciplinary self-understanding and our students' understanding of why we teach them to read the way we do, first and foremost because it's true. But situating our pedagogy and our scholarship within a genealogy of political reading, and acknowledging that trying to get politics "out of the classroom" is really trying to get a different politics into the classroom, might also help us understand and value that pedagogy and scholarship differently. And perhaps it would help us let go of a narrative about how method has endangered us and might save us, and instead would let us face together the systematic—and politically motivated, in a number of senses—defunding of higher education and endemic creation of unsustainable amounts of student debt that are the primary enemies of literary study, the humanities, and access to higher education itself.

Notes

1. For the role of literature in forming political identities as a tool of both colonialism and anti-colonialism, see Maryam Wasif Khan's chapter "Empires, Decolonization, and the Canon" in this volume.
2. Some notable exceptions exist. See for example Eric Bennett, *Workshops of Empire*; Abigail Droge, "Reading George Eliot with Victorian College Students"; Laura Fisher, *Reading for Reform: The Social Work of Literature in the Progressive Era;* Colleen Lye, "Identity Politics, Criticism, and Self-Criticism"; Nathanial Mills, "Aggravated into Writing: Margaret Walker, Iowa, and the Workshopping of African American Literature"; Sonya Posmentier, "Lyric Reading in the Black Ethnographic Archive; Jane Stanley, *The Rhetoric of Remediation*; Kate Stanley, *Practices of Surprise in American Literature After Emerson*; Gauri Viswanathan, *Masks of Conquest: Literary Study and British Rule in India.*
3. For more on the extent to which the notion of "political" criticism has been limited to and by the figure of Jameson, see Benjamin Kehlmann's chapter "Symptoms" in this volume.
4. While in the last decade or so critics including Joseph North, William Warner, and Clifford Siskin have felt the need to disabuse the discipline of a widespread consensus that New Historicism was a politically left or radical project, this assessment misses how debated NH's politics were by literary scholars at the time.
5. For more on the "Canon Wars" of the 1980s and 1990s, see Ian Afflerbach's chapter "On or about 1989" in this volume.

Works Cited

Bennett, Eric. *Workshops of Empire: Stegner, Engle, and American Creative Writing During the Cold War.* U of Iowa P, 2015.

Bérubé, Michael. *What's Liberal About the Liberal Arts?: Classroom Politics and "Bias" in Higher Education.* W. W. Norton & Company, 2007.

Best, Stephen, and Sharon Marcus. "Surface Reading: An Introduction." *Representations*, vol. 108, no. 1, 2009, pp. 1–21.

Brooks, Cleanth. *The Well Wrought Urn: Studies in the Structure of Poetry.* First edition, Mariner Books, 1956.

Buurma, Rachel Sagner, and Laura Heffernan. *The Teaching Archive: A New History for Literary Study.* U of Chicago P, 2021.

Collier, Patrick. *Teaching Literature in the Real World: A Practical Guide.* Bloomsbury Academic, 2021.

Culler, Jonathan. *Structuralist Poetics: Structuralism, Linguistics and the Study of Literature.* 2nd edition. Routledge, 2002.

Droge, Abigail. "Reading George Eliot with Victorian College Students." *Victorian Studies*, vol. 63, no. 2, 2021, pp. 224–245.

Eagleton, Terry. *Criticism and Ideology: A Study in Marxist Literary Theory.* Verso Books, 2006, p. 191.

Felski, Rita. "From Literary Theory to Critical Method." *Profession*, 2008, pp. 108–16.

Fisher, Laura R. *Reading for Reform : the Social Work of Literature in the Progressive Era.* U of Minnesota P, 2019.

Gannett, William C. *Studies in Longfellow, Whittier, Holmes and Lowell; Outlines and Topics for Study with Questions and References.* Boston, [c1898].

Garber, Marjorie. "Good to Think With." *Profession*, 2008, pp. 11–20.

Graff, Gerald. *Professing Literature: An Institutional History, Twentieth Anniversary Edition.* U of Chicago P, 2008.

Guillory, John. "The Very Idea of Pedagogy." *Profession*, 2002, pp. 164–71.

Hader, John Jay. *What Do Workers Study?: An Analysis of the Content of Workers' Education in the United States and Great Britain for the Years 1920 to 1927 Inclusive, with Some Comparative Notes of Workers' Education in Germany.* Workers' Education Bureau Press, 1929.

Hampton Bulletin. Hampton Institute, May 1941.

Harpham, Geoffrey Galt. "The Depths of the Heights: Reading Conrad with America's Soldiers." *Profession*, 2008, pp. 74–82.

Hines, Andy. "Reading for Self-Defense." *Reception: Texts, Readers, Audiences, History*, vol. 13, no. 1, July 2021, pp. 15–23. *scholarlypublishingcollective.org.*

Jameson, Fredric. *Marxism and Form: Twentieth-Century Dialectical Theories of Literature*. Princeton UP, 1974.

Kurnick, David. "A Few Lies: Queer Theory and Our Method Melodramas." *ELH*, vol. 87, no. 2, 2020, pp. 349–74.

Lye, Colleen. "Identity Politics, Criticism, and Self-Criticism." *The South Atlantic Quarterly*, vol. 119, no. 4, 2020, p. 701.

Matthew, Patricia A., and Jonathan Greenberg. "The Ideology of the Mermaid." *Pedagogy*, vol. 9, no. 2, Apr. 2009, pp. 217–33.

Miller, Nancy K. "On Being Wrong." *Profession*, 2008, pp. 54–65.

Mills, Nathaniel. "Aggravated into Writing: Margaret Walker, Iowa, and the Workshopping of African American Literature." *American Quarterly*, vol. 73, no. 2, 2021, pp. 233–259.

Posmentier, Sonya. "Lyric Reading in the Black Ethnographic Archive." *American Literary History*, vol. 30, no. 1, Jan. 2018, pp. 55–84.

Redding, J. Saunders. English 364: The Negro in American Literature, box 24, folder 10, Jay Saunders Redding Papers, John Hay Library, Brown University.

Robinson, James Harvey. *The Mind in the Making*. 1921. *Internet Archive*, http://archive.org/details/in.ernet.dli.2015.262617.

Royster, James Finch. *Contemporary Literature: A Program for Women's Clubs*. Chapel Hill, NC, [c1922]

Savonick, Danica. "Changing the Subject: Adrienne Rich and the Poetics of Activist Pedagogy." *American Literature*, vol. 89, no. 2, June 2017, pp. 305–29.

Spillers, Hortense. "Critical Theory in Times of Crisis." *South Atlantic Quarterly*, vol. 119, no. 4, Oct. 2020, pp. 681–83.

Stanley, Jane. *The Rhetoric of Remediation*. U of Pittsburgh P, 2010.

Stanley, Kate. *Practices of Surprise in American Literature After Emerson*. Cambridge UP, 2018.

Viswanathan, Gauri. *Masks of Conquest: Literary Study and British Rule in India*. Columbia UP, 1989.

Veeser, Harold, editor. *The New Historicism*. 1st edition. Routledge, 1989.

INDEX

Note: *Italic* page numbers refer to figures and page numbers followed by "n" denote endnotes.

1619 Project, The 188–191

abortion 19, 243
action: act 3–5, 12, 16, 24, 32, 38, 47, 68, 77, 95, 113, 116, 120, 138, 146, 153, 154, 175, 176, 184, 198, 206, 208, 215, 259, 270, 294, 295, 306, 309, 313, 316, 319, 341, 358–360, 390, 395, 402, 415; actor 2–6, 54, 56, 59–61, 68, 112, 116, 136, 138, 139, 140, 173, 181, 195, 380, 390, 391, 427; agency 12, 47, 319; agent≈4
activism 43–45, 122, 316, 346, 403, 420, 444; climate change 420; environmental 388, 403–404; #MeToo 71; political 47, 444; before "political unconscious" 43–45; scholar-activism 343; student 444
Adiga, Aravind 132, 202
Adorno, Theodor 250, 253
aesthetic/aesthetics 11–20, 24, 39, 79, 262, 267, 295, 366–368, 447; bodies that gather 15–18; Cosmopolitan 145; crisis of relationality 13–15; formalism 35–40; literary 248; Marxist 249–250; of logistics 381; of the Popular Front 141; queer belonging as design problem 18–19; scene theory 13–15
Aesthetics and Politics 250, 366
affect 11–20, 45, 134–136, 178, 188, 210, 212, 216–218, 232, 344; bodies that gather 15–18; crisis of relationality 13–15; queer belonging as design problem 18–19; scene theory 13–15; spaces and subjects 372–373; theory 11–15, 19, 343
Africa (African) 28, 69, 87–94, 120, 121, 122, 155, 167, 185, 186, 188, 212, 214, 221, 222, 243, 244, 264, 274, 275, 276

African Americans 70, 89, 92–93, 96, 119, 123, 124, 133, 226, 230, 241, 262–266, 317, 394; *see also* Black
Afro-American Novel and Its Tradition, The (Bell) 241
Agamben, Giorgio 22, 23, 25, 26, 28, 29
agency 11, 12, 14, 19, 23, 44, 45, 47, 59, 60, 70, 99, 115, 119, 125, 177, 180, 201, 295, 303, 304, 308, 319, 320, 342–345, 353, 356, 358, 360, 403, 448
Age of Anxiety, The (Auden) 228, 229, 231–232
Ahmed, Sara 58
AIDS epidemic 241
AI technologies *see* artificial intelligence (AI) technologies
Akkad, Omar El 138
Alaimo, Stacy 388, 403
Alarcón, Norma 411, 413
Alchemy of Race and Rights, The (Williams) 66
Alexie, Sherman 242
Alighieri, Dante 172
alternate period vocabularies 227–228
alternative networks 221–223
Althusser, Louis 43–45, 49–50, 51n3, 447
America is in the Heart (Bulosan) 126
American Moor (Cobb) 53, 58–62
Anand, Mulk Raj 286–287, 289n2
anarchism 204, 210, 212
Anderson, Benedict 149, 154, 218
Angelou, Maya 96
Angels in America: A Gay Fantasia on National Themes (Kushner) 241
Anglophone 46, 150, 155, 242, 244, 272; academics 238; fiction 239, 241; literary history 226, 237, 239; literary studies 151, 214, 227, 239; literature 227

Index

"Anglo-Saxon" 165–167, 166; masculinity 168; myth 165; period 162; race 168; roots 167; studies 165–168; superiority 165–166
Animal Claim, The (Menely) 198, 391
animals 2, 23, 109–117, 325–327, 332, 357, 432; Animals Act of 1835 110; anthropomorphic representation 114, 115; Disneyfication of 114; political animals 109–111; protect the rights of 198; sympathy and imagination 114–117; wild animal politics 111–114; Wild Animals in Captivity Act of 1900 110
Anker, Elizabeth S. 70, 72n4
Ankersmit, F. R. 237
anthropomorphism (anthropomorphic) 113–116, 199, 399
Anthropocene 112, 116, 399, 403
Anthropogenic climate change 112, 352, 398, 402, 403, 405, 422
Antinomies of Realism, The (Jameson) 35, 40n3, 250
Anti-Thuggee Campaign 206, 212n2
anxiety 80, 106, 107, 125, 185, 228, 229, 231, 232, 314, 318, 319, 331, 435, 437
Anzaldúa, Gloria 242, 409, 411, 413
Appadurai, Arjun 227
Apter, Emily 315, 320
Aravamudan, Srinivas 209
Archaeologies of the Future: The Desire Called Utopia and Other Science Fictions (Jameson) 40n4, 439
architecture (architectural) 16, 35–40, 207, 238, 367, 368, 436
archives 3, 5, 168, 275, 341–349, 398, 443; archival turns 342–345; speculative methods 345–346; writing histories 346–349
Arendt, Hannah 68, 110, 138, 140, 195, 300
Aristotle 3, 22–26, 32, 109, 112–113, 172; philosophy of forms 23; theory of hylomorphism 25
art 11–12, 18, 23, 89, 210, 219, 255, 270, 282–288, 291, 295–298; "art for art's sake" 24; "the flat ephemeral pamphlet" 46; literary art 172, 332–333; as a "modest refuge" 145–146; monuments and treasures of 211; and propaganda 280–288; role of 210; Soviet art theory 49; and truth 280–288
Art of Charlie Chan Hock Chye, The (Liew) 334–335
"Art of Fiction, The" (James) 210
artificial intelligence (AI) technologies 98, 100–103, 106–107, 107n1
ASNC (Anglo-Saxon, Norse, and Celtic) 165
Atlas of the World's Languages in Danger 315
Attridge, Derek 300
Atwood, Margaret 132, 241, 252, 427, 438, 439
Auden, W. H. 46, 138, 229, 231–232, 234, 283, 284
Auerbach, Erich 75–78, 276, 277, 278

Aurora (Robinson) 425–426
Austen, Jane 132, 197, 198, 242, 400
"Autumn on Nan-Yüeh" (Empson) 47, 48
Azoulay, Ariella 274–275

Baker, Houston A. 265–266
Baker, Kyle 334
Bakhtin, Mikhail 80
Bakunin, Mikhail 210, 212n5, 425
Baldwin, James 241, 266
Balestrini, Nanni 49, 50
Balibar, Étienne 148, 149, 151, 152, 413
Bangavasi trial 217, 223n4
Banks, Russell 138, 146n2
Baraka, Amiri 264–265
Barthes, Roland 57, 270, 273, 274
Battle of Hastings 5, 164, 165
Battle of Waterloo 200
Baudelaire, Charles 368
Baudrillard, Jean 238
Beckett, Samuel 239
Bede, Ven 162, 165, 167, 168n7
Bellamy, Edward 432, 435
Beloved (Morrison) 88, 241, 333
Benjamin, Walter 57, 250, 270, 274, 277
Bentham, Jeremy 110–111
Beowulf 167–168, 169n21
Berger, John 138, 139, 144–146, 272
Berlant, Lauren 13–15, 58, 378
Berlin, Irving 263, 267
Bernays, Edward 282, 285
Best, Stephen 51n2, 252–254, 344
Between St. Dennis and St. George (Ford) 281
Between the Acts (Woolf) 283
Bhabha, Homi K. 150
Bible 88, 118, 187
Biden, Joe 96, 317
Big Short: Inside the Doomsday Machine, The (Lewis) 130, 132
Bildungsroman 40n5, 68–69, 210
biopolitics 12, 22, 25–30, 138, 150, 154, 178, 308; anatomical 28; feminization of 308; Foucauldian and Agambenian histories of 26; in modernity 25; norms and forms 25–26; oppressive 29; personal 27; repressive 26; and Western political thought 25
Black 36, 58, 60, 61, 67, 70, 88, 90, 92–96, 123–126, 188, 190, 196, 199, 217, 241, 244, 264, 271, 278, 346, 389, 394, 401, 403, 424, 444, 447, 448; Black-Americans 35, 38; Black consciousness 60; Black culture 93, 265; Black music 29, 265; Black studies 101, 265, 343, 401, 443, 444, 447, 448; de-composition 263; phonic substance 266; sounds 263–267; see also African-Americans
Black Atlantic, The (Gilroy) 398
"Black Box" 302–309, 310n8

454

Index

Black Lives Matter movement 247, 375, 379
Black Skyscraper, The (Brown) 372, 377
Blake, William 196
blame 103, 173–181, 252, 447, 449; Chaucerian 174–176; resurrecting, to decolonize Jesus 180–181; in *SGGK* 176–180; and snare of political 172–173
Blindspot (Cole) 269, *270*
Bloch, Ernst 250, 253, 436–437
Bloom, Allan 242, 441
Bloom, Harold 242
Blue Fasa (Mackey) 28
blue humanities 398–400, 404
Blum, Hester 399, 401
Bodies That Matter (Butler) 241
body/bodies 2, 11–16, 18–20, 24, 27–31, 47, 60, 61, 66. 68, 70, 71, 74, 75, 79, 82, 87–96, 98, 99, 104, 106, 107, 115, 120, 121, 124, 125, 135, 136, 164, 167, 176, 177, 180–181, 190, 196, 198, 201, 208, 223, 238, 242, 253, 267, 271, 272, 281, 307, 317, 329, 333, 347, 369, 375, 379, 383, 387, 392, 397, 399, 401, 408, 409, 415, 420, 421, 435, 448; embodiment 11, 14, 68–70, 99, 100, 105–107, 309
Boer War 221–222
Bolaño, Roberto 71
Bolívar, Simón 152–155, 156n11, 200
Borderlands/La Frontera: The New Mestiza (Anzaldúa) 242, 409
borders 4, 66, 68, 110, 112, 140, 143, 148–154, 195, 209, 355, 408–417; of border theory 412–414; border theory and Indigenous studies 414–416; inescapable 416–417; re-bordering 410–412
Bowen, Elizabeth 225, 287
Bradford, William 89–93, 243
Brathwaite, Kamau 402
Brave New World (Huxley) 369, 438
Brecht, Bertolt 140, 250
Brief and Wondrous Life of Oscar Wao, The (Diaz) 251
Britton, Dennis 188
Brooks, Cleanth 442
Brooks, Gwendolyn 230, 231, 234
Brown, Adrienne 372, 377
Brown, Wendy 64–65
Brown Girl, Brownstones (Marshall) 33, 35–40, 40n5
Browning, Elizabeth Barrett 22, 27, 28, 30–31
Browning, Robert 27, 28
Bulosan, Carlos 126
Burgess, Anthony 438
Burke, Edmund 195, 196, 204, 206, 208, 210
Burroughs, Edgar Rice 422
Bush, George W. 305
Butler, Judith 241
Butler, Octavia E. 88, 241, 424, 439

Cade, Jack 53–56, 58
Call of the Wild, The (London) 391, 394
canon (canonical) 44, 45, 47, 49, 74, 75, 77, 79, 80, 81, 82, 227, 231, 237, 239, 240, 243, 366, 385n1, 392, 400; decolonization 74–83; empires 74–83; English canon 445; "Canon Wars" 33, 441, 445, 448; Western 74–76
Canterbury Tales (Chaucer) 173–176, 181
capital (capitalism, capitalist) 12, 34, 36–39, 118–126, 134–136, 239, 240, 247, 248, 252–253, 255, 260, 317–320, 361, 369, 370, 372, 375, 378, 384, 385, 390, 395, 397, 398, 401, 404, 405, 437; imperial 130–134; industrial 236; modernity 239; symbolic 134–136
Capital (Marx) 132; as literature 118–123; and literature of workers 123–125
Carby, Hazel 241, 267
Caribbean 35–37, 87, 91, 92, 122, 172, 260, 264, 402
Carson, Rachel 112
Carter, Jimmy 96, 341
Casamassima (James) 210–212
catalogue 64, 65, 66, 68, 70, 71, 344; catalogue form 70–72
Catholicism 187, 207, 208
Caudwell, Christopher 47, 49
causality/cause 15, 43, 44, 46–50, 106, 138, 141, 144, 153, 206, 208, 218, 220, 281, 296, 367, 402, 431, 432; theorizing 14, 43–47, 49–51
Cavendish, Margaret 432
Caxton, William 173
censorship 78, 79, 187, 215, 217–220, 222, 227, 287, 329, 331; *The Adventures of Obadiah Oldbuck* 333; *Animal Farm* 326; *The Art of Charlie Chan Hock Chye* 334, 335; *Barefoot Gen* 334; *Blasé* 329; *Breakdowns* 329, *332*; *The Complete Maus: A Survivor's Tale* Volume I & II 323–336; *Counterlife* 333; *Dallas Morning News* 334; *Histoire de M. Vieux Bois* 333; imperial 217–218; *Krazy Kat* 325–327; *Mad* 329; *My Favorite Things Is Monsters* 335; *The Nib* 335, 336; *Norton Anthology of American Literature* 241, 333; *Seduction of the Innocent: The Influence of Comic Books on Today's Youth* 331; *Texas History Movies* 334; *Understanding Comics* 334; wartime 218–219
Ceremony (Silko) 16, 96, 115, 242
Chamberlain, Neville 244
Charles I, King 54
Chatterjee, Partha 218
Chaucer, Geoffrey 5, 172, 174–176, 180
Chaucerian blame 174–176
Chaucer's Retraction 175–176, 180
Chesterton, G. K. 288n1
"Chicano border narratives" 410
Chin, Frank 241–242

455

Index

Christianity 58, 89, 92, 163, 243, 416; Church 164, 173, 187, 243; Jesus 19, 144, 174, 180–181
Churchill, Winston 163, 229; "Sinews of Peace" address 229
Chute, Hillary 329, 333
Cicero, Marcus Tullius 24
Cisneros, Ernesto 408, 410–412
Cisneros, Sandra 242
cities 4, 80–82, 232, 276, 364–373, 376–379, 416; affectable spaces/subjects 372–373; as object of knowledge 366–367; politics of modernization 367–370; social contradictions of urban life 370–372
Citizen 13660 (Okubo) 334
Citizen: An American Lyric (Rankine) 271–272, 275
citizens 24, 79, 82, 87–96, 140, 142–144, 155, 231, 232, 288, 405, 433
citizenship 68, 70, 87–96, 123, 126, 139, 140, 143, 144, 146, 150, 217, 230, 275, 413; original citizens 88–96; origin stories 88–96, 102, 165
Civil Rights movement 335–336
Civil War 54, 55, 95, 141, 153, 195, 445
classrooms 2, 5, 315, 331, 336, 441–449; comics in 333–336; English as apolitical 443–445; longer history of politics in literature 445–448; politics and classroom imaginary 441–443; scene today 448–449
Class Struggle in France (Marx) 125
Claybaugh, Amanda 55, 151–152
climate 35, 106, 149, 248, 249, 255, 287, 303, 336, 352, 353, 355, 360, 361, 377, 378, 390, 398, 402–405, 420, 424, 427, 439; climate change 353, 360, 361, 403
Clinton, Bill 96, 247
Clockwork Orange, A (Burgess) 438
Clune, Michael 298–299
Cobb, Keith Hamilton 53, 59–61
coda 49–51, 385
Coetzee, J. M. 114–115, 244
Cohen, Jeffrey Jerome 357, 415
Cold War 125, 139, 145, 226, 228, 231, 232, 236, 239, 264, 314, 336, 355, 401; seeking refuge in 143–144
Cole, Teju 269, *270,* 317
collective 3, 4, 13, 15–17, 34, 35, 58, 66, 67, 69, 87, 88, 91–93, 105, 107, 123, 124, 138, 146, 148, 149, 153, 163, 211, 228, 232, 234, 252, 262, 267, 283, 308, 313, 316, 319, 320, 388, 402–404, 423
Collins, Patricia Hill 241
colony/colonialism/ coloniality colonial 2, 32, 35, 36, 68, 69, 74, 77, 78, 82, 83n1, 87, 89–92, 101, 122, 125, 152–155, 161, 162, 166, 181, 184–186, 188, 197, 205–209, 211, 212, 215, 217, 218, 221–223, 242, 244, 259, 260, 262, 266, 273, 275, 281, 288, 289n5, 299, 303, 314, 334, 345, 353, 354, 357, 360, 369, 371–372, 375, 377, 382, 384, 394, 395, 397, 401, 404, 405, 408, 414, 423–425, 431, 435, 437, 443, 444, 450n1; decolonization 74–83, 132, 180–181, 227, 264, 274, 344, 372, 415, 417; "early England" and imperial legacy of 162–165; postcolonial/postcolonialism 36, 67, 68, 74, 77–82, 150, 227, 244, 273, 314, 334, 344, 371, 385n1, 401, 402, 409; and terrorism 205–209; see also empire; imperialism
"Colony: Its Guilty Secret and its Accursed Share, The" (Mbembe) 206
Color Purple, The (Walker) 241
comics 2, 323–336; in the classroom 333–336; funny animal 325–327; as literary art 332–333; underground 327–332
commodities 118, 119, 120, 121, 122, 124, 134, 135, 315, 318, 376, 377, 378, 379, 380
common sense 196, 262, 267, 294, 366, 373
Common Sense (Paine) 55
computer-aided translation (CAT) 319
Conrad, Joseph 44
consensus future 422–427
contact zones 34, 40, 409, 416
Crenshaw, Kimberlé Williams 241
Crisis, The 285
crisis of relationality 13–15, 18, 19
"Criteria of Negro Art" 285
critical methods 70, 253, 293, 297, 299, 300; action, politics 295–296; in literature 68–70; politics of 293–295, in rights 68–70
Critical Race Theory 11, 67, 241, 243, 245, 293, 331, 441
criticism 1, 2, 47, 123, 218, 260, 271, 272, 291–300; Anglo-American literary 292; British rule 215; cultural criticism 293, 409; evaluative criticisms 298–299; feminist criticism 369, 442, 443; formalisms 297–298; literary 1, 5, 6, 32, 80, 252, 293, 366; Marxist criticism 443; phenomenological criticisms 299–300; photography 273; political criticism 253–254; politics of critical method 293–295; politics of critical method in action 295–296; post-colonial criticism 314; rival methods 297–300; sympathetic identification 68, 293; teaching literature 1; tradition of 34; usual story 292–293; vitriolic criticism 242
critique 14, 26, 35–37, 39, 42, 45, 55, 59, 68, 72, 77, 78, 80, 92, 94, 95, 102, 104, 105, 107, 118, 120, 121, 122, 140, 151, 181, 199, 207, 209, 211, 216–218, 222, 231–233, 245, 248–255, 260, 266, 272, 273, 281, 292–294, 296, 297, 299, 300, 326, 241, 343, 344, 355, 369, 388, 390, 411, 412, 415, 417, 424, 431, 433, 435; end of 252–254

456

"Cry of the Children, The" (Victorian era) 22, 27, 30
culture/cultural 13, 33, 118, 135, 150, 167, 176, 187, 189, 218, 237, 238, 239, 240, 243, 244, 267, 298, 317, 345, 366, 368, 399, 409, 410, 412, 430, 436; cultural studies 11, 42, 229, 266, 366, 375, 408
Cvetkovich, Ann 122

Dallas Morning News 334
Dante 118, 172
Das, Santanu 215, 221–222
Davis, Angela 267
Davis, Kathleen 161
Davis, Mike 370
Dawes, James 72n4
Dawes Act of 1887 414
debt 128, 129, 130, 131, 132, 133, 134, 135, 136
debtors 128–136; realism and imperial capitalism 130–134; symbolic capitalism 134–136
Decline in the Birth-Rate, The (Webb) 433
decolonization 74–83, 264, 372
Defence of the Realm Act 280
Defense of Judgment, A (Clune) 298
De Landa, Manuel 357
Deleuze, Gilles 11, 135, 387
DeLillo, Don 333
DeLoughrey, Elizabeth 354, 397, 399, 400, 402
democracy (democratic, democratize) 2, 3, 6, 76, 78, 89, 92–95, 112, 134, 140, 142, 146, 175, 195, 200, 217, 225, 226, 228, 230, 236–237, 245, 264, 389–391, 394, 397, 405
Democracy (Didion) 144
Democratic Party 247, 248
Derrida, Jacques 109, 135, 236–239, 266, 342, 387, 391
Descartes, René 11, 387
Detransition, Baby (Peters) 13, 18–19
Dewey, John 236, 292
Dickens, Charles 32, 55, 132, 202, 286, 289n3, 348, 446
Dictionary of Untranslatables: A Philosophical Lexicon 320
Didion, Joan 138, 144
digital platforms 302–309; "Black Box" 306–308; digital age 303; digital counterterrorism 306–308; networked reader, reembodying 308–309; reading as digital counterterrorism 306–308; translation in digital age 318–320; Twitter and platform national security 304–306
Dimaline, Cherie 414–417
Disraeli, Benjamin 148
Don Juan (Byron) 200–201
Douglass, Frederick 94–96, 150, 261–262
Downtown Eastside (DTES) 376, 381, 383–384
drones 79, 82, 98, 129, 223

Du Bois, W. E. B. 262–265, 285, 413
Duchamp, Marcel 333

"early England" and imperial legacy of colonialism 162–165
earth 101, 102, 103, 116, 146, 353, 357, 419, 421, 423, 425, 426, 427
ecocriticism (ecocritical) 5, 189–190, 387–391, 394–395
ecology 352, 359, 371, 381, 390, 394, 395
Edgeworth, Maria 197, 207
education 2, 37, 67, 187, 240, 242, 250, 289n5, 297–299, 323, 334, 391, 441–444, 446, 448, 449
Efrén Divided (Cisneros) 408, 410, 417
Egan, Jennifer 251, 308, 309, 310n8
Eggers, Dave 138, 146n2, 251
Eliot, George 32
Eliot, T. S. 263, 282, 283–285, 289n2, 447
Elizabeth Costello (Coetzee) 114–115
Elizabeth I 54, 185, 187
Ellison, Ralph 95, 264–266
"Emergency Skin" (Jemisin) 100–103, 105
Empire of Wild (Dimaline, Cherie) 414–415
empires 74–83, 149, 214, 215, 216, 218, 219, 220, 221, 222, 314, 404, 415, 450; imperial/imperialist 74, 113, 130–134, 149, 181, 200, 214, 221, 222, 365, 416, 419, 422, 427
Empson, William 47, 48, 286
"End of History?, The" (Fukuyama) 236, 237, 273
End of History and the Last Man, The 236–237
Eng, Mercedes 376, 383, 384
Engels, Friedrich 434
England 53, 54, 161, 162, 163, 164, 165, 166, 167, 194, 195, 196, 243, 244, 281; English 6, 139, 152, 155, 165, 166, 173, 174, 181, 207, 226, 227, 230, 231, 244, 314, 320, 334, 372, 432, 441, 442; Englishness 165, 183, 185
Enlightenment 68, 88, 208, 209, 294, 432, 444
enslaved person 23, 87, 196, 199, 200
enslavement 87–96, 122, 262
environment (environmental) 5, 33, 37, 39, 111, 112, 113, 132, 207, 237, 276, 353, 353, 355, 360, 365, 366, 368–373, 375, 377, 381, 383, 390, 393, 394, 398, 401, 403–405, 424, 426, 438; environmental activism 388, 403–404; environmental humanities 389, 399
Equiano, Olaudah 196
Erasure 248–249
Erdrich, Louise 242
Eros and Civilization (Marcuse) 437
Esty, Jed 35, 239
ethics (ethical) 3, 4, 24, 68, 70, 74, 76, 77, 88, 89, 95, 146, 168, 173, 174, 175, 177, 178, 179, 180, 181, 190, 231, 233, 282, 284, 293, 296, 298, 313, 395, 398, 423

ethics of politics 176–180
eugenics 105, 149, 433, 438
European Union 149, 184
Eustace Diamonds, The (Trollope) 131–132
Everett, Percival 248
evidence 42, 216, 217, 221, 247, 249, 341, 342, 343, 345, 348, 442, 445
exceptionalism 58, 89, 90, 183–184, 360, 390, 412; 1616/1619 188–191; and race 183–184; and Shakespeare 183–184
Exit West (Hamid) 272, 278n1, 364–365, 372, 378
experience 2, 4, 6, 11, 14, 16, 17, 34–37, 39, 42, 49, 58, 61, 66, 67, 70, 78, 92, 93, 95, 98, 106, 111, 126, 152, 188, 189, 232, 240, 249, 250, 262, 272, 281, 284, 295, 300, 317–320, 336, 365–369, 375, 402
"Eyes of Asia, The" stories 214, 215, 220, 222

Fabian, Johannes 259, 433
Fabianism 433
Fanon, Frantz 218
Fascism 75–78, 139, 141, 145, 233, 250, 283, 284, 288, 330, 331, 336, 434; Fascist 25, 75, 78, 149, 225, 248, 282
feeling (feelings) 4, 11, 12, 15, 16, 19, 45, 125, 138, 141, 148, 195–199, 201, 209, 218, 226, 228, 229, 231, 232, 249–252, 254, 260, 263, 272, 308, 320, 347, 377, 434
Felski, Rita 42, 43, 46, 51, 51n2, 252–254, 442, 448
feminism (feminist) 11, 67, 76, 191, 248, 283, 303, 307, 344, 368, 369, 389, 399, 409, 442, 443
fiction 2, 6, 33, 35, 37, 56, 69, 70, 80, 88, 94, 100, 103, 104, 105, 107, 110, 113–115, 131, 133, 136, 138, 148–155, 172, 174, 198, 202, 204–211, 216, 217, 220, 222, 225, 227, 233, 239, 244, 248–251, 255, 272, 275–278, 283, 295, 296, 302, 304, 306–310, 335, 342, 346–349, 365, 388, 389, 395, 400, 408, 412, 419, 420, 422, 423–425, 427, 439, 444, 447; colonial terrorism in 206–209
Foreign Intelligence Surveillance Act (FISA) 306, 309n5
forms (formal, formalism, formalist) 24, 35, 145, 253, 291, 293, 296–300, 444, 445; aesthetic 35–40; biopolitics 25–26; brief account of 22–24; literary politics and persistence of 24–25; poetic forms-of-life 27–31
Forms (Levine) 297
Forster, E. M. 228, 230, 289n2
Foucault, Michel 25, 26, 28, 150, 238, 239, 316, 367, 411
Franco, Francisco 282
Frankenstein (Shelley) 198–199
Frankfurt School 249–250, 253, 436, 437
Franzen, Jonathan 248–252, 254
Fraser, Nancy 240
Freedgood, Elaine 32–34, 36, 40n3
French Revolution 5, 55, 194–196, 198, 202, 205, 206, 211
Freud, Sigmund (Freudian) 14, 15, 342, 436
Frost, Robert 357, 447
Fukuyama, Francis 236–237, 240
future 5, 18, 19, 38, 66, 67, 95, 103, 117, 128, 132, 136, 138–146; 195, 196, 241, 265, 270–278, 281, 283, 308, 318, 336, 343, 345, 352, 362, 365, 372, 402, 403, 419, 421, 422, 425–428; 432, 434, 439; activist struggles 50; as emotional memory 57–58; futurity/futurism 14, 33, 49, 105, 138, 206, 273, 275, 306, 308, 345, 366, 371, 423; pre-packaged convenience 360; rebellion 58; as recuperation 57–58

Gaddis, William 239
Gellhorn, Martha 138–139
gender/gendered 5, 13, 17, 33, 65, 68, 71, 72, 98, 100, 101, 102, 105, 126, 129, 168, 172, 174, 177, 178, 180, 186, 189, 190, 197, 233, 234, 238–242, 249, 260, 298, 303, 309, 331, 365, 369, 377, 387, 401, 409, 435, 444, 449
Geneva Conventions of 1949 143, 229
genre 2, 4, 22, 23, 32, 46, 48, 55, 65, 68, 69–71, 80, 94, 98, 102, 105, 121, 123, 125, 130, 154, 155, 174, 179, 187, 189, 207, 209–212, 232, 251, 255, 273, 285, 304, 309, 327, 335, 346, 348, 365, 400, 419, 421, 430–432, 438, 442, 447
Ghosh, Amitav 218
Gilroy, Paul 151, 267, 398
Glissant, Édouard 387, 402
Global Bank 133–134
globalization 318, 320; and its discontents 243–245; as world literature 314–316
Global North 360, 419, 426
Global South 69, 364, 370–372, 426
Godwin, Francis 198, 420
Godwin, William 198–199
Gold, Mike 46, 126
Goldblatt, David 275–278
Goldsmith, Kenneth 318–319
Google 305, 318, 319
Goonewardena, Kanishka 375, 385n2
Gordimer, Nadine 244, 276
Gorman, Amanda 96, 96n2, 317
Gramsci, Antonio 366
Greenblatt, Stephen 54, 58–59, 185
Grewal, Inderpal 68, 303, 307
Guattari, Félix 11, 387
Guidotti-Hernández, Nicole 408, 412
Guillory, John 33, 442

Habermas, Jürgen 238, 244–245
Haley, Alex 88, 241
Hall, Kim F. 61–62, 186, 190, 191
Hamid, Mohsin 132, 138, 146n1, 255, 272, 278n1, 364–365, 369, 372, 378
Handmaid's Tale, The (Atwood) 241, 438
Haraway, Donna 98, 116, 359, 387
Hardt, Michael 178, 179
Hartman, Saidiya V. 70, 72n3, 266, 342, 345, 349n4
Hayles, N. Katherine 98–100, 106, 309
Hegel, G. W. F. (Hegelian) 236, 265
heterotopia 367, 411, 412
Hicks, D. Emily 410
"Hill We Climb, The" (Gorman) 96, 317
historiography, historiographical 43, 45, 79, 87, 161, 346, 402; historiographic metafiction 239
history/historical/historicism 33, 34, 43, 45, 48, 49, 50, 53, 54, 55, 69, 87–90, 129, 145, 150, 154, 161, 207, 208, 225, 226, 241, 267, 273, 293, 295, 297, 315, 316, 334, 335, 336, 347, 348, 379, 383, 404, 419, 446, 448; Anglo-American literary criticism 392; anthropomorphism 114; Black women celebrities 70; British rule in India 215; Christian salvation 181; of class division 53; of critical theory 50; English scholars 166; humanitarianism 139; literary 4, 43, 44, 45, 46, 75, 88, 183, 226, 227, 237, 238, 239, 240, 312, 347; literary criticism 291; literary history 4, 44, 238; political philosophy 4; political 4, 155, 181, 296; politics in the literature classroom 445–448; of racism 37–38; radical religious rebellion 208; social 161; writing of 57
Hobsbawm, Eric 149, 154
Homer 27, 74, 75, 78–81, 83n2, 430
homes 82, 115, 145, 352–362, 428n5
hooks, bell 93, 241
Hueffer, Ford Madox *see* Ford, Madox Ford
Hughes, Langston 133, 262
humanism 76, 78, 98–100, 102, 107, 112, 114, 239; origins of 76–77; Western 76
humans 4, 16, 82, 98–107, 109–115, 139, 299, 319, 352, 358, 391, 405, 419–422, 425, 427; (humanism *see* humanism)
Human Shore: Seacoasts in History, The (Gillis) 404
Hurston, Zora Neale 263–264
Hutcheon, Linda 238, 239
Huxley, Aldous 369, 438

Iden, Alexander 54
Iliad, The (Homer) 78–81
imagination 28, 68, 91, 92, 94, 114, 135, 206, 210, 211, 227, 261, 273–275, 292, 293, 297, 345, 346, 353, 361, 365, 377, 388, 389, 390, 397, 405, 435, 438, 441; animals 114–117; and sympathy 114–117
imperialism 24, 74, 75, 149, 165, 166, 174, 185, 200; imperial capitalism 130–134; imperial censorship 215, 217–218
India 74, 77, 79, 82, 206, 208, 214–222, 243, 244, 285, 286, 287, 288, 427; disaffection in 217–218; imperial censorship 217–218
Indigenous/Indigeneity 69, 89, 118, 122, 149, 151, 153–155, 165, 166, 168, 185, 190, 221, 242, 346, 354, 357, 375, 376, 379, 383, 389, 394, 399, 401, 414–416, 431, 432; border theory and 414–416; studies 185, 190
individual 2, 6, 16, 26, 27, 34, 35, 44, 50, 60, 64, 65, 67, 69, 70, 87, 99, 106, 135, 139, 148, 172–174, 176, 180, 181, 195, 232, 236, 240, 245, 249, 251, 252, 254, 264, 266, 282, 284, 288, 297, 313, 317, 319, 343, 347–348, 360, 362, 365, 367, 368, 371, 381, 402, 423, 438, 442, 448
Inferno (Dante) 80, 118, 121
infrastructure 19, 44, 154, 250, 304, 307, 313, 319, 365, 367, 368, 371, 377–381, 383
"interdisciplinary" 5, 67–69, 344, 387, 398, 444
Interesting Narrative of the Life of Olaudah Equiano, The (Equiano, Olaudah) 196
Ireland (Irish) 164, 185, 197–199, 204–212, 220, 287
Irish nationalism 204, 205, 207
Iron Curtain 143, 144, 229
Isherwood, Christopher 46, 139, 284
Ishiguro, Kazuo 104, 244

Jack Cade's Rebellion 53–55
Jackson, Zakiyyah Iman 72n3, 72n4, 101–102, 106
Jacobin, 204–210
Jaji, Tsitsi Ella 267
James, C. L. R. 126, 401
James, Henry 32, 210, 241, 272
Jameson, Frederic (Jamesonian) 34, 35, 36, 40n3, 40n4, 43–46, 49, 50, 51n3, 54, 55, 58, 121–123, 125, 238, 239, 250, 253, 431, 436–437, 439, 444, 448
Jesus 19, 144, 174; resurrecting blame to decolonize 180–181
Jetñil-Kijiner, Kathy 353–356, 358–360, 362n2
Jews 25, 126, 139, 181, 323, 433
Johnson, James Weldon 133, 262, 263
Jonson, Ben 183
Joyce, James 308, 368

Kant, Immanuel 11, 260, 264, 266, 267, 268n1
Keats, John 286–288
Khomeini, Ayatollah 243, 317
Kim (Mukherjee) 216, 220
kinship 6, 13, 17–19, 67, 69, 116, 221, 359, 401

Kipling, Rudyard 214–216, 219–222, 281, 288n1
knowledge 6, 38, 54, 68, 72, 76, 174, 175, 180, 181, 232, 238, 251, 260, 288, 291, 293, 295, 296, 298–300, 318, 345, 346, 355, 357, 368, 369, 371, 411, 431, 444, 448, 449; city as object of 366–367
Koestler, Arthur 138–140
Krazy Kat 325–327
Kushner, Tony 27, 241

labor 90–92, 118–122, 124, 125, 368, 369, 375, 376, 378, 434, 435, 437, 438; work 44, 74, 75, 151, 183, 184, 188, 190, 191, 249, 251, 252, 253, 254, 255, 283, 306, 343; workers 118, 119, 120, 121, 122, 123, 124, 125, 126, 133, 134, 135, 378, 379
Lacan, Jacques 238, 390, 394
Lahiri, Jhumpa 69, 241
Lalla Rookh 209, 211–212
language (linguistic, linguistics) 6, 13, 14, 24, 26, 34, 42, 46, 48, 55, 57–59, 62, 66–68, 79, 82, 88, 95, 113, 122, 130, 131, 134–136, 140, 142, 145, 148, 152, 161, 164–166, 168, 173, 174, 176, 180, 181, 184, 186, 188, 190, 196, 198, 204, 205, 216, 219, 222, 226, 230, 231, 233, 239, 241, 244, 245, 255, 259, 260, 261, 266, 267, 272, 273, 295, 308, 312–315, 317, 318, 320, 321, 330, 331, 358, 364, 368, 372, 376, 387, 389, 390–392, 397, 402, 408–411, 413, 426, 442, 448; and nation-state 152–155
Lasswell, Harold 1, 282
late-1940s literature: *Age of Anxiety* 231–232; alternate period vocabularies 227–228; late-1940s currency of "the recent war" 229–231; midcentury mark, arbitrariness of 228–229; periodic contortions 226–227; against "the good war" 232–234; World War II 232–234
late capitalism 239, 252, 378
Latour, Bruno 387, 388–390, 395
laws 25, 26, 43, 44, 67, 69, 70, 206, 208, 217, 218, 397, 431
Lefebvre, Henri 367, 375, 379–380
Le Guin, Ursula K. 420, 439
Leopold, Aldo 111–112, 426
Levine, Caroline 17, 23, 151, 156n8, 297
Levitas, Ruth 434, 436
Lewis, Cecil Day 230, 283
Lezra, Jacques 320
liberalism/liberal 25, 99, 100, 107, 155, 217, 218, 232, 236, 237, 239, 240, 243, 368, 444; at the end of history 236–237; liberal pluralism 236–237, 243; liberal subject 34, 100, 267, 308
Limits of Critique, The (Felski) 42, 51n2, 252–253
literary history 4, 44, 75, 183, 226, 227, 234, 237–240, 312, 325

literary pluralism: and recognition 240–243
London, Jack 123, 391–394
Looking Backward (Bellamy) 369, 432, 435
Lord Byron 198, 200, 201, 209
Lukács, Georg/György 34, 250, 348
lumpenproletariat 119, 125–126

Machado, Carmen Maria 71–72
machine translation (MT) 319
Mackey, Nathaniel 22, 24, 28–31
Manifest Destiny 91, 405, 422
maps 5, 46, 149, 152, 155, 202, 249, 259, 261, 357, 376, 380, 381, 408, 414, 416; mapping 185, 250, 357, 376, 379, 397, 415–417
Marcus, Sharon 51n2, 252–254
Marcuse, Herbert 437–438
Marshall, Paule 33, 35–40
Marx, Karl (Marxist, Marxian) 42, 44, 45, 50, 56, 57, 64, 118–122, 124–126, 131, 135, 136, 137n2, 179, 236, 239, 249, 250, 253, 293, 366, 368, 390, 400, 401, 432, 433, 434, 436, 437, 443–448
Massachusetts Bay 87, 90
"Mass Declamation" 46, 48, 51n5
Massey, Doreen 369, 399
Massumi, Brian 12–15
materialism 11, 23, 50, 255, 390, 402; aleatory materialism 50; idealist materialism 50
"Materialism and Revolution" (Sartre) 47
Maus (Spiegelman) 323, 325, 327, 329–334, 336
Mayflower Compact, The 89–90
Mbembe, Achille 206
McCarthy, Cormac 251, 439
McDonald, Rónán 293, 299, 300
McKibben, Bill 353–355
Mee, John 55, 196
Melville, Herman 241, 400*Memoirs of Captain Rock* (Moore) 207
memory 6, 55–58, 61, 92, 104, 202, 227, 241, 260, 276, 325, 333, 341, 342, 344, 392, 401, 402; emotional 57–58; revolution and 55–56
Menchú, Rigoberto 69
Menely, Tobias 198, 391
#MeToo movement 70–72
Midnight's Children (Rushdie) 243–244
Midsommar 13, 15–19
migration 6, 148, 162, 167, 169, 317, 365; immigrant 36, 38, 76, 90, 123, 125, 132, 244, 263, 372, 421; immigration 154, 222, 237, 265, 446; migrant 122, 126
Miller, Nancy K. 230, 442
Milton, John 54, 132, 286
mimesis (mimetic) 32, 35, 36, 75, 76
Moby Dick (Melville) 400, 401
modern: early-modern 60, 61, 189, 191, 376, 382; postmodern 36, 227, 237, 238, 239, 240, 333, 449; pre-modern 26, 190

Index

modernism (modernist) 24, 26, 35, 36, 46, 50, 68, 123, 126, 133, 145, 183, 188, 189, 204, 214, 226, 238–240, 368; academic 234n4; activist 47–49; artistic 24; late modernism 239; literary 227; meta-modernism 239
modernization: politics of 365, 367–370, 404
modern "truth" 288
Moi, Toril 51, 294
"monstrosity" 199, 201
Moore, Thomas 207, 209
Morales, Alejandro 411–412
More, Thomas 430–433
Morris, William 369, 432, 434
Morrison, Toni 88, 93, 241, 252, 333
Morton, Stephen 207, 361
Moten, Fred 7n2, 266, 379
Mufti, Aamir 75, 156n10
music (song) 27, 29, 76, 81, 82, 92, 93, 118, 201, 217, 259–267, 280, 343, 377, 436

Nakamura, Lisa 303, 308
Napoleon 56, 194, 200
narratives (narratology) 14, 15, 17, 18, 90, 92, 102, 150, 154, 237, 239, 261, 365, 367, 371
nation/national 2, 4, 6, 39, 58, 65, 68, 75, 78, 82, 88, 90, 92, 94–96, 125, 129, 130, 133, 138–146, 148–156, 165, 166, 172, 174, 184–186, 188, 201, 209, 210, 218, 227, 228, 233, 240, 242, 244, 245, 255, 261, 262, 263, 265, 267, 269, 270, 273, 281, 284, 302–308, 312, 320, 331, 334, 336, 352, 353, 368, 372, 379, 400, 401, 405, 408, 411, 413, 414, 431, 435; Irish nationalism 204, 205, 207; language 152–155; metonymic nationalism 150; nationalism 48, 80, 154, 218, 221, 397, 401
nation-state 67, 69, 78, 139, 143, 149–155, 208, 243–245, 397, 400, 401, 412–416, 426; national security 303–309
Native American 89, 242, 443; *see also* Indigenous/Indigeneity
nature 56, 60, 65, 71, 74, 78, 80, 93, 109, 111, 112, 114, 116, 152, 175, 178, 204, 206, 210, 217, 229, 242, 260, 293, 305, 307, 313, 320, 346, 347, 361, 366, 387–395, 398, 399, 410, 413, 415, 422, 425, 431, 432, 444; ecocriticism 387–388
naturalism 33, 118
nature 56, 71, 112, 260, 387, 388, 389, 390, 391, 393, 394, 395, 410
Neal, Larry 264–265
Negri, Antonio 135, 136, 178, 179
New Criticism/New Critics/New Critical 1, 45, 46, 292, 296, 297, 442, 445; Brooks, Cleanth 442
News from Nowhere (Morris) 369, 432, 434, 435
Nguyen, Viet Thanh 138, 146, 255
Nietzsche, Friedrich 128

Norman Conquest of 1066 161–168
norms (normal, normative) 3, 17, 23, 25, 26, 42, 68, 87, 98, 105, 106, 146, 216, 218, 239, 254, 267, 294, 296, 303, 307, 315, 357, 434

oceans 151, 354, 397–405, 413; blue humanities 398–400; coastal zone 404–405; critical ocean studies 398–400; oceanic studies 398–400; oceans of resistance 405; ship of state 400–401; sea 38, 96, 111, 353–359, 361, 385, 395, 397–405, 421; undersea crossings 401–404
O'Connor, Flannery 138, 144, 146n2
October Cities (Rotella) 377
"Ode on a Grecian Urn" (Keats) 288
On Beauty (Smith, Zadie) 295–297
Orwell, George 45, 225, 230–231, 284, 285–286, 438
Owen, Wilfred 281, 283
Owenson, Sydney 197, 207, 211
Oxford English Dictionary 394, 420

Padilla Peralta, Dan-el 76–77
Pakistan 74, 77, 78, 79, 81, 82, 243
Parker, Noel 190, 413
Patriot Act 303, 305, 306
Patterson, Orlando 68, 241
period (periodic, periodization) 4, 6, 24, 36, 45, 46, 53–56, 68, 88, 133, 139, 140, 155n7, 161–166, 168, 187–190, 195–196, 204, 205, 207, 208, 210, 211, 222, 225–228, 231, 234, 239, 240, 247–249, 252, 273, 300, 312, 319, 327, 329, 342, 346, 366, 376, 379, 401, 432, 433, 446
peripheries 124, 239, 377, 383, 409; Western canon in 77–78
philosophy: aesthetic 11, 24, 42, 117, 266, 301n4, 447; political 4, 23, 187, 420, 433; sensation 11, 211
photography (photographic) 269–278, 319, 325, 381, 426; depth of field 274–275; focal point 270–274; and literature 269–278; in practice 275–278; and time 269–278
planets 100, 102, 112, 114, 116, 117, 236, 343, 352, 353, 355, 361, 362, 387, 398, 399, 403, 419–428; early planets 420–421; revisionist planetology 424–426; thinking like 426–428; twentieth-century visions 421–424
Plato 2, 23, 260, 388, 389, 397, 400, 430, 433
Pluralism 239, 240, 244–245; liberal 236–237; literary 240–243
poetry (poet, poetic) 2, 3, 6, 22–31, 46–48, 54, 55, 71, 79, 82, 93, 96, 115, 116, 132, 133, 142, 144, 175, 179, 181, 183, 185, 187–189, 194, 196, 198, 200, 201, 202, 209, 217, 221, 225, 230, 242, 259–267, 271, 280–289, 302, 313, 317, 352, 353, 355–361, 365, 368, 376, 379, 383–384, 385, 397, 402, 405, 409, 442, 445–448

461

polis 3, 23, 25, 26, 183, 195, 365
Poovey, Mary 38, 130–131
Pope, Jessie 280–281
posthumans/posthumanism 4, 11, 98–107, 117n1, 309, 389–390; moving beyond 100–107
postmodernism (postmodern, postmodernist) 12, 14, 35, 36, 227, 237–240, 333, 449
Pound, Ezra 24–25, 51n6, 225
power 3, 4, 6, 11–13, 19, 23–27, 31, 32–39, 44, 53–60, 62, 64, 65, 68, 70, 74, 76, 79, 82, 88, 90, 93, 98–101, 104, 106, 107, 111, 113–116, 119–121, 123, 125, 129, 131, 133, 136, 137, 140, 142, 149, 150, 153, 155, 162–164, 166, 172–180, 184–186, 190, 195, 198–200, 202, 204, 207, 213, 215, 218, 231, 247, 248, 253, 266, 267, 278, 286, 288, 292–306, 341–349, 353–357, 360, 362, 364–370, 378, 390, 401–405, 408–410, 413, 414, 417, 425, 427, 434, 435, 438, 444, 445, 447, 449
Powers, Richard 251, 255
practice: aesthetic 1, 2, 6, 20, 22, 23, 77, 116, 264, 295, 298, 366, 367, 371, 372, 447, 448; literary 1, 6, 23, 34, 43, 89, 188, 226, 227, 237, 239, 248, 269, 273, 292, 352, 366, 430, 449; political 430; social 20, 34, 273, 277, 278
Pratt, Mary Louise 409–410, 414
propaganda 25, 214–216, 219–221, 280–288; and art 280–288; modern "truth" 288; political writing 282–284; and truth 280–288; wartime 219–221; writing as 284–287
Pynchon, Thomas 239, 252

queer 13, 18, 19, 67, 343, 346, 348, 388, 389, 403, 409race/racist/racial 2, 5, 11–13, 15, 24, 37, 39, 43, 59, 60, 64, 65, 67, 72, 88, 90, 92, 95, 100, 101, 102, 105, 106, 110–112, 116, 120, 121, 123–126, 129, 143, 148, 150, 164–168, 169n20, 181, 183–186, 188–191, 199, 209, 215, 218, 221, 233, 239–241, 248, 249, 260, 262–266, 293, 327, 332, 335, 378, 394, 410, 423, 431, 443, 447, 448; capitalism 100, 189, 247, 317, 378, 385, 395; and exceptionalism 183–184; hierarchies 37, 221, 230, 343, 377; and Shakespeare 183–184; *see also* Black

Rancière, Jacques 12, 24, 25, 43, 116, 117, 391
Rankine, Claudia 271–272, 275, 317
reader 3–6, 24, 27, 34, 39, 42, 49, 59, 66, 69, 74, 75, 77–79, 80, 82, 89, 90, 93, 95, 96, 101, 107, 119, 126, 131, 141, 167, 172, 174–176, 196, 199, 210, 216, 219, 221, 230, 233, 237, 238, 242, 249, 252, 261, 265, 271, 275, 277, 278, 280–285, 295, 296, 297–299, 300, 302–304, 307–309, 312, 315, 323, 325, 329, 333, 335, 352, 391, 392, 394, 411, 415, 424, 427, 431, 436

Reagan, Ronald 45, 47, 202, 242, 245, 441
realism/real 1, 23, 32, 33, 34, 35, 36, 37, 38, 39, 44, 51, 53, 55, 56, 94, 130, 133, 135, 136, 149, 152, 153, 187, 204, 205, 210, 211, 212, 220, 232, 236, 250, 264, 271, 274, 277–278, 296, 297, 302, 304, 330, 335, 346, 358, 366, 376–378, 382, 388–390, 395, 408, 412, 417, 434; and imperial capitalism 130–134; importance of 33–35; literary 35–40; and representation 32–40; social realism 250, 365; theorizing, after millennium 33–35
rebellion (rebel) 54, 58, 59, 61, 68, 82, 164, 173, 207, 208
recognition 58, 67, 68, 75, 141, 143, 236, 237, 240, 242, 359, 360; and literary pluralism 240–243
"Reformation, The" 58, 62, 187
refugees 3, 138–146, 167, 244, 272, 316, 364, 372; 1930s and 1940s 139–140; John Berger 144–146; Muriel Rukeyser 140–143; *A Painter of His Time* 144–146; refugee futures 146; seeking refuge in the Cold War 143–144; sovereignty 139–140; sympathy 139–140
representation 3–5, 12, 14, 15, 22, 32–40, 68–70, 91, 99, 101, 102, 110, 114–116, 118, 119, 121, 122, 125, 128–133, 135, 138, 139, 148, 150, 183, 190, 208, 214, 231, 233, 238–241, 243, 252, 253, 255, 262, 271–275, 285, 286, 295, 327, 331–335, 344, 365, 367–369, 370, 379, 394, 398, 400, 402, 408, 414, 430, 442, 444, 447; aesthetic formalism 35–40; *Brown Girl, Brownstones* 35–40; literary realism 35–40; theorizing realism after millennium 33–35
repression 12, 27, 31, 42, 194, 199, 200, 218, 437, 438, 438
revolution: America 195; French 5, 55, 194–196, 198, 202, 205, 206, 211; Haiti 199–200; Hungary 144; Ireland 210
rights 2, 64–72, 76, 87, 88, 90, 92–95, 103, 110, 111, 113, 116, 119, 140, 143, 155, 198, 230, 231, 240, 248, 267, 317, 335, 377, 398, 416, 443; catalogue 64–72; critical methods in 68–70
Robinson, Kim Stanley 132, 424–426, 439
romanticism (romantic) 12, 33, 36, 116, 145, 155, 178, 198, 217, 260, 288, 371, 388, 394, 425
Roots (Haley) 88, 241
Rousseau, Jean-Jacques 195, 196, 298
Rukeyser, Muriel 138, 139, 140–143
Rushdie, Salman 2, 243, 245n1, 317, 321n1

Said, Edward 75, 76–78, 80, 145, 168, 244
Sartre, Jean-Paul 47, 218, 225, 313, 394
Sedgwick, Eve Kosofsky 15, 42, 45, 51n2, 241–242, 387, 391, 394
Seghers, Anna 140

Sellout, The (Beatty) 255
Seltzer, Mark 55
Senghor, Léopold Sédar 244
Senior, Olive 172, 178
Sense and Sensibility (Austen) 197
sentiment (sentimentalism) 28, 29, 33, 48, 55, 68, 70, 123, 131, 139, 196–201, 216,218, 219, 295, 445
Sentimental Journey, A (Sterne) 196–197
September 11, 2001 attacks 78, 305, 441
Serviss, Garrett P. 422
settler colonialism 91, 190, 377, 378, 414, 415
Sewell, Anna 110
Sexing the Cherry (Winterson) 241
sex (sexual, sexuality) 2, 5, 13, 16, 18, 25, 64, 65, 71, 100, 105, 172, 179, 189, 190, 196, 228, 239, 240, 241, 323, 331, 335, 376, 383, 443, 449; sex work 376, 383
Shakespeare, William 24, 53–56, 58–62, 183–189, 286, 288, 442; and exceptionalism 183–184; *Henry VI, Part 2* 53; *Merchant of Venice, The* 186; *Othello* 58; and race 183–184; *Richard II* 54
Sharpe, Christina 271, 387, 401
Shelley, Percy Bysshe 53, 200
Sinclair, Upton 119, 123–125
Sir Gawain and the Green Knight (SGGK) 174, 176; blame in 176–180; ethics of politics in 176–180; shame in 176–180
slavery/slave/enslavement 25, 66, 87, 88, 89, 91, 92, 94, 95, 96, 118, 119, 120, 121, 122, 123, 184, 186, 199, 261, 445; bondage 93, 196; enslaved person 23, 87, 196, 199, 200; enslavement 87–96, 122, 262
Smith, Adam 121–122, 196, 404
"Song of the Andoumboulou" 22, 28–31
Sophocles *(Antigone)* 27, 397
sovereignty 4, 25, 70, 134, 138–143, 149, 152, 154, 173, 177, 178, 185, 190, 206–208, 217, 264, 296, 346, 355, 397, 413, 414, 416
speculation/speculative 6, 129, 130, 342, 345, 346, 395; speculative fiction 100, 105, 365, 372, 439
Spiegelman, Art 323–325, 328–330, 332
Spillers, Hortense J. 70, 266–267, 401, 443
Spinoza, Baruch 11, 20
Spivak, Gayatri Chakravorty 72n4, 244, 419
Star Trek 319, 321n2, 423, 434
state 27, 64, 67, 77, 79, 80, 81, 82, 121, 136, 149, 150, 151, 153, 155, 185, 205, 231, 280, 286, 288, 307, 308, 309, 400, 401
streets and highways 375–385; of "autocartography" 385; coda 385; experience 377–380; infrastructure 377–380; levels in concrete 377–380; logistical lyrics 383–384; logistics 377–380; textual maps of the street 380–383

"Surface Reading: An Introduction" (Best and Marcus) 51n2, 252
sympathy 4, 68, 114, 115, 138, 141, 143, 145, 148, 196, 198, 199, 206, 285; animals 114–117; and imagination 114–117; refugees 139–140
symptom (symptomatic) 12, 42–51, 55, 121, 123, 126, 293, 299, 300; activist modernism 47–49; coda 49–51; interwar literary politics 45–47; literature and activism before political unconscious 43–45; politics of despair 45; symptomatic reading as 45; symptomatic reading as symptom 45; theorizing causality 43–45

Taliban 79, 82
Taylor, Charles 240, 243
Taylor, Philip Meadows 208
terror/terrorism 82, 121, 181, 204–206, 212n3, 237, 303, 306, 308, 369; colonial 206–209; and the colony 205–206; and genre 209–210; Victorian novels of terror 210–212
thagi 206, 208, 212n2
Thatcher, Margaret 45, 47, 202, 242
theorizing 412, 413; causality 43–45; realism after the millennium 33–35
theory: affect 11–15, 19, 343; critical race 11, 67, 241, 243, 245, 293, 331, 344, 441; gender 71, 238, 241; economic 404; literary 5, 45, 50, 442; political 7n2, 25, 105, 113, 140, 173, 177, 231, 275, 393, 431; queer 11, 241, 242, 443; social 273
Thompson, E. P. 47, 49, 366
thug 205, 208, 210, 212n2
time 17–19, 60, 62, 74–81, 116, 118, 120, 128, 129, 131, 136, 140, 141, 144–146, 150, 155, 161, 162, 164, 165, 195, 197, 198, 205, 209, 210, 215, 225, 226, 228, 229, 231, 232, 239, 241, 243, 244, 250, 252, 263, 266, 267, 269, 270, 272–278, 281, 283, 288, 299, 302–304, 307, 309, 313, 314, 316, 317, 319, 325, 329, 333, 335, 341, 344, 345, 352, 353, 356–359, 361, 367, 373, 379, 384, 392, 442; and photography 269–278
Tolkien, J. R. R. 167, 420
totalitarianism 287, 438
Toyoshima Yoshio 227, 230
Tran, Vu 138, 146
translation 6, 46, 69, 81, 82, 101, 152, 155, 184, 195, 209, 210, 234n1, 254, 261, 333, 334, 358, 411, 427, 449; globalization as world literature 314–316; and literature 312–314; and politics 312–314; politics of translation 320–321; translation in the digital age 318–320; visibility of translation 316–318
Trollope, Anthony 131, 132, 433
Trump, Donald 2, 169n20, 184, 245, 247

truth 2, 34, 38, 40, 65, 68, 80, 82, 102, 103, 163, 174, 202, 210, 215, 242, 271, 280–288, 341, 360, 384, 388, 438, 445; and art 280–288; modern 288; and propaganda 280–288
Twitter 70, 302–309; and platform national security 304–306

Ulysses (Joyce) 308, 368
Uncle Tom's Cabin (Stowe) 55, 123
United Irishmen 197, 207, 212n1
United Kingdom 58, 87, 96, 161, 197, 228, 422, 443, 448
United Nations (UN) 143, 154, 155, 397, 427
United States 6, 38, 61, 76, 79, 87–92, 94–96, 118, 122, 129, 130, 144, 148, 150, 151, 153, 188, 220, 225, 228, 231, 232, 233, 305, 323, 325, 331, 336, 367, 371, 401, 404, 409, 410, 412–414, 421, 422, 435, 438, 441, 443, 445, 448; Capitol riots 24; conflicts 96; legacy of plantocracy 89; national cultures 152; national security 303
university/universities 33, 45, 48, 77–80, 240, 265, 292, 293, 299, 300, 315, 318, 441–444, 447, 448; academy 43, 47, 66, 74–90, 82, 88, 252, 443; colleges 39, 114, 276, 333, 442, 443, 444, 446, 447, 448
Upward, Edward 46, 48–49
urban life 368, 370, 375, 376, 384; social contradictions of 370–372
U.S. 1 (Rukeyser) 142
utopia/utopian 4, 16, 17, 19, 34, 35, 36, 37, 39, 40, 45, 49, 54, 90, 103, 131, 136, 198, 199, 206, 253, 316, 321n2, 367, 369, 370, 372, 420, 423, 425, 430–439; beginnings 430–432; nineteenth century 432–435; twentieth century and beyond 436–439

value 3, 5, 33, 35, 60, 64, 65, 72, 89, 101–103, 105, 119–122, 124, 128–136, 168, 172, 176, 178–180, 211, 220, 229, 239, 242, 243, 245, 254, 265, 266, 287, 291–300, 308, 313, 325, 330, 343, 345, 347, 367, 390, 391, 409, 435, 441, 442, 446, 447, 449
vernacular 74, 77, 79, 83, 164, 166, 172, 173, 174, 181, 220, 266, 257, 278, 444
Victorian 27, 32–37, 131, 132, 151, 152, 165, 204, 209, 214, 221, 348, 368, 434, 435, 438; gothicism 204; novels of terror 210–212; realism 33, 34, 37
Viet Thanh Nguyen 138, 146, 255

Walcott, Derek 401–402
Walker, Alice 241
Walker, David 94, 95
Walkowitz, Rebecca 312, 315
war: Boer War 221; Civil War 54, 95, 141, 153, 445; Cold War 125, 139, 143–144, 145, 226, 236, 239, 264, 314, 336; English Civil War 195; Pequot War 91; Spanish Civil War 139, 140, 141; U.S. Civil War 55; War on Terror 79, 303; World War I/WWI 125, 139, 214, 215, 221, 223, 226, 229, 230, 280, 281, 282, 283, 286, 334; World War II/WWII 36, 112, 119, 132, 141, 142, 143, 144, 225, 226, 227, 228, 229, 230, 231, 232, 233, 234, 244, 282, 283, 286, 287, 333, 334
Wa Thiong'o, Ngũgĩ 133–134
Weheliye, Alexander G. 70, 72n3, 267
Wells, H. G. 288n1, 369, 420–421, 423, 433, 438
West (Western) 2, 23, 24–29, 68, 69, 74, 75, 76, 78, 80, 82, 92, 102, 109, 110, 122, 132, 139, 140, 161, 166, 205, 208, 209, 211, 214, 215, 217, 222, 240, 243, 266, 312, 327, 357, 360, 361, 384, 400, 402, 405, 427, 430
Western canon 74–76, 79, 80, 82, 242, 400; in the peripheries 77–78
Wharton, Edith 32, 33, 40n2
Whitehead, Colson 251, 255, 378
white/white supremacy 2, 4, 12, 17–19, 36–40, 58–60, 65, 67, 74, 76, 88, 89, 92–96, 102, 107n3, 121, 123–126, 154, 161, 164–168, 169n7, 188, 190, 191, 221, 231, 233, 249, 263, 267, 272, 327, 341, 369, 389, 447
White Tiger (Adiga) 132–133, 202
wild (wilderness) 110, 115, 197, 382, 394, 395
Williams, Patricia J. 66–67
Williams, Raymond 229, 387
Winthrop, John 90–93
Wizard of the Crow (Thiong'o) 133–134
Wollstonecraft, Mary 197, 198
Woloch, Alex 45
Wood, James 251–252, 254
Wood, Michael 320
Woolf, Virginia 75, 272, 280, 308, 368
Wordsworth, William 194–202, 260–262, 264, 266, 442
workers 2, 27, 113, 118–126, 133, 134, 135, 136, 173, 181, 260, 378, 379, 383, 401, 434; *Capital* and literature of workers 123–125; *Capital* as literature 118–123; lumpenproletariat 125–126
world literature 77, 156n10; globalization as 314–316
World War I 125, 139, 214, 215, 221, 223, 226, 230, 280, 281–282, 283, 286, 420
World War II 36, 112, 119, 132, 141–144, 225, 226, 228, 229–230, 232–234, 264, 282, 284, 286–287, 333, 334, 423
Wright, Richard: *Native Son* 119, 125–126; *12 Million Black Voices* 272
writer/author 2–5, 24, 33, 36, 46–48, 50, 57, 70, 95, 116, 120, 123, 133, 136, 139, 140,

146, 172–175, 198, 206, 211, 225–231, 238, 240–244, 250–252, 255, 262, 275, 276, 281, 283, 285–288, 303, 383, 400, 402, 414, 417, 423, 444, 447

writing 1, 2, 14, 18, 28, 36, 45–48, 51, 55–57, 68–71, 76, 88, 92, 93, 111, 116, 122, 131, 138, 139, 141, 154, 165, 172, 174, 175, 198, 201, 207, 217, 219, 220–223, 226, 227, 230, 237, 249, 251, 255, 262, 264, 266, 267, 269, 271, 273, 275, 281–288, 345–347, 381, 384, 399, 400, 404, 410, 431, 432, 434, 436, 438, 441, 442, 444, 447; histories 346–349; political 282–284; as propaganda 284–287

Yellow Peril hysteria 222

Zukofsky, Louis 259, 267